Lecture Notes in Computer Science 9207

More information about this series at http://www.springer.com/series/7407

Daniel Kroening · Corina S. Păsăreanu (Eds.)

Computer Aided Verification

27th International Conference, CAV 2015
San Francisco, CA, USA, July 18–24, 2015
Proceedings, Part II

Editors
Daniel Kroening
University of Oxford
Oxford
UK

Corina S. Păsăreanu
Carnegie Mellon University
Moffett Field, CA
USA

ISSN 0302-9743 ISSN 1611-3349 (electronic)
Lecture Notes in Computer Science
ISBN 978-3-319-21667-6 ISBN 978-3-319-21668-3 (eBook)
DOI 10.1007/978-3-319-21668-3

Library of Congress Control Number: 2015943799

LNCS Sublibrary: SL1 – Theoretical Computer Science and General Issues

Springer Cham Heidelberg New York Dordrecht London

Printed on acid-free paper

Springer International Publishing AG Switzerland is part of Springer Science+Business Media
(www.springer.com)

Preface

It is our great pleasure to welcome you to CAV 2015, the 27th International Conference on Computer-Aided Verification, held in San Francisco, California, during July 18–24, 2015.

The CAV conference series is dedicated to the advancement of the theory and practice of computer-aided formal analysis methods for hardware and software systems. The conference covers the spectrum from theoretical results to concrete applications, with an emphasis on practical verification tools and the algorithms and techniques that are needed for their implementation. CAV considers it vital to continue spurring advances in hardware and software verification while expanding to new domains such as biological systems and computer security.

The CAV 2015 program included five keynotes, technical papers (58 long and 11 short papers accepted out of 252 submissions), 11 co-located events (VSTTE – Verified Software: Theories, Tools, and Experiments; SMT – Satisfiability Modulo Theories, EC2, IPRA – Interpolation: From Proofs to Applications; SYNT – Synthesis; VeriSure – Verification and Assurance; HCVS – Horn Clauses for Verification and Synthesis; VMW – Verification Mentoring Workshop, REORDER, SNR – Symbolic and Numerical Methods for Reachability Analysis; VEMDP – Verification of Engineered Molecular Devices and Programs), the Artifact Evaluation as well as briefings from the SMT and Synthesis competitions.

The invited keynote speakers were Philippa Gardner (Imperial College London), Leslie Lamport (Microsoft Research), Bob Kurshan (Cadence), William Hung (Synopsys), and Peter O'Hearn (University College London and Facebook).

Many people worked hard to make CAV 2015 a success. We thank the authors and the keynote speakers for providing the excellent technical material, the Program Committee for their thorough reviews and the time spent on evaluating all the submissions and discussing them during the on-line discussion period, and the Steering Committee for their guidance throughout the planning for CAV 2015.

We also thank Temesghen Kahsai, Local Chair, for his dedication and help with CAV 2015 planning and Hana Chockler, Sponsorship Chair, for helping to bring much needed financial support to the conference; Dirk Beyer, Workshop Chair, and all the organizers of the co-located events for bringing their events to the CAV week; Elizabeth Polgreen for the program and proceedings; Arie Gurfinkel, Temesghen Kahsai, Michael Tautschnig, and the Artifact Evaluation Committee for their work on evaluating the artifacts submitted.

We gratefully acknowledge NSF for providing financial support for student participants. We sincerely thank the CAV sponsors for their generous contributions:

- Google (Platinum sponsor)
- NASA, Fujitsu, SGT, Facebook, Microsoft (Gold sponsors)
- IBM, Cadence (Silver sponsors)
- Intel, Samsung (Bronze sponsors)

We also thank Carnegie Mellon University Silicon Valley and the University of Oxford for their support.

Finally, we hope you find the proceedings of CAV 2015 intellectually stimulating and practically valuable.

May 2015

Corina S. Păsăreanu
Daniel Kroening

Organization

Program Committee

Aws Albarghouthi	University of Toronto, Canada
Jade Alglave	University College London, UK
Domagoj Babic	Google
Armin Biere	Johannes Kepler University, Austria
Roderick Bloem	Graz University of Technology, Austria
Ahmed Bouajjani	LIAFA, University of Paris Diderot, France
Marius Bozga	Verimag/CNRS, France
Aaron Bradley	Mentor Graphics
David Brumley	Carnegie Mellon University, USA
Tevfik Bultan	University of California at Santa Barbara, USA
Krishnendu Chatterjee	Institute of Science and Technology (IST)
Swarat Chaudhuri	Rice University, USA
Marsha Chechik	University of Toronto, Canada
Hana Chockler	King's College London, UK
Byron Cook	Microsoft Research
Isil Dillig	Stanford University, USA
Dino Distefano	Facebook
Alastair Donaldson	Imperial College London, UK
Azadeh Farzan	University of Toronto, Canada
Antonio Filieri	University of Stuttgart, Germany
Jasmin Fisher	Microsoft Research
Indradeep Ghosh	Fujitsu Labs of America
Patrice Godefroid	Microsoft Research
Aarti Gupta	Princeton University, USA
Arie Gurfinkel	Software Engineering Institute, CMU, USA
Gerard Holzmann	NASA/JPL, USA
Warren Hunt	University of Texas, USA
Ranjit Jhala	University of California San Diego, USA
Barbara Jobstmann	EPFL, Jasper DA, and CNRS-Verimag, Switzerland/France
Joost-Pieter Katoen	RWTH Aachen University, Germany
Daniel Kroening	University of Oxford, UK
Marta Kwiatkowska	University of Oxford, UK
Akash Lal	Microsoft Research, India
Darko Marinov	University of Illinois at Urbana-Champaign, USA
Ken McMillan	Microsoft Research
Kedar Namjoshi	Bell Labs

David Parker	University of Birmingham, UK
Corina Pasareanu	CMU/NASA Ames Research Center, USA
André Platzer	Carnegie Mellon University, USA
Zvonimir Rakamaric	University of Utah, USA
Grigore Rosu	University of Illinois at Urbana-Champaign, USA
Philipp Ruemmer	Uppsala University, Sweden
Mooly Sagiv	Tel Aviv University, Israel
Sriram Sankaranarayanan	University of Colorado, Boulder, USA
Koushik Sen	University of California, Berkeley, USA
Natarajan Shankar	SRI International
Natasha Sharygina	Università della Svizzera Italiana, Italy
Sharon Shoham	Technion, Israel
Nishant Sinha	IBM Research Labs
Fabio Somenzi	University of Colorado at Boulder, USA
Manu Sridharan	Samsung Research America
Ofer Strichman	Technion, Israel
Zhendong Su	UC Davis, USA
Cesare Tinelli	The University of Iowa, USA
Emina Torlak	U.C. Berkeley, USA
Tayssir Touili	LIAFA, CNRS and University Paris Diderot, France
Thomas Wahl	Northeastern University, USA
Georg Weissenbacher	Vienna University of Technology, Austria
Eran Yahav	Technion, Israel

Additional Reviewers

Abdelkader, Karam
Abdullah, Syed Md. Jakaria
Abraham, Erika
Aiswarya, C.
Akshay, S.
Alberti, Francesco
Alt, Leonardo
André, Etienne
Arechiga, Nikos
Asarin, Eugene
Astefanoaei, Lacramioara
Athanasiou, Konstantinos
Aydin, Abdulbaki
Backeman, Peter
Balakrishnan, Gogul
Bang, Lucas
Barbot, Benoit
Barrett, Clark
Bartocci, Ezio
Basset, Nicolas
Ben Sassi, Mohamed Amin
Ben-David, Shoham
Benes, Nikola
Berdine, Josh
Bertrand, Nathalie
Bhatt, Devesh
Blackshear, Sam
Bocic, Ivan
Bogomolov, Sergiy
Bornholt, James
Bortz, David
Brain, Martin
Brockschmidt, Marc
Brotherston, James
Bruns, Glenn
Bushnell, David
Calcagno, Cristiano
Ceska, Milan
Chakarov, Aleksandar
Chakravarthy, Venkat
Chan, May T.M.
Chapman, Martin
Chau, Cuong
Chen, Xin
Chen, Yuting
Cherini, Renato
Chiang, Wei-Fan
Chmelik, Martin
Choi, Wontae
Cimatti, Alessandro
Ciobaca, Stefan
Clancy, Kevin
Combaz, Jacques
Cox, Arlen
D'Antoni, Loris

D'Silva, Vijay
Dan, Andrei Marian
Dang, Thao
Darulova, Eva
David, Cristina
De Niz, Dionisio
Degorre, Aldric
Dehnert, Christian
Dhok, Monika
Diaz, Marcio
Dimjasevic, Marko
Dor, Nurit
Doyen, Laurent
Dragoi, Cezara
Dutertre, Bruno
Dutra, Rafael
Ebtekar, Aram
Ehlers, Rüdiger
Eide, Eric
Eisner, Cindy
Enea, Constantin
Fainekos, Georgios
Falcone, Ylies
Fedyukovich, Grigory
Feret, Jerome
Ferrere, Thomas
Fisman, Dana
Forejt, Vojtech
Fraer, Ranan
Frehse, Goran
Fu, Xiang
Fu, Zhoulai
Fuhs, Carsten
Fulton, Nathan
Gao, Sicun
Garg, Pranav
Garoche, Pierre-Loic
Gascon, Adria
Gerard, Leonard
Ghorbal, Khalil
Giacobbe, Mirco
Girard, Antoine
Gligoric, Milos
Goel, Shilpi
Gong, Liang
Gordon, Colin S.
Gotsman, Alexey
Gretz, Friedrich
Griesmayer, Andreas
Grinchtein, Olga
Grumberg, Orna
Gu, Yijia
Guck, Dennis
Gupta, Ashutosh
Gvero, Tihomir
Gyori, Alex
Günther, Henning
Haase, Christoph
Hadarean, Liana
Hahn, Ernst Moritz
Hall, Ben
Hall, Benjamin
Hallé, Sylvain
Hamza, Jad
He, Shaobo
Heizmann, Matthias
Henriques, David
Henry, Julien
Heule, Marijn
Hofferek, Georg
Horn, Alexander
Hyvärinen, Antti
Ivancic, Franjo
Ivrii, Alexander
Jain, Mitesh
Jansen, Nils
Jeannin, Jean-Baptiste
Ji, Ran
Jovanovic, Aleksandra
Jovanović, Dejan
Kafle, Bishoksan
Kahsai, Temesghen
Kahveci, Tuba
Kaminski, Benjamin Lucien
Kannan, Jayanthkumar
Kapinski, James
Karbyshev, Aleksandr
Karimi, Derrick
Keidar-Barner, Sharon
Keller, Chantal
Kennedy, Andrew
Khalimov, Ayrat
Khlaaf, Heidy
Kiefer, Stefan
Kim, Chang Hwan Peter
Kincaid, Zachary
King, Andy
King, Tim
Kini, Keshav
Koenighofer, Robert
Komuravelli, Anvesh
Konnov, Igor
Koskinen, Eric
Kretinsky, Jan
Kugler, Hillel
Kuncak, Viktor
Laarman, Alfons
Lahav, Ori
Lahiri, Shuvendu
Lampka, Kai
Lange, Martin
Lano, Kevin
Lawford, Mark
Le, Vu
Legay, Axel
Li, Goudong
Li, Guodong
Li, Peng
Li, Wenchao
Li, Yi
Liang, Tianyi
Lin, Yu
Liu, Peizun
Loos, Sarah
Luo, Qingzhou
Maler, Oded
Marescotti, Matteo
Martins, João G.
Martins, Ruben
Meel, Kuldeep
Mehne, Ben
Meller, Yael
Mereacre, Alexandru
Meshman, Yuri
Miné, Antoine
Misailovic, Sasa
Mitra, Sayan

Mitsch, Stefan
Moore, Brandon
Moses, Yoram
Mover, Sergio
Moy, Matthieu
Mukherjee, Rajdeep
Mukherjee, Suvam
Musuvathi, Madanlal
Müller, Andreas
Nadel, Alexander
Naiman, Lev
Natraj, Ashutosh
Navas, Jorge A
Neider, Daniel
Nellen, Johanna
Nguyen, Huu Vu
Nickovic, Dejan
Nimal, Vincent
Nori, Aditya
Norman, Gethin
O'Hearn, Peter
Ober, Iulian
Oehlerking, Jens
Olivo, Oswaldo
Olmedo, Federico
Ong, Luke
Otop, Jan
Ouaknine, Joel
Owre, Sam
Padon, Oded
Palikareva, Hristina
Paoletti, Nicola
Papavasileiou, Vasilis
Park, Daejun
Partush, Nimrod
Pek, Edgar
Peleg, Hila
Piterman, Nir
Podelski, Andreas
Pommellet, Adrien
Pous, Damien
Prasad, Mukul
Prähofer, Herbert
Puggelli, Alberto
Qian, Xuehai
Qiu, Xiaokang
Quesel, Jan-David
Radoi, Cosmin
Ramachandran, Jaideep
Ratschan, Stefan
Ray, Sayak
Rinetzky, Noam
Rodríguez Carbonell, Enric
Roeck, Franz
Rungta, Neha
Ryvchin, Vadim
Safránek, David
Salay, Rick
Sawaya, Geof
Schewe, Sven
Schlaipfer, Matthias
Scholl, Christoph
Schrammel, Peter
Schäf, Martin
Schäfer, Andreas
See, Abigail
Seidl, Martina
Selfridge, Ben
Serbanuta, Traian Florin
Sethi, Divjyot
Sharma, Rahul
Sheinvald, Sarai
Shi, August
Shmulevich, Ilya
Sinz, Carsten
Slivovsky, Friedrich
Sogokon, Andrew
Solovyev, Alexey
Sousa Pinto, Joao
Srivathsan, B
Stefanescu, Andrei
Stefanescu, Gheorghe
Sticksel, Christoph
Suda, Martin
Sun, Chengnian
Sun, Yutian
Szekeres, Laszlo
Taghdiri, Mana
Tautschnig, Michael
Thakur, Aditya
Tiwari, Ashish
Tonetta, Stefano
Topcu, Ufuk
Tracol, Mathieu
Tsiskaridze, Nestan
Tzoref-Brill, Rachel
Ulbrich, Mattias
Urban, Caterina
Urban, Christian
Vafeiadis, Viktor
Veitsman, Maor
Velner, Yaron
Vizel, Yakir
Voelzer, Hagen
Von Essen, Christian
Völp, Marcus
Wachter, Björn
Wang, Zilong
Wehrman, Ian
Wei, Ou
Wetzler, Nathan
Whalen, Mike
Wickerson, John
Wiltsche, Clemens
Wintersteiger, Christoph
Wolf, Karsten
Wolf, Verena
Wu, Zhilin
Yorav, Karen
Yorsh, Greta
Yoshida, Hiroaki
Younes, Håkan L.S.
Yu, Fang
Zawadzki, Erik
Zeljić, Aleksandar
Zhang, Qirun
Zhang, Yi
Zheng, Yunhui
Zutshi, Aditya

Contents – Part II

SMT Techniques and Applications

HW Verification

Synthesis

Contents – Part I

Invited Paper

Model Checking and Refinements

Quantitative Reasoning

Lightning Talks

SMT Techniques and Applications

POLING: SMT Aided Linearizability Proofs

He Zhu(✉), Gustavo Petri, and Suresh Jagannathan

Purdue University, West Lafayette, USA
zhuhemail@gmail.com

Abstract. Proofs of linearizability of concurrent data structures generally rely on identifying linearization points to establish a simulation argument between the implementation and the specification. However, for many linearizable data structure operations, the linearization points may not correspond to their internal static code locations; for example, they might reside in the code of another concurrent operation. To overcome this limitation, we identify important program patterns that expose such instances, and describe a tool (POLING) that automatically verifies the linearizability of implementations that conform to these patterns.

1 Introduction

Linearizability [13] is the de facto correctness condition for the implementation of concurrent data structures. In a nutshell, linearizability establishes an observational equivalence between a multi-step fine-grained implementation, and an atomic coarse-grained specification of the data structure [7]. Thus, linearizability implies that each *operation* of a data structure implementation can be considered as executing atomically with respect to other concurrent operations.

While the definition of linearizability is intuitively simple, its proofs tend to be complex, and oftentimes depend on complicated simulation relations between the *abstraction* and the *implementation* (eg. [3,18]). A common strategy to define linearizability simulations is to identify program points in the implementation of the data structure – known as *linearization points* (LP) – upon whose execution an operation can be considered to have happened atomically [21]. Technically, a linearization point indicates in a weak simulation argument a unique and atomic step in the execution of the implementation at which the specification and the implementation match their behaviors.

In this paper, we present a lightweight technique which reduces this complex task into a property checking problem. In our approach, the abstract specification of a data structure operation is defined using *recursive functions* on heaplets (assertions describing a portion of the heap). We model these assertions as a set of memory locations following [17], enabling the use of SMT solvers to discharge our proof obligations. For example, at a linearization point (LP) of a *stack push* method, the *set of locations conforming the stack* after the execution of LP, should be equal to the set of locations conforming the stack before the push, plus an additional location containing the new value pushed. The validity of the formulae relating these two states of this linearizability argument (over *sets*) is

D. Kroening and C.S. Păsăreanu (Eds.): CAV 2015, Part II, LNCS 9207, pp. 3–19, 2015.
DOI: 10.1007/978-3-319-21668-3_1

decidable because they can be translated to quantifier-free formulas over integers and functions, and can be solved by using SMT solvers.

Tools like CAVE [22] are succesful at automatically proving linearizability for data structures where the linearization points – static program locations – can be affixed to static program locations within each operation implementation. Unfortunately, a large class of lock-free linearizable data structures resist proofs by identifying such linearization points [3,11,16]. This should not be surprising since the definition of linearizability only requires the existence of a linearization for each invocation, which is intrinsically a *semantical* property of the implementation. Such a linearization needs not always correspond to the execution of predefined instructions within the code of the operation implementation. Our work extends previous efforts on the automation of linearizability proofs leveraging internal linearization points [22], by identifying data structure implementations whose linearization points may reside in code belonging to a concurrent operation.

We do so by identifying two common *patterns*, occurring in fine-grained concurrent algorithms which cannot be verified using linearization points. Our ideas extend the state of the art in automatic linearizability verification by extending CAVE [22] beyond linearization points. To the verification of linearizability by linearization points, POLING adds the following three notable features.

- Firstly, POLING converges faster than CAVE in all the benchmarks that both tools can handle. This can be attributed to the fact that POLING reasons about separation logic (SL) verification conditions by interpreting them as *sets* of memory locations, following [17], with efficient SMT solvers.
- Secondly, POLING can verify linearizability for implementations that use *helping* [14], a mechanism that allows an operation performed by one thread to be completed by a concurrent operation of a different thread.
- Finally, POLING is sensitive to *hindsight* [16], a specific pattern in which the linearization of operations that do not update the state (called *pure*) can only be established *a posteriori* of their execution, and it might depend on other threads operations.

2 Overview

In the tradition of CAVE, we focus on the linearizability of concurrent data structures implemented using linked lists. Some examples of such data structures are: stacks, queues and sets (see [12]). In our work we assume a garbage collected environment. Our approach is defined with respect to the *most general client* (MGC) program in which an unbounded number of threads interact though a single shared instance of the data structure [21], hence generalizing any possible client.

To introduce POLING, consider the implementation of a lock-free stack due to Treiber [19] shown in Fig. 1. The stack is organized as a linked list of nodes containing a payload (`val`), and a `next` pointer to the following node in the list. The head of the list is saved in the field `first` of a shared global variable

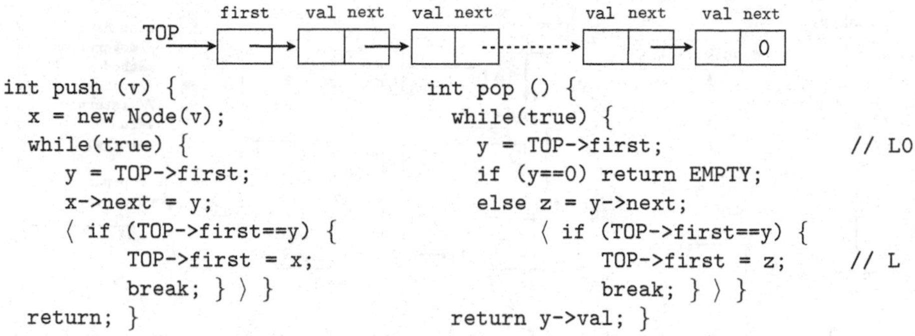


```
int push (v) {                        int pop () {
  x = new Node(v);                      while(true) {
  while(true) {                           y = TOP->first;                 // L0
     y = TOP->first;                      if (y==0) return EMPTY;
     x->next = y;                         else z = y->next;
     ⟨ if (TOP->first==y) {                  ⟨ if (TOP->first==y) {
          TOP->first = x;                         TOP->first = z;         // L
          break; } ⟩ }                            break; } ⟩ }
  return; }                             return y->val; }
```

Fig. 1. Treiber stack.

TOP, which serves as the synchronization point for competing threads. Thus, TOP->first points to the last-in node, when there is one, and it contains 0 if the stack is empty. The operations push and pop are presented. As customary, we group blocks that should be executed atomically with "⟨" and "⟩" (in this case they represent an inline of a cas instruction). The operation push creates a new node - it reads the head of the linked list, and then tries to atomically update it. If some other thread modifies TOP->first between the read and the write, the update is aborted and the process is reiterated. A similar argument applies to pop.

Since linearizability relates the implementation to a specification, the programmer must provide the specification. In the case of CAVE this is done by means of a simple language with primitives for the interpretation of lists and sets. The programmer can use these primitives to operationally specify the data structure. On the other hand, in POLING the specification is done declaratively using *recursive functions*. The *specification* of pop is defined declaratively as:

$$\begin{array}{lcl} \texttt{vals}(\sigma, \texttt{TOP->first}) = r :: \texttt{vals}(\sigma', \texttt{TOP->first}) & \iff & \texttt{pop}() = r \\ \texttt{vals}(\sigma, \texttt{TOP->first}) = [\,] & \iff & \texttt{pop}() = \texttt{Empty} \end{array}$$

In these equations, TOP and first are program variables. The keyword vals is a primitive used to abstractly refer to the contents of a data structure, where the argument σ represents the current state, and the argument TOP->first is a program expression pointing to the first element of the list. The state resulting from executing pop is represented by the symbol σ'. Finally, the return value of pop is denoted by r. Then, the specification of pop establishes the relation between the abstract state of the list before and after its execution. In this example, POLING interprets vals(σ, TOP->first) as a *recursive function* [17], defining the values stored in the locations reachable from TOP->first in σ. Recursive functions will be formalized in Sect. 3.

In Fig. 1, the program point marked with L0 corresponds to the linearization point of pop when the list is empty. The specification for the non-empty case is satisfied at the program point L, because the set of values of locations reachable

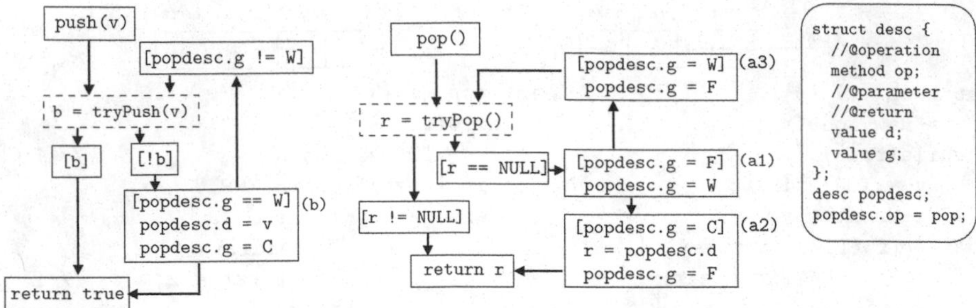

Fig. 2. Elimination based stack. The formulae in square brackets are assumes and each node denotes an atomic block. Struct `desc` is an annotated descriptor.

from `TOP->first` in a state σ (before the execution of the statement at `L`) equals to the set of values reachable in the resulting state (σ') plus the element pointed by `y`, which is `pop`'s return value. Importantly no other point in `pop` changes the values of the reachable locations. POLING using the set of memory locations at `L` calls an SMT solver to automatically check whether the update to these locations, before and after `L`, respects the specification of `pop`. We present verification details in Sect. 4.

The example shown in Fig. 2 (adapted from [6]) is a simplification of the HSY stack [10]. The stack uses an underlying Treiber implementation, but improves its performance for high-contention scenarios through an elimination layer, an occurrence of the *helping mechanism.* The example allows pairs of overlapping instances of pop and push to exchange their values without accessing the list. Each operation attempts an iteration of the Treiber implementation, and if it fails it applies the helping mechanism. The process is iterated until the operation succeeds. Helping is implemented by storing a descriptor of a pending pop into the shared state variable `popdesc`. In the descriptor, if the value of `g` is W(aiting) in location $\mathtt{a}_1$, there is an invocation of pop ready to be helped. If the value of `g` is C(ollided), then a pair of push and pop invocations is in the process of exchanging the value through `g` in location `b`. The helping completes or gives up when `pop` sets the value of `g` back to F(ree), in locations $\mathtt{a}_2$ and $\mathtt{a}_3$, so that another instance of helping can happen. Importantly, the linearization of `pop` can happen in the code of a concurrent `push` in location `b` and, in location $\mathtt{a}_2$, the `pop` can witness that it has been helped because the transition through $\mathtt{a}_1$ to $\mathtt{a}_2$ can only be caused by an action that happened in location `b` of a `push` thread, where it was linearized.

We exploit this witnessing strategy in our linearization proofs. When an operation is linearized by another operation that helps it, we record the state at which the operation was linearized. Then, in the verification of the helped operation, we can use the recorded state as a witness to check that it was indeed helped by a concurrent operation. We observe that the witnessing is carried out through the descriptors (`popdesc`). To verify how a `push` can find and then help a pending `pop`, we allow programmers to use JML-style markers to annotate the descriptor data structure, indicating for an operation's name, the parameters and the return value (in Fig. 2 denoted via `@operation`, `@parameter` and `@return` respectively). We cover the details of the verification in Sect. 4.

3 Formal Model

We define a data structure $\mathtt{D}$ as a pair $(\mathtt{D}_\Sigma, \mathtt{D}_\mathtt{M})$ consisting of $\mathtt{D}_\Sigma$, the domain of the data structure; and $\mathtt{D}_\mathtt{M}$ a set of method names, or *primitive operations* in the terminology of [13]. We call an *invocation* of the method $\mathtt{m}$ simply an *operation*, and use the metavariable $op_\mathtt{m}$ to range over the set $\mathcal{O}ps$ of all possible invocations. In turn, operations can be decomposed into a tuple $op_\mathtt{m} = (\mathtt{m}, t, v, r)$ containing a thread identifier $t \in \mathcal{T}id$, a vector with the arguments v, and if the operation is completed, a return value r.

Program Model. We omit a description of the program state and operational semantics of the programming language, assumed to be a standard first-order, shared-memory, concurrent, imperative language. We assume a set of states $\sigma \in \mathtt{D}_\Sigma$, and an operational semantics with execution steps between states labeled by events $ev \in \mathcal{E}vs$ following the judgment: $\sigma \xrightarrow{t,ev} \sigma'$. Events capture data and control-flow actions (loads, stores, conditionals, etc.) with the addition of *invocation* and *response* events of operation $op_\mathtt{m}$, denoted $\mathsf{inv}(op_\mathtt{m})$ and $\mathsf{res}(op_\mathtt{m})$ respectively. These latter two kinds of events serve to delimit the "duration" of operation invocations. We assume the obvious extension of this step judgment to traces of events ranged by $\mathsf{tr} \in \mathcal{E}vs^*$, denoted $\sigma \xrightarrow{\mathsf{tr}} \sigma'$, with the obvious inductive definition. Where unnecessary, we also omit the intermediate states.

Linearizability. Following [21], and without loss of generality, we assume a thread makes at most one invocation to an operation of the data structure. We then overload the notations for invocations and responses as $\mathsf{inv}(t)$ and $\mathsf{res}(t)$, for thread t. We define $\mathsf{history}(\mathsf{tr})$ to be the projection of invocation and response events in trace tr. Traces induce a partial order between operations. We say that a operation t precedes operation t' in tr t'intr ($t \prec_\mathsf{tr} t'$) as defined below[1]:

$$t \prec_\mathsf{tr} t' \iff \exists\ \mathsf{tr}_0\ \mathsf{tr}_1\ \mathsf{tr}_2,\ \mathsf{tr} = \mathsf{tr}_0 \cdot \mathsf{res}(t) \cdot \mathsf{tr}_1 \cdot \mathsf{inv}(t') \cdot \mathsf{tr}_2$$

We say that a history is *sequential* if each invocation event $\mathsf{inv}(t)$ is immediately followed by its corresponding response event $\mathsf{res}(t)$.

Definition 1 (Linearizable History). *A history h is linearizable w.r.t. the specification of a data structure $\mathtt{D}$ if, and only if, there exists a sequential trace h_s of $\mathtt{D}$ such that $\prec_h \subseteq \prec_{H_s}$, and the set of operations of h and h_s coincide.*

This notion is trivially lifted to implementations by requiring every implementation trace to have a linearizable history.

[1] We eschew treating uncompleted invocations [13], which is a simple extension.

Set Specification. As hinted in Sect. 2, we abstract the data structure through an abstraction function: $\mathtt{vals}(\sigma, \mathtt{x})$, which for a given state σ represents the set of values stored in the data structure pointed by the program variable $\mathtt{x}$. This allows us to express the abstract data structure specification as an equation relating the initial state σ and final state σ'. Then for *Set* data structures implemented as an ordered list, where we assume that the global variable $\mathsf{head}(Set)$ points to the beginning of the list, we write:

$$\begin{aligned} \mathtt{vals}(\sigma', \mathsf{head}(Set)) &= \{v\} \cup \mathtt{vals}(\sigma, \mathsf{head}(Set)) &&\iff \mathtt{add}(v) = \text{true} \\ \mathtt{vals}(\sigma', \mathsf{head}(Set)) \cup \{v\} &= \mathtt{vals}(\sigma, \mathsf{head}(Set)) &&\iff \mathtt{contains}(v) = \text{true} \\ v &\notin \mathtt{vals}(\sigma, \mathsf{head}(Set)) &&\iff \mathtt{contains}(v) = \text{false} \end{aligned}$$

Order Preserving Specifications. Using the concatenation operator (::) instead of union (∪) as above, we can capture the behavior of data structures whose temporal behavior imposes an ordering. For example a stack pop should always return the "last" value pushed. Assuming that $\mathsf{head}(\mathtt{D})$ is the global variable pointing to the first element of the list, we can specify pop and $\mathtt{dequeue}$ – where we omit all other methods – as:

$$\begin{aligned} \mathtt{vals}(\sigma, \mathsf{head}(Stk)) &= r :: \mathtt{vals}(\sigma', \mathsf{head}(Stk)) &&\iff \mathsf{pop}() = r \\ \mathtt{vals}(\sigma, \mathsf{head}(Queue)) &= \mathtt{vals}(\sigma', \mathsf{head}(Queue)) :: r &&\iff \mathtt{dequeue}() = r \end{aligned}$$

State Abstraction. Since we use RGSep [21], we abstract the program state σ using separation logic formulae, denoted by a metavariable ψ. The syntax of these formulae is given by the following grammars, where $\approx$ ranges over binary relations of expression.

$$\begin{aligned} \psi &::= P * \boxed{P'} \mid \psi \vee \psi' & \Pi &::= \mathtt{true} \mid \mathtt{false} \mid E \approx E' \mid (\Pi \wedge \Pi') \\ P &::= \Pi \wedge \Gamma & \Gamma &::= \mathsf{emp} \mid E_{tl} \mapsto \rho \mid \Gamma * \Gamma' \mid \mathtt{lseg}_{tl,\rho}(E, E) \end{aligned}$$

We briefly describe these assertions (details can be found in [21]): 1. The formulae are given in disjunctive normal form, representing the different possible states reachable through different paths, 2. Each of the disjuncts has two parts, the local state, P predicating over the state local to the thread, and a shared state $\boxed{P'}$ – demarcated by a box [21] – which predicates over the state accessible to all threads, 3. Further, each of these states can be separated into a *pure* part Π, only concerned with stack allocated variables, and a *spatial* part Γ, which describes the heap, 4. Finally, heap assertions include the standard separation logic operators, where $E_{tl} \mapsto \rho$ denotes that the location E contains a record ρ (a mapping from field names to values), where the special field tl points to the next node in a linked list, and $\mathtt{lseg}_{tl,\rho}(E, E')$ denotes a linked list segment starting at location E and ending at E'. The same convention applies to tl. All the nodes in this list segment share a same field-value mapping described in ρ.

Data Structure Abstraction. We use the method of [17] to discharge proof obligations about the state using an SMT solver. In [17] SL assertions are encoded as predicates on sets of memory locations. To that end, we define in Fig. 3 a data structure abstraction function that takes an RGSep assertion, and transforms it into a set of values. This is the function $(\!|\mathsf{vals}|\!)(\psi_\sigma, \mathtt{x})$, which is the symbolic

$$(\!|\mathsf{vals}|\!)(P * \boxed{\Pi \wedge \Gamma}, \mathsf{E}) = \mathsf{val}_{\mathsf{aux}}(\Gamma, \mathsf{Find}(\Gamma, \mathsf{E}))$$

where

$$\mathsf{val}_{\mathsf{aux}}(\Gamma, \mathsf{E}_{tl} \mapsto \rho) = \mathtt{VAL}(E) \cup (\!|\mathsf{vals}|\!)(\boxed{\Gamma}, \rho(tl))$$
$$\mathsf{val}_{\mathsf{aux}}(\Gamma, \mathsf{lseg}_{tl,\rho}(\mathsf{E}, \mathsf{E}')) = \mathtt{VALS}(E, E') \cup (\!|\mathsf{vals}|\!)(\boxed{\Gamma}, \mathsf{E}')$$

Fig. 3. Recursive abstraction definition

counterpart to the function $\mathtt{vals}(\sigma, \mathtt{x})$ used for specifications. This recursive abstraction definition represents the set of elements that inhabit the data structure. The function $\mathsf{Find}(\Gamma, \mathsf{E})$, simply finds the syntactic atomic occurrence of a node or a list starting from E in the spacial formula Γ. We omit its trivial recursive definition over RGSep formulae. Here, the capitalized expressions `VALS` are uninterpreted functions in the logic of the underlying theorem provers we use [17]. Finally, notice that if we substitute the concatenation operator (::) for all the occurrences of the union operator ($\cup$) in Fig. 3, we obtain a recursive definition for lists instead of sets. A refined definition of our data structure abstraction is given in [25] (that also considers reachable locations that are logically detached).

4 Verification

Our verification begins after a pass of the frontend of CAVE [22], which given the implementation of a data structure `D`, uses symbolic execution and shape analysis to produce `D`'s data structure invariant [4] and RGSep [21] rely-guarantee actions. To aid the verification of the helping mechanism, POLING requires the programmer to instrument descriptors (as exemplified in Fig. 2). A simple analysis could be implemented to instrument the descriptors automatically, or an interface could be implemented to indicate the thread descriptors, but we omit this unrelated step to simplify our development.

Central to our development are *LP (linearization point) functions.*

Definition 2 (Valid LP). *Assume a trace* $\mathsf{tr} : \sigma_i \xrightarrow{\mathsf{tr}} \sigma_f$ *of the data structure* `D`, *and a function* $\varrho : \mathcal{O}ps \to \mathtt{D}_\Sigma$, *mapping each operation op of* tr *to the state in* tr *exactly prior to the linearization of op. We say that* ϱ *is a* valid linearization point *function for* tr *with respect to an abstract specification* φ *if:*

1. *every operation* $op \in \mathsf{tr}$, *has an LP state (i.e.* $\varrho(op)$*) strictly between its invocation (*$\mathsf{inv}(op)$*) and its response (*$\mathsf{res}(op)$*). Formally:*

$$\exists\ \mathsf{tr}_{(1:4)},\ \sigma_i \xrightarrow{\mathsf{tr}} \sigma_f = \sigma_i \xrightarrow{\mathsf{tr}_1} \cdot \xrightarrow{\mathsf{inv}(op)} \cdot \xrightarrow{\mathsf{tr}_2} \varrho(op) \xrightarrow{\mathsf{tr}_3} \cdot \xrightarrow{\mathsf{res}(op)} \cdot \xrightarrow{\mathsf{tr}_4} \sigma_f$$

2. *only the states that linearize operations can affect the abstract data structure:*

$$\sigma_1 \notin \{\varrho(op) \mid op \in \mathsf{tr}\} \ \mathit{and}\ \sigma_i \xrightarrow{\mathsf{tr}} \sigma_f = \sigma_i \xrightarrow{\mathsf{tr}_1} \sigma_1 \xrightarrow{ev} \sigma_2 \xrightarrow{\mathsf{tr}_2} \sigma_f$$
$$\Rightarrow \mathtt{vals}(\sigma_1, \mathsf{head}(\mathtt{D})) = \mathtt{vals}(\sigma_2, \mathsf{head}(\mathtt{D}))$$

3. *for each operation* $op \in \mathtt{tr}$*, we have that the LP state, and its subsequent state are related by the data structure specification* φ*. Formally, if the abstract specification of* $op = (\mathtt{m}, t, v, r)$ *is* φ*, for a trace of op:* $\sigma_i \xrightarrow{\mathsf{tr}} \sigma_f = \sigma_i \xrightarrow{\mathsf{tr}_1} \varrho(op) \xrightarrow{ev} \hat{\sigma} \xrightarrow{\mathsf{tr}_2} \cdot \xrightarrow{\mathsf{res}(op)} \sigma_r \xrightarrow{\mathsf{tr}_3} \sigma_f$ *where* $(\mathtt{m}(v) = \sigma_r(r))$*:*
(1) *if op is the only operation linearized in* $\varrho(op)$ *(i.e. there does not exist another* op'*, such that* $op' \neq op \wedge \varrho(op') = \varrho(op)$*) then*

$$[\varrho(op)/\sigma][\hat{\sigma}/\sigma']\varphi$$

(2) *if there does exist one* op' *whose abstract specification is* φ'*, such that* $op' \neq op \wedge \varrho(op') = \varrho(op)$[2] *then, for any (ghost) state* σ_g*,*

$$([\varrho(op)/\sigma][\sigma_g/\sigma']\varphi \Rightarrow [\sigma_g/\sigma][\hat{\sigma}/\sigma']\varphi') \vee ([\varrho(op)/\sigma][\sigma_g/\sigma']\varphi' \Rightarrow [\sigma_g/\sigma][\hat{\sigma}/\sigma']\varphi)$$

In condition 3, to verify whether an operation *op* can be linearized when *op* is the single operation linearized in state $\varrho(op)$, we prove that the specification $[\varrho(op)/\sigma][\hat{\sigma}/\sigma']\varphi$ is respected by the execution step from the LP state $\varrho(op)$. In the substitution, the parametric pre state σ and post state σ' of the specification φ, are replaced with the LP state and its post state $\hat{\sigma}$. However, in the case of helping, many operations can be linearized in a single step (e.g. a push and a pop exemplified in Fig. 2). We handle this case by introducing *ghost states*. For example, if an event $\varrho(op) \xrightarrow{ev} \hat{\sigma}$ linearizes two operations; say $\varrho(op) = \varrho(op')$, we check that there exists an intermediate state σ_g such that $\varrho(op)$ and σ_g satisfy the specification of *op* and σ_g and $\hat{\sigma}$ satisfy the specification of op', or viceversa. Intuitively this mediates and orders the linearization of the two operations.

Theorem 1. *A data structure implementation* D *is linearizable with respect to an abstract specification* φ*, if for every trace* tr *of the implementation, there exists a* valid D-LP *function with respect to the specification* φ*.*[3]

Witness States. Definition 2 paired with Theorem 1 provides us with a way of checking linearizability by constructing valid LP functions. However, since LP functions map operations to states, it could be the case that the LP state of a certain operation may precede an event from a thread other than the one whose operation is linearized. The same argument applies when multiple operations are linearized in a single step. This is true for the helping mechanism of Fig. 2. In this case, we define *witness states* as states from which one thread can make sure that it has been linearized, i.e. that a prior LP state ($\varrho(op)$) exists. For the simple case where the linearization point of an operation can be identified with its own program statement, the witness state is exactly the state before executing this statement. We prove linearizability by identifying *witness states*. In our approach, we distinguish effectful witness states where the abstract data structure is altered (like L in Fig. 1), from pure (or effect-less) witness state that leave the abstract data structure intact (like L0 in Fig. 1).

---

[2] Definition 2 is defined for at most two operations linearized in one step. It can be extended to handle the case when finitely many operations are helped in one step.
[3] Theorems are proved in [25].

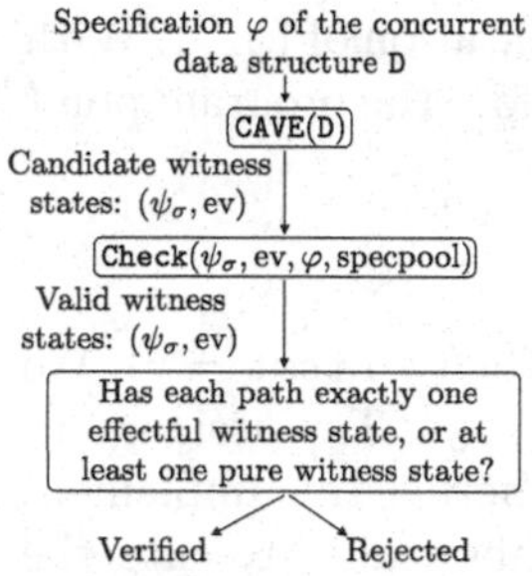

Specification φ of the concurrent data structure D

CAVE(D)

Candidate witness states: (ψ_σ, ev)

Check(ψ_σ, ev, φ, specpool)

Valid witness states: (ψ_σ, ev)

Has each path exactly one effectful witness state, or at least one pure witness state?

Verified

Rejected

```
1: Check(ψσ, ev, φ, specpool) =
2:   let ψσ' = symb-exec(ψσ, ev) in
3:     if (smt-check(φ[σ ↦ ψσ, σ' ↦ ψσ'])) then ✓
4:     else if (helps(ψσ, ψσ', specpool)) then ✓
5:     else if (helped(ψσ, ψσ', specpool)) then ✓
6:     else if (hindsight(ψσ')) then ✓
7:     else if ((|vals|)(ψσ, head(D)) = (|vals|)(ψσ', head(D)))
8:       then ✗
9:       else (abort "not linearizable")
```

Fig. 4. General framework. (The full pseudo code is provided in [25]).

Algorithm. We present our overall verification strategy in Fig. 4. We first use heuristics derived from CAVE to identify a set of states as candidate witness states (ψ_σ), paired with the event (ev) to be executed next; such events include all the memory reads or writes. The abstract states (ψ_σ) are obtained through the symbolic execution of CAVE. The function `Check` verifies whether in a symbolic state ψ_σ the linearization of the operation can be witnessed w.r.t. its abstract specification φ. Programmers provide φ through the definition $\texttt{vals}(\sigma, \mathsf{head}(\mathtt{D}))$ which is translated into the symbolic version $(\!|\mathsf{vals}|\!)(\psi_\sigma, \mathsf{head}(\mathtt{D}))$.

Consider the pseudo-code of `Check` (given in Fig. 4). In line 2 we symbolically execute the event ev from the state ψ_σ. To check if the abstract specification φ is fulfilled, in line 3, we replace the initial and final state with the ones obtained by symbolic execution and then unroll the definitions $(\!|\mathsf{vals}|\!)(\psi_\sigma, \mathbf{head}(\mathtt{D}))$ and $(\!|\mathsf{vals}|\!)(\psi_{\sigma'}, \mathbf{head}(\mathtt{D}))$ that are mentioned in the specification of the method, and encode them using first order logic (FOL) with set theories following [17]. We feed the unrolled formulae to an SMT solver (the arguments v and return values r in the specification are also replaced with proper program variables, not shown here). Notice that satisfiability of quantifier-free formulas over sets/multisets with set union ($\cup$) is decidable. Concatenation (::) is considered as uninterpreted. If the formula is provable we have identified a witness state.

This strategy only applies to the case when linearization can be syntactically associated to instructions of the operation's own code, i.e. LPs. Lines 4-6 deal with the cases when the linearization point might reside in operations of concurrent threads, which will be covered in the subsequent sections. If we are not able to prove φ in ψ_σ after these checks, at line 7, before reporting this state is not a candidate witness, we check that the abstract data structure did not change. We recall that we assume that only linearization events can modify the abstract state of the data structure. Hence, if the state did change, we abort the process in line 9, and report that the implementation could not be proved linearizable. After all the witness states are validated, following the strategy in [22], we use a simple data-flow analysis to verify each program path has either exactly one witness state or at least one pure witness.

Example 1. Consider the pop method of the stack implementation of Fig. 1. With the method delineated above we obtain a symbolic state before the program point L (we only show the shared state):

$$\texttt{TOP} \mapsto (\texttt{first} : \texttt{y}) * \texttt{y} \mapsto \texttt{z} * \mathsf{lseg}_{\texttt{next}}(\texttt{z}, 0)$$

This state is rendered from the successful test in the pop ($\texttt{TOP} \mapsto \texttt{first} = \texttt{y}$). We will consider this state to be the witness state of pop (i.e. ψ_σ). The assignment of z to TOP->first would then be performed. To verify whether this implementation is faithful to the Stack specification, we first symbolically execute the instruction at L to render the post state after L (i.e. $\psi_{\sigma'}$):

$$\texttt{TOP} \mapsto (\texttt{first} : \texttt{z}) * \mathsf{lseg}_{\texttt{next}}(\texttt{z}, 0) * \texttt{y} \mapsto \texttt{z}$$

According to the abstract specification of pop (Definition 3), we have to prove:

$$(\!|\mathsf{vals}|\!)(\psi_\sigma, \texttt{TOP} \mapsto (\texttt{first})) = r :: (\!|\mathsf{vals}|\!)(\psi_{\sigma'}, \texttt{TOP} \mapsto (\texttt{first}))$$

After unfolding, and substituting the special return symbol r with the actual return value, we obtain:

$$\texttt{VAL(y)::VALS(z,0)} = \texttt{VAL(y)::VALS(z,0)}$$

which is clearly provable. Moreover,

$$(\!|\mathsf{vals}|\!)(\psi_\sigma, \texttt{TOP} \mapsto (\texttt{first})) = (\!|\mathsf{vals}|\!)(\psi_{\sigma'}, \texttt{TOP} \mapsto (\texttt{first}))$$

holds for all the other states of pop. After all these verification steps, our method concludes that the program state before L is a valid effectful witness state.

Helping Verification. Consider a trace $\sigma_i \xrightarrow{\mathsf{tr}_1} \varrho(op') \xrightarrow{t,ev} \sigma \xrightarrow{\mathsf{tr}_2} \sigma_f$ corresponding to an execution of a data structure where op' is specified as $(\mathtt{m}, t', v, r)$. This trace is typical of algorithms implementing the helping mechanism. Here, the event (ev) that linearizes thread t' (the thread executing op') is taken by a concurrent thread t. A key ingredient of this pattern are the *descriptors*, which are used to keep information about ongoing invocations performed by different threads (c.f. popdesc in Fig. 2). A thread can acknowledge its concurrent threads through its descriptors which are used by the concurrent threads to complete helping. In our proof, a thread under verification can retrieve the specifications of the other concurrent operations through their descriptors.

To exploit such descriptors, we add to the symbolic state, a set that represents helped operations. We call this set the *Spec Pool*, and use it to keep track of the synchronization entailed through the descriptors. Operations that perform helping are assumed to affect the Spec Pool. In the Spec Pool, each helped operation is equipped with (1) the condition that must hold upon its linearization and (2) the rely actions (used by the helper thread) that linearize it.

We provide a pictorial description of the process in Fig. 5. Here we consider an event $\varrho(op') \xrightarrow{t,ev} \sigma$ from thread t which helps a concurrent operation op'. This event modifies the Spec Pool by inserting a tuple (op', $\alpha(\psi_\sigma)$, RG) indicating

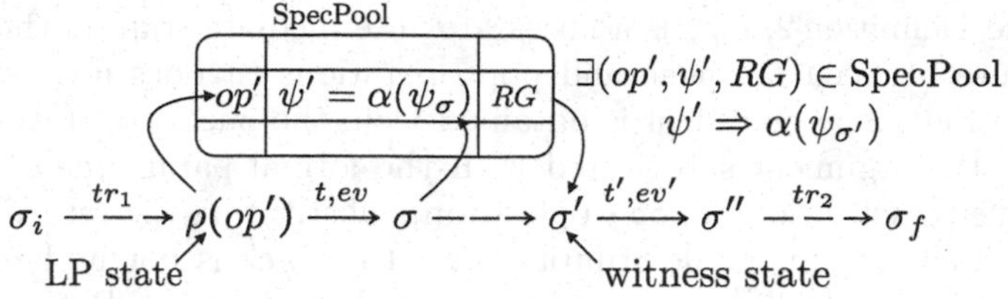

Fig. 5. Spec pool.

that *op*′ has been helped at a state σ, and RG is the rely-guarantee actions extracted from this step [23], where α is a function that encodes a SL formula ψ_σ into a FOL formula. A verification step from *op*′ (i.e. t') can observe the effects of t at state σ' (by checking a first order logical implication between $\alpha(\psi_\sigma)$ and $\alpha(\psi_{\sigma'})$). When verifying *op*′ we also need to check that σ' can only be reached with the help of the rely action RG, absent of which σ' would be unreachable for t'. If the check is successful, σ' is considered as the witness state for *op*′. Figure 6 presents the definition of $\alpha(\psi)$. Simply stated, we keep the pure part of the SL formula and forget about the list segments. We encode the field-value mapping of a memory location ($\mathsf{E}_{\mathsf{tls}} \mapsto \rho$) into a conjunction of equations; each equation encodes the value $\rho(\mathsf{pf})$ of a field pf on the location E. We encode E only if it is marked as a descriptor (local variables are implicitly existentially quantified).

Our approach hence reduces the problem of verifying linearizability to the following proof obligations: (a) we must check *how* an operation can be helped at the valid LP state in Fig. 5 (i.e. linearized by another thread); this corresponds to the `helps` function in Fig. 4, (b) for the thread that is helped, we must check the code that detects *whether* the operation has been helped at the valid witness state in Fig. 5; this corresponds to the `helped` function in Fig. 4, and (c) we must check that the helped operation is linearized exactly once.

For (a) we prove whether a given execution step in thread t can linearize another thread t' (with $t' \neq t$), directly following Definition 2. Let us consider how this proof works for `push` and `pop` of Fig. 2. At the statement `b` of `push` we detect the descriptor `popdesc`, representing a concurrent `pop` thread. Assuming `head`(Stk) = `TOP`, we check:

$$\forall \psi_{gst},\ \big(\ (\!|\mathsf{vals}|\!)(\psi_{gst}, \mathtt{TOP}) = \mathsf{v} :: (\!|\mathsf{vals}|\!)(\psi_\sigma, \mathtt{TOP}) \Rightarrow (\!|\mathsf{vals}|\!)(\psi_{gst}, \mathtt{TOP}) = \mathsf{popdesc.d} :: (\!|\mathsf{vals}|\!)(\psi_{\sigma'}, \mathtt{TOP})\ \big)$$

$$\alpha(P * \boxed{\Pi \wedge \Gamma}) = \Pi \wedge \alpha_\Gamma(\Gamma)$$

$$\alpha_\Gamma(\Gamma' * \Gamma'') = \alpha_\Gamma(\Gamma'') \wedge \begin{cases} \bigwedge_{\mathsf{pf} \in \mathsf{dom}(\rho)} \mathsf{pf}(\mathsf{E}) = \rho(\mathsf{pf}) & \text{if } \Gamma' = \mathsf{E}_{\mathsf{tls}} \mapsto \rho\ \&\ \mathtt{Isdesc}(E) \\ \mathsf{true} & \text{otherwise} \end{cases}$$

Fig. 6. Data abstraction from SL formula to FOL formula.

According to Definition 2, ψ_{gst} is a necessary intermediate state in the abstract data structure between the push and pop operations (it does not exist in the actual execution). The precedent is obtained from the `push`'s operation specification, with the argument substituted with the formal parameter `v`. The consequent is the specification of `pop`'s operation, substituting the return value for `popdesc.d`, known from the descriptor. Since the stack is not updated by the instruction `b`, after unrolling we can prove the above formula. Both operations are linearized in this step. After verifying that `pop` is helped, we create a Spec Pool item (op', ψ', RG), representing the result of helping at statement `b`:

$$(\texttt{pop},\ \exists \texttt{v}.\texttt{popdes.g} = \texttt{C} \wedge \texttt{popdes.d} = \texttt{v},\ \texttt{popdes} \mapsto (\texttt{g}:\texttt{W}) \rightsquigarrow \texttt{popdes} \mapsto (\texttt{g}:\texttt{C}))$$

As stated, ψ' is the data abstraction of state σ' while RG here only shows the key rely-guarantee action ([21]), i.e., `g` is changed from W(aiting) to C(ollided).

We prove (b) by showing that if a thread t' is linearized by another thread t, this fact is manifest through the Spec Pool. To prove that t' has been helped in a state $\psi_{\sigma'}$, we need to find a pool element (op', ψ', RG) such that the operation of t' is with the same method name to op', and prove with an SMT solver that:

$$(\psi' \Rightarrow \alpha(\psi_{\sigma'})) \wedge \neg(\psi' \wedge \alpha(\psi_{\sigma' \setminus RG}))$$

The first conjunct implies that op' may have been linearized by another thread, and the second one ensures that this could only result from other threads' interference RG. To check that this linearization could not have been possible without the interference from another thread's helps, we compute the state $\psi_{\sigma' \setminus RG}$ by symbolically executing the method (using CAVE) to the code location of σ' dropping the rely action RG. Then the conditions recorded in the Spec Pool (the conditions hold upon helping) must contradict $\psi_{\sigma' \setminus RG}$. Consider the path reaching the statement `a2` in `pop` in Fig. 2. The conditions in the Spec Pool for `pop` (ψ') entail the data abstraction of state at `a2` (abstracted as `popdesc.g` = `C`). The only possible way to satisfy this assertion is by the rely RG, since originally we had `popdesc.g` = `W` at `a1`. We conclude that the `pop` was linearized by RG, the action made by a concurrent `push`. We also need to ensure a program path that witnesses helping must return the value of the return-field instrumented in the descriptor (e.g. return `popdesc.d` at `a2`).

We prove (c) by checking that an operation can only be helped once (e.g. helping for thread t' should be prohibited from state σ'' in the trace in Fig. 5). We leave the details in [25].

Our verification procedure maintains the Spec Pool as part of the abstract state, and calls function `Check` of Fig. 4 twice. In the first pass, we construct the Spec Pool by identifying helping scenarios; in the second pass, we exploit the Spec Pool to identify helped operations. Specifically, in Fig. 4, when a candidate state fails to fulfill the specification at line 3, we attempt to prove (a), calling function `helps` at line 4, which identifies a set of descriptors in the state that enable helping. If successful, the corresponding pool items are created (in the first pass). Otherwise, at line 5, by calling function `helped`, we attempt proof obligation b to check if the operation has been helped (in the second pass).

Verification with Hindsight. This pattern is based on the Hindsight Lemma of [16]. In the interest of space we shall avoid presenting a full example like `Lazy_set` [9] (see [25]), which implements a set with an optimistic lock free *contains* operations using a linked list. As in the picture below, each node contains three fields: a value, a mark bit representing whether the item has been removed from the list (marked with grey), and a link (denoted as n) to the following node.

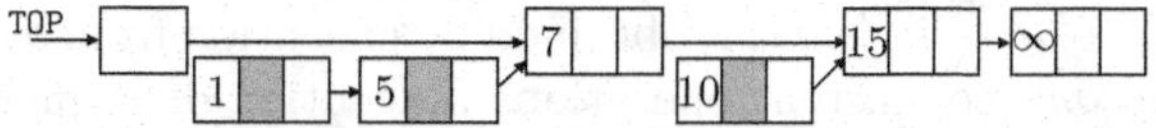

The fundamental invariants for this algorithm are: 1. the elements in the set are *ordered* for fast lookups through the lock-free *contains* method, 2. the elements *in* the list are all reachable from the `TOP` pointer, and are not marked, 3. removed elements are marked before being unlinked, and 4. the next pointer of a removed node never changes, hence it might still point to a node in the data structure, until this node is in turn removed. In the figure, the set contains the elements 7 and 15, but from the removed nodes we know that it contained the elements 1, 5 and 10 at some point in the past. A concurrent *contains* operation, which started before the elements were removed, may assume 1, 5 and 10 are still *contained*. Following [16], we shall call nodes that are reachable from `TOP` (including those that are marked) *backbone nodes* (e.g. 7 and 15). Conversely, nodes that cannot be reached from `TOP` are called *exterior nodes* (e.g. 1, 5 and 10).

Lemma 1 (Hindsight [16]). *Let* tr *be an execution of the set data structure presented above satisfying:*

1. *An exterior node never becomes a backbone node.*
2. *The successor of an exterior node will never change.*
3. *If the successor of a backbone node changes, the node remains a backbone node in the immediate following state.*

Then, for any states $\sigma_i = \mathsf{tr}(i)$, $\sigma_k = \mathsf{tr}(k)$ *such that* $0 \leq i \leq k < |\mathsf{tr}|$ *and for any nodes* u, v, w *such that* $u.n \mapsto v$ *is a backbone link in* σ_i, *and* $v.n \mapsto w$ *is a link (not necessarily in the backbone) in* σ_k, *there exists a state* $\sigma_j = \mathsf{tr}(j)$ *such that* $i \leq j \leq k$ *and* $v.n \mapsto w$ *is a backbone link in* σ_j.

Lemma 1 allows us to use exterior nodes and links in the current state to infer that there existed a past state in which the exterior nodes were in the backbone. Using this information we attempt to linearize the *contains* method, even if the found node is, in the current state, an exterior node. However, Lemma 1 cannot be used directly because, although an exterior link $v.n \mapsto w$ might be found in the current state, its premise, that a link $u.n \mapsto v$ was present in the backbone in a previous state, cannot be immediately established by looking at the current state in the symbolic execution. To resolve this problem we propose Theorem 2 which we exploit to automate the application of Lemma 1 in POLING.

Theorem 2. *If there is an exterior link $v.n \mapsto w$ in σ, a past state of σ in which the link is a backbone link exists provided the following conditions:*

1. *The premises of Lemma 1 hold, and*
2. `Reach`*($head$(`D`), v) can be proved in the sequential state σ^{seq}.*[4]

The sequential counterpart σ^{seq} of a state σ in a trace of an operation *op*, $\sigma_i \xrightarrow{\mathsf{inv}(op)} \cdot \xrightarrow{\mathsf{tr}_2} \sigma \xrightarrow{\mathsf{tr}_3} \cdot \xrightarrow{\mathsf{res}(op)} \sigma_f$, is obtained by execution from σ_i to σ dropping all the steps from *op*'s concurrent operations (executing *op* sequentially).

Note that the second condition ensures a temporal traversal to v (see [16]) and hence guarantees that $v.n \mapsto w$ was once a backbone link. The verification of this pattern (e.g. *contains* operation) is implemented in the `hindsight` function in line 6 in the `Check` function (Fig. 4). In this function, exploiting Theorem 2, if an exterior link $v.n \mapsto w$ is found in a candidate state σ and `Reach(head(D)`, v) holds in σ^{seq} (we compute $\psi_{\sigma^{seq}}$ by utilizing symbolic execution with an empty set of rely-guarantee actions in the implementation), we construct a past state σ_p and substitute it for σ when verifying the method's specification. If the verification succeeds, σ is a pure witness state for the verifying thread's linearization, that is, we can deduce the existence of LP state (σ_p) from witness state σ. We also customize the symbolic execution engine to verify all the three premises in Lemma 1: for each execution step $\sigma \xrightarrow{t,ev} \sigma'$, we collect exterior nodes (symbolically) in σ (ψ_σ), and verify that the step ev does not change their successors and they do not become reachable from `head(D)`; we also collect backbone nodes and check, if their successors are changed by ev, then they remain reachable from `head(D)` in σ' (ψ'_σ). If any of these checks fails, the `hindsight` function (Fig. 4) returns false.

$$\frac{\psi^{\mathtt{D}}_{Inv} : \bigvee_i \Pi_i \wedge \Gamma_i \qquad v.n \mapsto w \in \sigma}{\sigma_p \equiv \bigvee_i (\bigvee_{S \in \Gamma_i} \Pi_i \wedge \mathsf{exp}(v, w, S) * (\Gamma_i \backslash S))}$$

$$\begin{aligned} \mathsf{exp}(v, w, \mathsf{true}) &= v.n \mapsto w * \mathsf{true} \\ \mathsf{exp}(v, w, z \mapsto z') &= v = z \wedge v \mapsto z' \\ \mathsf{exp}(v, w, lseg(z, z')) &= lseg(z, v) * v.n \mapsto w * lseg(w, z') \end{aligned}$$

Fig. 7. Hindsight application rule.

To reconstruct a past state σ_p as above, we introduce the Hindsight Lemma application rule in Fig. 7. The rule is an adaptation of May-subtraction [23]. Intuitively, May-Subtract(P, Q) considers the ways in which an RGSep assertion Q can be removed from another assertion P. Our application rule works as May-Subtract($\psi^{\mathtt{D}}_{Inv}$, $v.n \mapsto w$) to subtract an exterior link out of data structure invariant, and return the remaining state with the link added back. The auxiliary function `exp` (expose) considers all the ways in which v can be matched to a `node` or `linked list` assertion. Notice that since the only thing that is assumed in the rule (the hypotheses) is the data structure shape invariant $\psi^{\mathtt{D}}_{Inv}$ (derived from CAVE), the resulting symbolic state is an abstraction of an actual past state. The correctness of this rule is guaranteed by the proof of Theorem 2.

[4] `Reach` is the obvious reachability predicate over SL formulas.

Limitations. Although POLING can automatically handle concurrent data structures with non-internal linearization points, we acknowledge that it cannot verify a class of concurrent data structure whose linearization points depend on future behaviors [11]. We expect to extend POLING to support this class of programs in the future.

5 Experimental Results

We evaluated POLING[5] on 11 examples, divided into 3 categories shown in the tables of Fig. 8. In the first table we present algorithms provable using internal linearization points. We compare the times that CAVE (version 2.1) and POLING take to verify the algorithms and notice that for all these programs POLING outperforms CAVE. This can be attributed to our usage of SMT solvers following [17] to efficiently discharge linearizability proof obligations.

The second table presents algorithms falling under the hindsight pattern. We considered set implementation algorithms that perform an optimistic `contains` (or `lookup`) operation. Optimistic_set [16] traverses the list optimistically (without acquiring any locks, or synchronizing with other threads) to find a node. In contrast, Lazy_set [9], and its variant Vechev_CAS_set [24] use a bit for marking nodes before deletion.

The last table includes programs that implement the helping mechanism. Conditional compare-and-swap (CCAS) [20] is a simplified version of the well known RDCSS algorithm [8]. If a CCAS method finds a (thread) descriptor in its targeting shared memory location, they attempt to help complete the operation in that descriptor before performing its own. Finally, HSY_stack is the full HSY stack implementation [10]. Our running time in this complex example is comparable to a rewriting technique illustrated in [6]. As expected, CAVE cannot prove all the programs in the second and third categories.

Linearization Points

Program	CAVE	POLING
LockCoupling_set [12]	13.28s	4.01s
Vechev_DCAS_set [24]	73.90s	3.15s
2lock_queue [15]	2.91s	2.51s
Treiber [19]	0.28s	0.06s
MSqueue [15]	7.66s	1.12s
DGLMqueue [5]	9.40s	1.47s

Hindsight

Program	POLING
Vechev_CAS_set [24]	868.44s
Optimistic_set [16]	27.51s
Lazy_set [9]	321.78s

Helping

Program	POLING
CCAS [20]	0.82s
HSY_stack [10]	5.98s

Fig. 8. Experimental results.

6 Related Work and Conclusion

Related Work. Most techniques on linearizability verification (e.g., [1,2]) are based on forward simulation arguments, and typically only work for methods

[5] Project page: https://www.cs.purdue.edu/homes/zhu103/poling/index.html.

with internal linearization points local to their own code locations. To deal with external linearization points, [3] proposed a technique limited to the case where only read-only operations may have external linearization points.

Complete backward simulation strategies have been proposed in [18]. However, they are often difficult to automate. Other methods combine both forward and backward simulations, using history and/or prophecy variables [21], instrumenting the program with auxiliary state [14], or using logical relations to construct relational proofs [20]. A general and modular proof strategy is proposed in [14], that, along with lightweight instrumentation, leverages rely-guarantee reasoning to manually verify algorithms with external linearization points. In contrast, our method exploits witness states to infer a proof automatically. The helping mechanism is also considered in [6] (which does not deal with the hindsight pattern) by rewriting the implementation so that all operations have their linearization points within their rewritten code. Our technique does not rely on rewritings because the relevant witness is found within the Spec Pool.

Our technique can be considered an adaptation of [17] which verifies sequential data structures using recursive definitions on heaplets. Similar to POLING, the automata based approach [1] is also a property checking algorithm which formalizes linearizability specifications as automata, and checks the cross-product of a symbolic encoding of the program with the specification automata for safety. The main difference between POLING and [1] resides in the verification of implementations with external linearization points.

Conclusion. We describe a procedure and a tool POLING that automatically checks the linearizability of fine-grained concurrent data structures. POLING abstracts concurrent data structure into sets of locations following [17] and considers linearizability verification as a property checking technique, which are efficiently solved with an SMT solver. POLING extends prior art by incorporating important concurrent programming patterns: algorithms using *helping*, and algorithms that can be proved using the *hindsight* lemma [16]. Our experimental results provide evidence of the effectiveness of our tool.

References

1. Abdulla, P.A., Haziza, F., Holík, L., Jonsson, B., Rezine, A.: An integrated specification and verification technique for highly concurrent data structures. In: Piterman, N., Smolka, S.A. (eds.) TACAS 2013 (ETAPS 2013). LNCS, vol. 7795, pp. 324–338. Springer, Heidelberg (2013)
2. Amit, D., Rinetzky, N., Reps, T., Sagiv, M., Yahav, E.: Comparison under abstraction for verifying linearizability. In: Damm, W., Hermanns, H. (eds.) CAV 2007. LNCS, vol. 4590, pp. 477–490. Springer, Heidelberg (2007)
3. Derrick, J., Schellhorn, G., Wehrheim, H.: Verifying linearisability with potential linearisation points. In: Butler, M., Schulte, W. (eds.) FM 2011. LNCS, vol. 6664, pp. 323–337. Springer, Heidelberg (2011)
4. Distefano, D., O'Hearn, P.W., Yang, H.: A local shape analysis based on separation logic. In: Hermanns, H., Palsberg, J. (eds.) TACAS 2006. LNCS, vol. 3920, pp. 287–302. Springer, Heidelberg (2006)

5. Doherty, S., Groves, L., Luchangco, V., Moir, M.: Formal verification of a practical lock-free queue algorithm. In: de Frutos-Escrig, D., Núñez, M. (eds.) FORTE 2004. LNCS, vol. 3235, pp. 97–114. Springer, Heidelberg (2004)
6. Drăgoi, C., Gupta, A., Henzinger, T.A.: Automatic linearizability proofs of concurrent objects with cooperating updates. In: Sharygina, N., Veith, H. (eds.) CAV 2013. LNCS, vol. 8044, pp. 174–190. Springer, Heidelberg (2013)
7. Filipovic, I., O'Hearn, P.W., Rinetzky, N., Yang, H.: Abstraction for concurrent objects. Theor. Comput. Sci. **411**, 252–266 (2010)
8. Harris, T.L., Fraser, K., Pratt, I.A.: A practical multi-word compare-and-swap operation. In: Malkhi, D. (ed.) DISC 2002. LNCS, vol. 2508, pp. 265–279. Springer, Heidelberg (2002)
9. Heller, S., Herlihy, M.P., Luchangco, V., Moir, M., Scherer III, W.N., Shavit, N.N.: A lazy concurrent list-based set algorithm. In: Anderson, J.H., Prencipe, G., Wattenhofer, R. (eds.) OPODIS 2005. LNCS, vol. 3974, pp. 3–16. Springer, Heidelberg (2006)
10. Hendler, D., Shavit, N., Yerushalmi, L.: A scalable lock-free stack algorithm. In: SPAA (2004)
11. Henzinger, T.A., Sezgin, A., Vafeiadis, V.: Aspect-oriented linearizability proofs. In: D'Argenio, P.R., Melgratti, H. (eds.) CONCUR 2013 – Concurrency Theory. LNCS, vol. 8052, pp. 242–256. Springer, Heidelberg (2013)
12. Herlihy, M., Shavit, N.: The Art of Multiporcessor Programming. MorganKaufmann, San Francisco (2008)
13. Herlihy, M., Wing, J.: Linearizability: a correctness condition for concurrent objects. ACM TOPLAS **12**(3), 463–492 (1990)
14. Liang, H., Feng, X.: Modular verification of linearizability with non-fixed linearization points. In: PLDI (2013)
15. Michael, M., Scott, M.: Simple, fast, and practical non-blocking and blocking concurrent queue algorithms. In: PODC (1996)
16. O'Hearn, P., Rinetzky, N., Vechev, M., Yahav, E., Yorsh, G.: Verifying linearizability with hindsight. In: PODC (2010)
17. Qiu, X., Garg, P., Stefanescu, A., Madhusudan, P.: Natural proofs for structure, data, and separation. In: PLDI (2013)
18. Schellhorn, G., Wehrheim, H., Derrick, J.: How to prove algorithms linearisable. In: Madhusudan, P., Seshia, S.A. (eds.) CAV 2012. LNCS, vol. 7358, pp. 243–259. Springer, Heidelberg (2012)
19. Treiber, P.: System programming: coping with parallelism. In: Technique report RJ 5118, IBM Almaden Research Center (1986)
20. Turon, A., Thamsborg, J., Ahmed, A., Birkedal, L., Dreyer, D.: Logical relations for fine-grained concurrency. In: POPL (2013)
21. Vafeiadis, V.: Modular fine-grained concurrency verification. Ph.D. thesis, University of Cambridge (2008)
22. Vafeiadis, V.: Automatically proving linearizability. In: Touili, T., Cook, B., Jackson, P. (eds.) CAV 2010. LNCS, vol. 6174, pp. 450–464. Springer, Heidelberg (2010)
23. Vafeiadis, V.: RGSep action inference. In: Barthe, G., Hermenegildo, M. (eds.) VMCAI 2010. LNCS, vol. 5944, pp. 345–361. Springer, Heidelberg (2010)
24. Vechev, M., Yahav, E.: Deriving linerizable fine-grained concurrent objects. In: PLDI (2008)
25. Zhu, H., Petri, G., Jagannathan, S.: Poling: Smt aided linearizability proofs. Technical report, Purdue Univsersity (2015). https://www.cs.purdue.edu/homes/zhu103/poling/tech.pdf

Finding Bounded Path in Graph Using SMT for Automatic Clock Routing

Amit Erez(✉) and Alexander Nadel

Intel Corporation, P.O. Box 1659, 31015 Haifa, Israel
{amit.erez,alexander.nadel}@intel.com

Abstract. Automating the routing process is essential for the semiconductor industry to reduce time-to-market and increase productivity. This study sprang from the need to automate the following critical task in clock routing: given a set of nets, each net consisting of a driver and a receiver, connect each driver to its receiver, where the delay should be almost the same across the nets. We demonstrate that this problem can be reduced to bounded-path, that is, the NP-hard problem of finding a simple path, whose cost is bounded by a given range, connecting two given vertices in an undirected positively weighted graph. Furthermore, we show that bounded-path can be reduced to bit-vector reasoning and solved with a SAT-based bit-vector SMT solver. In order to render our solution scalable, we override the SAT solver's decision strategy with a novel graph-aware strategy and augment conflict analysis with a graph-aware procedure. Our solution scales to graphs having millions of edges and vertices. It has been deployed at Intel for clock routing automation.

1 Introduction

Integrated circuits (IC) are made up of a large number of transistors forming logical gates connected by *nets*. The process of finding the geometrical layout of all the nets is called *routing*. Routing is an essential stage of the physical design process [25]. A clock is a control signal that synchronizes data transfer in the circuit. Specialized algorithms are required for routing the clock nets as opposed to other types of nets [26]. This is because the clock must arrive at all functional units at almost the same time. Clock nets must be routed before the other nets (except the power nets), hence rapid clock routing is critical for decreasing the time-to-market of semiconductor products. In clock routing, the following requirement must often be met for a set of nets, each net consisting of a driver and a receiver: wires connecting the driver to the receiver must have almost the same delay across the nets. This type of routing is called *matching constrained routing (MCR)*. This paper shows how to automate MCR.

Section 2 reviews related work and provides some preliminaries. We define the *bounded path problem* (or, simply, *bounded-path*) as follows: given a positively weighted undirected graph, a source s and a target t, find a *bounded path* (that is, a simple path, whose cost lays within a given cost range) from s to t. Section 3 shows that MCR can be reduced to bounded-path in a grid graph.

D. Kroening and C.S. Păsăreanu (Eds.): CAV 2015, Part II, LNCS 9207, pp. 20–36, 2015.
DOI: 10.1007/978-3-319-21668-3_2

Section 4 demonstrates that bounded-path is NP-hard even for a grid graph. It also shows how to reduce bounded-path to bit-vector (BV) logic. Solving bounded-path instances originating in MCR with a BV solver does not scale to industrial instances. Section 5 remedies this situation by proposing a new problem-aware approach to solving bounded-path within an eager BV solver [9,14]. First, we override the decision strategy of the SAT solver with a graph-aware strategy, which builds a bounded path from source to target explicitly. Second, we augment conflict analysis with graph-aware reasoning.

The main conceptual novelty of our approach w.r.t the decision procedure, independent of the particular problem, is the pivotal role of the decision strategy. While custom SAT decision heuristics have been applied previously [3,24], our decision strategy *replaces constraints*, that is, it guarantees that the algorithm is sound even after we remove the heaviest part of the constraints used in our initial reduction to BV logic. In addition, we use the decision strategy rather than constraints for heuristically optimizing the solution (w.r.t track utilization).

Furthermore, the underlying ideas behind graph-aware reasoning can be used to speed-up SAT-based approaches to other graph reachability problems, such as routing in the presence of design patterns [23] and cooperative path finding [28].

Section 6 of this work presents experimental results. We study the impact various aspects of our approach have on crafted bounded-path instances (available in [11]). In addition, we demonstrate that our approach solves a family of instances originating in the clock routing of modern Intel designs. Section 7 concludes our work.

2 Related Work and Preliminaries

The term clock routing is often associated with a routing scenario where the driver needs to be connected to *multiple* receivers within *the same net*, forming a tree wherein the delay from the driver to each receiver should be almost identical [13,31]. This scenario does not fall within the scope of this work.

The current solutions for MCR in IC [16,22] are designed for handling analog and mixed designs with exactly zero allowed skew (where *skew* is deviation in delay). The solution space explored in [16,22] is limited to cases where the number of wire segments in all nets is identical, and the length, layer and width of respective wires are identical. These limitations guarantee that the zero allowed skew requirement is met but are too restrictive for our setting. In particular, if the routing area is not rectangular (a common phenomenon in hierarchical designs with non-rectangular hierarchical block boundaries), none of the valid routing solutions are expected to conform to these limitations in a variety of test-cases. In addition, in our setting the allowed skew is greater than zero.

A propositional formula in Conjunctive Normal Form (CNF) is a conjunction/set of Boolean clauses, where each clause is a disjunction of literals and a literal is a Boolean variable or its negation. A SAT solver [8,20,27] receives a CNF formula and returns a satisfying assignment to its variables, if one exists. An eager BV solver [9,14] works by preprocessing the given BV formula [9,14,21], bit-blasting it to CNF and solving with SAT. We assume that the reader is familiar with the basics of modern SAT and eager BV solving. See [17] for a recent overview.

Propositional satisfiability has been applied to solving the NP-complete problem of FPGA routing since [30]. From [30] we borrow the idea of using connectivity constraints to ensure that two given nodes are connected. The core problem in MCR of routing with almost the same delay does not exist in FPGA routing.

A DPLL(T) [15] theory solver for reasoning about costs to ensure that any satisfying assignment lays within some user-given cost bound has been proposed in [10]. Conceptually, the added value of our approach lies in: (a) introducing the concept of a decision strategy which replaces constraints and *guides* the solver towards a good solution while meeting additional optimization goals, and (b) introducing graph-aware reasoning.

We need some graph theory-related notations. Given an undirected graph $G = (V, E)$, where each edge $e \in E$ is associated with a positive cost c_e, a source node $s \in V$, a target node $t \in V$, and a simple path π from s to t of cost c (where the cost of a path is the sum of the costs of its edges), π is the *longest* path if there is no path from s to t of cost greater than c. π is *bounded* in the given cost range $[c_{min}, c_{max}]$, if $c_{min} \leq c \leq c_{max}$. A vertex $v \in V$ is *internal* if it is neither a source nor a target. We denote by $S = \sum_{e \in E} c_e$ the sum of the costs of all the edges in the graph. Let $m = (c_{max} + c_{min})/2$ be the middle of the cost range. Then the *actual skew* $k = |c - m|/(c_{max} - m)$ is the deviation of the generated path's cost from the middle. Sometimes the cost range is provided as a pair consisting of the *target cost* tc and the *allowed skew* a, which is equivalent to the cost range $[(1 - a) * tc, (1 + a) * tc]$.

We define a grid graph next. Let I be the infinite graph whose vertex set consists of all points of the plane with integer coordinates and in which two vertices are connected if the Euclidean distance between them is equal to 1. A *grid graph* is a finite, node-induced sub-graph of I. A vertex v in a grid graph is uniquely determined by its coordinates (v_x, v_y). A *vertical tracki* or a *horizontal tracki* comprises vertices whose x-coordinate or y-coordinate, respectively, is i. The maximal degree of a vertex in a grid graph is 4. An edge in a grid graph is either *vertical*, if the x-coordinates of its vertices are identical, or, otherwise, *horizontal*. The grid graph G is *mainly vertical* if most of its edges are vertical, otherwise it is *mainly horizontal*. Figure 4a on page 13 is an example of a mainly vertical grid graph. A vertex $v = (v_x, v_y)$ is to the `north/south/east/west` of $u = (u_x, u_y)$ if $v_y > u_y / v_y < u_y / v_x > u_x / v_x < u_x$, respectively.

Finally, we provide some relevant complexity results. Let *longest-path* be the problem of finding a longest path. Longest-path is NP-hard even for an unweighted graph, since Hamiltonian-path is trivially reducible to longest-path (see, e.g., [18]). Moreover, Hamiltonian-path, and thus longest-path, is NP-hard even for an unweighted grid graph [19]. Clearly, finding a longest path in a weighted graph and a weighted grid graph is also NP-hard. Longest-path is polynomial for some special grid graph classes, including *solid* grid graphs, where all of the bounded faces have area one (that is, the grid has no "holes") [29].

3 Matching Constrained Routing in Clock Routing

Let *net* be a subset of vertices in a 3-dimensional grid. *Routing* is about connecting all the vertices for each net with wires, where intersecting and/or touching wires which belong to different nets is not allowed (once the vertices have been connected the wiring is also considered to be part of the net).

Consider our more specific setting. Let $\{n_0, n_1, \ldots, n_k\}$ be a set of nets, where each net comprises the *driver* (source vertex) and the *receiver* (target vertex). First, as in any routing, in MCR one must connect the driver to the receiver for each net without intersection. Second, in MCR the delay must be similar for each net up to an allowed skew, where the *delay* is the amount of time it takes for the signal to travel from the driver to the receiver.

In our setting, the routing can use two adjacent x-y planes of the 3-dimensional grid only, where one plane is called the *horizontal metal* and the other is the *vertical metal.* The wires in the horizontal/vertical metal must lay along the horizontal/vertical tracks only, respectively. The two metals can be connected (with so-called *vias*). Superimposing the two metals reduces the problem space to a two-dimensional grid graph, where each intersection between available sub-tracks induces a vertex as shown in Fig. 1.

The routing delay depends on the length of the wires and the physical properties of the metals used. To model the similar delay requirement, we associate each edge with a cost proportional to the length of the wire represented by the edge, multiplied by a constant C_h or C_v, depending on whether the edge is horizontal or vertical. The ratio between constants C_h and C_v represents the difference in delay between the horizontal and vertical metals.

To generate routing with similar delay for the given set of nets, we proceed as follows. For each net independently we find the shortest path connecting its driver to its receiver. We then select as a *reference cost (RC)* the cost of the *longest* shortest path π_{rc} connecting the driver to the receiver for some net n_{rc}. π_{rc} comprises the solution for n_{rc}. Then, for each remaining net we formulate and solve a *separate* bounded-path instance, with the target cost being the RC and the allowed skew being user given (e.g., 2.5 %), where sub-tracks occupied by previously laid out nets are not part of the problem, as shown in Fig. 1. Hence the resulting grid graphs are normally not solid.

Moreover, as is the case with other routing algorithms, the router is requested to use as few tracks as possible. It is also desirable to minimize the actual skew. Both of these requirements are naturally translated into similar requirements for the bounded-path solver. Both are not strict in the sense that a good enough rather than the optimal solution is required.

4 Reducing Bounded-Path to Bit-Vector Reasoning

This section shows that bounded-path is NP-hard, and provides an encoding of bounded-path into BV logic. We start with Proposition 1, which shows that bounded-path is NP-hard by reducing longest-path to a binary search over

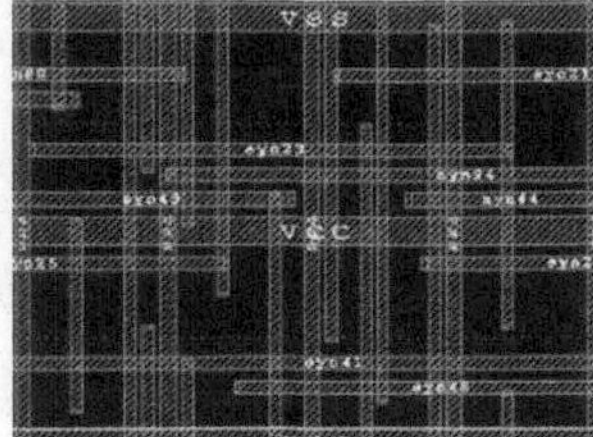

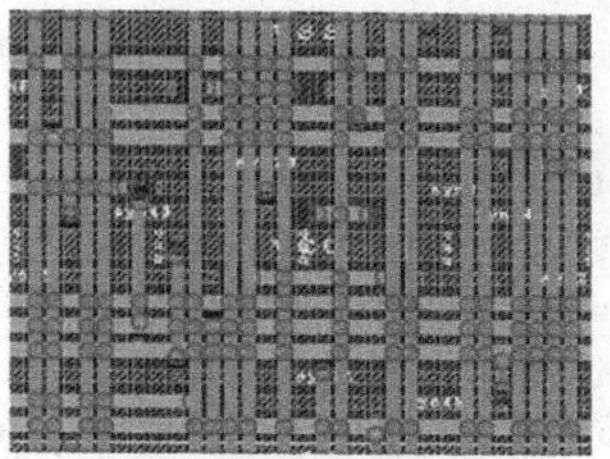

Fig. 1. Reducing the physical design problem (left) to a grid graph (right). On the left we see a bird's-eye view on a piece of layout with some of the vertical and horizontal tracks already occupied by wires. On the right we see the grid graph generation process. Legal sub-tracks are formed in non-occupied track parts, not too close to wires ends. Intersections and edge points of the legal sub-tracks are the vertices in the resulting grid graph. Edges are induced by the connections between the vertices.

the entire cost range, where each invocation solves bounded-path. Proposition 1 holds for any graph class for which longest-path is NP-hard, including weighted grid graphs induced by MCR. The extended version of this work [12] details the proof of Proposition 1 and provides lower-level examples of our encoding, which is introduced next.

Proposition 1. *The bounded path problem is NP-hard.*

We propose a reduction of bounded-path to bit-vector (BV) logic. Given an instance of bounded-path, our encoding ensures that a BV solver will output SAT and return a bounded path iff such exists.

We call an edge/vertex *active* iff it appears on the path from s to t and *inactive* otherwise. Consider now Fig. 2.

First, we associate each edge e and vertex v with a Boolean variable a_e and a_v, respectively, to represent whether the edge or the vertex, respectively, is active (items 1a and 1b in Fig. 2). The set of active vertices and edges comprise the bounded path returned by the solver for a satisfiable problem. The variables c_v and dir_e, discussed next, are intended to contain meaningful values for active edges and vertices only.

Second, each vertex v is associated with a BV variable c_v which represents the cost of the path from the source s to v if v is active (item 2a in Fig. 2). The width of c_v for each v is set to $\lceil log_2 S \rceil + 1$ to be able, in the worst case, to accommodate the cost of all the edges S without overflow.

Third, each edge e is associated with a Boolean variable representing its direction dir_e (item 2b in Fig. 2). The direction dir_e is intended to contain 0 for $e = (v, u)$ iff v is closer to s than u on the constructed path from s to t, in which case we say that e is *v-outgoing* and *u-incoming*. The other option is that $dir_e = 1$, and we say that e is *u-outgoing* and *v-incoming*.

Next, we introduce the constraints. They can be classified into connectivity constraints and cost constraints.

Connectivity constraints guarantee that a valid path of an arbitrary cost from s to t is constructed by the solver. Given a vertex v, let the set of v's *neighbors* be the set of edges touching v. Constraint 3a ensures that if an edge $e = (v, u)$ is active, then both v and u are active, while constraint 3b ensures that each vertex has a proper number of active neighbors. Specifically, an inactive vertex has no active neighbors. The source and the target vertices have one active neighbor each, while an internal active vertex has two active neighbors.

Figure 2 contains a high-level representation of constraint 3b's encoding. The actual encoding requires a solver supporting *conditional cardinality constraints* of the form $a \rightarrow \texttt{exactly}_k N$ (that is, if a Boolean a holds, then exactly k out of the set of Boolean variables N hold), where k is either 0, 1, or, 2 and N can be as large as the maximal vertex degree. While such constraints are not part of the standard BV language [4], an eager SMT solver can easily be extended to support them. This can be done by encoding the cardinality constraint $\texttt{exactly}_k N$ as a set of clauses (the problem is well-studied; see [7] for an overview) and then adding the selector literal $\neg a$ to each clause. Note that in a grid graph, the maximal degree of any vertex is 4, hence conditional cardinality constraints can be expressed with just a few clauses.

Consider now the cost constraints. They ensure that the cost of the constructed path falls within the specified cost range.

Constraints 4a to 4c guarantee that the direction is set correctly for any active edge. Namely, constraint 4a ensures that the active edge touching the source s must be s-outgoing, while constraint 4b ensures that the active edge touching the target t must be t-incoming (note that connectivity constraints guarantee that there is one and only one active edge touching the source and the target). Constraint 4c guarantees that if an internal vertex v is active, it has one v-incoming and one v-outgoing edge.

Finally, constraints 4d to 4f ensure that the eventual cost falls within the specified range. The cost is 0 for the source (constraint 4d) and it falls within the user-given range for the target (constraint 4f). The cost is propagated through the path's vertices taking advantage of the fact that the previous vertex is available through the direction of the incoming edge (constraint 4e).

5 Graph-Aware Solving

This section introduces graph-aware reasoning that enhances the eager approach to BV solving. In our new approach, the BV solver is provided with the connectivity variables and constraints only; the cost variables and constraints are omitted, thus substantially reducing the size of the problem. Our graph-aware decision strategy ensures that the path returned will still be bounded.

5.1 Graph-Aware Solving with Augmented Conflict Analysis

Consider Algorithm 1 which comprises the algorithmic framework of our approach. The algorithm contains five functions:

Algorithm 1. Graph-Aware Solving

```
function SOLVE(Graph G, Source s, Target t, Cost c_min, Cost c_max)
    For every vertex v, compute the minimal cost m(v) to t with Dijkstra
    Generate connectivity constraints and bit-blast to SAT
    tc:=(c_max + c_min)/2
    P:= []; l:=s; curr_cost:=0; stage:=init
    loop
        s:= Run the SAT solver
        if s = SAT then
            return P
        else if s = UNSAT then
            return No path exists
        else                                                ▷ s = UNKNOWN
            Refine by providing the clause ¬P to the SAT solver and restart the SAT solver

function ONDECISION(Decision level d)
    if stage ≠ shortestp and curr_cost + m(l) ≥ tc then
        stage:=shortestp
    if stage = shortestp then
        N:= unassigned edges in nbors(l)
        return e ∈ N minimizing c_e + m(other_ver(e, l))
    e:= NEXTEDGE
    l:=PATHPUSHBACK(e,d)
    return a_e

function ONIMPLICATION(Literal l)
    if l ≡ a_e for e = (l, v) then
        l:= PATHPUSHBACK(e, not_a_decision)

function ONBACKTRACK(Decision level d)
    {P, l, curr_cost, stage} :=backtrack_point(d)

function PATHPUSHBACK(Edge e, Decision level d)
    if d ≠ not_a_decision then
        backtrack_point(d):= {P, l, curr_cost, stage}
    curr_cost:=curr_cost + c_e
    Push e to the back of P
    u:=other_ver(e, l)
    if curr_cost + m(u) > c_max or (u = t and curr_cost < c_min) then
        Stop the SAT solver and have it return UNKNOWN
    if u = t then
        Stop the SAT solver and have it return SAT
    return u
```

Algorithm 2. Grid-Aware Strategies

```
function GetUnassignedEdge(Direction d)
    if e = (l, u) or e = (u, l) ∈ E, such that u is to the d from v, exists and unassigned then
        return e
    else
        return ∅
function ChooseDirOrdered
    for all d ∈ D do
        if GetUnassignedEdge(d) ≠ ∅ then
            return GetUnassignedEdge(d)
    return ∅
function GridAwareNextEdge
    if stage = init then
        if ChooseDirOrdered({south, west}) ≠ ∅ then
            return ChooseDirOrdered(south, west)
        stage:=spend
    if stage = spend then
        if l_x = t_x then
            stage:=sec_init
            sec_init_main_dir:= s to the south of t ? south : north
        else
            d:= ChooseDirOrdered({north, south, east, west})
            if d = west and there is no simple path from l to t then
                Stop the SAT solver and have it return unknown
            return d
    if stage = sec_init then
        if ChooseDirOrdered({sec_init_main_dir, east}) ≠ ∅ then
            return ChooseDirOrdered({sec_init_main_dir, east})
        stage:=sec_spend
    if stage = sec_spend then
        d:= ChooseDirOrdered({north, south, west, east})
        if d = east and there is no simple path from l to t then
            Stop the SAT solver and have it return unknown
        return d
```

1. Solve: the main function invoked by the user.
2. OnDecision: this function is invoked by the underlying SAT solver to get a decision literal when it has to take a decision.
3. OnImplication: invoked by the SAT solver whenever it derives a new implication (that is, whenever a value for a variable is forced by propagation).
4. OnBacktrack: invoked by the SAT solver whenever it backtracks.
5. PathPushBack: a multi-functional auxiliary function, explained later.

Solve receives the graph G, the source s, the target t, the minimal cost c_{min} and the maximal cost c_{max}. It returns a path P from s to t, whose cost is bounded by $[c_{min}, c_{max}]$, if available. The function starts at line 2 by computing

1. Connectivity variables
   (a) Boolean a_e: a_e is 1 iff $e \in E$ is active.
   (b) Boolean a_v: a_v is 1 iff $v \in V$ is active.
2. Cost variables
   (a) BV c_v: the cost of the path from s to v
   (b) Boolean dir_e: the direction of $e \in E$
3. Connectivity constraints
   (a) a_e implies a_v and a_u, where $e = (v, u)$
   (b) Each vertex v has exactly n active neighbor edges, where:
      i. n=0 if the vertex is inactive
      ii. n=1 if v is the source or the target
      iii. n=2 if v is an active internal vertex
4. Cost constraints
   (a) The active edge touching the source s is s-outgoing
   (b) The active edge touching the target t is t-incoming
   (c) For every active internal vertex v, there must be one v-outgoing and one v-incoming active edge
   (d) $c_s = 0$
   (e) $c_v = c_e + c_u$, given an active internal vertex v, where e, touching v and u, is the v-incoming edge
   (f) $c_{min} \leq c_t \leq c_{max}$

Fig. 2. Translating bounded-path to BV

the minimal cost $m(v)$ from each node v to the target t with one invocation of the Dijkstra algorithm. As we will see, the minimal costs are required for the decision strategies and conflict analysis. At line 3, connectivity constraints are generated and bit-blasted to SAT (word-level preprocessing can also be applied before bit-blasting). The SAT solver is not yet invoked at this stage. At line 4, the target cost tc, comprising the middle of the range $[c_{min}, c_{max}]$, is computed. The algorithm will try to build a path from s to t whose cost is as close as possible to tc (in accordance with the actual skew minimization requirement).

The main loop of the algorithm starts at line 6. It uses the following variables, initialized at line 5:

1. P holds the edges of a simple path starting at s. If the algorithm completes successfully, P will hold a path from s to t bounded by $[c_{min}, c_{max}]$.
2. l contains the latest vertex of the generated path from s to t.
3. *curr_cost* contains the overall cost of (the edges of) P so far.
4. *stage* contains the current stage of the decision strategy (explained later in Sects. 5.2 and 5.3).

The main loop invokes the SAT solver at line 7. The solver may return three possible results. If the solver returns SAT, then P is guaranteed to contain a bounded path from s to t; thus P is returned to the user. If it returns UNSAT, there is no solution, and a special value is returned to the user.

In addition, the solver may return the value UNKNOWN, meaning that a graph conflict was encountered and refinement is required. A *graph conflict* is a situation where no path from s to t with prefix P and cost bounded by $[c_{min}, c_{max}]$ exists. Our algorithm may identify three types of graph conflicts, shown in Fig. 3 and discussed later. When a graph conflict is encountered, the algorithm refines the problem by adding a new *graph conflict clause* which prevents regeneration of the current path P. The graph conflict clause contains activation variables corresponding to the edges in the path P, negated (the clause can be optionally minimized by removing edges from its tail as long as the conflict still occurs). Then the algorithm continues to the next iteration of the loop. After restarting (where by restarting we mean backtracking to decision level 0), the algorithm will pick the same decisions until but not including the latest edge, which has to be different in order to satisfy the graph conflict clause.

5.2 Interactive SAT Solving

We continue the presentation of Algorithm 1. Given a vertex v, let $nbors(v)$ be the set of v's neighbors (recall that v's neighbors are the edges touching v). Given a vertex v and an edge $e \in nbors(v)$, the *other vertex* of e, $other\_ver(e, v)$, is the vertex $u \neq v$, touched by e.

Consider the function ONDECISION, invoked by the SAT solver to pick the next decision. It receives the current decision level d and returns an unassigned literal, which is picked by the SAT solver as the next decision literal.

At each stage of the algorithm, let the *cost low bound (CLB)* be $c(P) + m(l)$, that is, the cost of the current path P from s to the latest vertex l plus the pre-computed minimal cost from l to t. Once CLB is greater than or equal to the target cost, the algorithm enters the *shortest path stage* `shortestp` (see lines 15 to 16), where the cost of any path from s to t with prefix P cannot be lower than the target cost. Hence, the algorithm picks an edge so as to have CLB as low as possible after the edge is picked (lines 17 to 19). Note that if the pre-computed shortest path is still not occupied, the algorithm will arrive at t, where the path cost is exactly the target cost. If the shortest path stage is not entered, ONDECISION invokes a core decision strategy (described in Sect. 5.3) to pick the next unassigned decision literal. The choice is crucial for performance, but does not alter the correctness.

After an edge is picked, ONDECISION invokes the auxiliary function PATHPUSHBACK, providing it the edge e and the decision level d. Normally, PATHPUSHBACK pushes e to the end of P and returns the new latest vertex l, and then ONDECISION returns a_e as the next decision literal (all this is unless PATHPUSHBACK discovers a graph conflict or finds that the problem is satisfied). We will get back to the functionality of PATHPUSHBACK a bit later.

The function ONIMPLICATION is invoked by the SAT solver whenever its Boolean Constraint Propagation (BCP) learns a new implication. It receives the implied literal. If the literal activates an edge e touching the latest vertex l, then e is pushed to P using PATHPUSHBACK and l is updated accordingly.

Now consider PATHPUSHBACK. First, if the function is invoked when a new decision is taken, it creates a backtrack point at decision level d (lines 29 to 30) so as to let the algorithm (or, more specifically, function ONBACKTRACK) restore all the relevant variables when (and if) the SAT solver backtracks to decision level d. Creating the backtrack point and backtracking whenever required is essential to maintaining the consistency of the algorithm. Then PATHPUSHBACK updates the current cost *curr_cost* and pushes e to the end of P.

Line 34 of PATHPUSHBACK checks conditions 1 and 2 in Fig. 3 that might trigger a graph conflict (condition 3 is discussed in Sect. 5.3). First, a graph conflict occurs when the target t is reached, but the cost is not bounded. Note that triggering a graph conflict on this occasion is essential to guaranteeing the soundness of the algorithm. Second, a graph conflict is identified when CLB exceeds the maximal value c_{max} for any non-target vertex. This is not necessary for soundness, but advisable for pruning the search space, thus improving performance. If a graph conflict is identified, PATHPUSHBACK stops the SAT solver and asks it to return UNKNOWN.

If no graph conflict is identified, the algorithm checks whether the target is reached within the required cost, in which case it stops the SAT solver and has it return SAT. Finally, if none of the stopping conditions were triggered, PATHPUSHBACK returns the new latest vertex on the path.

1. P connects s to t, but P's cost is not within $[c_{min}, c_{max}]$
2. The CLB $c(P) + m(l)$ exceeds the maximal value c_{max} and $l \neq t$
3. The target t is no longer reachable (see an example in Fig. 4a)

Fig. 3. Graph conflict conditions

5.3 Core Decision Strategies

This section proposes the core decision strategies for Algorithm 1. We start by proposing the following simple *graph-aware* strategy, applicable to finding a bounded path in any graph: *go away from the target until the shortest path stage is entered.* This is done by always preferring an edge e such that CLB, after picking e, is the lowest possible. Unfortunately, this simple strategy cannot be used for MCR in our setting, since it ignores the track minimization requirement.

Recall the grid graph related definitions from Sect. 2. We propose a *grid-aware* decision strategy for the problem of finding a bounded path from $s = (s_x, s_y)$ to $t = (t_x, t_y)$ in a grid graph G, where the maximal x-coordinate/y-coordinate is X/Y, respectively. We make the following assumptions regarding the input problem without restricting the generality: (a) G is mainly vertical; (b) $s_y < t_y$ or ($s_y = t_y$ and $|s_y| \leq |Y - s_y|$); (c) $s_x \leq t_x$. Any grid graph can be transformed to meet these conditions by rotating G by $90°$, if necessary, to meet the first condition, and choosing the point (0,0) out of the 4 corners to meet the last two conditions.

Our grid-aware strategy is designed to find a bounded path in a grid graph, keeping two main goals in mind:

1. *Graph conflicts-awareness*: try to avoid graph-aware conflicts and identify them when they cannot be avoided.
2. *Track minimization*: try to minimize the number of tracks in the path.

The function GRIDAWARENEXTEDGE in Algorithm 2 implements the strategy (it is intended to be called at line 20 in Algorithm 1). The algorithm has five stages, where the shortest path stage `shortestp` is entered whenever CLB is greater than or equal to the target cost at any other stage as discussed in Sect. 5.2 and shown in Algorithm 1. The remaining four stages are explained below.

During the initial stage `init`, the algorithm goes towards the corner $(0, 0)$, that is, southwards and westwards, whenever possible. See Fig. 4a for an illustration and lines 12 to 15 in Algorithm 2 for the implementation of stage `init`. The implementation applies an auxiliary function CHOOSEDIRORDERED, which receives an ordered sequence of directions $D = \{d_1, d_2, \ldots\}$. It returns an unassigned edge e touching l, such that $other\_ver(e, l)$ is to the d_i of l, where i is the lowest possible index, such that e exists and is unassigned. After the `init` stage, the algorithm enters the `spend` stage.

During the `spend` stage, the algorithm tries to "spend the cost" using as few tracks as possible by moving along the vertical tracks coast-to-coast whenever possible (recall that the vertical tracks have more edges than the horizontal tracks by our convention). When moving along a vertical track is no longer possible, the algorithm turns towards the target t (in order not to block the way to t). This stage can finish with the following possible outcomes:

1. The algorithm is turned away to the west by the SAT solver's propagation and there is no longer any path from l to t (line 22), where the latter condition is checked using DFS. In this case, a graph conflict corresponding to condition 3 in Fig. 3 is triggered, and the algorithm stops the SAT solver. An example of such an outcome is shown in Fig. 4a. In this case, a conflict clause is generated by Algorithm 1. After restarting the SAT solver, the algorithm follows the same path as before until an implication in the new conflict clause turns it to the east and the graph conflict is avoided, as shown in Fig. 4b.
2. PATHPUSHBACK in Algorithm 1 halts the main loop of Algorithm 1 due to a graph conflict or when a bounded path from s to t is found (the latter is an unlikely corner case).
3. The shortest path stage `shortestp` is entered.
4. The vertical track of t is reached (line 17), in which case the second initialization stage `sec_init` is entered.

During the second initial stage `sec_init` (lines 25 to 28), the algorithm goes to one of the eastern corners according to the relative position of l with respect to t. When moving to the corner is no longer possible, the algorithm enters the second spend stage **sec_spend**.

During the second spend stage **sec_spend** (lines 29 to 33), the algorithm spends the cost similarly to the first spend stage **spend**, except that it moves eastwards and does not stop when the vertical track of t is reached. In our example in Fig. 4b, stage **sec_spend** is finished when CLB becomes equal to the target cost and the shortest path stage is entered.

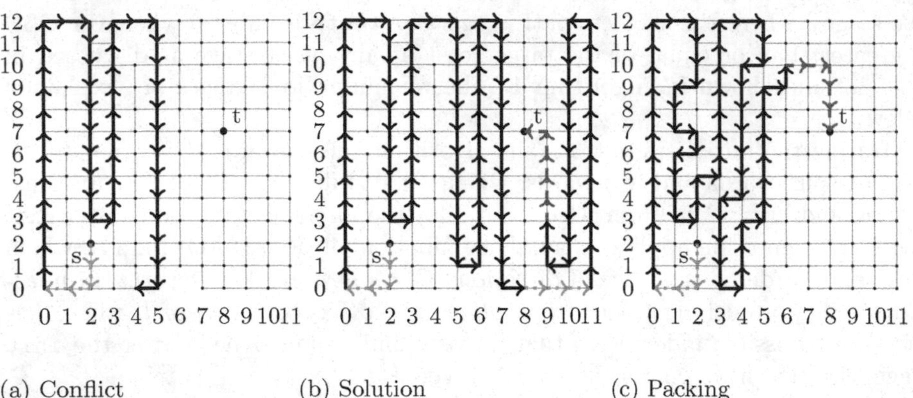

(a) Conflict (b) Solution (c) Packing

Fig. 4. Application of the grid-aware strategies. Assume the cost of each edge is 1 and the requested cost range is [70, 80]. The red dotted edges correspond to the initial stages **init** and **sec_init**, the black solid edges correspond to the cost spend stages **spend** and **sec_spend**, while the blue dashed edges correspond to the shortest path stage **shortestp**. A graph conflict situation is shown in Fig. 4a; the eventual solution after the conflict is handled is shown in Fig. 4b; the packing effect is shown in Fig. 4c.

Remark 1. Assume the grid-aware strategy can go either eastwards or along the vertical track during the **spend** stage after circumventing an obstacle. Consider the choices at vertex (2, 9) in Fig. 4a for an example. Algorithm 2 prefers continuing along the vertical track. An alternative would be preferring to go westwards (implementation-wise, that would require replacing the parameters to ChooseDirOrdered at line 21 in Algorithm 2 by {**west**, **north**, **south**, **east**}). Similarly, such an algorithm would prefer going eastwards whenever possible during the **sec_spend** stage. We call this alternative approach *packing*. Its impact is shown in Fig. 4c. Packing is designed to use all the available space in the grid graph, thus it is better suited to cases where there are many obstacles or the target cost is high. However, it comes at the price of excessive track usage. Note the "ripple effect" of occupying the horizontal tracks 6,5 and 4, created by the turn westwards at point (2, 6).

Remark 2. Our approach is expected to generate non-optimal results in terms of track minimization for a generic rectilinear polygon as compared to a (possibly holed) mainly vertical rectangle, since some of the polygon's rectangles might be mainly horizontal (even though, *most* of the edges are vertical). We leave designing an adaptive strategy that would change the explored dimension on-the-fly to future work.

6 Experimental Results

First, we present experiments conducted on artificially generated test benchmarks. The benchmarks and detailed results are available in [11]. The benchmarks comprise diversified parametrized instances of bounded-path in grid graphs, generated as follows:

for all $t \in \{10^1, 10^2, 10^3\}$ **do**
  for all $d \in \{0, 0.25, 0.5, 0.75, 1\}$ **do**
    for all $vcost \in \{102, 104, 106, 108, 110, 112, 114, 116, 118, 120\}$ **do**
      for all $r \in \{0.1, 0.2, 0.3, 0.4, 0.5\}$ **do**
        $c{:=}S \times r$ ▷ S is the overall edges cost
        Generate a square grid of size $t{\times}t$ with randomly set source and target. Remove any node v (along with the edges $nbors(v)$) with probability d/t. Set the cost of each horizontal and vertical edge to 100 and $vcost$, respectively. Set the target cost to c and the allowed skew to 2.5 %.

The parameters were selected as follows so as to diversify the instances and to be able to analyze various aspects of the algorithms' performance: (a) t stands for the number of tracks along each dimension, hence $t \times t$ is the grid size; (b) d determines the dilution rate. We remove $(d/t)t^2 = dt$ vertices on average at random, so as to defragment the grid graph. (c) $vcost$ determines the vertical cost, while the horizontal cost is static; (d) r determines the target cost as a function of the overall edges cost S.

We compared the following algorithms, implemented on top of Intel's eager SMT solver Hazel: (a) `BV`: reduction to BV, described in Sect. 4. (b) `Graph`: Algorithm 1 with the graph-aware strategy described in the first paragraph of Sect. 5.3. (c) `Grid`: Algorithm 1 with the grid-aware strategy in Algorithm 2 (d) `GridP`: Algorithm 1 with the grid-aware strategy Algorithm 2 and packing (recall Remark 1 in Sect. 5.3).

We used machines with 32Gb of memory running Intel® Xeon® processors with 3Ghz CPU frequency. The time-out was set to 600 sec.

Table 1 presents the number of instances solved within the time-out per grid size. Table 2 shows the overall number of tracks used for all the algorithms (except `BV`) on benchmarks solved by all these algorithms. Tables 3 and 4 show the number of instances `Grid` and `GridP`, respectively, solve per each combination of r and d values for $s = 10^2$. The main conclusions are as follows.

Plain translation to BV does not scale even to $100{\times}100$ grids. To validate that this result is independent of the underlying solver, in an additional experiment, we verified that the two leading SAT solvers Lingeling [5,6] and Glucose 4.0 [1,2] can solve none of the CNF instances corresponding to benchmarks with $t = 100$ and $d \in \{0, 1\}$. The CNF instances, available in [11], were dumped by Hazel

Table 1. Solved per grid size

s	#	BV	Graph	GridP	Grid
10	250	138	217	223	200
100	250	0	171	226	151
1000	250	0	158	194	154
Sum	750	138	546	643	505

Table 2. Tracks used in %

s	Graph	GridP	Grid
10	58	56	45
100	44	59	22
1000	43	51	21

Table 3. `Grid`: solved out of 10 instances per cell, given $r\&d$ for $s = 10^2$

r/d	0	0.25	0.5	0.75	1
0.1	10	9	9	8	10
0.2	10	10	8	7	7
0.3	10	9	8	6	2
0.4	10	8	0	0	0
0.5	10	0	0	0	0

Table 4. `GridP`: solved out of 10 instances per cell, given $r\&d$ for $s = 10^2$

r/d	0	0.25	0.5	0.75	1
0.1	10	10	10	10	10
0.2	10	10	10	10	10
0.3	10	10	10	10	10
0.4	10	10	10	10	10
0.5	10	7	5	3	1

after the world-level preprocessing stage. We could not run external BV solvers as is, since they do not support conditional cardinality constraints.

`GridP` is the most robust strategy as it solves the most test instances. Moreover, when the target cost is not too high ($r < 0.5$), `GridP` solves all the instances for $s = 10^2$. `Grid` cannot solve instances with high target costs and/or dilution rates. Hence, as expected, packing is useful for handling grids with many obstacles. The performance of `Graph` is surprisingly good for such a simple strategy.

As expected, `Grid` is by far the best algorithm in terms of track minimization.

We also conducted experiments on a family of real-world instances generated by Intel's clock routing flow. The family has 51 benchmarks. The number of edges in the benchmarks ranges from 70,492 to 4,436,948, with an average of 1,203,631, while the number of vertices ranges between 44,320 and 2,837,800 with the average of 780,782. The results can be summarized as follows: (a) `BV` solved none of the 51 instances, `Grid` and `Graph` solved all the instances, while `GridP` solved 49 instances. (b) `Grid` used 285 tracks overall, `Graph` used 863 tracks, while `GridP` used 387 tracks. Hence, unlike in the case of randomized test instances, it pays to use `Grid` on real-world instances. `Grid` is successfully applied for clock routing automation at Intel.

7 Conclusion

We have presented an SMT-based approach to automating the matching constrained routing problem that has emerged in the clock routing of integrated circuits. We reduced the problem to bounded-path, that is, the problem of finding a simple path, whose cost is bounded by a user-given range, connecting two given vertices in an undirected positively weighted graph. We have shown that bounded-path can be solved by applying an eager bit-vector solver, but only if the solver is enhanced with a dedicated graph-aware decision strategy and graph-aware conflict analysis. Our solution scales to graphs having millions of edges and vertices. It has been successfully deployed at Intel as part of the core engine for automatic clock routing.

Acknowledgments. We are grateful to Nachum Dershowitz for suggesting and proving that bounded-path is NP-hard (the paper's proof differs from Nachum's proof). We thank Paul Inbar, Eran Talmor, and Vadim Ryvchin for their useful comments.

References

1. Audemard, G., Simon, L.: The Glucose SAT Solver. http://www.labri.fr/perso/lsimon/glucose/. Accessed: 05–January–2015
2. Audemard, G., Simon, L.: GLUCOSE 2.1: aggressive, but reactive, clause database management, dynamic restarts (system description). In: Pragmatics of SAT 2012 (POS 2012), June 2012
3. Barrett, C., Donham, J.: Combining SAT methods with non-clausal decision heuristics. Electr. Notes Theor. Comput. Sci. **125**(3), 3–12 (2005)
4. Barrett, C., Stump, A., Tinelli, C.: The SMT-LIB Standard: version 2.0. In: Gupta, A., Kroening, D., (eds.) Proceedings of the 8th International Workshop on Satisfiability Modulo Theories, Edinburgh (2010)
5. Biere, A.: Lingeling, Plingeling and Treengeling. http://fmv.jku.at/lingeling/. Accessed: 05–January–2015
6. Biere, A.: Lingeling, plingeling and treengeling entering the SAT competition. In: Proceedings of SAT Competition 2013, p. 51 (2013)
7. Biere, A., Le Berre, D., Lonca, E., Manthey, N.: Detecting cardinality constraints in CNF. In: Sinz, C., Egly, U. (eds.) SAT 2014. LNCS, vol. 8561, pp. 285–301. Springer, Heidelberg (2014)
8. Biere, A., Heule, M., Van Maaren, H., Walsh, T.: Handbook of Satisfiability, volume 185 of Frontiers in Artificial Intelligence and Applications. IOS Press, Amsterdam (2009)
9. Brummayer, R., Biere, A.: Boolector: An efficient SMT solver for bit-vectors and arrays. In: Kowalewski, S., Philippou, A. (eds.) TACAS 2009. LNCS, vol. 5505, pp. 174–177. Springer, Heidelberg (2009)
10. Cimatti, A., Franzén, A., Griggio, A., Sebastiani, R., Stenico, C.: Satisfiability modulo the theory of costs: foundations and applications. In: Esparza, J., Majumdar, R. (eds.) TACAS 2010. LNCS, vol. 6015, pp. 99–113. Springer, Heidelberg (2010)
11. Erez, A., Nadel, A.: Finding bounded path in graph using SMT for automatic clock routing: Benchmarks and detailed results. http://goo.gl/sM4xxz
12. Amit Erez and Alexander Nadel. Finding bounded path in graph using SMT for automatic clock routing: Extended version. https://goo.gl/jtq669
13. Fishburn, J.P.: Clock skew optimization. IEEE Trans. Comput. **39**(7), 945–951 (1990)
14. Ganesh, V., Dill, D.L.: A decision procedure for bit-vectors and arrays. In: Damm, W., Hermanns, H. (eds.) CAV 2007. LNCS, vol. 4590, pp. 519–531. Springer, Heidelberg (2007)
15. Ganzinger, H., Hagen, G., Nieuwenhuis, R., Oliveras, A., Tinelli, C.: DPLL(T): fast decision procedures. In: Alur, R., Peled, D.A. (eds.) CAV 2004. LNCS, vol. 3114, pp. 175–188. Springer, Heidelberg (2004)

16. Gao, Q., Yao, H., Zhou, Q., Cai, Y.: A novel detailed routing algorithm with exact matching constraint for analog and mixed signal circuits. In: Proceedings of the 12th International Symposium on Quality Electronic Design (ISQED 2011), pp. 36–41. IEEE, Santa Clara, 14–16 March 2011
17. Hadarean, L.: An Efficient and Trustworthy Theory Solver for Bit-vectors in Satisfiability Modulo Theories. dissertation, New York University (2015)
18. Ioannidou, K., Nikolopoulos, S.D.: The longest path problem is polynomial on cocomparability graphs. Algorithmica **65**(1), 177–205 (2013)
19. Itai, A., Papadimitriou, C.H., Szwarcfiter, J.L.: Hamilton paths in grid graphs. SIAM J. Comput. **11**(4), 676–686 (1982)
20. Moskewicz, M.W., Madigan, C.F., Zhao, Y., Zhang, L., Chaff, S.M.: Engineering an efficient SAT solver. In: Proceedings of the 38th Design Automation Conference (DAC 2001), pp. 530–535. ACM, Las Vegas, 18–22 June 2001
21. Nadel, A.: Bit-vector rewriting with automatic rule generation. In: Biere, A., Bloem, R. (eds.) CAV 2014. LNCS, vol. 8559, pp. 663–679. Springer, Heidelberg (2014)
22. Ozdal, M.M., Hentschke, R.F.: Maze routing algorithms with exact matching constraints for analog and mixed signal designs. In: 2012 IEEE/ACM International Conference on Computer-Aided Design (ICCAD 2012), pp. 130–136. IEEE, San Jose, 5–8 November 2012
23. Ryzhenko, N., Burns, S.: Standard cell routing via boolean satisfiability. In: Groeneveld, P., Sciuto, D., Hassoun, S., (eds.) The 49th Annual Design Automation Conference DAC 2012, pp. 603–612. ACM, San Francisco, 3–7 June 2012
24. Sabharwal, A.: Symchaff: a structure-aware satisfiability solver. In: Veloso, M.M., Kambhampati, S., (eds.) Proceedings, The Twentieth National Conference on Artificial Intelligence and the Seventeenth Innovative Applications of Artificial Intelligence Conference, pp. 467–474. AAAI Press / The MIT Press, Pittsburgh, 9–13 July 2005
25. Sherwani, N.A.: Algorithms for VLSI Physical Design Automation, Chap. 8, 3rd edn. Kluwer, The Netherlands (1998)
26. Sherwani, N.A.: Algorithms for VLSI Physical Design Automation, Chap. 11. Kluwer, The Netherlands (1988)
27. Marques Silva, J.P., Sakallah, K.A.: GRASP: a search algorithm for propositional satisfiability. IEEE Trans. Comput. **48**(5), 506–521 (1999)
28. Surynek, P.: A simple approach to solving cooperative path-finding as propositional satisfiability works well. In: Pham, D.-N., Park, S.-B. (eds.) PRICAI 2014. LNCS, vol. 8862, pp. 827–833. Springer, Heidelberg (2014)
29. Umans, C., Lenhart, W.: Hamiltonian cycles in solid grid graphs. In: Proceedings of the 38th Annual Symposium on Foundations of Computer Science 1997, pp. 496–505, October 1997
30. Wood, R.G., Rutenbar, R.A.: FPGA routing and routability estimation via Boolean satisfiability. pp. 222–231 (1998)
31. Wu, G., Jia, S., Wang, Y., Zhang, G.: An efficient clock tree synthesis method in physical design. In: IEEE International Conference of Electron Devices and Solid-State Circuits (EDSSC 2009), pp. 190–193, December 2009

Cutting the Mix

Jürgen Christ[1,2](✉) and Jochen Hoenicke[1]

[1] Department of Computer Science, University of Freiburg, Freiburg im Breisgau, Germany
{christj,hoenicke}@informatik.uni-freiburg.de

[2] Max Planck Institute for Software Systems (MPI-SWS), Kaiserslautern, Germany

Abstract. While linear arithmetic has been studied in the context of SMT individually for reals and integers, mixed linear arithmetic allowing comparisons between integer and real variables has not received much attention. For linear integer arithmetic, the cuts from proofs algorithm has proven to have superior performance on many benchmarks. In this paper we extend this algorithm to the mixed case where real and integer variables occur in the same linear constraint. Our algorithm allows for an easy integration into existing SMT solvers. Experimental evaluation of our prototype implementation inside the SMT solver SMTInterpol shows that this algorithm is successful on benchmarks that are hard for all existing solvers.

1 Introduction

The theory of linear arithmetic is fundamental in system modelling and verification. SMT solvers supported this theory from the beginning. In recent years, lots of work has been devoted to improve the support and performance for this theory [9,12,13,17]. Usually, two theories are supported for linear arithmetic: linear arithmetic over the rational/real numbers (LRA), and linear arithmetic over integers (LIA). While the first theory can be solved by the Simplex algorithm the latter needs more techniques to ensure that the solution has integer values. While each of the two theories has many applications for itself, some applications require both theories. An example for this is the verification of timed automata or hybrid systems where continuous variables are used for physical entities and integer variables for control. Also planning and scheduling problems require mixed integer and real arithmetic. While there exists some support for this theory, there is still room for improvement.

Boosting performance on satisfiability modulo mixed linear arithmetic broadens the applicability of SMT solvers. For linear integer arithmetic, the cuts from proofs algorithm [7] greatly improved the state of the art. On SMTLIB benchmarks with many real but few or no integer solutions, the algorithm significantly

This work is supported by the German Research Council (DFG) as part of the Transregional Collaborative Research Center "Automatic Verification and Analysis of Complex Systems" (SFB/TR14 AVACS).

D. Kroening and C.S. Păsăreanu (Eds.): CAV 2015, Part II, LNCS 9207, pp. 37–52, 2015.
DOI: 10.1007/978-3-319-21668-3_3

outperforms traditional techniques like the Omega test [18] or cutting plane techniques based on Gomory cuts. Improving the performance on mixed linear arithmetic is a next logical step to increase applicability of modern SMT solvers.

In this paper, we lift the cuts from proof algorithm from linear arithmetic over the integers to mixed linear arithmetic. We give a new technique to derive cuts in mixed linear arithmetic based on a basis transformation of the constraint system. We experimentally compare our implementation with other SMT solvers that support mixed linear arithmetic. This evaluation shows that our new technique is able to solve problems that cannot be solved by existing techniques.

Related Work. Only very few publications address mixed linear arithmetic in the context of SMT. Berezin et al. [3] present an extension of the Omega test to mixed arithmetic. The decision procedure splits the variables into real-valued variables and integer-valued variables. Then, it uses Fourier-Motzkin elimination for the real-valued variables and the Omega-test to eliminate the integer variables. The Fourier-Motzkin elimination usually produces an exponential blow-up of the input problem. The technique is therefore more memory intensive than our technique.

Dutertre and de Moura [9] present a way to compute mixed Gomory cuts in the context of the state of the art Simplex-based theory solver for linear arithmetic. The derivation is based on the current assignment, a row in the Simplex tableau, and non-trivial reasoning. Since Gomory cuts are used as theory lemmas in the proof of unsatisfiability, they have to be justified. This is especially important for proof producing or interpolating solvers. The derivation of Gomory cuts is much more involved than the simple technique presented here based on extended branches.

A lot of research exists in the context of MILP solvers. These solvers use a variety of different cuts (see [14,19] for details). MILP solvers use floating-point arithmetic making them imprecise and unstable [16]. Our technique is designed for integration into SMT solvers that typically use arbitrary precision arithmetic to ensure soundness. In the evaluation section, we do not compare against MILP solvers since these can be unsound due to rounding problems.

There are several techniques for solving linear integer arithmetic [4,10,11], some of which can be extended to mixed arithmetic, although we are not aware of any publications. A variation of the algorithm from [10] is used in MathSAT and CVC4. This is similar to ours but use a diophantine equation solver to generate the branch instead of the Hermite normal form.

2 Notation and Preliminaries

The algorithms in this paper are used to solve a system of linear inequalities. We use $\boldsymbol{x}$ to denote a vector of variables $x_1, \ldots, x_n$. Given a matrix $A \in \mathbb{Q}^{m \times n}$ and a vector $\boldsymbol{b} \in \mathbb{Q}^m$ we solve the problem $A\boldsymbol{x} \leq \boldsymbol{b}$. Here $\leq$ on vectors is defined component-wise. Strict inequalities can be expressed by allowing infinitesimal numbers in $\boldsymbol{b}$. However, we ignore strict inequalities in this paper to keep the presentation simple.

The variables $x_1, \ldots, x_n$ can be (depending on the problem) real or integer valued, i. e., we are interested in integer or real solutions of the above system. It is easy to see that for every real solution there is also a rational solution, so it is enough to distinguish between solutions in $\mathbb{Q}$ and $\mathbb{Z}$. We note that $A\boldsymbol{x} \leq \boldsymbol{b}$ is equivalent to $\lambda A\boldsymbol{x} \leq \lambda\boldsymbol{b}$ for $\lambda > 0$. Therefore we can w.l.o.g. assume that A is an integer matrix.

In the case of mixed arithmetic, we distinguish between rational-valued variables $x_1, \ldots, x_{n_1}$ and integer-valued variables $x_{n_1+1}, \ldots, x_n$. The goal is to find a rational solution for the first n_1 variables and an integer solution for the second $n_2 = n - n_1$ variables. Thus, the vector $\boldsymbol{x}$ is a vector consisting of real-valued variables and integer-valued variables.

In this paper we need the notion of nonsingular and unimodular matrices and the Hermite normal form. A matrix $U \in \mathbb{Q}^{n\times n}$ is *nonsingular* if $\det(U) \neq 0$. A matrix $U \in \mathbb{Z}^{n\times n}$ is *unimodular* if $|det(U)| = 1$. We remind the reader that a matrix is nonsingular if and only if it has an inverse $U^{-1} \in \mathbb{Q}^{n\times n}$ with $UU^{-1} = U^{-1}U = Id$, where Id denote the identity matrix. Moreover, a matrix $U \in \mathbb{Z}^{n\times n}$ is unimodular if and only if it has an inverse U^{-1} that is also an integer matrix.

A matrix $H \in \mathbb{Q}^{n\times n}$ is in *Hermite normal form*[1] if (i) H is lower triangular, (ii) $h_{ii} > 0$ for $1 \leq i \leq n$, and (iii) $h_{ij} \leq 0$ and $|h_{ij}| < h_{ii}$ for $j < i \leq n$. For every nonsingular integer matrix A there is a unique unimodular matrix U and a unique matrix H in Hermite normal form with $H = AU$. This also holds for rational matrices: If a nonsingular $A \in \mathbb{Q}^{n\times n}$ is given we can multiply it with $\lambda > 0$ such that $\lambda A \in \mathbb{Z}^{n\times n}$. Then the unique H', U with $H' = \lambda AU$ results in a unique $H = (1/\lambda)H'$ with $H = AU$. Note that since U is unimodular, the matrix H is an integer matrix if and only if A is an integer matrix.

3 Solving Linear Integer Arithmetic and Mixed Linear Arithmetic

We first review the state of the art in satisfiability solving modulo the theory of linear integer arithmetic. Let $A \in \mathbb{Z}^{n\times m}$ and $\boldsymbol{b} \in \mathbb{Z}^m$. To find an integer solution of $A\boldsymbol{x} \leq \boldsymbol{b}$, SMT solvers first compute a rational solution of $A\boldsymbol{x} \leq \boldsymbol{b}$, which is called the LP relaxation. If the relaxation is unsatisfiable, the original formula is unsatisfiable, too. Otherwise let $\boldsymbol{x}_0 = (x_{01}, \ldots, x_{0n})$ be the values assigned to the variables in the solutions to the relaxation. If all x_{0i} are integral, the original formula is satisfiable. Otherwise the relaxation is refined by means of branches $x_i \leq \lfloor x_{0i} \rfloor \vee x_i \geq \lceil x_{0i} \rceil$ in a *branch-and-bound* solver or by cuts in a *branch-and-cut* solver. Both techniques remove the current non-integral solution from the relaxation. For a detailed overview and derivations of different cuts we refer to [19].

[1] We follow [7] and use column-style Hermite normal form with negative coefficients in the lower left triangle for nonsingular square matrices.

Instead of branches, modern solvers introduce extended branches. These are defined by a vector $\boldsymbol{r} \in \mathbb{Z}^n$ and branch on $\boldsymbol{r}\cdot\boldsymbol{x} \leq \lfloor \boldsymbol{r}\cdot\boldsymbol{x}_0 \rfloor \vee \boldsymbol{r}\cdot\boldsymbol{x} \geq \lceil \boldsymbol{r}\cdot\boldsymbol{x}_0 \rceil$. Thus, an extended branch does not have to be along one of the variables. Most SMT solvers come with a DPLL engine, that can be used to decide on the branch. In this case the theory solver can ask the DPLL engine to decide on the new literal and add it to the constraint system. This procedure is repeated until the LP relaxation becomes unsatisfiable or an assignment satisfies both, the LP relaxation and the integer constraints of the variables. When the LP relaxation becomes unsatisfiable a conflict is produced and the DPLL engine will explore the other branch. When all branches have been explored the original system is known to be unsatisfiable. This is the technique used in our solver SMTInterpol.

Another technique introduces cuts. These are constraints of the form $\boldsymbol{r}\cdot\boldsymbol{x} \leq c$ that are implied by the current constraint system $A\boldsymbol{x} \leq \boldsymbol{b}$ and exclude the current rational solution in the LP relaxation. An example are Gomory cuts [9]. Cuts have the advantage that they can be propagated and no backtracking is necessary. While they exclude only non-integer solutions, their negation can still be satisfiable in conjunction with the LP relaxation. Thus, cut constraints need a specialised proof rule. An interpolating SMT solver also needs a specialised procedure to interpolate these cuts. Branches on the other hand are simple case splits. A way to achieve the best of both worlds is the cuts from proofs algorithm [7]. This algorithm computes extended branches. But as we will see in the next section, one of the two cases is trivially unsatisfiable. Thus, the other case can be propagated by the theory and no backtracking is necessary. This algorithm combines the strength of cuts with the simplicity of branches.

4 Cuts from Proofs

We will now give a short overview of the cuts from proofs algorithm. We focus on the main ideas needed for our adaptation to mixed arithmetic. In this chapter we assume that $\boldsymbol{x}$ only contains integer variables.

The algorithm is based on the Simplex algorithm. The solution space forms a polyhedron in $\mathbb{Q}^n$. If the solution space is non-empty, the Simplex algorithm returns a solution of $A\boldsymbol{x} \leq b$. We further assume that the returned solution $\boldsymbol{x}_0$ is a vertex of the polyhedron, i.e., there is a nonsingular square submatrix A' and a corresponding vector b', such that $A'\boldsymbol{x}_0 = \boldsymbol{b}$'. We call $A'\boldsymbol{x} \leq \boldsymbol{b}'$ the *defining constraints* of the vertex. If the returned solution is not on a vertex we introduce artificial branches on input variables into A and use these branches as defining constraints. These branches are rarely needed in practise.

The main idea is to bring the constraint system $A'\boldsymbol{x} \leq \boldsymbol{b}'$ into a Hermite normal form H and to compute the unimodular matrix U with $A'U = H$. The Hermite normal form is uniquely defined. The constraint system $A'\boldsymbol{x} \leq \boldsymbol{b}'$ is equivalent to $H\boldsymbol{y} \leq \boldsymbol{b}'$ with $\boldsymbol{y} := U^{-1}\boldsymbol{x}$. Since the solution $\boldsymbol{x}_0$ of $A'\boldsymbol{x}_0 = \boldsymbol{b}'$ is not integral, the corresponding vector $\boldsymbol{y}_0 = U^{-1}\boldsymbol{x}_0$ is not integral, either. The cuts from proofs algorithm creates an extended branch on one of the components y_i of $\boldsymbol{y}$, i.e., $y_i \leq \lfloor y_{0i} \rfloor$ or $y_i \geq \lceil y_{0i} \rceil$.

Although the description in Dillig et al. [7] looks different, they really do the same. They introduce the notion of *proof of unsatisfiability*, which they define as an equation $d\boldsymbol{r} \cdot \boldsymbol{x} = n$ where $\boldsymbol{r}$ is an integer vector, n, d are integers, and d does not divide n. It is clear that this equation cannot have integer solutions for $\boldsymbol{x}$. In particular, they define $\boldsymbol{r}$ as the i-th row of $H^{-1}A'$ and n/d as the i-th entry of $H^{-1}b$. From this proof of unsatisfiability they generate the extended branch

$$1/g(d_i \boldsymbol{r}_i \cdot \boldsymbol{x}) \leq \lfloor n_i/g \rfloor \vee 1/g(d_i \boldsymbol{r}_i \cdot \boldsymbol{x}) \geq \lceil n_i/g \rceil$$

where g is the greatest common divisor of the components of $d_i \boldsymbol{r}_i$. However, $g = d_i$ since $\boldsymbol{r}_i$ is a row of the unimodular matrix U^{-1}. Thus, they branch on $y_i \leq \lfloor y_{0i} \rfloor$ or $y_i \geq \lceil y_{0i} \rceil$.

Due to the special shape of the Hermite normal form used here and in [7], the constraint $H\boldsymbol{y} \leq \boldsymbol{b}'$ implies that $\boldsymbol{y} \leq \boldsymbol{y}_0$. This means that the second branch can be omitted, i. e., one can introduce the cut $y_i \leq \lfloor y_{0i} \rfloor$. This is shown in the following lemma.

Lemma 1. *Let* $A\boldsymbol{x}_0 = b$ *and* $H = AU$ *the Hermite normal form of* A. *Let* $\boldsymbol{y}_0 = U^{-1}\boldsymbol{x}_0$. *Then*

$$A\boldsymbol{x} \leq \boldsymbol{b} \textit{ implies that } U^{-1}\boldsymbol{x} \leq \boldsymbol{y}_0$$

Proof. We assume $A\boldsymbol{x} \leq \boldsymbol{b}$ and show for every row i that $(U^{-1}\boldsymbol{x})_i \leq y_{0i}$ by induction over i. Let $i \geq 1$. Since $(HU^{-1}\boldsymbol{x})_i = (A\boldsymbol{x})_i \leq b_i$,

$$\sum_{j=1}^{n} h_{ij}(U^{-1}\boldsymbol{x})_j = (HU^{-1}\boldsymbol{x})_i \leq b_i = (A\boldsymbol{x}_0)_i = (H\boldsymbol{y}_0)_i = \sum_{j=1}^{n} h_{ij} y_{0j}.$$

Isolating $h_{ii}(U^{-1}\boldsymbol{x})_i$ on the left hand side, we get (note that $h_{ij} = 0$ for $j > i$)

$$h_{ii}(U^{-1}\boldsymbol{x})_i \leq h_{ii} y_{0i} + \sum_{j=1}^{i-1} h_{ij}(y_{0j} - (U^{-1}\boldsymbol{x})_j).$$

From the induction hypothesis $(U^{-1}\boldsymbol{x})_j \leq y_{0j}$ and $h_{ij} \leq 0$ for $j < i$ we derive $h_{ii}(U^{-1}\boldsymbol{x})_i \leq h_{ii} y_{0i}$. Now $(U^{-1}\boldsymbol{x})_i \leq y_{0i}$ follows, since $h_{ii} > 0$. □

Example 1. The following example stems from Pugh [18]. Given the constraint system $27 \leq 11x + 13y \leq 45$ and $-10 \leq 7x - 9y \leq 4$. Figure 1 shows that these constraints form a parallelogram that does not contain any integer solution. The Simplex algorithm may choose as defining constraints the upper bounds (which are the thick lines in the diagram):

$$\begin{bmatrix} 11 & 13 \\ 7 & -9 \end{bmatrix} \begin{bmatrix} x \\ y \end{bmatrix} = \begin{bmatrix} 45 \\ 4 \end{bmatrix}$$

This gives a non-integer solution for x and y. The algorithm then proceeds by computing the Hermite normal form as

$$H = \begin{bmatrix} 1 & 0 \\ -103 & 190 \end{bmatrix} = \begin{bmatrix} 11 & 13 \\ 7 & -9 \end{bmatrix} \begin{bmatrix} -7 & 13 \\ 6 & -11 \end{bmatrix} = AU.$$

From this it computes the cuts as

$$U^{-1}\begin{bmatrix}x\\y\end{bmatrix} \leq H^{-1}b \Leftrightarrow \begin{bmatrix}11x+13y\\6x+7y\end{bmatrix} \leq \begin{bmatrix}45\\\lfloor\frac{4639}{190}\rfloor\end{bmatrix} = \begin{bmatrix}45\\24\end{bmatrix}.$$

The second cut $6x + 7y \leq 24$ is now added to the system. It follows from the original constraints because

$$\frac{103}{190}\cdot(11x+13y \leq 45) + \frac{1}{190}(7x - 9y \leq 4) \text{ gives } 6x + 7y \leq \frac{4639}{190}.$$

The figure depicts this cut graphically. Although this cut removes only a small part of the solution space, it replaces the constraint $11x + 13y \leq 45$ by a constraint with smaller coefficients. Continuing with this constraint, the same algorithm will produce the second cut $x + y \leq \lfloor\frac{388}{103}\rfloor = 3$. This cut then replaces the previous cut in the defining constraints and the third cut is $x \leq \lfloor\frac{31}{16}\rfloor = 1$. For the fourth and last cut the Simplex algorithm chooses another constraint, e. g., $-10 \leq 7x - 9y$, since the lower right constraint is not inside the solution space anymore. This produces the cut $y \leq \lfloor\frac{17}{9}\rfloor = 1$. The solution space is now empty, which means the system is unsatisfiable. □

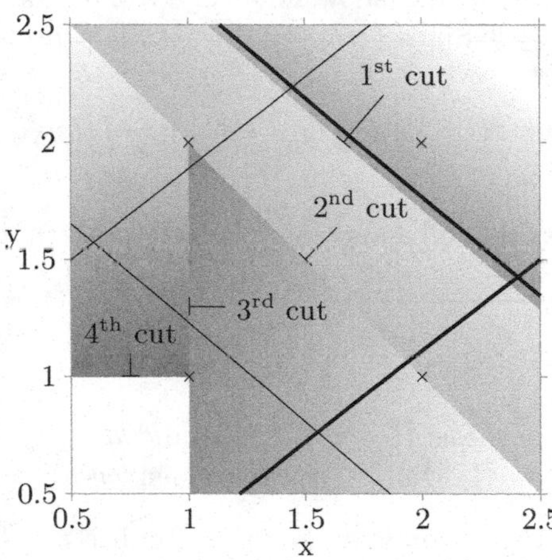

Fig. 1. Run of the cuts from proofs algorithm on Example 1. The black lines are the constraints, which form a parallelogram without integer solutions. The thick lines on the right denote the defining constraints for the first cut. The second cut is computed from the first cut and the lower right constraint and so on. The fourth cut shows that there are no integer solutions.

Why is $y_i \leq \lfloor y_{0i} \rfloor$ a good cut? It is not clear how to answer this question. One can argue that one replaces the variables $\boldsymbol{x}$ with new variables $\boldsymbol{y}$ and solves a very simple constraint system $H\boldsymbol{y} \leq \boldsymbol{b}$ by doing cuts on the $\boldsymbol{y}$ variables. Also, it can be seen that if the constraint $y_i \leq \lfloor y_{0i} \rfloor$ replaces the corresponding i-th row in the defining constraint for every cut (which is what under certain condition the Bland heuristic [19] would do), the resulting constraint system has an integer solution. But the best answer is that it empirically works.

Although the Hermite normal form is unique there is still an important way the produced cuts can be influenced. The order of the defining constraints directly determines the quality of the produced cuts. As a heuristic, the constraints that are most unlikely to change should come first. For this reason we put equality constraints first in the matrix A'. Other than this, we put the rows in the reverse order in which they would be chosen by the Bland heuristic.

Our view of the algorithm is that it transforms the basis $\boldsymbol{x}$ using a unimodular matrix U to a basis $\boldsymbol{y}$, such that the constraint system $A\boldsymbol{x} \leq \boldsymbol{b}$ has a much simpler representation $H\boldsymbol{y} \leq \boldsymbol{b}$ in the new constraint system. Then it creates cuts on the coordinates of the new basis $\boldsymbol{y}$ that are not yet integral. In the next section we want to extend this idea to mixed problems where some variables are real variables and some variables are integer variables.

5 Mixed Cuts from Proofs

As mentioned in the previous section, the basic idea of the cuts from proof algorithm can be described by a transformation of the basis $\boldsymbol{x}$ to a new basis $\boldsymbol{y}$ where the current constraint system is simpler. In this section we extend this idea to mixed real/integer arithmetic.

For mixed arithmetic the basis $\boldsymbol{x} = (x_1 \ldots, x_{n_1}, x_{n_1+1}, \ldots, x_n)$ is split into n_1 real variables and $n_2 = n - n_1$ integer variables. The transformed basis $\boldsymbol{y} = U\boldsymbol{x}$ should have the same number of real and integer variables. To achieve this the matrix must have the form

$$U = \begin{bmatrix} U_{(r)} & V \\ 0 & U_{(i)} \end{bmatrix}$$

where all coefficients of $U_{(i)}$ are integral.

We further require that every valid solution of $\boldsymbol{y}$ should correspond to a valid solution of $\boldsymbol{x}$. Therefore, the matrix U must be invertible and its inverse should have again this form. The inverse of U is

$$U^{-1} = \begin{bmatrix} U_{(r)}^{-1} & -U_{(r)}^{-1} V U_{(i)}^{-1} \\ 0 & U_{(i)}^{-1} \end{bmatrix}$$

We require that $U_{(i)}^{-1} \in \mathbb{Z}^{n_2 \times n_2}$ (hence $U_{(i)}$ must be unimodular) and that $U_{(r)}$ is nonsingular. We call a matrix of this form a mixed transformation matrix.

Definition 1. *Given a mixed problem with n_1 real and n_2 integer variables and $n = n_1 + n_2$. A matrix $U \in \mathbb{Q}^{n \times n}$ is a* mixed transformation matrix *if there are a nonsingular $U_{(r)} \in \mathbb{Q}^{n_1 \times n_1}$, a unimodular $U_{(i)} \in \mathbb{Z}^{n_2 \times n_2}$, and $V \in \mathbb{Q}^{n_1 \times n_2}$, such that*

$$U = \begin{bmatrix} U_{(r)} & V \\ 0 & U_{(i)} \end{bmatrix}.$$

By the above observation the mixed transformation matrices form a subgroup of $\mathbb{Q}^{n\times n}$, i. e., the inverse of a mixed transformation matrix is again a mixed transformation matrix. Thus, we have the following lemma stating that a valid solution for the original system corresponds to a valid solution of the transformed coordinate system.

Lemma 2. *Let U be a mixed transformation matrix. Then*

$$\boldsymbol{x} \in (\mathbb{Q}^{n_1} \times \mathbb{Z}^{n_2}) \textit{ if and only if } U\boldsymbol{x} \in (\mathbb{Q}^{n_1} \times \mathbb{Z}^{n_2}).$$

Proof. Follows directly from the shape of U and U^{-1}. □

Again we bring the matrix A of defining constraints into a normal form H with $H = AU$ where U is a mixed transformation matrix. We call this the mixed normal form. A matrix H is in mixed normal form if

$$H = \begin{bmatrix} Id & 0 \\ * & H_{(i)} \end{bmatrix}$$

where $Id \in \mathbb{Q}^{n_1\times n_1}$ is the identity matrix, $*$ is an arbitrary $\mathbb{Q}^{n_2\times n_1}$ matrix, and $H_{(i)} \in \mathbb{Q}^{n_2\times n_2}$ is in Hermite normal form.

A matrix has a normal form if and only if the first n_1 constraints are linear independent on the real variables. Thus we may have to reorder the matrix A to put these rows first. Since the matrix A is nonsingular, it is always possible to reorder the rows of A such that the top-left $n_1 \times n_1$ submatrix is nonsingular.

Lemma 3. *Let $A \in \mathbb{Q}^{n\times n}$, such that the upper left $n_1 \times n_1$ submatrix is nonsingular. Then A has a unique mixed normal form $H = AU$, such that U is a mixed transformation matrix.*

Proof. Existence. We subdivide A into

$$\begin{bmatrix} A_{11} & A_{12} \\ A_{21} & A_{22} \end{bmatrix}$$

and note that A_{11} is invertible in $\mathbb{Q}^{n_1\times n_1}$. We set $U_{(r)} = A_{11}^{-1}$. Then we transform the matrix $A_{22} - A_{21}U_{(r)}A_{12}$ into Hermite Normal Form $H_{(i)}$ with

$$H_{(i)} = (A_{22} - A_{21}U_{(r)}A_{12})U_{(i)}.$$

The mixed normal form is

$$H = \begin{bmatrix} Id & 0 \\ A_{21}U_{(r)} & H_{(i)} \end{bmatrix} = \begin{bmatrix} A_{11} & A_{12} \\ A_{21} & A_{22} \end{bmatrix} \begin{bmatrix} U_{(r)} & -U_{(r)}A_{12}U_{(i)} \\ 0 & U_{(i)} \end{bmatrix}.$$

Uniqueness. Assume that $H = AU$ with

$$H = \begin{bmatrix} Id & 0 \\ H_{21} & H_{22} \end{bmatrix}, A = \begin{bmatrix} A_{11} & A_{12} \\ A_{21} & A_{22} \end{bmatrix}, U = \begin{bmatrix} U_{11} & U_{12} \\ 0 & U_{22} \end{bmatrix}$$

where H_{22} is in Hermite normal form and U_{22} is unimodular. The top left corner of H gives $Id = A_{11}U_{11}$, thus $U_{11} = A_{11}^{-1}$ is unique. The top right corner of H gives $0 = A_{11}U_{12} + A_{12}U_{22}$, thus $U_{12} = -A_{11}^{-1}A_{12}U_{22}$. Inserting this into the equation for the bottom right corner of H gives

$$H_{22} = (-A_{21}A_{11}^{-1}A_{12} + A_{22})U_{22}$$

Thus, H_{22} is the unique Hermite normal form of $-A_{21}A_{11}^{-1}A_{12} + A_{22}$ and U_{22} is also unique. This shows that U is unique and therefore also $H = AU$. □

Example 2. We change the constraint system of Example 1 and make the variable x real-valued. Secondly, we require that $x - \lfloor x \rfloor \leq 0.2$. To express this we introduce an integer variable z representing $\lfloor x \rfloor$. The constraint system is

$$\begin{aligned} 27 \leq\ & 11x + 13y \leq 45 \\ -10 \leq\ & 7x - 9y \leq 4 \\ 0 \leq\ & x - z \leq 0.2 \end{aligned}$$

Figure 2 depicts the solution space. The integer points are denoted by crosses; x, y must lie in one of the horizontal thick lines for z, y to be integer and the last constraint to be satisfied. Also x, y must lie in the parallelogram. As can be seen from the figure, there is a solution, e. g., $x = 1.2, y = 2, z = 1$. Our algorithm uses the Simplex algorithm to find a vertex in the solution space. We assume it uses as defining constraints

$$\begin{aligned} 11x + 13y &\leq 45 \\ -7x + 9y &\leq 10 \\ z - x &\leq 0 \end{aligned}$$

with the solution $x = z = \frac{55}{38}, y = \frac{85}{38}$. The mixed normal form is

$$H = \begin{bmatrix} 1 & 0 & 0 \\ -7/11 & 100/11 & 0 \\ -1/11 & -9/11 & 1 \end{bmatrix} = \begin{bmatrix} 11 & 13 & 0 \\ -7 & 9 & 0 \\ -1 & 0 & 1 \end{bmatrix} \begin{bmatrix} 1/11 & -13/11 & 0 \\ 0 & 1 & 0 \\ 0 & -2 & 1 \end{bmatrix} = AU$$

From this it computes the cuts as

$$U^{-1}\begin{bmatrix} x \\ y \\ z \end{bmatrix} \leq H^{-1}b \Leftrightarrow \begin{bmatrix} 11x + 13y \\ y \\ 2y + z \end{bmatrix} \leq \begin{bmatrix} 45 \\ \lfloor 85/38 \rfloor \\ \lfloor 225/38 \rfloor \end{bmatrix} = \begin{bmatrix} 45 \\ 2 \\ 5 \end{bmatrix}.$$

The figure visualises the cuts. Note that the cut $2y + z \leq 5$ is for the z variable, so x may still be in the differently shaded area right of this cut. When the two cuts $y \leq 2$ and $2y + z \leq 5$ are introduced, the Simplex algorithm will search for a new vertex, e. g., $x = \frac{8}{7}, y = 2, z = 1$ with the defining constraints

$$\begin{aligned} -7x + 9y &\leq 10, \\ y &\leq 2, \\ 2y + z &\leq 5. \end{aligned}$$

This solution has integer values for y and z and the algorithm terminates with this solution.

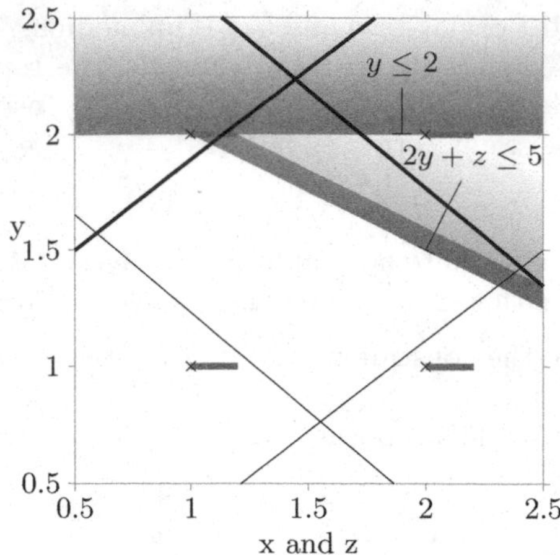

Fig. 2. Run of our algorithm on Example 2. The thick lines on the top denote the defining constraints. From the constraints two cuts are computed. These cuts meet at the vertex $y = 2, z = 1$, which can be extended to a feasible solution with $x = 8/7$.

Our algorithm introduces extended branches $y_i \leq \lfloor y_{0i} \rfloor \vee y_i \geq \lceil y_{0i} \rceil$. As in Lemma 1, one can see that these branches are cuts if the matrix H contains only nonpositive values in the lower left triangle. However, Lemma 3 shows that $H_{21} = A_{21}A_{11}^{-1}$ and there are examples where the coefficients of this matrix are positive. Moreover, since the mixed normal form is unique, there is no simple fix. In the above example we had to carefully choose the defining constraints to get cuts instead of branches. In our implementation of the algorithm we usually get several extended branches until the defining constraints contain enough integer constraints, which means that there are only few non-zero entries in H_{21}. Then usually cuts are generated.

6 Implementation and Evaluation

We implemented the technique presented in this paper in the SMT solver SMT-Interpol [5]. When experimenting, we discovered that most of the time spent by SMTInterpol was not in the cut engine, but in trying to find a solution to the LP relaxation and deciding on already created extended branches. In the runs we investigated further, SMTInterpol quickly creates several extended branches and cuts and then spends hours in the DPLL engine and the Simplex algorithm to solve the LP relaxation. In the end, the benchmark is solved without adding a new branch or cut. The main problem is that our implementation keeps all branches and cuts generated by the technique proposed here and even decides on them. To rectify this problem, we created a second version of SMTInterpol that removes cuts and branches that did not help to close the current branch in the decision tree of the DPLL engine. This version is still experimental and part of ongoing work.

We evaluated the technique on a number of benchmarks. We used hard conjunctive benchmarks, since we aimed at evaluating the cut engine and not the DPLL engine. Since SMTLIB [2] currently does not contain a logic for mixed linear arithmetic without arrays or quantifiers, we created the logic QF_LIRA. This logic is also supported by CVC4 [1], MathSAT 5 [6], yices 2 [8], and Z3 [15][2].

In the evaluation we include a *virtual solver* that combines yices 2 and both versions of SMTInterpol. We do not report times on this solver, but only the number of benchmarks that would be solved by a portfolio of the combined solvers. We chose yices 2 since it is the best performing solver on our benchmark set (closely followed by MathSAT).

The evaluation was performed on StarExec[3] using a timeout of 600 seconds for both CPU and wall time. Memory was limited to 8 GB. We created some benchmarks based on existing benchmarks for linear integer arithmetic, especially those that test the cut generation engine. In the following, we will discuss the benchmarks and the results.

Family Cut_Lemmas Biased. To generate this set of benchmarks, we used all benchmarks from the cut_lemmas family from QF_LIA that are flagged as unsatisfiable. We systematically switched the sort of the variables in the order of their declaration. After we switched one variable, we ran SMTInterpol for five minutes to check if the benchmark was still unsatisfiable. If it was we kept the modification. Otherwise we reverted to the last unsatisfiable modification. The goal is to create a hard unsatisfiable and a few hard satisfiable benchmarks by finding the limit where the satisfiability of the benchmarks changes. Since the modification was guided by SMTInterpol, we call this family *biased*. The chosen modifications depend on which solver we initially used to solve the benchmark. We created a total of 1575 benchmarks. Even though we could know the status of most of these benchmarks, we did not include it in the file[4]. But we checked that if two or more solvers solved the same benchmark, they agreed on the status.

The results are shown in Table 1. The difference between wall time and CPU time for SMTInterpol is caused by the Java virtual machine. SMTInterpol itself is single threaded, but, e. g., the garbage collection runs in parallel. We remark that the virtual solver (combination of yices 2 and both variants of SMTInterpol) solves all but 22 benchmarks. One of the remaining benchmarks can be solved by both CVC4 and MathSAT 5 which additionally solves three more benchmarks. The remaining 18 cannot be solved by any of the solvers used in the evaluation. Furthermore, both versions of SMTInterpol could solve benchmarks that no competing solver (CVC4, MathSAT 5, yices 2, or Z3) could solve.

Figure 3 shows scatter plots that compare yices 2 resp. MathSAT 5 and the version of SMTInterpol that forgets literals. The white area at the bottom of each

[2] Z3 actually warns the user that it does not know this logic. The solver works nevertheless and interprets the logic as expected.

[3] See https://www.starexec.org/starexec/secure/explore/spaces.jsp?id=62799 using username `public` and password `public`.

[4] This causes StarExec to report both results *sat* and *unsat* as wrong.

Table 1. Results of the evaluation on the benchmarks from the biased family. For each solver we report the number of solved benchmarks, the number of satisfiable resp. unsatisfiable benchmarks, the wall and CPU time and the number of benchmarks that could not be solved by any competing solver.

Solver	# solved	# sat	# unsat	wall time	CPU time	# only
SMTInterpol	1107/1575	447	660	64079	68397	42
SMTInterpol forget	1226/1575	465	761	94262	99743	57
CVC4	1309/1575	483	826	63338	63359	0
MathSAT 5	1404/1575	521	883	59959	60000	3
yices 2	1427/1575	509	918	29272	29289	10
Z3	1147/1575	511	636	71688	71736	0
virtual	1553/1575	539	1014			

plot is caused by the startup overhead of the Java virtual machine. Both plots show that there are several problems on which yices 2 and MathSAT 5 time out while SMTInterpol solves them in less than a second. Overall the difficulty of a problem for yices 2 and MathSAT 5 is quite unrelated to the difficulty for SMTInterpol. This undermines the thesis that these solver complement each other well. It is also reflected in the number of benchmarks solved by the virtual solver.

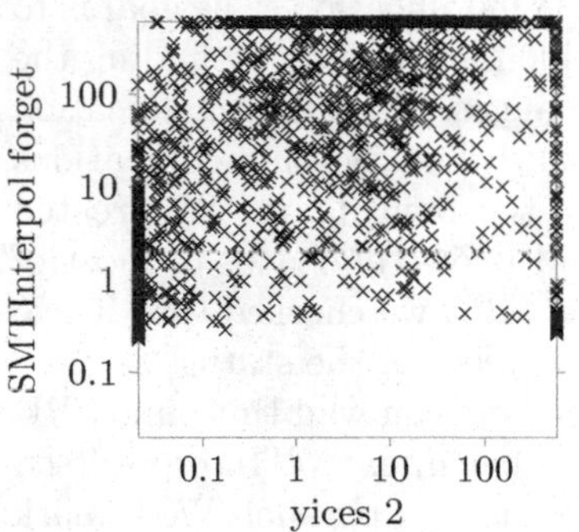

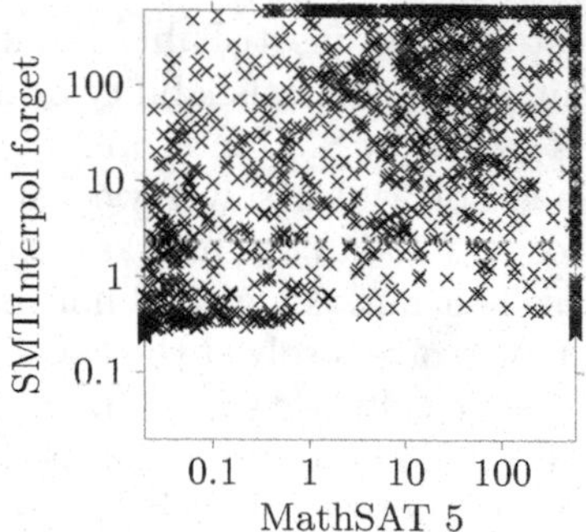

Fig. 3. Scatter plot comparing yices 2 resp. MathSAT 5 and the version of SMTInterpol that forgets literals on the biased family.

Family Cut_Lemmas Unbiased. Again, we used all benchmarks from the cut_lemmas family that are flagged as unsatisfiable. This time, we created 10 new benchmarks from each of these benchmarks by randomly changing the sort of 20 % of the variables from integer to real. We chose that percentage because it creates roughly the same number of unsat and sat benchmarks. This family does not use any solver in the creation and should thus not be biased to a specific solver. We created a total of 930 benchmarks in this division. Since we do not know the status of these benchmarks, no status information is recorded in the generated files. But, again, whenever two solvers solved the same benchmark, they agreed on the status.

Table 2. Results of the evaluation on the benchmarks from the unbiased family. For each solver we report the number of solved benchmarks, the number of satisfiable resp. unsatisfiable benchmarks, the wall and CPU time, and the number of benchmarks that could not be solved by any competing solver.

Solver	# solved	# sat	# unsat	wall time	CPU time	# only
SMTInterpol	697/930	218	479	33421	35936	27
SMTInterpol forget	751/930	236	515	43473	46340	29
CVC4	785/930	239	546	35037	35109	0
MathSAT 5	832/930	259	573	28686	28695	3
yices 2	831/930	250	581	22260	22267	7
Z3	708/930	239	469	38762	38779	0
virtual	915/930	270	645			

The results are shown in Table 2. From the 15 benchmarks that could not be solved by the virtual solver, three could only be solved by MathSAT 5. Both versions of SMTInterpol solve several benchmarks that cannot be solved by CVC4, MathSAT 5, yices 2, or Z3.

The scatter plots comparing yices 2 resp. MathSAT 5 to the forget version of SMTInterpol look almost identical to the ones shown in Fig. 3.

Table 3. Results of the evaluation on the benchmarks from the dillig family. For each solver we report the number of solved benchmarks, the number of satisfiable resp. unsatisfiable benchmarks, the wall and CPU time and the number of benchmarks that could not be solved by any competing solver.

Solver	# solved	# sat	# unsat	wall time	CPU time	# only
SMTInterpol	2204/2330	2187	17	10858	14710	0
SMTInterpol forget	2194/2330	2176	18	13303	17319	1
CVC4	1967/2330	1938	29	44360	44372	0
MathSAT 5	2317/2330	2288	29	17309	17333	0
yices 2	2302/2330	2273	29	17115	17132	0
Z3	2101/2330	2072	29	69255	69344	0
virtual	2330/2330	2301	29			

Family Dillig. The benchmarks from the cuts from proofs paper [7] are available in the SMTLIB in QF_LIA in the dillig family. For each of these benchmarks, we created 10 new benchmarks where we randomly changed the sort of 20 % of the variables from integer to real. This lead to a total of 2330 benchmarks. Since the benchmarks are randomly generated, we do not know the status. But the solvers agreed on the status of those benchmarks that could be solved by multiple solvers.

The results for the dillig family are shown in Table 3. The virtual solver solves *all* benchmarks in this family even though no single solver could solve all benchmarks.

The scatter plots from Fig. 4 compare yices 2 resp. MathSAT 5 and the forget version of SMTInterpol. This time there seems to be a strange line at slightly more than one second. Either SMTInterpol solves a benchmark in this time or it does not solve the benchmark at all.

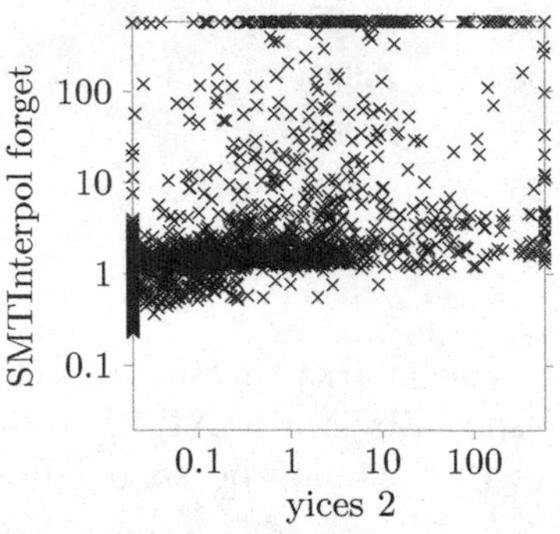

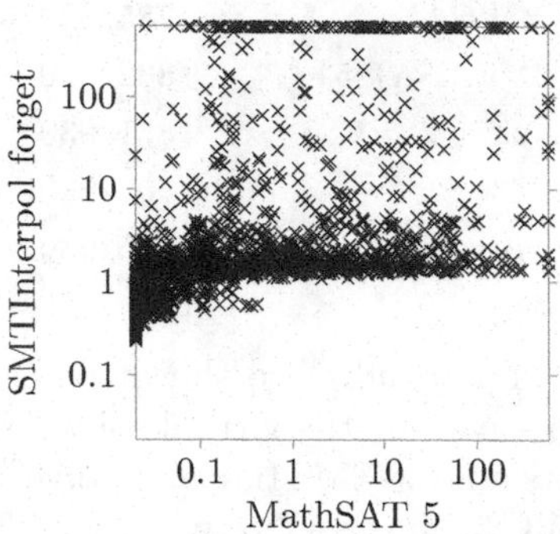

Fig. 4. Scatter plots comparing yices 2 resp. MathSAT 5 and the version of SMTInterpol that forgets literals on the dillig family.

Family Tightrhombus. We created 44 benchmarks specifically designed to test the cut engine. These benchmarks are inspired by the tightrhombus benchmarks used to test the cut engine for QF_LIA. They encode a tight rhombus in the following way. Choose coefficients $c_x > 0$, $c_y > 0$ and scale $s > 0$. The rhombus for QF_LIA is created as

$$0 \le (c_x \cdot s)x - (c_y \cdot s + 1)y \le s - 1 \ \wedge\ 1 \le (c_x \cdot s + 1)x - (c_y \cdot s)y \le s$$

for integer variables x and y. For mixed arithmetic, we use a real-valued variable y and bound the distance between y and the nearest integer point. The bound can be computed for each rhombus. Since yices 2 does not support the `to_int` construct from SMTLIB, we encode it using a fresh integer variable z. We created benchmarks for $c_x = 273, c_y = 245$ resp. $c_x = 283, c_y = 245$ for scales $s = 10^{i+1}$, $0 \le i \le 10$. We carefully chose the bound on the distance between y and z such that the benchmark is barely satisfiable. To create unsatisfiable benchmarks, we subtracted a small value from the bound. We chose 10^{-13} to not create trivially unsatisfiable benchmarks since the minimal distance between y and z for scale 10^{11} is very small.

The results for this family are shown in Table 4. We omit the virtual solvers since both version of SMTInterpol solve all the benchmarks. While CVC4 only solves benchmarks with scale up to 4, MathSAT solves all satisfiable benchmarks with $c_x = 273$, but has problems on the other set. Similarly, Z3 solves almost all satisfiable benchmarks with $c_x = 283$ (except for scale $s = 10^{11}$) but has

Table 4. Results of the evaluation on the benchmarks from the tightrhombus family. For each solver we report the number of solved benchmarks, the number of satisfiable resp. unsatisfiable benchmarks, the wall and CPU time and the number of benchmarks that could not be solved by any competing solver.

Solver	# solved	# sat	# unsat	wall time	CPU time	# only
SMTInterpol	44/44	22	22	15	20	12
SMTInterpol forget	44/44	22	22	15	20	12
CVC4	20/44	10	10	585	585	0
MathSAT 5	21/44	15	6	326	326	0
yices 2	18/44	10	8	514	514	0
Z3	21/44	15	6	364	365	0

problems on the other set. Also note that 12 benchmarks were solved only by either of the variants of SMTInterpol, but not by the other solvers.

This evaluation shows that the clear winner is a combination of the (to our knowledge unpublished) technique used by yices 2 with the technique presented in this paper. Such a combination advances the state of the art in mixed linear arithmetic solving in the SMT context. Furthermore, the technique presented in this paper is able to solve some benchmarks that no other technique can solve. The comparison between the performances of the different versions of SMTInterpol shows that removal of literals that do not contribute to closing of a decision branch sometimes is beneficial.

7 Conclusion and Future Work

We presented a novel method to compute cuts in mixed linear arithmetic solving in the context of SMT. The method is inspired by the cuts from proofs algorithm used to solve integer linear arithmetic. It transforms the original constraint system into a simpler one. This is achieved by transforming the basis of the original constraint system into a new one. Cuts and branches are then created for the new basis. We showed in some experiments that this new technique is able to solve benchmarks that cannot be solved by state-of-the-art solvers.

The evaluation showed that the cut engine is not the bottleneck. Instead SMTInterpol spends most time in the Simplex algorithm and the DPLL engine deciding on the extended branches. An investigation when and which branches and cuts should be removed from the solver is part of future work.

References

1. Barrett, C., Conway, C.L., Deters, M., Hadarean, L., Jovanović, D., King, T., Reynolds, A., Tinelli, C.: CVC4. In: Gopalakrishnan, G., Qadeer, S. (eds.) CAV 2011. LNCS, vol. 6806, pp. 171–177. Springer, Heidelberg (2011)

2. Barrett, C., Stump, A., Tinelli, C.: The SMT-LIB Standard: 2.0. In: SMT (2010)
3. Berezin, S., Ganesh, V., Dill, D.L.: An online proof-producing decision procedure for mixed-integer linear arithmetic. In: Garavel, H., Hatcliff, J. (eds.) TACAS 2003. LNCS, vol. 2619, pp. 521–536. Springer, Heidelberg (2003)
4. Bobot, F., Conchon, S., Contejean, E., Iguernelala, M., Mahboubi, A., Mebsout, A., Melquiond, G.: A simplex-based extension of fourier-motzkin for solving linear integer arithmetic. In: Gramlich, B., Miller, D., Sattler, U. (eds.) IJCAR 2012. LNCS, vol. 7364, pp. 67–81. Springer, Heidelberg (2012)
5. Christ, J., Hoenicke, J., Nutz, A.: SMTInterpol: an interpolating smt solver. In: Donaldson, A., Parker, D. (eds.) SPIN 2012. LNCS, vol. 7385, pp. 248–254. Springer, Heidelberg (2012)
6. Cimatti, A., Griggio, A., Schaafsma, B.J., Sebastiani, R.: The MathSAT5 SMT solver. In: Piterman, N., Smolka, S.A. (eds.) TACAS 2013 (ETAPS 2013). LNCS, vol. 7795, pp. 93–107. Springer, Heidelberg (2013)
7. Dillig, I., Dillig, T., Aiken, A.: Cuts from proofs: a complete and practical technique for solving linear inequalities over integers. In: Bouajjani, A., Maler, O. (eds.) CAV 2009. LNCS, vol. 5643, pp. 233–247. Springer, Heidelberg (2009)
8. Dutertre, B.: Yices 2.2. In: Biere, A., Bloem, R. (eds.) CAV 2014. LNCS, vol. 8559, pp. 737–744. Springer, Heidelberg (2014)
9. Dutertre, B., de Moura, L.: Integrating simplex with DPLL(T). Technical report, CSL, SRI INTERNATIONAL (2006)
10. Griggio, A.: A practical approach to satisfiability modulo linear integer arithmetic. JSAT **8**(1/2), 1–27 (2012)
11. Jovanović, D., de Moura, L.: Cutting to the chase solving linear integer arithmetic. In: Bjørner, N., Sofronie-Stokkermans, V. (eds.) CADE 2011. LNCS, vol. 6803, pp. 338–353. Springer, Heidelberg (2011)
12. King, T., Barrett, C., Dutertre, B.: Simplex with sum of infeasibilities for SMT. In: FMCAD, pp. 189–196. IEEE (2013)
13. King, T., Barrett, C.W., Tinelli, C.: Leveraging linear and mixed integer programming for SMT. In: FMCAD, pp. 139–146. IEEE (2014)
14. Martin, A.: General mixed integer programming: computational issues for branch-and-cut algorithms. In: Jünger, M., Naddef, D. (eds.) Computational Combinatorial Optimization. LNCS, vol. 2241, p. 1. Springer, Heidelberg (2001)
15. de Moura, L., Bjørner, N.S.: Z3: an efficient SMT solver. In: Ramakrishnan, C.R., Rehof, J. (eds.) TACAS 2008. LNCS, vol. 4963, pp. 337–340. Springer, Heidelberg (2008)
16. Neumaier, A., Shcherbina, O.: Safe bounds in linear and mixed-integer linear programming. Math. Program. **92**(2), 283–296 (2004)
17. de Oliveira, D.C.B., Monniaux, D.: Experiments on the feasibility of using a floating-point simplex in an SMT solver. In: PAAR-2012, pp. 19–28. EasyChair (2012)
18. Pugh, W.: The omega test: a fast and practical integer programming algorithm for dependence analysis. Commun. ACM **8**, 4–13 (1992)
19. Schrijver, A.: Theory of Linear and Integer Programming. John Wiley & Sons, Chichester (1986)

The Inez Mathematical Programming Modulo Theories Framework

Panagiotis Manolios(✉), Jorge Pais, and Vasilis Papavasileiou

Northeastern University, Boston, USA
{pete,jpais,vpap}@ccs.neu.edu

Abstract. Our Mathematical Programming Modulo Theories (MPMT) constraint solving framework extends Mathematical Programming technology with techniques from the field of Automated Reasoning, *e.g.*, solvers for first-order theories. In previous work, we used MPMT to synthesize system architectures for Boeing's Dreamliner and we studied the theoretical aspects of MPMT by means of the Branch and Cut Modulo T (BC(T)) transition system. BC(T) can be thought of as a blueprint for MPMT solvers. This paper provides a more practical and algorithmic view of BC(T). We elaborate on the design and features of Inez, our BC(T) constraint solver. Inez is an open-source, freely available superset of the OCaml programming language that uses the SCIP Branch and Cut framework to extend OCaml with MPMT capability. Inez allows users to write programs that arbitrarily interweave general computation with MPMT constraint solving.

1 Introduction

The ILP (or, more generally, Mathematical Programming) Modulo Theories (IMT or MPMT) framework accommodates Mathematical Programming (MP) instances, where some variable symbols have meaning in background first-order theories [21]. In previous work, we used this approach to solve systems architectural synthesis problems with hard real-time constraints for Boeing and we introduced the Branch and Cut Modulo T (BC(T)) architecture for solving MPMT [17,21]. BC(T) combines Branch and Cut (B&C) with theory reasoning. B&C is the most established family of algorithms for solving ILP instances, empowering such powerful solvers as CPLEX [2], Gurobi [3], and SCIP [8].

We have formalized BC(T) as a highly non-deterministic transition system [21]. By abstracting away solver implementation details, the BC(T) transition system captures a wide range of possible implementations, and facilitates theoretical analysis. BC(T) can be thought of a design space for MPMT solvers. Implementing an MPMT solver involves zooming in on a region of this design space, with assorted performance trade-offs. To inform efficient solver design, this paper provides an algorithmic (and more deterministic) view of BC(T).

This research was supported in part by DARPA under AFRL Cooperative Agreement No. FA8750-10-2–0233 and by NSF grants CCF-1117184 and CCF-1319580.

D. Kroening and C.S. Păsăreanu (Eds.): CAV 2015, Part II, LNCS 9207, pp. 53–69, 2015.
DOI: 10.1007/978-3-319-21668-3_4

Inez[1] extends the SCIP [8] solver and we show how to implement MPMT on top of a B&C-based solver. We explain as much of the operation of the B&C core as needed to demonstrate where theory solvers fit, with an emphasis on the interface between theory solvers and B&C. We do not cover purely internal operations of either side. For example, we treat Simplex (which handles real relaxations within B&C) purely as a black box. We use congruence closure (CC) as an example of a background procedure. Given that the core operations of CC are well-known [27], our discussion only covers the BC(T)-specific aspects. Our choice of CC is motivated by its wide applicability and by the relatively simple (but not trivial) constraints and algorithms involved.

We provide an overview of the features of Inez. Notably, Inez provides database techniques for reasoning in the presence of data [22]. Inez additionally supports user-provided axioms through *local theory extensions* [30]. Inez is implemented in OCaml, and makes extensive use of OCaml language constructs and technologies. In fact, the standard way of interacting with the solver is via scripts in a superset of OCaml. Programming with Inez is qualitatively different from programming in a standard programming language because Inez allows us to write programs that arbitrarily interleave general computation with MPMT constraint solving. To our knowledge, Inez is the first system that allows expressing constraints over uninterpreted functions within a programming language, with minimal syntactic overhead, while providing type-safety.

The rest of the paper is organized as follows. Section 2 introduces our superset of the OCaml language through a worked example, and explains how OCaml facilitates our implementation efforts. Section 3 describes the core BC(T) setup as a set of algorithms, while Sect. 4 discusses extensions on top of this setup. Section 5 provides an overview of related work. We conclude with Sect. 6. In the interest of space, we do not provide experimental results. We refer the interested readers to our previous work for a comparison of Inez against SMT solvers on instances from the SMT-LIB [21], and also on database problems [22].

2 The Inez Language

In this section, we introduce some of the most notable features of Inez by means of a worked example. We focus on the user-facing aspects of Inez, *i.e.*, on its input language, which is a superset of OCaml. Our extensions over OCaml are language constructs (and supporting APIs) for easily expressing logical constraints and seamlessly integrating with the underlying constraint solver. Building on top of OCaml allows us to provide a mixed functional and constraint language that users can utilize to express their models in a compact and self-contained way.

Inez utilizes the Camlp4 framework [1] to extend OCaml by assigning meaning to programs that are *syntactically valid* (*i.e.*, recognized by the unmodified OCaml grammar) but *semantically invalid*. The semantics of programs accepted by unmodified OCaml do not change under Inez. This design decision has multiple benefits. First, the syntax of Inez programs is natural, given that these

[1] https://github.com/vasilisp/inez.

programs are syntactically valid OCaml anyway. Also, there are no additional syntactic constructs to cause trouble for editors and other tools. Finally, the implementation is cleaner, because all that it does is transform Abstract Syntax Trees (ASTs) produced by the Camlp4 parser.

Our integration of OCaml and constraints has great impact from a user perspective. For instance, consider a problem that depends on raw data defined and stored in a different location than the problem code, *e.g.*, in a plain text file, spreadsheet, database or web service. With Inez, data retrieval, data processing, and constraint solving can all happen side by side, in the same environment. We present concrete Inez code that obtains data from a database, defines data structures to store and manipulate this data, and finally produces and solves an MPMT instance. In the interest of succinctness, we omit the data retrieval code. A complete implementation (based on MySQL [4] and the `mysql_protocol` [5] library) can be found online.[2]

The example is based on a facility location problem [10]. We are given a finite set of locations and a finite set of cities. Each city requires a certain number of units of some product. We have to decide where to place facilities in order to satisfy the needs of the cities, while maximizing our earnings.

```
1 open Script ;;
2 open Core.Std ;;
3
4 let n_cities = db_get_n_cities() ;;
5 let locations = db_get_locations() ;;
6 let revenue = db_get_revenue() ;;
7 let capacity = db_get_capacity() ;;
8 let demand = db_get_demand() ;;
9 let n_locations = Array.length locations ;;
```

Lines 1 and 2 are a typical preamble for Inez scripts. The module `Script` contains useful functions for interacting with Inez, while `Core.Std` refers to Jane Street Core, which is a featureful alternative to INRIA's OCaml base library. Inez uses Jane Street Core internally, and we recommend that Inez scripts also use this library. Lines 4 to 8 perform queries to a database instance to obtain data relevant to the problem: (4) an integer `n_cities` with the number of cities we plan to serve; (5) an array `locations` where each position corresponds to the ZIP code of a potential location; (6) a matrix `revenue`, such that for $0 \leq i <$ `n_cities` and $0 \leq j <$ `n_locations`, `revenue.`(i)`.`(j) represents the revenue of selling to city i a unit of product fabricated at location j; (7) an array `capacity`, where for $0 \leq j <$ `n_locations`, `capacity.`(j) is the production capacity for a factory in location j; and (8) an array `demand` that represents the demand, in units of product, from each city. Finally, we define `n_locations` as the size of the array `locations`, *i.e.*, the number of potential locations.

[2] http://www.ccs.neu.edu/home/pete/2015/cav-example.zip.

```
10 let build =
11   let f _ = fresh_bool_var () in Array.init n_locations ~f ;;
12
13 let production =
14   let f _ =
15     let f _ =
16       let v = fresh_int_var () in
17       constrain (~logic (v >= 0)); v in
18     Array.init n_locations ~f in
19   Array.init n_cities ~f ;;
```

Each city is identified by an integer $c \in [0 \ldots n\_cities - 1]$. Each location is identified by the corresponding ZIP code in the `locations` array. Line 10 defines an array of size `n_locations`, where each element is an Inez Boolean variable, created by the function `fresh_bool_var`. The library function `Array.init` initializes each element of the array, by calling its `f` argument (a function) with the corresponding index as the argument. (In our case, the argument to `f` is ignored, hence the underscore.) Each Boolean variable corresponds to a location and represents whether a facility is built there or not. Similarly, line 13 defines a two-dimensional matrix of Inez integer variables. The two dimensions correspond to cities and locations: for each possible pair of city c and location l, `production.(c).(l)` represents the planned production (in units of product) of a factory to-be-built in location l destined to city c. The Inez-provided function `constrain` adds a formula to the solver context. In line 17 we constrain each integer variable so that it only takes positive values.

For expressing these constraints, we utilize the `~logic` keyword. `~logic` allows expressing terms and formulas with minimal syntactic overhead. We utilize Camlp4 infrastructure to preprocess applications of `~logic` to ensure that the intended meaning over terms and formulas applies. Specifically, (a) integer literals become Inez integer terms; (b) the literals `true` and `false` become formulas; and (c) operators like `+` and `&&` obtain meaning over terms and formulas (as opposed to their standard meaning over OCaml integers and Booleans, respectively). For instance, given integer variables `x` and `y`, `~logic (x + 1)` is an Inez term, while `~logic (1 <= y && x <= 0)` is an Inez formula. Inez integer terms and formulas are regular OCaml values that can be passed around.

```
20 let cost (_ : Int) = (~free : Int) ;;
21
22 for i = 0 to n_locations - 1 do
23   let i = toi i in
24   constrain (~logic (cost i >= hist_lb i &&
25                      cost i <= hist_ub i))
26 done ;;
```

Now consider the following situation. During an early planning phase, the exact cost of building a facility on a given location may be unknown. However, experience from similar previous developments could provide bounds for these costs. We use an uninterpreted function (UF) to express this. Given an integer representing the ID of a location, the UF `cost` (Line 20) returns an integer that corresponds to the cost of building a facility on that location. The syntax for UFs follows closely the standard syntax for defining OCaml functions. Inez recognizes the declaration of `cost` as its own responsibility because of the keyword `~free` in the function body. The declaration produces an actual OCaml function `cost` from integer terms to integer terms. (*Integer terms* belong to an OCaml datatype that describes symbolic integer expressions; integer terms differ from OCaml integers.) Functions can also operate over Booleans. (The `Int` annotations could have been omitted, because integer is the default.)

The function `toi` (Line 23) converts an OCaml integer to an integer term. We use `constrain` to bound the return values of `cost` (Line 25). The upper (respectively lower) bound for each location is computed by the OCaml function `hist_ub` (respectively `hist_lb`), which retrieves historical construction data from a database and analyzes the current situation in order to provide estimate bounds for the cost of building. We impose this constraint across all locations by means of a standard OCaml `for` loop (Lines 22-26).

Also, suppose that we have some knowledge about the global building costs for each location and how they compare to one another. That is, given two ZIP codes, we can determine where it is cheaper to build a factory. This knowledge allows us to define an ordering among ZIP codes, and thus assign to each a unique identifier in the range $[0 \ldots n\_locations - 1]$ such that the ZIP code with *id* 0 is the cheapest location and the one with *id* $n\_locations - 1$ is the most expensive. Given such ids, `cost` is monotonically increasing. Monotonicity can be expressed in Inez by means of an axiom, as follows:

```
27 assert_axiom
28   (~forall x (~forall y ([x <= y], cost x <= cost y))) ;;
```

The function `assert_axiom` is used to introduce an axiom. The keyword `~forall` defines two universally quantified variables `x` and `y`. We subsequently provide a list of assumptions (in this case just `x <= y`), followed by a conclusion (`cost x <= cost y`). We provide details on our implementation of axioms in Sect. 4.2.

We subsequently add constraints to ensure that the units produced by each factory that is built will not exceed its capacity, *i.e.*, that

$$\forall l \in locations. \left[\left(\sum_{c \in cities} production[c][l] \right) \leq build[l] * capacity[l] \right].$$

The Inez encoding is

```
29 for l = 0 to n_locations - 1 do
30  constrain
31    (let cities = List.init n_cities ~f:Fn.id
32     and f c = production.(c).(l) in
33     ~logic
```

```
34         (sum cities ~f <= iite build.(l) (toi capacity.(l)) 0))
35 done ;;
```

We notably use the Inez-provided function `sum` (Line 34), to express the sum of Inez terms resulting from the application of the function `f` on each element of the list `cities`. Additionally, we use the function `iite` (Line 34) that encodes an if-then-else condition. The first argument to `iite` is an Inez formula, while the second and third are Inez integer expressions for each possible case. Our application of `iite` ensures that, if a factory is built on location `l`, then we obtain the capacity from the corresponding array, otherwise the capacity is zero.

Our concrete example additionally enforces that the demands of each city are satisfied, which can be expressed mathematically as:

$$\forall c \in \mathit{cities}. \left[\left(\sum_{l \in \mathit{locations}} \mathit{production}[c][l] \right) = \mathit{demand}[c] \right]$$

In the interest of brevity, we omit the corresponding Inez code.

Finally, we define an objective function, which is to maximize the earnings, *i.e.*, the total revenue minus the cost of building the factories. The corresponding Inez code specifies the optimization criterion by means of the `maximize` function (and re-uses constructs that we have described already):

```
36 maximize
37   (let cities    = List.init n_cities ~f:Fn.id
38    and locations = List.init n_locations ~f:Fn.id in
39    let s1 =
40      ~logic (sum cities ~f:(fun c -> sum locations ~f:(fun l ->
41        revenue.(c).(l) * production.(c).(l))))
42    and s2 =
43      ~logic (sum locations ~f:(fun l ->
44        iite build.(l) (cost (toi l)) 0)) in
45    ~logic (s1 - s2)) ;;
46
47 solve_print_result () ;;
```

Line 47 starts the solving process and prints the result (which can be one of `opt`, `sat`, `unsat`, `unbounded`, or `unknown`) to the standard output. Note that our example builds a single set of constraints, and calls the underlying solver once. In general, Inez provides an incremental *push*/*pop* interface that allows the user to add and remove constraints, and perform multiple queries. As an example, consider that for the presented problem we had two different optimization criteria: first maximize the earnings and second minimize the number of factories. One could achieve this by *push*-ing the first maximization criterion, solving the problem, registering the maximum value obtained, and finally *pop*-ing the criterion. One could then add a constrain that restricts the first criterion to be equal to the registered value and minimize the second criterion. The full power of OCaml is available to determine future steps by examining intermediate results. Inez thus provides a framework for constraint-based algorithms.

We conclude this section with an overview of the OCaml features that we have utilized to provide the functionality described in this section. Interestingly, (a) *Generalized Algebraic Data Types (GADTs)* [18] allow us to represent terms and formulas in a type-safe way; (b) the extensibility of Inez is reflected on the *module system*, *i.e.*, extending the backend amounts to instantiating a *functor* that given a theory solver (wrapped up as a module) produces a solver for the resulting logic (*i.e.*, another module); (c) the *toplevel system* allows us to build custom read-evaluate-print loops that interactively interpret OCaml plus our logic fragments; finally, (d) `camlidl` enables relatively seamless interaction with C/C++ code (like SCIP and our implementation of CC).

3 An Algorithmic View of BC(T)

This section provides a set of interconnected algorithms that together implement BC(T). We thus document the architecture empowering the backend of Inez. The algorithms primarily operate upon *nodes* and sets thereof. Each node is described by a set of *integer linear constraints*, *i.e.*, constraints of the form $c_1 \cdot v_1 + \cdots + c_n \cdot v_n \; \{< \mid \leq \mid = \mid \geq \mid >\} \; c$, where c_i are integer constants, v_i are variable symbols, and the right-hand side c is an integer constant. While we provide support for *mixed integer linear constraints* (*i.e.*, integer and real variables side-by-side) through an experimental version of Inez, our discussion focuses on the integer case for simplicity. A node characterizes an open subproblem that needs to be explored. Nodes also carry metadata, like known variable bounds.

In addition to the integer linear constraints, the input to the solver contains uninterpreted function (UF) constraints. We assume that variable abstraction [20] has happened as a preprocessing step, resulting in linear constraints that do not involve UF terms. The definitions symbol that is used in the pseudocode stands for a collection of atomic formulas of the form $v = f(l)$, where v is a variable symbol, f is a UF symbol, and l is a list of arguments of the form $w + k$, where w is a variable symbol and k is an integer constant. Entirely concrete terms are a special case that can be encoded with a single integer variable fixed to zero. UF terms thus involve limited arithmetic, as is common practice [27]. definitions is an immutable global constant.

Our pseudocode uses *sum types* (also known as *tagged unions*) for some of the variables. Sum types have multiple *constructors* that correspond to different cases for the values carried. The constructor of a particular element serves as a tag denoting which case the element belongs in. Furthermore, the magic constant $*$ stands for non-deterministic Boolean choice. $*$ is used in conditionals where heuristics apply. $\langle e \rangle$ denotes that standard operators within e are to be interpreted over syntactic objects, *e.g.*, $\langle v - w \rangle$ is not a concrete integer or real, but a term representing the subtraction of w from v. We follow a generally applicative style, *e.g.*, operations that modify a node (by producing new linear constraints and bounds) produce a new node. Our presentation is top-down.

Our CC solver is implemented by the functions with suffix `_cc` (`check_cc`, `enforce_cc`, `propagate_cc`, and `branch_cc`). These are the functions that need to be replaced (or enhanced) for supporting a theory other than $\emptyset$.

```
function bc(p : node) : (Unsat|Optimal(assignment))
    P ← {p}
    α ← None
    while P ≠ ∅ do
        q ← pick(P)
        P ← P \ {q}
        match solve_node(q, obj(α)) with
            case Unsat
                noop() // do nothing
            case Solved(β)
                α ← Some(β)
            case Branched(Q)
                P ← P ∪ Q
    match α with
        case None
            return Unsat
        case Some(β)
            return Optimal(β)
```

3.1 High-Level Functions

The top-level B&C procedure, bc, accepts as its argument a set of integer linear constraints, p. p corresponds to the root node of the B&C search tree. bckeeps track of a set P of nodes to be examined (initialized with $\{p\}$). α carries a candidate satisfying (integer) assignment. α, belonging in a sum type, is of the form Some(β) if an assignment β is known; α is None otherwise. The loop body in bcpicks one of the remaining nodes in P and processes it by calling solve_node. The implementation of pick(not provided) may involve sophisticated heuristics for the choice of next node to be examined. A bias towards the children of the node that was more recently branched upon (*i.e.*, depth-first search) is common.

solve_nodereceives as arguments the node p to be processed, in addition to an upper bound l for the objective values of the solutions of interest. l corresponds to an already-known solution. (We assume that the function obj that computes l and our comparisons with l take care of the possibility of no known solution or unbounded solution, by supporting the special constants $+\infty, -\infty$.) solve_node performs three processing stages: (a) propagation (Sect. 3.2); (b) solving a continuous relaxation of the linear constraints; and (c) enforcing constraints against a relaxation-obtained solution (Sect. 3.3). Enforcing may result in branching (Sect. 3.4). The aforementioned stages operate on one node at a time, always called p in the respective functions, while their output may be multiple nodes, as a result of branching.

```
function
solve_node(p : node, l : int) : (Unsat|Solved(assignment)|Branched({node}))
    match propagate (p) with
        case Unsat
            return Unsat
        case Unmodified
            noop()
        case Modified(p')
            p ← p'
    match solve_relaxation(p) with
        case Unsat
            return Unsat
        case Modified(p')
            return solve_node(p', l)
        case Solved(α)
            if obj(α) ≥ l then
                return Unsat
            else
                match enforce(p, α) with
                    case Sat
                        return Solved(α)
                    case Unsat
                        return Unsat
                    case Modified(p')
                        return solve_node(p', l)
                    case Branched(P)
                        return Branched(P)
```

3.2 Propagation

The function `propagate` attempts to reduce the domain of variables. In the process of doing so, it may detect infeasibility (response Unsat); if it succeeds, `propagate` returns a version p' of the original node p modified with new bounds (Modified(p')); Unmodified means that no propagation was possible, neither was the function able to detect infeasibility. The implementation we provide combines ILP (`propagate_ilp`) and CC (`propagate_cc`) propagation techniques. We do not explain `propagate_ilp`, which is internal to the ILP solver, and as such orthogonal to BC(T). Either kind of propagation can be skipped. We repeatedly perform propagation, until a fixpoint is reached, or until a heuristic for termination returns true, *e.g.*, after a fixed number of rounds. In practice, SCIP employs various *constraint handlers* that provide propagation procedures of different *priority*. The top-level propagation procedure takes into account priorities to combine the sub-procedures.

```
function propagate (p : node) : (Unsat|Modified(node)|Unmodified)
    m ← false
    while * do
        if * then
            match propagate_ilp(p) with
                case Unsat
                    return Unsat
                case Modified(p')
                    p ← p'
                    m ← true
                case Unmodified
                    noop()
        if * then
            match propagate_cc(p) with
                case Unsat
                    return Unsat
                case Modified(p')
                    p ← p'
                    m ← true
                case Unmodified
                    noop()
    return m ? Modified(p) : Unmodified
```

propagate_cc is described in a declarative way. Our concrete implementation is similar to the CC procedures in SMT, and therefore takes offsets into account [27]. equalities(p) stands for known equalities of the form $v = w + k$, where v and w are integer variables and k is an integer constant. We implement this by defining an auxiliary variable $d_{v,w} = v - w$ for every interesting pair of variables v and w. We can subsequently query whether $d_{v,w}$ is fixed. For any equality $v = w + k$ implied by the already known equalities (conjoined with definitions), we try to fix the upper and lower bound of $v - w$ to k (via the functions set_lb and set_ub that provide an interface to the ILP solver), and report unsatisfiability if this is impossible. The outer forall statement should be read as a declarative specification (*i.e.*, we range over all relevant v, w), not as a suggestion for efficient implementation.

3.3 Enforcing Continuous Relaxations

In solve_node, propagation is followed by solving a continuous relaxation. A response Unsat for the relaxation implies that the integer constraints of the node (which are strictly harder than the real constraints of the relaxation) are also unsatisfiable. If solve_relaxation returns an assignment α (case Solved(α)), solve_node first checks whether α is better than the already known solution (obj(α) $< l$), and does not further process the node if not; integer solutions can be

```
function propagate_cc(p : node) : (Unsat|Modified(node)|Unmodified)
    m ← false
    forall v, w ∈ variables(p) do
        if equalities(p) ∧ definitions ⊨_Z v = w + k for some k ∈ ℤ then
            match set_lb(p, ⟨v − w⟩, k) with
                case Unsat
                    return Unsat
                case Modified(p′)
                    m ← true
                    p ← p′
                case Unmodified
                    noop()
            match set_ub(p, ⟨v − w⟩, k) with
                case Unsat
                    return Unsat
                case Modified(p′)
                    m ← true
                    p ← p′
                case Unmodified
                    noop()
    return m ? Modified(p) : Unmodified
```

at most as good as the solution to the relaxation. Otherwise, `enforce` is executed. If α is not integer, or if it is theory-inconsistent, `enforce` is responsible for explaining why, *e.g.*, by introducing implied linear constraints violated by α. `enforce` may determine that α satisfies all constraints (response Sat), or that the node (and not just α) is infeasible (response Unsat). In either of these cases, `solve_node` has solved p. Enforcing may result in learning new linear constraints or bounds (case Modified(p')), in which case `solve_node` re-processes the node.

`enforce` combines different kinds of enforcement, in much the same way that `propagate` combines different kinds of propagation. The part of enforcement that is related to integrality (`enforce_ilp`) may branch around a real solution, or apply cut generation techniques [12,15]. ILP cut generation techniques are beyond the scope of this paper. Conversely, the implementation of `enforce_ilp` is not shown. We proceed to describe CC enforcement (`enforce_cc`). First, `enforce_cc` calls `check_cc` to check whether α is theory-consistent. `check_cc` reports that α does not satisfy the UF constraints if there exist calls $v = f(l)$ and $v' = f(l')$ of some function f, such that all arguments in the respective positions of the lists of arguments l and l' have the same value under α, but $\alpha(v) \neq \alpha(v')$. `check_cc` then returns the *conflict* (f, v, v', l, l') to explain what is wrong with α. If no conflict is found, bcreceives α, and α becomes the new candidate solution. In case `check_cc` returns a conflict, `enforce_cc` ensures that

```
function
enforce(p : node, α : assignment) : (Sat|Unsat|Modified(node)|Branched({node}))
    match enforce_ilp(p, α) with
        case Sat
            return enforce_cc(p, α)
        case Unsat
            return Unsat
        case Modified(p')
            return Modified(p')
        case Branched(P)
            return Branched(P)
```

```
function enforce_cc(p : node, α : assignment) :
(Sat|Unsat|Modified(node)|Branched({node}))
    match check_cc(p, α) with
        case Conflict(c)
            match propagate_cc(p) with
                case Unsat
                    return Unsat
                case Modified(p')
                    return Modified(p')
                case Unmodified
                    return Branched(branch_cc(p, c))
        case Sat
            return Sat
```

propagation has happened by calling `propagate_cc`again. The latter function may have been skipped during the propagation stage. `enforce_cc` only needs to act further if propagation can neither detect unsatisfiability, nor produce new information. In this case, `enforce_cc` proceeds by branching.

Note that CC enforcement happens after the corresponding method for the ILP constraints. CC enforcement thus only ever deals with integer assignments, which yields cleaner implementation. Additionally, this design prioritizes ILP-related over theory-related operations, thus emphasizing ILP-heavy problems.

3.4 Branching

Branching is what our CC implementation performs when all else fails. Concretely, the following invariant holds when we get to `branch_cc`. There exists an integer solution for the non-theory constraints of p (given that integrality enforcement has succeeded), but the integer bounds that hold for p do not allow any information to be propagated, neither can we deduce unsatisfiability of p.

```
function check_cc(p : node, α : assignment) : (Sat|Conflict(conflict))
    m ← {} // m is a map
    foreach ⟨v = f(l)⟩ ∈ definitions do
        c ← [α(w) + k|⟨w + k⟩ in l] // list comprehension over l
        if (f, c) ∈ keys(m) then
            (v', l') ← m[(f, c)]
            if α(v) ≠ α(v') then
                return Conflict(f, v, v', l, l')
        else
            m[(f, c)] ← (v, l)
    return Sat
```

When we call `branch_cc`from `enforce_cc`, we have access to a conflict (f, v, v', l, l'). Note that there must be some position $i \in [0, \mathtt{arity}(f) - 1]$ such that the equality $l[i] = l'[i]$ is not implied by the bounds visible to `propagate_cc`. Otherwise, all arguments would have been equal, and `propagate_cc` would have produced the equality $v = v'$, which is violated. It is always possible to branch on whether $l[i] < l'[i]$, $l[i] = l'[i]$, or $l[i] > l'[i]$. If, according to the bounds on $v - v'$, $v = v'$ is a possibility, then we may instead choose to branch on whether $v < v'$, $v = v'$, or $v > v'$. Our branching involves very little guesswork. A conflict (f, v, v', l, l') provides a witness for the gap between the assignment under examination α (which is not feasible with respect to UF) and the more limited information that is available as bounds in p (which do not entail infeasibility). In order to steer the ILP solver away from the problematic assignment α (and other assignments similar to it), we have to examine the aforementioned gap. We do so by branching driven by the conflict.

The branching strategy we outlined is in alignment with the Nelson-Oppen (NO) scheme for combining decision procedures [20,25]. We branch on pairs of variables that are shared between ILP and UF, *i.e.*, make progress towards an *arrangement* of the shared variables. Such branching will eventually produce subproblems for which CC has all the information on the shared variables that it needs to determine (in)feasibility of the UF constraints (in definitions); similarly, for the UF-feasible subproblems, the ILP solver (with no more input possible from CC) has all the information it needs to apply complete techniques and determine feasibility. We thus guarantee termination of the combination.

4 Extensions

4.1 Propositional Structure

We have so far not discussed integer linear constraints that appear under arbitrary propositional structure. Inez provides such support by utilizing *indicator constraints.* Such constraints have the form $l \Rightarrow \Sigma_{0 \leq i < n}[c_i \cdot x_i] \leq c$, where l is a

```
function branch_cc(p : node, (f, v, v', l, l') : conflict) : {node}
    if * ∧ lb(p, ⟨v − v'⟩) ≤ 0 ∧ ub(p, ⟨v − v'⟩) ≥ 0 then
        P ← {⟨p ∧ v = v'⟩}
        if lb(p, ⟨v − v'⟩) < 0 then
            P ← P ∪ {⟨p ∧ v < v'⟩}
        if ub(p, ⟨v − v'⟩) > 0 then
            P ← P ∪ {⟨p ∧ v > v'⟩}
        return P
    for i ∈ [0, arity(f) − 1] do
        if α(l[i]) = α(l'[i]) then
            if lb(p, ⟨l[i] − l'[i]⟩) < 0 ∨ ub(p, ⟨l[i] − l'[i]⟩) > 0 then
                P ← {⟨p ∧ l[i] = l'[i]⟩}
                if lb(p, ⟨l[i] − l'[i]⟩) < 0 then
                    P ← P ∪ {⟨p ∧ l[i] < l'[i]⟩}
                if ub(p, ⟨l[i] − l'[i]⟩) > 0 then
                    P ← P ∪ {⟨p ∧ l[i] > l'[i]⟩}
                return P
    assert(false) // unreachable
```

possibly negated Boolean variable, c_i and c are constants, and v_i are variables. Indicator constraints can establish equivalence between a Boolean variable b and an inequality $\Sigma_{0 \leq i<n}[c_i \cdot x_i] \leq c$ via the constraints $b \Rightarrow \Sigma_{0 \leq i<n}[c_i \cdot x_i] \leq c$ and $\neg b \Rightarrow -\Sigma_{0 \leq i<n}[c_i \cdot x_i] \leq -c-1$. Once we have Boolean variables like b, encoding propositional structure can be done via clauses (which are a special case of integer linear inequalities) in a Tseitin-like fashion.

Indicator constraints can be encoded in terms of integer linear constraints [21], based on a technique that is known as Big-M. SCIP deals with indicator constraints via a specialized *constraint handler* (rather than via Big-M). This handler implements indicator constraints through propagation, enforcing, and branching functions that fit in BC(T) just like their CC counterparts (Sect. 3).

4.2 Local Theory Extensions

We demonstrate how to support user-provided axioms within BC(T) and Inez. Such axioms constrain newly defined function symbols (beyond the ones in the signature $\Sigma_{\mathbb{Z}}$ of Linear Integer Arithmetic, *e.g.*, +). We thus *extend* QFLIA by axiomatizing new functions. Throughout this section, we assume a first-order signature Σ, comprised of the axiomatized function symbols.

An example of the kinds of axioms we support was given via the axiom in Line 28 of our introductory example. Our axiom is only meaningful as an *extension* of (Integer Linear) Arithmetic. The intended meaning (monotonicity of `cost`) is only achieved because $\leq$ is already constrained by Arithmetic. More generally, we support axioms that are universally quantified disjunctions of inequalities that may contain function symbols. Our focus on clauses is not a restriction; collections of clausal axioms can be used to encode axioms with more complex structure.

Our implementation of axioms in Inez builds upon results on *local theory extensions* [30] that allow us to replace axioms with a finite set of instances thereof (computed based on the set of terms that appear in the formula). In our case, the instantiation procedure produces clauses, where the literals involve arithmetic and the Σ-function symbols.

While in principle we can simply encode the axiom instances of interest as part of the input formula (Sect. 4.1), our implementation applies a specialized procedure that retains the clausal structure. The literals are inequalities, *e.g.*, for our monotonicity example we have inequalities of the form $x \leq y$ and $\texttt{cost}(x) \leq \texttt{cost}(y)$ over x and y that appear in the input as arguments to `cost`. By introducing fresh variables, we simplify these literals by rewriting them to the form $v \leq c$, where v is a variable and c is a constant. We then employ a SCIP handler for constraints of the form $\bigvee_i v_i \leq c_i$, that notably employs SAT-like techniques for clauses [6].

4.3 Databases

Inez provides an extension aimed at database analysis [22]. The workhorse of this extension is what we call *table membership* constraints, which have the form

$$(x_1+c_1, \ldots, x_k+c_k) \in \{(y_{1,1}+d_{1,1}, \ldots, y_{1,k}+d_{1,k}), \ldots, (y_{l,1}+d_{l,1}, \ldots, y_{l,k}+d_{l,k})\},$$

where x_i, $y_{i,j}$ are variables and c_i, $d_{i,j}$ are (integer) constants. On top of table membership, Inez provides higher-level database-inspired modeling constructs.

Table membership fits in BC(T) just like CC. Functions `propagate_db` and `enforce_db` replace (or enhance) the corresponding CC functions, while everything else remains unchanged. Design decisions in `enforce_db` resemble the ones in `enforce_cc`, *e.g.*, branching (driven by the data) happens only as a last resort.

5 Related Work

Frontend: Existing projects that enhance programming languages with constraints [7,19,31] differ from Inez both with respect to the language constructs that they provide and the underlying constraint technology.

Backend: Inez seeks to combine the strengths of MP solvers [2,3,8] and solvers for first-order theories [24,25,29], *e.g.*, as implemented within Lazy SMT [28]. Previous work on similar combinations has focused on improving the arithmetic capabilities [13,16] of SMT solvers by integrating MP engines [9,14,23], and on extending SMT for optimization [11,26]. MPMT differs by having as its core an MP solver, as opposed to a SAT solver.

6 Conclusions

We provided an overview of the techniques that empower the Inez constraint solver. Inez is an open-source, freely available system that instantiates the BC(T) architecture for Mathematical Programming Modulo Theories. We described the concrete algorithms used to in Inez to efficiently implement BC(T). Inez is an extension of OCaml that allows users to write programs that orchestrate arbitrary interleaving between general computation and MPMT constraint solving.

References

1. Camlp4. https://github.com/ocaml/camlp4/wiki
2. CPLEX. http://www-01.ibm.com/software/integration/optimization/cplex-optimizer/
3. Gurobi. http://www.gurobi.com
4. MySQL. https://www.mysql.com/
5. mysql_protocol. https://github.com/slegrand45/mysql_protocol
6. SCIP Constraint Handler for Bound Disjunction Constraints. http://scip.zib.de/doc-3.1.1/html/cons__bounddisjunction_8h.php
7. Z3py. http://rise4fun.com/z3py/tutorial
8. Achterberg, T.: SCIP: solving constraint integer programs. Math. Program. Comput. **1**(1), 1–41 (2009)
9. Besson, F.: On using an inexact floating-point LP solver for deciding linear arithmetic in an SMT solver. In: SMT (2010)
10. Castillo, E., Conejo, A., Pedregal, P., Garca, R., Alguacil, N.: Building and Solving Mathematical Programming Models in Engineering and Science. Wiley, Hoboken (2002)
11. Cimatti, A., Franzén, A., Griggio, A., Sebastiani, R., Stenico, C.: Satisfiability modulo the theory of costs: foundations and applications. In: Esparza, J., Majumdar, R. (eds.) TACAS 2010. LNCS, vol. 6015, pp. 99–113. Springer, Heidelberg (2010)
12. Cornuejols, G.: Valid inequalities for mixed integer linear programs. Math. Program. **112**(1), 3–44 (2008)
13. Dutertre, B., de Moura, L.: A fast linear-arithmetic solver for DPLL(T). In: Ball, T., Jones, R.B. (eds.) CAV 2006. LNCS, vol. 4144, pp. 81–94. Springer, Heidelberg (2006)
14. Faure, G., Nieuwenhuis, R., Oliveras, A., Rodríguez-Carbonell, E.: SAT modulo the theory of linear arithmetic: exact, inexact and commercial solvers. In: Kleine Büning, H., Zhao, X. (eds.) SAT 2008. LNCS, vol. 4996, pp. 77–90. Springer, Heidelberg (2008)
15. Gomory, R.E.: Outline of an algorithm for integer solutions to linear programs. Bull. AMS **64**, 275–278 (1958)
16. Griggio, A.: A practical approach to satisfiability modulo linear integer arithmetic. JSAT **8**, 1–27 (2012)
17. Hang, C., Manolios, P., Papavasileiou, V.: Synthesizing cyber-physical architectural models with real-time constraints. In: Gopalakrishnan, G., Qadeer, S. (eds.) CAV 2011. LNCS, vol. 6806, pp. 441–456. Springer, Heidelberg (2011)
18. Jones, S.P., Vytiniotis, D., Weirich, S., Washburn, G.: Simple unification-based type inference for GADTs. In: ICFP (2006)

19. Koksal, A.S., Kuncak, V., Suter, P.: Constraints as Control. In: POPL (2012)
20. Manna, Z., Zarba, C.: Combining Decision Procedures. In: 10th Anniversary Colloquium of UNU/IIST (2002)
21. Manolios, P., Papavasileiou, V.: ILP modulo theories. In: Sharygina, N., Veith, H. (eds.) CAV 2013. LNCS, vol. 8044, pp. 662–677. Springer, Heidelberg (2013)
22. Manolios, P., Papavasileiou, V., Riedewald, M.: ILP Modulo Data. In: FMCAD (2014)
23. Monniaux, D.: On using floating-point computations to help an exact linear arithmetic decision procedure. In: Bouajjani, A., Maler, O. (eds.) CAV 2009. LNCS, vol. 5643, pp. 570–583. Springer, Heidelberg (2009)
24. Nelson, G., Oppen, D.: Fast Decision Algorithms Based on Union and Find (1977)
25. Nelson, G., Oppen, D.C.: Simplification by cooperating decision procedures. TOPLAS **1**, 245–257 (1979)
26. Nieuwenhuis, R., Oliveras, A.: On SAT modulo theories and optimization problems. In: Biere, A., Gomes, C.P. (eds.) SAT 2006. LNCS, vol. 4121, pp. 156–169. Springer, Heidelberg (2006)
27. Nieuwenhuis, R., Oliveras, A.: Fast congruence closure and extensions. Inf. Comput. **205**, 557–580 (2007)
28. Nieuwenhuis, R., Oliveras, A., Tinelli, C.: Solving SAT and SAT modulo theories: from an abstract davis-putnam-logemann-loveland procedure to DPLL(T). JACM **53**(6), 937–977 (2006)
29. Shostak, R.: A practical decision procedure for arithmetic with function symbols. JACM **26**(2), 351–360 (1979)
30. Sofronie-Stokkermans, V.: Hierarchic reasoning in local theory extensions. In: Nieuwenhuis, R. (ed.) CADE 2005. LNCS (LNAI), vol. 3632, pp. 219–234. Springer, Heidelberg (2005)
31. Torlak, E., Bodik, R.: A lightweight symbolic virtual machine for solver-aided host languages. In: PLDI (2014)

Using Minimal Correction Sets to More Efficiently Compute Minimal Unsatisfiable Sets

Fahiem Bacchus[1(✉)] and George Katsirelos[2]

[1] Department of Computer Science, University of Toronto, Toronto, ON, Canada
fbacchus@cs.toronto.edu

[2] MIAT, INRA, Toulouse, France
george.katsirelos@toulouse.inra.fr

Abstract. An unsatisfiable set is a set of formulas whose conjunction is unsatisfiable. Every unsatisfiable set can be corrected, i.e., made satisfiable, by removing a subset of its members. The subset whose removal yields satisfiability is called a correction subset. Given an unsatisfiable set $\mathcal{F}$ there is a well known hitting set duality between the unsatisfiable subsets of $\mathcal{F}$ and the correction subsets of $\mathcal{F}$: every unsatisfiable subset hits (has a non-empty intersection with) every correction subset, and, dually, every correction subset hits every unsatisfiable subset. An important problem with many applications in practice is to find a minimal unsatisfiable subset (MUS) of $\mathcal{F}$, i.e., an unsatisfiable subset all of whose proper subsets are satisfiable. A number of algorithms for this important problem have been proposed. In this paper we present new algorithms for finding a single MUS and for finding all MUSES. Our algorithms exploit in a new way the duality between correction subsets and unsatisfiable subsets. We show that our algorithms advance the state of the art, enabling more effective computation of MUSES.

1 Introduction

A set of formulas is said to be unsatisfiable if the conjunction of its members has no model (is unsatisfiable). A minimal unsatisfiable set (a MUS) has the additional property that every proper subset of it is satisfiable.

Given an unsatisfiable set $\mathcal{F}$ the task of computing a MUS contained in $\mathcal{F}$ (a MUS of $\mathcal{F}$) has long been an important problem for a range of verification applications related to diagnosis and debugging, e.g., program type debugging, circuit diagnosis, production configuration (see [6]).

MUSES have become even more important with the increasing applications of SAT based approaches in system analysis and verification. In [23] a number of ways that MUSES can be used in SAT based bounded model checking (BMC) are presented. For example, a MUS might tell the user that the property being checked did not play a role in deriving *unsat*, thus indicating that the system specification is unconstrained. MUSES also play an important role in applications that exploit unsatisfiable sets (sometimes called unsatisfiable cores).

D. Kroening and C.S. Păsăreanu (Eds.): CAV 2015, Part II, LNCS 9207, pp. 70–86, 2015.
DOI: 10.1007/978-3-319-21668-3_5

As discussed in [6] many of these application can benefit significantly from computing MUSES rather than just using the default unsatisfiable core returned by the solver. Formal equivalence checking, proof-based abstraction refinement, and boolean function bi-decomposition are three important applications in which computing a MUS has proved to be beneficial [6]. Belov et al. [4] present some more recent results quantifying the benefits of computing MUSES in the hybrid counterexample/proof-based abstraction engine GLA implemented in the ABC verification tool [9]. A more recent application of MUSES arises in the FrankenBit verifier [12] where MUSES are used to compute invariants [13].

With this range of applications it is not surprising that there has been an extensive amount of research into developing more effective algorithms for computing MUSES, e.g., [5,6,11,14,18–20] (see [6] for a more extensive list).

In this paper we continue this line of research and present new algorithms for computing MUSES. Our new algorithms exploit the well known hitting set duality between the unsatisfiable subsets of an unsatisfiable set $\mathcal{F}$ and the correction subsets of $\mathcal{F}$. Our algorithms work in particular with *minimal subsets*—the duality also holds between minimal unsatisfiable subsets and minimal correction subsets. This duality has been exploited before to compute all MUSES in the CAMUS system [16]. However, in CAMUS the first step was to compute the set of all MCSES, *AllMcses*, from which all MUSES can be extracted by finding all minimal hitting sets of *AllMcses*. Unfortunately in practice it is often impossible to complete the first step of computing *AllMcses*.

We find new ways to exploit the MUS/MCS connection in order to compute a single MUS and to incrementally compute all MUSES. Our method does not require computing *AllMcses*. We show empirically that our new algorithms advance the state of the art in MUS computation, and thus can potentially enhance a range of applications in formal methods that rely on computing MUSES.

2 Background

Let $\mathbb{T}$ be some background theory and $\mathcal{F}$ be a set of $\mathbb{T}$-formulas such that the **conjunction** of these formulas is $\mathbb{T}$-*unsat*, i.e., their conjunction has no $\mathbb{T}$-*model*. In many applications it is useful to identify a smaller subset of $\mathcal{F}$ that is $\mathbb{T}$-*unsat*. In practice, if the $\mathbb{T}$-*sat* status of various subsets of $\mathcal{F}$ can be effectively determined, then finding a **minimal** subset of $\mathcal{F}$ that is $\mathbb{T}$-*unsat* is often achievable.

In this paper we will always regard a set of formulas $\mathcal{F}$ as representing the conjunction of its members. So, e.g., $\mathcal{F}$ is $\mathbb{T}$-*unsat* means $\bigwedge_{f\in\mathcal{F}} f$ is $\mathbb{T}$-*unsat*.

Definition 1 (MUS). An unsatisfiable subset U of $\mathcal{F}$ is a subset of $\mathcal{F}$ that is $\mathbb{T}$-*unsat*. A **Minimal Unsatisfiable Set** (MUS) of $\mathcal{F}$ is a unsatisfiable subset $M \subseteq \mathcal{F}$ that is minimal w.r.t. set inclusion. That is, M is $\mathbb{T}$-*unsat* and every proper subset $S \subsetneq M$, S is $\mathbb{T}$-*sat*.

Definition 2 (MSS). A satisfiable subset of $\mathcal{F}$ is a subset of $\mathcal{F}$ that is $\mathbb{T}$-*sat*. A **Maximal Satisfiable Subset** (MSS) of $\mathcal{F}$ is a satisfiable subset $S \subseteq \mathcal{F}$ that is maximal w.r.t set inclusion. That is, S is $\mathbb{T}$-*sat* and for every proper superset $U \supsetneq S$ such that $U \subseteq \mathcal{F}$, U is $\mathbb{T}$-*unsat*.

Definition 3 (MCS). A correction subset of $\mathcal{F}$ is a subset of $\mathcal{F}$ whose complement in $\mathcal{F}$ is $\mathbb{T}$-*sat*. A **Minimal Correction Subset** (MCS) of $\mathcal{F}$ is a correction subset $C \subseteq \mathcal{F}$ that is minimal w.r.t. set inclusion, i.e., $\mathcal{F} \setminus C$ is an MSS of $\mathcal{F}$.

Definition 4. A formula $f \in \mathcal{F}$ is said to be **critical** (or a *transition* formula [7]) for $\mathcal{F}$ when $\mathcal{F}$ is $\mathbb{T}$-*unsat* and $\mathcal{F} - \{f\}$ is $\mathbb{T}$-*sat*.

Intuitively, a MUS is an unsatisfiable set that cannot be reduced without causing it to become satisfiable; a MSS is a satisfiable set that cannot be added to without causing it to become unsatisfiable; and an MCS is a minimal set of removals from $\mathcal{F}$ that causes $\mathcal{F}$ to become satisfiable.

A critical formula for $\mathcal{F}$ is one whose removal from $\mathcal{F}$ causes $\mathcal{F}$ to become satisfiable. It should be noted if f is critical for $\mathcal{F}$ then (a) f must be contained in every MUS of $\mathcal{F}$ and (b) $\{f\}$ is an MCS of $\mathcal{F}$. Furthermore, it can be observed that M is a MUS if and only if every $f \in M$ is critical for M. Note that a formula f that is critical for a set S is not necessarily critical for a superset $S' \supset S$. In particular, S' might contain other MUSES that do not contain f.

Duality. There is a well known hitting set duality between MUSES and MCSES that to the best of our knowledge was first presented formally by Reiter [22] in the context of diagnosis problems.

A hitting set H of a collection of sets $\mathcal{C}$ is a set that "hits" every set in $\mathcal{C}$ in the sense that it has a non empty intersection with each such set: $\forall C \in \mathcal{C}. H \cap C \neq \emptyset$. A hitting set H is minimal (or irreducible) if no subset of H is a hitting set.

Let *AllMuses*($\mathcal{F}$) (*AllMcses*($\mathcal{F}$)) be the set containing all MUSES (MCSES) of $\mathcal{F}$. Then Reiter's result can be recast to show that $M \in$ *AllMuses*($\mathcal{F}$) iff M is a minimal hitting set of *AllMcses*($\mathcal{F}$), and dually, $\mathcal{C} \in$ *AllMcses*($\mathcal{F}$) iff C is a minimal hitting set of *AllMuses*($\mathcal{F}$). Intuitively, we can see that if a MUS M fails to hit an MCS C, then $M \subseteq \mathcal{F}-C$, i.e., M is a subset of a satisfiable set and hence can't be unsatisfiable. Similarly, if an MCS C fails to hit a MUS M then $\mathcal{F}-C \supseteq M$ is a superset of an unsatisfiable set and hence can't be satisfiable. It is also not hard to see that the duality between MCSES and MUSES also holds for non-minimal sets. That is, every correction subset (not necessarily minimal) hits all unsatisfiable subsets and vice versa.

Although we have discussed MUSES and MCSES in the context of a fixed set of formulas $\mathcal{F}$ we will also be working with subsets of $\mathcal{F}$. It is useful to point out that if $\mathcal{F}' \subseteq \mathcal{F}$, then *AllMuses*($\mathcal{F}'$) $\subseteq$ *AllMuses*($\mathcal{F}$) and in general *AllMuses*($\mathcal{F}'$) $\neq$ *AllMuses*($\mathcal{F}$). Hence, if f is critical for $\mathcal{F}$ it is critical for all unsatisfiable subsets of $\mathcal{F}$ (f is critical iff it is contained in every MUS).

An MCS C' of $\mathcal{F}' \subset \mathcal{F}$ is not necessarily an MCS of $\mathcal{F}$, however C' can always be extended to an MCS C of $\mathcal{F}$. In particular, we can add the formulas of $\mathcal{F} \setminus \mathcal{F}'$ to $\mathcal{F}'$ one at a time. If C' is no longer a correction subset of $\mathcal{F}' \cup \{f\}$ we add f to C'. At each stage the augmented C' is an MCS of the augmented $\mathcal{F}'$, and at the end C' has been extended to be an MCS of $\mathcal{F}$. Since we have not seen this observation previously in the literature, and its proof is illustrative of concepts needed in our algorithms, we provide a proof here.

Proposition 1. *Let $C' \in$ AllMcses$(\mathcal{F}')$ and $f \in \mathcal{F} \setminus \mathcal{F}'$. If C' is a correction subset of $\mathcal{F}' \cup \{f\}$ it is an* MCS *of $\mathcal{F}' \cup \{f\}$, and if it is not then $C' \cup \{f\}$ is an* MCS *of $\mathcal{F}' \cup \{f\}$.*

Proof. C' is a minimal correction subset of $\mathcal{F}'$ if and only if for every $a \in C'$ there exists a MUS $M \in$ *AllMuses*$(\mathcal{F}')$ such that $M \cap C' = \{a\}$. That is, M is only hit by a, hence C' will no longer be a correction subset if we remove a. M serves as a witness that a is needed in C', and C' is minimal iff every member of C' has a witness. Since *AllMuses*$(\mathcal{F}') \subseteq$ *AllMuses*$(\mathcal{F}' \cup \{f\})$, the witnesses for C' remain valid after adding f to $\mathcal{F}'$ and if C' corrects $\mathcal{F}' \cup \{f\}$ it must be an MCS of $\mathcal{F}' \cup \{f\}$. If C' does not correct $\mathcal{F}' \cup \{f\}$ then there are some MUSES in *AllMuses*$(\mathcal{F}' \cup \{f\})$ that are not hit by C'. But since C' hits all muses in *AllMuses*$(\mathcal{F}')$ these un-hit MUSES must contain f. So $C' \cup \{f\}$ is a correction subset of $\mathcal{F}' \cup \{f\}$. Furthermore, any of these new MUSES can serve as a witness for f, and for every $a \in C$ there is a witness for a in *AllMuses*$(\mathcal{F}')$ which cannot contain f. Hence, these witnesses remain valid when f is added to C', and $C' \cup \{f\}$ is an MCS of $\mathcal{F}' \cup \{f\}$. □

Although we have given the above definitions in terms of an arbitrary theory $\mathbb{T}$, in the rest of this paper we will work with $\mathbb{T}$ being ordinary propositional logic (*Prop*) and $\mathcal{F}$ being a set of clauses. In particular, our algorithms assume access to some basic facilities of modern SAT solvers. Some of these facilities are also available in modern SMT solvers, and thus some of our ideas could be lifted to theories handled by SMT solvers.

3 Prior MUS Algorithms

Current state-of-the-art algorithms for computing MUSES have converged on versions of Algorithm 1.

Algorithm 1 operates on a working set of clauses $W = (unkn \cup crits)$ with the clauses of unknown status, *unkn*, initially equal to $\mathcal{F}$. In the main **while** loop the status of each clause in *unkn* is resolved and its size reduced until $unkn = \emptyset$. At this point W consists only of a set of clauses, *crits*, all of which are known to be critical for W. As observed above this implies that $W = crits$ is a MUS.

The input assumption is that $W = \mathcal{F}$ is *unsat*, and this condition is an invariant of the algorithm. Each iteration of the main loop selects a clause of unknown status $c \in unkn$ and tests the satisfiability of $W \setminus \{c\}$. We have that $W \setminus \{c\} \models \neg c$, as W has no models. Hence, we can make the SAT test of $W \setminus \{c\}$ more efficient by adding the implied $\neg c$ (since c is a clause, $\neg c$ is a set of unit clauses which are particularly advantageous for a SAT solver).

If $W \setminus \{c\}$ is *sat* then we know that c is critical for W (and for all subsets of W that the algorithm subsequently works with). In this case we can additionally find more critical clauses by applying the technique of recursive model rotation (RMR) [7,24]. Note that the satisfying model π returned is such that $\pi \models (crits \cup unkn) \setminus \{c\}$ and $\pi \not\models c$, which is the condition required for RMR to work correctly.

Algorithm 1. findmus($\mathcal{F}$): Current state-of-the-art algorithm for computing a MUS

```
Input: F an unsatisfiable set of clauses
Output: a MUS of F
crits ← ∅
unkn ← F
while unkn ≠ ∅ do
    c ← choose c ∈ unkn
    unkn ← unkn \ {c}
    (sat?,π,κ) ← SatSolve(crits ∪ unkn ∪ {¬c})
    /* SatSolve returns the status (sat or unsat), a model π if sat, or an unsat
       subset κ of the input if unsat.                                        */
    if sat? then
        crits ← crits ∪ {c}
        C ← ERMR (c, crits, unkn, π)
        crits ← crits ∪ C
        unkn ← unkn \ C
    else
        if κ ⊆ (crits ∪ unkn) then
            unkn ← unkn ∩ κ
return crits
```

Every newly identified critical clause is removed from *unkn* and added to *crits* thus reducing the number of iterations of the main loop.

If $W \setminus \{c\}$ is *unsat* then there is some MUS of W that does not contain c. The algorithm then focuses on finding one of these MUSES by removing c from W. Note that there might also be MUSES of W that do contain c so the final MUS found depends on the order in which clauses of *unkn* are tested. One final optimization is that we can obtain an *unsat* core, κ, from the *sat* solver. If that core did not depend on the added $\neg c$ clauses then we can reduce W by setting it to κ. In this case it must be that $crits \subseteq \kappa$: all the clauses of *crits* are critical for $W \setminus \{c\}$. Hence, to make $W = \kappa$ we simply need to remove from *unkn* all clauses not in κ. This optimization is called clause set refinement [20].

Algorithm 1 is used in state of the art MUS finding algorithms like [8, 20], and these systems also add a number of other lower level optimizations as described in [20]. The main difference between these MUS finding systems is that some use a modified SAT solver that keeps track of the resolution proof used to derive *unsat* [20]—the unsatisfiable subset κ is extracted from that proof—while others use selector variables for the input clauses and the technique of SAT solving under assumptions to obtain κ [10].

4 MCS Based MUS Finding

In this section we present our new algorithms for finding MUSES. Our algorithms are based on the duality between MCSES and MUSES mentioned in Sect. 2. This duality has been exploited in previous work, in particular in the CAMUS system [16]. However, in that prior work the first step was to compute all MCSES of the input formula $\mathcal{F}$, $AllMcses(\mathcal{F})$, after which MUSES were found by finding minimal hitting sets of $AllMcses(\mathcal{F})$. This first step is very expensive, and sometimes cannot be completed since there can be exponential number of MCSES. So CAMUS is not very effective for the task of finding a single MUS. In this work we revisit this duality to arrive at algorithms that do not require an exhaustive enumeration of all MCSES.

4.1 Finding a Single MUS

Algorithm 2 is our new algorithm for finding a single MUS. Like Algorithm 1, it operates on the working set of clauses $W = (unkn \cup crits)$ with the clauses of unknown status, *unkn*, initially equal to $\mathcal{F}$. In the main **while** loop a minimal correction subset of W is computed using Algorithm 3. Algorithm 3 works to find not just any MCS: it searches for an MCS contained entirely in *unkn*. Every clause in the set *crits* is critical for W, and thus every clause in *crits* is a singleton MCS. We are not interested in finding these MCSES. If there is no MCS in *unkn* it must be the case that W remains *unsat* even if all of *unkn* is removed from it. That is, *crits* is an unsatisfiable set all of whose members are critical—it is a MUS.

If we do find an MCS, CS, we then choose some clause from it, c, add c to *crits* and remove all of CS from *unkn*. Algorithm 3 also returns the satisfying solution, π it found for $W \setminus CS$ (verifying that CS is a correction subset). This solution can be used to find more criticals using RMR. Note that since CS is a minimal correction subset it must be the case that $\pi \not\models a$ for every $a \in CS$. Thus, $\pi \models (crits \cup unkn) \setminus \{c\}$ and $\pi \not\models c$, which is the condition required for RMR to work correctly. As will be described below we have developed an extension of standard RMR, **em-rmr**, that can find even more new criticals.

Clause set refinement can be used within this algorithm. Algorithm 3 (**find-mcs**) computes an unsatisfiable core whenever $|CS| \geq 1$. From this core an unsatisfiable set $\kappa \subseteq crits \cup unkn$ can be extracted and used as in Algorithm 1 to reduce *unkn* to $unkn \cap \kappa$. A simpler solution, however, is to do another SAT call on the unsatisfiable set $crits \cup unkn$ whenever $|CS| > 1$. In this case the SAT solver has just refuted a closely related formula in **find-mcs** and can exploit its previously learned clauses to quickly refute $crits \cup unkn$. The core it returns can then be intersected with *unkn*. In our experiments, we confirmed that in the vast majority of cases the cost of this step is negligible typically taking less than a second cumulatively.

However, in those cases where the instance contains only one MUS all MCSES will have size 1, and we would never get to perform clause set refinement. We address this deficiency by forcing a SAT call on $crits \cup unkn$ whenever clause set refinement has not been performed for some time. The logic of when to do the SAT call and returning a reduced *unkn* set is encapsulated in the **refine-clause-set** subroutine.

Theorem 1. *If its input formula $\mathcal{F}$ is unsat,* ***find-mcs*** *correctly returns an* MCS *of $crits \cup unkn$ contained in unkn if any exist,* ***em-rmr*** *correctly returns a set of clauses critical for $crits \cup unkn$, and* ***refine-clause-set*** *correctly returns*

Algorithm 2. MCS-MUS($\mathcal{F}$): Find a MUS of $\mathcal{F}$ using MCS duality.

Input: $\mathcal{F}$ an **unsatisfiable** set of clauses
Output: a MUS of $\mathcal{F}$

$crits \leftarrow \emptyset$
$unkn \leftarrow \mathcal{F}$
while *true* **do**
  $(CS, \pi) \leftarrow$ **find-mcs**$(crits, unkn)$ // *Find CS, an* MCS *contained in unkn.*
  if $CS = null$ **then**
    return *crits*
  $c \leftarrow$ **choose** $c \in CS$
  $crits \leftarrow crits \cup \{c\}$
  $unkn \leftarrow unkn \setminus CS$
  $C \leftarrow$ **em-rmr** $(c, crits, unkn, \pi)$
  $crits \leftarrow crits \cup C$
  $unkn \leftarrow unkn \setminus C$
  $unkn \leftarrow$ **refine-clause-set**$(crits, unkn, |CS| > 1)$

an unsatisfiable subset of $crits \cup unkn$*, then Algorithm 2 will return a* MUS *of its input formula* $\mathcal{F}$.

Proof. We show that two invariants hold in the main loop of Algorithm 2: (1) $crits \cup unkn$ is unsat and (2) every clause in *crits* is critical for $crits \cup unkn$.

Algorithm 2 terminates when **find-mcs** is unable to find a correction subset in *unkn*. This happens when $crits \cup unkn$ remains *unsat* even after all the clauses of *unkn* are removed, i.e., when it detects that *crits* is *unsat* (see Algorithm 3). In this case, we know that *crits* is an *unsat* set of clauses and from invariant (2) all of its members are critical, i.e., it is a MUS. Hence, the correctness of Algorithm 2 follows from the invariants.

Initially $crits = \emptyset$ and $unkn = \mathcal{F}$, and $\mathcal{F}$ is *unsat* by assumption. So the invariants hold at the start of the main loop. Assume that they hold up until the $i-1$'th iteration of the main loop. If in the i'th iteration we fail to find an MCS contained in *unkn*, then *crits* is *unsat* and unchanged from the $i-1$'th iteration. So invariant (1) holds and by induction so does invariant (2).

Otherwise, let CS be the MCS returned by **find-mcs** with $CS \subseteq unkn$. CS is an MCS of $W = crits \cup unkn$, therefore there is a witness $M \in AllMuses(W)$ for every $c \in CS$ with $M \cap CS = \{c\}$. Algorithm 2 updates *crits* to $crits \cup \{c\}$ (for some $c \in CS$) and *unkn* to $unkn \setminus CS$. Let this updated set $crits \cup unkn$ be $W' = W \setminus CS \cup \{c\}$. We have that $M \subseteq W'$ so invariant (1) continues to hold. Furthermore, let $M' \in AllMuses(W')$ be any MUS of W'. Since $AllMuses(W') \subseteq AllMuses(W)$, M' is also a MUS of W. Hence M' must be hit by the MCS CS and since W' only contains c from CS we must have $c \in M'$. This shows that c hits all MUSES of W', i.e., removing it from W' removes all MUSES from W' making W' *sat*. That is, c is critical for $W' = crits \cup unkn$, and invariant (2) continues to hold.

Finally since we are assuming that **em-rmr** is correct, the invariants are preserved after **em-rmr** moves some clauses from *unkn* to *crits*. The call to **refine-clause-set** cannot affect invariant (2) and since we assume that it is correct, it preserves also invariant (1). ∎

Algorithm 3. findmcs(*crits*, *unkn*): Find an MCS of $crits \cup unkn$ entirely contained in *unkn*.

```
Input: (crits, unkn) Two sets of clauses whose union is unsatisfiable.
Output: CS an MCS of crits ∪ unkn that is contained in unkn and a model π
        such that π ⊨ (crits ∪ unkn) \ CS
(sat?, π, κ) ← SatSolve(crits)
if not sat? then
    return null
CS ← {c ∈ unkn | π ⊭ c}
while |CS| > 1 do
    (sat?, π′, κ) ← SatSolve(crits ∪ (unkn \ CS) ∪ atLeastOneIsTrue(CS))
    if sat? then
        CS ← {c ∈ CS | π′ ⊭ c}
        π ← π′
    else
        return (CS, π)
return (CS, π)
```

Finding a Constrained MCS. There are two state of the art algorithms for finding MCSES, CLD [17] and Relaxation Search [3]. Both can be modified to find an MCS in a particular subset of the input clauses. We tried Relaxation Search but found that an approach that is similar to CLD, but not identical, worked best for our purposes. The resulting Algorithm 3 finds an MCS of the union of its two input clause sets, *crits* and *unkn* that is constrained to be contained in *unkn*.

Initially a SAT test is performed on *crits*. If *crits* is *unsat*, then there is no correction subset contained in *unkn* so the algorithm returns **null**. Otherwise, we have a satisfying model π of *crits*. The set of clauses falsified by any model is always a correction subset, and for π this correction subset, *CS*, is contained in *unkn*. The algorithm makes *CS* minimal by a sequence of SAT calls, each one asking the SAT solver to find a new model that falsifies a proper subset of clauses from the previous model. At each iteration, *CS* is updated to be the reduced set of falsified clauses. This continues until a model cannot be found or *CS* is reduced down to one clause. If a model cannot be found this means that adding any clause of *CS* to $(crits \cup unkn) \setminus CS$ yields an unsatisfiable formula, i.e., *CS* is an MCS. If *CS* is reduced to one clause then that clause must be an MCS since $crits \cup unkn$ is unsatisfiable, and an invariant of the algorithm is that *CS* is always a correction set of $crits \cup unkn$.

The main difference between Algorithm 3 and CLD of [17] lies in the encoding of *atLeastOneIsTrue*(*CS*) constraint passed to the SAT solver. In CLD this constraint is encoded as one large clause that is the disjunction of all of the clauses in *CS*. π falsifies all clauses of *CS*, so it must falsify their disjunction, therefore this disjunction is not a tautology. Furthermore, when the disjunction is satisfied at least one more clause of *CS* must also be satisfied. In Algorithm 3 we instead add a **selection variable** to each clause of *CS*. That is, each clause $c_i \in CS$ is transformed into the clause $c_i^+ = c_i \vee \neg s_i$, where s_i is a new variable not appearing elsewhere in the formula. Making s_i true strengthens c_i^+ back to c_i, while making it false satisfies c_i^+, effectively removing it from the CNF. With these selector variables *atLeastOneIsTrue*(*CS*) can be encoded as a clause containing all of the selector variables: $\bigvee_{c_i \in CS} s_i$.

In addition, we found that in 90 % of cases when the SAT call is able to find an improving model it was able to do so without backtracking (no conflicts were found). Hence, a lot of the time of the solver is spent in descending a single branch that changes little between iterations of Algorithm 3. This time can be significantly reduced if we backtrack only to the point where the branches diverge. This is similar to techniques used already in general SAT solving for improving restarts [21] and in incremental SAT solving for reducing the overhead of assumptions [1]. We found that these two simple changes had a surprisingly positive effect on efficiency.

Recursive Model Rotation (RMR). If $\mathcal{F}$ is unsatisfiable then it follows from the definition that a clause c is critical for $\mathcal{F}$ if and only if there exists a model π such that $\pi \models \mathcal{F} \setminus \{c\}$. Hence, if in Algorithm 1 or Algorithm 2, we find for the current set of working clauses $W = (unkn \cup crits)$ a model π such that $\pi \models W \setminus \{c\}$ we know that c is critical for W.

The technique of RMR [7] is to examine models that differ from π by only one assignment to see if we can find a model that witnesses the criticality of a clause different from c whose status is still undetermined. This is accomplished by flipping π's assignments to the variables of c one by one. Each such flipped model satisfies c and can be checked to see if it falsifies only one other unknown clause. If such a clause c' is found, then c' is now known to be critical, and we can recursively flip the model that witnesses its criticality. Recursive model rotation has been found to be very effective in MUS finding, eliminating many SAT tests. *Eager* model rotation (ERMR) [20] improves RMR by allowing it to falsify a critical clause, which may enable further rotations.

We have found that we can effectively find more critical clauses than ERMR using Algorithm 4. This algorithm first runs ERMR and then uses a SAT solver to find a model that witnesses the criticality of a clause of unknown status. This is done by using a standard encoding of an "at most one" constraint over the negation of the selector variables of the clauses currently in *unkn*. This forces the model to satisfy all clauses of $crits \cup unkn$ except one. (The model must falsify that remaining clause as $crits \cup unkn$ is unsatisfiable). This sequence of SAT calls can in principle find all critical clauses, but it can sometimes take too long. In practice, we put a strict time bound on the SAT call, and found that within that bound we could still find a useful number of additional critical clauses. As we will show in Sect. 5, this method can sometimes hinder performance, but also allows us to solve some instances that were otherwise too hard.

4.2 Finding All MUSES

We have also developed an algorithm for finding all MUSES. Our algorithm exploits the idea of using a SAT formula to represent a constrained collection

Algorithm 4. em-rmr(c, *crits*, *unkn*, π) find more criticals than ERMR

Input: (c, *crits*, *unkn*, π): *crits* $\cup$ *unkn* is *unsat*; all clauses of *crits* are critical for *crits* $\cup$ *unkn*, $c \in$ *crits*; $\pi \not\models c$, and $\pi \models (crits \cup unkn) \setminus \{c\}$.

Output: Returns an additional set of clauses critical for *crits* $\cup$ *unkn*.

```
while true do
    crits' ← crits ∪ ERMR (c, crits, unkn, π)
    unkn' ← unkn \ crits'
    (sat?, π, κ) ← SatSolve(crits' ∪ atMostOne({¬s_i | c_i ∈ unkn'}))
    if sat? then
        c ← the single c_i ∈ unkn' such that π ⊨ ¬s_i
        crits' ← crits' ∪ {c}
        unkn' ← unkn' \ {c}
    else
        return (crits' \ crits)
```

of sets. This idea was also used in the MARCO system which also enumerates all MUSES [15]. Specifically, if we regard each propositional variable as being a set element, then the set of variables made true by any model can be viewed as being a set. The set of satisfying models then represents a collection of sets.

In MARCO, all MUSES are enumerated by maintaining a SAT formula *ClsSets* which contains a variable s_i for each clause $c_i \in \mathcal{F}$. Clauses are added to *ClsSets* to exclude all already found MUSES as well as all supersets of these MUSES. For example, if $M = \{c_1, c_3, c_4\}$ is a known MUS then the clause $(\neg s_1 \vee \neg s_3 \vee \neg s_4)$ ensures that every satisfying model of *ClsSets* excludes at least one clause of M—this blocks M and all supersets of M from being solutions to *ClsSets*. A SAT test is preformed on *ClsSets* which extracts a subset $\mathcal{F}'$ of $\mathcal{F}$ not containing any known MUS. If $\mathcal{F}'$ is *unsat* one of its MUSES is extracted using Algorithm 1 and then blocked in *ClsSets*, otherwise MARCO grows $\mathcal{F}'$ into an MSS-MCS pair $\langle S, \mathcal{F} \setminus S\rangle$ and a clause is added to *ClsSets* to block $\mathcal{F} \setminus S$ and all of its supersets. For example, for a correction subset $C = \{c_1, c_3, c_4\}$ the clause $(s_1 \vee s_3 \vee s_4)$ is added to *ClsSets*. When *ClsSets* becomes *unsat*, all MUSES have been enumerated.

Algorithm 5 is our new algorithm for enumerating all MUSES of an unsatisfiable formula $\mathcal{F}$. The high level structure of Algorithm 5 is similar to that of MARCO but rather than treating the MUS extraction procedure as a black box, it records the (not necessarily minimal) correction subsets discovered during the MUS procedure and uses them to accelerate the extraction of future MUSES. In particular, MUSES and MCSES are blocked in the same way as in MARCO. Hence, at any stage the set $\mathcal{F}'$ obtained from a SAT solution of *ClsSets* has the properties (a) $\mathcal{F}'$ does not contain any known MUSES and (b) $\mathcal{F}'$ hits all known correction subsets. We want $\mathcal{F}'$ to hit all known correction subsets as otherwise $\mathcal{F}'$ cannot contain a MUS. When *ClsSets* becomes unsatisfiable all MUSES have been enumerated (and blocked).

Given a SAT solution $\mathcal{F}'$ of *ClsSets*, we extract a MUS using a procedure similar to Algorithm 2. In addition, however, we mirror the removal of clauses from *unkn* by setting the corresponding variable in *ClsSets* to *false*. Unit propagation in *ClsSets* may then give us more variables that can be moved to *crits*, because

Algorithm 5. MCS-MUS-ALL($\mathcal{F}$): Enumerate all MUSES of $\mathcal{F}$ using MCS duality.

```
Input: F an unsatisfiable set of clauses
Output: enumerate all MUSES of F
ClsSets ← empty set of clauses and the set of variables {s_i | c_i ∈ F}
while true do
    (sat?, π, κ) ← SatSolve(ClsSets)                 // Setting all decisions to true
    if not sat? then
        return                                        // All MUSES enumerated
    F' ← {c_i | c_i ∈ F ∧ π ⊨ s_i}
    F^c ← F \ F'
    (sat?, π, κ) ← SatSolve(F')
    if sat? then
        ClsSets ← ClsSets ∪ (⋁_{c_i ∈ F^c} s_i) // MCS
    else
        crits ← {c_i | s_i ∈ UP(ClsSets ∪ {(¬s_j)|c_j ∈ F^c}}
        unkn ← F' \ crits
        while true do
            (CS, π) ← find-mcs(crits, unkn)
            if CS = null then
                enumerate(crits)                      // crits is a MUS
                ClsSets ← ClsSets ∪ (⋁_{c_i ∈ crits} ¬s_i)   // Block this MUS
                break
            else
                c ← choose c ∈ CS
                CS^F ← extend-cs (CS, π, F', F^c)
                ClsSets ← ClsSets ∪ (⋁_{c_i ∈ CS^F} s_i) // Correction set
                F^c ← F^c ∪ (CS \ {c})
                crits ← crits ∪ {c} ∪ {c_i | s_i ∈ UP(ClsSets ∪ {(¬s_j)|c_j ∈ F^c}}
                unkn ← unkn \ (CS ∪ crits)
                crits ← em-rmr (c,crits,unkn,π)
                unkn ← refine-clause-set(crits, unkn, |CS| > 1),
```

previously discovered correction sets must be hit. Once a MUS is constructed, all these assignments to *ClsSets* are retracted.

One complication that arises in comparison to Algorithm 2 is that when we discover an MCS, it is only an MCS of $crits \cup unkn$, but we can only add MCSES of $\mathcal{F}$ to *ClsSets*. Therefore, we need to extend each MCS that we discover to an MCS of $\mathcal{F}$. The function **extend-cs** does this by adding to CS all clauses of $\mathcal{F} \setminus (crits \cup unkn)$ that were violated by π. We choose not to minimize this CS, as it can be costly especially if $\mathcal{F}$ is much bigger than $crits \cup unkn$.

An additional insight arising from the ideas of Relaxation Search [3] is that if while solving *ClsSets* we force the SAT solver to always set its decision variables to *true*, then the set $\mathcal{F}'$ we obtain will be a *maximal* set satisfying (a) and (b) above. Thus the set of excluded clauses $\mathcal{F}^c = \mathcal{F} \setminus \mathcal{F}'$ must be a *minimal* hitting set of the set of known MUSES. Each known MUS in *ClsSets* forces the exclusion of at least one clause. Thus $\mathcal{F}^c$, is a hitting set of the known MUSES. Since setting all decision variables to *true* causes the inclusion of clauses, all exclusions must be forced by unit propagation. This means that each excluded clause arises from a MUS all of whose other clauses have already been included in $\mathcal{F}'$. That is, for each excluded clause c in $\mathcal{F}^c$ there is some known MUS M such that $M \cap \mathcal{F}^c = \{c\}$. This shows that $\mathcal{F}^c$ is minimal.

Theorem 2. *If its input formula $\mathcal{F}$ is unsat, All-MCS-MUS returns all MUSes of its input formula $\mathcal{F}$.*

Proof (Sketch). First note that all MUSES and all MSSES are solutions of *ClsSets*. At each iteration, it produces either a satisfiable set, whose complement is an MCS, or an unsatisfiable set which is reduced to a MUS. Each is subsequently blocked so cannot be reported again, nor can any of its supersets. Additionally, the inner loop generates correction subsets, which it blocks in *ClsSets*, without checking if they are MCSES of $\mathcal{F}$. If these are MCSES then they will not be produced as solutions of *ClsSets*. So the algorithm will produce only MUSES and MCSES before *ClsSets* becomes unsat. Additionally, it will produce all MUSES, as this is the only way to block such solutions.

It remains to show that it produces correct MCSES and MUSES. For MCSES, it follows from the fact that the formula is satisfiable and the solution is maximal. For MUSES, we only need to show that unit propagation in *ClsSets* produces critical clauses. Indeed, all correction sets that are blocked in *ClsSets* are either produced by solutions of *ClsSets* itself or as MCSES of some subset of $\mathcal{F}$, extended to a correction set of $\mathcal{F}$. When such a blocking clause becomes unit, it means that exactly one of the clauses of the corresponding correction set remains in $crits \cup unkn$. A MUS must hit all correction sets, so the sole remaining clause is critical for $crits \cup unkn$. The correctness of the rest of the MUS extraction procedure follows from the correctness of Algorithm 2. ■

5 Empirical Evaluation

We implemented all of our new algorithms C++, and evaluated them against state-of-the-art algorithms for the corresponding tasks. We ran all experiments on a cluster of 48-core Opteron 6176 nodes at 2.3 GHz having 378 GB RAM.

Discovering MCSES. The state of the art in discovering MCSES is CLD [17] and Relaxation Search (RS) [3]. We compared Algorithm 3, (denoted MCSCL) using MINISAT as the *sat* solver without preprocessing [10], against CLD and RS in the tasks of identifying a single MCS and generating all MCSES of a formula, on a set comprising 1343 industrial instances from SAT competitions and structured MAXSAT instances from MAXSAT evaluations [17]. We show cactus plots comparing the three algorithms in both tasks in Fig. 1, with a timeout of 1800 seconds.

We first note that there is a relatively small window in which the algorithms may differentiate. In the case of discovering a single MCS, more than 1200 instances are solved instantaneously by all 3 algorithms, while some 20 of

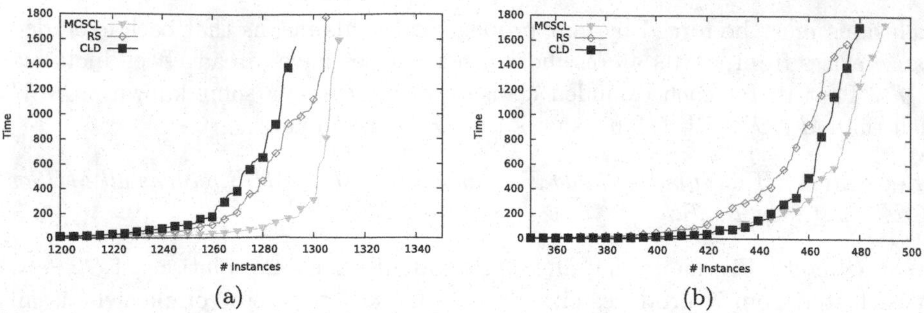

Fig. 1. Number of solved instances against time for (a) generating a single MCS and (b) generating all MCSES of a formula.

them are out of reach for all. Regardless, MCSCL is faster than the other two algorithms, for easy instances as well as hard ones and finds an MCS in 17 more instances than CLD and 5 more instances than RS. Similarly, in the case of discovering all MCSES, all 3 algorithms solve approximately 400 instances in less than a second, while 700 have too many MCSES to enumerate. In this case, MCSCL again outperforms both the other alternatives, finding all MCSES in 15 more instances than RS and 9 more instances than CLD.

Discovering a Single MUS. For this task, we used a set of 324 instances assembled by Belov et al. [5] for the evaluation of the tool DMUSER. We tested implementations of MCS-MUS that used either MINISAT or GLUCOSE [2] as the backend *sat* solver both with preprocessing enabled. We modified these solvers to bound time spent in preprocessing to 5 % of total runtime. We evaluated MCS-MUS with **em-rmr** or with only eager model rotation. We compared against MUSER [8] using MINISAT and using GLUCOSE, and against HAIFA-MUC [20] (based on MINISAT). For all algorithms, we preprocess the instances by *trimming* them using GLUCOSE and the tool DRAT-TRIM, which is a particularly effective heuristic clause set refinement method, but which cannot prove minimality and rarely produces a minimal MUS. We also compare against DMUSER [5] a system that augments a "core" MUS extraction algorithms with more elaborate trimming techniques. DMUSER yields significant improvements to MUSER and HAIFA-MUC and potentially could also improve MCS-MUS. However, we have not, as yet, integrated MCS-MUS into DMUSER to test this. The timeout in this experiment—including trimming—was set to 3600 seconds. Results are shown in Fig. 2.

Our first observation is that the combination of MINISAT and assumption-based solving is deficient, as is evident by the very poor performance of MUSER with MINISAT. Nevertheless, MCS-MUS with MINISAT is comparable to both HAIFA-MUC and MUSER with glucose[1]. We also see that **em-rmr** improves performance

[1] Our results seem to contradict the findings of Belov et al. [5], who found that MUSER with GLUCOSE was worse than HAIFA-MUC. It is unclear why this is the case.

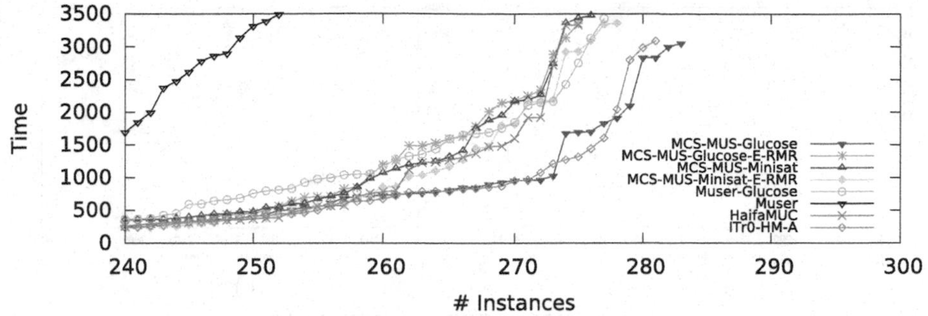

Fig. 2. Number of solved instances against time for extracting a single MUS.

overall in this case, yielding the second best combination among core algorithms. When paired with its GLUCOSE backend, MCS-MUS becomes the overall best algorithm for this task, surpassing even ITr-HM-A, the best configuration of DMUSER reported in [5]. However, the improvement of MCS-MUS when moving from MINISAT to GLUCOSE is not as dramatic as that of MUSER. It is, however, clearly ahead of other core algorithms and although it solves just 6 more instances than the next closest algorithm it does so significantly faster and even solves 2 more instances than DMUSER. Interestingly, **em-rmr** improves MCS-MUS with MINISAT but makes things worse when GLUCOSE is used.

Discovering All MUSES. Here we compare Algorithm 5 (MCS-MUS-ALL) against the state of the art for discovering multiple (potentially all) MUSES, MARCO [15]. We use only the MINISAT backend, as that is what MARCO is based on, with the additional optimization that for every unsatisfiable subset that we minimize, we create a copy of the SAT solver in which we can do destructive updates. This is implicit in MARCO, which uses an external tool for extracting a MUS.

We used the set of benchmarks from the MUS track of the 2011 SAT competition[2] (without trimming) and ran both algorithms for 3600 seconds on each instance. In Fig. 3 we show scatter plots of the time taken by each algorithm to generate the first MUS, of the time taken to differentiate between an instance with one MUS or many and of the number of MUSES generated within the timeout. Determining whether an instance contains one MUS or many involves either successfully terminating generation or generating a second MUS.

We see that MCS-MUS-ALL is more effective than MARCO at generating the first MUS and differentiating between instances with a single MUS or many MUSES. Indeed, it finds a MUS in 20 more instances than MARCO and differentiates 17 more instances. However, when MARCO can generate several MUSES, it is typically more efficient at doing so, especially for very large numbers of MUSES. We conjecture that in these cases, extracting a single MUS is so efficient, that the

[2] http://www.satcompetition.org/2011.

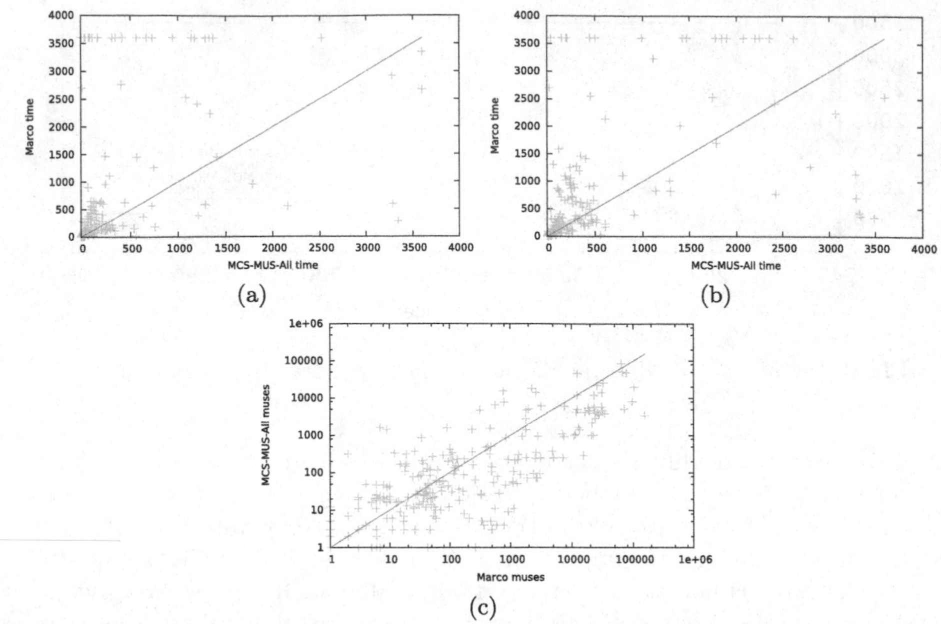

Fig. 3. (a) Time for finding a single MUS, (b) Time to differentiate between single-MUS and multiple-MUS instances, (c) number of MUSES generated, *in logscale*. In all cases, points above the line indicate MCS-MUS-ALL was better.

overhead of keeping track of the correction sets that MCS-MUS-ALL generates outweighs their potential benefit. This means that when the objective is to generate a variety of MUSES quickly on instances of moderate difficulty, MCS-MUS-ALL is to be preferred, but for large numbers of MUSES in easy instances, MARCO is preferable.

6 Conclusions

We have proposed a novel approach to extracting MUSES from unsatisfiable formulas. We exploited the well-known hitting set duality between correction sets and unsatisfiable subsets and used a greedy approach which, given an unhit MCS, can extend a set of clauses so that they are guaranteed to be a subset of a MUS. We further extended this algorithm to generating all MUSES. These developments hinge in part on our new very efficient MCS extraction algorithm. In all cases, we have demonstrated that the new algorithms outperform the state of the art. Despite this, there is little tuning or low level optimizations in our implementation, in contrast to the current state of the art [20]. This suggests that in future work we explore such optimizations to widen the gap.

References

1. Audemard, G., Lagniez, J.-M., Simon, L.: Improving glucose for incremental SAT solving with assumptions: application to MUS extraction. In: Järvisalo, M., Van Gelder, A. (eds.) SAT 2013. LNCS, vol. 7962, pp. 309–317. Springer, Heidelberg (2013)
2. Audemard, G., Simon, L.: Predicting learnt clauses quality in modern SAT solvers. In: Proceedings of the International Joint Conference on Artifical Intelligence (IJCAI), pp. 399–404 (2009)
3. Bacchus, F., Davies, J., Tsimpoukelli, M., Katsirelos, G.: Relaxation search: a simple way of managing optional clauses. In: Proceedings of the AAAI National Conference (AAAI), pp. 835–841 (2014)
4. Belov, A., Chen, H., Mishchenko, A., Marques-Silva, J.: Core minimization in sat-based abstraction. In: Design, Automation and Test in Europe (DATE), pp. 1411–1416 (2013)
5. Belov, A., Heule, M.J.H., Marques-Silva, J.: MUS extraction using clausal proofs. In: Sinz, C., Egly, U. (eds.) SAT 2014. LNCS, vol. 8561, pp. 48–57. Springer, Heidelberg (2014)
6. Belov, A., Lynce, I., Marques-Silva, J.: Towards efficient MUS extraction. AI Commun. **25**(2), 97–116 (2012)
7. Belov, A., Marques-Silva, J.: Accelerating MUS extraction with recursive model rotation. In: Formal Methods in Computer-Aided Design (FMCAD), pp. 37–40 (2011)
8. Belov, A., Marques-Silva, J.: Muser2: an efficient MUS extractor. JSAT **8**(1/2), 123–128 (2012)
9. Brayton, R., Mishchenko, A.: ABC: an academic industrial-strength verification tool. In: Touili, T., Cook, B., Jackson, P. (eds.) CAV 2010. LNCS, vol. 6174, pp. 24–40. Springer, Heidelberg (2010)
10. Eén, N., Sörensson, N.: An extensible SAT-solver. In: Giunchiglia, E., Tacchella, A. (eds.) SAT 2003. LNCS, vol. 2919, pp. 502–518. Springer, Heidelberg (2004)
11. Grégoire, É., Mazure, B., Piette, C.: On approaches to explaining infeasibility of sets of boolean clauses. In: International Conference on Tools with Artificial Intelligence (ICTAI), pp. 74–83 (2008)
12. Gurfinkel, A., Belov, A.: FrankenBit: bit-precise verification with many bits. In: Ábrahám, E., Havelund, K. (eds.) TACAS 2014 (ETAPS). LNCS, vol. 8413, pp. 408–411. Springer, Heidelberg (2014)
13. Gurfinkel, A., Belov, A., Marques-Silva, J.: Synthesizing Safe Bit-Precise Invariants. In: Ábrahám, E., Havelund, K. (eds.) TACAS 2014 (ETAPS). LNCS, vol. 8413, pp. 93–108. Springer, Heidelberg (2014)
14. Lagniez, J.-M., Biere, A.: Factoring out assumptions to speed up MUS extraction. In: Järvisalo, M., Van Gelder, A. (eds.) SAT 2013. LNCS, vol. 7962, pp. 276–292. Springer, Heidelberg (2013)
15. Liffiton, M.H., Malik, A.: Enumerating infeasibility: finding multiple MUSes quickly. In: Gomes, C., Sellmann, M. (eds.) CPAIOR 2013. LNCS, vol. 7874, pp. 160–175. Springer, Heidelberg (2013)
16. Liffiton, M.H., Sakallah, K.A.: Algorithms for computing minimal unsatisfiable subsets of constraints. J. Autom. Reasoning **40**(1), 1–33 (2008)
17. Marques-Silva, J., Heras, F., Janota, M., Previti, A., Belov, A.: On computing minimal correction subsets. In: Proceedings of the International Joint Conference on Artifical Intelligence (IJCAI), pp. 615–622 (2013)

18. Marques-Silva, J., Janota, M., Belov, A.: Minimal sets over monotone predicates in boolean formulae. In: Sharygina, N., Veith, H. (eds.) CAV 2013. LNCS, vol. 8044, pp. 592–607. Springer, Heidelberg (2013)
19. Nadel, A., Ryvchin, V., Strichman, O.: Efficient MUS extraction with resolution. In: Formal Methods in Computer-Aided Design (FMCAD), pp. 197–200 (2013)
20. Nadel, A., Ryvchin, V., Strichman, O.: Accelerated deletion-based extraction of minimal unsatisfiable cores. J. Satisfiability Boolean Model. Comput. (JSAT) **9**, 27–51 (2014)
21. Ramos, A., van der Tak, P., Heule, M.J.H.: Between restarts and backjumps. In: Sakallah, K.A., Simon, L. (eds.) SAT 2011. LNCS, vol. 6695, pp. 216–229. Springer, Heidelberg (2011)
22. Reiter, R.: A theory of diagnosis from first principles. Artif. Intell. **32**(1), 57–95 (1987)
23. Torlak, E., Chang, F.S.-H., Jackson, D.: Finding minimal unsatisfiable cores of declarative specifications. In: Proceedings of the International Symposium on Formal Methods (FM), pp. 326–341 (2008)
24. Wieringa, S.: Understanding, improving and parallelizing mus finding using model rotation. In: Milano, M. (ed.) CP 2012. LNCS, vol. 7514, pp. 672–687. Springer, Heidelberg (2012)

Deciding Local Theory Extensions via E-matching

Kshitij Bansal[1], Andrew Reynolds[2], Tim King[3], Clark Barrett[1], and Thomas Wies[1(✉)]

[1] NYU, New York, USA
wies@cs.nyu.edu
[2] EPFL, Lausanne, Switzerland
[3] Verimag, Gieres, France

Abstract. Satisfiability Modulo Theories (SMT) solvers incorporate decision procedures for theories of data types that commonly occur in software. This makes them important tools for automating verification problems. A limitation frequently encountered is that verification problems are often not fully expressible in the theories supported natively by the solvers. Many solvers allow the specification of application-specific theories as quantified axioms, but their handling is incomplete outside of narrow special cases.

In this work, we show how SMT solvers can be used to obtain complete decision procedures for local theory extensions, an important class of theories that are decidable using finite instantiation of axioms. We present an algorithm that uses E-matching to generate instances incrementally during the search, significantly reducing the number of generated instances compared to eager instantiation strategies. We have used two SMT solvers to implement this algorithm and conducted an extensive experimental evaluation on benchmarks derived from verification conditions for heap-manipulating programs. We believe that our results are of interest to both the users of SMT solvers as well as their developers.

1 Introduction

Satisfiability Modulo Theories (SMT) solvers are a cornerstone of today's verification technology. Common applications of SMT include checking verification conditions in deductive verification [14,26], computing program abstractions in software model checking [1,9,27], and synthesizing code fragments in software synthesis [5,6]. Ultimately, all these tasks can be reduced to satisfiability of formulas in certain first-order theories that model the semantics of prevalent data types and software constructs, such as integers, bitvectors, and arrays. The appeal of SMT solvers is that they implement decision procedures for efficiently reasoning about formulas in these theories. Thus, they can often be used off the shelf as automated back-end solvers in verification tools.

To the memory of Morgan Deters.

D. Kroening and C.S. Păsăreanu (Eds.): CAV 2015, Part II, LNCS 9207, pp. 87–105, 2015.
DOI: 10.1007/978-3-319-21668-3_6

Some verification tasks involve reasoning about universally quantified formulas, which goes beyond the capabilities of the solvers' core decision procedures. Typical examples include verification of programs with complex data structures and concurrency, yielding formulas that quantify over unbounded sets of memory locations or thread identifiers. From a logical perspective, these quantified formulas can be thought of as axioms of application-specific theories. In practice, such theories often remain within decidable fragments of first-order logic [2,7,9,23]. However, their narrow scope (which is typically restricted to a specific program) does not justify the implementation of a dedicated decision procedure inside the SMT solver. Instead, many solvers allow theory axioms to be specified directly in the input constraints. The solver then provides a quantifier module that is designed to heuristically instantiate these axioms. These heuristics are in general incomplete and the user is given little control over the instance generation. Thus, even if there exists a finite instantiation strategy that yields a decision procedure for a specific set of axioms, the communication of strategies and tactics to SMT solvers is a challenge [12]. Further, the user cannot communicate the completeness of such a strategy. In this situation, the user is left with two alternatives: either she gives up on completeness, which may lead to usability issues in the verification tool, or she implements her own instantiation engine as a preprocessor to the SMT solver, leading to duplication of effort and reduced solver performance.

The contributions of this paper are two-fold. First, we provide a better understanding of how complete decision procedures for application-specific theories can be realized with the quantifier modules that are implemented in SMT solvers. Second, we explore several extensions of the capabilities of these modules to better serve the needs of verification tool developers. The focus of our exploration is on *local theory extensions* [21,36]. A theory extension extends a given base theory with additional symbols and axioms. Local theory extensions are a class of such extensions that can be decided using finite quantifier instantiation of the extension axioms. This class is attractive because it is characterized by proof and model-theoretic properties that abstract from the intricacies of specific quantifier instantiation techniques [15,20,36]. Also, many well-known theories that are important in verification but not commonly supported by SMT solvers are in fact local theory extensions, even if they have not been presented as such in the literature. Examples include the array property fragment [8], the theory of reachability in linked lists [25,32], and the theories of finite sets [39] and multisets [38].

We present a general decision procedure for local theory extensions that relies on E-matching, one of the core components of the quantifier modules in SMT solvers. We have implemented our decision procedure using the SMT solvers CVC4 [3] and Z3 [11] and applied it to a large set of SMT benchmarks coming from the deductive software verification tool GRASShopper [29,31]. These benchmarks use a hierarchical combination of local theory extensions to encode verification conditions that express correctness properties of programs manipulating complex heap-allocated data structures. Guided by our experiments, we developed generic optimizations in CVC4 that improve the performance of our base-line decision procedure. Some of these optimizations required us to implement extensions in the solver's quantifier module. We believe that our results are of interest to both the users of SMT solvers as well as their developers. For users we provide simple ways of realizing complete decision procedures for application-specific theories with today's SMT solvers. For developers we provide interesting insights that can help them further improve the completeness and performance of today's quantifier instantiation modules.

Related Work. Sofronie-Stokkermans [36] introduced local theory extensions as a generalization of locality in equational theories [15,18]. Further generalizations include Psi-local theories [21], which can describe arbitrary theory extensions that admit finite quantifier instantiation. The formalization of our algorithm targets local theory extensions, but we briefly describe how it can be generalized to handle Psi-locality. The original decision procedure for local theory extensions presented in [36], which is implemented in H-Pilot [22], eagerly generates all instances of extension axioms upfront, before the base theory solver is called. As we show in our experiments, eager instantiation is prohibitively expensive for many local theory extensions that are of interest in verification because it results in a high degree polynomial blowup in the problem size.

In [24], Swen Jacobs proposed an incremental instantiation algorithm for local theory extensions. The algorithm is a variant of model-based quantifier instantiation (MBQI). It uses the base theory solver to incrementally generate partial models from which relevant axiom instances are extracted. The algorithm was implemented as a plug-in to Z3 and experiments showed that it helps to reduce the overall number of axiom instances that need to be considered. However, the benchmarks were artificially generated. Jacob's algorithm is orthogonal to ours as the focus of this paper is on how to use SMT solvers for deciding local theory extensions without adding new substantial functionality to the solvers. A combination with this approach is feasible as we discuss in more detail below.

Other variants of MBQI include its use in the context of finite model finding [33], and the algorithm described in [17], which is implemented in Z3. This algorithm is complete for the so-called almost uninterpreted fragment of first-order logic. While this fragment is not sufficiently expressive for the local theory extensions that appear in our benchmarks, it includes important fragments such as Effectively Propositional Logic (EPR). In fact, we have also experimented with a hybrid approach that uses our E-matching-based algorithm to reduce the benchmarks first to EPR and then solves them with Z3's MBQI algorithm.

E-matching was first described in [28], and since has been implemented in various SMT solvers [10,16]. In practice, user-provided *triggers* can be given as hints for finer grained control over quantifier instantiations in these implementations. More recent work [13] has made progress towards formalizing the semantics of triggers for the purposes of specifying decision procedures for a number of theories. A more general but incomplete technique [34] addresses the prohibitively large number of instantiations produced by E-matching by prioritizing instantiations that lead to ground conflicts.

2 Example

We start our discussion with a simple example that illustrates the basic idea behind local theory extensions. Consider the following set of ground literals

$$G = \{a + b = 1,\ f(a) + f(b) = 0\}.$$

We interpret G in the theory of linear integer arithmetic and a monotonically increasing function $f : \mathbb{Z} \to \mathbb{Z}$. One satisfying assignment for G is:

$$a = 0,\ b = 1,\ f(x) = \{-1 \text{ if } x \leq 0, 1 \text{ if } x > 0\}. \tag{1}$$

We now explain how we can use an SMT solver to conclude that G is indeed satisfiable in the above theory.

SMT solvers commonly provide inbuilt decision procedures for common theories such as the theory of linear integer arithmetic (`LIA`) and the theory of equality over uninterpreted functions (`UF`). However, they do not natively support the theory of monotone functions. The standard way to enforce f to be monotonic is to axiomatize this property,

$$K = \forall x, y.\ x \leq y \implies f(x) \leq f(y), \tag{2}$$

and then let the SMT solver check if $G \cup \{K\}$ is satisfiable via a reduction to its natively supported theories. In our example, the reduction target is the combination of `LIA` and `UF`, which we refer to as the *base theory*, denoted by $\mathcal{T}_0$. We refer to the axiom K as a *theory extension* of the base theory and to the function symbol f as an *extension symbol.*

Most SMT solvers divide the work of deciding ground formulas G in a base theory $\mathcal{T}_0$ and axioms $\mathcal{K}$ of theory extensions between different modules. A quantifier module looks for substitutions to the variables within an axiom K, x and y, to some ground terms, t_1 and t_2. We denote such a substitution as $\sigma = \{x \mapsto t_1, y \mapsto t_2\}$ and the instance of an axiom K with respect to this substitution as $K\sigma$. The quantifier module iteratively adds the generated ground instances $K\sigma$ as lemmas to G until the base theory solver derives a contradiction. However, if G is satisfiable, as in our case, then the quantifier module does not know when to stop generating instances of K, and the solver may diverge, effectively enumerating an infinite model of G.

For a local theory extension, we can syntactically restrict the instances $K\sigma$ that need to be considered before concluding that G is satisfiable to a finite set of candidates. More precisely, a theory extension is called *local* if in order to decide satisfiability of $G \cup \{K\}$, it is sufficient to consider only those instances $K\sigma$ in which all ground terms already occur in G and K. The monotonicity axiom K is a local theory extension of $\mathcal{T}_0$. The local instances of K and G are:

$$\begin{aligned}
K\sigma_1 &= a \leq b \implies f(a) \leq f(b) \text{ where } \sigma_1 = \{x \mapsto a, y \mapsto b\},\\
K\sigma_2 &= b \leq a \implies f(b) \leq f(a) \text{ where } \sigma_2 = \{x \mapsto b, y \mapsto a\},\\
K\sigma_3 &= a \leq a \implies f(a) \leq f(a) \text{ where } \sigma_3 = \{x \mapsto a, y \mapsto a\}, \text{ and}\\
K\sigma_4 &= b \leq b \implies f(b) \leq f(b) \text{ where } \sigma_4 = \{x \mapsto b, y \mapsto b\}.
\end{aligned}$$

Note that we do not need to instantiate x and y with other ground terms in G, such as 0 and 1. Adding the above instances to G yields

$$G' = G \cup \{K\sigma_1, K\sigma_2, K\sigma_3, K\sigma_4\}.$$

which is satisfiable in the base theory. Since K is a local theory extension, we can immediately conclude that $G \cup \{K\}$ is also satisfiable.

Recognizing Local Theory Extensions. There are two useful characterizations of local theory extensions that can help users of SMT solvers in designing axiomatization that are local. The first one is model-theoretic [15,36]. Consider again the set of ground clauses G'. When checking satisfiability of G' in the base theory, the SMT solver may produce the following model:

$$a = 0,\ b = 1,\ f(x) = \{-1 \text{ if } x = 0,\ 1 \text{ if } x = 1,\ \text{-1 otherwise}\}. \tag{3}$$

This is not a model of the original $G \cup \{K\}$. However, if we restrict the interpretation of the extension symbol f in this model to the ground terms in $G \cup \{K\}$, we obtain the *partial model*

$$a = 0,\ b = 1,\ f(x) = \{-1 \text{ if } x = 0,\ 1 \text{ if } x = 1,\ \text{undefined otherwise}\}. \tag{4}$$

This partial model can now be embedded into the model (1) of the theory extension. If such embeddings of partial models of G' to total models of $G \cup \{K\}$ always exist for all sets of ground literals G, then K is a local theory extension of $\mathcal{T}_0$. The second characterization of local theory extensions is proof-theoretic and states that a set of axioms is a local theory extension if it is saturated under (ordered) resolution [4]. This characterization can be used to automatically compute local theory extensions from non-local ones [20].

Note that the locality property depends both on the base theory as well as the specific axiomatization of the theory extension. For example, the following axiomatization of a monotone function f over the integers, which is logically equivalent to Eq. (2) in $\mathcal{T}_0$, is not local:

$$K = \forall x.\, f(x) \leq f(x+1).$$

Similarly, if we replace all inequalities in Eq. (2) by strict inequalities, then the extension is no longer local for the base theory $\mathcal{T}_0$. However, if we replace $\mathcal{T}_0$ by a theory in which $\leq$ is a dense order (such as in linear real arithmetic), then the strict version of the monotonicity axiom is again a local theory extension.

In the next two sections, we show how we can use the existing technology implemented in quantifier modules of SMT solvers to decide local theory extensions. In particular, we show how E-matching can be used to further reduce the number of axiom instances that need to be considered before we can conclude that a given set of ground literals G is satisfiable.

3 Preliminaries

Sorted First-Order Logic. We present our problem in sorted first-order logic with equality. A *signature* Σ is a tuple $(\mathsf{Sorts}, \Omega, \Pi)$, where Sorts is a countable set of sorts and Ω and Π are countable sets of function and predicate symbols, respectively. Each function symbol $f \in \Omega$ has an associated arity $n \geq 0$ and associated sort $s_1 \times \cdots \times s_n \to s_0$ with $s_i \in \mathsf{Sorts}$ for all $i \leq n$. Function symbols of arity 0 are called *constant symbols.* Similarly, predicate symbols $P \in \Pi$ have an arity $n \geq 0$ and sort $s_1 \times \cdots \times s_n$. We assume dedicated equality symbols $\approx_s \in \Pi$ with the sort $s \times s$ for all sorts $s \in \mathsf{Sorts}$, though we typically drop the explicit subscript. Terms are built from the function symbols in Ω and (sorted) variables taken from a countably infinite set X that is disjoint from Ω. We denote by $t : s$ that term t has sort s.

A Σ-atom A is of the form $P(t_1, \ldots, t_n)$ where $P \in \Pi$ is a predicate symbol of sort $s_1 \times \cdots \times s_n$ and the t_i are terms with $t_i : s_i$. A *Σ-formula* F is either a Σ-atom A, $\neg F_1$, $F_1 \wedge F_2$, $F_1 \vee F_2$, or $\forall x : s.F_1$ where F_1 and F_2 are Σ-formulas. A *Σ-literal* L is either A or $\neg A$ for a Σ-atom A. A *Σ-clause* C is a disjunction of Σ-literals. A Σ-term, atom, or formula is said to be *ground*, if no variable appears in it. For a set of formulas $\mathcal{K}$, we denote by $\mathsf{st}(\mathcal{K})$ the set of all ground subterms that appear in $\mathcal{K}$.

A Σ-sentence is a Σ-formula with no free variables where the free variables of a formula are defined in the standard fashion. We typically omit Σ if it is clear from the context.

Structures. Given a signature $\Sigma = (\mathsf{Sorts}, \Omega, \Pi)$, a *$\Sigma$-structure* M is a function that maps each sort $s \in \mathsf{Sorts}$ to a non-empty set $M(s)$, each function symbol $f \in \Omega$ of sort $s_1 \times \cdots \times s_n \to s_0$ to a function $M(f) : M(s_1) \times \cdots \times M(s_n) \to M(s_0)$, and each predicate symbol $P \in \Pi$ of sort $s_1 \times \cdots \times s_n$ to a relation $M(s_1) \times \cdots \times M(s_n)$. We assume that all structures M interpret each symbol $\approx_s$ by the equality relation on $M(s)$. For a Σ-structure M where Σ extends a signature Σ_0 with additional sorts and function symbols, we write $M|_{\Sigma_0}$ for the Σ_0-structure obtained by restricting M to Σ_0.

Given a structure M and a *variable assignment* $\nu : X \to M$, the evaluation $t^{M,\nu}$ of a term t in M, ν is defined as usual. For a structure M and an atom A of the form $P(t_1, \ldots, t_n)$, (M, ν) satisfies A iff $(t_1^{M,\nu}, \ldots, t_n^{M,\nu}) \in M(P)$. This is written as $(M, \nu) \models A$. From this satisfaction relation of atoms and Σ-structures, we can derive the standard notions of the satisfiability of a formula, satisfying a set of formulas $(M, \nu) \models \{F_i\}$, validity $\models F$, and entailment $F_1 \models F_2$. If a Σ-structure M satisfies a Σ-sentence F, we call M a model of F.

Theories and Theory Extensions. A *theory* $\mathcal{T}$ over signature Σ is a set of Σ-structures. We call a Σ-sentence K an *axiom* if it is the universal closure of a Σ-clause, and we denote a set of Σ-axioms as $\mathcal{K}$. We consider theories $\mathcal{T}$ defined as a class of Σ-structures that are models of a given set of Σ-sentences $\mathcal{K}$.

Let $\Sigma_0 = (\mathsf{Sorts}_0, \Omega_0, \Pi)$ be a signature and assume that the signature $\Sigma_1 = (\mathsf{Sorts}_0 \cup \mathsf{Sorts}_e, \Omega_0 \cup \Omega_e, \Pi)$ extends Σ_0 by new sorts Sorts_e and function symbols Ω_e. We call the elements of Ω_e *extension symbols* and terms starting with extension symbols *extension terms.* Given a Σ_0-theory $\mathcal{T}_0$ and Σ_1-axioms $\mathcal{K}_e$, we call $(\mathcal{T}_0, \mathcal{K}_e, \mathcal{T}_1)$ the *theory extension* of $\mathcal{T}_0$ with $\mathcal{K}_e$, where $\mathcal{T}_1$ is the set of all Σ_1-structures M that are models of $\mathcal{K}_e$ and whose reducts $M|_{\Sigma_0}$ are in $\mathcal{T}_0$. We often identify the theory extension with the theory $\mathcal{T}_1$.

4 Problem

We formally define the problem of satisfiability modulo theory and the notion of local theory extensions in this section.

Let $\mathcal{T}$ be a theory over signature Σ. Given a Σ-formula ϕ, we say ϕ is satisfiable modulo $\mathcal{T}$ if there exists a structure M in $\mathcal{T}$ and an assignment ν of the variables in ϕ such that $(M, \nu) \models \phi$. We define the ground satisfiability modulo theory problem as the corresponding decision problem for quantifier-free formulas.

Problem 1 (Ground satisfiability problem for Σ-theory $\mathcal{T}$).

input: A quantifier-free Σ-formula ϕ.
output: sat if ϕ is satisfiable modulo $\mathcal{T}$, unsat otherwise.

We say the satisfiability problem for $\mathcal{T}$ is *decidable* if there exists a procedure for the above problem which always terminates with sat or unsat. We write entailment modulo a theory as $\phi \models_{\mathcal{T}} \psi$.

We say an axiom of a theory extension is *linear* if all the variables occur under at most one extension term. We say it is *flat* if there there is no nesting of terms containing variables. It is easy to linearize and flatten the axioms by using additional variables and equality. As an example, $\forall x.\phi$ with $f(x)$ and $f(g(x))$ as terms in F may be written as

$$\forall xyz. x \approx y \land z \approx g(y) \implies F'$$

where F' is obtained from F by replacing $f(g(x))$ with $f(z)$. For the remainder of the paper, we assume that all extension axioms $\mathcal{K}_e$ are flat and linear. For the simplicity of the presentation, we assume that if a variable appears below a function symbol then that symbol must be an extension symbol.

Definition 2 (Local Theory Extensions). *A theory extension $(\mathcal{T}_0, \mathcal{K}_e, \mathcal{T}_1)$ is* local *if for any set of ground Σ_1-literals G: G is satisfiable modulo $\mathcal{T}_1$ if and only if $G \cup \mathcal{K}_e[G]$ is satisfiable modulo $\mathcal{T}_0$ extended with free function symbols. Here $\mathcal{K}_e[G]$ is the set of instances of $\mathcal{K}_e$ where the subterms of the instantiation are all subterms of G or $\mathcal{K}_e$ (in other words, they do not introduce new terms).*

For simplicity, in the rest of this paper, we work with theories $\mathcal{T}_0$ which have decision procedures for not just $\mathcal{T}_0$ but also $\mathcal{T}_0$ extended with free function symbols. Thus, we sometimes talk of satisfiability of a Σ_1-formula with respect a Σ_0-theory $\mathcal{T}_0$, to mean satisfiability in the $\mathcal{T}_0$ with the extension symbols in Σ_1

treated as free function symbols. In terms of SMT, we only talk of extensions of theories containing uninterpreted functions (UF).

A naive decision procedure for ground SMT of a local theory extension $\mathcal{T}_1$ is thus to generate all possible instances of the axioms $\mathcal{K}_e$ that do not introduce new ground terms, thereby reducing to the ground SMT problem of $\mathcal{T}_0$ extended with free functions.

Hierarchical Extensions. Note that local theory extensions can be stacked to form hierarchies $((\ldots((\mathcal{T}_0, \mathcal{K}_1, \mathcal{T}_1), \mathcal{K}_2, \mathcal{T}_2), \ldots), \mathcal{K}_n, \mathcal{T}_n)$. Such a hierarchical arrangement of extension axioms is often useful to modularize locality proofs. In such cases, the condition that variables are only allowed to occur below extension symbols (of the current extension) can be relaxed to any extension symbol of the current level or below. The resulting theory extension can be decided by composing procedures for the individual extensions. Alternatively, one can use a monolithic decision procedure for the resulting theory $\mathcal{T}_n$, which can also be viewed as a single local theory extension $(\mathcal{T}_0, \mathcal{K}_1 \cup \cdots \cup \mathcal{K}_n, \mathcal{T}_n)$. In our experimental evaluation, which involved hierarchical extensions, we followed the latter approach.

5 Algorithm

In this section, we describe a decision procedure for a local theory extension, say $(\mathcal{T}_0, \mathcal{K}_e, \mathcal{T}_1)$, which can be easily implemented in most SMT solvers with quantifier instantiation support. We describe our procedure $\mathfrak{D}_{\mathcal{T}_1}$ as a theory module in a typical SMT solver architecture. For simplicity, we separate out the interaction between theory solver and core SMT solver. We describe the procedure abstractly as taking as input:

- the original formula ϕ,
- a set of extension axioms $\mathcal{K}_e$,
- a set of instantiations of axioms that have already been made, Z, and
- a set of $\mathcal{T}_0$ satisfiable ground literals G such that $G \models \phi \wedge (\bigwedge_{\psi \in Z} \psi)$, and
- a set equalities $E \subseteq G$ between terms.

It either returns

- sat, denoting that G is $\mathcal{T}_1$ satisfiable; or
- a new set of instantiations of the axioms, Z'.

For completeness, we describe briefly the way we envisage the interaction mechanism of this module in a DPLL(T) SMT solver. Let the input problem be ϕ. The SAT solver along with the theory solvers for $\mathcal{T}_0$ will find a subset of literals G from $\phi \wedge (\bigwedge_{\psi \in Z} \psi)$ such that its conjunction is satisfiable modulo $\mathcal{T}_0$. If no such satisfying assignment exists, the SMT solver stops with unsat. One can think of G as being simply the literals in ϕ on the SAT solver trail. G will be sent to $\mathfrak{D}_{\mathcal{T}_1}$ along with information known about equalities between terms. The set Z can be also thought of as internal state maintained by the $\mathcal{T}_1$-theory solver module, with new instances Z' sent out as theory lemmas and Z updated to $Z \cup Z'$ after each call to $\mathfrak{D}_{\mathcal{T}_1}$. If $\mathfrak{D}_{\mathcal{T}_1}$ returns sat, so does the SMT solver and stops. On the other hand, if it returns a new set of instances, the SMT solver continues the search to additionally satisfy these.

E-matching. In order to describe our procedure, we introduce the well-studied E-matching problem. Given a universally quantified Σ-sentence K, let $X(K)$ denote the quantified variables. Define a Σ-substitution σ of K to be a mapping from variables $X(K)$ to Σ-terms of corresponding sort. Given a Σ-term p, let $p\sigma$ denote the term obtained by substituting variables in p by the substitutions provided in σ. Two substitutions σ_1, σ_2 with the same domain X are equivalent modulo a set of equalities E if $\forall x \in X. E \models \sigma_1(x) \approx \sigma_2(x)$. We denote this as $\sigma_1 \sim_E \sigma_2$.

Problem 3 (E-matching).

input: A set of ground equalities E, a set of Σ-terms G, and patterns P.
output: The set of substitutions σ over the variables in p, modulo E, such that for all $p \in P$ there exists a $t \in G$ with $E \models t \approx p\sigma$.

E-matching is a well-studied problem, specifically in the context of SMT. An algorithm for E-matching that is efficient and backtrackable is described in [10]. We denote this procedure by $\mathfrak{E}$.

The procedure $\mathfrak{D}_{\mathcal{T}_1}(\phi, \mathcal{K}_e, Z, G, E)$ is given in Fig. 1. Intuitively, it adds all the new instances along the current search path that are required for local theory reasoning as given in Definition 2, but modulo equality. For each axiom K in $\mathcal{K}_e$, the algorithm looks for function symbols containing variables. For example, if we think of the monotonicity axiom in Sect. 2, these would be the terms $f(x)$ and $f(y)$. These terms serve as patterns for the E-matching procedure. Next, with the help of the E-matching algorithm, all *new* instances are computed (to be more precise, all instances for the axiom K in Z which are equivalent modulo $\sim_E$ are skipped). If there are no new instances for any axiom in $\mathcal{K}_e$, and the set G of literals implies ϕ, we stop with sat. as effectively we have that $G \cup \mathcal{K}_e[G]$ is satisfiable modulo $\mathcal{T}_0$. Otherwise, we return this set.

We note that though the algorithm $\mathfrak{D}_{\mathcal{T}_1}$ may *look* inefficient because of the presence of nested loops, keeping track of which substitutions have already happened, and which substitutions are new. However, in actual implementations all of this is taken care of by the E-matching algorithm. There has been significant research on fast, incremental algorithms for E-matching in the context of SMT, and one advantage of our approach is to be able to leverage this work.

Correctness. The correctness argument relies on two aspects: one, that if the SMT solver says sat (resp. unsat) then ϕ is satisfiable (resp. unsatisfiable) modulo $\mathcal{T}_1$, and second, that it terminates.

For the case where the output is unsat, the correctness follows from the fact that Z only contains instances of $\mathcal{K}_e$. The sat case is more tricky, but the main idea is that the set of instances made by $\mathfrak{D}_{\mathcal{T}_1}(\phi, \mathcal{K}_e, Z, G, E)$ are logically

$\mathfrak{D}_{\mathcal{T}_1}(\phi, \mathcal{K}_e, Z, G, E)$
Local variable: Z', initially an empty set.

1. For each $K \in \mathcal{K}_e$:
   (a) Define the set of patterns P to be the function symbols in K containing variables. We observe that because the axioms are linear and flat, these patterns are always of the form $f(x_1, \ldots, x_n)$ where f is an extension symbol and the x_i are quantified variables.
   (b) Run $\mathfrak{E}(E, G, P)$ obtaining substitutions $\mathcal{S}$. Without loss of generality, assume that $\sigma \in \mathcal{S}$ returned by the algorithm are such that $\mathsf{st}(K\sigma) \subseteq \mathsf{st}(G \cup \mathcal{K}_e)$. For the special case of the patterns in (a), for any σ not respecting the condition there exists one in the equivalence class that respects the condition. Formally, $\forall \sigma. \exists \sigma'. \sigma' \sim_E \sigma \wedge \mathsf{st}(K\sigma') \subseteq \mathsf{st}(G \cup \mathcal{K}_e)$. We make this assumption only for simplicity of arguments later in the paper. If one uses an E-matching procedure not respecting this constraint, our procedure will still be terminating and correct (albeit total number of instantiations suboptimal).
   (c) For each $\sigma \in \mathcal{S}$, if there exists no $K\sigma'$ in Z such that $\sigma \sim_E \sigma'$, then add $K\sigma$ to Z' as a new instantiation to be made.
2. If Z' is empty, return sat, else return Z'.

Fig. 1. Procedure $\mathfrak{D}_{\mathcal{T}_1}$

equivalent to $\mathcal{K}_e[G]$. Thus, when the solver stops, $G \cup \mathcal{K}_e[G]$ is satisfiable modulo $\mathcal{T}_0$. As a consequence, G is satisfiable modulo $\mathcal{T}_1$. Since $G \models \phi$, we have that ϕ is satisfiable modulo $\mathcal{T}_1$.

The termination relies on the fact that the instantiations returned by procedure $\mathfrak{D}_{\mathcal{T}_1}(\phi, \mathcal{K}_e, Z, G, E)$ do not add new terms, and they are always a subset of $\mathcal{K}_e[\phi]$. Since, $\mathcal{K}_e[\phi]$ is finite, eventually $\mathfrak{D}$ will stop making new instantiations. Assuming that we have a terminating decision procedure for the ground SMT problem of $\mathcal{T}_0$, we get a terminating decision procedure for $\mathcal{T}_1$.

Theorem 4. *An SMT solver with theory module $\mathfrak{D}_{\mathcal{T}_1}$ is a decision procedure for the satisfiability problem modulo $\mathcal{T}_1$.*

Psi-Local Theories. We briefly explain how our approach can be extended to the more general notion of Psi-local theory extensions [21]. Sometimes, it is not sufficient to consider only local instances of extension axioms to decide satisfiability modulo a theory extension. For example, consider the following set of ground literals:

$$G = \{f(a) = f(b), a \neq b\}$$

Suppose we interpret G in a theory of an injective function $f : S \to S$ with a partial inverse $g : S \to S$ for some set S. We can axiomatize this theory as a theory extension of the theory of uninterpreted functions using the axiom

$$K = \forall x, y.\, f(x) = y \implies g(y) = x.$$

G is unsatisfiable in the theory extension, but the local instances of K with respect to the ground terms $\mathsf{st}(G) = \{a, b, f(a), f(b)\}$ are insufficient to yield a contradiction in the base theory. However, if we consider the local instances with respect to the larger set of ground terms

$$\Psi(\mathsf{st}(G)) = \{a, b, f(a), f(b), g(f(a)), g(f(b))\},$$

then we obtain, among others, the instances

$$f(a) = f(b) \implies g(f(b)) = a \quad \text{and} \quad f(b) = f(a) \implies g(f(a)) = b.$$

Together with G, these instances are unsatisfiable in the base theory.

The set $\Psi(\mathsf{st}(G))$ is computed as follows:

$$\Psi(\mathsf{st}(G)) = \mathsf{st}(G) \cup \{\, g(f(t)) \mid t \in \mathsf{st}(G)\,\}$$

It turns out that considering local instances with respect to $\Psi(\mathsf{st}(G))$ is sufficient to check satisfiability modulo the theory extension K for arbitrary sets of ground clauses G. Moreover, $\Psi(\mathsf{st}(G))$ is always finite. Thus, we still obtain a decision procedure for the theory extension via finite instantiation of extension axioms. Psi-local theory extensions formalize this idea. In particular, if Ψ satisfies certain properties including monotonicity and idempotence, one can again provide a model-theoretic characterization of completeness in terms of embeddings of partial models. We refer the reader to [21] for the technical details.

To use our algorithm for deciding satisfiability of a set of ground literals G modulo a Psi-local theory extension $(\mathcal{T}_0, \mathcal{K}_e, \mathcal{T}_1)$, we simply need to add an additional preprocessing step in which we compute $\Psi(\mathsf{st}(G))$ and define $G' = G \cup \{\, \mathtt{instclosure}(t) \mid t \in \Psi(\mathsf{st}(G))\,\}$ where `instclosure` is a fresh predicate symbol. Then calling our procedure for $\mathcal{T}_1$ with G' decides satisfiability of G modulo $\mathcal{T}_1$.

6 Implementation and Experimental Results

Benchmarks. We evaluated our techniques on a set of benchmarks generated by the deductive verification tool GRASShopper [19]. The benchmarks encode memory safety and functional correctness properties of programs that manipulate complex heap-allocated data structures. The programs are written in a type-safe imperative language without garbage collection. The tool makes no simplifying assumptions about these programs like acyclicity of heap structures.

GRASShopper supports mixed specifications in (classical) first-order logic and separation logic (SL) [35]. The tool reduces the program and specification to verification conditions that are encoded in a hierarchical combination of (Psi-) local theory extensions. This hierarchy of extensions is organized as follows:

1. *Base theory:* at the lowest level we have `UFLIA`, the theory of uninterpreted functions and linear integer arithmetic, which is directly supported by SMT solvers.

2. *GRASS:* the first extension layer consists of the theory of graph reachability and stratified sets. This theory is a disjoint combination of two local theory extensions: the theory of linked lists with reachability [25] and the theory of sets over interpreted elements [39].
3. *Frame axioms:* the second extension layer consists of axioms that encode the frame rule of separation logic. This theory extension includes arrays as a subtheory.
4. *Program-specific extensions:* The final extension layer consists of a combination of local extensions that encode properties specific to the program and data structures under consideration. These include:
   - axioms defining memory footprints of SL specifications,
   - axioms defining structural constraints on the shape of data structures,
   - sorted constraints, and
   - axioms defining partial inverses of certain functions, e.g., to express injectivity of functions and to specify the content of data structures.

We refer the interested reader to [29–31] for further details about the encoding.

The programs considered include sorting algorithms, common data structure operations, such as inserting and removing elements, as well as complex operations on abstract data types. Our selection of data structures consists of singly and doubly-linked lists, sorted lists, nested linked lists with head pointers, binary search trees, skew heaps, and a union find data structure. The input programs comprise 108 procedures with a total of 2000 lines of code, 260 lines of procedure contracts and loop invariants, and 250 lines of data structure specifications (including some duplicate specifications that could be shared across data structures). The verification of these specifications are reduced by GRASShopper to 816 SMT queries, each serves as one benchmark in our experiments. 802 benchmarks are unsatisfiable. The remaining 14 satisfiable benchmarks stem from programs that have bugs in their implementation or specification. All of these are genuine bugs that users of GRASShopper made while writing the programs.[1] We considered several versions of each benchmark, which we describe in more detail below. Each of these versions is encoded as an SMT-LIB 2 input file.

Experimental Setup. All experiments were conducted on the StarExec platform [37] with a CPU time limit of one hour and a memory limit of 100 GB. We focus on the SMT solvers CVC4 [3] and Z3 [11][2] as both support `UFLIA` and quantifiers via E-matching. This version of CVC4 is a fork of v1.4 with special support for quantifiers.[3]

In order to be able to test our approach with both CVC4 and Z3, wherever possible we transformed the benchmarks to simulate our algorithm. We describe these transformations in this paragraph. First, the quantified formulas in the benchmarks were linearized and flattened, and annotated with patterns to simulate Step 1(a) of our algorithm (this was done by GRASShopper in our

[1] See www.cs.nyu.edu/~kshitij/localtheories/ for the programs and benchmarks used.

[2] We used the version of Z3 downloaded from the git master branch at http://z3.codeplex.com on Jan 17, 2015.

[3] This version is available at www.github.com/kbansal/CVC4/tree/cav14-lte-draft.

experiments, but may also be handled by an SMT solver aware of local theories). Both CVC4 and Z3 support using these annotations for controlling instantiations in their E-matching procedures. In order to handle Psi-local theories, the additional terms required for completeness were provided as dummy assertions, so that these appear as ground terms to the solver. In CVC4, we also made some changes internally so as to treat these assertions specially and apply certain additional optimizations which we describe later in this section.

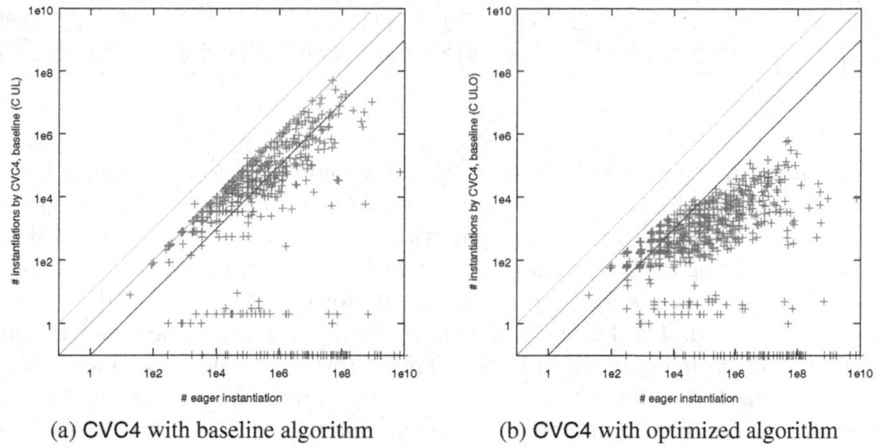

(a) CVC4 with baseline algorithm (b) CVC4 with optimized algorithm

Fig. 2. # of eager instantiations vs. E-matching instantiations inside the solver

Experiment 1. Our first experiment aims at comparing the effectiveness of eager instantiation versus incremental instantiation up to congruence (as done by E-matching). Figure 2 charts the number of eager instantiations versus the number of E-matching instantiations for each query in a logarithmic plot.[4] Points lying on the central line have an equal number of instantiations in both series while points lying on the lower line have 10 times as many eager instantiations as E-matching instantiations. (The upper line corresponds to $\frac{1}{10}$.) Most benchmarks require substantially more eager instantiations. We instrumented GRASShopper to eagerly instantiate all axioms. Subfigure (a) compares upfront instantiations with a baseline implementation of our E-matching algorithm. Points along the x-axis required no instantiations in CVC4 to conclude unsat. We have plotted the above charts up to 10e10 instantiations. There were four outlying benchmarks where upfront instantiations had between 10e10 and up to 10e14 instances. E-matching had zero instantiations for all four. Subfigure (b) compares against an optimized version of our algorithm implemented in CVC4. It shows that incremental solving reduces the number of instantiations significantly, often by several orders of magnitude. The details of these optimizations are given later in the section.

[4] Figure 2 does not include timeouts for CVC4.

Table 1. Comparison of solvers on uninstantiated benchmarks (time in sec.)

		C UD		C UL		C ULO		Z3 UD		Z3 UL		Z3 ULO	
family	#	#	time	#	time	#	time	#	time	#	time	#	time
sl lists	139	127	70	139	383	**139**	**17**	138	1955	138	1950	139	68
dl lists	70	66	1717	70	843	**70**	**33**	56	11375	56	11358	70	2555
sl nested	63	63	1060	63	307	**63**	**13**	52	6999	52	6982	59	1992
sls lists	208	181	6046	204	11230	**208**	**3401**	182	20596	182	20354	207	4486
trees	243	229	2121	228	22042	**239**	**7187**	183	41208	183	40619	236	27095
soundness	79	76	17	79	1533	**79**	**70**	76	7996	76	8000	79	336
sat	14	-	-	14	670	**14**	**12**	-	-	10	3964	14	898
total	816	742	11032	797	37009	**812**	**10732**	687	90130	697	93228	804	37430

Experiment 2. Next, we did a more thorough comparison on running times and number of benchmarks solved for *uninstantiated benchmarks*. These results are in Table 1. The benchmarks are partitioned according to the types of data structures occurring in the programs from which the benchmarks have been generated. Here, "sl" stands for singly-linked, "dl" for double-linked, and "sls" for sorted singly-linked. The binary search tree, skew heap, and union find benchmarks have all been summarized in the "trees" row. The row "soundness" contains unsatisfiable benchmarks that come from programs with incorrect code or specifications. These programs manipulate various types of data structures. The actual satisfiable queries that reveal the bugs in these programs are summarized in the "sat" row.

We simulated our algorithm and ran these experiments on both CVC4 (C) and Z3 obtaining similar improvements with both. We ran each with three configurations:

UD Default. For comparison purposes, we ran the solvers with default options. CVC4's default solver uses an E-matching based heuristic instantiation procedure, whereas Z3's uses both E-matching and model-based quantifier instantiation (MBQI). For both of the solvers, the default procedures are incomplete for our benchmarks.

UL These columns refer to the E-matching based complete procedure for local theory extensions (algorithm in Fig. 1).[5]

ULO Doing instantiations inside the solver instead of upfront, opens the room for optimizations wherein one tries some instantiations before others, or reduces the number of instantiations using other heuristics that do not affect completeness. The results in these columns show the effect of all such optimizations.

As noted above, the UL and ULO procedures are both complete, whereas UD is not. This is also reflected in the "sat" row in Table 1. Incomplete Instantiation-based procedures cannot hope to answer "sat". A significant improvement can

[5] The configuration C UL had one memory out on a benchmark in the tree family.

be seen between the UL and ULO columns. The general thrust of the optimizations was to avoid blowup of instantiations by doing ground theory checks on a subset of instantiations. Our intuition is that the theory lemmas learned from these checks eliminate large parts of the search space before we do further instantiations.

For example, we used a heuristic for Psi-local theories inspired from the observation that the axioms involving Psi-terms are needed mostly for completeness, and that we can prove unsatisfiable without instantiating axioms with these terms most of the time. We tried an approach where the instantiations were staged. First, the instantiations were done according to the algorithm in Fig. 1 for locality with respect to ground terms from the original query. Only when those were saturated, the instantiations for the auxiliary Psi-terms were generated. We found this to be very helpful. Since this required non-trivial changes inside the solver, we only implemented this optimization in CVC4; but we think that staging instantiations for Psi-local theories is a good strategy in general.

A second optimization, again with the idea of cutting instantiations, was adding assertions in the benchmarks of the form $(a = b) \vee (a \neq b)$ where a, b are ground terms. This forces an arbitrary arrangement over the ground terms before the instantiation procedure kicks in. Intuitively, the solver first does checks with many terms equal to each other (and hence fewer instantiations) eliminating as much of the search space as possible. Only when equality or disequality is relevant to the reasoning is the solver forced to instantiate with terms disequal to each other. One may contrast this with ideas being used successfully in the care-graph-based theory combination framework in SMT where one needs to try all possible arrangements of equalities over terms. It has been observed that equality or disequality is sometimes relevant only for a subset of pairs of terms. Whereas in theory combination this idea is used to cut down the number of arrangements that need to be considered, we use it to reduce the number of unnecessary instantiations. We found this really helped CVC4 on many benchmarks.

Another optimization was instantiating special cases of the axioms first by enforcing equalities between variables of the same sort, before doing a full instantiation. We did this for axioms that yield a particularly large number of instances (instantiations growing with the fourth power of the number of ground terms). Again, we believe this could be a good heuristic in general.

Experiment 3. Effective propositional Logic (EPR) is the fragment of first order-logic consisting of formulas of the shape $\exists \boldsymbol{x} \forall \boldsymbol{y}. G$ with G quantifier-free and where none of the universally quantified variables $\boldsymbol{y}$ appears below a function symbol in G. Theory extensions that fall into EPR are always local. Our third exploration is to see if we can exploit dedicated procedures for this fragment when such fragments occur in the benchmarks. For the EPR fragment, Z3 has a complete decision procedure that uses model-based quantifier instantiation. We therefore implemented a hybrid approach wherein we did upfront partial instantiation to the EPR fragment using E-matching with respect to top-level equalities (as described in our algorithm). The resulting EPR benchmark is then decided using Z3's MBQI mode. This approach can only be expect to help where

Table 2. Comparison of solvers on partially instantiated benchmarks (time in sec.)

		C	PL	C	PLO	Z3	PM	Z3	PL	Z3	PLO
family	#	#	time	#	time	#	time	#	time	#	time
sl lists	139	139	664	139	20	**139**	**9**	139	683	139	29
dl lists	70	70	3352	70	50	**70**	**41**	67	12552	70	423
sl nested	63	63	2819	63	427	**63**	**182**	56	7068	62	804
sls lists	208	206	14222	207	3086	**208**	**37**	203	17245	208	1954
trees	243	232	7185	243	6558	**243**	**663**	222	34519	242	8089
soundness	79	78	156	79	49	**79**	**23**	79	2781	79	39
sat	14	14	85	**14**	**22**	13	21	12	1329	14	109
total	816	802	28484	**815**	10213	**815**	**976**	778	76177	814	11447

there are EPR-like axioms in the benchmarks, and we did have some which were heavier on these. We found that on singly linked list and tree benchmarks this hybrid algorithm significantly outperforms all other solver configurations that we have tried in our experiments. On the other hand, on nested list benchmarks, which make more heavy use of purely equational axioms, this technique does not help compared to only using E-matching because the partial instantiation already yields ground formulas.

The results with our hybrid algorithm are summarized in Column Z3 PM of Table 2. Since EPR is a special case of local theories, we also tried our E-matching based algorithm on these benchmarks. We found that the staged instantiation improves performance on these as well. The optimization that help on the uninstantiated benchmarks also work here. These results are summarized in the same table.

Overall, our experiments indicate that there is a lot of potential in the design of quantifier modules to further improve the performance of SMT solvers, and at the same time make them complete on more expressive decidable fragments.

7 Conclusion

We have presented a new algorithm for deciding local theory extensions, a class of theories that plays an important role in verification applications. Our algorithm relies on existing SMT solver technology so that it can be easily implemented in today's solvers. In its simplest form, the algorithm does not require any modifications to the solver itself but only trivial syntactic modifications to its input. These are: (1) flattening and linearizing the extension axioms; and (2) adding trigger annotations to encode locality constraints for E-matching. In our evaluation we have experimented with different configurations of two SMT solvers, implementing a number of optimizations of our base line algorithm. Our results suggest interesting directions to further improve the quantifier modules of current SMT solvers, promising better performance and usability for applications in automated verification.

Acknowledgments. We would like to thank the anonymous reviewers for their insightful comments and suggestions. This work was supported in part by the National Science Foundation under grants CNS-1228768 and CCF-1320583.

This work was also supported by the European Research Council under the European Union's Seventh Framework Programme (FP/2007-2013) / ERC Grant Agreement nr. 306595 "STATOR".

References

1. Albarghouthi, A., Li, Y., Gurfinkel, A., Chechik, M.: UFO: a framework for abstraction- and interpolation-based software verification. In: Madhusudan, P., Seshia, S.A. (eds.) CAV 2012. LNCS, vol. 7358, pp. 672–678. Springer, Heidelberg (2012)
2. Alberti, F., Ghilardi, S., Sharygina, N.: Decision procedures for flat array properties. In: Ábrahám, E., Havelund, K. (eds.) TACAS 2014 (ETAPS). LNCS, vol. 8413, pp. 15–30. Springer, Heidelberg (2014)
3. Barrett, C., Conway, C.L., Deters, M., Hadarean, L., Jovanović, D., King, T., Reynolds, A., Tinelli, C.: CVC4. In: Gopalakrishnan, G., Qadeer, S. (eds.) CAV 2011. LNCS, vol. 6806, pp. 171–177. Springer, Heidelberg (2011)
4. Basin, D.A., Ganzinger, H.: Complexity analysis based on ordered resolution. In: Proceedings, 11th Annual IEEE Symposium on Logic in Computer Science, pp. 456–465. IEEE. New Brunswick, New Jersey, USA, July 27–30 1996
5. Beyene, T.A., Chaudhuri, S., Popeea, C., Rybalchenko, A.: A constraint-based approach to solving games on infinite graphs. In: POPL, pp. 221–234. ACM (2014)
6. Bodik, R., Torlak, E.: Synthesizing programs with constraint solvers. In: Madhusudan, P., Seshia, S.A. (eds.) CAV 2012. LNCS, vol. 7358, pp. 3–3. Springer, Heidelberg (2012)
7. Bouajjani, A., Drăgoi, C., Enea, C., Sighireanu, M.: Accurate invariant checking for programs manipulating lists and arrays with infinite data. In: Chakraborty, S., Mukund, M. (eds.) ATVA 2012. LNCS, vol. 7561, pp. 167–182. Springer, Heidelberg (2012)
8. Bradley, A.R., Manna, Z., Sipma, H.B.: What's decidable about arrays? In: Emerson, E.A., Namjoshi, K.S. (eds.) VMCAI 2006. LNCS, vol. 3855, pp. 427–442. Springer, Heidelberg (2006)
9. Brillout, A., Kroening, D., Rümmer, P., Wahl, T.: An interpolating sequent calculus for quantifier-free presburger arithmetic. J. Autom. Reasoning **47**(4), 341–367 (2011)
10. de Moura, L., Bjørner, N.S.: Efficient e-matching for SMT solvers. In: Pfenning, F. (ed.) CADE 2007. LNCS (LNAI), vol. 4603, pp. 183–198. Springer, Heidelberg (2007)
11. de Moura, L., Bjørner, N.S.: Z3: an efficient SMT solver. In: Ramakrishnan, C.R., Rehof, J. (eds.) TACAS 2008. LNCS, vol. 4963, pp. 337–340. Springer, Heidelberg (2008)
12. de Moura, L., Passmore, G.O.: The strategy challenge in SMT solving. In: Bonacina, M.P., Stickel, M.E. (eds.) Automated Reasoning and Mathematics. LNCS, vol. 7788, pp. 15–44. Springer, Heidelberg (2013)
13. Dross, C., Conchon, S., Kanig, J., Paskevich, A.: Reasoning with triggers. In: Fontaine, P., Goel, A. (eds.) SMT 2012, vol. 20. EPiC Series, pp. 22–31. EasyChair (2013)

14. Filliâtre, J.-C., Paskevich, A.: Why3 — where programs meet provers. In: Felleisen, M., Gardner, P. (eds.) ESOP 2013. LNCS, vol. 7792, pp. 125–128. Springer, Heidelberg (2013)
15. Ganzinger, H.: Relating semantic and proof-theoretic concepts for polynomial time decidability of uniform word problems. In: Proceedings of the 16th Annual IEEE Symposium on Logic in Computer Science, 2001, pp. 81–90 (2001)
16. Ge, Y., Barrett, C., Tinelli, C.: Solving quantified verification conditions using satisfiability modulo theories. Annals of Mathematics and Artificial Intelligence **55**(1–2), 101–122 (2009)
17. Ge, Y., de Moura, L.: Complete instantiation for quantified formulas in satisfiabiliby modulo theories. In: Bouajjani, A., Maler, O. (eds.) CAV 2009. LNCS, vol. 5643, pp. 306–320. Springer, Heidelberg (2009)
18. Givan, R., McAllester, D.A.: New results on local inference relations. In: KR, pp. 403–412. Morgan Kaufmann (1992)
19. GRASShopper tool web page. http://cs.nyu.edu/wies/software/grasshopper. Accessed Febuary 2015
20. Horbach, M., Sofronie-Stokkermans, V.: Obtaining finite local theory axiomatizations via saturation. In: Fontaine, P., Ringeissen, C., Schmidt, R.A. (eds.) FroCoS 2013. LNCS, vol. 8152, pp. 198–213. Springer, Heidelberg (2013)
21. Ihlemann, C., Jacobs, S., Sofronie-Stokkermans, V.: On local reasoning in verification. In: Ramakrishnan, C.R., Rehof, J. (eds.) TACAS 2008. LNCS, vol. 4963, pp. 265–281. Springer, Heidelberg (2008)
22. Ihlemann, C., Sofronie-Stokkermans, V.: System description: H-PILoT. In: Schmidt, R.A. (ed.) CADE-22. LNCS, vol. 5663, pp. 131–139. Springer, Heidelberg (2009)
23. Itzhaky, S., Banerjee, A., Immerman, N., Lahav, O., Nanevski, N., Sagiv, M.: Modular reasoning about heap paths via effectively propositional formulas. In: POPL, pp. 385–396. ACM (2014)
24. Jacobs, S.: Incremental instance generation in local reasoning. In: Bouajjani, A., Maler, O. (eds.) CAV 2009. LNCS, vol. 5643, pp. 368–382. Springer, Heidelberg (2009)
25. Lahiri, S.K., Qadeer, S.: Back to the future: revisiting precise program verification using SMT solvers. In: POPL, pp. 171–182 (2008)
26. Leino, K.R.M.: Dafny: an automatic program verifier for functional correctness. In: Clarke, E.M., Voronkov, A. (eds.) LPAR-16 2010. LNCS, vol. 6355, pp. 348–370. Springer, Heidelberg (2010)
27. McMillan, K.L.: Interpolants from Z3 proofs. In: International Conference on Formal Methods in Computer-Aided Design, FMCAD 2011, Austin, TX, USA, October 30 - November 02, 2011, pp. 19–27 (2011)
28. Nelson, C.G.: Techniques for Program Verification. Ph.D. thesis, Stanford, CA, USA (1980). AAI8011683
29. Piskac, R., Wies, T., Zufferey, D.: Automating separation logic using SMT. In: Sharygina, N., Veith, H. (eds.) CAV 2013. LNCS, vol. 8044, pp. 773–789. Springer, Heidelberg (2013)
30. Piskac, R., Wies, T., Zufferey, D.: Automating separation logic with trees and data. In: Biere, A., Bloem, R. (eds.) CAV 2014. LNCS, vol. 8559, pp. 711–728. Springer, Heidelberg (2014)
31. Piskac, R., Wies, T., Zufferey, D.: GRASShopper: complete heap verification with mixed specifications. In: TACAS. Springer (2014)

32. Rakamarić, Z., Bingham, J.D., Hu, A.J.: An inference-rule-based decision procedure for verification of heap-manipulating programs with mutable data and cyclic data structures. In: Cook, B., Podelski, A. (eds.) VMCAI 2007. LNCS, vol. 4349, pp. 106–121. Springer, Heidelberg (2007)
33. Reynolds, A., Tinelli, C., Goel, A., Krstić, S., Deters, M., Barrett, C.: Quantifier instantiation techniques for finite model finding in SMT. In: Bonacina, M.P. (ed.) CADE 2013. LNCS, vol. 7898, pp. 377–391. Springer, Heidelberg (2013)
34. Reynolds, A., Tinelli, C., De Moura, L.: Finding conflicting instances of quantified formulas in SMT. In: Formal Methods in Computer-Aided Design, FMCAD (2014)
35. Reynolds, J.C.: Separation logic: a logic for shared mutable data structures. In: LICS, pp. 55–74 (2002)
36. Sofronie-Stokkermans, V.: Hierarchic reasoning in local theory extensions. In: Nieuwenhuis, R. (ed.) CADE 2005. LNCS (LNAI), vol. 3632, pp. 219–234. Springer, Heidelberg (2005)
37. Stump, A., Sutcliffe, G., Tinelli, C.: StarExec: a cross-community infrastructure for logic solving. In: Demri, S., Kapur, D., Weidenbach, C. (eds.) IJCAR 2014. LNCS, vol. 8562, pp. 367–373. Springer, Heidelberg (2014)
38. Zarba, C.G.: Combining multisets with integers. In: Voronkov, A. (ed.) CADE-18, vol. 2392, pp. 363–376. Springer, Heidelberg (2002)
39. Zarba, C.G.: Combining sets with elements. In: Dershowitz, N. (ed.) Verification: Theory and Practice. LNCS, vol. 2772, pp. 762–782. Springer, Heidelberg (2004)

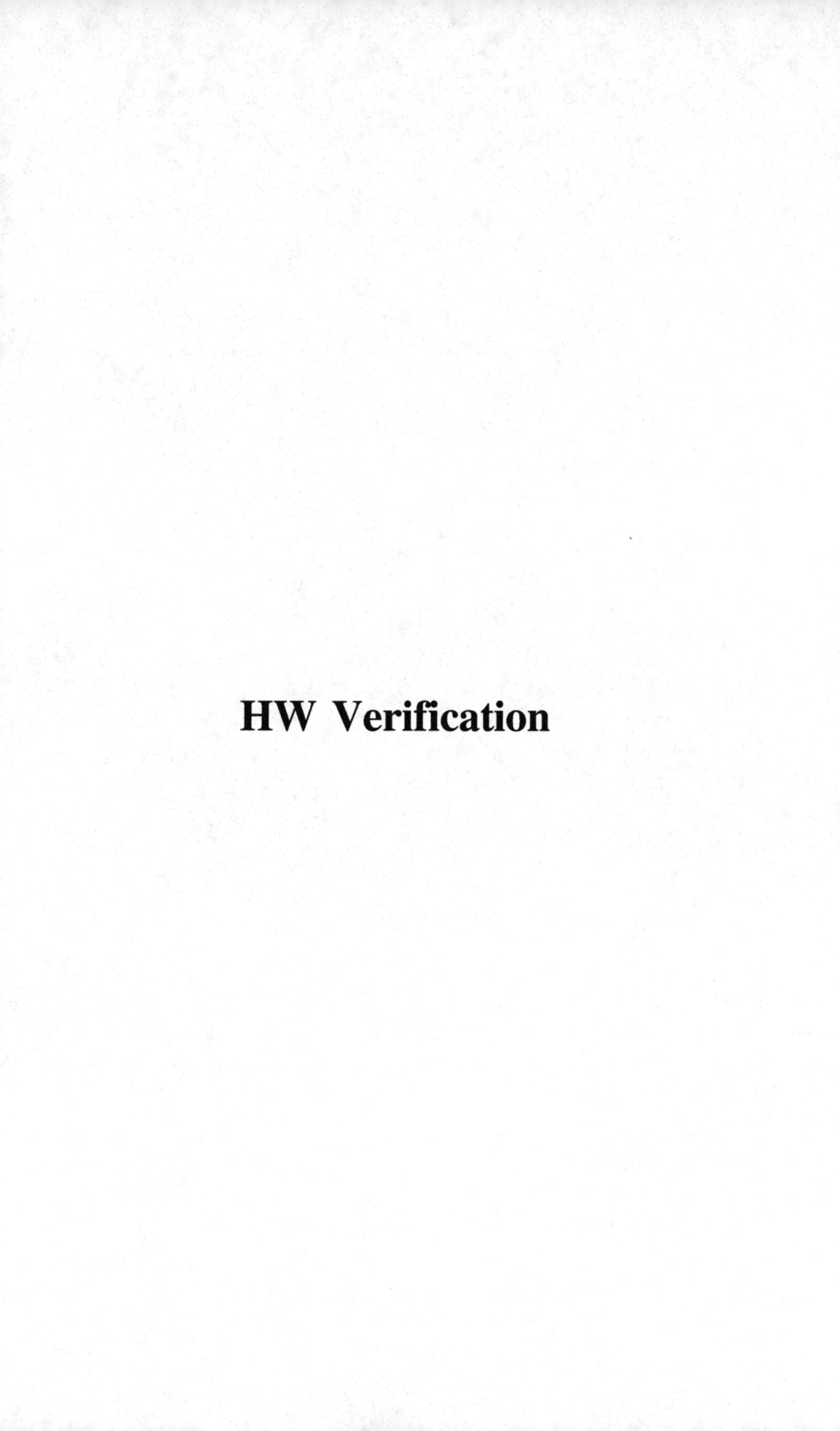

HW Verification

Modular Deductive Verification of Multiprocessor Hardware Designs

Muralidaran Vijayaraghavan[1](✉), Adam Chlipala[1], Arvind[1], and Nirav Dave[2]

[1] MIT, Cambridge, USA
{vmurali,adamc,arvind}@csail.mit.edu
[2] SRI International, Menlo Park, USA
ndave@csl.sri.com

Abstract. We present a new framework for modular verification of hardware designs in the style of the Bluespec language. That is, we formalize the idea of components in a hardware design, with well-defined input and output channels; and we show how to specify and verify components individually, with machine-checked proofs in the Coq proof assistant. As a demonstration, we verify a fairly realistic implementation of a multicore shared-memory system with two types of components: memory system and processor. Both components include nontrivial optimizations, with the memory system employing an arbitrary hierarchy of cache nodes that communicate with each other concurrently, and with the processor doing speculative execution of many concurrent read operations. Nonetheless, we prove that the combined system implements sequential consistency. To our knowledge, our memory-system proof is the first machine verification of a cache-coherence protocol parameterized over an arbitrary cache hierarchy, and our full-system proof is the first machine verification of sequential consistency for a multicore hardware design that includes caches and speculative processors.

1 Introduction

A modern high-performance, cache-coherent, distributed-memory hardware system is inherently complex. Such systems by their nature are highly concurrent and nondeterministic. The goal of this work is to provide a framework for full verification of complex hardware systems.

Modularity has long been understood as a key property for effective design and verification in this domain, decomposing systems into pieces that can be specified and verified independently. In our design, processors and memory systems independently employ intricate optimizations that exploit opportunities for parallelism. We are able to prove that each of these two main components still provides strong guarantees to support sequential consistency (SC) [25], and then compose those proofs into a result for the full system. Either component may be optimized further without requiring any changes to the implementation, specification, or proof of the other. Our concrete optimizations include speculation in processors and using a hierarchy of caches in memory.

D. Kroening and C.S. Păsăreanu (Eds.): CAV 2015, Part II, LNCS 9207, pp. 109–127, 2015.
DOI: 10.1007/978-3-319-21668-3_7

We thus present **the first mechanized proof of correctness of a realistic multiprocessor, shared-memory hardware system**, including **the first mechanized correctness proof of a directory-based cache-coherence protocol for arbitrary cache hierarchies**, *i.e.*, the proof is parameterized over an unknown number of processors connected to an unknown number of caches in an unknown number of levels (*e.g.*, L1, L2). Our proof has been carried out in the Coq proof assistant and is available at http://github.com/vmurali/SeqConsistency. Since our technique is based on proof assistants, the computational complexity of verification remains constant for any choice of parameters. In the process, we introduce **a methodology for modular verification of hardware designs**, based on the theory of labeled transition systems (LTSes).

LTSes as hardware descriptions are an established idea [2,17,18], for which there are compilers that convert LTSes into efficient hardware. Our work is based on the Bluespec language [3,6], whose semantics match the formalism of this paper. Bluespec specifies hardware components as atomic rules of a transition system over state elements, and its commercial compiler synthesizes these specs into circuits (*i.e.*, Verilog code) with competitive performance. The model that we verify is close to literally transliterated from real Bluespec designs that have been compiled to hardware. Our cache-coherent memory system is based on a Bluespec implementation [13] used to implement an FPGA-based simulator for a cache-coherent multiprocessor PowerPC system [23]. The hardware synthesized from that implementation is rather efficient: an 8-core system with a 2-level cache hierarchy can run 55 million instructions per second on the BEE FPGA board [10]. Within Coq we adopt a semantics style very close to Bluespec, using inductive definitions of state transition systems, where each transition rule corresponds to an atomic Bluespec rule.

Our high-level agenda here is to import to the hardware-verification domain good ideas from the worlds of programming-language semantics and formal software verification, and to demonstrate some advantages of human-guided deductive techniques over model-checking techniques that less readily support modularity and generalization over infinite families of systems, and which may provide less insight to hardware designers (*e.g.*, by not yielding human-understandable invariants about systems).

Paper Organization: We begin with a discussion of related work in Sect. 2. Section 3 introduces our flavor of the labeled transition systems formalism, including a definition of trace refinement. Section 4 shows a generic decomposition of any multiprocessor system, independently of the memory model that it implements, and discusses the store atomicity property of the memory subcomponent. Section 5 gives a simple formal model of sequential consistency. The following sections refine the two main subcomponents of our multiprocessor system. Section 7 discusses definition and verification of a speculative processor model, and Sect. 8 defines and proves our hierarchical cache-coherence protocol. Finally, Sect. 9 shows the whole-system modular proof of our complex system and ends with some conclusions in Sect. 10.

2 Related Work

Hardware verification is dominated by model checking – for example, processor verification [8,29] and (more recently) Intel's execution cluster verification [22]. Many abstraction techniques are used to reduce designs to finite state spaces, which can be explored exhaustively. There are limits to the construction of sound abstractions, so verifications of protocols such as cache-coherence have mostly treated systems with concrete topologies, involving particular finite numbers of caches and processors. For instance, explicit-state model checking tools like Murphi [15] or TLC [21,26] are able to handle only single-level cache hierarchies with fewer than ten addresses and ten CPUs, as opposed to the billions of addresses in a real system, or the ever-growing number of CPUs. Symbolic model-checking techniques have fared better: McMillan *et al.* have verified a two-level MSI protocol based on the Gigamax distributed multiprocessor using SMV [31]. Optimizations on these techniques (*e.g.*, partial-order reduction [4], symmetry reduction [5,11,12,16,19,37], compositional reasoning [20,28,30], extended-FSM [14]) also scale the approach, verifying up to two levels of cache hierarchy, but are unable to handle multi-level hierarchical protocols. In fact, related work by Zhang et al. [37] insists that parameterization should be restricted to single dimensions for the state-of-the-art tools to scale practically. In all these cases, finding invariants automatically is actually hard. Chou et al. [12] require manual insertion of extra invariants, called "non-interference lemmas", to eliminate counterexamples that violate the required property. Flow-based methodology [35] gives yet another way of manually specifying invariants. In general, we believe that the level of complexity of the manually specified invariants between those approaches and ours is similar. Moreover, we might hope to achieve higher assurance and understanding of design ideas by verifying *infinite families* of hardware designs, which resist reduction to finite-state models. Past work by Zhang et al. [37] has involved model-checking hierarchical cache-coherence protocols [38], with a restriction to *binary* trees of caches only, relying on paper-and-pencil proofs about the behavior of fractal-like systems. Those authors agree that, as a result, the protocol suffers from a serious performance handicap. Our cache protocol in this paper is chosen to support more realistic performance scaling.

Theorem provers have also been used to verify microprocessors, *e.g.*, HOL to verify an academic microprocessor AVI-1 [36]. Cache-coherence proofs have also used mechanized theorem provers, though all previous work has verified only single-level hierarchies. Examples include using ACL2 for verifying a bus-based snoop protocol [32], using a combination of model-checking and PVS [33] to verify the FLASH protocol [24], and using PVS to mechanize some portions of a paper-and-pencil proof verifying that the Cachet cache-coherence protocol [34] does not violate the CRF memory model. The first two of these works do not provide insights that can be used to design and verify other protocols. The last falls short of proving a "full functional correctness" property of a memory system. In this paper, we verify that property for a complex cache protocol, based on human-meaningful invariants that generalize to related protocols.

3 Labeled Transition Systems

We make extensive use of the general theory of labeled transition systems, a semantics approach especially relevant to communicating concurrent systems. As we are formalizing processors for Turing-complete machine languages, it is challenging to prove that a system preserves almost any aspect of processor behavior from a model such as SC. To focus our theorems, we pick the time-honored property of *termination*. An optimized system should terminate or diverge iff the reference system could also terminate or diverge, respectively. All sorts of other interesting program properties are reducible to this one, in the style of computability theory. Our basic definitions of transition systems build in special treatment of halting, so that we need not mention it explicitly in most of the following contexts.

Definition 1. *A* ***labeled transition system (LTS)*** *is a ternary relation, over* $\mathcal{S}^H \times \mathcal{L}^\epsilon \times \mathcal{S}^H$, *for some sets* $\mathcal{S}$ *of states and* $\mathcal{L}$ *of labels. We usually do not mention these sets explicitly, as they tend to be clear from context. We write* X^ϵ *for lifting of a set* X *to have an extra "empty" element* ϵ *(like an* `option` *type in ML). We write* X^H *for lifting of a set* X *to have an extra "halt" element* H*. We also implicitly consider each LTS to be associated with an* initial *state in* $\mathcal{S}$*.*

For LTS A, we write $(s) \xrightarrow[\text{A}]{\ell} (s')$ as shorthand for $(s, \ell, s') \in A$, and we write A_0 for A's initial state. The intuition is that A is one process within a concurrent system. The label ℓ from set $\mathcal{L}$ of labels is produced when A participates in some IO exchange with another process; otherwise it is an empty or "silent" label ϵ. For brevity, we may omit labels for ϵ steps.

3.1 Basic Constructions on LTSes

From an LTS representing single-step system evolution, we can build an LTS capturing arbitrary-length evolutions.

Definition 2. *The* ***transitive-reflexive closure*** *of* A*, written* A^**, is a derived LTS. Where* A*'s states and labels are* $\mathcal{S}$ *and* $\mathcal{L}$*, the states of* A^* *are* $\mathcal{S}$*, and the labels are* $\mathcal{L}^*$*, or* sequences *of labels from the original system.* A^* *steps from* s *to* s' *when there exist zero or more transitions in* A *that move from* s *to* s'*. The label of this transition is the* concatenation *of all labels generated in* A*, where the empty or "silent" label* ϵ *is treated as an identity element for concatenation.*

We also want to compose n copies of an LTS together, with no explicit communication between them. We apply this construction later to lift a single-CPU system to a multi-CPU system.

Definition 3. *The* n***-repetition*** *of* A*, written* A^n*, is a derived LTS. Where* A*'s states and labels are* $\mathcal{S}$ *and* $\mathcal{L}$*, the states of* A^n *are* $\mathcal{S}^n$*, and the labels are* $[1, n] \times \mathcal{L}$*, or pairs that* tag *labels with which component system generated them. These labels are generated only when the component system generates a label. The whole system halts whenever one of the components halts.*

Eventually, we need processes to be able to communicate with each other, which we formalize via the + composition operator that connects same-label transitions in the two systems, treating the label as a cooperative communication event that may now be hidden from the outside world, as an ϵ label.

Definition 4. *Where A and B are two LTSes sharing labels set $\mathcal{L}$, and with state sets $\mathcal{S}_A$ and $\mathcal{S}_B$ respectively, the* **communicating composition** *$A+B$ is a new LTS with states $\mathcal{S}_A \times \mathcal{S}_B$ and an empty label set, defined as follows:*

$$A\frac{(a)\xrightarrow[A]{}(a') \quad a' \neq H}{(a,b)\xrightarrow[A+B]{}(a',b)} \qquad B\frac{(b)\xrightarrow[B]{}(b') \quad b' \neq H}{(a,b)\xrightarrow[A+B]{}(a,b')} \qquad H_A\frac{(a)\xrightarrow[A]{}(H)}{(a,b)\xrightarrow[A+B]{}(H)}$$

$$H_B\frac{(b)\xrightarrow[B]{}(H)}{(a,b)\xrightarrow[A+B]{}(H)} \qquad Join\frac{(a)\xrightarrow[A]{\ell}(a') \quad (b)\xrightarrow[B]{\ell}(b') \quad a',b' \neq H}{(a,b)\xrightarrow[A+B]{}(a',b')}$$

3.2 Refinement Between LTSes

We need a notion of when one LTS "implements" another. Intuitively, transition labels and halting are all that the outside world can observe. Two systems that produce identical labels and termination behavior under all circumstances can be considered as safe substitutes for one another. We need only an asymmetrical notion of compatibility:

Definition 5. *For some label domain $\mathcal{L}$, let $f : \mathcal{L} \rightarrow \mathcal{L}^\epsilon$ be a function that is able to replace labels with alternative labels, or erase them altogether. Let LTSes A and B have the same label set $\mathcal{L}$. We say that A* **trace-refines** *B* **w.r.t.** *f, or $A \sqsubseteq_f B$, if:*

$$\forall s_A, \eta.\ (A_0)\xrightarrow[A^*]{\eta}(s_A) \Rightarrow \exists s_B.\ (B_0)\xrightarrow[B^*]{f(\eta)}(s_B) \wedge (s_A = H \Leftrightarrow s_B = H)$$

Each label in the trace is replaced by the mapping of f on it, and labels mapped to ϵ by f are dropped. f is overloaded to denote the multilabel version when applied to η.

For brevity, we write $A \sqsubseteq B$ for $A \sqsubseteq_{\mathsf{id}} B$, for identity function id, forcing traces in the two systems to match exactly. Under this notion of identical traces, we say that A is sound w.r.t. B. That case matches traditional notions of trace refinement, often proved with simulation arguments, which we also adopt.

3.3 A Few Useful Lemmas

We need the following theorems in our proof.

Theorem 1. *$\sqsubseteq$ is reflexive and transitive.*

Theorem 2. *If $A \sqsubseteq_f B$, then $A^n \sqsubseteq_{f^n} B^n$, where f^n is f lifted appropriately to deal with indices ($f^n(i,\ell) = (i,\ell')$ when $f(\ell) = \ell'$, and $f^n(i,\ell) = \epsilon$ when $f(\ell) = \epsilon$).*

Theorem 3. *If $A \sqsubseteq_f A'$ and $B \sqsubseteq_f B'$, then $A+B \sqsubseteq_{\mathsf{id}} A'+B'$.*

All these theorems can be proved using standard techniques.

4 Decomposing a Shared-Memory Multiprocessor System

Any conventional multiprocessor system can be divided logically into three components, as shown in Fig. 1. The top-level system design is shown in the middle, while the details of its components, the memory system and the processor (P_i), are shown in the magnified boxes. The processor component P_i can be implemented in a variety of ways, from one executing instructions one-by-one in program order, to a complex one speculatively executing many instructions concurrently to exploit parallelism. The memory component is normally implemented using a hierarchy of caches, in order to increase the performance of the overall system, because the latency of accessing memory directly is large compared to that of accessing a much smaller cache. Between each processor and the global memory subsystem appears some local buffer, LB_i, each specific to processor P_i.

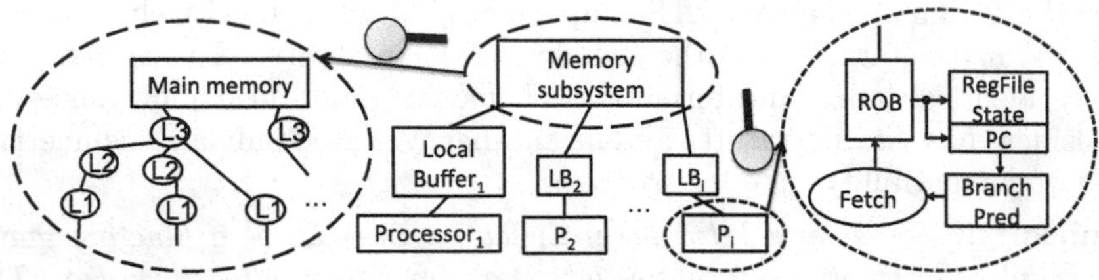

Fig. 1. Components of a multiprocessor system

Popular ISAs, such as Intel x86, ARM, and PowerPC, do not guarantee sequential consistency. However, we want to emphasize that, in every weak-memory system we are aware of, *the main memory still exposes atomic loads and stores*! Weaker semantics in a core P_i arise only because of (1) reordering of memory instructions by the core and/or (2) the properties of the local buffers LB_i connected to P_i.

Consequently, we focus on this opportunity to simplify proof decomposition. We prove that our main memory component satisfies an intuitive *store atomicity* property – which is an appropriate specification of the memory component even for implementations of weaker memory models. Store atomicity can be understood via the operational semantics of Fig. 2, describing an LTS that receives load and store requests (Ld and St) from processors and sends back load responses (LdRp). The transfer happens via input buffers $ins(p)$ from processor p and output buffers $outs(p)$ to processor p. Note that this model allows the memory system to answer pending memory requests in any order (as indicated by the bag union operator $\uplus$), even potentially reordering requests from a single processor, so long as, whenever it does process a request, that action appears to take place *atomically*.

$$\textbf{Ins}\ \frac{}{\begin{pmatrix} ins, \\ outs, m \end{pmatrix} \xrightarrow[M_m]{p,\,\mathrm{ToM}(q)} \begin{pmatrix} ins[p := \{q\} \uplus \\ ins(p)], outs, m \end{pmatrix}} \qquad \textbf{Rm}\ \frac{outs(p) = rs \uplus \{r\}}{\begin{pmatrix} ins, \\ outs, m \end{pmatrix} \xrightarrow[M_m]{p,\,\mathrm{ToP}(r)} \begin{pmatrix} ins, outs[\\ p := rs], m \end{pmatrix}}$$

$$\textbf{Ld}\ \frac{ins(p) = qs \uplus \{t, \mathsf{Ld}, a\}}{(ins, outs, m) \xrightarrow[M_m]{} (ins[p := qs], outs[p := (t, \mathsf{Ld}, m(a)) \uplus outs(p)], m)}$$

$$\textbf{St}\ \frac{ins(p) = qs \uplus \{\mathsf{St}, a, v\}}{(ins, outs, m) \xrightarrow[M_m]{} (ins[p := qs], outs[p := (\mathsf{St}) \uplus outs(p)], m[a := v])}$$

Fig. 2. LTS for a simple memory

Figure 2 provides our first example of a hardware component specified as an LTS via a set of inference rules. Such notation may seem far from the domain of synthesizable hardware, but it is actually extremely close to Bluespec notation, and the Bluespec compiler translates automatically to hardware circuits in Verilog [1].

The memory component is composed of a *hierarchy of caches*, with cache nodes labeled like "L1," "L2," etc., to avoid the latency of round trips with main memory. Therefore, it is the responsibility of the hierarchy of caches (which forms the memory subcomponent) to implement the store atomicity property. In fact, as we prove in Sect. 8, the purpose of the cache-coherence protocol is to establish this invariant for the memory subcomponent. Concretely, we have verified a *directory-based* protocol for coordinating an arbitrary tree of caches, where each node stores a conservative approximation of its children's states.

As an instance of the above decomposition, we prove that a multiprocessor system with no local buffering in between the processor and the memory components indeed implements SC. We implement a highly speculative processor that executes instructions and issues loads out of order, but commits instructions (once some "verification" is done) in order.

The processor itself can be decomposed into several components. In the zoomed-in version of Fig. 1, we show a highly speculative out-of-order-issue processor. We have the normal architectural state, such as values of registers. Our proofs are generic over *a family of instruction set architectures*, with parameters for opcode sets and functions for executing opcodes and decoding them from memory. Other key components are a *branch predictor*, which guesses at the control-flow path that a processor will follow, to facilitate speculation; and a *reorder buffer (ROB)*, which decides which instructions along that path to try executing ahead of schedule. Our proofs apply to an arbitrary branch predictor and any reorder buffer satisfying a simple semantic condition.

Our framework establishes theorems of the form "if system A has a run with some particular observable behavior, then system B also has a run with the same behavior." In this sense, we say that A correctly implements B. Other important properties, such as *deadlock freedom* for A (which might get stuck without producing any useful behavior), are left for future work.

5 Specifying Sequential Consistency

Our final theorem in this paper establishes that a particular complex hardware system implements sequential consistency (SC) properly. We state the theorem in terms of the trace refinement relation $\sqsubseteq$ developed in Sect. 3. Therefore, we need to define an LTS embodying SC. The simpler this system, the better. We need not worry about its performance, since we prove that an optimized system remains faithful to it.

Figure 3 defines an LTS for an n-processor system that is sequentially consistent, parameterized over details of the ISA. In particular, the ISA gives us some domains of architectural states s (e.g., register files) and of program counters pc. A function $\mathsf{dec}(s, pc)$ figures out which instruction pc references in the current state, returning the instruction's "decoded" form. A companion function $\mathsf{exec}(s, pc, d)$ actually executes the instruction, returning a new state s' and the next program counter pc'.

$$\text{Halt}\ \frac{\theta(i) = (s, pc) \quad \mathsf{dec}(s, pc) = H}{(\theta, m) \xrightarrow[\mathsf{SC}]{} (H)} \qquad \text{NonMem}\ \frac{\theta(i) = (s, pc) \quad \mathsf{dec}(s, pc) = (\mathsf{Nm}, x) \quad \mathsf{exec}(s, pc, (\mathsf{Nm}, x)) = (s', pc')}{(\theta, m) \xrightarrow[\mathsf{SC}]{} (\theta[i := (s', pc')], m)}$$

$$\text{Load}\ \frac{\theta(i) = (s, pc) \quad \mathsf{dec}(s, pc) = (\mathsf{Ld}, x, a) \quad \mathsf{exec}(s, pc, (\mathsf{Ld}, x, m(a))) = (s', pc')}{(\theta, m) \xrightarrow[\mathsf{SC}]{} (\theta[i := (s', pc')], m)}$$

$$\text{Store}\ \frac{\theta(i) = (s, pc) \quad \mathsf{dec}(s, pc) = (\mathsf{St}, a, v) \quad \mathsf{exec}(s, pc, (\mathsf{St})) = (s', pc')}{(\theta, m) \xrightarrow[\mathsf{SC}]{} (\theta[i := (s', pc')], m[a := v])}$$

Fig. 3. LTS for SC with n simple processors

The legal instruction forms, which are outputs of dec, are (Nm, x), for an operation not accessing memory; (Ld, x, a), for a memory load from address a; (St, a, v), for a memory store of value v to address a; and H, for a "halt" instruction that moves the LTS to state H. The parameter x above represents the rest of the instruction, including the opcode, registers, constants, *etc.*

The legal inputs to exec encode both a decoded instruction and any relevant responses from the memory system. These inputs are (Nm, x) and St, which need no extra input from the memory; and (Ld, x, v), where v gives the contents of the requested memory cell.

We define the initial state of SC as (θ_0, m_0), where m_0 is some initial memory fixed throughout our development, mapping every address to value v_0; and θ_0 maps every processor ID to (s_0, pc_0), using architecture-specific default values s_0 and pc_0.

This LTS encodes Lamport's notion of SC, where processors take turns executing nondeterministically in a simple interleaving. Note that, in this setting, an operational specification such as the LTS for SC is precisely the proper characterization of *full functional correctness* for a hardware design, much as a precondition-postcondition pair does that in a partial-correctness Hoare logic.

Our SC LTS fully constrains observable behavior of a system to remain consistent with simple interleaving. Similar operational models are possible as top-level specifications for systems following weaker memory models, by giving the LTS for the *local buffer* component and composing the three components simultaneously.

Our final, optimized system is parameterized over an ISA in the same way as SC is. In the course of the rest of this paper, we define an optimized system O and prove $O \sqsubseteq \text{SC}$. To support a modular proof decomposition, however, we need to introduce a few intermediate systems first.

$$\textbf{Halt}\ \frac{\mathsf{dec}(s, pc) = H}{(s, pc, \bot) \xrightarrow[\text{P}_{\text{ref}}]{} (H)} \qquad \textbf{NM}\ \frac{\mathsf{dec}(s, pc) = (\mathsf{Nm}, x) \quad \mathsf{exec}(s, pc, (\mathsf{Nm}, x)) = (s', pc')}{(s, pc, \bot) \xrightarrow[\text{P}_{\text{ref}}]{} (s', pc', \bot)}$$

$$\textbf{LdRq}\ \frac{\mathsf{dec}(s, pc) = (\mathsf{Ld}, x, a)}{(s, pc, \bot) \xrightarrow[\text{P}_{\text{ref}}]{\text{ToM}(\epsilon, \mathsf{Ld}, a)} (s, pc, \top)} \qquad \textbf{StRq}\ \frac{\mathsf{dec}(s, pc) = (\mathsf{St}, a, v)}{(s, pc, \bot) \xrightarrow[\text{P}_{\text{ref}}]{\text{ToM}(\mathsf{St}, a, v)} (s, pc, \top)}$$

$$\textbf{LdRp}\ \frac{\begin{array}{c}\mathsf{dec}(s, pc) = (\mathsf{Ld}, x, a) \\ \mathsf{exec}(s, pc, (\mathsf{Ld}, x, v)) = (s', pc')\end{array}}{(s, pc, \top) \xrightarrow[\text{P}_{\text{ref}}]{\text{ToP}(\epsilon, \mathsf{Ld}, v)} (s', pc', \bot)} \qquad \textbf{StRp}\ \frac{\begin{array}{c}\mathsf{dec}(s, pc) = (\mathsf{St}, a, v) \\ \mathsf{exec}(s, pc, (\mathsf{St})) = (s', pc')\end{array}}{(s, pc, \top) \xrightarrow[\text{P}_{\text{ref}}]{\text{ToP}(\mathsf{St})} (s', pc', \bot)}$$

Fig. 4. LTS for a simple decoupled processor (P_{ref})

6 Respecifying Sequential Consistency with Communication

Realistic hardware systems do not implement the monolithic SC of Fig. 3 directly. Instead, there is usually a split between processors and memory. Here we formalize that split using LTSes that compose to produce a system refining the SC model.

Figure 4 defines an LTS for a simple *decoupled* processor (P_{ref}). Memory does not appear within a processor's state. Instead, to load from or store to an address, *requests* are sent to the memory system and *responses* are received. Both kinds of messages are encoded as labels: ToM for requests to memory and ToP for responses from memory back to the processor.

A state of P_{ref} is a triple $(s, pc, wait)$, giving the current architectural state s and program counter pc, as well as a Boolean flag $wait$ indicating whether the processor is blocked waiting for a response from the memory system. As in the SC model, the state of the processor is changed to H whenever dec returns H.

As initial state for system P_{ref}, we use $(s_0, pc_0, \bot)$.

The simple memory defined earlier in Fig. 2 is meant to be composed with P_{ref} processors. A request to memory like (t, Ld, a) asks for the value of memory cell a, associating a *tag* t that the processor can use to match responses to requests. Those responses take the form (t, Ld, v), giving the value v of the requested memory address.

A memory state is a triple $(ins, outs, m)$, giving not just the memory m itself, but also buffers ins and $outs$ for receiving processor requests and batching up responses to processors, respectively. We define the initial state of the M_m LTS as $(\emptyset, \emptyset, m_0)$, with empty queues.

Now we can compose these LTSes to produce an implementation of SC.

For a system of n processors, our decoupled SC implementation is $\mathrm{P}^n_{\mathrm{ref}} + M_m$.

Theorem 4. $P^n_{ref} + M_m \sqsubseteq SC$

Proof. By induction on traces of the decoupled system, relating them to those of the SC reference (similar to the technique in WEB refinement [27]). We need to choose an abstraction function f from states of the complex system to states of the simple system. This function must be inductive in the appropriate sense: a step from s to s' on the left of the simulation relation must be matched by sequences of steps on the right from $f(s)$ to $f(s')$. We choose f that just preserves state components in states with no pending memory-to-processor responses. When such responses exist, f first executes them on the appropriate processors. □

7 Speculative Out-of-Order Processor

We implement a *speculative* processor, which may create many simultaneous outstanding requests to the memory – as an optimization to increase parallelism. Our processor proof is in some sense generic over correct speculation strategies. We parameterize over two key components of a processor design: a *branch predictor* (which makes guesses about processor-local control flow in advance of resolving conditional jumps) and a *reorder buffer* (which decides what speculative instructions – such as memory loads – are worth issuing at which moments, in effect *reordering* later instructions to happen before earlier instructions have finished).

The branch predictor is the simpler of the two components, whose state is indicated with metavariable bp. The operations on such state are $\mathsf{curPpc}(bp)$ (to extract the current program-counter prediction); $\mathsf{nextPpc}(bp)$ (to advance to predicting the next instruction); and $\mathsf{setNextPpc}(bp, pc)$ (to reset prediction to begin at a known-accurate position pc). We need not impose any explicit correctness criterion on branch predictors; the processor uses predictions only as hints, and it always resets the predictor using setNextPpc after detecting an inaccurate hint.

The interface and formal contract of a reorder buffer are more involved. We write rob as a metavariable for reorder-buffer state, and ϕ denotes the state of an empty buffer. The operations associated with rob are:

- $\mathsf{insert}(pc, rob)$, which appends the program instruction at location pc to the list of instructions that the buffer is allowed to consider executing.
- $\mathsf{compute}(rob)$, which models a step of computation inside the buffer, returning both an updated state and an optional speculative load to issue. For instance,

$$\textbf{Fetch}\ \frac{}{(s, pc, wait, rob, bp) \xrightarrow[\mathrm{P_{so}}]{} (s, pc, wait, \mathsf{insert}(\mathsf{curPpc}(bp), rob), \mathsf{nextPpc}(bp))}$$

$$\textbf{Comp}\ \frac{\mathsf{compute}(rob) = (rob', \epsilon)}{\begin{pmatrix} s, pc, wait, \\ rob, bp \end{pmatrix} \xrightarrow[\mathrm{P_{so}}]{} \begin{pmatrix} s, pc, wait, \\ rob', bp \end{pmatrix}} \qquad \textbf{SpLdRq}\ \frac{\mathsf{compute}(rob) = (rob', (\mathsf{SpecLd}, t, a))}{\begin{pmatrix} s, pc, wait, \\ rob, bp \end{pmatrix} \xrightarrow[\mathrm{P_{so}}]{\mathsf{ToM}(t, \mathsf{Ld}, a)} \begin{pmatrix} s, pc, wait, \\ rob', bp \end{pmatrix}}$$

$$\textbf{SpLdRp}\ \frac{t \neq \epsilon}{(s, pc, wait, rob, bp) \xrightarrow[\mathrm{P_{so}}]{\mathsf{ToP}(t, \mathsf{Ld}, v)} (s, pc, wait, \mathsf{updLd}(rob, t, v), bp)}$$

$$\textbf{Abort}\ \frac{\mathsf{commit}(rob) = (pc', \_, \_) \quad pc' \neq pc}{(s, pc, wait, rob, bp) \xrightarrow[\mathrm{P_{so}}]{} (s, pc, wait, \phi, \mathsf{setNextPpc}(bp, pc))}$$

$$\textbf{Halt}\ \frac{\mathsf{commit}(rob) = H}{(s, pc, \bot, rob, bp) \xrightarrow[\mathrm{P_{so}}]{} (H)} \qquad \textbf{Nm}\ \frac{\mathsf{commit}(rob) = (pc, pc', (\mathsf{Nm}, s'))}{(s, pc, \bot, rob, bp) \xrightarrow[\mathrm{P_{so}}]{} (s', pc', \bot, \mathsf{retire}(rob), bp)}$$

$$\textbf{StRq}\ \frac{\mathsf{commit}(rob) = (pc, pc', (\mathsf{St}, a, v, s'))}{\begin{pmatrix} s, pc, \bot, \\ rob, bp \end{pmatrix} \xrightarrow[\mathrm{P_{so}}]{\mathsf{ToM}(\mathsf{St}, a, v)} \begin{pmatrix} s, pc, \top, \\ rob, bp \end{pmatrix}} \qquad \textbf{LdRq}\ \frac{\mathsf{commit}(rob) = (pc, pc', (\mathsf{Ld}, x, a, v, s'))}{\begin{pmatrix} s, pc, \bot, \\ rob, bp \end{pmatrix} \xrightarrow[\mathrm{P_{so}}]{\mathsf{ToM}(\epsilon, \mathsf{Ld}, a)} \begin{pmatrix} s, pc, \top, \\ rob, bp \end{pmatrix}}$$

$$\textbf{StRp}\ \frac{\mathsf{commit}(rob) = (pc, pc', (\mathsf{St}, a, v, s'))}{\begin{pmatrix} s, pc, \top, \\ rob, bp \end{pmatrix} \xrightarrow[\mathrm{P_{so}}]{\mathsf{ToP}(\mathsf{St})} \begin{pmatrix} s', pc', \bot, \\ \mathsf{retire}(rob), bp \end{pmatrix}} \qquad \textbf{LdRpGd}\ \frac{\mathsf{commit}(rob) = (pc, pc', (\mathsf{Ld}, x, a, v, s'))}{\begin{pmatrix} s, pc, \top, \\ rob, bp \end{pmatrix} \xrightarrow[\mathrm{P_{so}}]{\mathsf{ToP}(\epsilon, \mathsf{Ld}, v)} \begin{pmatrix} s', pc', \bot, \\ \mathsf{retire}(rob), bp \end{pmatrix}}$$

$$\textbf{LdRpBad}\ \frac{\mathsf{commit}(rob) = (pc, pc', (\mathsf{Ld}, x, a, v', s')) \quad v' \neq v \quad \mathsf{exec}(s, pc, (\mathsf{Ld}, x, v)) = (s'', pc'')}{(s, pc, \top, rob, bp) \xrightarrow[\mathrm{P_{so}}]{\mathsf{ToP}(\epsilon, \mathsf{Ld}, v)} (s'', pc'', \bot, \phi, \mathsf{setNextPpc}(bp, pc''))}$$

Fig. 5. Speculating, out-of-order issue processor

it invokes the dec and exec functions (as defined for SC) internally to obtain the next program counter, state, *etc.* (but the actual states are not updated).

- updLd(rob, t, v), which informs the buffer that the memory has returned result value v for the speculative load with tag $t \neq \epsilon$.
- commit(rob), which returns the next instruction in serial program order, if we have accumulated enough memory responses to execute it accurately, or returns ϵ otherwise. When commit returns an instruction, it also returns the associated program counter plus the next program counter to which it would advance afterward. Furthermore, the instruction is extended with any relevant response from memory (used only for load instructions, obtained through updLd) and with the new architectural state (*e.g.*, register file) after execution.
- retire(rob), which informs the buffer that its commit instruction was executed successfully, so it is time to move on to the next instruction.

Figure 5 defines the speculative processor LTS $\mathrm{P_{so}}$. This processor may issue arbitrary speculative loads, but it *commits* only the instruction that comes next in serial program order. The processor will issue two kinds of loads, a speculative load (whose tag is not ϵ) and a commit or real load (whose tag is ϵ). To maintain SC, every speculative load must have a matching verification load later on, and we maintain the illusion that the program depends only on the results of verification loads, which, along with stores, *must be issued in serial program order.*

When committing a previously issued speculative load instruction, the associated speculative memory load response is verified against the new commit load response. If the resulting values do not match, the processor terminates all past uncommitted speculation, by emptying the reorder buffer and resetting the next predicted program counter in the branch predictor to the correct next value. In common cases, performance of executing loads twice is good, because it is likely that the verification load finds the address already in a local cache – thanks to the recent processing of the speculative load. Moreover, 60 % to 90 % of verification loads can be avoided by tracking speculative loads [9]; in the future we will extend our proofs to include such optimizations.

A full processor state is $(s, pc, wait, rob, bp)$, comprising architectural state, the program counter, a Boolean flag indicating whether the processor is waiting for a memory response about an instruction being committed, and the reorder-buffer and branch-predictor states. Its initial state is given by $(s_0, pc_0, \bot, \phi, bp_0)$. The interface of this processor with memory (*i.e.*, communication labels with $\mathsf{ToM}, \mathsf{ToP}$) is identical to that of the reference processor.

Finally, we impose a general correctness condition on reorder buffers (Fig. 6). Intuitively, whenever the buffer claims (via a commit output) that a particular instruction is next to execute (thus causing certain state changes), that instruction must really be next in line according to how the program runs in the SC system, and its execution must really cause those state changes.

ROB-invariant: If P_{so} reaches a state $(s, pc, wait, rob, bp)$,

$$\begin{cases} \mathsf{commit}(rob) = (pc, pc', (\mathsf{Nm}, s')) & \Rightarrow \exists x.\ \mathsf{dec}(s, pc) = (\mathsf{Nm}, x) \wedge \mathsf{exec}(s, pc, (\mathsf{Nm}, x)) = (s', pc') \\ \mathsf{commit}(rob) = (pc, pc', (\mathsf{Ld}, x, a, v, s')) & \Rightarrow \mathsf{dec}(s, pc) = (\mathsf{Ld}, x, a) \wedge \mathsf{exec}(s, pc, (\mathsf{Ld}, x, v)) = (s', pc') \\ \mathsf{commit}(rob) = (pc, pc', (\mathsf{St}, a, v, s')) & \Rightarrow \mathsf{dec}(s, pc) = (\mathsf{St}, a, v) \wedge \mathsf{exec}(s, pc, (\mathsf{St})) = (s', pc') \\ \mathsf{commit}(rob) = H & \Rightarrow \mathsf{dec}(s, pc) = H \end{cases}$$

Fig. 6. Correctness of reorder buffer

When this condition holds, we may conclude the correctness theorem for out-of-order processors. We use a trace-transformation function noSpec that drops all speculative-load requests and responses (*i.e.*, those load requests and responses whose tags are not ϵ). See Definition 5 for a review of how we use such functions in framing trace refinement. Intuitively, we prove that any behavior by the speculating processor can be matched by the simple processor, with speculative messages erased.

Theorem 5. $P_{so} \sqsubseteq_{\mathsf{noSpec}} P_{ref}$

Proof. By induction on $\mathrm{P_{so}}$ traces, using an abstraction function that drops the speculative messages and the *rob* and *bp* states to relate the two systems. The reorder-buffer correctness condition is crucial to relate its behavior with the simple in-order execution of $\mathrm{P_{ref}}$. □

Corollary 1. $P_{so}^n \sqsubseteq_{\mathsf{noSpec}^n} P_{ref}^n$

Proof. Direct consequence of Theorems 5 and 2 (the latter is about n-repetition). □

8 Cache-Based Memory System

We now turn our attention to a more efficient implementation of memory. With the cache hierarchy of Fig. 1, we have concurrent interaction of many processors with many caches, and the relationship with the original M_m system is far from direct. However, this intricate concurrent execution is crucial to hiding the latency of main-memory access. Figure 7 formalizes as an LTS M_c the algorithm we implemented (based on a published implementation [13]) for providing the memory abstraction on top of a cache hierarchy. We have what is called an *invalidating directory-based hierarchical cache-coherence protocol.*

We describe a state of the system using fields d, ch, cs, dir, w, $dirw$, ins, $outs$. The ins and $outs$ sets are the interfaces to the processors and are exactly the same as in M_m (Fig. 2). We use $parent(c, p)$ to denote that p is the parent of c.

A coherence state is M, S, or I, broadly representing permissions to modify, read, or do nothing with an address, respectively, the decreasing permissions denoted by $M > S > I$. More precisely, if a node n is in coherence state M or S for some address, then there might be some node in n's subtree that has write or read permissions, respectively, for that address. Coherence state of cache c for address a is denoted by $cs(c, a)$. $d(c, a)$ represents the data in cache c for address a.

$w(c, a)$ stores the permission an address a in cache c is waiting for, if any. That is, cache c has decided to *upgrade* its coherence state for address a to a more permissive value, but it is waiting for acknowledgment from its parent before upgrading.

$dir(p, c, a)$ represents the parent p's notion of the coherence state of the child c for address a. We later prove that this notion is always conservative, *i.e.*, if the parent assumes that a child does not have a particular permission, then it is guaranteed in this system that the child will not have that permission. $dirw(p, c, a)$ denotes whether the parent p is waiting for any downgrade response from its child c for address a, and if so, the coherence state that the child must downgrade to as well.

There are three types of communication channels in the system: (i) $ch(p, c, \mathsf{RR})$ (which carries both downgrade request and upgrade response messages from parent p to its child c), (ii) $ch(c, p, \mathsf{Rq})$ (which carries upgrade request messages from child c to its parent p) and (iii) $ch(c, p, \mathsf{Rp})$ (which carries downgrade response messages from child c to its parent p). While the $ch(c, p, \mathsf{Rp})$ and $ch(p, c, \mathsf{RR})$ channels deliver messages between the same pair of nodes in the same order in which the messages were injected (*i.e.*, they obey the FIFO property, indicated by the use of :: in Fig. 7), $ch(c, p, \mathsf{Rq})$ need not obey such a property (indicated by the use of $\uplus$ for unordered bags in Fig. 7). This asymmetry arises because only one downgrade request can be outstanding for one parent-child pair for an address.

Here is an intuition on how the transitions work in the common case. A cache can spontaneously decide to upgrade its coherence state, in which case it sends an upgrade request to its parent. The parent then makes a local decision on whether to send a response to the requesting child or not, based on its directory

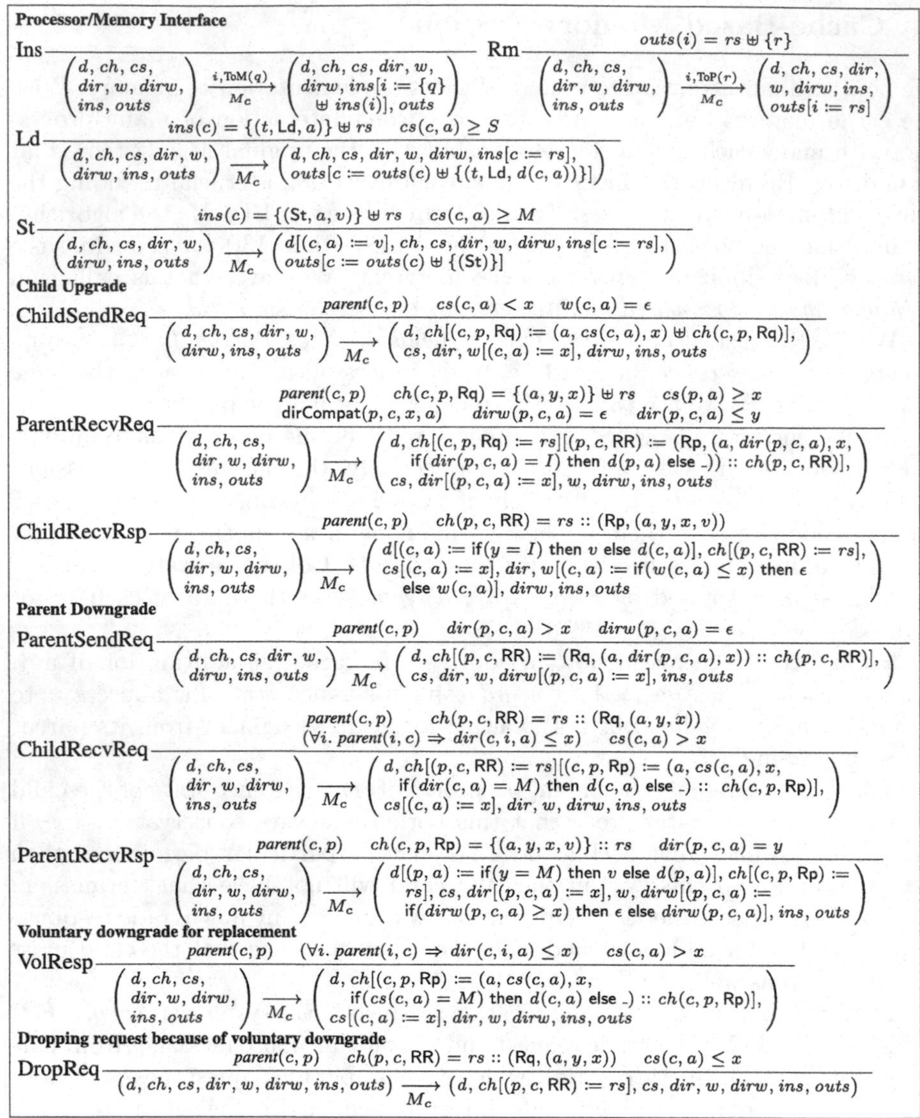

Fig. 7. LTS for cache-coherent shared-memory system

approximation and its own coherence state cs. If cs is lower than the requested upgrade, then it cannot handle the request, and instead must decide to upgrade cs. Once the parent's cs is not lower than the requested upgrade, it makes sure that the rest of its children are "compatible" with the requested upgrade (given by the $\mathsf{dirCompat}$ definition below). If not, the parent must send requests to the incompatible children to downgrade. Finally, when the cs's upgrade and children's downgrade responses are all received, the original request can be responded to. A request in *ins* can be processed by an L1 cache only if it is in the appropriate state, otherwise it has to request an upgrade for that address.

Definition 6. $\mathsf{dirCompat}(p, c, x, a) = \begin{cases} x = M \Rightarrow \forall c' \neq c.\ dir(p, c', a) = I \\ x = S \ \Rightarrow \forall c' \neq c.\ dir(p, c', a) \leq S \end{cases}$

A complication arises because a cache can voluntarily decide to downgrade its state. This transition is used to model invalidation of cache lines to make room for a different location. As a result, the parent's *dir* and the corresponding *cs* of the child may go out of sync, leading to the parent requesting a child to downgrade when it already has. To handle this situation, the child has to drop the downgrade request when it has already downgraded to the required state (Rule DropReq in Fig. 7), to avoid deadlocks by not dequeuing the request.

8.1 Proving M_c is Store Atomic

We must prove the following theorem, *i.e.*, the cache-based system is sound with respect to the simple memory.

Theorem 6. $M_c \sqsubseteq M_m$

We present the key theorem needed for this proof below. Throughout this section, we say *time* to denote the number of transitions that occurred before reaching the specified state.

Theorem 7. *A is store atomic, i.e.,* $A \sqsubseteq M_m$ *and* $M_m \sqsubseteq A$ *iff for any load request* $\mathsf{ToM}(t, \mathsf{Ld}, a)$ *received, the response* $\mathsf{ToP}(t, \mathsf{Ld}, v)$ *sent at time* T *is such that*

1. $v = v_0$ *(the initial value of any memory address) and no store request* $\mathsf{ToM}(\mathsf{St}, a, v')$ *has been processed at any time* T' *such that* $T' < T$ *or*
2. *There is a store request* $\mathsf{ToM}(\mathsf{St}, a, v)$ *that was processed at time* T_q *such that* $T_q < T$ *and no other store request* $\mathsf{ToM}(\mathsf{St}, a, v')$ *was processed at any time* T' *such that* $T_q < T' < T$.

The proof that M_c obeys the properties in Theorem 7 is involved enough that we state only key lemmas that we used.

Lemma 1. *At any time* T*, if address* a *in cache* c *obeys* $cs(c, a) \geq S$ *and* $\forall i.\ dir(c, i, a) \leq S$*, then* a *will have the* ***latest value****, i.e.,*

1. $d(c, a) = v_0$ *and no store request* $\mathsf{ToM}(\mathsf{St}, a, v)$ *has been processed at any time* T' *such that* $T' < T$ *or*
2. *There is a store request* $\mathsf{ToM}(\mathsf{St}, a, v)$ *that was processed at time* T_q *such that* $T_q < T \wedge d(c, a) = v$ *and no other store request* $\mathsf{ToM}(\mathsf{St}, a, v')$ *was processed at any time* T' *such that* $T_q < T' < T$.

It is relatively straightforward to prove the properties of Theorem 7, given Lemma 1. To prove Lemma 1, it has to be decomposed further into the following, each of which holds at any time.

Lemma 2. *If some response m for an address a is in transit (i.e., we are considering any time T such that $T_s \leq T \leq T_r$ where T_s is the time of sending m and T_r the time of receiving m), then no cache can process store requests for a, and m must be sent from a cache c where $cs(c, a) \geq S$ and $\forall i.\ dir(c, i, a) \leq S$.*

Lemma 3. *At any time, $\forall p, \forall c, \forall a.\ parent(c, p) \Rightarrow$*

$$cs(c, a) \leq dir(p, c, a) \wedge \mathsf{dirCompat}(p, c, dir(p, c, a), a) \wedge dir(p, c, a) \leq cs(p, a)$$

The same proof structure can be used to prove other invalidation-based protocols with inclusive caches (where any address present in a cache will also be present in its parent) like MESI, MOSI, and MOESI; we omit the discussion of extending this proof to these for space reasons. The MSI proof is about 12,000 lines of Coq code, of which 80 % can be reused as-is for the other protocols.

9 The Final Result

With our two main results about optimized processors and memories, we can complete the correctness proof of the composed optimized system.

First, we need to know that, whenever the simple memory can generate some trace of messages, it could also generate the same trace with all speculative messages removed. We need this property to justify the introduction of speculation, during our final series of refinements from the optimized system to SC.

Theorem 8. $M_m \sqsubseteq_{\mathsf{noSpec}^n} M_m$

Proof. By induction on traces, with an identity abstraction function. □

That theorem turns out to be the crucial ingredient to justify placing a speculative processor in-context with simple memory.

Theorem 9. $P^n_{so} + M_m \sqsubseteq P^n_{ref} + M_m$

Proof. Follows from Theorem 3 (our result about +), Corollary 1, and Theorem 8. □

The last theorem kept the memory the same while refining the processor. The next one does the opposite, switching out memory.

Theorem 10. $P^n_{so} + M_c \sqsubseteq P^n_{so} + M_m$

Proof. Follows from Theorems 6 and 3 plus reflexivity of $\sqsubseteq$ (Theorem 1). □

Theorem 11. $P^n_{so} + M_c \sqsubseteq SC$

Proof. We twice apply $\sqsubseteq$ transitivity (Theorem 1) to connect Theorems 10, 9, and 4 □

10 Conclusions and Future Work

In this paper, we developed a mechanized modular proof of a parametric hierarchical cache-coherence protocol in Coq and use this proof modularly for a verification of sequential consistency for a complete system containing out-of-order processors. Our proof modularization corresponds naturally to the modularization seen in hardware implementations, allowing verification to be carried out in tandem with the design. Our overall goal is to enable design of formally verified hardware systems. To this end, we have been working on a DSL in Coq for translating to and from Bluespec, and we are developing appropriate libraries and proof automation, extending the work of Braibant *et al.* [7] with support for modular specification and verification, systematizing some elements of this paper's Coq development that are specialized to our particular proof.

While we provide a clean interface for an SC system, we are also working on encompassing relaxed memory models commonly used in modern processors.

Acknowledgments. This work was supported in part by NSF grant CCF-1253229 and in part by the Defense Advanced Research Projects Agency (DARPA) and the United States Air Force, under Contract No. FA8750-11-C-0249. Any opinions, findings, and conclusions or recommendations expressed in this material are those of the authors and do not necessarily reflect the views of the Department of Defense or the U.S. Government.

References

1. Arvind, Nikhil, R.S., Rosenband, D.L., Dave, N.: High-level synthesis: an essential ingredient for designing complex ASICs. In: Proceedings of ICCAD 2004, San Jose, CA (2004)
2. Arvind, Shen, X.: Using term rewriting systems to design and verify processors. Micro, IEEE **19**(3), 36–46 (1999)
3. Augustsson, L., Schwarz, J., Nikhil, R.S.: Bluespec Language definition, Sandburst Corp (2001)
4. Bhattacharya, R., German, S.M., Gopalakrishnan, G.C.: Symbolic partial order reduction for rule based transition systems. In: Borrione, D., Paul, W. (eds.) CHARME 2005. LNCS, vol. 3725, pp. 332–335. Springer, Heidelberg (2005)
5. Bhattacharya, R., German, S.M., Gopalakrishnan, G.C.: Exploiting symmetry and transactions for partial order reduction of rule based specifications. In: Valmari, A. (ed.) SPIN 2006. LNCS, vol. 3925, pp. 252–270. Springer, Heidelberg (2006)
6. Bluespec Inc, Waltham, M.A.: Bluespec SystemVerilog Version 3.8 Reference Guide, November 2004
7. Braibant, T., Chlipala, A.: Formal verification of hardware synthesis. In: Sharygina, N., Veith, H. (eds.) CAV 2013. LNCS, vol. 8044, pp. 213–228. Springer, Heidelberg (2013)
8. Burch, J.R., Dill, D.L.: Automatic verification of pipelined microprocessor control. In: Dill, D.L. (ed.) Computer Aided Verification. LNCS, pp. 68–80. Springer, Heidelberg (1994)

9. Cain, H.W., Lipasti, M.H.: Memory ordering: a value-based approach. In: Proceedings of the 31st Annual International Symposium on Computer Architecture, 2004, pp. 90–101, June 2004
10. Chang, C., Wawrzynek, J., Brodersen, R.W.: Bee2: a high-end reconfigurable computing system. Des. Test Comput. IEEE **22**(2), 114–125 (2005)
11. Xiaofang Chen, Y., Yang, G.G., Chou, C.-T.: Efficient methods for formally verifying safety properties of hierarchical cache coherence protocols. Form. Methods Syst. Des. **36**(1), 37–64 (2010)
12. Chou, C.-T., Mannava, P.K., Park, S.: A simple method for parameterized verification of cache coherence protocols. In: Formal Methods in Computer Aided Design, pp. 382–398. Springer (2004)
13. Dave, N., Ng, M.C., Arvind.: Automatic synthesis of cache-coherence protocol processors using bluespec. In: Proceedings of Formal Methods and Models for Codesign, MEMOCODE, Verona, Italy (2005)
14. Delzanno, G.: Automatic verification of parameterized cache coherence protocols. In: Emerson, E.A., Sistla, A.P. (eds.) Computer Aided Verification. LNCS, vol. 1855, pp. 53–68. Springer, Heidelberg (2000)
15. Dill, D.L., Drexler, A.J., Hu, A.J., Yang, C.H.: Protocol verification as a hardware design aid. In: Proceedings of the IEEE 1992 International Conference on Computer Design: VLSI in Computers and Processors, ICCD 1992, pp. 522–525, October 1992
16. Emerson, E.A., Kahlon, V.: Exact and efficient verification of parameterized cache coherence protocols. In: Geist, D., Tronci, E. (eds.) CHARME 2003. LNCS, vol. 2860, pp. 247–262. Springer, Heidelberg (2003)
17. Hoe, J.C., Arvind.: Synthesis of operation-centric hardware descriptions. In: Proceedings of ICCAD 2000, pp. 511–518, San Jose, CA (2000)
18. Hoe, J.C., Arvind.: Operation-centric hardware description and synthesis. IEEE Trans. Comput. Aided Des. Integr. Circuits Syst. **23**(9), 1277–1288 (2004)
19. Norris Ip, C., Dill, D.L., Mitchell, J.C.: State reduction methods for automatic formal verification (1996)
20. Jhala, R., McMillan, K.L.: Microarchitecture verification by compositional model checking. In: Berry, G., Comon, H., Finkel, A. (eds.) CAV 2001. LNCS, vol. 2102, pp. 396–410. Springer, Heidelberg (2001)
21. Joshi, R., Lamport, L., Matthews, J., Tasiran, S., Tuttle, M.R., Yuan, Y.: Checking cache-coherence protocols with TLA^+. Formal Methods Syst. Des. **22**(2), 125–131 (2003)
22. Kaivola, R., Ghughal, R., Narasimhan, N., Telfer, A., Whittemore, J., Pandav, S., Slobodová, A., Taylor, C., Frolov, V., Reeber, E., et al.: Replacing testing with formal verification in Intel® Core^{tm} i7 processor execution engine validation. In: Bouajjani, A., Maler, O. (eds.) Computer Aided Verification, vol. 5643, pp. 414–429. Springer, Heidelberg (2009)
23. Khan, A., Vijayaraghavan, M., Boyd-Wickizer, S., Arvind: Fast and cycle-accurate modeling of a multicore processor. In: 2012 IEEE International Symposium on Performance Analysis of Systems & Software, pp. 178–187, New Brunswick, NJ, USA, April 1–3, 2012
24. Kuskin, J., Ofelt, D., Heinrich, M., Heinlein, J., Simoni, R., Gharachorloo, K., Chapin, J., Nakahira, D., Baxter, J., Horowitz, M.A., Gupta, A.M., Rosenblum, M., Hennessy, J.: The stanford FLASH multiprocessor. In: Proceedings of the 21st Annual International Symposium on Computer Architecture, pp. 302–313, April 1994

25. Lamport, L.: How to make a multiprocessor computer that correctly executes multiprocess programs. IEEE Trans. Comput. **100**(9), 690–691 (1979)
26. Lamport, L.: Specifying Systems: The TLA+ Language and Tools for Hardware and Software Engineers. Addison-Wesley Longman Publishing Co., Inc., Boston (2002)
27. Manolios, P., Srinivasan, S.K.: Automatic verification of safety and liveness for pipelined machines using WEB refinement. ACM Trans. Des. Autom. Electron. Syst. 45:1–45:19 (2008)
28. McMillan, K.L.: Parameterized verification of the FLASH cache coherence protocol by compositional model checking. In: Margaria, T., Melham, T.F. (eds.) CHARME 2001. LNCS, vol. 2144, pp. 179–195. Springer, Heidelberg (2001)
29. McMillan, K.L.: Verification of an implementation of Tomasulo's algorithm by compositional model checking. In: Hu, A.J., Vardi, M.Y. (eds.) Computer Aided Verification, pp. 110–121. Springer, Heidelberg (1998)
30. McMillan, K.L.: Verification of infinite state systems by compositional model checking. In: Pierre, L., Kropf, T. (eds.) CHARME 1999. LNCS, vol. 1703, pp. 219–237. Springer, Heidelberg (1999)
31. McMillan, K.L., Schwalbe, J.: Formal verification of the Gigamax cache consistency protocol. In: Proceedings of the International Symposium on Shared Memory Multiprocessing, pp. 111–134 (1992)
32. Moore, J.S.: An ACL2 proof of write invalidate cache coherence. In: Hu, A.J., Vardi, M.Y. (eds.) Computer Aided Verification. LNCS, vol. 1427, pp. 29–38. Springer, Heidelberg (1998)
33. Park, S., Dill, D.L.: Verification of FLASH cache coherence protocol by aggregation of distributed transactions. In: Proceedings of the 8th Annual ACM Symposium on Parallel Algorithms and Architectures, pp. 288–296. ACM Press (1996)
34. Shen, X., Arvind, Rudolph, L.: Commit-reconcile & fences (CRF): a new memory model for architects and compiler writers. In: Proceedings of the 26th annual international symposium on Computer architecture, pp. 150–161. IEEE Computer Society (1999)
35. Talupur, M., Tuttle, M.R.: Going with the flow: parameterized verification using message flows. In: Formal Methods in Computer-Aided Design, FMCAD 2008, pp. 1–8, November 2008
36. Windley, P.J.: Formal modeling and verification of microprocessors. IEEE Trans. Comput. **44**(1), 54–72 (1995)
37. Zhang, M., Bingham, J.D., Erickson, J., Sorin, D.J.: Pvcoherence: designing flat coherence protocols for scalable verification. In: 20th IEEE International Symposium on High Performance Computer Architecture, HPCA 2014, pp. 392–403. IEEE Computer Society, Orlando, FL, USA, February 15–19 (2014)
38. Zhang, M., Lebeck, A.R., Sorin. D.J.: Fractal coherence: scalably verifiable cache coherence. In: Proceedings of the 2010 43rd Annual IEEE/ACM International Symposium on Microarchitecture, MICRO '43, pp. 471–482. IEEE Computer Society, Washington, DC, USA (2010)

Word-Level Symbolic Trajectory Evaluation

Supratik Chakraborty[1(✉)], Zurab Khasidashvili[2], Carl-Johan H. Seger[3], Rajkumar Gajavelly[1], Tanmay Haldankar[1], Dinesh Chhatani[1], and Rakesh Mistry[1]

[1] IIT Bombay, Mumbai, India
supratik@cse.iitb.ac.in
[2] Intel IDC, Haifa, Israel
[3] Intel, Portland, OR, USA

Abstract. Symbolic trajectory evaluation (STE) is a model checking technique that has been successfully used to verify industrial designs. Existing implementations of STE, however, reason at the level of bits, allowing signals to take values in $\{0, 1, X\}$. This limits the amount of abstraction that can be achieved, and presents inherent limitations to scaling. The main contribution of this paper is to show how much more abstract lattices can be derived automatically from RTL descriptions, and how a model checker for the general theory of STE instantiated with such abstract lattices can be implemented in practice. This gives us the first practical word-level STE engine, called STEWord. Experiments on a set of designs similar to those used in industry show that STEWord scales better than word-level BMC and also bit-level STE.

1 Introduction

Symbolic Trajectory Evaluation (STE) is a model checking technique that grew out of multi-valued logic simulation on the one hand, and symbolic simulation on the other hand [2]. Among various formal verification techniques in use today, STE comes closest to functional simulation and is among the most successful formal verifiation techniques used in the industry. In STE, specifications take the form of symbolic trajectory formulas that mix Boolean expressions and the temporal next-time operator. The Boolean expressions provide a convenient means of describing different operating conditions in a circuit in a compact form. By allowing only the most elementary of temporal operators, the class of properties that can be expressed is fairly restricted as compared to other temporal logics (see [4] for a nice survey). Nonetheless, experience has shown that many important aspects of synchronous digital systems at various levels of abstraction can be captured using this restricted logic. For example, it is quite adequate for expressing many of the subtleties of system operation, including clocking schemas, pipelining control, as well as complex data computations [7,8,12].

R. Gajavelly, T. Haldankar and D. Chhatani contributed to this work when they were in IIT Bombay.

D. Kroening and C.S. Păsăreanu (Eds.): CAV 2015, Part II, LNCS 9207, pp. 128–143, 2015.
DOI: 10.1007/978-3-319-21668-3_8

In return for the restricted expressiveness of STE specifications, the STE model checking algorithm provides siginificant computational efficiency. As a result, STE can be applied to much larger designs than any other model checking technique. For example, STE is routinely used in the industry today to carry out complete formal input-output verification of designs with several hundred thousand latches [7,8]. Unfortunately, this still falls short of providing an automated technique for formally verifying modern system-on-chip designs, and there is clearly a need to scale up the capacity of STE even further.

The first approach that was pursued in this direction was structural decomposition. In this approach, the user must break down a verification task into smaller sub-tasks, each involving a distinct STE run. After this, a deductive system can be used to reason about the collections of STE runs and verify that they together imply the desired property of the overall design [6]. In theory, structural decomposition allows verification of arbitrarily complex designs. However, in practice, the difficulty and tedium of breaking down a property into small enough sub-properties that can be verified with an STE engine limits the usefulness of this approach significantly. In addition, managing the structural decomposition in the face of rapidly changing RTL limits the applicability of structural decomposition even further.

A different approach to increase the scale of designs that can be verified is to use aggressive abstraction beyond what is provided automatically by current STE implementations. If we ensure that our abstract model satisfies the requirements of the general theory of STE, then a property that is verified on the abstract model holds on the original model as well. Although the general theory of STE allows a very general circuit model [11], all STE implementations so far have used a three-valued circuit model. Thus, every bit-level signal is allowed to have one of three values: 0, 1 or X, where X represents "either 0 or 1". This limits the amount of abstraction that can be achieved. The main contribution of this paper is to show how much more abstract lattices can be derived automatically from RTL descriptions, and how the general theory of STE can be instantiated with these lattices to give a practical word-level STE engine that provides significant gains in capacity and efficiency on a set of benchmarks.

Operationally, word-level STE bears similarities with word-level bounded model checking (BMC). However, there are important differences, the most significant one being the use of X-based abstractions on slices of words, called *atoms*, in word-level STE. This allows a wide range of abstraction possibilities, including a combination of user-specified and automatic abstractions – often a necessity for complex verification tasks. Our preliminary experimental results indicate that by carefully using X-based abstractions in word-level STE, it is indeed possible to strike a good balance between accuracy (cautious propagation of X) and performance (liberal propagation of X).

The remainder of the paper is organized as follows. We discuss how words in an RTL design can be split into atoms in Sect. 2. Atoms form the basis of abstracting groups of bits. In Sect. 3, we elaborate on the lattice of values that this abstraction generates, and Sect. 4 presents a new way of encoding values of atoms in this lattice. We also discuss how to symbolically simulate

RTL operators and compute least upper bounds using this encoding. Section 5 presents an instantiation of the general theory of STE using the above lattice, and discusses an implementation. Experimental results on a set of RTL benchmarks are presented in Sect. 6, and we conclude in Sect. 7.

2 Atomizing Words

In bit-level STE [2,12], every variable is allowed to take values from $\{0, 1, X\}$, where X denotes "either 0 or 1". The ordering of information in the values 0, 1 and X is shown in the lattice in Fig. 1, where a value lower in the order has "less information" than one higher up in the order. The element $\top$ is added to complete the lattice, and represents an unachievable over-constrained value. Tools that implement bit-level STE usually use dual-rail encoding to reason about ternary values of variables. In dual-rail encoding, every bit-level variable v is encoded using two binary variables v_0 and v_1. Intuitively, v_i indicates whether v can take the value i, for i in $\{0, 1\}$. Thus, 0, 1 and X are encoded by the valuations $(0, 1)$, $(1, 0)$ and $(1, 1)$, respectively, of (v_0, v_1). By convention, $(v_0, v_1) = (0, 0)$ denotes $\top$. An undesired consequence of dual-rail encoding is the doubling of binary variables in the encoded system. This can pose serious scalability issues when verifying designs with wide datapaths, large memories, etc. Attempts to scale STE to large designs must therefore raise the level of abstraction beyond that of individual bits.

In principle, one could go to the other extreme, and run STE at the level of words as defined in the RTL design. This requires defining a lattice of values of words, and instantiating the general theory of STE [11] with this lattice. The difficulty with this approach lies in implementing it in practice. The lattice of values of an m-bit word, where each bit in the word can take values in $\{0, 1, X\}$, is of size at least 3^m. Symbolically representing values from such a large lattice and reasoning about them is likely to incur overheads similar to that incurred in bit-level STE. Therefore, STE at the level of words (as defined in the RTL design) does not appear to be a practical proposition for scaling.

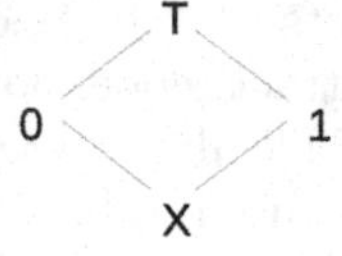

Fig. 1. Ternary lattice

The idea of splitting words into sub-words for the purpose of simplifying analysis is not new (see e.g. [5]). An aggressive approach to splitting (an extreme example being bit-blasting) can lead to proliferation of narrow sub-words, making our technique vulnerable to the same scalability problems that arise with dual-rail encoding. Therefore, we adopt a more controlled approach to splitting. Specifically, we wish to split words in such a way that we can speak of an entire sub-word having the value X without having to worry about which individual bits in the sub-word have the value X. Towards this end, we partition every word in an RTL design into sub-words, which we henceforth call *atoms*, such that every RTL statement that reads or updates a word either does so for all bits in an atom, or for no bit in an atom. In other words, no RTL statement (except the few discussed at the end of this section) reads or updates an atom partially.

The above discussion leads to a fairly straightforward algorithm for identifying atoms in an RTL design. We refer the reader to the full version of the paper [3] for details of our atomization technique, and illustrate it on a simple example below. Figure 2(a) shows a System-Verilog code fragment, and Fig. 2(b) shows an atomization of words, where the solid vertical bars represent the boundaries of atoms. Note that every System-Verilog statement in Fig. 2(a) either reads or writes all bits in an atom, or no bit in an atom. Since we wish to reason at the granularity of atoms, we must interpret word-level reads and writes in terms of the corresponding atom-level reads and writes. This can be done either by modifying the RTL, or by taking appropriate care when symbolically simulating the RTL. For simplicity of presentation, we show in Fig. 2(c) how the code fragment in Fig. 2(b) would appear if we were to use only the atoms identified in Fig. 2(b). Note that no statement in the modified RTL updates or reads a slice of an atom. However, a statement may be required to read a slice of the result obtained by applying an RTL operator to atoms (see, for example, Fig. 2(c) where we read a slice of the result obtained by adding concatenated atoms). In our implementation, we do not modify the RTL. Instead, we symbolically simulate the original RTL, but generate the expressions for various atoms that would result from simulating the modified RTL.

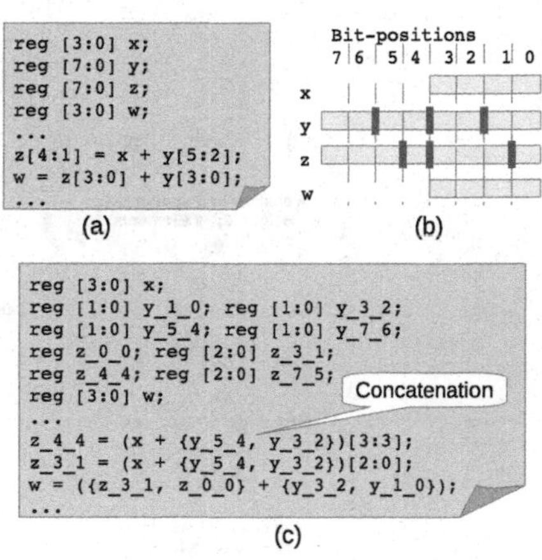

Fig. 2. Illustrating atomization

Once the boundaries of all atoms are determined, we choose to disregard values of atoms in which some bits are set to X, and the others are set to 0 or 1. This choice is justified since all bits in an atom are read or written together. Thus, either all bits in an atom are considered to have values in $\{0, 1\}$, or all of them are considered to have the value X. This implies that values of an m-bit atom can be encoded using $m + 1$ bits, instead of using $2m$ bits as in dual-rail encoding. Specifically, we can associate an additional "invalid" bit with every m-bit atom. Whenever the "invalid" bit is set, all bits in the atom are assumed to have the value X. Otherwise, all bits are assumed to have values in $\{0, 1\}$. We show later in Sects. 4.1 and 4.2 how the value and invalid bit of an atom can be recursively computed from the values and invalid bits of the atoms on which it depends.

Memories and arrays in an RTL design are usually indexed by variables instead of by constants. This makes it difficult to atomize memories and arrays statically, and we do not atomize them. Similarly, if a design has a logical shift operation, where the shift length is specified by a variable, it is difficult to statically identify subwords that are not split by the shift operation. We ignore all such RTL operations during atomizaion, and instead use extensional arrays [13] to model and reason about them. Section 4.2 briefly discusses the modeling of memory/array reads and writes in this manner. A more detailed description is available in the full version of the paper [3].

3 Lattice of Atom Values

Recall that the primary motivation for atomizing words is to identify the right granularity at which an entire sub-word (atom) can be assigned the value X without worrying about which bits in the sub-word have the value X. Therefore, an m-bit atom a takes values from the set $\{\overbrace{0\cdots00}^{\text{m bits}}, \ldots \overbrace{1\cdots11}^{\text{m bits}}, \mathbf{X}\}$, where $\mathbf{X}$ is a single abstract value that denotes an assignment of X to at least one bit of a. Note the conspicuous absence of values like $0X1\cdots0$ in the above set. Figure 3(a) shows the lattice of values for a 3-bit atom, ordered by information content. The $\top$ element is added to complete the lattice, and represents an unachievable over-constrained value. Figure 3(b) shows the lattice of values of the same atom if we allow each bit to take values in $\{0, 1, X\}$. Clearly, the lattice in Fig. 3(a) is shallower and sparser than that in Fig. 3(b).

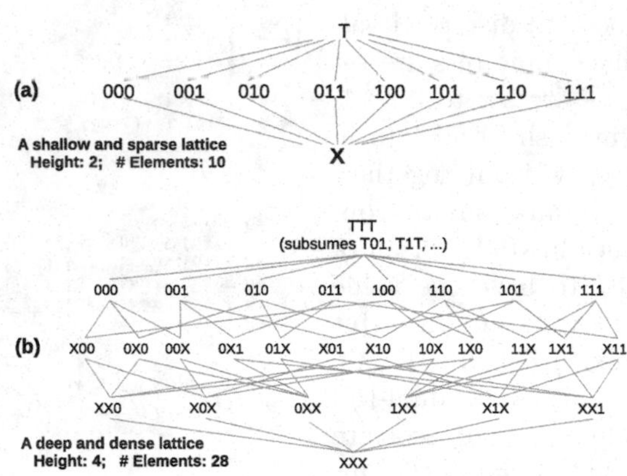

Fig. 3. Atom-level and bit-level lattices

Consider an m-bit word w that has been partitioned into non-overlapping atoms of widths $m_1, \ldots m_r$, where $\sum_{j=1}^{r} m_j = m$. The lattice of values of w is given by the product of r lattices, each corresponding to the values of an atom of w. For convenience of representation, we simplify the product lattice by collapsing all values that have at least one atom set to $\top$ (and therefore represent unachievable over-constrained values), to a single $\top$ element. It can be verified that the height of the product lattice (after the above simplification) is given by $r + 1$, the total number of elements in it is given by $\prod_{j=1}^{r} \left(2^{m_j} + 1\right) + 1$ and the number of elements at level i from the bottom is given by $\binom{m}{i} \prod_{j=1}^{i} 2^{m_j}$, where $0 < i \leq r$. It is not hard to see from these expressions that atomization using few wide atoms (i.e., small values of r and large values of m_j) gives shallow and sparse lattices compared to atomization using many narrow atoms (i.e., large values of r and small values of m_j). The special case of a bit-blasted lattice (see Fig. 3(b)) is obtained when $r = m$ and $m_j = 1$ for every $j \in \{1, \ldots r\}$.

Using a sparse lattice is advantageous in symbolic reasoning since we need to encode a small set of values. Using a shallow lattice helps in converging fast when computing least upper bounds – an operation that is crucially needed when performing symbolic trajectory evaluation. However, making the lattice of values sparse and shallow comes at the cost of losing precision of reasoning. By atomizing words based on their actual usage in an RTL design, and by abstracting values of atoms wherein some bits are set to X and the others are set to 0 or 1, we strike a balance between depth and density of the lattice of values on one hand, and precision of reasoning on the other.

4 Symbolic Simulation with Invalid-Bit Encoding

As mentioned earlier, an m-bit atom can be encoded with $m + 1$ bits by associating an "invalid bit" with the atom. For notational convenience, we use $\mathsf{val}(a)$ to denote the value of the m bits constituting atom a, and $\mathsf{inv}(a)$ to denote the value of its invalid bit. Thus, an m-bit atom a is encoded as a pair $(\mathsf{val}(a), \mathsf{inv}(a))$, where $\mathsf{val}(a)$ is a bit-vector of width m, and $\mathsf{inv}(a)$ is of Boolean type. Given $(\mathsf{val}(a), \mathsf{inv}(a))$, the value of a is given by $\mathsf{ite}(\mathsf{inv}(a), \mathbf{X}, \mathsf{val}(a))$, where "ite" denotes the usual "if-then-else" operator. For clarity of exposition, we call this encoding "invalid-bit encoding". Note that invalid-bit encoding differs from dual-rail encoding even when $m = 1$. Specifically, if a 1-bit atom a has the value X, we can use either $(0, \mathsf{true})$ or $(1, \mathsf{true})$ for $(\mathsf{val}(a), \mathsf{inv}(a))$ in invalid-bit encoding. In contrast, there is a single value, namely $(a_0, a_1) = (1, 1)$, that encodes the value X of a in dual-rail encoding. We will see in Sect. 4.2 how this degree of freedom in invalid-bit encoding of X can be exploited to simplify the symbolic simulation of word-level operations on invalid-bit-encoded operands, and also to simplify the computation of least upper bounds.

Symbolic simulation is a key component of symbolic trajectory evaluation. In order to symbolically simulate an RTL design in which every atom is invalid-bit encoded, we must first determine the semantics of word-level RTL operators with respect to invalid-bit encoding. Towards this end, we describe below a generic technique for computing the value component of the invalid-bit encoding of the result of applying a word-level RTL operator. Subsequently, we discuss how the invalid-bit component of the encoding is computed.

4.1 Symbolically Simulating Values

Let op be a word-level RTL operator of arity k, and let res be the result of applying op on $v_1, v_2, \ldots v_k$, i.e., $res = \mathsf{op}(v_1, v_2, \ldots v_k)$. For each i in $\{1, \ldots k\}$, suppose the bit-width of operand v_i is m_i, and suppose the bit-width of res is m_{res}.

We assume that each operand is invalid-bit encoded, and we are interested in computing the invalid-bit encoding of a specified slice of the result, say $res[q:p]$, where $0 \leq p \leq q \leq m_{res} - 1$. Let $\langle \mathsf{op} \rangle : \{0,1\}^{m_1} \times \cdots \times \{0,1\}^{m_k} \rightarrow \{0,1\}^{m_{res}}$ denote the RTL semantics of op. For example, if op denotes 32-bit unsigned addition, then $\langle \mathsf{op} \rangle$ is the function that takes two 32-bit operands and returns their 32-bit unsigned sum. The following lemma states that $\mathsf{val}(res[q:p])$ can be computed if we know $\langle \mathsf{op} \rangle$ and $\mathsf{val}(v_i)$, for every $i \in \{1, \ldots k\}$. Significantly, we do not need $\mathsf{inv}(v_i)$ for any $i \in \{1, \ldots k\}$ to compute $\mathsf{val}(res[q:p])$.

Lemma 1. *Let* $v = \left(\langle \mathsf{op} \rangle (\mathsf{val}(v_1), \mathsf{val}(v_2), \ldots \mathsf{val}(v_k))\right)[q:p]$*. Then* $\mathsf{val}(res[q:p])$ *is given by* v*, where* $res = \mathsf{op}(v_1, v_2, \ldots v_k)$*.*

The proof of Lemma 1, given in [3], exploits the observation that if $\mathsf{inv}(res[q:p])$ is true, then the value of $\mathsf{val}(res[q:p])$ does not matter. Lemma 1 tells us that when computing $\mathsf{val}(res[q:p])$, we can effectively assume that invalid-bit encoding is not used. This simplifies symbolic simulation with invalid-bit encoding significantly. Note that this simplification would not have been possible had we not had the freedom to ignore $\mathsf{val}(res[q:p])$ when $\mathsf{inv}(res[q:p])$ is true.

4.2 Symbolically Simulating Invalid Bits

We now turn to computing $\mathsf{inv}(res[q:p])$. Unfortunately, computing $\mathsf{inv}(res[q:p])$ precisely is difficult and involves operator-specific functions that are often complicated. We therefore choose to approximate $\mathsf{inv}(res[q:p])$ in a sound manner with functions that are relatively easy to compute. Specifically, we allow $\mathsf{inv}(res[q:p])$ to evaluate to true (denoting $res[q:p] = \mathbf{X}$) even in cases where a careful calculation would have shown that $\mathsf{op}(v_1, v_2, \ldots v_k)$ is not $\mathbf{X}$. However, we never set $\mathsf{inv}(res[q:p])$ to false if any bit in $res[q:p]$ can take the value X in a bit-blasted evaluation of res. Striking a fine balance between the precision and computational efficiency of the sound approximations is key to building a practically useful symbolic simulator using invalid-bit encoding. Our experience indicates that simple and sound approximations of $\mathsf{inv}(res[q:p])$ can often be carefully chosen to serve our purpose. While we have derived templates for approximating $\mathsf{inv}(res[q:p])$ for res obtained by applying all word-level RTL operators that appear in our benchmarks, we cannot present all of them in detail here due to space constraints. We present below a discussion of how $\mathsf{inv}(res[q:p])$ is approximated for a subset of important RTL operators. Importantly, we use a recursive formulation for computing $\mathsf{inv}(res[q:p])$. This allows us to recursively compute invalid bits of atoms obtained by applying complex sequences of word-level operations to a base set of atoms.

Word-Level Addition: Let $+_m$ denote an m-bit addition operator. Thus, if a and b are m-bit operands, $a +_m b$ generates an m-bit sum and a 1-bit $carry$. Let the carry generated after adding the least significant r bits of the operands be denoted $carry_r$. We discuss below how to compute sound approximations of $\mathsf{inv}(sum[q:p])$ and $\mathsf{inv}(carry_r)$, where $0 \leq p \leq q \leq m-1$ and $1 \leq r \leq m$.

It is easy to see that the value of $sum[q : p]$ is completely determined by $a[q : p]$, $b[q : p]$ and $carry_p$. Therefore, we can approximate $\mathsf{inv}(sum[q : p])$ as follows: $\mathsf{inv}(sum[q : p]) = \mathsf{inv}(a[q : p]) \vee \mathsf{inv}(b[q : p]) \vee \mathsf{inv}(carry_p)$.

To see why the above approximation is sound, note that if all of $\mathsf{inv}(a[q : p])$, $\mathsf{inv}(b[q : p])$ and $\mathsf{inv}(carry_p)$ are false, then $a[q : p]$, $b[q : p]$ and $carry_p$ must have non-$\mathbf{X}$ values. Hence, there is no uncertainty in the value of $sum[q : p]$ and $\mathsf{inv}(sum[q : p]) = \mathsf{false}$. On the other hand, if any of $\mathsf{inv}(a[q : p]$, $\mathsf{inv}(b[q : p])$ or $\mathsf{inv}(carry_p)$ is true, there is uncertainty in the value of $sum[q : p]$.

The computation of $\mathsf{inv}(carry_p)$ (or $\mathsf{inv}(carry_r)$) is interesting, and deserves special attention. We identify three cases below, and argue that $\mathsf{inv}(carry_p)$ is false in each of these cases. In the following, $\mathbf{0}$ denotes the p-bit constant $00 \cdots 0$.

1. If $\big(\mathsf{inv}(a[p-1 : 0]) \vee \mathsf{inv}(b[p-1 : 0])\big) = \mathsf{false}$, then both $\mathsf{inv}(a[p-1 : 0])$ and $\mathsf{inv}(b[p-1 : 0])$ must be false. Therefore, there is no uncertainty in the values of either $a[p-1 : 0]$ or $b[p-1 : 0]$, and $\mathsf{inv}(carry_p) = \mathsf{false}$.
2. If $\big(\neg\mathsf{inv}(a[p-1 : 0]) \wedge (\mathsf{val}(a[p-1 : 0]) = \mathbf{0})\big) = \mathsf{true}$, then the least significant p bits of $\mathsf{val}(a)$ are all 0. Regardless of $\mathsf{val}(b)$, it is easy to see that in this case, $\mathsf{val}(carry_p) = 0$ and $\mathsf{inv}(carry_p) = \mathsf{false}$.
3. This is the symmetric counterpart of the case above, i.e., $\big(\neg\mathsf{inv}(b[p-1 : 0]) \wedge (\mathsf{val}(b[p-1 : 0]) = \mathbf{0})\big) = \mathsf{true}$.

We now approximate $\mathsf{inv}(carry_p)$ by combining the conditions corresponding to the three cases above. In other words,

$$\begin{aligned}\mathsf{inv}(carry_p) = {} & \big(\mathsf{inv}(a[p-1 : 0]) \vee \mathsf{inv}(b[p-1 : 0])\big) \wedge \\ & \big(\mathsf{inv}(a[p-1 : 0]) \vee (\mathsf{val}(a[p-1 : 0]) \neq \mathbf{0})\big) \wedge \\ & \big(\mathsf{inv}(b[p-1 : 0]) \vee (\mathsf{val}(b[p-1 : 0]) \neq \mathbf{0})\big)\end{aligned}$$

Word-Level Division: Let $\div_m$ denote an m-bit division operator. This is among the most complicated word-level RTL operators for which we have derived an approximation of the invalid bit. If a and b are m-bit operands, $a \div_m b$ generates an m-bit quotient, say $quot$, and an m-bit remainder, say rem. We wish to compute $\mathsf{inv}(quot[q : p])$ and $\mathsf{inv}(rem[q : p])$, where $0 \leq p \leq q \leq m-1$. We assume that if $\mathsf{inv}(b)$ is false, then $\mathsf{val} \neq 0$; the case of $a \div_m b$ with $(\mathsf{val}(b), \mathsf{inv}(b)) = (0, \mathsf{false})$ leads to a "divide-by-zero" exception, and is assumed to be handled separately.

The following expressions give sound approximations for $\mathsf{inv}(quot[q : p])$ and $\mathsf{inv}(rem[q : p])$. In these expressions, we assume that i is a non-negative integer such that $2^i \leq \mathsf{val}(b) < 2^{i+1}$. We defer the argument for soundness of these approximations to the full version of the paper [3], for lack of space.

$$\begin{aligned}&\mathsf{inv}(quot[q : p]) = \mathsf{ite}(\mathsf{inv}(b), temp_1, temp_2), \text{ where}\\ &\qquad temp_1 = \mathsf{inv}(a) \vee (\mathsf{val}(a[m-1 : p]) \neq \mathbf{0}) \text{ and}\\ &\qquad temp_2 = \mathsf{ite}(\mathsf{val}(b) = 2^i, temp_3, (i < p) \vee \mathsf{inv}(a[m-1 : p])), \text{ where}\\ &\qquad temp_3 = (p + i \leq m-1) \wedge \mathsf{inv}(a[\min(q+i, m-1) : p+i]))\\ &\mathsf{inv}(rem[q : p]) = \mathsf{inv}(b) \vee \mathsf{ite}(\mathsf{val}(b) = 2^i, (i > p) \wedge \mathsf{inv}(a[\min(q, i-1) : p]), i \geq p)\end{aligned}$$

Note that the constraint $2^i \leq \mathsf{val}(b) < 2^{i+1}$ in the above formulation refers to a fresh variable i that does not appear in the RTL. We will see later in Sect. 5 that a word-level STE problem is solved by generating a set of word-level constraints, every satisfying assignment of which gives a counter-example to the verification problem. We add constraints like $2^i \leq \mathsf{val}(b) < 2^{i+1}$ in the above formulation, to the set of word-level constraints generated for an STE problem. This ensures that every assignment of i in a counterexample satisfies the required constraints on i.

If-then-else: Consider a conditional assignment statement "`if (BoolExpr) then x = Exp1; else x = Exp2;`". Symbolically simulating this statement gives $x = \mathsf{ite}(\mathsf{BoolExpr}, \mathsf{Exp1}, \mathsf{Exp2})$. The following gives a sound approximation of $\mathsf{inv}(x[q:p])$; the proof of soundness is given in the full version of the paper [3].

$$\begin{aligned}
\mathsf{inv}(x[q:p]) &= \mathsf{ite}(\mathsf{inv}(\mathsf{BoolExpr}), temp_1, temp_2), \text{ where} \\
temp_1 &= \mathsf{inv}(\mathsf{Exp1}[q:p]) \vee \mathsf{inv}(\mathsf{Exp2}[q:p]) \vee (\mathsf{val}(\mathsf{Exp1}[q:p]) \neq \mathsf{val}(\mathsf{Exp2}[q:p])) \\
temp_2 &= \mathsf{ite}(\mathsf{val}(\mathsf{BoolExpr}), \mathsf{inv}(\mathsf{Exp1}[q:p]), \mathsf{inv}(\mathsf{Exp2}[q:p]))
\end{aligned}$$

Bit-Wise Logical Operations: Let $\neg_m$ and $\wedge_m$ denote bit-wise negation and conjunction operators respectively, for m-bit words. If a, b, c and d are m-bit words such that $c = \neg_m a$ and $d = a \wedge_m b$, it is easy to see that the following give sound approximations of $\mathsf{inv}(c)$ and $\mathsf{inv}(d)$.

$$\begin{aligned}
\mathsf{inv}(c[q:p]) &= \mathsf{inv}(a[q:p]) \\
\mathsf{inv}(d[q:p]) &= \big(\mathsf{inv}(a[q:p]) \vee \mathsf{inv}(b[q:p])\big) \wedge \big(\mathsf{inv}(a[q:p]) \vee (\mathsf{val}(a[q:p]) \neq \mathbf{0})\big) \wedge \\
&\qquad \big(\mathsf{inv}(b[q:p]) \vee (\mathsf{val}(b[q:p]) \neq \mathbf{0})\big)
\end{aligned}$$

The invalid bits of other bit-wise logical operators (like disjunction, xor, nor, nand, etc.) can be obtained by first expressing them in terms of $\neg_m$ and $\wedge_m$ and then using the above approximations.

Memory/Array Reads and Updates: Let A be a 1-dimensional array, i be an index expression, and x be a variable and Exp be an expression of the base type of A. For notational convenience, we will use A to refer to both the array, and the (array-typed) expression for the value of the array. On symbolically simulating the RTL statement "`x = A[i];`", we update the value of x to read(A, i), where the read operator is as in the extensional theory of arrays (see [13] for details). Similarly, on symbolically simulating the RTL statement "`A[i] = Exp`", we update the value of array A to update($\mathsf{A}_{\mathsf{orig}}$, i, Exp), where $\mathsf{A}_{\mathsf{orig}}$ is the (array-typed) expression for A prior to simulating the statement, and the update operator is as in the extensional theory of arrays.

Since the expression for a variable or array obtained by symbolic simulation may now have read and/or update operators, we must find ways to compute sound approximations of the invalid bit for expressions of the form read(A, i)$[q:p]$. Note that since A is an array, the symbolic expression for A is either (i) $\mathsf{A}_{\mathsf{init}}$, i.e. the initial value of A at the start of symbolic simulation, or (ii) update(A′, i′, Exp′) for some expressions A′, i′ and Exp′, where A′ has the same array-type as A, i′ has an index type, and Exp' has the base type of A. For simplicity of exposition, we assume that all arrays are either completely initialized or completely uninitialized at the start of symbolic simulation. The invalid bit of $\mathsf{read}(\mathsf{A},\mathsf{i})[q:p]$ in case (i) is then easily seen to be true if $\mathsf{A}_{\mathsf{init}}$ denotes an uninitialized array, and false otherwise. In case (ii), let v denote $\mathsf{read}(\mathsf{A},\mathsf{i})$. The invalid bit of $v[q:p]$ can then be approximated as:

$$\mathsf{inv}(v[q:p]) = \mathsf{inv}(\mathsf{i}) \vee \mathsf{inv}(\mathsf{i}') \vee \mathsf{ite}\left(\mathsf{val}(\mathsf{i}) = \mathsf{val}(\mathsf{i}'), \mathsf{inv}(\mathsf{Exp}'[q:p]), \mathit{temp}\right), \text{ where}$$
$$\mathit{temp} = \mathsf{inv}(\mathsf{read}(\mathsf{A}',\mathsf{i})[q:p]).$$

We defer the argument for soundness of the above approximation to the full version of the paper [3].

4.3 Computing Least Upper Bounds

Let $a = (\mathsf{val}(a), \mathsf{inv}(a))$ and $b = (\mathsf{val}(b), \mathsf{inv}(b))$ be invalid-bit encoded elements in the lattice of values for an m-bit atom. We define $c = \mathit{lub}(a, b)$ as follows.

(a) If $(\neg\mathsf{inv}(a) \wedge \neg\mathsf{inv}(b) \wedge (\mathsf{val}(a) \neq \mathsf{val}(b))$, then $c = \top$.
(b) Otherwise, $\mathsf{inv}(c) = \mathsf{inv}(a) \wedge \mathsf{inv}(b)$ and $\mathsf{val}(c) = \mathsf{ite}(\mathsf{inv}(a), \mathsf{val}(b), \mathsf{val}(a))$ (or equivalently $\mathsf{val}(c) = \mathsf{ite}(\mathsf{inv}(b), \mathsf{val}(a), \mathsf{val}(b)))$.

Note the freedom in defining $\mathsf{val}(c)$ in case (b) above. This freedom comes from the observation that if $\mathsf{inv}(c) = \mathsf{true}$, the value of $\mathsf{val}(c)$ is irrelevant. Furthermore, if the condition in case (a) is not satisfied and if both $\mathsf{inv}(a)$ and $\mathsf{inv}(b)$ are false, then $\mathsf{val}(a) = \mathsf{val}(b)$. This allows us to simplify the expression for $\mathsf{val}(c)$ on-the-fly by replacing it with $\mathsf{val}(b)$, if needed.

5 Word-Level STE

In this section, we briefly review the general theory of STE [11] instantiated to the lattice of values of atoms. An RTL design C consists of inputs, outputs and internal words. We treat bit-level signals as 1-bit words, and uniformly talk of words. Every input, output and internal word is assumed to be atomized as described in Sect. 2. Every atom of bit-width m takes values from the set $\{\mathbf{0} \ldots \mathbf{2^m - 1}, \mathbf{X}\}$, where constant bit-vectors have been represented by their integer values. The values themselves are ordered in a lattice as discussed in Sect. 3. Let $\leq_m$ denote the ordering relation and $\sqcup_m$ denote the lub operator in the lattice of values for an m-bit atom. The lattice of values for a word is the product of lattices corresponding to every atom in the word. Let $\mathcal{A}$ denote the collection of all atoms in the design, and let $\mathcal{D}$ denote the collection of values of all atoms in $\mathcal{A}$. A state of the design is a mapping $s : \mathcal{A} \rightarrow \mathcal{D} \cup \top$ such that if $a \in \mathcal{A}$ is an m-bit atom, then $s(a)$ is a value in the set $\{\mathbf{0}, \ldots \mathbf{2^m} - \mathbf{1}, \mathbf{X}, \top\}$. Let $\mathcal{S}$ denote the set of all states of the design, and let $(\mathcal{S}, \sqsubseteq, \sqcup)$ be a lattice that is isomorphic to the product of lattices corresponding to the atoms in $\mathcal{A}$.

Given a design C, let $\mathsf{Tr}_C : \mathcal{S} \to \mathcal{S}$ define the transition function of C. Thus, given a state s of C at time t, the next state of the design at time $t+1$ is given by $\mathsf{Tr}_C(s)$. To model the behavior of a design over time, we define a *sequence* of states as a mapping $\sigma : \mathbb{N} \to \mathcal{S}$, where $\mathbb{N}$ denotes the set of natural numbers. A *trajectory* for a design C is a sequence σ such that for all $t \in \mathbb{N}$, $\mathsf{Tr}_C(\sigma(t)) \sqsubseteq \sigma(t+1)$. Given two sequences σ_1 and σ_2, we abuse notation and say that $\sigma_1 \sqsubseteq \sigma_2$ iff for every $t \in \mathbb{N}$, $\sigma_1(t) \sqsubseteq \sigma_2(t)$.

The general *trajectory evaluation logic* of Seger and Bryant [11] can be instantiated to words as follows. A *trajectory formula* is a formula generated by the grammar $\varphi ::= \mathsf{a} \text{ is } \mathsf{val} \mid \varphi \text{ and } \varphi \mid P \to \varphi \mid N\varphi$, where a is an atom of C, val is a non-X, non-$\top$ value in the lattice of values for a, and P is a quantifier-free formula in the theory of bit-vectors. Formulas like P in the grammar above are also called *guards* in STE parlance.

We use Seger et al's [2,12] definitions for the *defining sequence* of a trajectory formula ψ given the assignment ϕ, denoted $[\psi]^\phi$, and for the *defining trajectory* of ψ with respect to a design C, denoted $[\![\psi]\!]_C^\phi$. Details of these definitions may be found in the full version of the paper [3]. In symbolic trajectory evaluation, we are given an antecedent Ant and a consequent Cons in trajectory evaluation logic. We are also given a quantifier-free formula Constr in the theory of bit-vectors with free variables that appear in the guards of Ant and/or Cons. We wish to determine if for every assignment ϕ that satisfies Constr, we have $[\mathsf{Cons}]^\phi \sqsubseteq [\![\mathsf{Ant}]\!]_C^\phi$.

5.1 Implementation

We have developed a tool called $\mathsf{STEWord}$ that uses symbolic simulation with invalid-bit encoding and SMT solving to perform STE. Each antecedent and consequent tuple has the format $(g, a, \mathit{vexpr}, \mathit{start}, \mathit{end})$, where g is a guard, a is the name of an atom in the design under verification, vexpr is a symbolic expression over constants and guard variables that specifies the value of a, and start and end denote time points such that $\mathit{end} \geq \mathit{start} + 1$.

An antecedent tuple $(g, a, \mathit{vexpr}, t_1, t_2)$ specifies that given an assignment ϕ of guard variables, if $\phi \models g$, then atom a is assigned the value of expression vexpr, evaluated on ϕ, for all time points in $\{t_1, \ldots t_2 - 1\}$. If, however, $\phi \not\models g$, atom a is assigned the value $\mathbf{X}$ for all time points in $\{t_1, \ldots t_2 - 1\}$. If a is an input atom, the antecedent tuple effectively specifies how it is driven from time t_1 through $t_2 - 1$. Using invalid-bit encoding, the above semantics is easily implemented by setting $\mathsf{inv}(a)$ to $\neg g$ and $\mathsf{val}(a)$ to vexpr from time t_1 through $t_2 - 1$. If a is an internal atom, the defining trajectory requires us to compute the lub of the value driven by the circuit on a and the value specified by the antecedent for a, at every time point in $\{t_1, \ldots t_2 - 1\}$. The value driven by the circuit on a at any time is computed by symbolic simulation using invalid-bit encoding, as explained in Sects. 4.1 and 4.2. The value driven by the antecedent can also be invalid-bit encoded, as described above. Therefore, the lub can be computed as described in Sect. 4.3. If the lub is not $\top$, $\mathsf{val}(a)$ and $\mathsf{inv}(a)$ can be set to the value and invalid-bit, respectively, of the lub. In practice, we assume that the lub is not $\top$ and proceed as above. The conditions under which the *lub* evaluates to $\top$ are collected separately, as described below. The values of all internal atoms that are not specified in any antecedent tuple are obtained by symbolically simulating the circuit using invalid-bit encoding.

If the *lub* computed above evaluates to $\top$, we must set atom a to an unachievable over-constrained value. This is called *antecedent failure* in STE parlance. In our implementation, we collect the constraints (formulas representing the condition for case (a) in Sect. 4.3) under which antecedent failure occurs for every antecedent tuple in a set AntFail. Depending on the mode of verification, we do one of the following:

- If the disjunction of formulas in AntFail is satisfiable, we conclude that there is an assignment of guard variables that leads to an antecedent failure. This can then be viewed as a failed run of verification.
- We may also wish to check if $[\mathsf{Cons}]^\phi \sqsubseteq [\![\mathsf{Ant}]\!]_C^\phi$ only for assignments ϕ that do not satisfy any formula in AntFail. In this case, we conjoin the negation of every formula in AntFail to obtain a formula, say NoAntFail, that defines all assignments ϕ of interest.

A consequent tuple $(g, a, vexpr, t_1, t_2)$ specifies that given an assignment ϕ of guard variables, if $\phi \models g$, then atom a must have its invalid bit set to false and value set to $vexpr$, (evaluated on ϕ) for all time points in $\{t_1, \ldots t_2-1\}$. If $\phi \not\models g$, a consequent tuple imposes no requirement on the value of atom a. Suppose that at time t, a consequent tuple specifies a guard g and a value expression $vexpr$ for an atom a. Suppose further that $(\mathsf{val}(a), \mathsf{inv}(a))$ gives the invalid-bit encoded value of this atom at time t, as obtained from symbolic simulation. Checking whether $[\mathsf{Cons}]^\phi(t)(a) \sqsubseteq [\![\mathsf{Ant}]\!]_C^\phi(t)(a)$ for all assignments ϕ reduces to checking the validity of the formula $\big(g \rightarrow (\neg \mathsf{inv}(a) \wedge (vexpr = \mathsf{val}(a)))\big)$. Let us call this formula $OK_{a,t}$. Let $\mathcal{T}$ denote the set of all time points specified in all consequent tuples, and let $\mathcal{A}$ denote the set of all atoms of the design. The overall verification goal then reduces to checking the validity of the formula $OK \triangleq \bigwedge_{t \in \mathcal{T},\, a \in \mathcal{A}} OK_{a,t}$. If we wish to focus only on assignments ϕ that do not cause any antecedent failure, our verification goal is modified to check the validity of NoAntFail $\rightarrow OK$. In our implementation, we use Boolector [1], a state-of-the-art solver for bit-vectors and the extensional theory of arrays, to check the validity (or satisfiability) of all verification formulas (or their negations) generated by STEWord.

6 Experiments

We used STEWord to verify properties of a set of System-Verilog word-level benchmark designs. Bit-level STE tools are often known to require user-guidance with respect to problem decomposition and variable ordering (for BDD based tools), when verifying properties of designs with moderate to wide datapaths. Similarly, BMC tools need to introduce a fresh variable for each input in each time frame when the value of the input is unspecified. Our benchmarks were intended to stress bit-level STE tools, and included designs with control and datapath logic, where the width of the datapath was parameterized. Our benchmarks were also intended to stress BMC tools by providing relatively long sequences of inputs that could either be X or a specified symbolic value, depending on a symbolic condition. In each case, we verified properties that were satisfied by the system and those that were not. For comparative evaluation, we implemented word-level bounded model checking as an additional feature of STEWord itself. Below, we first give a brief description of each design, followed by a discussion of our experiments.

Design 1: Our first design was a three-stage pipelined circuit that reads four pairs of k-bit words in each cycle, computed the absolute difference of each pair, and then added the absolute differences with a current running sum. Alternatively, if a reset signal was asserted, the pipeline stage that stored the sum was reset to the all-zero value, and the addition of absolute differences of pairs of inputs started afresh from the next cycle. In order to reduce the stage delays in the pipeline, the running sum was stored in a redundant format and carry-save-adders were used to perform all additions/subtractions. Only in the final stage was the non-redundant result computed. In addition, the design made extensive use of clock gating to reduce its dynamic power consumption – a characteristic of most modern designs that significantly complicates formal verification. Because of the non-trivial control and clock gating, the STE verification required a simple datapath invariant. Furthermore, in order to reduce the complexity in specifying the correctness, we broke down the overall verification goal into six properties, and verified these properties using multiple datapath widths.

Design 2: Our second design was a pipelined serial multiplier that reads two k-bit inputs serially from a single k-bit input port, multiplied them and made the result available on a $2k$-bit wide output port in the cycle after the second input was read. The entire multiplication cycle was then re-started afresh. By asserting and de-asserting special input flags, the control logic allowed the circuit to wait indefinitely between reading its first and second inputs, and also between reading its second input and making the result available. We verified several properties of this circuit, including checking whether the result computed was indeed the product of two values read from the inputs, whether the inputs and results were correctly stored in intermediate pipeline stages for various sequences of asserting and de-asserting of the input flags, etc. In each case, we tried the verification runs using different values of the bit-width k.

Design 3: Our third design was an implementation of the first stage in a typical digital camera pipeline. The design is fed the output of a single CCD/CMOS sensor array whose pixels have different color filters in front of them in a Bayer mosaic pattern [9]. The design takes these values and performs a "de-mosaicing" of the image, which basically uses a fairly sophisticated interpolation technique (including edge detection) to estimate the missing color values. The challenge here was not only verifying the computation, which entailed adding a fairly large number of scaled inputs, but also verifying that the correct pixel values were used. In fact, most non-STE based formal verification engines will encounter difficulty with this design since the final result depends on several hundreds of 8-bit quantities.

Design 4: Our fourth design was a more general version of Design 3, that takes as input a stream of values from a single sensor with a mosaic filter having alternating colors, and produces an interpolated red, green and blue stream as output. Here, we verified 36 different locations on the screen, which translates to 36 different locations in the input stream. Analyzing this example with BMC requires providing new inputs every cycle for over 200 cycles, leading to a blow-up in the number of variables used.

For each benchmark design, we experimented with a bug-free version, and with several buggy versions. For bit-level verification, we used both a BDD-based STE tool [12] and propositional SAT based STE tool [10]; specifically, the tool Forte was used for bit-level STE. We also ran word-level BMC to verify the same properties.

In all our benchmarks, we found that Forte and STEWord successfully verified the properties within a few seconds when the bitwidth was small (8 bits). However, the running time of Forte increased significantly with increasing bit-width, and for bit-widths of 16 and above, Forte could not verify the properties without serious user intervention. In contrast, STEWord required practically the same time to verify properties of circuits with wide datapaths, as was needed to verify properties of the same circuits with narrower datapaths, and required no user intervention. In fact, the word-level SMT constraints generated for a circuit with a narrow datapath were almost identical to those generated for the same circuit with a wider datapath, except for the bit-widths of atoms. This is not surprising, since once atomization is done, symbolic simulation is agnostic to the widths of various atoms. An advanced SMT solver like Boolector is often able to exploit the word-level structure of the final set of constraints and solve it without resorting to bit-blasting.

The BMC experiments involved adding a fresh variable in each time frame when the value of an input was not specified or conditionally specified. This resulted in a significant blow-up in the number of additional variables, especially when we had long sequences of conditionally driven inputs. This in turn adversely affected SMT-solving time, causing BMC to timeout in some cases.

To illustrate how the verification effort with STEWord compared with the effort required to verify the same property with a bit-level BDD- or SAT-based STE tool, and with word-level BMC, we present a sampling of our observations in Table 1, where no user intervention was allowed for any tool. Here "-" indicates more than 2 hours of running time, and all times are on an Intel Xeon 3GHz CPU, using a single core. In the column labeled "Benchmark", Design$i$-Pj corresponds to verifying property j (from a list of properties) on Design i. The column labeled "Word-level latches (# bits)" gives the number of word-level latches and the total number of bits in those latches for a given benchmark. The column labeled "Cycles of Simulation" gives the total number of time-frames for which STE and BMC was run. The column labeled "Atom Size (largest)" gives the largest size of an atom after our atomization step. Clearly, atomization did not bit-blast all words, allowing us to reason at the granularity of multi-bit atoms in STEWord.

Table 1. Comparing verification effort (time) with STEWord, Forte and BMC

Benchmark	STEWord	Forte (BDD and SAT)	BMC	Word-level latches (# bits)	Cycles of simulation	Atom size (largest)
Design1-P1 (32 bits)	2.38s	- -	3.71s	14 latches (235 bits wide)	12	31
Design1-P1 (64 bits)	2.77s	- -	4.53s	14 latches (463 bits wide)	12	64
Design2-P2 (16 bits)	1.56s	- -	1.50s	4 latches (64 bits wide)	6	32
Design2-P2 (32 bits)	1.65s	- -	1.52s	4 latches (128 bits wide)	6	64
Design3-P3 (16 bits)	24.06s	- -	-	54 latches (787 bits wide)	124	16
Design4-P4 (16 bits)	56.80s	- -	-	54 latches (787 bits wide)	260	16
Design4-P4 (32 bits)	55.65s	- -	-	54 latches (1555 bits wide)	260	32

Our experiments indicate that when a property is not satisfied by a circuit, Boolector finds a counterexample quickly due to powerful search heuristics implemented in modern SMT solvers. BDD-based bit-level STE engines are, however, likely to suffer from BDD size explosion in such cases, especially when the bit-widths are large. In cases where there are long sequences of conditionally driven inputs (e.g., design 4) BMC performs worse compared to STEWord, presumably beacause of the added complexity of solving constraints with significantly larger number of variables. In other cases, the performance of BMC is comparable to that of STEWord. An important observation is that the abstractions introduced by atomization and by approximations of invalid-bit expressions do not cause STEWord to produce conservative results in any of our experiments. Thus, STEWord strikes a good balance between accuracy and performance. Another interesting observation is that for correct designs and properties, SMT solvers (all we tried) sometimes fail to verify the correctness (by proving unsatisfiability of a formula). This points to the need for further developments in SMT solving, particularly for proving unsatisfiability of complex formulas. Overall, our experiments, though limited, show that word-level STE can be beneficial compared to both bit-level STE and word-level BMC in real-life verification problems.

We are currently unable to make the binaries or source of STEWord publicly available due to a part of the code being proprietary. A web-based interface to STEWord, along with a usage document and the benchmarks reported in this paper, is available at http://www.cfdvs.iitb.ac.in/WSTE/.

7 Conclusion

Increasing the level of abstraction from bits to words is a promising approach to scaling STE to large designs with wide datapaths. In this paper, we proposed a methodology and presented a tool to achieve this automatically. Our approach lends itself to a counterexample guided abstraction refinement (CEGAR) framework, where refinement corresponds to reducing the conservativeness in invalid-bit expressions, and to splitting existing atoms into finer bit-slices. We intend to build a CEGAR-style word-level STE tool as part of future work.

Acknowledgements. We thank Taly Hocherman and Dan Jacobi for their help in designing a System-Verilog symbolic simulator. We thank Ashutosh Kulkarni and Soumyajit Dey for their help in implementing and debugging STEWord. We thank all anonymous reviewers for the constructive and critical comments.

References

1. Brummayer, R., Biere, A.: Boolector: An efficient SMT solver for bit-vectors and arrays. In: Kowalewski, S., Philippou, A. (eds.) TACAS 2009. LNCS, vol. 5505, pp. 174–177. Springer, Heidelberg (2009)
2. Bryant, R.E., Seger, C.-J.H.: Formal verification of digital circuits using symbolic ternary system models. In: Clarke, E.M., Kurshan, R.P. (eds.) CAV 1990. LNCS, vol. 531, pp. 33–43. Springer, London (1990)
3. Chakraborty, S., Khasidashvili, Z., Seger, C-J. H., Gajavelly, R., Haldankar, T., Chhatani, D., Mistry, R.: Word-level symbolic trajectory evaluation. CoRR, Identifier: arXiv:1505.07916 [cs.LO], 2015. (http://www.arxiv.org/abs/1505.07916)
4. Emerson, E.A.: Temporal and modal logic. In: van Leeuwen, J. (ed.) Hanbook of Theoretical Computer Science, pp. 995–1072. Elsevier, Amsterdam (1995)
5. Johannsen, P.: Reducing bitvector satisfiability problems to scale down design sizes for RTL property checking. In: Proceedings of HLDVT, pp. 123–128 (2001)
6. Jones, R.B., O'Leary, J.W., Seger, C.-J.H., Aagaard, M., Melham, T.F.: Practical formal verification in microprocessor design. IEEE Des. Test Comput. **18**(4), 16–25 (2001)
7. Kaivola, R., Ghughal, R., Narasimhan, N., Telfer, A., Whittemore, J., Pandav, S., Slobodová, A., Taylor, C., Frolov, V., Reeber, E., Naik, A.: Replacing testing with formal verification in Intel Core^{TM} i7 processor execution engine validation. In: Bouajjani, A., Maler, O. (eds.) CAV 2009. LNCS, vol. 5643, pp. 414–429. Springer, Heidelberg (2009)
8. KiranKumar, V.M.A., Gupta, A., Ghughal, R.: Symbolic trajectory evaluation: The primary validation vehicle for next generation Intel® processor graphics FPU. In Proceedings of FMCAD, pp. 149–156 (2012)
9. Malvar, H.S., Li-Wei, H., Cutler, R.: High-quality linear interpolation for demosaicing of Bayer-patterned color images. Proceedings of ICASSP **3**, 485–488 (2004)
10. Roorda, J.-W., Claessen, K.: A new SAT-based algorithm for symbolic trajectory evaluation. In: Borrione, D., Paul, W. (eds.) CHARME 2005. LNCS, vol. 3725, pp. 238–253. Springer, Heidelberg (2005)
11. Seger, C.-J.H., Bryant, R.E.: Formal verification by symbolic evaluation of partially-ordered trajectories. Formal Methods Syst. Des. **6**(2), 147–189 (1995)
12. Seger, C.-J.H., Jones, R.B., O'Leary, J.W., Melham, T.F., Aagaard, M., Barrett, C., Syme, D.: An industrially effective environment for formal hardware verification. IEEE Trans. CAD Integr. Circuits Syst. **24**(9), 1381–1405 (2005)
13. Stump, A., Barrett, C.W., Dill, D.L.: A decision procedure for an extensional theory of arrays. In: Proceedings of LICS, pp. 29–37. IEEE Computer Society (2001)

Verifying Linearizability of Intel® Software Guard Extensions

Rebekah Leslie-Hurd[1(✉)], Dror Caspi[1], and Matthew Fernandez[2]

[1] Intel Corporation, Hillsboro, USA
{rebekah.leslie-hurd,dror.caspi}@intel.com
[2] NICTA and UNSW, Sydney, Australia
matthew.fernandez@nicta.com.au

Abstract. Intel® Software Guard Extensions (SGX) is a collection of CPU instructions that enable an application to create secure containers that are inaccessible to untrusted entities, including the operating system and other low-level software. Establishing that the design of these instructions provides security is critical to the success of the feature, however, SGX introduces complex concurrent interactions between the instructions and the shared hardware state used to enforce security, rendering traditional approaches to validation insufficient. In this paper, we introduce Accordion, a domain specific language and compiler for automatically verifying linearizability via model checking. The compiler determines an appropriate linearization point for each instruction, computes the required linearizability assertions, and supports experimentation with a variety of model configurations across multiple model checking tools. We show that this approach to verifying linearizability works well for validating SGX and that the compiler provides improved usability over encoding the problem in a model checker directly.

1 Introduction

When a programmer writes code to manipulate a computer, they have a mental model of the machine, involving a small set of registers with processors executing assembly instructions atomically. The reality of a modern multiprocessor is significantly more complex. The exposed registers are a small component of the internal processor state and execution of a single assembly instruction is not necessarily atomic with respect to other processors. This internal concurrency is particularly complex in the new Intel® Software Guard Extensions (SGX) [17], which introduce security critical internal processor state that is shared between privileged and user-mode instructions.

SGX is a collection of CPU instructions that enable an application to create secure containers within the application address space. These secure containers, called enclaves, provide strong integrity and confidentiality guarantees for the

NICTA is funded by the Australian Government through the Department of Communications and the Australian Research Council through the ICT Centre of Excellence Program.

D. Kroening and C.S. Păsăreanu (Eds.): CAV 2015, Part II, LNCS 9207, pp. 144–160, 2015.
DOI: 10.1007/978-3-319-21668-3_9

code and data pages that reside inside the enclave. Once placed in an enclave, memory pages are inaccessible to untrusted entities, including the operating system and other low-level software. SGX allows programmers to isolate the security-critical portion of their application, for example, to harden applications against vulnerabilities [15] or to protect their computation in an untrusted environment like the cloud [1].

To maximize compatibility with the existing software ecosystem, the SGX instructions work in tandem with the operating system (OS), trusting the OS to manage the system resources associated with enclave pages, such as page table mappings, but verifying that the OS never breaks the confidentiality and integrity guarantees of SGX. To this end, SGX tracks metadata for each enclave page to ensure that every access is secure. Accesses to this data structure, which is shared across all logical processors, must be appropriately synchronized to maintain security, while still maximizing parallelism for performance.

Finding the appropriate line between security and performance has been a particularly difficult aspect of the SGX architecture design and was a source of bugs that could have been devastating for the feature had they not been found soon enough. Applying formal verification techniques early in the design process enabled us to find pernicious concurrency bugs and to increase our confidence that we were not overlooking a critical error in the design. Though formal verification is commonly used at Intel® for arithmetic and protocol validation, SGX has more in common with software algorithms where multiple threads access a shared data structure and is not a natural fit for the hardware verification tools and methodologies that are currently in place.

Identifying this similarity to software algorithms led us to linearizability as a correctness condition. Linearizability [14] is a classic approach to reasoning about concurrent accesses to a shared data structure. A system is linearizable if each operation (in our case, instruction) appears to take effect atomically at some moment in time between its invocation and response, called its linearization point. In a linearizable system, we cannot observe the difference between a sequentialized trace where each instruction executes atomically at its linearization point and a real trace that arises in the concurrently executing system.

An important consequence of linearizability is that we can reason about operations on linearizable concurrent data structures as if they were atomic. As such, we can divide our verification challenge into two tasks: first, to prove that the SGX instructions uphold the desired security guarantees in a sequential (or single threaded) setting; and second, to prove that the system is linearizable. We have verified the sequential correctness of the instructions using DVF [13], but in this paper we focus on the second task, proving that SGX is linearizable.

We employ a standard technique for model checking linearizability [9,23] using a domain-specific heuristic for placing linearization points. Scalability presents a major challenge in our setting—there are 22 instructions that share the concurrent data structure, some of which contain as many as 50 interleaving points—and design changes during the early stages of development are frequent. The primary contribution of this paper is a domain specific language and compiler that supports automatic linearizability checking while providing fine-grained control over the generated model to improve scalability without the overhead of creating multiple models by hand. A secondary contribution of the paper is a demonstration of our approach on the industrial case study of SGX. We first describe how to prove that SGX is linearizable directly using model checking and then show how this process is improved by the use of Accordion. With this approach, we identified previously undiscovered concurrency bugs in a design that had already been intensively reviewed.

The remainder of the paper is organized as follows. In Sect. 2, we give an overview of the internal hardware data structures used by SGX, as well as the SGX instructions, to provide a basis for understanding the examples in the later sections. Section 3 describes our formal model of SGX in the iPave model checker and illustrates an architecture bug that was caught as a violation of linearizability. Section 4 introduces Accordion, our domain specific language and compiler for automatically proving linearizability. The remaining sections discuss related work (Sect. 5) and provide a summary (Sect. 6).

2 SGX Overview

SGX defines new processor internal state, outlined in Sect. 2.1, and a collection of instructions for creating, executing, and manipulating enclaves, covered in Sect. 2.2. In this paper, we focus on the instructions and processor state that directly affect the integrity and confidentiality guarantees of SGX, and thus, are particularly interesting targets of our linearizability analysis. For a complete overview of SGX, see the Programmer's Reference Manual [17].

2.1 Enclave Page Cache

The Enclave Page Cache (EPC) is a protected area of memory used to store enclave code and data as well as some additional management structures introduced by SGX. Each page of EPC memory has an associated entry in the Enclave Page Cache Map (EPCM), which tracks metadata for that page. The SGX instructions use this metadata to ensure that EPC memory pages are always accessed in a secure manner. The EPCM is also used in the address translation lookup algorithm for enclave memory accesses, providing a secure additional layer of access control on top of existing mechanisms such as segmentation, paging tables, and extended paging tables [16].

The EPCM is managed by the processor as part of SGX operation and is never directly accessible to software or to devices. The format of the EPCM is microarchitectural and implementation specific, but conceptually each EPCM entry contains the following fields:

`VALID` Unallocated EPC pages are considered to be invalid. Pages in this state cannot be read or written by enclave threads and can only be operated on by allocation instructions that specifically require an invalid page as an input. If the `VALID` bit is not set, the remaining fields should not be examined.

`OWNER` An enclave instance is identified by its enclave control structure, which is a special kind of EPC page called an SECS. Each EPC page is associated with a single enclave instance. We track membership in an enclave instance through the `OWNER` field in the EPCM, which points to the SECS page of the enclave to which the page belongs.

`PAGETYPE` The `PAGETYPE` field describes the kind of data that is stored in the EPC page. In this paper we discuss four types of enclave page contents: regular enclave code or data (`REG`), thread control structures (`TCS`), enclave control structures (`SECS`), and data that has been deallocated but not yet reclaimed (`TRIM`).

`LINADDR` Enclave pages are accessible through a single linear address that is fixed at allocation time. SGX ensures that all accesses to an EPC page are through the appropriate linear address by comparing the address of the access to the stored `LINADDR` value.

`RWX` EPC page permissions may be set independently from page table and extended page table permissions, resulting in the minimal common access rights. The `RWX` bits of the EPCM track these supplementary permissions.

`PENDING` When an EPC page is dynamically added to a running enclave, the enclave code approves the addition of the new page as a protection mechanism against malicious or buggy systems software (see Sect. 2.2). During this intermediate period when the page has been allocated but not approved, the `PENDING` bit is set to prevent enclave code from accessing the page.

`MODIFIED` When the EPCM attributes of a page are dynamically modified by systems software, such as the `PAGETYPE`, the enclave code acknowledges the change using a process similar to dynamic EPC page allocation. In this case, the `MODIFIED` bit is set to prevent enclave code from accessing the page.

See Sect. 2.2 for a description of how these fields are manipulated by the enclave instructions.

Figure 1 illustrates how the EPCM enforces security on enclave page accesses, even in the presence of incorrect OS behavior. In this example, the OS has incorrectly mapped a page belonging to enclave B to enclave A, but any attempt by A to access the page will be prevented by the SGX hardware due to the mismatch in the EPCM `OWNER` field.

2.2 Instructions

A summary of the SGX instructions is shown in Table 1. The remainder of this section will examine the behavior and usage of each instruction in more detail.

Enclave Creation. The enclave creation process begins with `ECREATE`, a supervisor instruction that allocates an enclave control structure from a free EPC page. As part of invoking the instruction, systems software selects the desired location in the EPC for the enclave control structure and a linear address range that will be associated with the enclave. A successful call to `ECREATE` sets the `VALID` bit for the page, sets the `OWNER` pointer to itself, sets the `PAGETYPE` to `SECS`, and the EPCM `RWX` bits to zero.

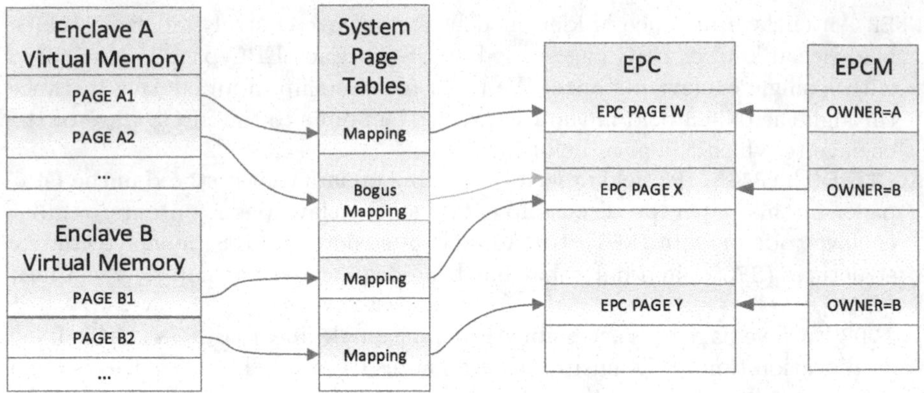

Fig. 1. Security protection in SGX. Systems software controls enclave memory with traditional structures like page tables, but cannot override the SGX security guarantees. Here, the OS maps enclave `A`'s virtual address `A2` to physical page `X`, which belongs to enclave `B`. Before allowing a memory access to `X`, the hardware checks the `OWNER` field, issuing a fault if the access does not come from enclave `B`. Here, this check prevents an unsecure access to `X` through the illegal mapping `A2`.

Enclave Initialization and Teardown. Once the SECS has been created, the enclave is initialized by copying data from normal memory pages into the EPC using `EADD`. A successful call to `EADD` sets the `VALID` bit for the page, associates the page with the specified enclave and sets the `OWNER` pointer to the appropriate SECS, sets the `PAGETYPE` to the specified type, and initializes the `RWX` bits. To destroy an enclave, system software deallocates all of its pages using `EREMOVE`.

Entering and Exiting an Enclave. SGX supports a standard call and return execution pattern through the instructions `EENTER` and `EEXIT`. The `EENTER` instruction puts the processor in a new enclave execution mode whereas `EEXIT` exits enclave mode and clears any enclave register state.

Dynamic Memory Management. Once an enclave is running, dynamic changes to its memory are performed as a collaborative effort between systems software and the enclave. The OS may allocate a new page (`EAUG`), deallocate a page or convert a `REG` page into a `TCS` (`EMODT`), and restrict the EPCM permissions available to the enclave (`EMODPR`). Without checks in place within the enclave, this could provide a vector for systems software to corrupt enclave data. To address this concern, we introduce the enclave-mode instruction `EACCEPT`, which an enclave executes to approve a change that was made by the OS. A successful call to `EACCEPT` finalizes the change by clearing the `PENDING` and `MODIFIED` bits. We also enable the enclave to perform dynamic changes itself where possible to reduce the number of enclave/kernel transitions. SGX currently supports enclave-mode permission extension (`EMODPE`) and a variant of `EACCEPT` that supports initialization of a newly allocated page (`EACCEPTCOPY`).

Table 1. Summary of the SGX instruction set. The table describes the instruction name, the processor mode from which the instruction should be called (supervisor, user, or enclave mode), and the usage of the instruction.

Name	Mode	Description
EACCEPT	enclave	Approve a dynamic memory change
EACCEPTCOPY	enclave	Approve and initialize a dynamically allocated page
EAUG	supervisor	Dynamically allocate a REG page
EADD	supervisor	Allocate a REG or TCS page
ECREATE	supervisor	Allocate SECS page and initialize control structure
EENTER	user	Call an enclave function
EEXIT	enclave	Return from enclave execution
EMODPE	enclave	Extend the EPCM permissions of a page
EMODPR	supervisor	Restrict the EPCM permissions of a page
EMODT	supervisor	Change the type of a page
EREMOVE	supervisor	Deallocate an enclave page

3 Proving SGX Is Linearizable in iPave

We encode linearizability as a model checking problem by inserting an assertion at the linearization point of each instruction. The assertion compares the current state of the EPCM (reached by some concurrent execution) with the known value that the EPCM would hold in a sequential execution. Any mismatch between the expected state and the actual state is caught by the model checker, and indicates that the instruction has observed an update by a concurrently executing instruction (that is, the instruction is not linearizable at that point). The linearization points are easy to identify in SGX because the instruction definitions all follow a similar pattern:

1. Pre-checking of parameters
2. Lock acquisition(s)
3. EPCM and other state checks
4. EPCM and other state updates
5. Lock release(s)

There is occasionally overlap between these steps, but it is always the case that a write is the last access to the EPCM and that this is a location where a correct SGX instruction implementation will have a linearization point.

We determine the appropriate linearization assertion on a per instruction basis by examining the EPCM state on which the instruction depends. We will see examples of this in the coming sections. In general, any EPCM value read by the instruction should not change between the time of the read and linearization point. The value of any EPCM field written by the instruction should not change between the time of the write and the linearization point. In some cases, tracking the value that was written requires the use of logic variables to remember intermediate values of the state.

3.1 Model Overview

We construct our formal model of SGX in iPave [10], a graphical specification language and SMT-based bounded model checker built on top of Boolector [4]. Similar to other modeling languages, an iPave model is specified as a finite state machine with guarded transitions between states. An example instruction specification in iPave is shown in Fig. 2. We can see that the EMODPE instruction shown in the figure follows the standard pattern, performing pre-checks on the EPCM to see if the running enclave may access the target page, acquiring a lock to synchronize accesses to the EPCM, checking that the state of the page is appropriate for the operation, and finally updating the RWX bits of the page.

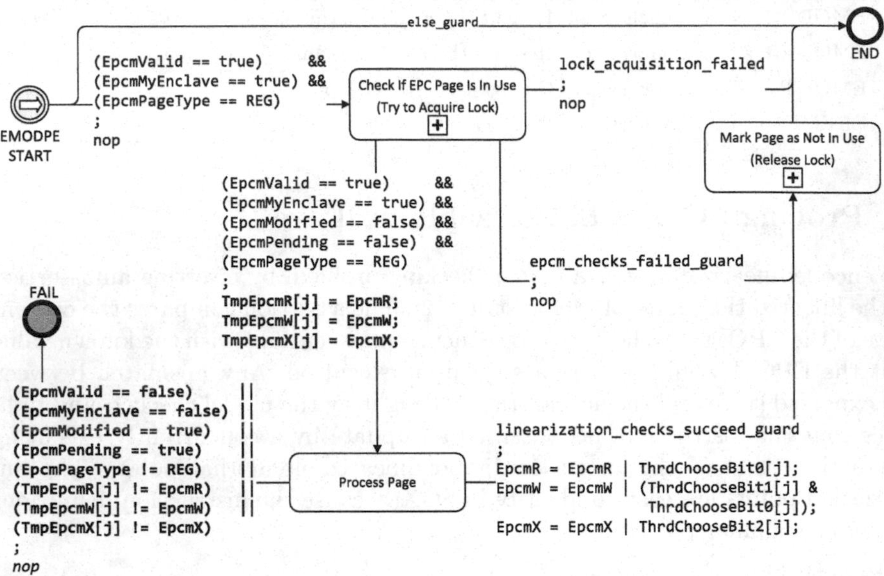

Fig. 2. Simplified EMODPE instruction specification in iPave. The model begins execution in the EMODPE START state in the upper left-hand corner of the diagram. Circles represent start or end states, rounded boxes represent intermediate states in the model's execution, and arrows represent transitions. Arrows may be labeled with guards and actions of the form **guard** ; **action**$_1$; ...; **action**$_n$;, which will only be executed if the guard is true. Either the guard or the action sequence may be empty; here the empty action sequence is represented by the effectless nop. Linearization checks and logic variable assignments are shown in bold.

The primary purpose of the iPave model is to verify that the SGX accesses to the EPCM are linearizable. To keep the problem tractable, the content of the model includes the minimum state necessary to describe the interaction between the instructions and the EPCM. The modeled state includes:

- A single concrete EPCM entry and its fields (see Sect. 2.1).
- An abstract representation of "the other" EPCM entries on the machine. Accesses to EPCM entries by SGX instructions are symmetric, so we employ this abstraction for improved performance.
- A single concrete enclave. Threads may enter this enclave and execute instructions on pages that belong to this enclave.
- An abstract representation of "the other" SGX enclaves.
- An array of logical processor states, which includes per hardware-thread data such as whether the processor is executing in enclave mode (and thus, allowed to access EPC pages) and other microarchitectural state.
- Metadata used to track model parameters and write assertions.

To improve the performance of the model checker, we initialize the state to an arbitrary reachable configuration, rather than a zeroed initial state. Though not all reachable states are known a priori, there is an easily calculable subset of the reachable states that can be used for initialization. In our experience, this significantly reduces the steps required to find interesting bugs. All of the SGX instructions described in Sect. 2.2 are modeled, as well as other relevant events such as memory accesses by enclave and non-enclave code.

3.2 Linearizability Assertions

We add linearizability checks to our iPave model according to the algorithm described at the beginning of the section, but optimize the insertion of the linearization point to reduce the number of possible interleavings. Our optimization is sound, but makes assumptions about the other instructions, making the approach less ideal than the general algorithm that we implement in Accordion. Examining Fig. 2, we see that the linearization checks are performed immediately before the state update to the `RWX` bits, avoiding the need to introduce an additional state after the `RWX` assignment. Immediately before the linearization point, we save the value of the `RWX` bits into logic variables. The intermediate state `Process Page` serves as a preemption point where other instructions could access the EPCM, after which we insert the linearization checks. In the case of `EMODPE`, the page must be valid, not pending, not modified, have the `REG` type, and belong to the currently running enclave. Furthermore, the values contained in the EPCM `RWX` bits should match the values saved in the logic variables. No other aspects of the state are accessed by the instruction, and thus no other fields need to be checked by our assertion.

3.3 Results

Our linearizability model in iPave uncovered architectural concurrency bugs that had not been discovered by manual inspection or testing, despite intensive review. We were also able to confirm a number of previously discovered bugs and increase overall confidence in the architecture design. Formal verification using iPave has been integrated into the SGX development and validation flow, where such methods were not previously common practice.

As an example of the kind of race that this methodology can detect, consider again the EMODPE example from Fig. 2. In that example, the PAGETYPE and OWNER of the page being modified by the instruction are checked twice: once before the EPC page lock is taken and once afterward. In an earlier version of the instruction definition, shown in Fig. 3, the OWNER is only checked before the lock acquisition and the PAGETYPE is only checked afterward. Due to an interaction with the EREMOVE instruction that is possible when a page has the type TRIM, this design allowed EMODPE to change the permissions of a page that did not belong to the running enclave, a clear violation of the SGX security guarantees. Though the bug might seem straightforward, it depends on a particular interleaving that is not easily triggered through testing.

```
(* Check security attributes of the EPC page *)
IF ((EPCM(DS:RCX).VALID = 0) or (EPCM(DS:RCX).OWNER != CR_ACTIVE_SECS))
   Then #PF(DS:RCX); FI;
(* Check the EPC page for concurrency *)
IF (EPC page in use by another SGX2 instruction) Then #GP(0); FI;
(* Re-check security attributes of the EPC page *)
IF ((EPCM(DS:RCX).PENDING != 0) or (EPCM(DS:RCX).MODIFIED != 0) or
     (EPCM(DS:RCX).PAGETYPE != REG) or (EPCM(DS:RCX).LINADDR != DS:RCX))
   Then #PF(DS:RCX); FI;
```

Fig. 3. Original EMODPE specification excerpt (Simplified)

The race condition found using iPave is shown in Table 2. The initial state for the model is that the concrete EPCM page belongs to the running enclave and is valid, not pending, not modified, and of the TRIM type. Examination of the race case revealed the root cause: the EPCM constraints in EMODPE were not sufficient to prevent the page from being removed during the instruction, nor was the removal detected as a failure mode of the instruction. The additional checks in the model shown in Fig. 2 prevent this race.

4 Automating the Process with Accordion

The iPave model was sufficient to demonstrate linearizability for a reasonably concrete model of SGX, but the modeling language and toolchain did not provide us with all of the features that we would like for our architecture explorations. We found that the graphical nature of the input language created a heavy translation burden from the original SGX specification. The translation process was a frequent source of modeling errors, and the disconnect between the specification and modeling language made it difficult for the architects to understand and evaluate the accuracy of the model. A further source of difficulty was the lack of abstraction mechanisms, such as functions, in the language. As a result, it was

Table 2. `EMODPE` race example

Step	Logical processor X	Logical processor Y
1	Start `EMODPE`	
2	Check `VALID` and `OWNER` fields	
3		Start `EREMOVE`
4		Check `PAGETYPE` and `MODIFIED` fields
5		Remove page; set `VALID=0`
6		End `EREMOVE`
7		Allocate page to another enclave with `VALID=1`, `MODIFIED=0`, `PENDING=0`, `PAGETYPE=REG`
8	Acquire exclusive access to page	
9	Perform post-lock EPCM checks	
10	Continue on another enclave's page!	

not easy to experiment with different SGX configurations (number of simultaneously running threads, number of memory pages, instructions to include in the verification run), and modifications required extensive manual effort.

To address the gaps in iPave for our usage, we designed and implemented Accordion, a domain specific language and compiler for proving linearizability. We focused on the following goals in the design of the language:

Mirror Existing Design Specification Language. Instruction set extensions are typically specified in a semi-formal notation that is not machine checkable. The Accordion language should match this syntax as closely as possible so that architects can comprehend the models easily, while also providing a machine checkable format with a defined semantics. The ultimate goal is that Accordion will supplant the informal specification language for SGX.

Support Rapid Prototyping. Design changes are frequent as a feature is extended and optimized. Bugs must be found as early in the design process as possible for verification to be worthwhile. Synchronization behavior is a particular source of experimentation, so the language should support a variety of locking primitives and should make varying the size and location of atomic blocks simple for the designer.

Enable Designers to Leverage a Variety of Analysis Tools. No tool consistently yields superior results. A single source avoids translation errors and provides significant time savings.

Support Experimentation within a Particular Analysis Tool. Model checkers and other verification tools can be sensitive to the size of the input problem. When analyzing a particular design, the validator needs to experiment with the configuration of the model to produce results in a timely fashion.

Automate Linearizability Analysis. Calculate the linearization points and generate linearizability assertions automatically in the compiler.

Facilitate Experimentation with Different Interleaving Semantics. In our experience, full interleaving semantics does not scale to models of the complete SGX architecture. To gain traction in our analysis, we would like to evaluate a collection of models with a variety of interleaving semantics, for example, analyzing atomic versions of enclave initialization instructions with fully interleaved versions of the dynamic memory management instructions.

In the remainder of this section, we will show how Accordion meets these goals by providing an overview of the language syntax, describing the compiler implementation in Haskell [18], and sketching the algorithm for automatically calculating linearization points and linearizability checks.

4.1 Language Syntax

The Accordion language supports a basic set of types including physical addresses, Boolean values, and unsigned integers. SGX data structures like the EPCM are built into the language as well, but ultimately we would like to introduce user-defined data structures to maximize extensibility to future hardware features. The expression language contains constants, variables, standard Boolean and arithmetic operations, structure accesses (for reading SGX data structures), and an address validation operation that performs SGX-specific checks on a physical address, such as membership in the EPC. The statement language includes variable assignments, conditionals, assertions, mutex and reader/writer lock acquire and release operations, abort statements, structure updates (for writing to SGX data structures), and atomic blocks (used to override the default grouping of statements into rules in the compiler; see Sect. 4.2).

Figure 4 shows the code for the `EMODPE` instruction in Accordion syntax and is analogous to the iPave specification shown in Fig. 2. As we will see in the next section, Accordion is implemented as an embedded domain specific language in Haskell, so aspects of the Haskell syntax are mixed with the Accordion syntax in the example. The instruction specification is written as a function with four arguments, only three of which are used by `EMODPE`. The argument `cr_active_secs` is a pointer to the enclave that is currently running, `rcx` contains the physical address of the EPC page to be modified, and `rbx` contains a data structure called a `secinfo` that specifies the desired permissions for the target EPC page. In hardware, and in the model produced by the Accordion compiler, these instruction parameters are provided implicitly as part of the system state.

Those familiar with Haskell will notice that the code is written in a monad using do-notation, but it is not essential to understand this mechanism in order to comprehend the code. The instruction content begins on Line 3 with a check that the target EPC page is accessible (valid, regular, and owned by the currently running enclave). If the check fails, execution will abort with page fault semantics (#PF). If the check succeeds, the instruction will continue with the

```
1  emodpe :: SGXInstruction
2  emodpe cr_active_secs rbx rcx _ = do
3   ift ((!)((epcm rcx).valid) ||
4        (epcm rcx).pagetype != REG ||
5        (epcm rcx).owner != cr_active_secs) (do
6     (#)PF rcx)
7   (epcm rcx).mutex.acquire() (do
8     (#)GP 0)
9   ift ((!)(epcm rcx).valid) || (epcm rcx).pt != REG ||
10       (epcm rcx).pending || (epcm rcx).modified ||
11       (epcm rcx).owner != cr_active_secs) (atomic $ do
12    (epcm rcx).mutex.release()
13    (#)PF rcx)
14  (epcm rcx).r =: (epcm rcx).r || (secinfo rbx).r
15  (epcm rcx).w =: (epcm rcx).w || (secinfo rbx).w
16  (epcm rcx).x =: (epcm rcx).x || (secinfo rbx).x
17  (epcm rcx).mutex.release()
18  end_of_flow
```

Fig. 4. Simplified `EMODPE` specification in accordion.

next statement at the leftmost level of indentation (Line 7). The rest of the code follows a similar pattern of execution. Except for the occurrences of `do`, `$`, and some case mismatches, the syntax shown here is very close to the informal specification language used by the SGX architects.

4.2 Compiler Implementation

We implemented Accordion as an embedded domain specific language (DSL) in Haskell [11]. When writing an embedded DSL, the language designer encodes the abstract syntax tree of the new language directly in the host language, allowing the designer to take advantage of the parser and type system of the host language in their DSL. This allowed us to get a version of Accordion running much faster than would have been possible with a standalone DSL. The disadvantage to using an embedded DSL is that there are certain syntactic aspects of the host language that cannot be overridden. For example, we cannot use the same symbol for assignment in Accordion as in the SGX specification, `:=`, because of the special treatment of colon in Haskell.

Model Generation. Our compiler supports two back-ends: one for generating Murphi syntax—which is compatible with the explicit state model checker CMurphi [7] and its distributed counterpart PReach [3]—and one for generating input to the symbolic bounded model checker SAL [2]. We found that running SAL with a relatively low bound performed well on many of our examples and was useful for finding early modeling bugs. PReach was slow to run but for small enough models (with either an abstract definition of the SGX instructions or a model that does not include the full instruction set) was able to give us a full proof of linearizability.

The full SGX architecture without any simplifying abstractions is too large to be fully verified, which is why it is so important for the compiler to provide support for generating models with a variety of configurations. We provide control over the number of threads, the number of memory pages, and the set of instructions to include in the generated model with compile time flags. Interleaving semantics are also specified at compile time on a per instruction basis. By default, every statement in an Accordion program becomes a rule in the resulting model. Sometimes, we are interested in evaluating the concurrent interaction between two or three instructions at this level, but are not interested in analyzing the initialization instructions that are necessary to drive the model into an interesting state. In those cases, we would compile the specification with full interleaving semantics for the instructions of interest but with atomic semantics, where the entire instruction becomes a single model transition, for the rest. The DSL also provides an `atomic` primitive for concurrency control between these extremes. Figure 4 shows an example of this primitive on Line 11, which will cause the lock release statement on Line 12 and the abort statement on Line 13 to compile to a single model checker rule.

Linearizability Inference. As discussed in Sect. 3, the SGX instruction definitions follow a common pattern that makes the location of the linearization point clear from a cursory inspection. In fact, this pattern is predictable enough that it can be computed, along with the precise set of checks that must be satisfied in order for the instruction to be linearizable.

Calculating the linearization point is relatively straightforward. We perform a backward walk through the control flow graph of the instruction, skipping past any abort statements (`end_of_flow` or a fault) or lock releases, until an SGX state update is found. We insert the linearization point here, after the final state update that the instruction performs. In our `EMODPE` example from Fig. 4, the linearization point would be placed in between Lines 16 and 17.

Once the linearization point has been identified, the compiler computes the assertion that should be placed there in the generated code. For this analysis, the compiler performs a forward walk over the control flow graph of the instruction, accumulating assumptions based on the portions of the SGX state that the instruction reads or writes. In Line 3 of `EMODPE`, for example, the instruction checks that the `VALID` bit is set, that the `PAGETYPE` is `REG`, and that the `OWNER` of the page matches the running enclave. This will generate an assertion that checks for that scenario at the linearization point. If another thread has modified the `VALID` bit, `PAGETYPE`, or `OWNER` of the page in the mean time, the assertion will fail. The full linearization assertion for `EMODPE` is:

assert((epcm rcx).valid ∧ (epcm rcx).pagetype = REG ∧
(epcm rcx).owner = cr_active_secs ∧
(!)(epcm rcx).pending ∧ (!)(epcm rcx).modified ∧
(epcm rcx).r = ((epcm rcx).r' || (secinfo rbx).r) ∧
(epcm rcx).w = ((epcm rcx).w' || (secinfo rbx).w) ∧
(epcm rcx).x = ((epcm rcx).x' || (secinfo rbx).x))

As outlined in Sect. 3, this assertion checks that any state accessed by the instruction does not change between the time of the access and the linearization point. The values `r'`, `w'`, and `x'` in the example are logic variables used to track the intermediate value of the EPCM.

Recall that the buggy version of `EMODPE` discussed in Sect. 3.3 checked the page owner before acquiring the lock but not afterward and only checked the page type afterward. This allowed the page to be removed and assigned to a different owner, without the ownership change being caught by the instruction. We can see that these automatically generated linearization assertions would catch this error, by identifying the requirement that the page owner remain unchanged from the moment of the first read until the linearization point.

Results. The models produced by the Accordion compiler are able to replicate the bugs that were found both by inspection and by formal verification using iPave. By making use of Accordion's model configuration facilities, we are able to construct experiments that find bugs in a matter of minutes and complete a total verification for a subset of instructions in a matter of hours, as opposed to the many hours or even days that iPave would require. These models are by no means equivalent, but for design-time analysis of new instructions the immediate feedback provided by the Accordion models is more useful than a long-running exhaustive verification. We can of course perform a full verification of SGX using Accordion as well.

No new bugs were found using Accordion because the SGX architecture was largely stable by the time our work on Accordion was complete. However, there are many ongoing projects within the SGX architecture team that would benefit from the sorts of analysis that Accordion provides.

5 Related Work

Model checking linearizability is not itself a new idea. Our algorithm for checking linearizability using a shadow state is equivalent to the algorithm for verifying commit-atomicity in [9]. In our case, we are able to calculate the shadow state within the Accordion compiler and generate the appropriate linearizability checks, avoiding the need to explicitly track the shadow state in the generated model. Much of the other work on linearizability to date has focused on general purpose concurrent data structures, such as lists [6,22,24]. There are also tools for automatically proving linearizability, such as CAVe [23] and Line-Up [5]. With SGX, our domain specific knowledge allows us to prove linearizability with a simpler approach, using off-the-shelf tools. We focus our efforts on the model generation code, which supports experimentation with a variety of tools and model configurations. Unlike other tools, Accordion provides fine grained control over the interleaving semantics in the generated model, allowing for a great deal of control over the possible schedules.

Similar to our work, CHESS [20] tackles the challenge of finding concurrency bugs in large systems that may not be amenable to full verification. The tool uses a happens-before analysis to analyze the concurrent execution of a system and exhaustively explores all interleavings in the program. This approach is not ideal for SGX because we do not use a standard set of concurrency primitives in our implementation. CHESS achieves scalability by bounding the number of context switches that may occur in a particular run of the system and by scoping the context switches to an area of interest in the program. These techniques for improving scalability would likely work well in our problem domain where races tend to involve a small number of context switches and where we have a strong sense for where races are likely to occur.

The Copilot DSL [21] is similar to our work on Accordion in that it is also embedded in Haskell and provides multiple formal verification back-ends. One back-end that Copilot compiles to is the Haskell SBV library [8], which supports reasoning about Haskell programs using SMT. This approach would be a valuable extension to Accordion. Currently our sequential verification proofs which use SMT and our linearization work using model checking are not connected via the same source. The two projects differ in the domain targeted by the DSLs: Copilot focuses on run-time monitoring for hard real-time programs, an area with very different considerations than SGX design. Other domain specific languages for hardware design exist, such as Kansas Lava [12] and Hawk [19], but these target low-level circuit designs rather than high-level features like SGX.

6 Summary

This paper introduced our approach to verifying SGX, a novel collection of hardware instructions for providing strong integrity and confidentiality guarantees in a highly concurrent setting. We identified linearizability as the relevant correctness condition for analyzing concurrent interactions between SGX instructions and described an algorithm for demonstrating linearizability using off-the-shelf model checking tools. Our work showed that this approach is capable of finding critical security bugs and underscored the importance of performing formal verification early in the design process of complex features like SGX. Building on the success of our verification in iPave, we outlined the development of the Accordion domain specific language and compiler, a tool that automatically proves linearizability for SGX instructions via model checking and supports experimentation with a wide variety of model configurations across multiple model checking tools.

References

1. Baumann, A., Peinado, M., Hunt, G.: Shielding applications from an untrusted cloud with Haven. In: 11th USENIX Symposium on Operating Systems Design and Implementation, OSDI 2014. USENIX Advanced Computing Systems Association, October 2014
2. Bensalem, S., Ganesh, V., Lakhnech, Y., Muñoz, C., Owre, S., Rueß, H., Rushby, J., Rusu, V., Saïdi, H., Shankar, N., Singerman, E., Tiwari, A.: An overview of SAL. In: LFM, pp. 187–196, Williamsburg, VA, USA (2000)
3. Bingham, B., Bingham, J., Paula, F.M.d., Erickson, J., Singh, G., Reitblatt, M.: Industrial strength distributed explicit state model checking. In: PDMC, pp. 28–36, Washington, DC, USA (2010)
4. Brummayer, R., Biere, A.: Boolector: an efficient SMT solver for bit-vectors and arrays. In: Kowalewski, S., Philippou, A. (eds.) TACAS 2009. LNCS, vol. 5505, pp. 174–177. Springer, Heidelberg (2009)
5. Burckhardt, S., Dern, C., Musuvathi, M., Tan, R.: Line-up: a complete and automatic linearizability checker. In: Programming Language Design and Implementation, PLDI 2010, June 2010
6. Černý, P., Radhakrishna, A., Zufferey, D., Chaudhuri, S., Alur, R.: Model checking of linearizability of concurrent list implementations. In: Touili, T., Cook, B., Jackson, P. (eds.) CAV 2010. LNCS, vol. 6174, pp. 465–479. Springer, Heidelberg (2010)
7. Dill, D.L., Drexler, A.J., Hu, A.J., Yang, C.H.: Protocol verification as a hardware design aid. In: ICCD, pp. 522–525, Cambridge, MA, USA (1992)
8. Erkök, L.: SBV: SMT based verification in Haskell. http://leventerkok.github.io/sbv/
9. Flanagan, C.: Verifying commit-atomicity using model-checking. In: Graf, S., Mounier, L. (eds.) SPIN 2004. LNCS, vol. 2989, pp. 252–266. Springer, Heidelberg (2004)
10. Fraer, R., Keren, D., Khasidashvili, Z., Novakovsky, A., Puder, A., Singerman, E., Talmor, E., Vardi, M., Yang, J.: From visual to logic formalisms for SoC validation. In: Formal Methods and Models for System Design, MEMOCODE 2014
11. Gill, A.: Domain-specific languages and code synthesis using Haskell. Queue **12**(4), 3030–3043 (2014)
12. Gill, A., Bull, T., Farmer, A., Kimmell, G., Komp, E.: Types and associated type families for hardware simulation and synthesis: the internals and externals of Kansas lava. In: Higher-Order and Symbolic Computation, pp. 1–20 (2013)
13. Goel, A., Krstić, S., Leslie, R., Tuttle, M.R.: SMT-based system verification with DVF. In: Satisfiability Modulo Theories, SMT 2012, pp. 32–43 (2012)
14. Herlihy, M.P., Wing, J.M.: Linearizability: a correctness condition for concurrent objects. ACM Trans. Program. Lang. Syst. (TOPLAS) **12**(3), 463–492 (1990)
15. Hoekstra, M., Lal, R., Pappachan, P., Phegade, V., Del Cuvillo, J.: Using innovative instructions to create trustworthy software solutions. In: Proceedings of the 2nd International Workshop on Hardware and Architectural Support for Security and Privacy, HASP 2013, ACM, New York, NY, USA (2013)
16. Intel Corporation, Santa Clara, CA, USA. Intel® 64 and IA-32 Architectures Software Developer's Manual, September 2014
17. Intel Corporation, Santa Clara, CA, USA. Intel® Software Guard Extensions Programming Reference, October 2014
18. Marlow, S.: Haskell 2010 language report 2010

19. Matthews, J., Cook, B., Launchbury, J.: Microprocessor specification in Hawk. In: Proceedings of the 1998 International Conference on Computer Languages, pp. 90–101. IEEE Computer Society Press (1998)
20. Musuvathi, M., Qadeer, S., Ball, T., Basler, G., Nainar, P.A., Neamtiu, I.: Finding and reproducing heisenbugs in concurrent programs. In: Eigth Symposium on Operating Systems Design and Implementation, OSDI 2008. USENIX, December 2008
21. Pike, L., Goodloe, A., Morisset, R., Niller, S.: Copilot: a hard real-time runtime monitor. In: Barringer, H., Falcone, Y., Finkbeiner, B., Havelund, K., Lee, I., Pace, G., Roşu, G., Sokolsky, O., Tillmann, N. (eds.) RV 2010. LNCS, vol. 6418, pp. 345–359. Springer, Heidelberg (2010)
22. Sethi, D., Talupur, M., Malik, S.: Model checking unbounded concurrent lists. In: Bartocci, E., Ramakrishnan, C.R. (eds.) SPIN 2013. LNCS, vol. 7976, pp. 320–340. Springer, Heidelberg (2013)
23. Vafeiadis, V.: Automatically proving linearizability. In: Touili, T., Cook, B., Jackson, P. (eds.) CAV 2010. LNCS, vol. 6174, pp. 450–464. Springer, Heidelberg (2010)
24. Vechev, M., Yahav, E., Yorsh, G.: Experience with model checking linearizability. In: Păsăreanu, C.S. (ed.) Model Checking Software. LNCS, vol. 5578, pp. 261–278. Springer, Heidelberg (2009)

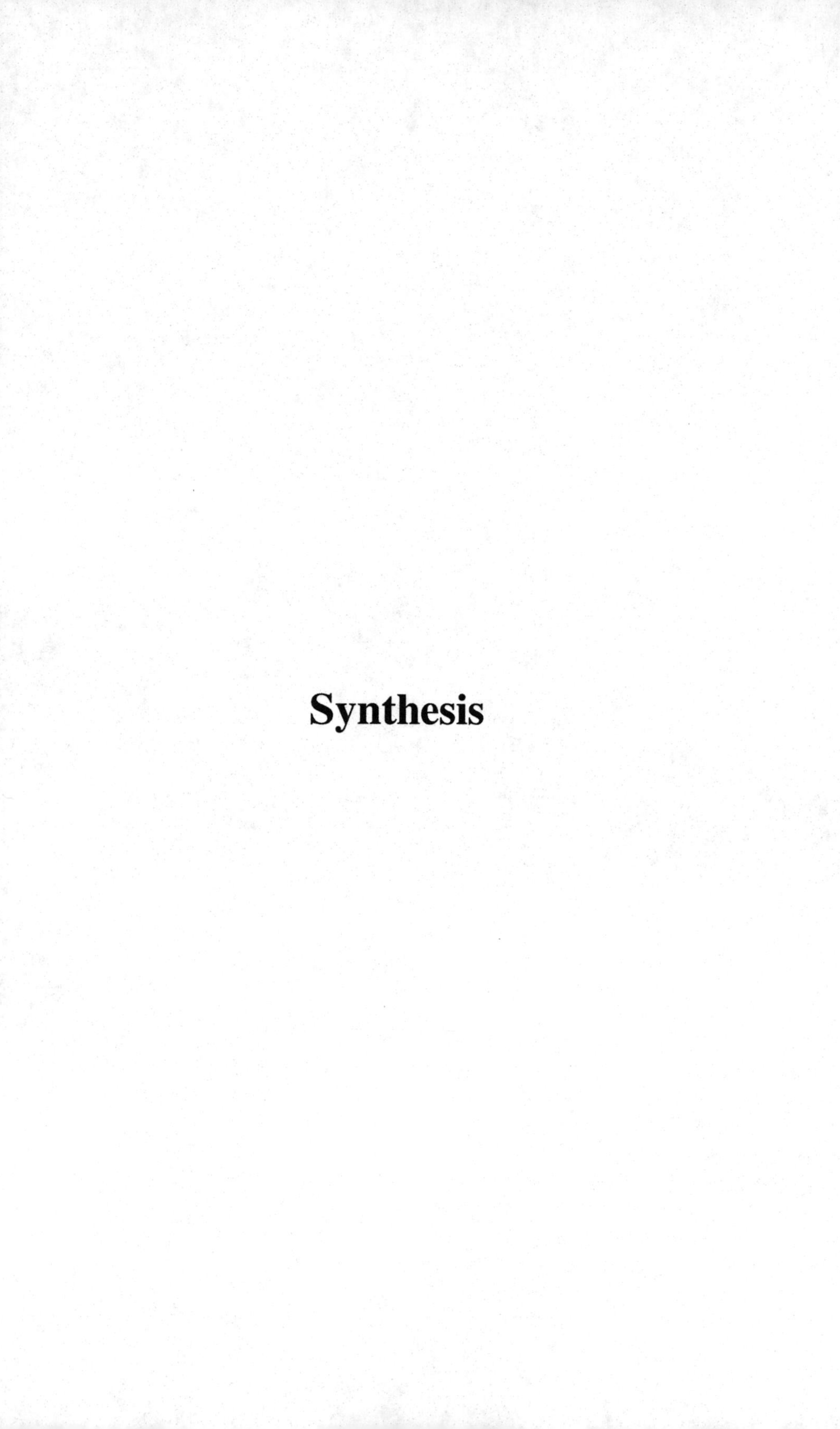

Synthesis

Synthesis Through Unification

Rajeev Alur[1], Pavol Černý[2], and Arjun Radhakrishna[1](✉)

[1] University of Pennsylvania, Philadelphia, USA
arjunrad@seas.upenn.edu
[2] University of Colorado Boulder, Boulder, USA

Abstract. Given a specification and a set of candidate programs (program space), the program synthesis problem is to find a candidate program that satisfies the specification. We present the synthesis through unification (STUN) approach, which is an extension of the counter-example guided inductive synthesis (CEGIS) approach. In CEGIS, the synthesizer maintains a subset S of inputs and a candidate program `Prog` that is correct for S. The synthesizer repeatedly checks if there exists a counterexample input c such that the execution of `Prog` is incorrect on c. If so, the synthesizer enlarges S to include c, and picks a program from the program space that is correct for the new set S.

The STUN approach extends CEGIS with the idea that given a program `Prog` that is correct for a subset of inputs, the synthesizer can try to find a program `Prog`′ that is correct for the rest of the inputs. If `Prog` and `Prog`′ can be *unified* into a program in the program space, then a solution has been found. We present a generic synthesis procedure based on the STUN approach and specialize it for three different domains by providing the appropriate unification operators. We implemented these specializations in prototype tools, and we show that our tools often performs significantly better on standard benchmarks than a tool based on a pure CEGIS approach.

1 Introduction

The task of program synthesis is to construct a program that satisfies a given declarative specification. The computer-augmented programming [2,17] approach allows the programmers to express their intent in different ways, for instance by providing a partial program, or by defining the space of candidate programs, or by providing positive and negative examples and scenarios. This approach to synthesis is becoming steadily more popular and successful [5].

We propose a novel algorithmic approach for the following problem: given a specification, a set of candidate programs (a program space), and a set of all possible inputs (an input space), find a candidate program that satisfies the specification on all inputs from the input space. The basic idea of our approach

This research was supported in part by the NSF under award CCF 1421752 and the peditions award CCF 1138996, by DARPA under agreement FA8750-14-2-0263, by the Simons Foundation, and by a gift from the Intel Corporation.

D. Kroening and C.S. Păsăreanu (Eds.): CAV 2015, Part II, LNCS 9207, pp. 163–179, 2015.
DOI: 10.1007/978-3-319-21668-3_10

is simple: if we have a candidate program that is correct only on a part of the input space, we can attempt to find a program that works on the rest of the input space, and then unify the two programs. The unification operator must ensure that the resulting program is in the program space.

The program space is syntactically restricted to a set which can be specified using a typed grammar. If this grammar contains `if` statements, and its expression language is expressive enough, then a simple unification operator exists. A program `Prog` for inputs that satisfy an expression C, and a program `Prog'` that works on the rest of the inputs can be unified into if (C) then `Prog` else `Prog'`. Even when if statements are not available, different unification operators may exist. These unification operators may be preferable to unification through if statements due to efficiency reasons. However, such unification operators may not be complete — it might not be possible to unify two given programs. We present an approach that deals with such cases with appropriate backtracking.

Our approach, which we dub STUN, works as follows: its first step is to choose a program `Prog` that works for a subset $\mathcal{I}_G$ of the input space. This step can be performed by any existing method, for instance by multiple rounds of the CEGIS loop [16]. The STUN procedure then makes a recursive call to itself to attempt to synthesize a program `Prog'` for inputs on which `Prog` is incorrect. An additional parameter is passed to the recursive call — unification constraints that ensure that the program `Prog'` obtained from the recursive call is unifiable with `Prog`. If the recursive call succeeds, programs `Prog` and `Prog'` can be unified, and the solution to the original problem was found. If the recursive call fails, then we need to backtrack, and choose another candidate for program `Prog`. In this case, we also use a form of conflict-driven learning.

Problem Domains. We instantiate the STUN approach to three different problem domains: bit-vector expressions, separable specifications for conditional linear arithmetic expressions, and non-separable specifications for conditional linear arithmetic expressions. In each domain, we provide a suitable unification operator, and we resolve the nondeterministic choices in the STUN algorithm.

We first consider the domain of bit-vector expressions. Here, the challenge is the absence of `if`-conditionals, which makes the unification operator harder to define. We represent bit-vector programs as $(\texttt{expr}, \rho)$, where `expr` is a bit-vector expression over input variables and additional auxiliary variables, and ρ is a constraint over the auxiliary variables. Two such pairs $(\texttt{expr}_1, \rho_1)$ and $(\texttt{expr}_2, \rho_2)$ can be unified if there exists a way to substitute the auxiliary variables in $\texttt{expr}_1$ and $\texttt{expr}_2$ to make the expressions equal, and the substitution satisfies the conjunction of ρ_1 and ρ_2. A solver based on such a unification operator has comparable performance on standard benchmarks [1] as existing solvers.

For the second and third domain we consider, the program space is the set of conditional linear-arithmetic expressions (CLEs) over rationals. The difference between the two domains is in the form of specifications. Separable specifications are those where the specification only relates an input and its corresponding output. In contrast, the non-separable specifications can place constraints over outputs that correspond to different inputs. For instance, $x > 0 \implies f(x+2) = f(x)+7$ is a non-separable specification, as it relates outputs for multiple inputs.

The second domain of separable specifications and CLEs over rationals is an ideal example for STUN, as the unification operator is easy to implement using conditions of CLEs. We obtain an efficient implementation where partial solutions are obtained by generalization of input-output examples, and such partial solutions are then unified. Our implementation of this procedure is order-of-magnitude faster on standard benchmarks than the existing solvers.

The third domain of non-separable specifications for CLEs requires solving constraints for which finding a solution might need an unbounded number of unification steps before convergence. We therefore implement a widening version of the unification operator, further demonstrating the generality of the STUN approach. Our implementation of this procedure performs on par with existing solvers on standard benchmarks.

Comparing CEGIS and STUN. The key conceptual difference between existing synthesis methods (CEGIS) and our STUN approach is as follows: CEGIS gradually collects a set of input-output examples (by querying the specification), and then finds a solution that matches all the examples. The STUN approach also collects input-output examples by querying the specification, but it finds a (general) solution for each of them separately, and then unifies the solutions. The STUN method has an advantage if solutions for different parts of the input space are different. In other words, CEGIS first combines subproblems, and then solves, while STUN first solves, and then combines solutions. The reason is that such solutions can be in many cases easily unifiable (if for instance the program space has `if` conditionals), but finding the whole solution at once for examples from the different parts of input space (as CEGIS requires) is difficult.

Summary. The main contributions of this work are two-fold. First, we propose a new approach to program synthesis based on unification of programs, and we develop a generic synthesis procedure using this approach. Second, we instantiate the STUN synthesis procedure to the domains of bit-vector expressions, and conditional linear expressions with separable and non-separable specifications. We show that in all cases, our solver has comparable performance to existing solvers, and in some cases (conditional linear-arithmetic expressions with separable specifications), the performance on standard benchmarks is several orders of magnitude better. This demonstrates the potential of the STUN approach.

2 Overview

In this section, we first present a simplified view of synthesis by unification (the UNIF loop), which works under very strong assumptions. We then describe what extensions are needed, and motivate our STUN approach.

UNIF Loop. Let us fix a specification *Spec*, a *program space* $\mathcal{P}$ (a set of candidate programs), and an *input space* $\mathcal{I}$. The program synthesis problem is to find a program in $\mathcal{P}$ that satisfies the specification for all inputs in $\mathcal{I}$.

A classical approach to synthesis is the counterexample-guided inductive synthesis (CEGIS) loop. We choose the following presentation for CEGIS in order to contrast it with UNIF. In CEGIS (depicted in Fig. 1), the synthesizer maintains a subset $\mathcal{J} \subseteq \mathcal{I}$ of inputs and a candidate program $\texttt{Prog} \in \mathcal{P}$ that is correct for $\mathcal{J}$. If $\mathcal{J} = \mathcal{I}$, i.e., if Prog is correct for all inputs in $\mathcal{I}$, the CEGIS loop terminates and returns Prog. If there is an input on which Prog is incorrect, the first step is to find such an input c. The second step is to find a program that is correct for both c and all the inputs in $\mathcal{J}$. In Fig. 1, this is done in the call to syntFitAll). This process is then repeated until $\mathcal{J}$ is equal to $\mathcal{I}$.

The unification approach to synthesis is based on a simple observation: if we have a program Prog that is correct for a subset $\mathcal{J}$ of inputs (as in CEGIS), the synthesizer can try to find a program Prog′ that is correct for some of the inputs in $\mathcal{I} \setminus \mathcal{J}$, and then attempt to unify Prog and Prog′ into a program in the program space $\mathcal{P}$. We call the latter option the UNIF loop. It is depicted in Fig. 2. In more detail, the UNIF loop works as follows. We first call syntFitSome in order to synthesize a program Prog′ that works for some inputs in $\mathcal{I}$ but not in $\mathcal{J}$. Let $\mathcal{J}'$ be the set of those inputs in $\mathcal{I} \setminus \mathcal{J}$ for which Prog′ satisfies *Spec*.

Next, we consider two programs $\mathcal{J} \cdot \texttt{Prog}$ and $\mathcal{J}' \cdot \texttt{Prog}$, where the notation $\mathcal{J} \cdot \texttt{Prog}$ denotes a program that on inputs in $\mathcal{J}$ behaves as Prog, and on other inputs its behavior is undefined. We need to unify the two programs to produce a program (in the program space $\mathcal{P}$) which is defined on $\mathcal{J} \cup \mathcal{J}'$. The unification operator denoted by $\oplus$, and the unified program is obtained as $\mathcal{J} \cdot \texttt{Prog} \oplus \mathcal{J}' \cdot \texttt{Prog}$. If the program space is closed under **if** conditionals, and if Prog and Prog′ are in $\mathcal{P}$, then the unification is easy. We obtain **if** $\mathcal{J}$ **then** Prog **else** **if** $\mathcal{J}'$ **then** Prog′ **else** $\perp$. Note that we abuse notation here: the symbols $\mathcal{J}$ and $\mathcal{J}'$, when used in programs, denote expressions that define the corresponding input spaces.

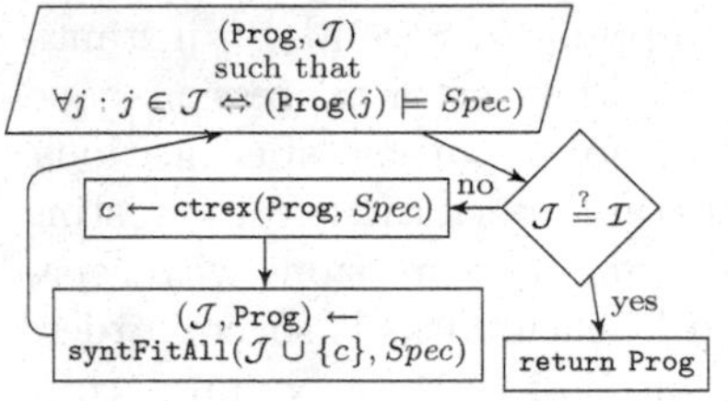

Fig. 1. CEGIS loop for input space $\mathcal{I}$ and specification *Spec*

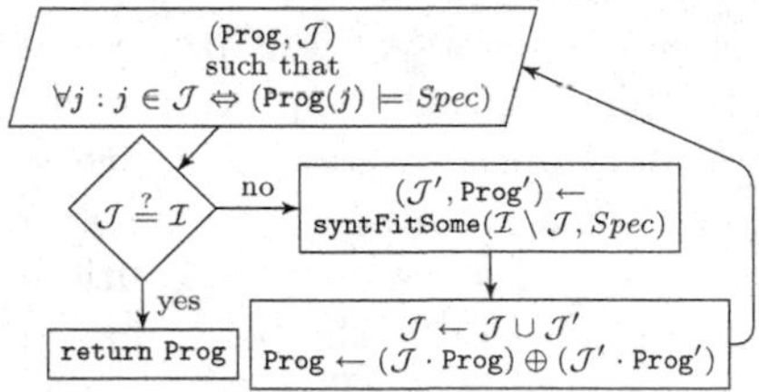

Fig. 2. UNIF loop for input space $\mathcal{I}$ and specification *Spec*

Example 1. Consider the following specification for the function max.

$$Spec = f(x,y) \geq x \wedge f(x,y) \geq y \wedge (f(x,y) = x \vee f(x,y) = y)$$

The input space $\mathcal{I}$ is the set of all pairs of integers. The program space $\mathcal{P}$ is the set of all programs in a simple if-language with linear-arithmetic expressions.

We demonstrate the UNIF loop (Fig. 2) on this example. We start with an empty program $\perp$. The program works for no inputs (i.e., the input space is $\emptyset$), so we start with the pair $(\bot, \emptyset)$ at the top of Fig. 2. As $\emptyset \neq \mathcal{I}$, we go to the right-hand side of Fig. 2, and call the procedure `syntFitSome`.

We now describe the procedure `syntFitSome`$(\mathcal{K}, \mathit{Spec})$ for the linear arithmetic domain. It takes two parameters: a set of inputs $\mathcal{K}$, and a specification *Spec*, and returns a pair $(\mathcal{J}', \mathtt{Prog}')$ consisting of a set $\emptyset \neq \mathcal{J}' \subseteq \mathcal{K}$ and a program $\mathtt{Prog}'$ which is correct on $\mathcal{J}'$. We pick an input-output example from the input space $\mathcal{K}$. This can be done by using a satisfiability solver to obtain a model of *Spec*. Let us assume that the specification is in CNF. An input-output example satisfies at least one atom in each clause. Let us pick those atoms. For instance, for the example $(2,3) \rightarrow 3$, we get the following conjunction G of atoms: $G \equiv f(x,y) \geq x \wedge f(x,y) \geq y \wedge f(x,y) = y$. We now generate a solution for the input-output example and G. For linear arithmetic, we could "solve for $f(x,y)$", i.e. replace $f(x,y)$ by t and solve for t. Let us assume that the solution $\mathtt{Prog}_0$ that we obtain is a function that on any input (x,y) returns y. We then plug the solution $\mathtt{Prog}_0$ to G, and simplify the resulting formula in order to obtain G_0, where G_0 is $y \geq x$. G_0 defines the set of inputs for which the solution is correct. We have thus effectively obtain the pair $(G_0, \mathtt{Prog}_0)$ that the function returns (this effectively represents the program **if** $y \geq x$ **then** y else $\bot$).

In the second iteration, we now call the function `syntFitSome`$(\mathcal{K}, \mathit{Spec})$ with the parameter $\mathcal{K} = \neg G_0$. We now ask for an input-output example where the input satisfies $\neg G_0$. Let us say we obtain $(5,4)$, with output 5. By a similar process as above, we obtain a program $\mathtt{Prog}_1$ that for all inputs (x,y) returns x, and works for all input that satisfy $G_1 \equiv x \geq y$.

The next step of the STUN loop asks us to perform the unification $(G_0 \cdot \mathtt{Prog}_0) \oplus (G_1 \cdot \mathtt{Prog}_1)$. Given that we have `if` conditionals in the language, this step is simple. We unify the two programs to obtain: if $y \geq x$ then y else x.

From the UNIF Loop to STUN. The main assumption that the UNIF loop makes is that the unification operator $\oplus$ always succeeds. We already mentioned that this is the case when the program space is closed under `if` conditionals. If the program space is not closed under `if` conditionals, or if we do not wish to use this form of unification for other reasons, then the UNIF loop needs to be extended. An example of a program space that is not closed under `if` conditionals, and that is an interesting synthesis target, are bit-vector expressions.

The STUN algorithm extends UNIF with backtracking (as explained in the introduction, this is needed since the unifcation can fail), and at each level, a CEGIS loop can be used in `syntFitSome`. The CEGIS and UNIF loops are thus combined, and the combination can be fine-tuned for individual domains.

3 Synthesis Through Unification Algorithm

Overview. The STUN procedure is presented in Algorithm 1. The input to the algorithm consists of a specification *Spec*, a program space $\mathcal{P}$, input space $\mathcal{I}$, and *outer unification constraints (OUCs)* ψ. OUCs are constraints on the program space which are needed if the synthesized program will need to be unified

Algorithm 1. The STUN (synthesis through unification) procedure

Input: Specification *Spec*, Program space $\mathcal{P}$, Input space $\mathcal{I}$, outer unification constraints (OUCs) ψ
Output: $\texttt{Prog} \in \mathcal{P}$ s.t. $\forall \texttt{inp} \in \mathcal{I} : \texttt{Prog}[\texttt{inp}] \models \mathit{Spec}$ and $\texttt{Prog} \models \psi$, or None
Global variables: learned unification constraints (LUCs) β, initialized to **true**

1: $\varphi \leftarrow \texttt{true}$ // CEGIS constraints
2: **if** $\mathcal{I} = \emptyset$ **return** $\top, \texttt{true}$ // input space is empty, base case of recursion
3: **while true do**
4: $(\texttt{Prog}, \texttt{timeOut}) \leftarrow \mathit{Generate}(\mathcal{P}, \mathit{Spec}, \mathcal{I}, \varphi, \psi, \beta)$ // generate next candidate
5: **if** $\texttt{Prog} = \texttt{None}$ **then**
6: **if** $\neg\texttt{timeOut}$ **then**
7: $\beta \leftarrow \beta \wedge \mathit{LearnFrom}(\mathit{Spec}, \psi, \beta)$ //learn unification constraints
8: **return** None //no solution exists
9: $\texttt{inp} \leftarrow \mathit{PickInput}(\mathcal{I}, \texttt{Prog})$ //take a positive- or a counter-example
10: **if** $\texttt{Prog}[\texttt{inp}] \not\models \mathit{Spec}$ **then**
11: $\varphi \leftarrow \varphi \wedge \mathit{project}(\mathit{Spec}, \texttt{inp})$ //get a constraint from a counter-example
12: **else**
13: $\mathcal{I}_G, \mathcal{I}_B \leftarrow \mathit{splitInpSpace}(\mathit{Spec}, \texttt{Prog}, \texttt{inp})$ // $\mathcal{I}_G \subseteq \{\texttt{inp}' \mid \texttt{Prog}[\texttt{inp}'] \models \mathit{Spec}\}$
// and $\texttt{inp} \in \mathcal{I}_G$, so $\mathcal{I}_B \subsetneq \mathcal{I}$ and we can make a recursive call
14: $\texttt{Prog}' \leftarrow \mathit{STUN}(\mathit{Spec}, \psi \wedge \mathit{UnifConstr}(\mathcal{I}_G, \texttt{Prog}), \mathcal{P}, \mathcal{I}_B)$ //recursive call
15: **if** $\texttt{Prog}' \neq \texttt{None}$ **return** $\mathcal{I}_G \cdot \texttt{Prog} \oplus \mathcal{I}_B \cdot \texttt{Prog}'$ //return the *unified* program

with an already created program. The algorithm is implemented as a recursive (backtracking) procedure STUN. At each level, a decision is tried: a candidate program that satisfies OUCs is generated, and passed to the recursive call. If the recursive call is successful, the returned program is unified with the current candidate. If the recursive call is unsuccessful, it records *learned unification constraint (LUCs)* to the global variable β, ensuring progress.

Algorithm Description. The algorithm first checks whether the input space is empty (this is the base case of our recursion). If so, we return a program $\top$ (Line 2), a program which can be unified with any other program.

If the input space $\mathcal{I}$ is not empty, we start the main loop (Line 3). In the loop, we need to generate a program Prog (Line 4) that works for a nonempty subset of $\mathcal{I}$. The generated program has to satisfy "CEGIS" constraints φ (that ensure that the program is correct on previously seen inputs at this level of recursion), OUCs ψ that ensure that the program is unifiable with programs already created in the upper levels of recursion, and LUCs β, which collects constraints learned from the lower levels of recursion. If the call to Generate fails (i.e., returns None), we exit this level of recursion, and learn constraints unification constraints that can be inferred from the failed exploration (Line 7). The only exception is when Generate fails due to a timeout, in which case we are not sure whether the task was unrealizable, and so no constraints are learned. Learning the constraints (computed by the function *LearnFrom*) is a form of conflict-driven learning.

Once a program Prog is generated, we need to check whether it works for all inputs in $\mathcal{I}$. If it does not, we need to decide whether to improve Prog (in a

CEGIS-like way), or generate a program `Prog'` that works for inputs on which `Prog` does not work. The decision is made as follows. We pick an input `inp` and check whether the program `Prog` is correct on `inp` (Line 10). If `Prog` is not correct on `inp`, then we have found a counterexample, and we use it to strengthen our CEGIS constraints (Line 11). We refer to this branch as CEGIS-like branch.

If `Prog` is correct on `inp`, then we know that `Prog` is correct for at least one input, and we can make a recursive call to generate a program that is correct for the inputs for which `Prog` is not. We refer to this branch as the UNIF-like branch. The first step is to split the input space $\mathcal{I}$ into the set $\mathcal{I}_G$ (an underapproximation of the set of inputs on which `Prog` works containing at least `inp`), and $\mathcal{I}_B$, the rest of the inputs (Line 13). We can now make the recursive call on $\mathcal{I}_B$ (Line 14). We pass the OUCs ψ to the recursive call, in addition to the information that the returned program will need to be unified with `Prog` (this is accomplished by adding $\mathit{UnifConstr}(\mathcal{I}_G, \texttt{Prog})$). If the recursive call does not find a program (i.e., returns $\texttt{Prog}' = \texttt{None}$), then the loop continues, and another candidate is generated. If the recursive call successfully returns a program `Prog'`, this program is unified with with `Prog` (Line 15). In more detail, we have a program `Prog` that works on inputs in $\mathcal{I}_G$, and a program `Prog'` that works on inputs in $\mathcal{I}_B$, and we unify them with the unification operator $\oplus$ to produce $\mathcal{I}_G \cdot \texttt{Prog} \oplus \mathcal{I}_B \cdot \texttt{Prog}'$. We know that the unification operator will succeed, as the unification constraint $\mathit{UnifConstr}(\mathcal{I}_G, \texttt{Prog})$ was passed to the recursive call.

The input choice (line 9), here nondeterministic, can be tuned for individual domains to favor positive- or counter-examples, and hence, CEGIS or UNIF.

Example 2. Consider a specification that requires that the right-most bit set to 1 in the input bit-vector is reset to 0. This problem comes from the Hacker's Delight collection [20]. A correct solution is, for instance, given by the expression $x \,\&\, (x-1)$. We illustrate the STUN procedure on this example. The full STUN procedure for the bit-vector domain will be presented in Sect. 4.

Unification. The unification operator $\mathcal{I}_G \cdot \texttt{Prog} \oplus \mathcal{I}_B \cdot \texttt{Prog}'$ works as follows. $\mathcal{I}_G \cdot \texttt{Prog}$ and $\mathcal{I}_B \cdot \texttt{Prog}'$ can be unified if there exists a way to substitute the constants c_i and c_i' occuring in `Prog` and `Prog'` with sub-expressions $\texttt{expr}_i$ and $\texttt{expr}_i'$ such that after the substitution, `Prog` and `Prog'` are equal to the same program $\texttt{Prog}^*$, and for all input in $\mathcal{I}_G$, $\texttt{expr}_i[i] = c_i$ and for all inputs in $\mathcal{I}_B$, $\texttt{expr}_i'[i] = c_i'$. Note that this is a (very) simplified version of the unification operator introduced in the next section. It is used here to illustrate the algorithm.

Unification Gone Wrong. Let us assume that the `Generate` function at Line 4 generates the program $x \,|\, 0$ (this can happen if say the simpler programs already failed). Note that $|$ is the bitwise or operator. Now let us assume that at Line 9, we pick the input 0. The program matches *Spec* at this input. The set $\mathcal{I}_G$ is $\{0\}$, and we go to the recursive call at Line 14 for the rest of the input space, with the constraint that the returned program must be unifiable with $x \,|\, 0$. In the recursive call, `Generate` is supposed to find a program that is unifiable with $x \,|\, 0$, i.e., of the form $x \,|\, c$ for some constant c. Further, for the recursive call to finally succeed (i.e., take the else branch at Line 12), we need this program to be correct on some input other than $x = 0$. However, as it can be seen, there is no such program and input. Hence, the procedure eventually backtracks while adding a constraint that enforces that the program $x \mid 0$ will no longer be attempted.

Unification Gone Right. After the backtracking, with the additional constraint, the program generation procedure is forbidden from generating the program $x \mid 0$. The `Generate` procedure instead generates say $x \,\&\, -1$. As before, for the recursive call to finally succeed, the program generation procedure is asked to find a program unifiable with $x \,\&\, -1$ (i.e., of the form $x \,\&\, c$) that works for an input other than 0. Let us assume that generated program in the next level of recursion is $x \,\&\, 4$; one input for which this is correct is $x = 5$. Attempting to unify these functions, the unification operator is asked to find an expression `expr` such that $\texttt{expr}[0/x] = -1$ and $\texttt{expr}[5/x] = 4$. One such candidate for `expr` is $x - 1$. This leads to a valid solution $x \,\&\, (x - 1)$ to the original synthesis problem.

Soundness. The procedure *splitInpSpace*(*Spec*, `Prog`, `inp`) is sound if for every invocation, it returns a pair $(\mathcal{I}_G, \mathcal{I}_B)$ such that $\{\texttt{inp}\} \subseteq \mathcal{I}_G \subseteq \{\texttt{inp}' \mid \texttt{Prog}[\texttt{inp}'] \models \mathit{Spec}\} \wedge \mathcal{I}_B = \mathcal{I} \setminus \mathcal{I}_G$. The unification operator $\oplus$ is sound w.r.t. *Spec* and $\mathcal{P}$ if for programs $\texttt{Prog}_1$ and $\texttt{Prog}_2$ satisfying *Spec* on inputs in $\mathcal{I}_1$ and $\mathcal{I}_2$, respectively, the program $\mathcal{I}_1 \cdot \texttt{Prog}_1 \oplus \mathcal{I}_2 \cdot \texttt{Prog}_2$ is in $\mathcal{P}$ and that it satisfies *Spec* on $\mathcal{I}_1 \cup \mathcal{I}_2$. The procedure STUN is *sound* if for all inputs $\mathcal{P}$, $\mathcal{I}$, *Spec*, ψ, it returns a program `Prog` such that $\texttt{Prog} \in \mathcal{P}$ and that $\forall \texttt{inp} \in \mathcal{I} : \texttt{Prog}[\texttt{inp}] \models \mathit{Spec}$.

Theorem 1. *Let us fix specification Spec and program space $\mathcal{P}$. If splitInpSpace and the unification operator $\oplus$ are sound, then the STUN procedure is sound.*

Domains and Specifications. We instantiate STUN approach to three domains: bit-vector expressions, separable specifications for conditional linear-arithmetic expressions, and non-separable specifications for conditional linear arithmetic expressions. Separable specifications are those where the specification relates an input and its corresponding output, but does not constrain outputs that correspond to different inputs. Formally, we define separable specifications syntactically — they are of the form $f(x) = o \wedge \Phi(o, x)$, where x is the tuple of all input variables, o is the output variable, f is the function being specified, and Φ is a formula. For example, the specification $\mathit{Spec} \equiv f(x, y) \geq x \wedge f(x, y) \geq y$ is separable as $\mathit{Spec} = (f(x, y) = o) \wedge (o \geq x \wedge o \geq y)$, and the specification $f(0) = 1 \vee f(1) = 1$ is a non-separable specification.

Notes About Implementation. We have implemented the STUN procedure for each of the three domains described above is a suite of tools. In each case, we evaluate our tool on the benchmarks from the SyGuS competition 2014 [1], and compare the performance of our tool against the enumerative solver ESOLVER [2,18]. The tool ESOLVER was the overall winner in the SyGuS competition 2014, and hence, is a good yardstick that represents the state of the art.

4 Domain: Bit-Vector Expressions

The first domain to which we apply the STUN approach is the domain of bit-vector expressions specified by separable specifications. Each bit-vector expression is either an input variable, a constant, or a standard bit-vector operator applied to two sub-expressions. This syntax does not have a top level `if-then-else` operator that allows unification of any two arbitrary programs.

Here, we instantiate the `Generate` procedure and the unification operator of Algorithm 1 to obtain a nondeterministic synthesis procedure (nondeterministic mainly in picking inputs that choose between the CEGIS-like and UNIF-like branches). Later, we present a practical deterministic version of the algorithm.

Representing Candidate Programs. In the following discussion, we represent programs using an alternative formalism that lets us lazily instantiate constants in the program. This representation is for convenience only—the procedure can be stated without using it. Formally, a *candidate bit-vector program* $\mathtt{Prog}$ over inputs $v_1, \ldots, v_n$ is a tuple $\langle \mathtt{expr}, \rho \rangle$ where: (a) $\mathtt{expr}$ is a bit-vector expression over $\{v_1, \ldots, v_n\}$ and auxiliary variables $\{\mathtt{SubProg}_0, \ldots, \mathtt{SubProg}_m\}$ such that each $\mathtt{SubProg}_i$ occurs exactly once in $\mathtt{expr}$; and (b) ρ is a satisfiable constraint over $\mathtt{SubProg}_i$'s. Variables $\mathtt{SubProg}_i$ represent constants of $\mathtt{expr}$ whose exact values are yet to be synthesized, and ρ is a constraint on their values. Intuitively, in the intermediate steps of the algorithm, instead of generating programs with explicit constants, we generate programs with symbolic constants along with constraints on them. A concrete program can be obtained by replacing the symbolic constants with values from some satisfying assignment of ρ.

Unification. As mentioned briefly in Sect. 3, two candidate programs are unifiable if the constants occurring in the expressions can be substituted with sub-expressions to obtain a common expression. However, the presence of symbolic constants requires a more involved definition of the unification operator. Further, note that the symbolic constants in the two programs do not have to be the same. Formally, programs $\mathtt{Prog} = \langle \mathtt{expr}, \rho \rangle$ and $\mathtt{Prog}' = \langle \mathtt{expr}', \rho' \rangle$ over input spaces $\mathcal{I}$ and $\mathcal{I}'$ are unifiable if:

- There exists an expression $\mathtt{expr}^*$ that can be obtained from $\mathtt{expr}$ by replacing each variable $\mathtt{SubProg}_i$ in $\mathtt{expr}$ by an expression $\mathtt{expr}_i$, over the formal inputs $\{v_1, \ldots, v_n\}$ and new auxiliary variables $\{\mathtt{SubProg}^*_1, \ldots, \mathtt{SubProg}^*_k\}$. Further, the same expression $\mathtt{expr}^*$ should also be obtainable from $\mathtt{expr}'$ by replacing each of its sub-programs $\mathtt{SubProg}'_i$ by an expression $\mathtt{expr}'_i$.
- Constraint $\rho^* = \bigwedge_{\mathcal{V}} \rho[\forall i.\mathtt{expr}_i[\mathcal{V}]/\mathtt{SubProg}_i] \wedge \bigwedge_{\mathcal{V}'} \rho'[\forall i.\mathtt{expr}'_i[\mathcal{V}']/\mathtt{SubProg}'_i]$ is satisfiable. Here, $\mathcal{V}$ and $\mathcal{V}'$ range over inputs from $\mathcal{I}$ and $\mathcal{I}'$, respectively.

If the above conditions hold, one possible unified program $\mathcal{I} \cdot \mathtt{Prog} \oplus \mathcal{I}' \cdot \mathtt{Prog}'$ is $\mathtt{Prog}^* = (\mathtt{expr}^*, \rho^*)$. Intuitively, in the unified program, each $\mathtt{SubProg}_i$ is replaced with a sub-expression $\mathtt{expr}_i$, and further, ρ^* ensures that the constraints from the individual programs on the value of these sub-expressions are satisfied.

Example 3. The programs $\mathtt{Prog} = (x \;\&\; \mathtt{SubProg}_0, \mathtt{SubProg}_0 = -1)$ and $\mathtt{Prog}' = (x \;\&\; \mathtt{SubProg}'_0, \mathtt{SubProg}'_0 = 4)$ over the input spaces $\mathcal{I} = (x = 0)$ and $\mathcal{I}' = (x = 5)$ can be unified into $(x \;\&\; (x - \mathtt{SubProg}^*_0), (0 - \mathtt{SubProg}^*_0 = -1) \wedge (5 - \mathtt{SubProg}^*_0 = 4))$. Here, both $\mathtt{SubProg}_0$ and $\mathtt{SubProg}'_0$ are replaced with $x - \mathtt{SubProg}^*_0$ and the constraints have been instantiated with inputs from corresponding input spaces.

Unification Constraints. In this domain, an outer unification constraint ψ is given by a candidate program $\texttt{Prog}_T$. Program $(\texttt{expr}, \rho) \models \psi$ if $\texttt{Prog}_T = (\texttt{expr}_T, \rho_T)$ and expr can be obtained from $\texttt{expr}_T$ by replacing each $\texttt{SubProg}_i^T$ with appropriate sub-expressions. A learned unification constraint β is given by $\bigwedge \texttt{Not}(\texttt{Prog}_F^i)$. Program $(\texttt{expr}, \rho) \models \beta$ if for each $\texttt{Prog}_F^i = (\texttt{expr}_F, \rho_F)$, there is no substitution of $\texttt{SubProg}_i^F$'s that transforms $\texttt{expr}_F$ to expr. Intuitively, a Prog satisfies $\psi = \texttt{Prog}_T$ and $\beta = \bigwedge \texttt{Not}(\texttt{Prog}_F^i)$ if Prog can be unified with $\texttt{Prog}_T$ and cannot be unified with any of $\texttt{Prog}_F^i$. Boolean combinations of unification constraints can be easily defined. In Algorithm 1, we define *UnifConstr*$(\mathcal{I}, \texttt{Prog}) = \texttt{Prog}$ and *LearnFrom*$(\mathit{Spec}, \psi, \beta) = \texttt{Not}(\psi)$. Note that using the alternate representation for programs having symbolic constants lets us have a very simple *LearnFrom* that just negates ψ – in general, a more complex *LearnFrom* might be needed.

Program Generation. A simple *Generate* procedure enumerates programs, ordered by size, and checks if the expression satisfies all the constraints.

Theorem 2. *Algorithm 1 instantiated with the procedures detailed above is a sound synthesis procedure for bit-vector expressions.*

A Practical Algorithm. We instantiate the non-deterministic choices in the procedure from Theorem 2 to obtain a deterministic procedure. Intuitively, this procedure maintains a set of candidate programs and explores them in a fixed order based on size. Further, we optimize the program generation procedure to only examine programs that satisfy the unification constraints, instead of following a generate-and-test procedure. Additionally, we eliminate the recursive call in Algorithm 1, and instead store the variables $\mathcal{I}_G$ locally with individual candidate programs. Essentially, we pass additional information to convert the recursive call into a tail call. Formally, we replace ρ in the candidate programs with $\{(\mathcal{V}_0, \rho_0), \ldots, (\mathcal{V}_k, \rho_k)\}$ where $\mathcal{V}_i$'s are input valuations that represent $\mathcal{I}_G$ from previous recursive calls. Initially, the list of candidate programs contains the program $(\texttt{SubProg}_0, \emptyset)$. In each step, we pick the first candidate (say $(\texttt{expr}, \{(\mathcal{V}_0, \rho_0), \ldots\})$) and concretize expr to $\texttt{expr}^*$ by substituting $\texttt{SubProg}_i$'s with values from a model of $\bigwedge_i \rho_i$. If $\texttt{expr}^*$ satisfies *Spec*, we return it.

Otherwise, there exists an input inp on which $\texttt{expr}^*$ is incorrect. We obtain a new constraint $\rho_{\texttt{inp}}$ on $\texttt{SubProg}_i$'s by substituting the input and the expression $\texttt{expr}^*$ in the specification *Spec*. If $\rho_{\texttt{inp}}$ is unsatisfiable, there are no expressions which can be substituted for $\texttt{SubProg}_i$'s to make expr correct on inp. Hence, the current candidate is eliminated–this is equivalent to a failing recursive call in the non-deterministic version.

Instead, if $\rho_{\texttt{inp}}$ is satisfiable, it is added to the candidate program. Now, if $\bigwedge \rho_i \wedge \rho_{\texttt{inp}}$ is unsatisfiable, the symbolic constants $\texttt{SubProg}_i$'s cannot be instantiated with explicit constants to make expr correct on all the seen inputs $\mathcal{V}_i$. However, $\texttt{SubProg}_i$'s can possibly be instantiated with other sub-expressions. Hence, we replace the current candidate with programs where each $\texttt{SubProg}_i$ is replaced with a small expression of the form *operator*(e_1, e_2) where e_1 and e_2 are either input variables or fresh $\texttt{SubProg}_i$ variables. Note that while substituting

Algorithm 2. A deterministic STUN algorithm for bit-vector expressions

$\mathit{Candidates} \leftarrow \langle(\mathtt{SubProg}_0, \emptyset)\rangle$
while true do
  $(\mathtt{expr}, \{(\mathcal{V}_0, \rho_0), \ldots, (\mathcal{V}_n, \rho_n)\}) \leftarrow \mathit{Candidates}[0]$
  $\mathtt{expr}^* \leftarrow \mathit{substitute}(\mathtt{expr}, \mathit{getModel}(\bigwedge_i \rho_i))$
  if $\nexists \mathtt{inp} : \mathtt{expr}^*[\mathtt{inp}] \not\models \mathit{Spec}$ **return** $\mathtt{expr}^*$
  $\rho_{\mathtt{inp}} \leftarrow \mathit{concretize}(\mathtt{expr}, \mathit{Spec}, \mathtt{inp})$ where $\mathtt{expr}^*[\mathtt{inp}] \not\models \mathit{Spec}$
  if $\neg \mathit{Satisfiable}(\rho_{\mathtt{inp}})$ **then**
    $\mathit{Candidates} \leftarrow \mathit{tail}(\mathit{Candidates})$
  else
    $\mathit{Candidates}[0] \leftarrow (\mathtt{expr}, \{(\mathcal{V}_0, \rho_0), \ldots, (\mathcal{V}_n, \rho_n)\} \cup \{(\mathcal{V}_{\mathtt{inp}}, \rho_{\mathtt{inp}})\})$
    if $\neg \mathit{Satisfiable}(\bigwedge \rho_i \wedge \rho_{\mathtt{inp}})$ **then**
      $\mathit{Candidates} \leftarrow \mathit{tail}(\mathit{Candidates})$
      for all $\mathtt{SubProg}_i \in \mathit{AuxVariables}(\mathtt{expr})$, $\mathtt{expr}' \leftarrow \mathit{LevelOneExprs}()$ **do**
        $\mathit{Candidates} \leftarrow \mathit{append}(\mathit{Candidates}, \mathit{substitute}(\mathtt{Prog}, (\mathtt{SubProg}_i, \mathtt{expr}')))$

these expression for $\mathtt{SubProg}_i$ in ρ_j, the input variables are replaced with the corresponding values from $\mathcal{V}_j$.

Informally, each $(\mathtt{expr}, \rho_i)$ is a candidate program generated at one level of the recursion in the non-deterministic algorithm and each valuation $\mathcal{V}_i$ is the corresponding input-space. An iteration where $\rho_{\mathtt{inp}}$ is unsatisfiable is a case where there is no program that is correct on inp is unifiable with the already generated program, and an iteration where $\bigwedge \rho_i \wedge \rho_{\mathtt{inp}}$ is unsatisfiable when the unification procedure cannot replace the symbolic constants with explicit constants, but instead has to search through more complex expressions for the substitution.

Theorem 3. *Algorithm 2 is a sound and complete synthesis procedure for bit-vector expressions.*

Experiments. We implemented Algorithm 2 in a tool called AUK and evaluated it on benchmarks from the bit-vector track of SyGuS competition 2014 [1]. For the full summary of results, see the full version [3]. For easy benchmarks (where both tools take < 1 second), ESOLVER is faster than AUK. However, on larger benchmarks, the performance of AUK is better. We believe that these results are due to ESOLVER being able to enumerate small solutions extremely fast, while AUK starts on the expensive theory reasoning. On larger benchmarks, AUK is able to eliminate larger sets of candidates due to the unification constraints while ESOLVER is slowed down by the sheer number of candidate programs.

5 Domain: CLEs with Separable Specifications

We now apply the STUN approach to the domain of conditional linear arithmetic expressions (CLEs). A program Prog in this domain is either a linear expression over the input variables or is if(cond) Prog else Prog′, where cond is a boolean combination of linear inequalities. This is an ideal domain for the UNIF loop due to the natural unification operator that uses the if-then-else construct. Here, we present our algorithm for the case where the variables range over rationals. Later, we discuss briefly how to extend the technique to integer variables.

Unification. Given two CLEs `Prog` and `Prog`′, and input spaces $\mathcal{I}$ and $\mathcal{I}'$, we define $\mathcal{I} \cdot \texttt{Prog} \oplus \mathcal{I}' \cdot \texttt{Prog}'$ to be the program if $(\mathcal{I})$ `Prog` else if $(\mathcal{I}')$ `Prog`′ else $\bot$. Note that we assume that $\mathcal{I}$ and $\mathcal{I}'$ are expressed as linear constraints. Here, since any two programs can be unified, unification constraints are not used.

Program Generation. Algorithm 3 is the program generation procedure *Generate* for CLEs for rational arithmetic specifications. Given a specification *Spec* and input space $\mathcal{I}$, it first generates a concrete input-output example such that the input is in $\mathcal{I}$ and the example satisfies *Spec*. Then, it generalizes the input-output pair to a program as follows. From each clause of *Spec*, we pick one disjunct that evaluates to true for the current input-output pair. Each disjunct that constrains the output can be expressed as $o \ \mathsf{op}\ \phi$ where $\mathsf{op} \in \{\leq, \geq, <, >\}$ and ϕ is a linear expression over the input variables. Recall from the definition of separable specifications that o is the output variable that represents the output of the function to be synthesized. Each such inequality gives us either an upper or a lower bound (in terms of input variables) on the output variable. These bounds are evaluated using the input-output example, and the strictest upper and lower bounds are chosen. The algorithm then returns an expression `Prog` that respects these strictest bounds. We define the *SplitInpSpace* procedure from Algorithm 1 as follows: input space $\mathcal{I}_G$ is obtained by substituting the program `Prog` into the disjuncts, and $\mathcal{I}_B$ is obtained as $\mathcal{I} \wedge \neg\mathcal{I}_G$.

Theorem 4. *Algorithm 1 instantiated with the procedures detailed above is a sound and complete synthesis procedure for conditional linear rational arithmetic expressions specified using separable specifications.*

Extension to Integers. The above procedure cannot be directly applied when variables range over integers instead of rationals. Here, each disjunct can be put into the form $c \cdot o \ \mathsf{op}\ \phi$ where c is a positive integer and ϕ is a linear integer expression over inputs. For rationals, this constraint can be normalized to obtain $o \ \mathsf{op}\ \frac{1}{c}\phi$. In the domain of integers, $\frac{1}{c}\phi$ is not necessarily an integer.

Algorithm 3. Procedure *Generate*

Require: Specification *Spec* in CNF, Input space $\mathcal{I}$
Ensure: Candidate program `Prog`

if $\mathcal{I} = \emptyset$ **return** $\top$
$pex \leftarrow getModel(\mathcal{I} \wedge Spec)$
$LB \leftarrow -\infty$, $UB \leftarrow \infty$
for all *Clause* of *Spec* **do**
  Pick *Disjunct* in *Clause* such that *Disjunct*[*pex*] holds
  if o occurs in *Disjunct* and $Disjunct \equiv (o \ \mathsf{op}\ \phi)$ **then**
    case $\mathsf{op} \in \{\leq, <\} \wedge UB[pex] > \phi[pex]$: $UB \leftarrow \phi$
    case $\mathsf{op} \in \{\geq, >\} \wedge LB[pex] < \phi[pex]$: $LB \leftarrow \phi$
return $(LB + UB)/2$

There are two possible ways to solve this problem. A simple solution is to modify the syntax of the programs to allow floor $\lfloor\cdot\rfloor$ and ceiling $\lceil\cdot\rceil$ functions. Then, $c \cdot o \leq \phi$ and $c \cdot o \geq \phi$ can be normalized as $o \leq \lfloor \phi/c \rfloor$ and $o \geq \lceil \phi/c \rceil$. The generation procedure can then proceed using these normalized expressions. The alternative approach is to use a full-fledged decision procedure for solving the constraints of the form $o \text{ op } \frac{1}{c}\phi$. However, this introduces divisibility constraints into the generated program. For a detailed explanation on this approach and techniques for eliminating the divisibility constraints, see [14].

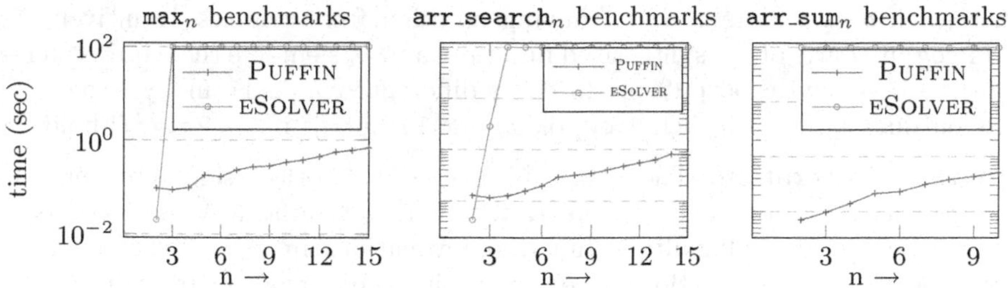

Fig. 3. Results on separable linear integer benchmarks

Experiments. We implemented the above procedure in a tool called PUFFIN and evaluated it on benchmarks from the linear integer arithmetic track with separable specifications from the SyGuS competition 2014. The results on three classes of benchmarks ($\texttt{max}_n$, $\texttt{array\_search}_n$, and $\texttt{array\_sum}_n$) have been summarized in Fig. 3. The $\texttt{max}_n$ benchmarks specify a function that outputs the maximum of n input variables (the illustrative example from Sect. 2 is max_2). Note that the SyGuS competition benchmarks only go up to max_5. The $\texttt{array\_search}_n$ and $\texttt{array\_sum}_n$ benchmarks respectively specify functions that search for a given input in an array, and check if the sum of two consecutive elements in an array is equal to a given value. In all these benchmarks, our tool significantly outperforms ESOLVER and other CEGIS-based solvers. This is because the CEGIS solvers try to generate the whole program at once, which is a complex expression, while our solver combines simple expressions generated for parts of the input spaces where the output expression is simple.

6 Domain: Non-Separable Specifications for CLEs

Here, we consider CLEs specified by non-separable specifications. While this domain allows for simple unification, non-separable specifications introduce complications. Further, unlike the previous domains, the problem itself is undecidable.

First, we define what it means for a program Prog to satisfy a non-separable specification on an input space $\mathcal{I}$. In further discussion, we assume that the program to be synthesized is represented by the function f in all specifications and formulae. We say that Prog satisfies *Spec* on $\mathcal{I}$ if *Spec* holds whenever the inputs to f in each occurrence in *Spec* belong to $\mathcal{I}$. For example, program $\texttt{Prog}(i)$

satisfies $Spec \equiv f(x) = 1 \wedge x' = x+1 \implies f(x') = 1$ on the input space $0 \leq i \leq 2$ if $(0 \leq x \leq 2 \wedge 0 \leq x' \leq 2) \implies Spec[f \leftarrow \texttt{Prog}]$ holds, i.e., we require *Spec* to hold when both x and x' belong to the input space.

Unification and Unification Constraints. The unification operator we use is the same as in Sect. 5. However, for non-separable specifications, the outputs produced by Prog on $\mathcal{I}$ may constrain the outputs of Prog′ on $\mathcal{I}'$, and hence, we need non-trivial unification constraints. An outer unification constraint ψ is a sequence $\langle(\mathcal{I}_0, \texttt{Prog}_0), (\mathcal{I}_1, \texttt{Prog}_1), \ldots\rangle$ where $\mathcal{I}_i$'s and $\texttt{Prog}_i$'s are input spaces and programs, respectively. A learned unification constraint β is given by $\bigwedge \rho_i$ where each ρ_i is a formula over f having no other free variables. Intuitively, $\mathcal{I}_i$ and $\texttt{Prog}_i$ fix parts of the synthesized function, and ρ_i's enforce the required relationships between the outputs produced by different $\texttt{Prog}_i$'s. Formally, $\texttt{Prog} \models \psi$ if its outputs agree with each $\texttt{Prog}_i$ on $\mathcal{I}_i$ and $\texttt{Prog} \models \beta$ if $\wedge \rho_i[\texttt{Prog}/f]$ holds.

Program Generation. The *Generate* procedure works using input-output examples as in the previous section. However, it is significantly more complex due to the presence of multiple function invocations in *Spec*. Intuitively, we replace all function invocations except one with the partial programs from the unification constraints and then solve the arising separable specification using techniques from the previous section. We explain the procedure in detail using an example.

Example 4. Consider the specification *Spec* given by $x \neq y \implies f(x) + f(y) = 10$. Here, the only solution is the constant function 5. Now, assume that the synthesis procedure has guessed that $\texttt{Prog}_0$ given by $\texttt{Prog}_0(i) = 0$ is a program that satisfies *Spec* for the input space $\mathcal{I}_0 \equiv i = 0$.

The unification constraint $\psi_0 = \langle(\texttt{Prog}_0, \mathcal{I}_0)\rangle$ is passed to the recursive call to ensure that the synthesized function satisfies $f(0) = 0$. The program generation unction in the recursive call works as follows: it replaces the invocation $f(x)$ in *Spec* with the partial function from ψ to obtain the constraint $(x = 0 \wedge x \neq y \implies \texttt{Prog}_0(0) + f(y) = 10)$. Solving to obtain the next program and input space, we get $\texttt{Prog}_1(i) = 10$ for the input space $\mathcal{I}_1 \equiv i = 1$. Now, the unification constraint passed to the next recursive call is $\psi = \langle(\texttt{Prog}_0, \mathcal{I}_0), (\texttt{Prog}_1, \mathcal{I}_1)\rangle$.

Again, instantiating $f(x)$ with $\texttt{Prog}_0$ and $\texttt{Prog}_1$ in the respective input spaces, we obtain the constraint $(x = 0 \wedge x \neq y \implies \texttt{Prog}_0(x) + f(y) = 10) \wedge (x = 1 \wedge x \neq y \implies \texttt{Prog}_1(x) + f(y) = 10)$. Now, this constraint does not have a solution—for $y = 2$, there is no possible value for $f(y)$. Here, a reason $\beta = \rho_0$ (say $\rho_0 \equiv f(1) = f(0)$) is learnt for the unsatisfiability and added to the learned constraint. Note that this conflict-driven learning is captured in the function *LearnFrom* in Algorithm 1. Now, in the parent call, no program satisfies β as well as $\psi = \langle(\texttt{Prog}_0, \mathcal{I}_0), (\texttt{Prog}_1, \mathcal{I}_1)\rangle$. By a similar unsatisfiability analysis, we get $\rho_1 \equiv f(0) = 5$ as the additional learned constraint. Finally, at the top level, with $\beta \equiv f(0) = f(1) \wedge f(0) = 5$, we synthesize the right value for $f(0)$.

Example 5 (Acceleration). Let $Spec \equiv (0 \leq x, y \leq 2 \implies f(x,y) = 1) \wedge (x = 4 \wedge y = 0 \implies f(x,y) = 0) \wedge (f(x,y) = 1 \wedge (x', y') = (x+2, y+2) \implies f(x', y') = 1)$.

The synthesis procedure first obtains the candidate program $\texttt{Prog}_0(i,j) = 1$ on the input space $\mathcal{I}_0 \equiv 0 \leq i \leq 1 \wedge 0 \leq j \leq 1$. The recursive call is passed

$(\texttt{Prog}_0, \mathcal{I}_0)$ as the unification constraint and generates the next program fragment $\texttt{Prog}_1(i,j) = 1$ on the input space $\mathcal{I}_1 \equiv 0 \leq i-2 \leq 2 \wedge 0 \leq j-2 \leq 2$. Similarly, each further recursive call generates $\texttt{Prog}_n(i,j) = 1$ on the input space $\mathcal{I}_n$ given by $0 \leq i-2*n \leq 2 \wedge 0 \leq j-2*n \leq 2$. The sequence of recursive calls do not terminate. To overcome this problem, we use an accelerating widening operator. Intuitively, it generalizes the programs and input spaces in the unification constraints to cover more inputs. In this case, the acceleration operator we define below produces the input space $\mathcal{I}^* \equiv 0 \leq i \wedge 0 \leq j \wedge -2 \leq i-j \leq 2$. Proceeding with this widened constraint lets us terminate with the solution program.

Acceleration. The *accelerating widening operator* ∇ operates on unification constraints. In Algorithm 1, we apply ∇ to the unification constraints being passed to the recursive call on line 14, i.e., we replace the expression $\psi \wedge \mathit{UnifConstr}(\mathcal{I}_G, \texttt{Prog})$ with $\nabla(\psi \wedge \mathit{UnifConstr}(\mathcal{I}_G, \texttt{Prog}), \beta)$.

While sophisticated accelerating widening operators are available for partial functions (see, for example, [9,11]), in our implementation, we use a simple one. Given an input unification constraint $\langle(\mathcal{I}_0, \texttt{Prog}_0), \ldots, (\mathcal{I}_n, \texttt{Prog}_n)\rangle$, the accelerating widening operator works as follows: (a) If $\texttt{Prog}_n \neq \texttt{Prog}_j$ for all $j < n$, it returns the input. (b) Otherwise, $\texttt{Prog}_n = \texttt{Prog}_j$ for some $j < n$ and we widen the domain where $\texttt{Prog}_n$ is applicable to $\mathcal{I}^*$ where $\mathcal{I}_j \cup \mathcal{I}_n \subseteq \mathcal{I}^*$. Intuitively, we do this by letting $\mathcal{I}^* = \nabla(\mathcal{I}_i, \mathcal{I}_j)$ where ∇ is the widening join operation for convex polyhedra abstract domain [10]. However, we additionally want $\texttt{Prog}_n$ on $\mathcal{I}^*$ to not cause any violation of the learned constraints $\beta = \bigwedge \rho_i$. Therefore, we use a widening operator with bounds on the convex polyhedral abstract domain instead of the generic widening operator. The bounds are obtained from the concrete constraints. We do not describe this procedure explicitly, but present an example below. The final output returned is $\langle(\mathcal{I}_0, \texttt{Prog}_0), \ldots, (\mathcal{I}^*, \texttt{Prog}_n)\rangle$.

Example 6. Consider the specification $\mathit{Spec} = f(0) = 1 \wedge (f(x) = 1 \wedge 0 \leq x \leq 10 \implies f(x+1) = 1) \wedge (f(12) = 0)$. After two recursive calls, we get the unification constraint $\psi = \langle(i = 0, \texttt{Prog}_0(i) = 1), (i = 1, \texttt{Prog}_1(i) = 1)\rangle$. Widening, we generalize the input spaces $i = 0$ and $i = 1$ to $\mathcal{I}^* = (i \geq 0)$. However, further synthesis fails due to the clause $f(12) = 0$ from *Spec*, and we obtain a learned unification constraint $\beta \equiv f(12) = 0$ at the parent call.

We then obtain an additional bound for the unification as replacing f by $\texttt{Prog}_1$ violates $f(12) = 0$. With this new bound, the widening operator returns the input space $\mathcal{I}^* = (12 > i \geq 0)$, which allows us to complete the synthesis.

Theorem 5. *Algorithm 1 instantiated with the procedures described above is a sound synthesis procedure for conditional linear expressions given by non-separable specifications.*

Experiments. We implemented the above procedure in a tool called RAZORBILL and evaluated it linear integer benchmarks with non-separable specifications from SyGuS competition 2014. For the full summary of results, see the full version [3]. As for the bit-vector benchmarks, on small benchmarks (where both tools finish in less than 1 second), ESOLVER is faster. However, on larger benchmarks, RAZORBILL can be much faster. As before, we hypothesize that this is due to ESOLVER quickly enumerating small solutions before the STUN based solver can perform any complex theory reasoning.

7 Concluding Remarks

Related Work. Algorithmic program synthesis became popular a decade ago with the introduction of CEGIS [17]. Much more recently, syntax-guided synthesis [2] framework, where the input to synthesis is a program space and a specification, was introduced, along with several types of solvers. Our synthesis problem falls into this framework, and our solvers solve SyGuS problem instances. Kuncak et al. [14] present another alternative (non-CEGIS) solver for linear arithmetic constraints.

STUN is a general approach to synthesis. For instance, in the domain of synthesis of synchronization [4,6,7,13,19], the algorithm used can be presented as an instantiation of STUN. The approach is based on an analysis of a counterexample trace that infers a fix in the form of additional synchronization. The bug fix works for the counterexample and possibly for some related traces. Such bug fixes are then unified similarly as in the STUN approach.

A synthesis technique related to STUN is based on version-space algebras [12,15]. There, the goal is to compose programs that works on a part of a single input (say a string) to a transformation that would work for the complete single input. In contrast, STUN unifies programs that work for different parts of the input space. The combination of the two approaches could thus be fruitful.

The widening operator has been introduced in [8], and has been widely used in program analysis, but not in synthesis. We proposed to use it to accelerate the process in which STUN finds solutions that cover parts of the input space. Use of other operators such as narrowing is worth investigating.

Limitations. We mentioned that the simple unification operator based on if statements might lead to inefficient code. In particular, if the specification is given only by input-output examples, the resulting program might be a sequence of conditionals with conditions corresponding to each example. That is why we proposed a different unification operator for the bit-vector domain, and we plan to investigate unification further. Furthermore, a limitation of STUN when compared to CEGIS is that designing unification operators requires domain knowledge (knowledge of the given program space).

Future Work. We believe STUN opens several new directions for future research. First, we plan to investigate unification operators for domains where the programs have loops or recursion. This seems a natural fit for STUN, because if for several different input we find that the length of the synthesized sequence of instructions in the solution depends on the size of the input, then the unification operator might propose a loop in the unified solution. Second, systems that at runtime prevent deadlocks or other problems can be thought of as finding solutions for parts of the input space. A number of such fixes could then be unified into a more general solution. Last, we plan to optimize the prototype solvers we presented. This is a promising direction, as even our current prototypes have comparable or significantly better performance than the existing solvers.

References

1. SyGuS competition 2014. http://www.sygus.org/SyGuS-COMP2014.html
2. Alur, R., Bodík, R., Juniwal, G., Martin, M., Raghothaman, M., Seshia, S., Singh, R., Solar-Lezama, A., Torlak, E., Udupa, A.: Syntax-guided synthesis. In: FMCAD, pp. 1–17 (2013)
3. Alur, R., Černý, P., Radhakrishna, A.: Synthesis through unification. CoRR abs/1505.05868 (2015). http://arxiv.org/abs/1104.4306
4. Bloem, R., Hofferek, G., Könighofer, B., Könighofer, R., Außerlechner, S., Spörk, R.: Synthesis of synchronization using uninterpreted functions. In: FMCAD, pp. 35–42 (2014)
5. Bodík, R., Jobstmann, B.: Algorithmic program synthesis: introduction. STTT **15**(5–6), 397–411 (2013)
6. Černý, P., Henzinger, T.A., Radhakrishna, A., Ryzhyk, L., Tarrach, T.: Efficient synthesis for concurrency by semantics-preserving transformations. In: Sharygina, N., Veith, H. (eds.) CAV 2013. LNCS, vol. 8044, pp. 951–967. Springer, Heidelberg (2013)
7. Černý, P., Henzinger, T.A., Radhakrishna, A., Ryzhyk, L., Tarrach, T.: Regression-free synthesis for concurrency. In: Biere, A., Bloem, R. (eds.) CAV 2014. LNCS, vol. 8559, pp. 568–584. Springer, Heidelberg (2014)
8. Cousot, P., Cousot, R.: Abstract interpretation: a unified lattice model for static analysis of programs by construction or approximation of fixpoints. In: POPL, pp. 238–252 (1977)
9. Cousot, P., Cousot, R.: An abstract interpretation framework for termination. In: POPL, pp. 245–258 (2012)
10. Cousot, P., Halbwachs, N.: Automatic discovery of linear restraints among variables of a program. In: POPL, pp. 84–96 (1978)
11. Cousot, P., Cousot, R.: Relational abstract interpretation of higher order functional programs (extended abstract). In: JTASPEFT/WSA, pp. 33–36 (1991)
12. Gulwani, S.: Automating string processing in spreadsheets using input-output examples. In: POPL, pp. 317–330 (2011)
13. Gupta, A., Henzinger, T., Radhakrishna, A., Samanta, R., Tarrach, T.: Succinct representation of concurrent trace sets. In: POPL15, pp. 433–444 (2015)
14. Kuncak, V., Mayer, M., Piskac, R., Suter, P.: Complete functional synthesis. In: PLDI, pp. 316–329 (2010)
15. Lau, T., Domingos, P., Weld, D.: Version space algebra and its application to programming by demonstration. In: ICML, pp. 527–534 (2000)
16. Solar-Lezama, A.: Program sketching. STTT **15**(5–6), 475–495 (2013)
17. Solar-Lezama, A., Tancau, L., Bodík, R., Seshia, S.A., Saraswat, V.A.: Combinatorial sketching for finite programs. In: ASPLOS, pp. 404–415 (2006)
18. Udupa, A., Raghavan, A., Deshmukh, J.V., Mador-Haim, S., Martin, M.M.K., Alur, R.: TRANSIT: specifying protocols with concolic snippets. In: PLDI, pp. 287–296 (2013)
19. Vechev, M.T., Yahav, E., Yorsh, G.: Abstraction-guided synthesis of synchronization. In: POPL, pp. 327–338 (2010)
20. Warren, H.S.: Hacker's Delight. Addison-Wesley Longman Publishing Co., Inc., Boston (2002)

From Non-preemptive to Preemptive Scheduling Using Synchronization Synthesis

Pavol Černý[1], Edmund M. Clarke[2], Thomas A. Henzinger[3], Arjun Radhakrishna[4], Leonid Ryzhyk[2], Roopsha Samanta[3], and Thorsten Tarrach[3](✉)

[1] University of Colorado Boulder, Boulder, Colorado
[2] Carnegie Mellon University, Pittsburgh, PA, USA
[3] IST Austria, Klosterneuburg, Austria
ttarrach@ist.ac.at
[4] University of Pennsylvania, Philadelphia, PA, USA

Abstract. We present a computer-aided programming approach to concurrency. The approach allows programmers to program assuming a friendly, non-preemptive scheduler, and our synthesis procedure inserts synchronization to ensure that the final program works even with a preemptive scheduler. The correctness specification is implicit, inferred from the non-preemptive behavior. Let us consider sequences of calls that the program makes to an external interface. The specification requires that any such sequence produced under a preemptive scheduler should be included in the set of such sequences produced under a non-preemptive scheduler. The solution is based on a finitary abstraction, an algorithm for bounded language inclusion modulo an independence relation, and rules for inserting synchronization. We apply the approach to device-driver programming, where the driver threads call the software interface of the device and the API provided by the operating system. Our experiments demonstrate that our synthesis method is precise and efficient, and, since it does not require explicit specifications, is more practical than the conventional approach based on user-provided assertions.

1 Introduction

Concurrent shared-memory programming is notoriously difficult and error-prone. Program synthesis for concurrency aims to mitigate this complexity by synthesizing synchronization code automatically [4,5,8,11]. However, specifying the programmer's intent may be a challenge in itself. Declarative mechanisms, such as assertions, suffer from the drawback that it is difficult to ensure that the specification is complete and fully captures the programmer's intent.

This research was supported in part by the European Research Council (ERC) under grant 267989 (QUAREM), by the Austrian Science Fund (FWF) under grants S11402-N23 (RiSE) and Z211-N23 (Wittgenstein Award), by NSF under award CCF 1421752 and the Expeditions award CCF 1138996, by the Simons Foundation, and by a gift from the Intel Corporation.

D. Kroening and C.S. Păsăreanu (Eds.): CAV 2015, Part II, LNCS 9207, pp. 180–197, 2015.
DOI: 10.1007/978-3-319-21668-3_11

We propose a solution where the specification is *implicit*. We observe that a core difficulty in concurrent programming originates from the fact that the scheduler can *preempt* the execution of a thread at any time. We therefore give the developer the option to program assuming a friendly, *non-preemptive*, scheduler. Our tool automatically synthesizes synchronization code to ensure that every behavior of the program under preemptive scheduling is included in the set of behaviors produced under non-preemptive scheduling. Thus, we use the non-preemptive semantics as an implicit correctness specification.

The non-preemptive scheduling model dramatically simplifies the development of concurrent software, including operating system (OS) kernels, network servers, database systems, etc. [13, 14]. In this model, a thread can only be descheduled by voluntarily yielding control, e.g., by invoking a blocking operation. Synchronization primitives may be used for communication between threads, e.g., a producer thread may use a semaphore to notify the consumer about availability of data. However, one does not need to worry about protecting accesses to shared state: a series of memory accesses executes atomically as long as the scheduled thread does not yield.

In defining behavioral equivalence between preemptive and non-preemptive executions, we focus on externally observable program behaviors: two program executions are *observationally equivalent* if they generate the same sequences of calls to interfaces of interest. This approach facilitates modular synthesis where a module's behavior is characterized in terms of its interaction with other modules. Given a multi-threaded program $\mathcal{C}$ and a synthesized program $\mathcal{C}'$ obtained by adding synchronization to $\mathcal{C}$, $\mathcal{C}'$ is *preemption-safe* w.r.t. $\mathcal{C}$ if for each execution of $\mathcal{C}'$ under a preemptive scheduler, there is an observationally equivalent non-preemptive execution of $\mathcal{C}$. Our synthesis goal is to automatically generate a preemption-safe version of the input program.

We rely on abstraction to achieve efficient synthesis of multi-threaded programs. We propose a simple, *data-oblivious* abstraction inspired by an analysis of synchronization patterns in OS code, which tend to be independent of data values. The abstraction tracks types of accesses (read or write) to each memory location while ignoring their values. In addition, the abstraction tracks branching choices. Calls to an external interface are modeled as writes to a special memory location, with independent interfaces modeled as separate locations. To the best of our knowledge, our proposed abstraction is yet to be explored in the verification and synthesis literature.

Two abstract program executions are observationally equivalent if they are equal modulo the classical independence relation I on memory accesses: accesses to different locations are independent, and accesses to the same location are independent iff they are both read accesses. Using this notion of equivalence, the notion of preemption-safety is extended to abstract programs.

Under abstraction, we model each thread as a nondeterministic finite automaton (NFA) over a finite alphabet, with each symbol corresponding to a read or a write to a particular variable. This enables us to construct NFAs N, representing the abstraction of the original program $\mathcal{C}$ under non-premptive scheduling, and P, representing the abstraction of the synthesized program $\mathcal{C}'$ under preemptive scheduling. We show that preemption-safety of $\mathcal{C}'$ w.r.t. $\mathcal{C}$ is implied by preemption-safety of the abstract synthesized program w.r.t. the abstract original program, which, in turn, is implied by language inclusion modulo I of NFAs P and N. While the problem of language inclusion modulo an independence relation is undecidable [2], we show that the antichain-based algorithm for standard language inclusion [9] can be adapted to decide a bounded version of language inclusion modulo an independence relation.

Our overall synthesis procedure works as follows: we run the algorithm for bounded language inclusion modulo I, iteratively increasing the bound, until it reports that the inclusion holds, or finds a counterexample, or reaches a timeout. In the first case, the synthesis procedure terminates successfully. In the second case, the counterexample is generalized to a set of counterexamples represented as a Boolean combination of ordering constraints over control-flow locations (as in [11]). These constraints are analyzed for patterns indicating the type of concurrency bug (atomicity, ordering violation) and the type of applicable fix (lock insertion, statement reordering). After applying the fix(es), the procedure is restarted from scratch; the process continues until we find a preemption-safe program, or reach a timeout.

We implemented our synthesis procedure in a new prototype tool called LISS (Language Inclusion-based Synchronization Synthesis) and evaluated it on a series of device driver benchmarks, including an Ethernet driver for Linux and the synchronization skeleton of a USB-to-serial controller driver. First, LISS was able to detect and eliminate all but two known race conditions in our examples; these included one race condition that we previously missed when synthesizing from explicit specifications [5], due to a missing assertion. Second, our abstraction proved highly efficient: LISS runs an order of magnitude faster on the more complicated examples than our previous synthesis tool based on the CBMC model checker. Third, our coarse abstraction proved surprisingly precise in practice: across all our benchmarks, we only encountered three program locations where manual abstraction refinement was needed to avoid the generation of unnecessary synchronization. Overall, our evaluation strongly supports the use of the implicit specification approach based on non-preemptive scheduling semantics as well as the use of the data-oblivious abstraction to achieve practical synthesis for real-world systems code.

Contributions. First, we propose a new specification-free approach to synchronization synthesis. Given a program written assuming a friendly, non-preemptive scheduler, we automatically generate a preemption-safe version of the program. Second, we introduce a novel abstraction scheme and use it to reduce preemption-safety to language inclusion modulo an independence relation. Third, we present the first language inclusion-based synchronization synthesis procedure and tool for concurrent programs. Our synthesis procedure includes a new algorithm for a bounded version of our inherently undecidable language inclusion problem. Finally, we evaluate our synthesis procedure on several examples. To the best of our knowledge, LISS is the first synthesis tool capable of handling realistic (albeit

```
void open_dev() {
while (*) {
  if (open==0) {
    power_up();
  }
  open=open+1;
 yield; } }
```

```
void close_dev() {
while (*) {
 if (open>0) {
   open=open-1;
   if (open==0) {
     power_down();
 } }
yield; } }
```

(a)

```
void open_dev_abs() {
while (*) {
(A) r open;
  if (*) {
    (B) w dev;
 }
(C) r open;
(D) w open;
yield; } }
```

```
void close_dev_abs() {
while (*) {
  (E) r open;
  if (*) {
    (F) r open;
    (G) w open;
    (H) r open;
    if (*) {
      (I) w dev;
} }
yield; } }
```

(b)

Fig. 1. Running example and its abstraction

simplified) device driver code, while previous tools were evaluated on small fragments of driver code or on manually extracted synchronization skeletons.

Related Work. Synthesis of synchronization is an active research area [3–6, 10–12, 15, 16]. Closest to our work is a recent paper by Bloem et al. [3], which uses implicit specifications for synchronization synthesis. While their specification is given by sequential behaviors, ours is given by non-preemptive behaviors. This makes our approach applicable to scenarios where threads need to communicate explicitly. Further, correctness in [3] is determined by comparing values at the end of the execution. In contrast, we compare sequences of events, which serves as a more suitable specification for infinitely-looping reactive systems.

Many efforts in synthesis of synchronization focus on user-provided specifications, such as assertions (our previous work [4, 5, 11]). However, it is hard to determine if a given set of assertions represents a complete specification. In this paper, we are solving language inclusion, a computationally harder problem than reachability. However, due to our abstraction, our tool performs significantly better than tools from [4, 5], which are based on a mature model checker (CBMC [7]). Our abstraction is reminiscent of previously used abstractions that track reads and writes to individual locations (e.g., [1, 17]). However, our abstraction is novel as it additionally tracks some control-flow information (specifically, the branches taken) giving us higher precision with almost negligible computational cost. The synthesis part of our approach is based on [11].

In [16] the authors rely on assertions for synchronization synthesis and include iterative abstraction refinement in their framework. This is an interesting extension to pursue for our abstraction. In other related work, CFix [12] can detect and fix concurrency bugs by identifying simple bug patterns in the code.

2 Illustrative Example

Fig. 1a contains our running example. Consider the case where the procedures `open_dev()` and `close_dev()` are invoked in parallel, possibly multiple times (modeled as a non-deterministic while loop). The functions `power_up()` and `power_down()` represent calls to a device. For the non-preemptive scheduler, the sequence of calls to the device will always be a repeating sequence of one call to `power_up()`, followed by one call to `power_down()`. Without additional synchronization, however, there could be two calls to `power_up()` in a row when executing it with a preemptive scheduler. Such a sequence is not observationally equivalent to any sequence that can be produced when executing with a non-preemptive scheduler.

Fig. 1b contains the abstracted versions (we omit tracking of branching choices in the example) of the two procedures, `open_dev_abs()` and `close_dev_abs()`. For instance, the instruction `open = open + 1` is abstracted to the two instructions labeled (C) and (D). The abstraction is coarse, but still captures the problem. Consider two threads `T1` and `T2` running the `open_dev_abs()` procedure. The following trace is possible under a preemptive scheduler, but not under a non-preemptive scheduler: `T1.A; T2.A; T1.B; T1.C; T1.D; T2.B; T2.C; T2.D`. Moreover, the trace cannot be transformed by swapping independent events into any trace possible under a non-preemptive scheduler. This is because instructions `A` and `D` are not independent. Hence, the abstract trace exhibits the problem of two successive calls to `power_up()` when executing with a preemptive scheduler. Our synthesis procedure finds this problem, and fixes it by introducing a lock in `open_dev()` (see Sect. 5).

3 Preliminaries and Problem Statement

Syntax. We assume that programs are written in a concurrent while language $\mathcal{W}$. A concurrent program $\mathcal{C}$ in $\mathcal{W}$ is a finite collection of threads $\langle \mathtt{T}_1, \ldots, \mathtt{T}_n \rangle$ where each thread is a statement written in the syntax from Fig. 2. All $\mathcal{W}$ variables (program variables `std_var`, lock variables `lock_var`, and condition variable `cond_var`) range over integers and each statement is labeled with a unique location identifier l. The only non-standard syntactic constructs in $\mathcal{W}$ relate to the *tags*. Intuitively, each tag is a communication channel between the program and an interface to an external system, and the input(tag) and output(tag, expr) statements read from and write to the channel. We assume that the program and the external system interface can only communicate through the channel. In practice, we use the tags to model device registers. In our presentation, we consider only a single external interface. Our implementation can handle communication with several interfaces.

```
expr ::= std_var | constant | operator(expr, expr, ..., expr)
lstmt ::= loc: stmt | lstmt; lstmt
stmt ::= skip | std_var := expr | std_var := havoc()
  | if (expr) lstmt else lstmt | while (expr) lstmt | std_var := input(tag)
  | output(tag, expr) | lock(lock_var)  | unlock(lock_var)
  | signal(cond_var)  | await(cond_var) | reset(cond_var) | yield
```

Fig. 2. Syntax of $\mathcal{W}$

Semantics. We begin by defining the semantics of a single thread in $\mathcal{W}$, and then extend the definition to concurrent non-preemptive and preemptive semantics. Note that in our work, reads and writes are assumed to execute atomically and further, we assume a sequentially consistent memory model.

Single-Thread Semantics. A program state is given by $\langle \mathcal{V}, P \rangle$ where $\mathcal{V}$ is a valuation of all program variables, and P is the statement that remains to be executed. Let us fix a thread identifier *tid*.

The operational semantics of a thread executing in isolation is given in Fig. 3. A single execution step $\langle \mathcal{V}, P \rangle \xrightarrow{\alpha} \langle \mathcal{V}', P' \rangle$ changes the program state from $\langle \mathcal{V}, P \rangle$ to $\langle \mathcal{V}', P' \rangle$ while optionally outputting an *observable symbol* α. The absence of a symbol is denoted using ϵ. Most rules from Fig. 3 are standard—the special rules are the Havoc, Input, and Output rules.

1. Havoc: Statement $l : x := \mathsf{havoc}$ assigns x a non-deterministic value (say k) and outputs the observable $(tid, \mathsf{havoc}, k, x)$.
2. Input, Output: $l : x := \mathsf{input}(t)$ and $l : \mathsf{output}(t, e)$ read and write values to the channel t, and output $(tid, \mathsf{input}, k, t)$ and $(tid, \mathsf{output}, k, t)$, where k is the value read or written, respectively.

Intuitively, the observables record the sequence of non-deterministic guesses, as well as the input/output interaction with the tagged channels. In the following, e represents an expression and $e[v/\mathcal{V}[v]]$ evaluates an expression by replacing all variables v with their values in $\mathcal{V}$.

$$\frac{e[v/\mathcal{V}[v]] = k}{\langle \mathcal{V}, l: x := e\rangle \xrightarrow{\epsilon} \langle \mathcal{V}[x := k], \mathsf{skip}\rangle}\textsc{Assign} \qquad \frac{k \in \mathbb{N} \quad \alpha = (tid, \mathsf{havoc}, k, x)}{\langle \mathcal{V}, l: x := \mathsf{havoc}\rangle \xrightarrow{\alpha} \langle \mathcal{V}[x := k], \mathsf{skip}\rangle}\textsc{Havoc}$$

$$\frac{e[v/\mathcal{V}[v]] = \mathsf{false}}{\langle \mathcal{V}, l: \mathsf{while}(e)\ s\rangle \xrightarrow{\epsilon} \langle \mathcal{V}, \mathsf{skip}\rangle}\textsc{While1} \qquad \frac{e[v/\mathcal{V}[v]] = \mathsf{true}}{\langle \mathcal{V}, l: \mathsf{while}(e)\ s\rangle \xrightarrow{\epsilon} \langle \mathcal{V}, s; \mathsf{while}(e)\ s\rangle}\textsc{While2}$$

$$\frac{e[v/\mathcal{V}[v]] = \mathsf{true}}{\langle \mathcal{V}, l: \mathsf{if}\ e\ \mathsf{then}\ s_1\ \mathsf{else}\ s_2\rangle \xrightarrow{\epsilon} \langle \mathcal{V}, s_1\rangle}\textsc{If1} \qquad \frac{e[v/\mathcal{V}[v]] = \mathsf{false}}{\langle \mathcal{V}, l: \mathsf{if}\ e\ \mathsf{then}\ s_1\ \mathsf{else}\ s_2\rangle \xrightarrow{\epsilon} \langle \mathcal{V}, s_2\rangle}\textsc{If2}$$

$$\frac{\langle \mathcal{V}, s_1\rangle \xrightarrow{\alpha} \langle \mathcal{V}', s_1'\rangle}{\langle \mathcal{V}, l: s_1; s_2\rangle \xrightarrow{\alpha} \langle \mathcal{V}', s_1'; s_2\rangle}\textsc{Sequence} \qquad \frac{k \in \mathbb{N} \quad \alpha = (tid, \mathsf{input}, k, t)}{\langle \mathcal{V}, l: x := \mathsf{input}(t)\rangle \xrightarrow{\alpha} \langle \mathcal{V}[x := k], \mathsf{skip}\rangle}\textsc{Input}$$

$$\frac{}{\langle \mathcal{V}, l: \mathsf{skip}; s_2\rangle \xrightarrow{\epsilon} \langle \mathcal{V}, s_2\rangle}\textsc{Skip} \qquad \frac{e[v/\mathcal{V}[v]] = k \quad \alpha = (tid, \mathsf{output}, k, t)}{\langle \mathcal{V}, l: \mathsf{output}(t, e)\rangle \xrightarrow{\alpha} \langle \mathcal{V}, \mathsf{skip}\rangle}\textsc{Output}$$

Fig. 3. Single thread semantics of $\mathcal{W}$

Non-Preemptive Semantics. The non-preemptive semantics of $\mathcal{W}$ is presented in the full version [18]. The non-preemptive semantics ensures that a single thread from the program keeps executing as detailed above until one of the following occurs: (a) the thread finishes execution, or it encounters (b) a yield statement, or (c) a lock statement and the lock is taken, or (d) an await statement and the condition variable is not set. In these cases, a context-switch is possible.

Preemptive Semantics. The preemptive semantics of a program is obtained from the non-preemptive semantics by relaxing the condition on context-switches, and allowing context-switches at all program points (see full version [18]).

3.1 Problem Statement

A *non-preemptive observation sequence* of a program $\mathcal{C}$ is a sequence $\alpha_0 \dots \alpha_k$ if there exist program states S_0^{pre}, S_0^{post}, ..., S_k^{pre}, S_k^{post} such that according to the non-preemptive semantics of $\mathcal{W}$, we have: (a) for each $0 \le i \le k$, $\langle S_i^{pre} \rangle \xrightarrow{\alpha_i} \langle S_i^{post} \rangle$, (b) for each $0 \le i < k$, $\langle S_i^{post} \rangle \xrightarrow{\epsilon}{}^* \langle S_{i+1}^{pre} \rangle$, and (c) for the initial state S_ι and a final state (i.e., where all threads have finished execution) S_f, $\langle S_\iota \rangle \xrightarrow{\epsilon}{}^* \langle S_0^{pre} \rangle$ and $\langle S_k^{post} \rangle \xrightarrow{\epsilon}{}^* \langle S_f \rangle$. Similarly, a *preemptive observation sequence* of a program $\mathcal{C}$ is a sequence $\alpha_0 \dots \alpha_k$ as above, with the non-preemptive semantics replaced with preemptive semantics. We denote the sets of non-preemptive and preemptive observation sequences of a program $\mathcal{C}$ by $[\![\mathcal{C}]\!]^{NP}$ and $[\![\mathcal{C}]\!]^{P}$, respectively.

We say that observation sequences $\alpha_0 \dots \alpha_k$ and $\beta_0 \dots \beta_k$ are *equivalent* if:

- The subsequences of $\alpha_0 \dots \alpha_k$ and $\beta_0 \dots \beta_k$ containing only symbols of the form $(tid, \mathsf{Input}, k, t)$ and $(tid, \mathsf{Output}, k, t)$ are equal, and
- For each thread identifier *tid*, the subsequences of $\alpha_0 \dots \alpha_k$ and $\beta_0 \dots \beta_k$ containing only symbols of the form $(tid, \mathsf{Havoc}, k, x)$ are equal.

Intuitively, observable sequences are equivalent if they have the same interaction with the interface, and the same non-deterministic choices in each thread. For sets of observable sequences $\mathcal{O}_1$ and $\mathcal{O}_2$, we write $\mathcal{O}_1 \subseteq \mathcal{O}_2$ to denote that each sequence in $\mathcal{O}_1$ has an equivalent sequence in $\mathcal{O}_2$. Given a concurrent program $\mathcal{C}$ and a synthesized program $\mathcal{C}'$ obtained by adding synchronization to $\mathcal{C}$, the program $\mathcal{C}'$ is *preemption-safe* w.r.t. $\mathcal{C}$ if $[\![\mathcal{C}']\!]^{P} \subseteq [\![\mathcal{C}]\!]^{NP}$.

We are now ready to state our synthesis problem. Given a concurrent program $\mathcal{C}$, the aim is to synthesize a program $\mathcal{C}'$, by adding synchronization to $\mathcal{C}$, such that $\mathcal{C}'$ is preemption-safe w.r.t. $\mathcal{C}$.

3.2 Language Inclusion Modulo an Independence Relation

We reduce the problem of checking if a synthesized solution is preemption-safe w.r.t. the original program to an automata-theoretic problem.

Abstract Semantics for $\mathcal{W}$. We first define a single-thread abstract semantics for $\mathcal{W}$ (Fig. 4), which tracks types of accesses (read or write) to each memory location while abstracting away their values. Inputs/outputs to an external interface are modeled as writes to a special memory location (`dev`). Even inputs are modeled as writes because in our applications we cannot assume that reads from the external interface are free of side-effects. Havocs become ordinary writes to the variable they are assigned to. Every branch is taken non-deterministically and tracked. The only constructs preserved are the lock and condition variables. The abstract program state consists of the valuations of the lock and condition variables and the statement that remains to be executed. In the abstraction, an observable is of the form $(tid, \{\mathsf{read}, \mathsf{write}, \mathsf{exit}, \mathsf{loop}, \mathsf{then}, \mathsf{else}\}, v, l)$ and observes the type of access (read/write) to variable v and records non-deterministic branching choices (exit/loop/then/else). The latter are not associated with any variable.

In Fig. 4, given expression e, the function $Reads(tid, e, l)$ represents the sequence $(tid, \mathsf{read}, v_1, l) \cdot \ldots \cdot (tid, \mathsf{read}, v_n, l)$ where $v_1, \ldots, v_n$ are the variables in e, in the order they are read to evaluate e.

$$\frac{\alpha = Reads(tid,e,l)\cdot(tid,\mathsf{write},x,l)}{\langle\mathcal{V}, l:\ x := \mathsf{e}\rangle \xrightarrow{\alpha} \langle\mathcal{V},\mathsf{skip}\rangle}\textsc{Assign} \qquad \frac{\alpha = (tid,\mathsf{write},x,l)}{\langle\mathcal{V}, l:\ x := \mathsf{havoc}\rangle \xrightarrow{\alpha} \langle\mathcal{V},\mathsf{skip}\rangle}\textsc{Havoc}$$

$$\frac{\alpha = Reads(tid,e,l)\cdot(tid,\mathsf{exit},\_,l)}{\langle\mathcal{V}, l:\ \mathsf{while}(e)\ s\rangle \xrightarrow{\alpha} \langle\mathcal{V},\mathsf{skip}\rangle}\textsc{While1} \qquad \frac{\alpha = Reads(tid,e,l)\cdot(tid,\mathsf{loop},\_,l)}{\langle\mathcal{V}, l:\ \mathsf{while}(e)\ s\rangle \xrightarrow{\alpha} \langle\mathcal{V},s;\mathsf{while}(e)\ s\rangle}\textsc{While2}$$

$$\frac{\alpha = Reads(tid,e,l)\cdot(tid,\mathsf{then},\_,l)}{\langle\mathcal{V}, l:\ \mathsf{if}\ e\ \mathsf{then}\ s_1\ \mathsf{else}\ s_2\rangle \xrightarrow{\alpha} \langle\mathcal{V},s_1\rangle}\textsc{If1} \qquad \frac{\alpha = Reads(tid,e,l)\cdot(tid,\mathsf{else},\_,l)}{\langle\mathcal{V}, l:\ \mathsf{if}\ e\ \mathsf{then}\ s_1\ \mathsf{else}\ s_2\rangle \xrightarrow{\alpha} \langle\mathcal{V},s_2\rangle}\textsc{If2}$$

$$\frac{\langle\mathcal{V},s_1\rangle \xrightarrow{\alpha} \langle\mathcal{V}',s_1'\rangle}{\langle\mathcal{V}, l:\ s_1;s_2\rangle \xrightarrow{\alpha} \langle\mathcal{V}',s_1';s_2\rangle}\textsc{Sequence} \qquad \frac{\alpha = (tid,\mathsf{write},\mathsf{dev},l)\cdot(tid,\mathsf{write},x,l)}{\langle l:\ x := \mathsf{input}(t)\rangle \xrightarrow{\alpha} \langle\mathsf{skip}\rangle}\textsc{Input}$$

$$\frac{}{\langle\mathcal{V}, l:\ \mathsf{skip};s_2\rangle \xrightarrow{\epsilon} \langle\mathcal{V},s_2\rangle}\textsc{Skip} \qquad \frac{\alpha = Reads(tid,e,l)\cdot(tid,\mathsf{write},\mathsf{dev},l)}{\langle\mathcal{V}, l:\ \mathsf{output}(t,e)\rangle \xrightarrow{\alpha} \langle\mathcal{V},\mathsf{skip}\rangle}\textsc{Output}$$

Fig. 4. Single thread abstract semantics of $\mathcal{W}$

The abstract program semantics is the same as the concrete program semantics where the single thread semantics is replaced by the abstract single thread semantics. Locks and conditionals and operations on them are not abstracted.

As with the concrete semantics of $\mathcal{W}$, we can define the non-preemptive and preemptive observable sequences for abstract semantics. For a concurrent program $\mathcal{C}$, we denote the sets of abstract preemptive and non-preemptive observable sequences by $[\![\mathcal{C}]\!]^P_{abs}$ and $[\![\mathcal{C}]\!]^{NP}_{abs}$, respectively.

Abstract observation sequences $\alpha_0 \ldots \alpha_k$ and $\beta_0 \ldots \beta_k$ are *equivalent* if:

- For each thread tid, the subsequences of $\alpha_0 \ldots \alpha_k$ and $\beta_0 \ldots \beta_k$ containing only symbols of the form (tid, a, v, l), with $a \in \{\mathsf{read}, \mathsf{write}, \mathsf{exit}, \mathsf{loop}, \mathsf{then}, \mathsf{else}\}$ are equal,
- For each variable v, the subsequences of $\alpha_0 \ldots \alpha_k$ and $\beta_0 \ldots \beta_k$ containing only write symbols (of the form $(tid, \mathsf{write}, v, l)$) are equal, and
- For each variable v, the multisets of symbols of the form $(tid, \mathsf{read}, v, l)$ between any two write symbols, as well as before the first write symbol and after the last write symbol are identical.

We first show that the abstract semantics is sound w.r.t. preemption-safety (see full version for the proof [18]).

Theorem 1. *Given concurrent program $\mathcal{C}$ and a synthesized program $\mathcal{C}'$ obtained by adding synchronization to $\mathcal{C}$, $[\![\mathcal{C}']\!]^{P}_{abs} \subseteq [\![\mathcal{C}]\!]^{NP}_{abs} \Rightarrow [\![\mathcal{C}']\!]^{P} \subseteq [\![\mathcal{C}]\!]^{NP}$.*

Abstract Semantics to Automata. An NFA $\mathcal{A}$ is a tuple $(Q, \Sigma, \Delta, Q_\iota, F)$ where Σ is a finite alphabet, Q, Q_ι, F are finite sets of states, initial states and final states, respectively and Δ is a set of transitions. A word $\sigma_0 \ldots \sigma_k \in \Sigma^*$ is *accepted* by $\mathcal{A}$ if there exists a sequence of states $q_0 \ldots q_{k+1}$ such that $q_0 \in Q_\iota$ and $q_{k+1} \in F$ and $\forall i : (q_i, \sigma_i, q_{i+1}) \in \Delta$. The set of all words accepted by $\mathcal{A}$ is called the language of $\mathcal{A}$ and is denoted $\mathcal{L}(\mathcal{A})$.

Given a program $\mathcal{C}$, we can construct automata $\mathcal{A}([\![\mathcal{C}]\!]^{\mathcal{NP}}_{\dashv\lfloor\int})$ and $\mathcal{A}([\![\mathcal{C}]\!]^{\mathcal{P}}_{\dashv\lfloor\int})$ that accept exactly the observable sequences under the respective semantics. We describe their construction informally. Each automaton state is a program state of the abstract semantics and the alphabet is the set of abstract observable symbols. There is a transition from one state to another on an observable symbol (or an ϵ) iff the program can execute one step under the corresponding semantics to reach the other state while outputting the observable symbol (on an ϵ).

Language Inclusion Modulo an Independence Relation. Let I be a non-reflexive, symmetric binary relation over an alphabet Σ. We refer to I as the *independence relation* and to elements of I as *independent* symbol pairs. We define a symmetric binary relation $\approx$ over words in Σ^*: for all words $\sigma, \sigma' \in \Sigma^*$ and $(\alpha, \beta) \in I$, $(\sigma \cdot \alpha\beta \cdot \sigma', \sigma \cdot \beta\alpha \cdot \sigma') \in \approx$. Let $\approx^t$ denote the reflexive transitive closure of $\approx$.[1] Given a language $\mathcal{L}$ over Σ, the closure of $\mathcal{L}$ w.r.t. I, denoted $\mathrm{Clo}_I(\mathcal{L})$, is the set $\{\sigma \in \Sigma^* \colon \exists \sigma' \in \mathcal{L} \text{ with } (\sigma, \sigma') \in \approx^t\}$. Thus, $\mathrm{Clo}_I(\mathcal{L})$ consists of all words that can be obtained from some word in $\mathcal{L}$ by repeatedly commuting adjacent independent symbol pairs from I.

Definition 1. (Language Inclusion Modulo an Independence Relation). *Given NFAs A, B over a common alphabet Σ and an independence relation I over Σ, the language inclusion problem modulo I is: $\mathcal{L}(A) \subseteq \mathrm{Clo}_I(\mathcal{L}(B))$?*

We reduce preemption-safety under the abstract semantics to language inclusion modulo an independence relation. The independence relation I we use is defined on the set of abstract observable symbols as follows: $((tid, a, v, l), (tid', a', v', l')) \in I$ iff $tid \neq tid'$, and one of the following holds: (a) $v \neq v'$ or (b) $a \neq \mathsf{write} \wedge a' \neq \mathsf{write}$.

Proposition 1. *Given concurrent programs $\mathcal{C}$ and $\mathcal{C}'$, $[\![\mathcal{C}']\!]^{P}_{abs} \subseteq [\![\mathcal{C}]\!]^{NP}_{abs}$ iff $\mathcal{L}(\mathcal{A}([\![\mathcal{C}']\!]^{\mathcal{P}}_{\dashv\lfloor\int})) \subseteq \mathrm{Clo}_{\mathcal{I}}(\mathcal{L}(\mathcal{A}([\![\mathcal{C}]\!]^{\mathcal{NP}}_{\dashv\lfloor\int})))$.*

4 Checking Language Inclusion

We first focus on the problem of language inclusion modulo an independence relation (Definition 1). This question corresponds to preemption-safety (Theorem. 1, Proposition 1) and its solution drives our synchronization synthesis (Sect. 5).

[1] The equivalence classes of $\approx^t$ are Mazurkiewicz traces.

Theorem 2. *For NFAs A, B over alphabet Σ and an independence relation $I \subseteq \Sigma \times \Sigma$, $\mathcal{L}(A) \subseteq \mathrm{Clo}_I(\mathcal{L}(B))$ is undecidable [2].*

Fortunately, a bounded version of the problem is decidable. Recall the relation $\approx$ over Σ^* from Sect. 3.2. We define a symmetric binary relation $\approx_i$ over Σ^*: $(\sigma, \sigma') \in \approx_i$ iff $\exists(\alpha, \beta) \in I$: $(\sigma, \sigma') \in \approx, \sigma[i] = \sigma'[i{+}1] = \alpha$ and $\sigma[i{+}1] = \sigma'[i] = \beta$. Thus $\approx^i$ consists of all words that can be optained from each other by commuting the symbols at positions i and $i+1$. We next define a symmetric binary relation $\asymp$ over Σ^*: $(\sigma, \sigma') \in \asymp$ iff $\exists \sigma_1, \ldots, \sigma_t$: $(\sigma, \sigma_1) \in \approx_{i_1}, \ldots, (\sigma_t, \sigma') \in \approx_{i_{t+1}}$ and $i_1 < \ldots < i_{t+1}$. The relation $\asymp$ intuitively consists of words obtained from each other by making a single forward pass commuting multiple pairs of adjacent symbols. Let $\asymp^k$ denote the k-composition of $\asymp$ with itself. Given a language $\mathcal{L}$ over Σ, we use $\mathrm{Clo}_{k,I}(\mathcal{L})$ to denote the set $\{\sigma \in \Sigma^* : \exists \sigma' \in \mathcal{L}$ with $(\sigma, \sigma') \in \asymp^k\}$. In other words, $\mathrm{Clo}_{k,I}(\mathcal{L})$ consists of all words which can be generated from $\mathcal{L}$ using a finite-state transducer that remembers at most k symbols of its input words in its states.

Definition 2. (Bounded Language Inclusion Modulo an Independence Relation). *Given NFAs A, B over Σ, $I \subseteq \Sigma \times \Sigma$ and a constant $k > 0$, the k-bounded language inclusion problem modulo I is: $\mathcal{L}(A) \subseteq \mathrm{Clo}_{k,I}(\mathcal{L}(B))$?*

Theorem 3. *For NFAs A, B over Σ, $I \subseteq \Sigma \times \Sigma$ and a constant $k > 0$, $\mathcal{L}(A) \subseteq \mathrm{Clo}_{k,I}(\mathcal{L}(B))$ is decidable.*

We present an algorithm to check k-bounded language inclusion modulo I, based on the antichain algorithm for standard language inclusion [9].

Antichain Algorithm for Language Inclusion. Given a partial order $(X, \sqsubseteq)$, an antichain over X is a set of elements of X that are incomparable w.r.t. $\sqsubseteq$. In order to check $\mathcal{L}(A) \subseteq \mathrm{Clo}_I(\mathcal{L}(B))$ for NFAs $A = (Q_A, \Sigma, \Delta_A, Q_{\iota,A}, F_A)$ and $B = (Q_B, \Sigma, \Delta_B, Q_{\iota,B}, F_B)$, the antichain algorithm proceeds by exploring A and B in lockstep. While A is explored nondeterministically, B is determinized on the fly for exploration. The algorithm maintains an antichain, consisting of tuples of the form (s_A, S_B), where $s_A \in Q_A$ and $S_B \subseteq Q_B$. The ordering relation $\sqsubseteq$ is given by $(s_A, S_B) \sqsubseteq (s'_A, S'_B)$ iff $s_A = s'_A$ and $S_B \subseteq S'_B$. The algorithm also maintains a *frontier* set of tuples *yet* to be explored.

Given state $s_A \in Q_A$ and a symbol $\alpha \in \Sigma$, let $succ_\alpha(s_A)$ denote $\{s'_A \in Q_A : (s_A, \alpha, s'_A) \in \Delta_A\}$. Given set of states $S_B \subseteq Q_B$, let $succ_\alpha(S_B)$ denote $\{s'_B \in Q_B : \exists s_B \in S_B :\ (s_B, \alpha, s'_B) \in \Delta_B\}$. Given tuple (s_A, S_B) in the frontier set, let $succ_\alpha(s_A, S_B)$ denote $\{(s'_A, S'_B) : s'_A \in succ_\alpha(s_A), S'_B = succ_\alpha(s_B)\}$.

In each step, the antichain algorithm explores A and B by computing α-successors of all tuples in its current frontier set for all possible symbols $\alpha \in \Sigma$. Whenever a tuple (s_A, S_B) is found with $s_A \in F_A$ and $S_B \cap F_B = \varnothing$, the algorithm reports a counterexample to language inclusion. Otherwise, the algorithm updates its frontier set and antichain to include the newly computed successors using the two rules enumerated below. Given a newly computed successor tuple p':

- Rule 1: if there exists a tuple p in the antichain with $p \sqsubseteq p'$, then p' is not added to the frontier set or antichain,
- Rule 2: else, if there exist tuples $p_1, \ldots, p_n$ in the antichain with $p' \sqsubseteq p_1, \ldots, p_n$, then $p_1, \ldots, p_n$ are removed from the antichain.

The algorithm terminates by either reporting a counterexample, or by declaring success when the frontier becomes empty.

Antichain Algorithm for k-Bounded Language Inclusion modulo I. This algorithm is essentially the same as the standard antichain algorithm, with the automaton B above replaced by an automaton $B_{k,I}$ accepting $\mathrm{Clo}_{k,I}(\mathcal{L}(\mathrm{B}))$. The set $Q_{B_{k,I}}$ of states of $B_{k,I}$ consists of triples (s_B, η_1, η_2), where $s_B \in Q_B$ and η_1, η_2 are k-length words over Σ. Intuitively, the words η_1 and η_2 store symbols that are expected to be matched later along a run. The set of initial states of $B_{k,I}$ is $\{(s_B, \varnothing, \varnothing) : s_B \in I_B\}$. The set of final states of $B_{k,I}$ is $\{(s_B, \varnothing, \varnothing) : s_B \in F_B\}$. The transition relation $\Delta_{B_{k,I}}$ is constructed by repeatedly applying the following rules, in order, for each state (s_B, η_1, η_2) and each symbol α. In what follows, $\eta[\backslash i]$ denotes the word obtained from η by removing its ith symbol.

1. Pick *new* s'_B and $\beta \in \Sigma$ such that $(s_B, \beta, s'_B) \in \Delta_B$
2. (a) If $\forall i$: $\eta_1[i] \neq \alpha$ and α is independent of all symbols in η_1, $\eta'_2 := \eta_2 \cdot \alpha$ and $\eta'_1 := \eta_1$, (b) else, if $\exists i$: $\eta_1[i] = \alpha$ and α is independent of all symbols in η_1 prior to i, $\eta'_1 := \eta_1[\backslash i]$ and $\eta'_2 := \eta_2$ (c) else, go to 1
3. (a) If $\forall i$: $\eta'_2[i] \neq \beta$ and β is independent of all symbols in η'_2, $\eta'_1 := \eta'_1 \cdot \beta$, (b) else, if $\exists i$: $\eta'_2[i] = \beta$ and β is independent of all symbols in η'_2 prior to i, $\eta'_2 := \eta'_2[\backslash i]$ (c) else, go to 1
4. Add $((s_B, \eta_1, \eta_2), \alpha, (s'_B, \eta'_1, \eta'_2))$ to $\Delta_{B_{k,I}}$ and go to 1.

Example 1. In Fig. 5, we have an NFA B with $\mathcal{L}(\mathrm{B}) = \{\alpha\beta, \beta\}$, $I = \{(\alpha, \beta)\}$ and $k = 1$. The states of $B_{k,I}$ are triples (q, η_1, η_2), where $q \in Q_B$ and $\eta_1, \eta_2 \in \{\varnothing, \alpha, \beta\}$. We explain the derivation of a couple of transitions of $B_{k,I}$. The transition shown in bold from $(q_0, \varnothing, \varnothing)$ on symbol β is obtained by applying the following rules once: 1. Pick q_1 since $(q_0, \alpha, q_1) \in \Delta_B$. 2(a). $\eta'_2 := \beta$, $\eta'_1 := \varnothing$. 3(a). $\eta'_1 := \alpha$. 4. Add $((q_0, \varnothing, \varnothing), \beta, (q_1, \alpha, \beta))$ to $\Delta_{B_{k,I}}$. The transition shown in bold from (q_1, α, β) on symbol α is obtained as follows: 1. Pick q_2 since $(q_1, \beta, q_2) \in \Delta_B$. 2(b). $\eta'_1 := \varnothing$, $\eta'_2 := \beta$. 3(b). $\eta'_2 := \varnothing$. 4. Add $((q_1, \alpha, \beta), \beta, (q_2, \varnothing, \varnothing))$ to $\Delta_{B_{k,I}}$. It can be seen that $B_{k,I}$ accepts the language $\{\alpha\beta, \beta\alpha, \beta\} = \mathrm{Clo}_{k,I}(B)$.

Proposition 2. *Given $k > 0$, NFA $B_{k,I}$ described above accepts* $\mathrm{Clo}_{k,I}(\mathcal{L}(B))$.

We develop a procedure to check language inclusion modulo I by iteratively increasing the bound k (see the full version [18] for the complete algorithm). The procedure is *incremental*: the check for $k+1$-bounded language inclusion modulo I only explores paths along which the bound k was exceeded in the previous iteration.

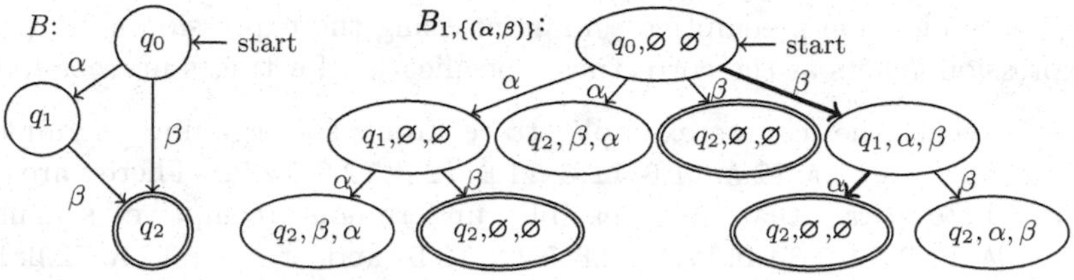

Fig. 5. Example for illustrating construction of $B_{k,I}$ for $k = 1$ and $I = \{(\alpha, \beta)\}$.

5 Synchronization Synthesis

We now present our iterative synchronization synthesis procedure, which is based on the procedure in [11]. The reader is referred to [11] for further details. The synthesis procedure starts with the original program $\mathcal{C}$ and in each iteration generates a candidate synthesized program $\mathcal{C}'$. The candidate $\mathcal{C}'$ is checked for preemption-safety w.r.t. $\mathcal{C}$ under the abstract semantics, using our procedure for bounded language inclusion modulo I. If $\mathcal{C}'$ is found preemption-safe w.r.t. $\mathcal{C}$ under the abstract semantics, the synthesis procedure outputs $\mathcal{C}'$. Otherwise, an abstract counterexample *cex* is obtained. The counterexample is analyzed to infer additional synchronization to be added to $\mathcal{C}'$ for generating a new synthesized candidate.

The counterexample trace *cex* is a sequence of event identifiers: $tid_0.l_0; \ldots ; tid_n.l_n$, where each l_i is a location identifier. We first analyze the *neighborhood* of *cex*, denoted *nhood*(*cex*), consisting of traces that are permutations of the events in *cex*. Note that each trace corresponds to an abstract observation sequence. Furthermore, note that preemption-safety requires the abstract observation sequence of any trace in *nhood*(*cex*) to be equivalent to that of some trace in *nhood*(*cex*) feasible under non-preemptive semantics. Let *bad traces* refer to the traces in *nhood*(*cex*) that are feasible under preemptive semantics and do not meet the preemption-safety requirement. The goal of our counterexample analysis is to characterize all bad traces in *nhood*(*cex*) in order to enable inference of synchronization fixes.

In order to succinctly represent subsets of *nhood*(*cex*), we use *ordering constraints.* Intuitively, ordering constraints are of the following forms: (a) atomic constraints $\Phi = A < B$ where A and B are events from *cex*. The constraint $A < B$ represents the set of traces in *nhood*(*cex*) where event A is scheduled before event B; (b) Boolean combinations of atomic constraints $\Phi_1 \wedge \Phi_2$, $\Phi_1 \vee \Phi_2$ and $\neg\Phi_1$. We have that $\Phi_1 \wedge \Phi_2$ and $\Phi_1 \vee \Phi_2$ respectively represent the intersection and union of the set of traces represented by Φ_1 and Φ_2, and that $\neg\Phi_1$ represents the complement (with respect to *nhood*(*cex*)) of the traces represented by Φ_1.

Non-preemptive Neighborhood. First, we generate all traces in *nhood*(*cex*) that are feasible under non-preemptive semantics. We represent a single trace π using an ordering constraint Φ_π that captures the ordering between non-independent accesses to variables in π. We represent all traces in *nhood*(*cex*) that are feasible under non-preemptive semantics using the expression $\Phi = \bigvee_\pi \Phi_\pi$. The expression Φ acts as the correctness specification for traces in *nhood*(*cex*).

Example. Recall the counterexample trace from the running example in Sect. 2: $cex = \texttt{T1.A;T2.A;T1.B;T1.C;T1.D;T2.B;T2.C;T2.D}$. There are two trace in *nhood*(*cex*) that are feasible under non-preemptive semantics: $\pi_1 = \texttt{T1.A;T1.B;T1.C;T1.D;T2.A;T2.B;T2.C;T2.D}$ and $\pi_2 = \texttt{T2.A;T2.B;T2.C;}$ $T2.D; T1.A; T1.B; T1.C; T1.D$. We represent π_1 as $\Phi(\pi_1) = \{\texttt{T1.A}, \texttt{T1.C}, \texttt{T1.D}\} < \texttt{T2.D} \wedge \texttt{T1.D} < \{\texttt{T2.A}, \texttt{T2.C}, \texttt{T2.D}\} \wedge \texttt{T1.B} < \texttt{T2.B}$ and π_2 as $\Phi(\pi_2) = \texttt{T2.D} < \{\texttt{T1.A}, \texttt{T1.C}, \texttt{T1.D}\} \wedge \{\texttt{T2.A}, \texttt{T2.C}, \texttt{T2.D}\} < \texttt{T1.D} \wedge \texttt{T2.B} < \texttt{T1.B}$. The correctness specification is $\Phi = \Phi(\pi_1) \vee \Phi(\pi_2)$.

Counterexample Generalization. We next build a quantifier-free first order formula Ψ over the event identifiers in *cex* such that any model of Ψ corresponds to a bad trace in *nhood*(*cex*). We iteratively enumerate models π of Ψ, building a constraint $\rho = \Phi(\pi)$ for each model π, and generalizing each ρ into ρ_g to represent a larger set of bad traces.

Example. Our trace *cex* from Sect. 2 would be generalized to $\texttt{T2.A} < \texttt{T1.D} \wedge \texttt{T1.D} < \texttt{T2.D}$. Any trace that fulfills this constraint is bad.

Inferring Fixes. From each generalized formula ρ_g described above, we infer possible synchronization fixes to eliminate all bad traces satisfying ρ_g. The key observation we exploit is that common concurrency bugs often show up in our formulas as simple patterns of ordering constraints between events. For example, the pattern $tid_1.l_1 < tid_2.l_2 \wedge tid_2.l'_2 < tid_1.l'_1$ indicates an atomicity violation and can be rewritten into $\texttt{lock}(tid_1.[l_1 : l'_1], tid_2.[l_2 : l'_2])$. The complete list of such rewrite rules is in the full version [18]. This list includes inference of locks and reordering of notify statements. The set of patterns we use for synchronization inference are not complete, i.e., there might be generalized formulae ρ_g that are not matched by any pattern. In practice, we found our current set of patterns to be adequate for most common concurrency bugs, including all bugs from the benchmarks in this paper. Our technique and tool can be easily extended with new patterns.

Example. The generalized constraint $\texttt{T2.A} < \texttt{T1.D} \wedge \texttt{T1.D} < \texttt{T2.D}$ matches the lock rule and yields $\texttt{lock}(\texttt{T2.[A : D]}, \texttt{T1.[D : D]})$. Since the lock involves events in the same function, the lock is merged into a single lock around instructions `A` and `D` in `open_dev_abs`. This lock is not sufficient to make the program preemption-safe. Another iteration of the synthesis procedure generates another counterexample for analysis and synchronization inference.

Proposition 3. *If our synthesis procedure generates a program* $\mathcal{C}'$*, then* $\mathcal{C}'$ *is preemption-safe with respect to* $\mathcal{C}$*.*

Note that our procedure does not guarantee that the synthesized program $\mathcal{C}'$ is deadlock-free. However, we avoid obvious deadlocks using heursitics such as merging overlapping locks. Further, our tool supports detection of any additional deadlocks introduced by synthesis, but relies on the user to fix them.

6 Implementation and Evaluation

We implemented our synthesis procedure in LISS. LISS is comprised of 5000 lines of C++ code and uses Clang/LLVM and Z3 as libraries. It is available as open-source software along with benchmarks at https://github.com/thorstent/Liss. The language inclusion algorithm is available separately as a library called LIMI (https://github.com/thorstent/Limi). LISS implements the synthesis method presented in this paper with several optimizations. For example, we take advantage of the fact that language inclusion violations can often be detected by exploring only a small fraction of the input automata by constructing $\mathcal{A}(\llbracket \mathcal{C} \rrbracket^{\mathcal{NP}}_{\dashv\lfloor f})$ and $\mathcal{A}(\llbracket \mathcal{C} \rrbracket^{\mathcal{P}}_{\dashv\lfloor f})$ on the fly.

Our prototype implementation has several limitations. First, LISS uses function inlining and therefore cannot handle recursive programs. Second, we do not implement any form of alias analysis, which can lead to unsound abstractions. For example, we abstract statements of the form "`*x = 0`" as writes to variable `x`, while in reality other variables can be affected due to pointer aliasing. We sidestep this issue by manually massaging input programs to eliminate aliasing.

Finally, LISS implements a simplistic lock insertion strategy. Inference rules (see Sect. 5) produce locks expressed as sets of instructions that should be inside a lock. Placing the actual lock and unlock instructions in the C code is challenging because the instructions in the trace may span several basic blocks or even functions. We follow a structural approach where we find the innermost common parent block for the first and last instructions of the lock and place the lock and unlock instruction there. This does not work if the code has gotos or returns that could cause control to jump over the unlock statement. At the moment, we simply report such situations to the user.

We evaluate our synthesis method against the following criteria: (1) Effectiveness of synthesis from implicit specifications; (2) Efficiency of the proposed synthesis procedure; (3) Precision of the proposed coarse abstraction scheme on real-world programs.

Implicit vs Explicit Synthesis. In order to evaluate the effectiveness of synthesis from implicit specifications, we apply LISS to the set of benchmarks used in our previous CONREPAIR tool for assertion-based synthesis [5]. In addition, we evaluate LISS and CONREPAIR on several *new* assertion-based benchmarks (Table 1). The set includes microbenchmarks modeling typical concurrency bug patterns in Linux drivers and the `usb-serial` macrobenchmark, which models a complete synchronization skeleton of the USB-to-serial adapter driver. We preprocess these benchmarks by eliminating assertions used as explicit specifications for synthesis. In addition, we replace statements of the form `assume(v)` with `await(v)`, redeclaring all variables `v` used in such statements as condition variables. This is necessary as our program syntax does not include `assume` statements.

We use LISS to synthesize a preemption-safe version of each benchmark. This method is based on the assumption that the benchmark is correct under non-preemptive scheduling and bugs can only arise due to preemptive scheduling.

Table 1. Experiments

Name	LOC	Th	It	MB	BF(s)	Syn(s)	Ver(s)	CR(s)
ConRepair benchmarks [5]								
ex1.c	18	2	1	1	< 1s	< 1s	< 1s	< 1s
ex2.c	23	2	1	1	< 1s	< 1s	< 1s	< 1s
ex3.c	37	2	1	1	< 1s	< 1s	< 1s	< 1s
ex5.c	42	2	3	1	< 1s	< 1s	2s	< 1s
lc-rc.c	35	4	0	1	-	-	< 1s	9s
dv1394.c	37	2	1	1	< 1s	< 1s	< 1s	17s
em28xx.c	20	2	1	1	< 1s	< 1s	< 1s	< 1s
f_acm.c	80	3	1	1	< 1s	< 1s	< 1s	1871.99s
i915_irq.c	17	2	1	1	< 1s	< 1s	< 1s	2.6s
ipath.c	23	2	1	1	< 1s	< 1s	< 1s	12s
iwl3945.c	26	3	1	1	< 1s	< 1s	< 1s	5s
md.c	35	2	1	1	< 1s	< 1s	< 1s	1.5s
myri10ge.c	60	4	0	1	-	-	< 1s	1.5s
usb-serial.bug1.c	357	7	2	1	0.4s	3.1s	3.4s	∞^b
usb-serial.bug2.c	355	7	1	3	0.7s	2.1s	12.9s	3563s
usb-serial.bug3.c	352	7	1	4	3.8s	1.3s	111.1s	∞^b
usb-serial.bug4.c	351	7	1	4	93.9s	2.4s	123.1s	∞^b
usb-serial.c[a]	357	7	0	4	-	-	103.2s	1200s
CPMAC driver benchmark								
cpmac.bug1.c	1275	5	1	1	1.3s	113.4s	21.9s	-
cpmac.bug2.c	1275	5	1	1	3.3s	68.4s	27.8s	-
cpmac.bug3.c	1270	5	1	1	5.4s	111.3s	8.7s	-
cpmac.bug4.c	1276	5	2	1	2.4s	124.8s	31.5s	-
cpmac.bug5.c	1275	5	1	1	2.8s	112.0s	58.0s	-
cpmac.c[a]	1276	5	0	1	-	-	17.4s	-

Th=Threads, It=Iterations, MB=Max bound, BF=Bug finding, Syn=Synthesis, Ver=Verification, Cr=ConRepair [a]a bug-free example [b]timeout after 3 hours

We discovered two benchmarks (`lc-rc.c` and `myri10ge.c`) that violated this assumption, i.e., they contained race conditions that manifested under non-preemptive scheduling; Liss did not detect these race conditions. Liss was able to detect and fix all other known races without relying on assertions. Furthermore, Liss detected a new race in the `usb-serial` family of benchmarks, which was not detected by ConRepair due to a missing assertion. We compared the output of Liss with manually placed synchronization (taken from real bug fixes) and found that the two versions were similar in most of our examples.

Performance and Precision. ConRepair uses CBMC for verification and counterexample generation. Due to the coarse abstraction we use, both steps are much cheaper with Liss. For example, verification of `usb-serial.c`, which was the most complex in our set of benchmarks, took Liss 103 s, whereas it took ConRepair 20 min [5].

The loss of precision due to abstraction may cause the inclusion check to return a counterexample that is spurious in the concrete program, leading to unnecessary synchronization being synthesized. On our existing benchmarks, this only occurred once in the `usb-serial` driver, where abstracting away the return value of a function led to an infeasible trace. We refined the abstraction manually by introducing a condition variable to model the return value.

While this result is encouraging, synthetic benchmarks are not necessarily representative of real-world performance. We therefore implemented another set of benchmarks based on a complete Linux driver for the TI AR7 CPMAC Ethernet controller. The benchmark was constructed as follows. We manually preprocessed driver source code to eliminate pointer aliasing. We combined the driver with a model of the OS API and the software interface of the device written in C. We modeled most OS API functions as writes to a special memory location. Groups of unrelated functions were modeled using separate locations. Slightly more complex models were required for API functions that affect thread synchronization. For example, the `free_irq` function, which disables the driver's interrupt handler, blocks waiting for any outstanding interrupts to finish. Drivers can rely on this behavior to avoid races. We introduced a condition variable to model this synchronization. Similarly, most device accesses were modeled as writes to a special `ioval` variable. Thus, the only part of the device that required a more accurate model was its interrupt enabling logic, which affects the behavior of the driver's interrupt handler thread.

Our original model consisted of eight threads. Liss ran out of memory on this model, so we simplified it to five threads by eliminating parts of driver functionality. Nevertheless, we believe that the resulting model represents the most complex synchronization synthesis case study, based on real-world code, reported in the literature.

The CPMAC driver used in this case study did not contain any known concurrency bugs, so we artificially simulated five typical race conditions that commonly occur in drivers of this type [4]. Liss was able to detect and automatically fix each of these defects (bottom part of Table 1). We only encountered two program locations where manual abstraction refinement was necessary.

We conclude that (1) our coarse abstraction is highly precise in practice; (2) manual effort involved in synchronization synthesis can be further reduced via automatic abstraction refinement; (3) additional work is required to improve the performance of our method to be able to handle real-world systems without simplification. In particular, our analysis indicates that significant speed-up can be obtained by incorporating a partial order reduction scheme into the language inclusion algorithm.

7 Conclusion

We believe our approach and the encouraging experimental results open several directions for future research. Combining the abstraction refinement, verification (checking language inclusion modulo an independence relation), and synthesis (inserting synchronization) more tightly could bring improvements in efficiency. An additional direction we plan on exploring is automated handling of deadlocks, i.e., extending our technique to automatically synthesize deadlock-free programs. Finally, we plan to further develop our prototype tool and apply it to other domains of concurrent systems code.

References

1. Alglave, J., Kroening, D., Nimal, V., Poetzl, D.: Don't sit on the fence. In: Biere, A., Bloem, R. (eds.) CAV 2014. LNCS, vol. 8559, pp. 508–524. Springer, Heidelberg (2014)
2. Bertoni, A., Mauri, G., Sabadini, N.: Equivalence and membership problems for regular trace languages. In: Nielsen, M., Schmidt, E.M. (eds.) Automata, Languages and Programming. LNCS, pp. 61–71. Springer, Heidelberg (1982)
3. Bloem, R., Hofferek, G., Könighofer, B., Könighofer, R., Außerlechner, S., Spörk, R.: Synthesis of synchronization using uninterpreted functions. In: FMCAD, pp. 35–42 (2014)
4. Černý, P., Henzinger, T.A., Radhakrishna, A., Ryzhyk, L., Tarrach, T.: Efficient synthesis for concurrency by semantics-preserving transformations. In: Sharygina, N., Veith, H. (eds.) CAV 2013. LNCS, vol. 8044, pp. 951–967. Springer, Heidelberg (2013)
5. Černý, P., Henzinger, T.A., Radhakrishna, A., Ryzhyk, L., Tarrach, T.: Regression-free synthesis for concurrency. In: Biere, A., Bloem, R. (eds.) CAV 2014. LNCS, vol. 8559, pp. 568–584. Springer, Heidelberg (2014)
6. Cherem, S., Chilimbi, T., Gulwani, S.: Inferring locks for atomic sections. In: PLDI, pp. 304–315 (2008)
7. Clarke, E., Kroning, D., Lerda, F.: A tool for checking ANSI-C programs. In: Jensen, K., Podelski, A. (eds.) TACAS 2004. LNCS, vol. 2988, pp. 168–176. Springer, Heidelberg (2004)
8. Clarke, E.M., Emerson, E.A.: Design and Synthesis of Synchronization Skeletons Using Branching Time Temporal Logic. Springer, Heidelberg (1982)
9. De Wulf, M., Doyen, L., Henzinger, T.A., Raskin, J.-F.: Antichains: a new algorithm for checking universality of finite automata. In: Ball, T., Jones, R.B. (eds.) CAV 2006. LNCS, vol. 4144, pp. 17–30. Springer, Heidelberg (2006)
10. Deshmukh, J., Ramalingam, G., Ranganath, V.-P., Vaswani, K.: Logical concurrency control from sequential proofs. In: Gordon, A.D. (ed.) ESOP 2010. LNCS, vol. 6012, pp. 226–245. Springer, Heidelberg (2010)
11. Gupta, A., Henzinger, T., Radhakrishna, A., Samanta, R., Tarrach, T.: Succinct representation of concurrent trace sets. In: POPL15, pp. 433–444 (2015)
12. Jin, G., Zhang, W., Deng, D., Liblit, B., Lu, S.: Automated Concurrency-Bug Fixing. In: OSDI, pp. 221–236 (2012)
13. Ryzhyk, L., Chubb, P., Kuz, I., Heiser, G.: Dingo: Taming device drivers. In: Eurosys April 2009

14. Sadowski, C., Yi, J.: User evaluation of correctness conditions: A case study of cooperability. In: PLATEAU, pp. 2:1–2:6 (2010)
15. Solar-Lezama, A., Jones, C., Bodík, R.: Sketching concurrent data structures. In: PLDI, pp. 136–148 (2008)
16. Vechev, M., Yahav, E., Yorsh, G.: Abstraction-guided synthesis of synchronization. In: POPL, pp. 327–338 (2010)
17. Vechev, M., Yahav, E., Raman, R., Sarkar, V.: Automatic verification of determinism for structured parallel programs. In: Cousot, R., Martel, M. (eds.) SAS 2010. LNCS, vol. 6337, pp. 455–471. Springer, Heidelberg (2010)
18. From Non-preemptive to Preemptive Scheduling using Synchronization Synthesis (full version). http://arxiv.org/abs/1505.04533

Counterexample-Guided Quantifier Instantiation for Synthesis in SMT

Andrew Reynolds[1(✉)], Morgan Deters[2], Viktor Kuncak[1], Cesare Tinelli[3], and Clark Barrett[2]

[1] École Polytechnique Fédérale de Lausanne (EPFL), Lausanne, Switzerland
andrew.j.reynolds@gmail.com
[2] Department of Computer Science, New York University, New York, USA
[3] Department of Computer Science, The University of Iowa, Iowa City, USA

Abstract. We introduce the first program synthesis engine implemented inside an SMT solver. We present an approach that extracts solution functions from unsatisfiability proofs of the negated form of synthesis conjectures. We also discuss novel counterexample-guided techniques for quantifier instantiation that we use to make finding such proofs practically feasible. A particularly important class of specifications are single-invocation properties, for which we present a dedicated algorithm. To support syntax restrictions on generated solutions, our approach can transform a solution found without restrictions into the desired syntactic form. As an alternative, we show how to use evaluation function axioms to embed syntactic restrictions into constraints over algebraic datatypes, and then use an algebraic datatype decision procedure to drive synthesis. Our experimental evaluation on syntax-guided synthesis benchmarks shows that our implementation in the CVC4 SMT solver is competitive with state-of-the-art tools for synthesis.

1 Introduction

The synthesis of functions that meet a given specification is a long-standing fundamental goal that has received great attention recently. This functionality directly applies to the synthesis of functional programs [17,18] but also translates to imperative programs through techniques that include bounding input space, verification condition generation, and invariant discovery [28–30]. Function synthesis is also an important subtask in the synthesis of protocols and reactive systems, especially when these systems are infinite-state [3,27]. The SyGuS

This work is supported in part by the European Research Council (ERC) Project *Implicit Programming* and Swiss National Science Foundation Grant *Constraint Solving Infrastructure for Program Analysis*.

This paper is dedicated to the memory of Morgan Deters who died unexpectedly in Jan 2015.

D. Kroening and C.S. Păsăreanu (Eds.): CAV 2015, Part II, LNCS 9207, pp. 198–216, 2015.
DOI: 10.1007/978-3-319-21668-3_12

format and competition [1,2,22] inspired by the success of the SMT-LIB and SMT-COMP efforts [5], has significantly improved and simplified the process of rigorously comparing different solvers on synthesis problems.

Connection between synthesis and theorem proving was established already in early work on the subject [12, 20]. It is notable that early research [20] found that the capabilities of theorem provers were the main bottleneck for synthesis. Taking lessons from automated software verification, recent work on synthesis has made use of advances in theorem proving, particularly in SAT and SMT solvers. However, that work avoids formulating the overall synthesis task as a theorem proving problem directly. Instead, existing work typically builds custom loops outside of an SMT or SAT solver, often using numerous variants of counterexample-guided synthesis. A typical role of the SMT solver has been to validate candidate solutions and provide counterexamples that guide subsequent search, although approaches such as symbolic term exploration [15] also use an SMT solver to explore a representation of the space of solutions. In existing approaches, SMT solvers thus receive a large number of separate queries, with limited communication between these different steps.

Contributions. In this paper, we revisit the formulation of the overall synthesis task as a theorem proving problem. We observe that SMT solvers already have some of the key functionality for synthesis; we show how to improve existing algorithms and introduce new ones to make SMT-based synthesis competitive. Specifically, we do the following.

- We show how to formulate an important class of synthesis problems as the problem of disproving universally quantified formulas, and how to synthesize functions automatically from selected instances of these formulas.
- We present counterexample-guided techniques for quantifier instantiation, which are crucial to obtain competitive performance on synthesis tasks.
- We discuss techniques to simplify the synthesized functions, to help ensure that they are small and adhere to specified syntactic requirements.
- We show how to encode syntactic restrictions using theories of algebraic datatypes and axiomatizable evaluation functions.
- We show that for an important class of single-invocation properties, the synthesis of functions from relations, the implementation of our approach in CVC4 significantly outperforms leading tools from the SyGuS competition.

Preliminaries. Since synthesis involves finding (and so proving the existence) of functions, we use notions from many-sorted *second-order* logic to define the general problem. We fix a set $\mathbf{S}$ of *sort symbols* and an (infix) equality predicate $\approx$ of type $\sigma \times \sigma$ for each $\sigma \in \mathbf{S}$. For every non-empty sort sequence $\boldsymbol{\sigma} \in \mathbf{S}^+$ with $\boldsymbol{\sigma} = \sigma_1 \cdots \sigma_n \sigma$, we fix an infinite set $\mathbf{X}_{\boldsymbol{\sigma}}$ of *variables* $x^{\sigma_1 \cdots \sigma_n \sigma}$ *of type* $\sigma_1 \times \cdots \times \sigma_n \to \sigma$. For each sort σ we identity the type $() \to \sigma$ with σ and call it a *first-order type*. We assume the sets $\mathbf{X}_{\boldsymbol{\sigma}}$ are pairwise disjoint and let $\mathbf{X}$ be their union. A *signature* Σ consists of a set $\Sigma^{\mathrm{s}} \subseteq \mathbf{S}$ of sort symbols and a set Σ^{f} of *function symbols* $f^{\sigma_1 \cdots \sigma_n \sigma}$ *of type* $\sigma_1 \times \cdots \times \sigma_n \to \sigma$, where $n \geq 0$ and $\sigma_1, \ldots, \sigma_n, \sigma \in \Sigma^{\mathrm{s}}$. We drop the sort superscript from variables or function symbols when it is clear from context or unimportant. We assume that signatures always include a Boolean sort Bool and constants $\top$ and $\bot$ of type Bool (respectively, for true and false). Given a many-sorted signature Σ together with quantifiers and lambda abstraction, the notion of well-sorted (Σ-)term, atom, literal, clause, and formula with variables in $\mathbf{X}$ are defined as usual in second-order logic. All atoms have the form $s \approx t$. Having $\approx$ as the only predicate symbol causes no loss of generality since we can model other predicate symbols as function symbols with return sort Bool. We will, however, write just t in place of the atom $t \approx \top$, to simplify the notation. A Σ-term/formula is *ground* if it has no variables, it is *first-order* if it has only *first-order variables*, that is, variables of first-order type. When $\boldsymbol{x} = (x_1, \ldots, x_n)$ is a tuple of variables and Q is either $\forall$ or $\exists$, we write $Q\boldsymbol{x}\,\varphi$ as an abbreviation of $Qx_1 \cdots Qx_n\,\varphi$. If e is a Σ-term or formula and $\boldsymbol{x} = (x_1, \ldots, x_n)$ has no repeated variables, we write $e[\boldsymbol{x}]$ to denote that all of e's free variables are from $\boldsymbol{x}$; if $\boldsymbol{t} = (t_1, \ldots, t_n)$ is a term tuple, we write $e[\boldsymbol{t}]$ for the term or formula obtained from e by simultaneously replacing, for all $i = 1, \ldots, n$, every occurrence of x_i in e by t_i. A *Σ-interpretation* $\mathcal{I}$ maps: each $\sigma \in \Sigma^{\mathrm{s}}$ to a non-empty set $\sigma^{\mathcal{I}}$, the *domain* of σ in $\mathcal{I}$, with $\mathsf{Bool}^{\mathcal{I}} = \{\top, \bot\}$; each $u^{\sigma_1 \cdots \sigma_n \sigma} \in \mathbf{X} \cup \Sigma^{\mathrm{f}}$ to a total function $u^{\mathcal{I}} : \sigma_1^{\mathcal{I}} \times \cdots \times \sigma_n^{\mathcal{I}} \to \sigma^{\mathcal{I}}$ when $n > 0$ and to an element of $\sigma^{\mathcal{I}}$ when $n = 0$. The interpretation $\mathcal{I}$ induces as usual a mapping from terms t of sort σ to elements $t^{\mathcal{I}}$ of $\sigma^{\mathcal{I}}$. If $x_1, \ldots, x_n$ are variables and $v_1, \ldots, v_n$ are well-typed values for them, we denote by $\mathcal{I}[x_1 \mapsto v_1, \ldots, x_n \mapsto v_n]$ the Σ-interpretation that maps each x_i to v_i and is otherwise identical to $\mathcal{I}$. A satisfiability relation between Σ-interpretations and Σ-formulas is defined inductively as usual.

A *theory* is a pair $T = (\Sigma, \mathbf{I})$ where Σ is a signature and $\mathbf{I}$ is a non-empty class of Σ-interpretations, the *models* of T, that is closed under variable reassignment (i.e., every Σ-interpretation that differs from one in $\mathbf{I}$ only in how it interprets the variables is also in $\mathbf{I}$) and isomorphism. A Σ-formula $\varphi[\boldsymbol{x}]$ is *T-satisfiable* (resp., *T-unsatisfiable*) if it is satisfied by some (resp., no) interpretation in $\mathbf{I}$. A satisfying interpretation for φ *models (or is a model of)* φ. A formula φ is *T-valid*, written $\models_T \varphi$, if every model of T is a model of φ. Given a fragment $\mathbf{L}$ of the language of Σ-formulas, a Σ-theory T is *satisfaction complete with respect to* $\mathbf{L}$ if every T-satisfiable formula of $\mathbf{L}$ is T-valid. In this paper we will consider only theories that are satisfaction complete wrt the formulas we are interested in. Most theories used in SMT (in particular, all theories of a specific structure such various theories of the integers, reals, strings, algebraic datatypes, bit vectors, and so on) are satisfaction complete with respect to the class of closed first-order Σ-formulas. Other theories, such as the theory of arrays, are satisfaction complete only with respect to considerably more restricted classes of formulas.

2 Synthesis Inside an SMT Solver

We are interested in synthesizing computable functions automatically from formal logical specifications stating properties of these functions. As we show later, under the right conditions, we can formulate a version of the synthesis problem in *first-order logic* alone, which allows us to tackle the problem using SMT solvers.

We consider the synthesis problem in the context of some theory T of signature Σ that allows us to provide the function's specification as a Σ-formula. Specifically, we consider *synthesis conjectures* expressed as (well-sorted) formulas of the form

$$\exists f^{\sigma_1 \cdots \sigma_n \sigma}\, \forall x_1^{\sigma_1} \cdots \forall x_n^{\sigma_n}\, P[f, x_1, \ldots, x_n] \tag{1}$$

or $\exists f\, \forall \boldsymbol{x}\, P[f, \boldsymbol{x}]$, for short, where the second-order variable f represents the function to be synthesized and P is a Σ-formula encoding properties that f must satisfy for all possible values of the input tuple $\boldsymbol{x} = (x_1, \ldots, x_n)$. In this setting, finding a witness for this satisfiability problem amounts to finding a function of type $\sigma_1 \times \cdots \times \sigma_n \rightarrow \sigma$ in some model of T that satisfies $\forall \boldsymbol{x}\, P[f, \boldsymbol{x}]$. Since we are interested in automatic synthesis, we the restrict ourselves here to methods that search over a subspace S of solutions representable syntactically as Σ-terms. We will say then that a synthesis conjecture is *solvable* if it has a syntactic solution in S.

In this paper we present two approaches that work with classes $\mathbf{L}$ of synthesis conjectures and Σ-theories T that are satisfaction complete wrt $\mathbf{L}$. In both approaches, we solve a synthesis conjecture $\exists f\, \forall \boldsymbol{x}\, P[f, \boldsymbol{x}]$ by relying on quantifier-instantiation techniques to produce a first-order Σ-term $t[\boldsymbol{x}]$ of sort σ such that $\forall \boldsymbol{x}\, P[t, \boldsymbol{x}]$ is T-satisfiable. When this t is found, the synthesized function is denoted by $\lambda \boldsymbol{x}.\, t$.

In principle, to determine the satisfiability of $\exists f\, \forall \boldsymbol{x}\, P[f, \boldsymbol{x}]$ an SMT solver supporting the theory T can consider the satisfiability of the (open) formula $\forall \boldsymbol{x}\, P[f, \boldsymbol{x}]$ by treating f as an uninterpreted function symbol. This sort of Skolemization is not usually a problem for SMT solvers as many of them can process formulas with uninterpreted symbols. The real challenge is the universal quantification over $\boldsymbol{x}$ because it requires the solver to construct internally (a finite representation of) an interpretation of f that is guaranteed to satisfy $P[f, \boldsymbol{x}]$ for every possible value of $\boldsymbol{x}$ [11,24].

More traditional SMT solver designs to handle universally quantified formulas have focused on instantiation-based methods to show *un*satisfiability. They generate ground instances of those formulas until a refutation is found at the ground level [10]. While these techniques are incomplete in general, they have been shown to be quite effective in practice [9,25]. For this reason, we advocate approaches to synthesis geared toward establishing the *unsatisfiability of the negation* of the synthesis conjecture:

$$\forall f\, \exists \boldsymbol{x}\, \neg P[f, \boldsymbol{x}] \tag{2}$$

Thanks to our restriction to satisfaction complete theories, (2) is T-unsatisfiable exactly when the original synthesis conjecture (1) is T-satisfiable.[1] Moreover, as

[1] Other approaches in the verification and synthesis literature also rely implicitly, and in some cases unwittingly, on this restriction or stronger ones. We make satisfaction completeness explicit here as a sufficient condition for reducing satisfiability problems to unsatisfiability ones.

we explain in this paper, a syntactic solution $\lambda x. t$ for (1) can be constructed from a refutation of (2), as opposed to being extracted from the valuation of f in a model of $\forall \boldsymbol{x}\, P[f, \boldsymbol{x}]$.

Two Synthesis Methods. Proving (2) unsatisfiable poses its own challenge to current SMT solvers, namely, dealing with the second-order universal quantification of f. To our knowledge, no SMT solvers so far had direct support for higher-order quantification. In the following, however, we describe two specialized methods to refute negated synthesis conjectures like (2) that build on existing capabilities of these solvers.

The first method applies to a restricted, but fairly common, case of synthesis problems $\exists f\, \forall \boldsymbol{x}\, P[f, \boldsymbol{x}]$ where every occurrence of f in P is in terms of the form $f(\boldsymbol{x})$. In this case, we can express the problem in the first-order form $\forall \boldsymbol{x}. \exists y. Q[\boldsymbol{x}, y]$ and then tackle its negation using appropriate quantifier instantiation techniques.

The second method follows the *syntax-guided synthesis* paradigm [1,2] where the synthesis conjecture is accompanied by an explicit syntactic restriction on the space of possible solutions. Our syntax-guided synthesis method is based on encoding the syntax of terms as first-order values. We use a deep embedding into an extension of the background theory T with a theory of algebraic data types, encoding the restrictions of a syntax-guided synthesis problem.

For the rest of the paper, we fix a Σ-theory T and a class $\mathbf{P}$ *of quantifier-free Σ-formulas $P[f, \boldsymbol{x}]$ such that T is satisfaction complete with respect to the class of synthesis conjectures* $\mathbf{L} := \{\exists f\, \forall \boldsymbol{x}\, P[f, \boldsymbol{x}] \mid P \in \mathbf{P}\}$.

3 Refutation-Based Synthesis

When axiomatizing properties of a desired function f of type $\sigma_1 \times \cdots \times \sigma_n \rightarrow \sigma$, a particularly well-behaved class are *single-invocation properties* (see, e.g., [13]). These properties include, in particular, standard function contracts, so they can be used to synthesize a function implementation given its postcondition as a relation between the arguments and the result of the function. This is also the form of the specification for synthesis problems considered in complete functional synthesis [16–18]. Note that, in our case, we aim to prove that the output exists for all inputs, as opposed to, more generally, computing the set of inputs for which the output exists.

A *single-invocation property* is any formula of the form $Q[\boldsymbol{x}, f(\boldsymbol{x})]$ obtained as an instance of a quantifier-free formula $Q[\boldsymbol{x}, y]$ not containing f. Note that the only occurrences of f in $Q[\boldsymbol{x}, f(\boldsymbol{x})]$ are in subterms of the form $f(\boldsymbol{x})$ with the *same* tuple $\boldsymbol{x}$ of *pairwise distinct* variables.[2] The conjecture $\exists f\, \forall \boldsymbol{x}\, Q[\boldsymbol{x}, f(\boldsymbol{x})]$ is logically equivalent to the *first-order* formula

$$\forall \boldsymbol{x}\, \exists y\, Q[\boldsymbol{x}, y] \tag{3}$$

[2] An example of a property that is *not* single-invocation is $\forall x_1\, x_2\, f(x_1, x_2) \approx f(x_2, x_1)$.

By the semantics of $\forall$ and $\exists$, finding a model $\mathcal{I}$ for it amounts (under the axioms of choice) to finding a function $h : \sigma_1^{\mathcal{I}} \times \cdots \times \sigma_n^{\mathcal{I}} \rightarrow \sigma^{\mathcal{I}}$ such that for all $\boldsymbol{s} \in \sigma_1^{\mathcal{I}} \times \cdots \times \sigma_n^{\mathcal{I}}$, the interpretation $\mathcal{I}[\boldsymbol{x} \mapsto \boldsymbol{s}, y \mapsto h(\boldsymbol{s})]$ satisfies $Q[\boldsymbol{x}, y]$. This section considers the case when **P** consists of single-invocation properties and describes a general approach for determining the satisfiability of formulas like (3) while computing a syntactic representation of a function like h in the process. For the latter, it will be convenient to assume that the language of functions contains an if-then-else operator ite of type $\mathsf{Bool} \times \sigma \times \sigma \rightarrow \sigma$ for each sort σ, with the usual semantics.

If (3) belongs to a fragment that admits quantifier elimination in T, such as the linear fragment of integer arithmetic, determining its satisfiability can be achieved using an efficient method for quantifier elimination [7,21]. Such cases have been examined in the context of software synthesis [17]. Here we propose instead an alternative instantiation-based approach aimed at establishing the unsatisfiability of the *negated* form of (3):

$$\exists \boldsymbol{x} \, \forall y \, \neg Q[\boldsymbol{x}, y] \tag{4}$$

or, equivalently, of a Skolemized version $\forall y \, \neg Q[\mathbf{k}, y]$ of (4) for some tuple $\mathbf{k}$ of fresh uninterpreted constants of the right sort. Finding a T-unsatisfiable finite set Γ of ground instances of $\neg Q[\boldsymbol{k}, y]$, which is what an SMT solver would do to prove the unsatisfiability of (4), suffices to solve the original synthesis problem. The reason is that, then, a solution for f can be constructed directly from Γ, as indicated by the following result.

Proposition 1. Suppose some set $\Gamma = \{\neg Q[\mathbf{k}, t_1[\mathbf{k}]], \ldots, \neg Q[\mathbf{k}, t_p[\mathbf{k}]]\}$ where $t_1[\boldsymbol{x}], \ldots, t_p[\boldsymbol{x}]$ are Σ-terms of sort σ is T-unsatisfiable. One solution for $\exists f \, \forall \boldsymbol{x} \, Q[\boldsymbol{x}, f(\boldsymbol{x})]$ is $\lambda \boldsymbol{x}. \, \mathsf{ite}(Q[\boldsymbol{x}, t_p], t_p, (\cdots \, \mathsf{ite}(Q[\boldsymbol{x}, t_2], t_2, t_1) \cdots))$.

Example 1. Let T be the theory of linear integer arithmetic with the usual signature and integer sort Int. Let $\boldsymbol{x} = (x_1, x_2)$. Now consider the property

$$P[f, \boldsymbol{x}] := f(\boldsymbol{x}) \geq x_1 \wedge f(\boldsymbol{x}) \geq x_2 \wedge (f(\boldsymbol{x}) \approx x_1 \vee f(\boldsymbol{x}) \approx x_2) \tag{5}$$

with f of type $\mathsf{Int} \times \mathsf{Int} \rightarrow \mathsf{Int}$ and x_1, x_2 of type Int. The synthesis problem $\exists f \, \forall \boldsymbol{x} \, P[f, \boldsymbol{x}]$ is solved exactly by the function that returns the maximum of its two inputs. Since P is a single-invocation property, we can solve that problem by proving the T-unsatisfiability of the conjecture $\exists \boldsymbol{x} \, \forall y \, \neg Q[\boldsymbol{x}, y]$ where

$$Q[\boldsymbol{x}, y] := y \geq x_1 \wedge y \geq x_2 \wedge (y \approx x_1 \vee y \approx x_2) \tag{6}$$

After Skolemization the conjecture becomes $\forall y \neg Q[\mathsf{a}, y]$ for fresh constants $\mathsf{a} = (\mathsf{a}_1, \mathsf{a}_2)$. When asked to determine the satisfiability of that conjecture an SMT solver may, for instance, instantiate it with a_1 and then a_2 for y, producing the T-unsatisfiable set $\{\neg Q[\mathsf{a}, \mathsf{a}_1], \neg Q[\mathsf{a}, \mathsf{a}_2]\}$. By Proposition 1, one solution for $\forall \boldsymbol{x} \, P[f, \boldsymbol{x}]$ is $f = \lambda \boldsymbol{x}. \, \mathsf{ite}(Q[\boldsymbol{x}, x_2], x_2, x_1)$, which simplifies to $\lambda \boldsymbol{x}. \, \mathsf{ite}(x_2 \geq x_1, x_2, x_1)$, representing the desired maximum function. ■

1. $\Gamma := \{\mathsf{G} \Rightarrow Q[\mathbf{k}, \mathsf{e}]\}$ where $\mathbf{k}$ consists of distinct fresh constants
2. Repeat
   If there is a model $\mathcal{I}$ of T satisfying Γ and G
   then let $\Gamma := \Gamma \cup \{\neg Q[\mathbf{k}, t[\mathbf{k}]]\}$ for some Σ-term $t[\boldsymbol{x}]$ such that $t[\mathbf{k}]^{\mathcal{I}} = \mathsf{e}^{\mathcal{I}}$;
   otherwise, return "no solution found"
   until Γ contains a T-unsatisfiable set $\{\neg Q[\mathbf{k}, t_1[\mathbf{k}]], \ldots, \neg Q[\mathbf{k}, t_p[\mathbf{k}]]\}$
3. Return $\lambda \boldsymbol{x}.\, \mathsf{ite}(Q[\boldsymbol{x}, t_p[\boldsymbol{x}]], t_p[\boldsymbol{x}], (\cdots \mathsf{ite}(Q[\boldsymbol{x}, t_2[\boldsymbol{x}]], t_2[\boldsymbol{x}], t_1[\boldsymbol{x}]) \cdots))$ for f

Fig. 1. A refutation-based synthesis procedure for single-invocation property $\exists f\, \forall \boldsymbol{x}\, Q[\boldsymbol{x}, f(\boldsymbol{x})]$.

Synthesis by Counterexample-Guided Quantifier Instantiation. Given Proposition 1, the main question is how to get the SMT solver to generate the necessary ground instances from $\forall y\, \neg Q[\mathbf{k}, y]$. Typically, SMT solvers that reason about quantified formulas use heuristic quantifier instantiation techniques based on E-matching [9], which instantiates universal quantifiers with terms occurring in some current set of ground terms built incrementally from the input formula. Using E-matching-based heuristic instantiation alone is unlikely to be effective in synthesis, where required terms need to be synthesized based on the semantics of the input specification. This is confirmed by our preliminary experiments, even for simple conjectures. We have developed instead a specialized new technique, which we refer to as *counterexample-guided quantifier instantiation*, that allows the SMT solver to quickly converge in many cases to the instantiations that refute the negated synthesis conjecture (4).

The new technique is similar to a popular scheme for synthesis known as counterexample-guided inductive synthesis, implemented in various synthesis approaches (e.g., [14,29]), but with the major difference of being built-in directly into the SMT solver. The technique is illustrated by the procedure in Fig. 1, which grows a set Γ of ground instances of $\neg Q[\mathbf{k}, y]$ starting with the formula $\mathsf{G} \Rightarrow Q[\mathbf{k}, \mathsf{e}]$ where G and e are fresh constants of sort Bool and σ, respectively. Intuitively, e represents a current, partial solution for the original synthesis conjecture $\exists f\, \forall \boldsymbol{x}\, Q[\boldsymbol{x}, f(\boldsymbol{x})]$, while G represents the possibility that the conjecture has a (syntactic) solution in the first place.

The procedure, which may not terminate in general, terminates either when Γ becomes unsatisfiable, in which case it has found a solution, or when Γ is still satisfiable but all of its models falsify G, in which case the search for a solution was inconclusive. The procedure is not *solution-complete*, that is, it is not guaranteed to return a solution whenever there is one. However, thanks to Proposition 1, it is *solution-sound*: every λ-term it returns is indeed a solution of the original synthesis problem.

Finding Instantiations. The choice of the term t in Step 2 of the procedure is intentionally left under Specified because it can be done in a number of ways. Having a good heuristic for such instantiations is, however, critical to the effectiveness of the procedure in practice. In a Σ-theory T, like integer arithmetic, with a fixed interpretation for symbols in Σ and a distinguished set of ground

Σ-terms denoting the elements of a sort, a simple, if naive, choice for t in Fig. 1 is the distinguished term denoting the element $\mathsf{e}^{\mathcal{I}}$. For instance, if σ is Int in integer arithmetic, t could be a concrete integer constant $(0, \pm 1, \pm 2, \ldots)$. This choice amounts to testing whether points in the codomain of the sought function f satisfy the original specification P.

More sophisticated choices for t, in particular where t contains the variables $\boldsymbol{x}$, may increase the generalization power of this procedure and hence its ability to find a solution. For instance, our present implementation in the CVC4 solver relies on the fact that the model $\mathcal{I}$ in Step 2 is constructed from a set of equivalence classes over terms computed by the solver during its search. The procedure selects the term t among those in the equivalence class of e, other than e itself. For instance, consider formula (6) from the previous example that encodes the single-invocation form of the specification for the max function. The DPLL(T) architecture, on which CVC4 is based, finds a model for $Q[\mathbf{a}, \mathsf{e}]$ with $\mathbf{a} = (\mathsf{a}_1, \mathsf{a}_2)$ only if it can first find a subset M of that formula's literals that collectively entail $Q[\mathbf{a}, \mathsf{e}]$ at the propositional level. Due to the last conjunct of (6), M must include either $\mathsf{e} \approx \mathsf{a}_1$ or $\mathsf{e} \approx \mathsf{a}_2$. Hence, whenever a model can be constructed for $Q[\mathbf{a}, e]$, the equivalence class containing e must contain either a_1 or a_2. Thus using the above selection heuristic, the procedure in Fig. 1 will, after at most two iterations of the loop in Step 2, add the instances $\neg Q[\mathbf{a}, \mathsf{a}_1]$ and $\neg Q[\mathbf{a}, \mathsf{a}_2]$ to Γ. As noted in Example 1, these two instances are jointly T-unsatisfiable. We expect that more sophisticated instantiation techniques can be incorporated. In particular, both quantifier elimination techniques [7,21] and approaches currently used to infer invariants from templates [8,19] are likely to be beneficial for certain classes of synthesis problems. The advantage of developing these techniques within an SMT solver is that they directly benefit both synthesis and verification in the presence of quantified conjectures, thus fostering cross-fertilization between different fields.

4 Refutation-Based Syntax-Guided Synthesis

In syntax-guided synthesis, the functional specification is strengthened by an accompanying set of syntactic restrictions on the form of the expected solutions. In a recent line of work [1,2,22] these restrictions are expressed by a grammar R (augmented with a kind of *let* binder) defining the language of solution terms, or *programs*, for the synthesis problem. In this section, we present a variant of the approach in the previous section that incorporates the syntactic restriction directly into the SMT solver via a deep embedding of the syntactic restriction R into the solver's logic. The main idea is to represent R as a set of algebraic datatypes and build into the solver an interpretation of these datatypes in terms of the original theory T.

While our approach is parametric in the background theory T and the restriction R, it is best explained here with a concrete example.

$$\begin{array}{ll}
\forall x\, y\, \mathsf{ev}(\mathsf{x}_1, x, y) \approx x & \forall s_1\, s_2\, x\, y\, \mathsf{ev}(\mathsf{leq}(s_1, s_2), x, y) \approx (\mathsf{ev}(s_1, x, y) \leq \mathsf{ev}(s_2, x, y)) \\
\forall x\, y\, \mathsf{ev}(\mathsf{x}_2, x, y) \approx y & \forall s_1\, s_2\, x\, y\, \mathsf{ev}(\mathsf{eq}(s_1, s_2), x, y) \approx (\mathsf{ev}(s_1, x, y) \approx \mathsf{ev}(s_2, x, y)) \\
\forall x\, y\, \mathsf{ev}(\mathsf{zero}, x, y) \approx 0 & \forall c_1\, c_2\, x\, y\, \mathsf{ev}(\mathsf{and}(c_1, c_2), x, y) \approx (\mathsf{ev}(c_1, x, y) \wedge \mathsf{ev}(c_2, x, y)) \\
\forall x\, y\, \mathsf{ev}(\mathsf{one}, x, y) \approx 1 & \forall c\, x\, y\, \mathsf{ev}(\mathsf{not}(c), x, y) \approx \neg \mathsf{ev}(c, x, y) \\
\multicolumn{2}{l}{\forall s_1\, s_2\, x\, y\, \mathsf{ev}(\mathsf{plus}(s_1, s_2), x, y) \approx \mathsf{ev}(s_1, x, y) + \mathsf{ev}(s_2, x, y)} \\
\multicolumn{2}{l}{\forall s_1\, s_2\, x\, y\, \mathsf{ev}(\mathsf{minus}(s_1, s_2), x, y) \approx \mathsf{ev}(s_1, x, y) - \mathsf{ev}(s_2, x, y)} \\
\multicolumn{2}{l}{\forall c\, s_1\, s_2\, x\, y\, \mathsf{ev}(\mathsf{if}(c, s_1, s_2), x, y) \approx \mathsf{ite}(\mathsf{ev}(c, x, y), \mathsf{ev}(s_1, x, y), \mathsf{ev}(s_2, x, y))}
\end{array}$$

Fig. 2. Axiomatization of the evaluation operators in grammar R from Example 2.

Example 2. Consider again the synthesis conjecture (6) from Example 1 but now with a syntactic restriction R for the solution space expressed by these algebraic datatypes:

$$\begin{array}{lll}
\mathsf{S} & := & \mathsf{x}_1 \mid \mathsf{x}_2 \mid \mathsf{zero} \mid \mathsf{one} \mid \mathsf{plus}(\mathsf{S}, \mathsf{S}) \mid \mathsf{minus}(\mathsf{S}, \mathsf{S}) \mid \mathsf{if}(\mathsf{C}, \mathsf{S}, \mathsf{S}) \\
\mathsf{C} & := & \mathsf{leq}(\mathsf{S}, \mathsf{S}) \mid \mathsf{eq}(\mathsf{S}, \mathsf{S}) \mid \mathsf{and}(\mathsf{C}, \mathsf{C}) \mid \mathsf{not}(\mathsf{C})
\end{array}$$

The datatypes are meant to encode a term signature that includes nullary constructors for the variables x_1 and x_2 of (6), and constructors for the symbols of the arithmetic theory T. Terms of sort S (resp., C) refer to theory terms of sort Int (resp., Bool).

Instead of the theory of linear integer arithmetic, we now consider its combination T_{D} with the theory of the datatypes above extended with two *evaluation operators*, that is, two function symbols $\mathsf{ev}^{\mathsf{S} \times \mathsf{Int} \times \mathsf{Int} \to \mathsf{Int}}$ and $\mathsf{ev}^{\mathsf{C} \times \mathsf{Int} \times \mathsf{Int} \to \mathsf{Bool}}$ respectively embedding S in Int and C in Bool. We define T_{D} so that all of its models satisfy the formulas in Fig. 2. The evaluation operators effectively define an interpreter for programs (i.e., terms of sort S and C) with input parameters x_1 and x_2.

It is possible to instrument an SMT solver that supports user-defined datatypes, quantifiers and linear arithmetic so that it constructs automatically from the syntactic restriction R both the datatypes S and C and the two evaluation operators. Reasoning about S and C is done by the built-in subsolver for datatypes. Reasoning about the evaluation operators is achieved by reducing ground terms of the form $\mathsf{ev}(d, t_1, t_2)$ to smaller terms by means of selected instantiations of the axioms from Fig. 2, with a number of instances proportional to the size of term d. It is also possible to show that T_{D} is satisfaction complete with respect to the class

$$\mathbf{L}_2 := \{\exists g\, \forall \boldsymbol{z}\, P[\lambda \boldsymbol{z}.\, \mathsf{ev}(g, \boldsymbol{z}), \boldsymbol{x}] \mid P[f, \boldsymbol{x}] \in \mathbf{P}\}$$

where instead of terms of the form $f(t_1, t_2)$ in P we have, modulo β-reductions, terms of the form $\mathsf{ev}(g, t_1, t_2)$.[3] For instance, the formula $P[f, \boldsymbol{x}]$ in Eq. (5) from Example 1 can be restated in T_{D} as the formula below where g is a variable of type S:

[3] We stress again, that both the instrumentation of the solver and the satisfaction completeness argument for the extended theory are generic with respect to the syntactic restriction on the synthesis problem and the original satisfaction complete theory T.

$$P_{\mathsf{ev}}[g, \boldsymbol{x}] := \mathsf{ev}(g, \boldsymbol{x}) \geq x_1 \wedge \mathsf{ev}(g, \boldsymbol{x}) \geq x_2 \wedge (\mathsf{ev}(g, \boldsymbol{x}) \approx x_1 \vee \mathsf{ev}(g, \boldsymbol{x}) \approx x_2)$$

In contrast to $P[f, \boldsymbol{x}]$, the new formula $P_{\mathsf{ev}}[g, \boldsymbol{x}]$ is first-order, with the role of the second-order variable f now played by the first-order variable g.

When asked for a solution for (5) under the restriction R, the instrumented SMT solver will try to determine instead the T_{D}-unsatisfiability of $\forall g\, \exists \boldsymbol{x}\, \neg P_{\mathsf{ev}}[g, \boldsymbol{x}]$. Instantiating g in the latter formula with $s :=$ $\mathsf{if}(\mathsf{leq}(\mathsf{x}_1, \mathsf{x}_2), \mathsf{x}_2, \mathsf{x}_1)$, say, produces a formula that the solver can prove to be T_{D}-unsatisfiable. This suffices to show that the program $\mathsf{ite}(x_1 \leq x_2, x_2, x_1)$, the analogue of s in the language of T, is a solution of the synthesis conjecture (5) under the syntactic restriction R. ■

1. $\Gamma := \emptyset$
2. Repeat
   (a) Let k be a tuple of distinct fresh constants.
   If there is a model $\mathcal{I}$ of T_{D} satisfying Γ *and* G, then $\Gamma := \Gamma \cup \{\neg P_{\mathsf{ev}}[\mathsf{e}^{\mathcal{I}}, \mathsf{k}]\}$;
   otherwise, return "no solution found"
   (b) If there is a model $\mathcal{J}$ of T_{D} satisfying Γ, then $\Gamma := \Gamma \cup \{\mathsf{G} \Rightarrow P_{\mathsf{ev}}[\mathsf{e}, \mathsf{k}^{\mathcal{J}}]\}$;
   otherwise, return $\mathsf{e}^{\mathcal{I}}$ as a solution

Fig. 3. A refutation-based syntax-guided synthesis procedure for $\exists f\, \forall \boldsymbol{x}\, P_{\mathsf{ev}}[f, \boldsymbol{x}]$.

To prove the unsatisfiability of formulas like $\forall g\, \exists \boldsymbol{x}\, \neg P_{\mathsf{ev}}[g, \boldsymbol{x}]$ in the example above we use a procedure similar to that in Sect. 3, but specialized to the extended theory T_{D}. The procedure is described in Fig. 3. Like the one in Fig. 1, it uses an uninterpreted constant e representing a solution candidate, and a Boolean variable G representing the existence of a solution. The main difference, of course, is that now e ranges over the datatype representing the restricted solution space. In any model of T_{D}, a term of datatype sort evaluates to a term built exclusively with constructor symbols. This is why the procedure returns in Step 2b the value of e in the model $\mathcal{I}$ found in Step 2a. As we showed in the previous example, a program that solves the original problem can then be reconstructed from the returned datatype term.

Implementation. We implemented the procedure in the CVC4 solver. Figure 4 shows a run of that implementation over the conjecture from Example 2. In this run, note that each model found for e satisfies all values of counterexamples found for previous candidates. After the sixth iteration of Step 2a, the procedure finds the candidate $\mathsf{if}(\mathsf{leq}(\mathsf{x}_1, \mathsf{x}_2), \mathsf{x}_2, \mathsf{x}_1)$, for which no counterexample exists, indicating that the procedure has found a solution for the synthesis conjecture. Currently, this problem can be solved in about 0.5 s in the latest development version of CVC4.

To make the procedure practical it is necessary to look for *small* solutions to synthesis conjectures. A simple way to limit the size of the candidate solutions is to consider smaller programs before larger ones. Adapting techniques for finding

Step	Model	Added Formula
$2a$	$\{\mathsf{e} \mapsto \mathsf{x}_1, \ldots\}$	$\neg P_{\mathsf{ev}}[\mathsf{x}_1, \mathsf{a}_1, \mathsf{b}_1]$
$2b$	$\{\mathsf{a}_1 \mapsto 0, \mathsf{b}_1 \mapsto 1, \ldots\}$	$\mathsf{G} \Rightarrow P_{\mathsf{ev}}[\mathsf{e}, 0, 1]$
$2a$	$\{\mathsf{e} \mapsto \mathsf{x}_2, \ldots\}$	$\neg P_{\mathsf{ev}}[\mathsf{x}_2, \mathsf{a}_2, \mathsf{b}_2]$
$2b$	$\{\mathsf{a}_2 \mapsto 1, \mathsf{b}_2 \mapsto 0, \ldots\}$	$\mathsf{G} \Rightarrow P_{\mathsf{ev}}[\mathsf{e}, 1, 0]$
$2a$	$\{\mathsf{e} \mapsto \mathsf{one}, \ldots\}$	$\neg P_{\mathsf{ev}}[\mathsf{one}, \mathsf{a}_3, \mathsf{b}_3]$
$2b$	$\{\mathsf{a}_3 \mapsto 2, \mathsf{b}_3 \mapsto 0, \ldots\}$	$\mathsf{G} \Rightarrow P_{\mathsf{ev}}[\mathsf{e}, 2, 0]$
$2a$	$\{\mathsf{e} \mapsto \mathsf{plus}(\mathsf{x}_1, \mathsf{x}_2), \ldots\}$	$\neg P_{\mathsf{ev}}[\mathsf{plus}(\mathsf{x}_1, \mathsf{x}_2), \mathsf{a}_4, \mathsf{b}_4]$
$2b$	$\{\mathsf{a}_4 \mapsto 1, \mathsf{b}_4 \mapsto 1, \ldots\}$	$\mathsf{G} \Rightarrow P_{\mathsf{ev}}[\mathsf{e}, 1, 1]$
$2a$	$\{\mathsf{e} \mapsto \mathsf{if}(\mathsf{leq}(\mathsf{x}_1, \mathsf{one}), \mathsf{one}, \mathsf{x}_1), \ldots\}$	$\neg P_{\mathsf{ev}}[\mathsf{if}(\mathsf{leq}(\mathsf{x}_1, \mathsf{one}), \mathsf{one}, \mathsf{x}_1), \mathsf{a}_5, \mathsf{b}_5]$
$2b$	$\{\mathsf{a}_5 \mapsto 1, \mathsf{b}_5 \mapsto 2, \ldots\}$	$\mathsf{G} \Rightarrow P_{\mathsf{ev}}[\mathsf{e}, 1, 2]$
$2a$	$\{\mathsf{e} \mapsto \mathsf{if}(\mathsf{leq}(\mathsf{x}_1, \mathsf{x}_2), \mathsf{x}_2, \mathsf{x}_1), \ldots\}$	$\neg P_{\mathsf{ev}}[\mathsf{if}(\mathsf{leq}(\mathsf{x}_1, \mathsf{x}_2), \mathsf{x}_2, \mathsf{x}_1), \mathsf{a}_6, \mathsf{b}_6]$
$2b$	none	

For $i = 1, \ldots, 6$, a_i and b_i are fresh constants of type Int.

Fig. 4. A run of the procedure from Fig. 3.

finite models of minimal size [26], we use a strategy that starting, from $n = 0$, searches for programs of size $n + 1$ only after its has exhausted the search for programs of size n. In solvers based on the DPLL(T) architecture, like CVC4, this can be accomplished by introducing a splitting lemma of the form $(\mathsf{size}(\mathsf{e}) \leq 0 \vee \neg \mathsf{size}(\mathsf{e}) \leq 0)$ and asserting $\mathsf{size}(\mathsf{e}) \leq 0$ as the first decision literal, where size is a function symbol of type $\sigma \rightarrow \mathsf{Int}$ for every datatype sort σ and stands for the function that maps each datatype value to its term size (i.e., the number of non-nullary constructor applications in the term). We do the same for $\mathsf{size}(\mathsf{e}) \leq 1$ if and when $\neg \mathsf{size}(\mathsf{e}) \leq 0$ becomes asserted. We extended the procedure for algebraic datatypes in CVC4 [6] to handle constraints involving size. The extended procedure remains a decision procedure for input problems with a concrete upper bound on terms of the form $\mathsf{size}(u)$, for each variable or uninterpreted constant u of datatype sort in the problem. This is enough for our purposes since the only term u like that in our synthesis procedure is e.

Proposition 2. With the search strategy above, the procedure in Fig. 3 has the following properties:

1. (Solution Soundness) Every term it returns can be mapped to a solution of the original synthesis conjecture $\exists f \, \forall \boldsymbol{x} \, P[f, \boldsymbol{x}]$ under the restriction R.
2. (Refutation Soundness) If it answers "no solution found", the original conjecture has no solutions under the restriction R.
3. (Solution Completeness) If the original conjecture has a solution under R, the procedure will find one.

Note that by this proposition the procedure can diverge only if the input synthesis conjecture has no solution. We refer the reader to a longer version of this paper for a proof of Proposition 2 [23]. For a general idea, the proof of solution soundness is based on the observation that when the procedure terminates at Step 2b, Γ has an unsatisfiable core with just one instance of $\neg P[g, \boldsymbol{x}]$. The procedure is refutation sound since when no model of Γ in Step 2a satisfies G, we have that even an arbitrary e cannot satisfy the current set of instances added to Γ in Step 2b. Finally, the procedure is solution complete first of all because Step 2a and 2b are effective thanks to the decidability of the background theory T_{D}. Each execution of Step 2a is guaranteed to produce a new candidate since T_{D} is also satisfaction complete. Thus, in the worst case, the procedure amounts to an enumeration of all possible programs until a solution is found.

5 Single Invocation Techniques for Syntax-Guided Problems

In this section, we considered the combined case of *single-invocation synthesis conjectures with syntactic restrictions.* Given a set R of syntactic restrictions expressed by a datatype S for programs and a datatype C for Boolean expressions, consider the case where (i) S contains the constructor $\mathsf{if} : \mathsf{C} \times \mathsf{S} \times \mathsf{S} \to \mathsf{S}$ (with the expected meaning) and (ii) the function to be synthesized is specified by a single-invocation property that can be expressed as a term of sort C. This is the case for the conjecture from Example 2 where the property $P_{\mathsf{ev}}[g, \boldsymbol{x}]$ can be rephrased as:

$$P_{\mathsf{C}}[g, \boldsymbol{x}] := \mathsf{ev}(\mathsf{and}(\mathsf{leq}(\mathsf{x}_1, g), \mathsf{and}(\mathsf{leq}(\mathsf{x}_2, g), \mathsf{or}(\mathsf{eq}(g, \mathsf{x}_1), \mathsf{eq}(g, \mathsf{x}_2)))), \boldsymbol{x}) \quad (7)$$

where again g has type S, $\boldsymbol{x} = (x_1, x_2)$, and x_1 and x_2 have type Int. The procedure in Fig. 1 can be readily modified to apply to this formula, with $P_{\mathsf{C}}[g, \mathbf{k}]$ and g taking the role respectively of $Q[\mathbf{k}, y]$ and y in that figure, since it generates solutions meeting our syntactic requirements. Running this modified procedure instead the one in Fig. 3 has the advantage that only the outputs of a solution need to be synthesized, not conditions in ite-terms. However, in our experimental evaluation found that the overhead of using an embedding into datatypes for syntax-guided problems is significant with respect to the performance of the solver on problems with no syntactic restrictions. For this reason, we advocate an approach for single-invocation synthesis conjectures with syntactic restrictions that runs the procedure from Fig. 1 as is, ignoring the syntactic restrictions R, and subsequently reconstructs from its returned solution one satisfying the restrictions. For that it is useful to assume that terms t in T can be effectively reduced to some (T-equivalent and unique) *normal form*, which we denote by $t\!\downarrow$.

Say the procedure from Fig. 1 returns a solution $\lambda \boldsymbol{x}.\, t$ for a function f. To construct from that a solution that meets the syntactic restrictions specified by datatype S, we run the iterative procedure described in Fig. 5. This procedure maintains an evolving set A of triples of the form (t, s, D), where D is a datatype, t is a term in normal form, s is a term satisfying the restrictions specified by D. The procedure incrementally makes calls to the subprocedure rcon, which takes a normal form term t, a datatype D and the set A above, and returns a pair (s, U) where s is a term equivalent to t in T, and U is a set of pairs (s', D') where

1. $A := \emptyset\,; t' := t\!\downarrow$
2. for $i = 1, 2, \ldots$
   (a) $(s, U) := \text{rcon}(t', \mathsf{S}, A)$;
   (b) if U is empty, return s; otherwise, for each datatype D_j occurring in U
   let d_i be the ith term in a fair enumeration of the elements of D_j
   let t_i be the analogue of d_i in the background theory T
   add $(t_i\!\downarrow, t_i, D_j)$ to A

rcon(t, D, A)
if $(t, s, D) \in A$, return $(s, \emptyset)$; otherwise, do one of the following:
(1) choose a $f(t_1, \ldots, t_n)$ s.t. $f(t_1, \ldots, t_n)\!\downarrow = t$ and f has an analogue $c^{D_1 \ldots D_n D}$ in D
let $(s_i, U_i) = \text{rcon}(t_i\!\downarrow, D_i, A)$ for $i = 1, \ldots, n$
return $(f(s_1, \ldots, s_n), U_1 \cup \ldots \cup U_n)$
(2) return $(t, \{(t, D)\})$

Fig. 5. A procedure for finding a term equivalent to t that meets the syntactic restrictions specified by datatype S.

s' is a subterm of s that fails to satisfy the syntactic restriction expressed by datatype D'. Overall, the procedure alternates between calling rcon and adding triples to A until rcon(t, D, A) returns a pair of the form $(s, \emptyset)$, in which case s is a solution satisfying the syntactic restrictions specified by S.

Example 3. Say we wish to construct a solution equivalent to $\lambda x_1\, x_2. x_1 + (2 * x_2)$ that meets restrictions specified by datatype S from Example 2. To do so, we let $A = \emptyset$, and call rcon$((x_1 + (2 * x_2))\!\downarrow, \mathsf{S}, A)$. Since A is empty and $+$ is the analogue of constructor $\mathsf{plus}^{\mathsf{SSS}}$ of S, assuming $(x_1 + (2 * x_2))\!\downarrow = x_1 + (2 * x_2)$, we may choose to return a pair based on the result of calling rcon on $x_1\!\downarrow$ and $(2 * x_2)\!\downarrow$. Since $\mathsf{x}_1^{\mathsf{S}}$ is a constructor of S and $x_1\!\downarrow = x_1$, rcon(x_1, S, A) returns $(x_1, \emptyset)$. Since S does not have a constructor for $*$, we must either choose a term t such that $t\!\downarrow = (2 * x_2)\!\downarrow$ where the topmost symbol of t is the analogue of a constructor in S, or otherwise return the pair $(2 * x_2, \{(2 * x_2, \mathsf{S})\})$. Suppose we do the latter, and thus rcon$(x_1 + (2 * x_2), \mathsf{S}, A)$ returns $(x_1 + (2 * x_2), \{(2 * x_2, \mathsf{S})\})$. Since the second component of this pair is not empty, we pick in Step 2b the first element of S, x_1 say, and add (x_1, x_1, S) to A. We then call rcon$((x_1 + (2 * x_2))\!\downarrow, \mathsf{S}, A)$ which by the same strategy above returns $(x_1 + (2 * x_2), \{(2 * x_2, \mathsf{S})\})$. This process continues until we pick, the term $\mathsf{plus}(\mathsf{x}_2, \mathsf{x}_2)$ say, whose analogue is $x_2 + x_2$. Assuming $(x_2 + x_2)\!\downarrow = (2 * x_2)\!\downarrow$, after adding the pair $(2 * x_2, x_2 + x_2, \mathsf{S})$ to A, rcon$((x_1 + (2 * x_2))\!\downarrow, \mathsf{S}, A)$ returns the pair $(x_1 + (x_2 + x_2), \emptyset)$, indicating that $\lambda x_1\, x_2. x_1 + (x_2 + x_2)$ is equivalent to $\lambda x_1\, x_2. x_1 + (2 * x_2)$, and meets the restrictions specified by S. ■

This procedure depends upon the use of normal forms for terms. It should be noted that, since the top symbol of t is generally ite, this normalization includes both low-level rewriting of literals within t, but also includes high-level rewriting techniques such as ite simplification, redundant subterm elimination and destructive equality resolution. Also, notice that we are not assuming that $t\!\downarrow = s\!\downarrow$ if and only if t is equivalent to s, and thus normal forms only underapproximate an equivalence relation between terms. Having a (more) consistent normal form for terms allows us to compute a (tighter) underapproximation, thus improving the performance of the reconstruction. In this procedure, we use the same normal form for terms that is used by the individual decision procedures of CVC4. This is unproblematic for theories such as linear arithmetic whose normal form for terms is a sorted list of monomials, but it can be problematic for theories such as bitvectors. As a consequence, we use several optimizations, omitted in the description of the procedure in Fig. 5, to increase the likelihood that the procedure terminates in a reasonable amount of time. For instance, in our implementation the return value of rcon is not recomputed every time A is updated. Instead, we maintain an evolving directed acyclic graph (dag), whose nodes are pairs (t, S) for term t and datatype S (the terms we have yet to reconstruct), and whose edges are the direct subchildren of that term. Datatype terms are enumerated for all datatypes in this dag, which is incrementally pruned as pairs are added to A until it becomes empty. Another optimization is that the procedure rcon may choose to try simultaneously to reconstruct *multiple* terms of the form $f(t_1, \ldots, t_n)$ when matching a term t to a syntactic specification S, reconstructing t when any such term can be reconstructed.

Although the overhead of this procedure can be significant when large subterms do not meet the syntactic restrictions, we found that in practice it quickly terminates successfully for a majority of the solutions we considered where reconstruction was possible, as we discuss in the next section. Furthermore, it makes our implementation more robust, since it effectively treats in the same way different properties that are equal modulo normalization (which is parametric in the built-in theories we consider).

6 Experimental Evaluation

We implemented the techniques from the previous sections in the SMT solver CVC4 [4], which has support for quantified formulas and a wide range of theories including arithmetic, bitvectors, and algebraic datatypes. We evaluated our implementation on 243 benchmarks used in the SyGuS 2014 competition [1] that were publicly available on the StarExec execution service [31]. The benchmarks are in a new format for specifying syntax-guided synthesis problems [22]. We added parsing support to CVC4 for most features of this format. All SyGuS benchmarks considered contain synthesis conjectures whose background theory is either linear integer arithmetic or bitvectors. We made some minor modifications to benchmarks to avoid naming conflicts, and to explicitly define several bitvector operators that are not supported natively by CVC4.

We considered multiple configurations of CVC4 corresponding to the techniques mentioned in this paper. Configuration **cvc4+sg** executes the syntax-guided procedure from Sect. 4, even in cases where the synthesis conjecture is single-invocation. Configuration **cvc4+si-r** executes the procedure from Sect. 3

	array (32)		**bv** (7)		**hd** (56)		**icfp** (50)		**int** (15)		**let** (8)		**multf** (8)		**Total** (176)	
	#	time	#	time	#	time	#	time	#	time	#	time	#	time	#	time
esolver	4	2250.7	2	71.2	50	878.5	0	0	5	1416.7	2	0.0	7	0.6	70	4617.7
cvc4+sg	1	3.1	0	0	34	4308.9	1	0.5	3	1.7	2	0.5	7	628.3	48	4943
cvc4+si-r	(32)	1.2	(6)	4.7	(56)	2.1	(43)	3403.5	(15)	0.6	(8)	1.0	(8)	0.2	(168)	3413.3
cvc4+si	30	1449.5	5	0.1	52	2322.9	0	0	6	0.1	2	0.5	7	0.1	102	3773.2

Fig. 6. Results for single-invocation synthesis conjectures, showing times (in seconds) and number of benchmarks solved by each solver and configuration over 8 benchmark classes with a 3600 s timeout. The number of benchmarks solved by configuration **cvc4+si-r** are in parentheses because its solutions do not necessarily satisfy the given syntactic restrictions.

on all benchmarks having conjectures that it can deduce are single-invocation. In total, it discovered that 176 of the 243 benchmarks could be rewritten into a form that was single-invocation. This configuration simply ignores any syntax restrictions on the expected solution. Finally, configuration **cvc4+si** uses the same procedure used by **cvc4+si-r** but then attempts to reconstruct any found solution as a term in required syntax, as described in Sect. 5.

We ran all configurations on all benchmarks on the StarExec cluster.[4] We provide comparative results here primarily against the enumerative CEGIS solver ESolver [32], the winner of the SyGuS 2014 competition. In our tests, we found that ESolver performed significantly better than the other entrants of that competition.

Benchmarks with Single-Invocation Synthesis Conjectures. The results for benchmarks with single-invocation properties are shown in Fig. 6. Configuration **cvc4+si-r** found a solution (although not necessarily in the required language) very quickly for a majority of benchmarks. It terminated successfully for 168 of 176 benchmarks, and in less than a second for 159 of those. Not all solutions found using this method met the syntactic restrictions. Nevertheless, our methods for reconstructing these solutions into the required grammar, implemented in configuration **cvc4+si**, succeeded in 102 cases, or 61 % of the total. This is 32 more benchmarks than the 70 solved by ESolver, the best known solver for these benchmarks so far. In total, **cvc4+si** solved 34 benchmarks that ESolver did not, while ESolver solved 2 that **cvc4+si** did not.

The solutions returned by **cvc4+si-r** were often large, having an order of 10 K subterms for harder benchmarks. However, after exhaustively applying simplification techniques during reconstruction with configuration **cvc4+si**, we found that the size of those solutions is comparable to other solvers, and in some cases even smaller. For instance, among the 68 benchmarks solved by both ESolver and **cvc4+si**, the former produced a smaller solution in 15 cases and the latter in 9. Only in 2 cases did **cvc4+si** produce a solution that had 10 more subterms than the solution produced by ESolver. This indicates that in addition to having a high precision, the techniques from Sect. 5 used for solution reconstruction are effective also at producing succinct solutions for this benchmark library.

[4] A detailed summary can be found at http://lara.epfl.ch/w/cvc4-synthesis.

	int (3)		invgu (28)		invg (28)		vctrl (8)		Total (67)	
	#	time	#	time	#	time	#	time	#	time
esolver	3	1.6	25	86.3	25	85.6	5	29.5	58	203.0
cvc4+sg	3	1476.0	23	811.6	22	2283.2	5	2933.1	53	7503.9

Fig. 7. Results for synthesis conjectures that are not single-invocation, showing times (in seconds) and numbers of benchmarks solved by CVC4 and ESOLVER over 4 benchmark classes with a 3600 s timeout.

Configuration **cvc4+sg** does not take advantage of the fact that a synthesis conjecture is single-invocation. However, it was able to solve 48 of these benchmarks, including a small number not solved by any other configuration, like one from the **icfp** class whose solution was a single argument function over bitvectors that shifted its input right by four bits. In addition to being solution complete, **cvc4+sg** always produces solutions of minimal term size, something not guaranteed by the other solvers and CVC4 configurations. Of the 47 benchmarks solved by both **cvc4+sg** and ESOLVER, the solution returned by **cvc4+sg** was smaller than the one returned by ESOLVER in 6 cases, and had the same size in the others. This provides an experimental confirmation that the fairness techniques for term size described in Sect. 4 ensure minimal size solutions.

Benchmarks with Non-single-invocation Synthesis Conjectures. Configuration **cvc4+sg** is the only CVC4 configuration that can process benchmarks with synthesis conjectures that are not single-invocation. The results for ESOLVER and **cvc4+sg** on such benchmarks from SyGuS 2014 are shown in Fig. 7. Configuration **cvc4+sg** solved 53 of them over a total of 67. ESOLVER solved 58 and additionally reported that 6 had no solution. In more detail, ESOLVER solved 7 benchmarks that **cvc4+sg** did not, while **cvc4+sg** solved 2 benchmarks (from the **vctrl** class) that ESOLVER could not solve. In terms of precision, **cvc4+sg** is quite competitive with the state of the art on these benchmarks. To give other points of comparison, at the SyGuS 2014 competition [1] the second best solver (the Stochastic solver) solved 40 of these benchmarks within a one hour limit and Sketch solved 23.

Overall Results. In total, over the entire SyGuS 2014 benchmark set, 155 benchmarks can be solved by a configuration of CVC4 that, whenever possible, runs the methods for single-invocation properties described in Sect. 3, and otherwise runs the method described in Sect. 4. This number is 27 higher than the 128 benchmarks solved in total by ESOLVER. Running both configuration **cvc4+sg** and **cvc4+si** in parallel[5] solves 156 benchmarks, indicating that CVC4 is highly competitive with state-of-the-art tools for syntax guided synthesis. CVC4's performance is noticeably better than ESOLVER on single-invocation properties, where our new quantifier instantiation techniques give it a distinct advantage.

Competitive Advantage on Single-Invocation Properties in the Presence of Ite. We conclude by observing that for certain classes of benchmarks,

[5] CVC4 has a *portfolio* mode that allows it to run multiple configurations at the same time.

n	2	3	4	5	6	7	8	9	10
esolver	0.01	1377.10	–	–	–	–	–	–	–
cvc4+si	0.01	0.02	0.03	0.05	0.1	0.3	1.6	8.9	81.5

Fig. 8. Results for parametric benchmarks class encoding the maximum of n integers. The columns show the run time for ESolver and cvc4 with a 3600 s timeout.

configuration **cvc4+si** scales significantly better than state-of-the-art synthesis tools. Figure 8 shows this in comparison with ESolver for the problem of synthesizing a function that computes the maximum of n integer inputs. As reported by Alur et al. [1], no solver in the SyGuS 2014 competition was able to synthesize such a function for $n = 5$ within one hour.

For benchmarks from the **array** class, whose solutions are loop-free programs that compute the first instance of an element in a sorted array, the best reported solver for these in [1] was Sketch, which solved a problem for an array of length 7 in approximately 30 minutes.[6] In contrast, **cvc4+si** was able to reconstruct solutions for arrays of size 15 (the largest benchmark in the class) in 0.3 s, and solved each of the benchmarks in the class but 8 within 1 s.

7 Conclusion

We have shown that SMT solvers, instead of just acting as subroutines for automated software synthesis tasks, can be instrumented to perform synthesis themselves. We have presented a few approaches for enabling SMT solvers to construct solutions for the broad class of syntax-guided synthesis problems and discussed their implementation in cvc4. This is, to the best of our knowledge, the first implementation of synthesis inside an SMT solver and it already shows considerable promise. Using a novel quantifier instantiation technique and a solution enumeration technique for the theory of algebraic datatypes, our implementation is competitive with the state of the art represented by the systems that participated in the 2014 syntax-guided synthesis competition. Moreover, for the important class of single-invocation problems when syntax restrictions permit the if-then-else operator, our implementation significantly outperforms those systems.

Acknowledgments. We would like to thank Liana Hadarean for helpful discussions on the normal form used in cvc4 for bit vector terms.

References

1. Alur, R., et al.: Syntax-guided synthesis. To Appear in Marktoberdrof NATO proceedings. (2014). http://sygus.seas.upenn.edu/files/sygus_extended.pdf. Accessed 06 February 2015

[6] These benchmarks, as contributed to the SyGuS benchmark set, use integer variables only; they were generated by expanding fixed-size arrays and contain no operations on arrays.

2. Alur, R., Bodík, R., Juniwal, G., Martin, M.M.K., Raghothaman, M., Seshia, S.A., Singh, R., Solar-Lezama, A., Torlak, E., Udupa, A.: Syntax-guided synthesis. In: FMCAD, pp. 1–17. IEEE (2013)
3. Alur, R., Martin, M., Raghothaman, M., Stergiou, C., Tripakis, S., Udupa, A.: Synthesizing finite-state protocols from scenarios and requirements. In: Yahav, E. (ed.) HVC 2014. LNCS, vol. 8855, pp. 75–91. Springer, Heidelberg (2014)
4. Barrett, C., Conway, C.L., Deters, M., Hadarean, L., Jovanović, D., King, T., Reynolds, A., Tinelli, C.: CVC4. In: Gopalakrishnan, G., Qadeer, S. (eds.) CAV 2011. LNCS, vol. 6806, pp. 171–177. Springer, Heidelberg (2011)
5. Barrett, C., Deters, M., de Moura, L.M., Oliveras, A., Stump, A.: 6 years of SMT-COMP. JAR **50**(3), 243–277 (2013)
6. Barrett, C., Shikanian, I., Tinelli, C.: An abstract decision procedure for satisfiability in the theory of inductive data types. J. Satisfiability Boolean Model. Comput. **3**, 21–46 (2007)
7. Bjørner, N.: Linear quantifier elimination as an abstract decision procedure. In: Giesl, J., Hähnle, R. (eds.) IJCAR 2010. LNCS, vol. 6173, pp. 316–330. Springer, Heidelberg (2010)
8. Cousot, P.: Proving program invariance and termination by parametric abstraction, lagrangian relaxation and semidefinite programming. In: Cousot, R. (ed.) VMCAI 2005. LNCS, vol. 3385, pp. 1–24. Springer, Heidelberg (2005)
9. de Moura, L., Bjørner, N.S.: Efficient e-Matching for SMT solvers. In: Pfenning, F. (ed.) CADE 2007. LNCS (LNAI), vol. 4603, pp. 183–198. Springer, Heidelberg (2007)
10. Detlefs, D., Nelson, G., Saxe, J.B.: Simplify: a theorem prover for program checking. J. ACM, Technical report (2003)
11. Ge, Y., de Moura, L.: Complete instantiation for quantified formulas in satisfiabiliby modulo theories. In: Bouajjani, A., Maler, O. (eds.) CAV 2009. LNCS, vol. 5643, pp. 306–320. Springer, Heidelberg (2009)
12. Green, C.C.: Application of theorem proving to problem solving. In: Walker, D.E., Norton, L.M. (eds.) IJCAI, pp. 219–240. William Kaufmann, San Francisco (1969)
13. Jacobs, S., Kuncak, V.: Towards complete reasoning about axiomatic specifications. In: Jhala, R., Schmidt, D. (eds.) Verification, Model Checking, and Abstract Interpretation. LNCS, vol. 6538, pp. 278–293. Springer, Heidelberg (2011)
14. Jha, S., Gulwani, S., Seshia, S.A., Tiwari, A.: Oracle-guided component-based program synthesis. In: Kramer, J., Bishop, J., Devanbu, P.T., Uchitel, S. (eds.) ICSE, pp. 215–224. ACM, New York (2010)
15. Kneuss, E., Kuraj, I., Kuncak, V., Suter, P.: Synthesis modulo recursive functions. In: Hosking, A.L., Eugster, P.T., Lopes, C.V. (eds.) OOPSLA, pp. 407–426. ACM, New York (2013)
16. Kuncak, V., Mayer, M., Piskac, R., Suter, P.: Complete functional synthesis. In: Zorn, B.G., Aiken, A. (eds.) PLDI, pp. 316–329. ACM, New York (2010)
17. Kuncak, V., Mayer, M., Piskac, R., Suter, P.: Software synthesis procedures. CACM **55**(2), 103–111 (2012)
18. Kuncak, V., Mayer, M., Piskac, R., Suter, P.: Functional synthesis for linear arithmetic and sets. STTT **15**(5–6), 455–474 (2013)
19. Madhavan, R., Kuncak, V.: Symbolic resource bound inference for functional programs. In: Biere, A., Bloem, R. (eds.) CAV 2014. LNCS, vol. 8559, pp. 762–778. Springer, Heidelberg (2014)
20. Manna, Z., Waldinger, R.J.: A deductive approach to program synthesis. TOPLAS **2**(1), 90–121 (1980)

21. Monniaux, D.: Quantifier elimination by lazy model enumeration. In: Touili, T., Cook, B., Jackson, P. (eds.) CAV 2010. LNCS, vol. 6174, pp. 585–599. Springer, Heidelberg (2010)
22. Raghothaman, M., Udupa, A.: Language to specify syntax-guided synthesis problems. In: CoRR, abs/1405.5590 (2014)
23. Reynolds, A., Deters, M., Kuncak, V., Tinelli, C., Barrett, C.W.: On counterexample guided quantifier instantiation for synthesis in CVC4. In: CoRR, abs/1502.04464, 2015. http://arxiv.org/abs/1502.04464
24. Reynolds, A., Tinelli, C., Goel, A., Krstić, S., Deters, M., Barrett, C.: Quantifier instantiation techniques for finite model finding in SMT. In: Bonacina, M.P. (ed.) CADE 2013. LNCS, vol. 7898, pp. 377–391. Springer, Heidelberg (2013)
25. Reynolds, A., Tinelli, C., Moura, L.D.: Finding conflicting instances of quantified formulas in SMT. In: Formal Methods in Computer-Aided Design, FMCAD (2014)
26. Reynolds, A.J.: Finite Model Finding in Satisfiability Modulo Theories. Ph.D. thesis, The University of Iowa (2013)
27. Ryzhyk, L., Walker, A., Keys, J., Legg, A., Raghunath, A., Stumm, M., Vij, M.: User-guided device driver synthesis. In: Flinn, J., Levy, H. (eds.) OSDI, pp. 661–676. USENIX Association, Berkeley (2014)
28. Solar-Lezama, A.: Program sketching. STTT **15**(5–6), 475–495 (2013)
29. Solar-Lezama, A., Tancau, L., Bodík, R., Seshia, S.A., Saraswat, V.A.: Combinatorial sketching for finite programs. In: Shen, J.P., Martonosi, M. (eds.) ASPLOS, pp. 404–415. ACM, New York (2006)
30. Srivastava, S., Gulwani, S., Foster, J.S.: Template-based program verification and program synthesis. STTT **15**(5–6), 497–518 (2013)
31. Stump, A., Sutcliffe, G., Tinelli, C.: StarExec: a cross-community infrastructure for logic solving. In: Demri, S., Kapur, D., Weidenbach, C. (eds.) IJCAR 2014. LNCS, vol. 8562, pp. 367–373. Springer, Heidelberg (2014)
32. Udupa, A., Raghavan, A., Deshmukh, J.V., Mador-Haim, S., Martin, M.M., Alur, R.: Transit: specifying protocols with concolic snippets. In: PLDI, pp. 287–296. ACM (2013)

Deductive Program Repair

Etienne Kneuss, Manos Koukoutos, and Viktor Kuncak[(✉)]

École Polytechnique Fédérale de Lausanne (EPFL),
Lausanne, Switzerland
viktor.kuncak@epfl.ch

Abstract. We present an approach to program repair and its application to programs with recursive functions over unbounded data types. Our approach formulates program repair in the framework of deductive synthesis that uses existing program structure as a hint to guide synthesis. We introduce a new specification construct for symbolic tests. We rely on such user-specified tests as well as automatically generated ones to localize the fault and speed up synthesis. Our implementation is able to eliminate errors within seconds from a variety of functional programs, including symbolic computation code and implementations of functional data structures. The resulting programs are formally verified by the Leon system.

1 Introduction

This paper explores the problem of automatically repairing programs written as a set of mutually recursive functions in a purely functional subset of Scala. We consider a function to be subject to repair if it does not satisfy its specification, expressed in the form of pre- and postcondition. The task of repair consists of automatically generating an alternative implementation that meets the specification. The repair problem has been studied in the past for reactive and pushdown systems [8,10,11,19,20,26]. We view repair as generalizing, for example, the *choose* construct of complete functional synthesis [15], sketching [21,22], and program templates [23], because the exact location and nature of expressions to be synthesized is left to the algorithm. Repair is thus related to localization of error causes [12,14,27]. To speed up our repair approach, we do use *coarse-grained* error localization based on derived test inputs. However, a more precise nature of the fault is in fact the *outcome* of our tool, because the repair identifies a particular change that makes the program correct. Using tests alone as a criterion for correctness is appealing for performance reasons [7,17,18], but this can lead to erroneous repairs. We therefore leverage prior work [13] on verifying and synthesizing recursive functional programs with *unbounded* data-types (trees, lists, integers) to provide strong correctness guarantees, while at the same time optimizing our technique to use automatically derived tests. By phrasing

V. Kuncak—This work is supported in part by the European Research Council (ERC) Project *Implicit Programming* and Swiss National Science Foundation Grant *Constraint Solving Infrastructure for Program Analysis.*

D. Kroening and C.S. Păsăreanu (Eds.): CAV 2015, Part II, LNCS 9207, pp. 217–233, 2015.
DOI: 10.1007/978-3-319-21668-3_13

the problem of repair as one of synthesis and introducing tailored deduction rules that use the original implementation as guide, we allow the repair-oriented synthesis procedure to automatically find correct fixes, in the worst case resorting to re-synthesizing the desired function from scratch. To make the repair approach practical, we found it beneficial to extend the power and generality of the synthesis engine itself, as well as to introduce explicit support for symbolic tests in the specification language and the repair algorithm.

Contributions. The overall contribution of this paper is a new repair algorithm and its implementation inside a deductive synthesis framework for recursive functional programs. The specific new techniques we contribute are the following.

- **Exploration of similar expressions**. We present an algorithm for expression repair based on a grammar for generating expressions *similar* to a given expression (according to an error model we propose). We use such grammars within our new generic symbolic term exploration routine, which leverages test inputs as well as an SMT solver, and efficiently explores the space of expressions that contain recursive calls whose evaluation depends on the expression being synthesized.
- **Fault localization**. To narrow down repair to a program fragment, we localize the error by doing dynamic analysis using test inputs generated automatically from specifications. We combine two automatic sources of inputs: enumeration techniques and SMT-based techniques. We collect traces leading to erroneous executions and compute common prefixes of branching decisions. We show that this localization is in practice sufficiently precise to repair sizeable functions efficiently.
- **Symbolic examples**. We propose an intuitive way of specifying possibly symbolic input-output examples using pattern matching of Scala. This allows the user to partially specify a function without necessarily having to provide full inputs and outputs. Additionally, it enables the developer to easily describe properties of generic (polymorphic) functions. We present an algorithm for deriving new examples from existing ones, which improves the usefulness of example sets for fault localization and repair.

  In our experience, the combination of formal specification and symbolic examples gives the user significant flexibility when specifying functions, and increases success rates when discovering and repairing program faults.
- **Integration into a deductive synthesis and verification framework**. Our repair system is part of a deductive verification system, so it can automatically produce new inputs from specification, prove correctness of code for all inputs ranging over an unbounded domain, and synthesize program fragments using deductive synthesis rules that include common recursion schemas.

The repair approach offers significant improvements compared with synthesis from scratch. Synthesis alone scales poorly when the expression to synthesize is large. Fault localization focuses synthesis on the smaller, invalid portions of the program and thus results in big performance gains. The source code of our tool and additional details are available from http://leon.epfl.ch as well as http://lara.epfl.ch/w/leon-repair.

```
abstract class Expr
case class Plus(lhs: Expr, rhs: Expr)
  extends Expr
... // 9 more subclasses

abstract class SExpr
case class SPlus(lhs: SExpr,
  rhs: SExpr) extends SExpr
... // 5 more subclasses

abstract class Type
case object IntType extends Type
case object BoolType extends Type

def typeOf(e: Expr): Option[Type] =
  ...

def semI(t: Expr): Int = {
require(typeOf(t)==Some(IntType))
  ...
}
def semB(t : Expr) : Boolean = {
require(typeOf(t)==Some(BoolType))
  ...
}
def simSem(e : SExpr) : Int = ...
```

```
def desugar(e: Expr) : SExpr = {
e match {
 case Plus (lhs, rhs) ⇒
   SPlus(desugar(lhs), desugar(rhs))
 case Minus(lhs, rhs) ⇒
   SPlus(desugar(lhs), Neg(desugar(rhs)))
 case And(lhs, rhs) ⇒
   SIte(desugar(lhs), desugar(rhs), SLiteral(0))
 case Or(lhs, rhs) ⇒
   SIte(desugar(lhs), SLiteral(1), desugar(rhs))
 case Not(e) ⇒
   SIte(desugar(e), SLiteral(0), SLiteral(1))
 case Ite(cond, thn, els) ⇒
   SIte(desugar(cond), desugar(els), desugar(thn))
 case IntLiteral(v) ⇒
   SLiteral(v)
 case BoolLiteral(b) ⇒
   SLiteral(if (b) 1 else 0)}
 ...
} ensuring { res ⇒ typeOf(e) match {
  case Some(IntType) ⇒
   simSem(res) == semI(e)
  case Some(BoolType) ⇒
   simSem(res) == if (semB(e)) 1 else 0
  case None() ⇒ true }
}
```

Fig. 1. The syntax tree translation in function desugar has a strong **ensuring** clause, requiring semantic equivalence of transformed and the original tree, as defined by several recursive evaluation functions. desugar contains an error. Our system finds it, repairs the function, and proves the resulting program correct.

Example. Consider the following functionality inspired by a part of a compiler. We wish to transform (desugar) an abstract syntax-tree of a typed expression language into a simpler untyped language, simplifying some of the constructs and changing the representation of some of the types, while preserving the semantics of the transformed expression. In Fig. 1, the original syntax trees are represented by the class Expr and its subclasses, whereas the resulting untyped language trees are given by SExpr. A syntax tree of Expr either evaluates to an integer, to a boolean, or to no value if it is not well typed. We capture this by defining a type-checking function typeOf, along with two separate semantic functions, semI and semB. SExpr, on the other hand, always evaluates to an integer, as defined by the simSem function. For brevity, most subclass definitions are omitted.

The desugar function translates a syntax tree of Expr into one of SExpr. We expect the function to ensure that the transformation preserves the semantics of the tree: originally integer-valued trees evaluate to the same value, boolean-valued trees now evaluate to 0 and 1, representing **false** and **true**, respectively, and mistyped trees are left unconstrained. This is expressed in the postcondition of desugar.

The implementation in Fig. 1 contains a bug: the thn and els branches of the Ite case have been accidentally switched. Using tests automatically generated using generic enumeration of small values, as well as from a verification attempt of desugar, our tool is able to find a coarse-grained location of the bug, as the body of the relevant case of the match statement. During repair, one of the rules performs a semantic exploration of expressions similar to the invalid one. It discovers that using the expression SIte(desugar(cond), desugar(thn), desugar(els)) instead of the invalid one makes the discovered tests pass. The system can then formally verify that the repaired program meets the specification for all inputs. If we try to introduce similar bugs in the correct desugar function, or to replace the entire body of a case with a dummy value, the system successfully recovers the intended case of the transformation. In some cases our system can repair multiple simultaneous errors; the mechanism behind that is explained in Sect. 2.2. Note that the developer communicates with our system only by writing code and specifications, both of which are functions in an existing functional programming language. This illustrates the potential of repair as a scalable and developer-friendly deployment of synthesis in software development.

2 Deductive Guided Repair

We next describe our deductive repair framework. The framework currently works under several assumptions, which we consider reasonable given the state of the art in repair of infinite-state programs. We consider the specifications of functions as correct; the code is assumed wrong if it cannot be proven correct with respect to this specification for all of the infinitely many inputs. If the specification includes input-output tests, it follows that the repaired function must have the same behavior on these tests. We do not guarantee that the output of the function is the same as the original one on tests not covered by the specification, though the repair algorithm tends to preserve some of the existing behaviors due to the local nature of repair. It is the responsibility of the developer to sufficiently specify the function being repaired. Although under-specified benchmarks may produce unexpected expressions as repair solutions, we found that even partial specifications often yield the desired repairs. A particularly effective specification style in our experience is to give a partial specification that depends on all components of the structure (for example, describes property of the set of stored elements), and then additionally provide a finite number of symbolic input-output tests. We assume that only one function of the program is invalid; the implementation of all other functions is considered valid as far as the repair of interest is concerned. Finally, we assume that all functions of the program, even the invalid one, terminate.

Stages of the Repair Algorithm. The function being repaired passes through the following stages, which we describe in the rest of the paper:

- **Test generation and verification**. We combine enumeration- and SMT-based techniques to either verify the validity of the function, or, if it is not valid, discover counterexamples (examples of misbehaviors).

- **Fault localization.** Our localization algorithm then selects the smallest expression executed in all failing tests, modulo recursion.
- **Synthesis of similar expressions.** This erroneous expression is replaced by a "program hole". The now-incomplete function is sent to synthesis, with the previous expression used as a synthesis hint. (Neither the notion of holes nor the notion of synthesis hints has been introduced in prior work on deductive synthesis [13]).
- **Verification of the solution.** Lastly, the system attempts to prove the validity of the discovered solution. Our results in Sect. 5, Fig. 4 indicate in which cases the synthesized function passed the verification.

Repair Framework. Our starting point is the deductive synthesis framework first introduced in [13]. We show how this framework can be applied to program repair by introducing dedicated rules, as well as special predicates. We reuse the notation for synthesis tasks $[\![\bar{a}\ \langle \Pi \rhd \phi \rangle\ \bar{x}]\!]$: $\bar{a}$ denotes the set of *input variables*, $\bar{x}$ denotes the set of *output variables*, ϕ is the *synthesis predicate*, and Π is the *path condition* to the synthesis problem. The framework relies on deduction rules that take such an input synthesis problem and either (1) solve it immediately by returning the tuple $\langle P \mid T \rangle$ where P corresponds to the precondition under which the term T is a solution, or (2) decompose it into sub-problems, and define a way to compute the overall solution from sub-solutions. We illustrate these rules as well as their notation with a rule for splitting a problem containing a top-level or:

$$\frac{[\![\bar{a}\ \langle \Pi \rhd \phi_1 \rangle\ \bar{x}]\!] \vdash \langle P_1 \mid T_1 \rangle \qquad [\![\bar{a}\ \langle \Pi \rhd \phi_2 \rangle\ \bar{x}]\!] \vdash \langle P_2 \mid T_2 \rangle}{[\![\bar{a}\ \langle \Pi \rhd \phi_1 \lor \phi_2 \rangle\ \bar{x}]\!] \vdash \langle P_1 \lor P_2 \mid \mathsf{if}(P_1)\ \{T_1\}\ \mathsf{else}\ \{T_2\} \rangle}$$

This rule should be interpreted as follows: from an input synthesis problem $[\![\bar{a}\ \langle \Pi \rhd \phi_1 \lor \phi_2 \rangle\ \bar{x}]\!]$, the rule decomposes it in two subproblems: $[\![\bar{a}\ \langle \Pi \rhd \phi_1 \rangle\ \bar{x}]\!]$ and $[\![\bar{a}\ \langle \Pi \rhd \phi_2 \rangle\ \bar{x}]\!]$. Given corresponding solutions $\langle P_1 \mid T_1 \rangle$ and $\langle P_2 \mid T_2 \rangle$, the rule solves the input problem with $\langle P_1 \lor P_2 \mid \mathsf{if}(P_1)\ \{T_1\}\ \mathsf{else}\ \{T_2\} \rangle$.

To track the original (incorrect) implementation along instantiations of our deductive synthesis rules, we introduce a *guiding predicate* into the path condition of the synthesis problem. We refer to this guiding predicate as $\odot[\mathsf{expr}]$, where expr represents the original expression. This predicate does not have any logical meaning in the path-condition (it is equivalent to **true**), but it provides syntactic information that can be used by repair-dedicated rules. These rules are covered in detail in Sects. 2.1, 2.2 and 3.

2.1 Fault Localization

A contribution of our system is the ability to focus the repair problem to a small sub-part of the function's body that is responsible for its erroneous behavior. The underlying hypothesis is that most of the original implementation is correct. This technique allows us to reuse as much of the original implementation as possible and minimizes the size of the expression given to subsequent more expensive techniques. Focusing also has the profitable side-effect of making repair more predictable, even in the presence of weak specifications: repaired implementation tends to produce programs that preserve some of the existing branches, and thus have the same behavior on the executions that use only these preserved branches. We rely on the list of examples that fail the function specification to lead us to the source of the problem: if all failing examples only use one branch of some branching expression in the program, then we assume that the error is contained in that branch. We define $\mathcal{F}$ as the set of all inputs of collected failing tests (see Sect. 4). We describe focusing using the following rules.

If-Focus. Given the input problem $[\![\bar{a}\ \langle \odot[\mathsf{if}(c)\ \{t\}\ \mathsf{else}\ \{e\}] \rhd \phi\rangle\ \bar{x}]\!]$ we first check if there is an alternative condition expression such that all failing tests succeed:

IF-FOCUS-CONDITION:

$$\frac{\exists C.\forall \bar{i} \in \mathcal{F}.\ \phi[\bar{x} \mapsto \mathsf{if}(C(\bar{a}))\ \{t\}\ \mathsf{else}\ \{e\}, \bar{a} \mapsto \bar{i}] \quad [\![\bar{a}\ \langle \odot[c] \wedge \Pi \rhd \phi[\bar{x} \mapsto \mathsf{if}(x')\ \{t\}\ \mathsf{else}\ \{e\}]\rangle\ x']\!] \vdash \langle P \mid T\rangle}{[\![\bar{a}\ \langle \odot[\mathsf{if}(c)\ \{t\}\ \mathsf{else}\ \{e\}] \wedge \Pi \rhd \phi\rangle\ \bar{x}]\!] \vdash \langle P \mid \mathsf{if}(T)\ \{t\}\ \mathsf{else}\ \{e\}\rangle}$$

Instead of solving this higher-order hypothesis, we execute the function and non-deterministically consider both branches of the **if** (and do so within recursive invocations as well). If a valid execution exists for each failing test, the formula is considered satisfiable enabling us to focus on the condition. Otherwise, we check whether c evaluates to either **true** or **false** for all failing inputs, allowing us to focus on the corresponding branch:

IF-FOCUS-THEN:

$$\frac{[\![\bar{a}\ \langle \odot[t] \wedge c \wedge \Pi \rhd \phi\rangle\ \bar{x}]\!] \vdash \langle P \mid T\rangle \qquad \forall \bar{i} \in \mathcal{F}.c[\bar{a} \mapsto \bar{i}]}{[\![\bar{a}\ \langle \odot[\mathsf{if}(c)\ \{t\}\ \mathsf{else}\ \{e\}] \wedge \Pi \rhd \phi\rangle\ \bar{x}]\!] \vdash \langle P \mid \mathsf{if}(c)\ \{T\}\ \mathsf{else}\ \{e\}\rangle}$$

IF-FOCUS-ELSE:

$$\frac{[\![\bar{a}\ \langle \odot[e] \wedge \neg c \wedge \Pi \rhd \phi\rangle\ \bar{x}]\!] \vdash \langle P \mid T\rangle \qquad \forall \bar{i} \in \mathcal{F}.\neg c[a \mapsto \bar{i}]}{[\![\bar{a}\ \langle \odot[\mathsf{if}(c)\ \{t\}\ \mathsf{else}\ \{e\}] \wedge \Pi \rhd \phi\rangle\ \bar{x}]\!] \vdash \langle P \mid \mathsf{if}(c)\ \{t\}\ \mathsf{else}\ \{T\}\rangle}$$

We use analogous rules to repair **match** expressions, which are ubiquitous in our programs. Here, if all failing tests lead to one particular branch of the **match**, we focus on that particular branch.

The above rules use tests to locally approximate the validity of branches. They are sound only if $\mathcal{F}$ is sufficiently large. Our system therefore performs an end-to-end verification for the complete solution, ensuring the overall soundness.

2.2 Guided Decompositions

In case focusing rules fail to identify a single branch of an **if**- or **match**-expression as responsible, we might still benefit from reusing most of the expression. In the case of **if**, reuse is limited to the **if**-condition, but for a **match**-expression, this may extend to multiple valid cases. To this end, we introduce rules analogous to focus, that do decompositions based on the guide.

IF-SPLIT:

$$\frac{[\![\bar{a}\ \langle \odot[t] \wedge c \wedge \Pi \rhd \phi\rangle\ \bar{x}]\!] \vdash \langle P_1 \mid T_1\rangle \qquad [\![\bar{a}\ \langle \odot[e] \wedge \neg c \wedge \Pi \rhd \phi\rangle\ \bar{x}]\!] \vdash \langle P_2 \mid T_2\rangle}{[\![\bar{a}\ \langle \odot[\mathsf{if}(c)\ \{t\}\ \mathsf{else}\ \{e\}] \wedge \Pi \rhd \phi\rangle\ \bar{x}]\!] \vdash \langle (c \wedge P_1) \vee (\neg c \wedge P_2) \mid \mathsf{if}(c)\ \{T_1\}\ \mathsf{else}\ \{T_2\}\rangle}$$

To reuse the valid branches of an **if** or a **match**-expression on which focus failed, we introduce a rule that solves the problem if the guiding expression satisfies the specification.

$$\text{GUIDED-VERIFY: } = \frac{\Pi \models \phi[\bar{x} \mapsto \mathsf{term}]}{[\![\bar{a}\ \langle \odot[term] \wedge \Pi \rhd \phi \rangle\ \bar{x}]\!] \vdash \langle \mathsf{true} \mid \mathsf{term} \rangle}$$

2.3 Generating Recursive Calls

Our purely functional language often requires us to synthesize recursive implementations. Consequently, the synthesizer must be able to generate calls to the function currently getting synthesized. However, we must take special care to avoid introducing calls resulting in a non-terminating implementation. (Such an erroneous implementation would be conceived as valid if it trivially satisfies the specification due to inductive hypothesis over a non-well-founded relation.)

Our technique consists of recording the arguments a at the entry point of the function, f, and keeping track of these arguments through the decompositions. We represent this information with a syntactic predicate $\Downarrow[\mathsf{f(a)}]$, similar to the guiding predicate from the previous sections. We then heuristically assume that reducing the arguments a will not introduce non-terminating calls.

We illustrate this mechanism by considering the desugar function shown in Fig. 1. We start by injecting the entry call information as

$$[\![e\ \langle \Downarrow[\mathsf{desugar(e)}] \wedge ... \rhd \phi \rangle\ x]\!]$$

This synthesis problem will then be decomposed by the various deduction rules available in the framework. An interesting case to consider is a decomposition by pattern-matching on e which specializes the problem to known variants of Expr. The specialized problem for the Plus variant will look as follows:

$$[\![e1\,, e2\ \langle \Downarrow[\mathsf{desugar(Plus(e1,\ e2))}] \wedge ... \rhd \phi \rangle\ x]\!]$$

As a result, we assume that the calls desugar(e1) and desugar(e2) are likely to terminate, so they are considered as candidate expressions when symbolically exploring terms, as explained in Sect. 3.

This relatively simple technique allows us to introduce recursive calls while filtering trivially non-terminating calls. In the case where it still introduces infinite recursion, we can discard the solution using a more expensive termination checker, though we found that this is seldom needed in practice.

2.4 Synthesis Within Repair

The repair-specific rules described earlier aim at solving repair problems according to the error model. Thanks to integration into the Leon synthesis framework, general synthesis rules also apply, which enables the repair of more intricate errors. This achieves an appealing combination between fast repairs for predictable errors and expressive, albeit slower, repairs for more complicated errors.

3 Counterexample-Guided Similar-Term Exploration

After following the overall structure of the original problem, it is often the case that the remaining erroneous branches can be fixed by applying small changes to their implementations. For instance, an expression calling a function might be wrong only in one of its arguments or have two of its arguments swapped. We exploit this assumption by considering different variations to the original expression. Due to the lack of a large code base in pure Scala subset that Leon handles, we cannot use statistically informed techniques such as [9], so we define an error model following our intuition and experience from previous work.

We use the notation $G(\mathsf{expr})$ to denote the space of variations of expr and define it in the form of a grammar as

$$G(\mathsf{expr}) ::= G_{swap}(\mathsf{expr}) \mid G_{arg}(\mathsf{expr}) \mid G_{*^2}(\mathsf{expr})$$

with the following forms of variations.

Swapping Arguments. We consider here all the variants of swapping two arguments that are compatible type-wise. For instance, for an operation with three operands of the same type:

$$G_{swap}(\mathsf{op(a,b,c)}) ::= \mathsf{op(b,a,c)} \mid \mathsf{op(a,c,b)} \mid \mathsf{op(c,b,a)}$$

Generalizing One Argument. This variation corresponds to making a mistake in only one argument of the operation we generalize:

$$G_{arg}(\mathsf{op(a,b,c)}) ::= \mathsf{op}(G(\mathsf{a}),\mathsf{b},\mathsf{c}) \mid \mathsf{op}(\mathsf{a},G(\mathsf{b}),\mathsf{c}) \mid \mathsf{op}(\mathsf{a},\mathsf{b},G(\mathsf{c}))$$

Bounded Arbitrary Expression. We consider a grammar of interesting expressions of the given type and of limited depth. This grammar considers all operations in scope as well as all input variables. It also considers safe recursive calls discovered in Sect. 2.3. Finally, it includes the guiding expression as a terminal, which corresponds to possibly wrapping the source expression in an operation. For example, given a predicate $\Downarrow[\mathsf{listSum(Cons(h,t))}]$ and a mod function $\mathsf{Int} \times \mathsf{Int} \rightarrow \mathsf{Int}$ in scope, an integer operation op(a,b,c) is generalized as:

$$\begin{aligned} G_{*^2}(\mathsf{op(a,b,c)}) &::= G_{Int2} \mid G_{Int1} \mid G_{Int0} & G_{Int1} &::= G_{Int0} + G_{Int0} \\ G_{Int2} &::= G_{Int1} + G_{Int1} & &\mid G_{Int0} - G_{Int0} \\ &\mid G_{Int1} - G_{Int1} & &\mid \mathsf{mod}(G_{Int0}, G_{Int0}) \\ &\mid \mathsf{mod}(G_{Int1}, G_{Int1}) & &\mid \mathsf{listSum(t)} \\ &\mid \mathsf{listSum(t)} & G_{Int0} &::= 0 \mid 1 \mid \mathsf{h} \mid \mathsf{op(a,b,c)} \end{aligned}$$

Our grammars cover a range of variations corresponding to common errors. During synthesis, the system generates a specific grammar for each invocation of this repair rule, and explores symbolically the space of all expressions in the grammar. We rely on a CEGIS-loop bootstrapped with our test inputs to explore these expressions. This can be abstractly represented by the following rule:

$$\text{CEGIS-GEN: } = \frac{\exists \mathsf{T} \in \mathcal{L}(G(\mathsf{term}))\ \forall \bar{a}.\Pi \implies \phi[\bar{x} \mapsto \mathsf{T}]}{[\![\bar{a}\ \langle \odot[term] \wedge \Pi \rhd \phi\rangle\ \bar{x}]\!] \vdash \langle \mathsf{true} \mid \mathsf{T}\rangle}$$

Even though this rule is inherently incomplete, it is able to fix common errors efficiently. Our deductive approach allows us to introduce such tailored rules without loss of generality: errors that go beyond this model may be repaired using more general, albeit slower synthesis rules.

Precise Handling of Recursive Calls in CEGIS. Our system uses a symbolic approach to avoid enumerating expressions explicitly [13]. When considering recursive calls among possible expressions within CEGIS, the interpretation of such calls needs to refer back to this same expression. Our previous approach [13] treats recursive invocations of the function under synthesis as satisfying only the postcondition, leading to spurious counter-examples. Our new solution first constructs a parametrized program explicitly representing the search space: given a grammar G at a certain unfolding level, we construct a function cTree($\bar{a}$, B) in which we describe non-terminals as values with each production guarded by a distinct entry of the B array, as in the following repair a case of the size function.

```
def cTree[T](h: T, t: List[T],
             B: Array[Boolean]) = {
  val c1 = if (B(0)) 0
           else if (B(1)) 1
           else if (B(2)) size(t, B)
           else _
  val c2 = if (B(3)) 0
           else if (B(4)) 1
           else if (B(5)) size(t, B)
           else _
  val c3 = if (B(6)) c1 + c2
           else if (B(7)) c1 − c2
           else _
  c3 }
```

```
def size[T](l: List[T],
            B: Array[Boolean]): Int = {
  l match {
    case Cons(h, t) ⇒ cTree(h, t, B)
    case Nil() ⇒ 0
  }
}
def nonEmpty(l: List[T],
             B: Array[Boolean]) = {
  size(l, B) > 0
}
```

In this new program, the function under repair is defined using the partial solution corresponding to the current deduction tree, in which we call cTree at the point of the CEGIS invocation. Other unsolved branches of the deduction tree become synthesis holes. We augment transitive callers with this additional B argument, passing it accordingly. This ensures that a specific valuation of B corresponds exactly to a program where the point of CEGIS invocation is replaced by the corresponding expression. We rely on tests collected in Sect. 4 to test individual valuations of B, removing failing expression from the search space. Finally, we perform CEGIS using symbolic term exploration with the SMT solver to find candidate expressions [13].

4 Generating and Using Tests for Repair

Tests play an essential role in our framework, allowing us to gather information about the valid and invalid parts of the function. In this section we elaborate on how we select, generate, and filter examples of inputs and possibly outputs. Several components of our system then make use of these examples. We distinguish two kinds of tests: input tests and input-output tests. Namely, input tests provide valid inputs for the function according to its precondition, while input-output tests also specify the exact output corresponding to each input.

Extraction and Generation of Tests. Our system relies on three main sources for tests that are used to make the repair process more efficient.

(1) User-provided symbolic input-output tests. It is often interesting for the user to specify how a function behaves by listing a few examples providing inputs and corresponding outputs. However, having to provide full inputs and outputs can be tedious and impractical. To make specifying families of tests convenient, we define a **passes** construct to express input-output examples, relying on pattern matching in our language to symbolically describe sets of inputs and their corresponding outputs. This gives us an expressive way of specifying classes of input-output examples. Not only may the pattern match more than one input, but the corresponding outputs are given by an expression which may depend on the pattern's variables. Wildcard patterns are particularly useful when the function does not depend on all aspects of its inputs. For instance, a function computing the size of a generic list does not inspect the values of individual list elements. Similarly, the sum of a list of integers could be specified concisely for all lists of sizes up to 2. Both examples are illustrated by Fig. 2.

```
def size[T](list: List[T]): Int = {
  list match {
    case Nil() ⇒ 0
    case Cons(h, t) ⇒ 1 + size(t)
  }
} ensuring { res ⇒
  (res ≥ 0) &&
  (list, res) passes {
    case Cons(_, Cons(_, Nil())) ⇒ 2
    case Cons(_, Nil()) ⇒ 1
    case Nil() ⇒ 0 } }
```

```
def sum(list: List[Int]): Int = {
  list match {
    case Nil() ⇒ 0
    case Cons(h, t) ⇒ h + sum(t)
  }
} ensuring { res ⇒
  (list, res) passes {
    case Cons(a, Cons(b, Nil())) ⇒ a + b
    case Cons(a, Nil()) ⇒ a
    case Nil() ⇒ 0 } }
```

Fig. 2. Partial specifications using the passes construct, allowing to match more than one inputs and providing the expected output as an expression.

Having partially symbolic input-output examples strikes a good balance between literal examples and full-functional specifications. From the symbolic tests, we generate concrete input-output examples by instantiating each pattern several times using enumeration techniques, and executing the output expression to yield an output value. For instance, from case Cons(a, Cons(b, Nil())) ⇒ a + b we will generate the following tests resulting from replacing a, b with all combinations of values from a finite set, including, for example, test with input Cons(1, Cons(2, Nil())) and output 3. We generate up to 5 distinct tests per pattern, when possible. These symbolic specifications are the only forms of tests provided by the developer; any other tests that our system uses are derived automatically.

(2) Generated input tests. We rely on the same enumeration technique to generate inputs satisfying the precondition of the function. Using a generate and test approach, we gather up to 400 valid input tests in the first 1000 enumerated.

(3) Solver-generated Tests. Lastly, we rely on the underlying solvers for recursive functions of Leon [25] to generate counter-examples. Given that the function is invalid and that it terminates, the solver (which is complete for counter-examples) is guaranteed to eventually provide us with at least one failing test.

Classifying and Minimizing Traces. We partition the set of collected tests into passing and failing sets. A test is considered as failing if it violates a precondition, a postcondition, or emits one of various other kinds of runtime errors when the function to repair is executed on it. In the presence of recursive functions, a given test may fail within one of its recursive invocations. It is interesting in such scenarios to consider the arguments of this specific sub-invocation: they are typically smaller than the original and are better representatives of the failure. To clarify this, consider the example in Fig. 3 (based on the program in Fig. 1):

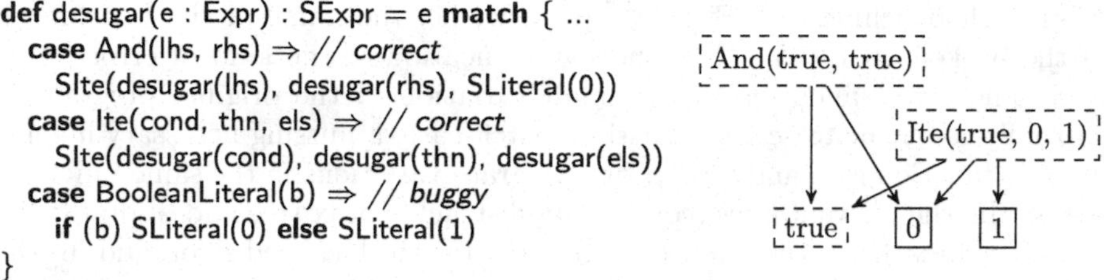

Fig. 3. Code and invocation graph for desugar. Solid borderlines stand for passing tests, dashed ones for failing ones. Type constructors for literals have been omitted.

Assume the tests collected are And(BooleanLiteral(**true**), BooleanLiteral(**true**)), Ite(BooleanLiteral(**true**), IntLiteral(0), IntLiteral(1)) and BooleanLiteral(**true**). When executed with these tests, the function produces the graph of eval invocations shown on the right of Fig. 3. A trivial classification tactic would label all three tests as faulty, even though it is obvious that all errors can be explained by the bug in BooleanLiteral, due to the dependencies between tests. More generally, *a failing test should also be blamed for the failure of all other tests that invoke it transitively.* Our framework deploys this smarter classification. Thus, in our example, it would only label BooleanLiteral(**true**) as a failing example, which would lead to correct localization of the problem on the faulty branch. Note that this process will discover new failing tests not present in the original test set, if they occur as recursive sub-invocations.

Our experience with incorporating tests into the Leon system indicate that they are proving time and again to be extremely important for the tool's efficiency, even though our system is in its spirit based on verification as opposed to testing alone. In addition to allowing us to detect errors sooner and filter out wrong synthesis candidates, tests also allow us to quickly find the approximate error location.

5 Evaluation

We evaluate our implementation on a set of benchmarks in which we manually injected errors (Fig. 4). The programs mainly focus on data structure implementations and syntax tree operations. Each benchmark is comprised of algebraic data-type definitions and recursive functions that manipulate them, specified using strong yet still partial preconditions and postconditions. We manually introduced errors of different types in each copy of the benchmarks. We ran our tool unassisted until completion to obtain a repair, providing it only with the name of the file and the name of the function to repair (typically the choice of the function could also have been localized automatically by running the verification on the entire file). The experiments were run on an Intel(R) Core(TM) i7-2600K CPU @ 3.40GHz with 16GB RAM, with 2GB given to the Java Virtual Machine. While the deductive reasoning supports parallelism in principle, our implementation is currently single-threaded.

For each benchmark of Fig. 4 we provide: (1) the name of the benchmark and the broken operation; (2) a short classification of the kind of error introduced. The error kinds include: a small variation of the original program, a completely faulty **match**-case, a missing **match**-case, a missing necessary **if**-split, a missing function call, and finally, two separate variations in the same function. We describe the relevant sizes (counted in abstract syntax tree nodes) of: (3) the overall benchmark, (4) the erroneous function, (5) the localized error, and (6) the repaired expression. The full size of the program is relevant because our repair algorithm may introduce calls to any function defined in the benchmark, and also because the verification of a function depends on other functions in the file (recall Fig. 1). We also include the time, in seconds, our tool took to: (7) collect and classify tests and (8) repair the broken expression. Finally, we report (9) if the system could formally (and automatically) prove the validity of the repaired implementation. Our examples are challenging to verify, let alone repair. They contain both functional and test-based specifications to capture the intended behavior. Many rely on unfolding procedure of [24,25] to handle contracts that contain other auxiliary recursive functions. The fast exponentiation algorithm of Numerical.power relies on non-linear reasoning of the Z3 SMT solver [4].

An immediate observation is that fault localization is often able to focus the repair to a small subset of the body. Combined with the symbolic term exploration, this translates to a fast repair if the error fell within the error model.

Operation	Error	Size				Time (sec)		Proof
		Prg	Fun	Err	Fix	Test	Repair	Success
Compiler.desugar1	full case	1335	81	3	5	1.2	2.2	✓
Compiler.desugar2	full case	1330	79	2	8	1.0	10.2	✓
Compiler.desugar3	variation	1324	83	7	7	0.9	1.6	✓
Compiler.desugar4	variation	1324	83	7	7	1.4	1.7	✓
Compiler.desugar5	2 variations	1458	83	83	83	1.4	14.0	✓
Compiler.simplify1	variation	1458	30	4	4	0.8	1.7	✓
Compiler.simplify2	variation	1464	30	2	2	0.8	1.7	✓
Heap.merge1	if cond	1084	36	3	3	1.9	3.0	✓
Heap.merge2	variation	1084	36	1	1	1.1	1.4	✓
Heap.merge3	if cond	1084	36	3	3	1.9	3.1	✓
Heap.merge4	variation	1084	36	6	6	1.2	2.4	✓
Heap.merge5	if cond	1086	38	5	7	1.2	3.0	✓
Heap.merge6	2 variations	1084	36	36	36	1.5	12.7	
Heap.insert	variation	1086	8	8	6	5.2	1.4	✓
Heap.makeNode	variation	1086	16	7	5	2.2	1.3	✓
List.pad	variation	1157	34	8	6	1.0	1.4	✓
List.++	variation	1153	9	3	5	2.5	1.1	✓
List.:+	full case	1161	11	1	3	1.8	1.2	✓
List.replace	full case	1172	14	3	13	1.8	11.2	✓
List.count	variation	1185	16	3	5	0.9	1.5	✓
List.find1	variation	1175	21	2	4	3.0	3.8	
List.find2	variation	1177	23	4	6	3.0	3.7	
List.find3	if cond	1178	24	18	17	4.8	5.9	
List.size	variation	1157	10	4	4	1.7	1.2	✓
List.sum	variation	1175	10	4	4	1.3	1.2	✓
List.delete	missing call	1162	16	1	3	1.5	1.1	✓
List.drop	2 variations	1166	21	21	27	1.5	16.6	✓
PropLogic.nnf1	missing call	915	51	1	3	0.7	1.3	✓
PropLogic.nnf2	missing case	911	47	1	13	0.9	3.4	✓
PropLogic.nnf3	variation	916	51	2	4	0.9	1.2	✓
PropLogic.nnf4	variation	920	52	5	5	0.8	1.3	✓
PropLogic.nnf5	full case	916	48	1	5	0.9	1.7	✓
Numerical.power	variation	133	23	5	7	0.3	1.2	✓
Numerical.moddiv	variation	186	30	3	3	0.3	1.1	✓
MergeSort.split	full case	221	28	3	7	2.0	3.3	✓
MergeSort.merge1	variation	951	32	5	5	1.7	1.3	✓
MergeSort.merge2	variation	951	32	3	3	1.8	1.9	✓
MergeSort.merge3	variation	949	30	3	5	1.5	1.5	✓
MergeSort.merge4	2 variations	951	32	32	32	1.8	21.1	

Fig. 4. Automatically repaired functions using our system. We provide for each operation: a small description of the kind of error introduced, the overall program size, the size of the invalid function, the size of the erroneous expression we locate and the size of the repaired version. We then provide the times our tool took to: gather and classify tests, and repair the erroneous expression. Finally, we mention if the resulting expression verifies. The source of all benchmarks can be found on http://lara.epfl.ch/w/leon-repair (see also http://leon.epfl.ch)

Among the hardest benchmarks are the ones labeled as having "2 variations". For example, Compiler.desugar5 is similar to one in Fig. 1 but contains two errors. In those cases, localization returns the entire **match** as the invalid expression. Our guided repair uses the existing **match** as the guide and successfully resynthesizes code that repairs both erroneous branches. Another challenging example is Heap.merge3, for which the more elaborate If-Focus-Condition rule of Sect. 2.1 kicks in to resynthesize the condition of the **if** expression.

The repairs listed in evaluation are not only valid according to their specification, but were also manually validated by us to match the intended behavior. A failing proof thus does not indicate a wrong repair, but rather that our system was not able to automatically derive a proof of its correctness, often due to insufficient inductive invariants. We identify three scenarios under which repair itself may not succeed: if the assumptions mentioned in Sect. 2 are violated, when the necessary repair is either too big or outside of the scope of general synthesis, or if test collection does not yield sufficiently many interesting failing tests to locate the error.

6 Further Related Work

Much of the prior work focused on imperative programming, without native support for algebraic data types, making it typically infeasible to even automatically verify data structure properties of the kind that our benchmarks contain. Syntax-guided synthesis format [1,2] does not support algebraic data types, or specific notion of repair (it could be used to specify some of the sub-problems that our system generates, such those of Sect. 3).

GenProg [7] and SemFix [17] accept as input a C program along with user-provided sets of passing and failing test cases, but no formal specification. Our technique for fault localization is not applicable to a sequential program with side-effects, and these tools employ statistical fault localization techniques, based on program executions. GenProg applies no code synthesis, but tries to repair the program by iteratively deleting, swapping, or duplicating program statements, according to a genetic algorithm. SemFix, on the other hand, uses synthesis, but does not take into account the faulty expression while synthesizing. AutoFix-E/E2 [18] operates on Eiffel programs equipped with formal contracts. Formal contracts are used to automatically generate a set of passing and failing test cases, but not to verify candidate solutions. AutoFix-E uses an elaborate mechanism for fault localization, which combines syntactic, control flow and statistical dynamic analysis. It follows a synthesis approach with repair schemas, which reuse the faulty statement (e.g. as a branch of a conditional). Samanta et al. [20] propose abstracting a C program with a boolean constraint, repairing this constraint so that all assertions in the program are satisfied by repeatedly applying to it update schemas according to a cost model, then concretize the boolean constraint back to a repaired C program. Their approach needs developer intervention to define the cost model for each program, as well as at the concretization step. Logozzo et al. [16] present a repair suggestion framework based on static analysis provided by the CodeContracts static checker [5]; the properties checked are typically simpler than those in our case. In [6], Gopinath et al. repair data structure operations by picking an input which exposes a suspicious statement, then using a SAT-solver to discover a corresponding concrete output that satisfies the specification. This concrete output is then abstracted to various possible expressions to yield candidate repairs, which are filtered with bounded verification. In their approach, Chandra et al. [3] consider an expression as a candidate for repair if substituting it with some concrete value fixes a failing test.

Repair has also been studied in the context of reactive and pushdown systems with otherwise finite control [8,10,11,19,20,26]. In [26], the authors generate repairs that preserve explicitly subsets of traces of the original program, in a way strengthening the specification automatically. We deal with the case of functions from inputs to outputs equipped with contracts. In case of a weak contract we provide only heuristic guarantees that the existing behaviors are preserved, arising from the tendency of our algorithm to reuse existing parts of the program.

7 Conclusions

We have presented an approach to program repair of mutually recursive functional programs, building on top of a deductive synthesis framework. The starting point gives it the ability to verify functions, find counterexamples, and synthesize small fragments of code. When doing repair, it has proven fruitful to first localize the error and then perform synthesis on a small fragment. Tests proved very useful in performing such localization, as well as for generally speeding up synthesis and repair. In addition to deriving tests by enumeration and verification, we have introduced a specification construct that uses pattern matching to describe symbolic tests, from which we efficiently derive concrete tests without invoking full-fledged verification. In case of tests for recursive functions, we perform dependency analysis and introduce new ones to better localize the cause of the error. While localization of errors within conditional control flow can be done by analyzing test runs, the challenge remains to localize change inside large expressions with nested function calls. We have introduced the notion of *guided synthesis* that uses the previous version of the code as a guide when searching for a small change to an existing large expression. The use of a guide is very flexible, and also allows us to repair multiple errors in some cases.

Our experiments with benchmarks of thousands of syntax tree nodes in size, including tree transformations and data structure operations confirm that repair is more tractable than synthesis for functional programs. The existing (incorrect) expression provides a hint on useful code fragments from which to build a correct solution. Compared to unguided synthesis, the common case of repair remains more predictable and scalable. At the same time, the developer need not learn a notation for specifying holes or templates. We thus believe that repair is a practical way to deploy synthesis in software development.

References

1. Alur, R., Bodik, R., Dallal, E., Fisman, D., Garg, P., Juniwal, G., Kress-Gazit, H., Madhusudan, P., Martin, M.M.K., Raghothaman, M., Saha, S., Seshia, S. A., Singh, R., Solar-Lezama, A., Torlak, E., Udupa, A.: Syntax-guided synthesis. To Appear in Marktoberdrof NATO proceedings, (2014). http://sygus.seas.upenn.edu/files/sygus_extended.pdf. Accessed 02 June 2015
2. Alur, R., Bodík, R., Juniwal, G., Martin, M.M.K., Raghothaman, M., Seshia, S. A., Singh, R., Solar-Lezama, A., Torlak, E., Udupa, A.: Syntax-guided synthesis. In: FMCAD, pp. 1–17. IEEE (2013)
3. Chandra, S., Torlak, E., Barman, S., Bodík, R.: Angelic debugging. In: Taylor, R.N., Gall, H.C., Medvidovic, N. (eds.) ICSE, pp. 121–130. ACM, New york (2011)
4. de Moura, L., Bjørner, N.S.: Z3: An efficient SMT solver. In: Ramakrishnan, C.R., Rehof, J. (eds.) TACAS 2008. LNCS, vol. 4963, pp. 337–340. Springer, Heidelberg (2008)
5. Fähndrich, M., Logozzo, F.: Static contract checking with abstract interpretation. In: Beckert, B., Marché, C. (eds.) FoVeOOS 2010. LNCS, vol. 6528, pp. 10–30. Springer, Heidelberg (2011)
6. Gopinath, D., Malik, M.Z., Khurshid, S.: Specification-Based Program Repair Using SAT. In: Abdulla, P.A., Leino, K.R.M. (eds.) TACAS 2011. LNCS, vol. 6605, pp. 173–188. Springer, Heidelberg (2011)
7. Goues, C.L., Nguyen, T., Forrest, S., Weimer, W.: Genprog: a generic method for automatic software repair. TSE **38**(1), 54–72 (2012)
8. Griesmayer, A., Bloem, R., Cook, B.: Repair of boolean programs with an application to C. In: Ball, T., Jones, R.B. (eds.) CAV 2006. LNCS, vol. 4144, pp. 358–371. Springer, Heidelberg (2006)
9. Gvero, T., Kuncak, V., Kuraj, I., Piskac, R., Complete completion using types and weights. In: PLDI, pp. 27–38 (2013)
10. Jobstmann, B., Griesmayer, A., Bloem, R.: Program repair as a game. In: Etessami, K., Rajamani, S.K. (eds.) CAV 2005. LNCS, vol. 3576, pp. 226–238. Springer, Heidelberg (2005)
11. Jobstmann, B., Staber, S., Griesmayer, A., Bloem, R.: Finding and fixing faults. JCSS **78**(2), 441–460 (2012)
12. Jose, M., Majumdar, R.: Cause clue clauses: error localization using maximum satisfiability. In: Hall, M.W., Padua, D.A. (eds.) PLDI, pp. 437–446. ACM, New york (2011)
13. Kneuss, E., Kuraj, I., Kuncak, V., Suter, P.: Synthesis modulo recursive functions. In: Hosking, A.L., Eugster, P.T., Lopes, C.V. (eds.) OOPSLA, pp. 407–426. ACM, New york (2013)
14. Könighofer, R., Bloem, R.: Automated error localization and correction for imperative programs. In: Bjesse, P., Slobodová, A. (eds.) FMCAD, pp. 91–100. FMCAD Inc, Austin (2011)
15. Kuncak, V., Mayer, M., Piskac, R., Suter, P.: Functional synthesis for linear arithmetic and sets. STTT **15**(5–6), 455–474 (2013)
16. Logozzo, F., Ball, T.: Modular and verified automatic program repair. In: Leavens, G.T., Dwyer, M.B. (eds.) OOPSLA, pp. 133–146. ACM, Newyork (2012)
17. Nguyen, H.D.T., Qi, D., Roychoudhury, A., Chandra, S.: Semfix: program repair via semantic analysis. In: Notkin, D., Cheng, B.H.C., Pohl, K. (eds.) ICSE, pp. 772–781. IEEE and ACM, New York (2013)

18. Pei, Y., Wei, Y., Furia, C.A., Nordio, M., Meyer, B.: Code-based automated program fixing. ArXiv e-prints (2011). arXiv:1102.1059
19. Samanta, R., Deshmukh, J.V., Emerson, E.A.: Automatic generation of local repairs for boolean programs. In: Cimatti, A., Jones, R.B. (eds.) FMCAD, pp. 1–10. IEEE, New York (2008)
20. Samanta, R., Olivo, O., Emerson, E.A.: Cost-aware automatic program repair. In: Müller-Olm, M., Seidl, H. (eds.) Static Analysis. LNCS, vol. 8723, pp. 268–284. Springer, Heidelberg (2014)
21. Solar-Lezama, A.: Program sketching. STTT **15**(5–6), 475–495 (2013)
22. Solar-Lezama, A., Tancau, L., Bodík, R., Seshia, S.A., Saraswat, V.A.: Combinatorial sketching for finite programs. In: ASPLOS, pp. 404–415 (2006)
23. Srivastava, S., Gulwani, S., Foster, J.S.: Template-based program verification and program synthesis. STTT **15**(5–6), 497–518 (2013)
24. Suter, P.: Programming with Specifications. Ph.D. thesis, EPFL, December 2012
25. Suter, P., Köksal, A.S., Kuncak, V.: Satisfiability modulo recursive programs. In: Yahav, E. (ed.) Static Analysis. LNCS, vol. 6887, pp. 298–315. Springer, Heidelberg (2011)
26. von Essen, C., Jobstmann, B.: Program repair without regret. In: Sharygina, N., Veith, H. (eds.) CAV 2013. LNCS, vol. 8044, pp. 896–911. Springer, Heidelberg (2013)
27. Zeller, A., Hildebrandt, R.: Simplifying and isolating failure-inducing input. TSE **28**(2), 183–200 (2002)

Quantifying Conformance Using the Skorokhod Metric

Jyotirmoy V. Deshmukh[1], Rupak Majumdar[2], and Vinayak S. Prabhu[2,3](✉)

[1] Toyota Technical Center, Los Angeles, USA
jyotirmoy.deshmukh@tema.toyota.com
[2] MPI-SWS, Kaiserslautern, Germany
{rupak,vinayak}@mpi-sws.org
[3] University of Porto, Porto, Portugal

Abstract. The conformance testing problem for dynamical systems asks, given two dynamical models (e.g., as Simulink diagrams), whether their behaviors are "close" to each other. In the semi-formal approach to conformance testing, the two systems are simulated on a large set of tests, and a metric, defined on pairs of real-valued, real-timed trajectories, is used to determine a lower bound on the distance. We show how the Skorokhod metric on continuous dynamical systems can be used as the foundation for conformance testing of complex dynamical models. The Skorokhod metric allows for both state value mismatches and timing distortions, and is thus well suited for checking conformance between idealized models of dynamical systems and their implementations. We demonstrate the robustness of the metric by proving a *transference theorem*: trajectories close under the Skorokhod metric satisfy "close" logical properties in the timed linear time logic TLTL augmented with a rich class of temporal and spatial constraint predicates. We provide an efficient window-based streaming algorithm to compute the Skorokhod metric, and use it as a basis for a conformance testing tool for Simulink. We experimentally demonstrate the effectiveness of our tool in finding discrepant behaviors on a set of control system benchmarks, including an industrial challenge problem.

1 Introduction

A fundamental question in model-based design is *conformance testing*: whether two models of a system display similar behavior. For discrete systems, this question is well-studied [19,20,28,29], and there is a rich theory of process equivalences based, e.g., on bisimilarity. For continuous and hybrid systems, however, the state of the art is somewhat unsatisfactory. While there is a straightforward generalization of process equivalences to the continuous case, in practice, equivalence notions such as bisimilarity are always too strong and most systems are not bisimilar. Since equivalence is a Boolean notion, one gets no additional information about the systems other than they are "not bisimilar." Further, even if two dynamical systems are bisimilar, they may still differ in many control-theoretic

This research was funded in part by a Humboldt foundation grant, FCT grant SFRHBPD902672012, and by a contract from Toyota Motors.

D. Kroening and C.S. Păsăreanu (Eds.): CAV 2015, Part II, LNCS 9207, pp. 234–250, 2015.
DOI: 10.1007/978-3-319-21668-3_14

properties. Thus, classical notions for equivalence and conformance have been of limited use in industrial practice.

In recent years, the notion of bisimulation has therefore been generalized to *metrics* on systems, which quantify the distance between them. For example, one approach is that of ϵ-bisimulation, which requires that the states of the two systems remain "close" forever (within an ϵ-ball), rather than coincide exactly. Under suitable stability assumptions on the dynamics, one can construct ϵ-bisimulations [17,18]. Unfortunately, proving the pre-requisites for the existence of ϵ-bisimulations for complex dynamical models, or coming up with suitable and practically tractable bisimulation functions is extremely difficult in practice. In addition, establishing ϵ-bisimulation requires full knowledge of the system dynamics making the scheme inapplicable where one system is an actual physical component with unknown dynamics. So, these notions have also been of limited industrial use so far.

Instead, a more pragmatic semi-formal approach has gained prominence in industrial practice. In this approach, the two systems are executed on the same input sequences and a metric on finite trajectories is used to evaluate the closeness of these trajectories. The key to this methodology is the selection of a *good* metric, with the following properties:

- *Transference.* Closeness in the metric must translate to preserving interesting classes of logical and functional specifications between systems, and
- *Tractability.* The metric should be efficiently computable.

In addition, there is the more informal requirement of *usability*: the metric should classify systems which the engineers consider close as being close, and conversely.

The simplest candidate metric is a *pointwise* metric that computes the maximum pointwise difference between two trajectories, sometimes generalized to apply a constant time-shift to one trajectory [15]. Unfortunately, for many practical models, two trajectories may be close only under variable time-shifts. This is the case, for example, for two dynamical models that may use different numerical integration techniques (e.g., fixed step versus adaptive step) or when some component in the implementation has some jitter. Thus, the pointwise metric spuriously reports large distances for "close" models. More nuanched hybrid distances have been proposed [1], but the transference properties of these metrics w.r.t. common temporal logics are not yet clear.

In this work we present a methodology for quantifying conformance between real-valued dynamical systems based on the *Skorokhod* metric [12]. The Skorokhod metric allows for mismatches in both the trace values and in the timeline, and quantifies temporal and spatial variation of the system dynamics under a unifying framework. The distortion of the timeline is specified by a *retiming* function r which is a continuous bijective strictly increasing function from $\mathbb{R}_+$ to $\mathbb{R}_+$. Using the retiming function, we obtain the *retimed trace* $x\left(\mathsf{r}(t)\right)$ from the original trace $x(t)$. Intuitively, in the retimed trace $x\left(\mathsf{r}(t)\right)$, we see exactly the same values as before, in exactly the same order, but the time duration between two values might now be different than the corresponding duration in the original trace. The amount of distortion for the retiming r is given by $\sup_{t\geq 0}|\mathsf{r}(t) - t|$. Using retiming functions, the Skorokhod distance between two traces x and y is defined to be the least value over all possible retimings r of:

$$\max\left(\sup_{t\in[0,T]} |\mathsf{r}(t)-t|,\ \sup_{t\in[0,T]} \mathcal{D}\big(x\left(\mathsf{r}(t)\right), y(t)\big)\right),$$

where $\mathcal{D}$ is a pointwise metric on values. In this formula, the first component quantifies the *timing discrepancy* of the timing distortion required to "match" two traces, and the second quantifies the *value mismatch* (in the metric space $\mathcal{O}$) of the values under the timing distortion. The Skorokhod metric was introduced as a theoretical basis for defining the semantics of hybrid systems by providing an appropriate hybrid topology [8,9]. We now demonstrate its usefulness in the context of conformance testing.

Transference. We show that the Skorokhod metric gives a robust quantification of system conformance by relating the metric to TLTL (timed LTL) enriched with (i) predicates of the form $f(x_1,\ldots,x_n) \geq 0$, as in Signal Temporal Logic [15], for specifying constraints on trace values; and (ii) *freeze quantifiers*, as in TPTL [4], for specifying temporal constraints (freeze quantifiers can express more complex timing constraints than bounded timing constraints, e.g., of MTL). TLTL subsumes MTL and STL [15]. We prove a *transference theorem*: flows (and propositional traces) which are close under the Skorokhod metric satisfy "close" TLTL formulae for a rich class of temporal and spatial predicates, where the untimed structure of the formulae remains unchanged, only the predicates are enlarged.

Tractability. We improve on recent polynomial-time algorithms for the Skorokhod metric [25] by taking advantage of the fact that, in practice, only retimings that map the times in one trace to "close" times in the other are of interest. This enables us to obtain a streaming sliding-window based monitoring procedure which takes only $O(W)$ time per sample, where W is the window size (assuming the dimension n of the system to be a constant).

Usability. Using the Skorokhod distance checking procedure as a subroutine, we have implemented a Simulink toolbox for conformance testing. Our tool integrates with Simulink's model-based design flow for control systems, and provides a stochastic search-based approach to find inputs which maximize the Skorokhod distance between systems under these inputs.

We present three case studies from the control domain, including industrial challenge problems; our empirical evaluation shows that our tool computes sharp estimates of the conformance distance reasonably fast on each of them. Our input models were complex enough that techniques such as ϵ-bisimulation functions are inapplicable. We conclude that the Skorokhod metric can be an effective foundation for semi-formal conformance testing for complex dynamical models. Proofs of the theorems are given in the accompanying technical report [13].

Related Work. The work of [1,2] is closely related to ours. In it, robustness properties of hybrid state sequences are derived with respect to a trace metric which also quantifies temporal and spatial variations. Our work differs in the following ways. First, we guarantee robustness properties over *flows* rather than only over (discrete) sequences. Second, the Skorokhod metric is a stronger form of the $(T, J, (\tau, \epsilon))$-closeness degree[1,2] (for systems which do not have hybrid time); and allows us to give stronger robustness transference guarantees. The Skorokhod metric requires order preservation of the timeline, which the $(T, J, (\tau, \epsilon))$-closeness function does not. Preservation of the timeline order allows us to (i) keep the untimed structure of the formulae the same (unlike in the transference theorem of [1]); (ii) show transference of a rich class of global timing constraints using freeze quantifiers (rather than only for the standard bounded time quantifiers of MTL/MITL). However, for implementations where the timeline order is not preserved, we have to settle for the less stronger guarantees provided by [1]. The work of [15] deals with spatial robustness of STL; the only temporal disturbances considered are constant time-shifts for the entire signal where the entire signal is moved to the past, or to the future by the same amount. In contrast, the Skorokhod metric incorporates variable time-shifts.

2 Conformance Testing with the Skorokhod Metric

2.1 Systems and Conformance Testing

Traces and Systems. A (finite) *trace* or a *signal* $\pi : [T_i, T_e] \mapsto \mathcal{O}$ is a mapping from a finite closed interval $[T_i, T_e]$ of $\mathbb{R}_+$, with $0 \leq T_i < T_e$, to some topological space $\mathcal{O}$. If $\mathcal{O}$ is a metric space, we refer to the associated metric on $\mathcal{O}$ as $\mathcal{D}_{\mathcal{O}}$. The time-domain of π, denoted $\mathsf{tdom}(\pi)$, is the time interval $[T_i, T_e]$ over which it is defined. The time-duration of π, denoted $\mathsf{tlen}(\pi)$, is $\sup(\mathsf{tdom}(\pi))$. The t-suffix of π for $t \in \mathsf{tdom}(\pi)$, denoted π^t, is the trace π restricted to the interval $(\mathsf{tdom}(\pi) \cap [t, \mathsf{tlen}(\pi)]$. We denote by $\pi_{\downarrow T'_e}$ the prefix trace obtained from π by restricting the domain to $[T_i, T'_e] \subseteq \mathsf{tdom}(\pi)$.

A (continuous-time) *system* $\mathfrak{A} : \left(\mathbb{R}_+^{[\,]} \mapsto \mathcal{O}_{\mathsf{ip}}\right) \mapsto \left(\mathbb{R}_+^{[\,]} \mapsto \mathcal{O}_{\mathsf{op}}\right)$, where $\mathbb{R}_+^{[\,]}$ is the set of finite closed intervals of $\mathbb{R}_+$, transforms input traces $\pi_{\mathsf{ip}} : [T_i, T_e] \mapsto \mathcal{O}_{\mathsf{ip}}$ into output traces $\pi_{\mathsf{op}} : [T_i, T_e] \mapsto \mathcal{O}_{\mathsf{op}}$ (over the same time domain). We require that the system is *causal*: if $\mathfrak{A}(\pi_{\mathsf{ip}}) \mapsto \pi_{\mathsf{op}}$, then for every $\min \mathsf{tdom}(\pi) \leq T'_e < \max \mathsf{tdom}(\pi)$, the system $\mathfrak{A}$ maps $\pi_{\mathsf{ip}\downarrow T'_e}$ to $\pi_{\mathsf{op}\downarrow T'_e}$. Common examples of such systems are (causal) dynamical and hybrid dynamical systems [7,30].

Conformance Testing. Let $\mathfrak{A}_1$ and $\mathfrak{A}_2$ be systems and let $\mathcal{D}_{\mathcal{TR}}$ be a metric over output traces. For a set Π_{ip} of input traces, we define the *(quantitative) conformance* between $\mathfrak{A}_1$ and $\mathfrak{A}_2$ w.r.t. Π_{ip} as $\sup_{\pi_{\mathsf{ip}} \in \Pi_{\mathsf{ip}}} \mathcal{D}_{\mathcal{TR}}\left(\mathfrak{A}_1(\pi_{\mathsf{ip}}), \mathfrak{A}_2(\pi_{\mathsf{ip}})\right)$ The conformance between $\mathfrak{A}_1$ and $\mathfrak{A}_2$ is their conformance w.r.t. the set of all input traces.

The conformance testing problem asks, given systems $\mathfrak{A}_1, \mathfrak{A}_2$, a trace metric $\mathcal{D}_{\mathcal{TR}}$, a tolerance δ, and a set of test input traces Π_{test}, if the quantitative conformance between $\mathfrak{A}_1$ and $\mathfrak{A}_2$ w.r.t. Π_{test} is more than δ. Clearly, conformance w.r.t. Π_{test} is a lower bound on the conformance between $\mathfrak{A}_1$ and $\mathfrak{A}_2$.

[1] Instead of having two separate parameters τ and ϵ for time and state variation, we pre-scale time and the n state components with $n+1$ constants, and have a single value quantifying closeness of the scaled traces.

[2] Informally, two signals x, y are $(T, J, (\tau, \epsilon))$-close if for each point $x(t)$, there is a point $y(t')$ with $|t - t'| < \tau$ such that $\mathcal{D}(x(t), y(t')) < \epsilon$; and similarly for $y(t)$.

Algorithm 1. Algorithm for conformance testing

Input: Systems $\mathfrak{A}_1$, $\mathfrak{A}_2$, trace metric $\mathcal{D}_{\mathcal{TR}}$, time horizon T, input parameterization F, termination criterion `terminate?`
Output: Input u that achieves maximum distance between $\mathfrak{A}_1$ and $\mathfrak{A}_2$

1 $d \leftarrow 0$, $u \leftarrow \perp$, $dmax \leftarrow 0$, $umax \leftarrow \perp$
2 **while** not(`terminate?`) **do**
3     $u \leftarrow$ `pickNewInputs`(F, T, d)
4     $y_1 \leftarrow$ `simulate`$(\mathfrak{A}_1, u, T)$ and $y_2 \leftarrow$ `simulate`$(\mathfrak{A}_2, u, T)$
5     $d \leftarrow \mathcal{D}_{\mathcal{TR}}(y_1, y_2)$
6   **if** $d > dmax$ **then** $dmax \leftarrow d$, $umax \leftarrow u$
7 **end**
8 **return** *"on input umax, outputs* $\mathfrak{A}_1(umax)$ *and* $\mathfrak{A}_2(umax)$ *differ by dmax by time T"*

Algorithm 1 is a standard optimization-guided adaptive testing algorithm. To define the set Π_{test} of test inputs, we use a fixed finite parameterization of the input space using a finite set F of *basis functions* and fix a time horizon T. We only generate inputs obtained as a linear combination $\sum_{f \in F} p_f \cdot f$ of basis functions over the interval $[0, T]$, where the coefficients $\{p_f \mid f \in F\}$ come from a closed convex subset of $\mathbb{R}^{|F|}$.

In each step, Algorithm 1 picks an input signal u and computes the distance between the corresponding outputs $y_1 = \mathfrak{A}_1(u)$ and $y_2 = \mathfrak{A}_2(u)$. Based on heuristics that rely on the current distance, and a possibly bounded history of costs, the procedure then picks a new value for u by choosing new values for the coefficients $\{p_f \mid f \in F\}$. For instance, in a gradient-ascent based procedure, the new value of u is chosen by estimating the local gradient in each direction in the input-parameter space, and then picking the direction that has the largest (positive) gradient. In our implementation, we use the Nelder-Mead (or nonlinear simplex) algorithm to pick new inputs.

On termination (e.g., when some maximum number of iterations is reached), the algorithm returns the conformance distance between $\mathfrak{A}_1$ and $\mathfrak{A}_2$ w.r.t. the set of tests generated. One can compare the distance to some tolerance δ chosen based on engineering requirements.

Sampling and Polygonal Traces. In practice, the output behaviors of the systems are observed with a sampling process, thus y_1 and y_2 on line 4 are discrete time-sampled *sequences*. We go from these sequences to output traces by linearly interpolating between the sampled time points.

Formally, a *polygonal trace* $\pi : I_\pi \mapsto \mathcal{O}$ where $\mathcal{O}$ is a vector space with the scalar field $\mathbb{R}$ is a continuous trace such that there exists a finite sequence $\min I_\pi = t_0 < t_1 < \cdots < t_m = \max I_\pi$ of time-points such that the trace segment between t_k and t_{k+1} is affine for all $0 \le k < m$, *i.e.*, for $t_k \le t \le t_{k+1}$ we have $\pi(t) = \pi(t_k) + \frac{t - t_k}{t_{k+1} - t_k} \cdot (\pi(t_{k+1}) - \pi(t_k))$.

Given a timed trace sequence tseq, let $[\![\mathsf{tseq}]\!]_{\mathsf{LI}}$ denote the polygonal trace obtained from tseq by linear interpolation. Let $\mathsf{tseq}_\pi, \mathsf{tseq}_{\pi'}$ be two corresponding samplings of the traces π, π', respectively. For a trace metric $\mathcal{D}_{\mathcal{TR}}$, we have:

$$\mathcal{D}_{\mathcal{TR}}(\pi, \pi') \le \mathcal{D}_{\mathcal{TR}}\left([\![\mathsf{tseq}_\pi]\!]_{\mathsf{LI}}, [\![\mathsf{tseq}_{\pi'}]\!]_{\mathsf{LI}}\right) + \mathcal{D}_{\mathcal{TR}}\left([\![\mathsf{tseq}_\pi]\!]_{\mathsf{LI}}, \pi\right) + \mathcal{D}_{\mathcal{TR}}\left([\![\mathsf{tseq}_{\pi'}]\!]_{\mathsf{LI}}, \pi'\right).$$

If Δ_{samerr} is a bound on the distance between a trace and an interpolated completion of its sampling, we have that $\mathcal{D}_{\mathcal{TR}}(\pi, \pi') \leq \mathcal{D}_{\mathcal{TR}}([\![\mathsf{tseq}_\pi]\!]_{\mathsf{LI}}, [\![\mathsf{tseq}_{\pi'}]\!]_{\mathsf{LI}}) + 2 \cdot \Delta_{\mathsf{samerr}}$. Thus, a value of $2 \cdot \Delta_{\mathsf{samerr}}$ needs to be added in the testing algorithm to account for the error due to polygonal approximations.

2.2 The Skorokhod Metric

We now define the Skorokhod metric, which we use as the metric in Algorithm 1. A *retiming* $\mathsf{r} : I \mapsto I'$, for closed intervals I, I' of $\mathbb{R}_+$ is an order-preserving (i.e., monotone) continuous bijective function from I to I'; thus if $t < t'$ then $\mathsf{r}(t) < \mathsf{r}(t')$. Let $\mathsf{R}_{I \mapsto I'}$ be the class of retiming functions from I to I' and let $\mathcal{I}$ be the identity retiming. Intuitively, retiming can be thought of as follows: imagine a stretchable and compressible timeline; a retiming of the original timeline gives a new timeline where some parts have been stretched, and some compressed, without the timeline having been broken. Given a trace $\pi : I_\pi \rightarrow \mathcal{O}$, and a retiming $\mathsf{r} : I \mapsto I_\pi$; the function $\pi \circ \mathsf{r}$ is another trace from I to $\mathcal{O}$.

Definition 1 (Skorokhod Metric). *Given a retiming* $\mathsf{r} : I \mapsto I'$, *let* $||\mathsf{r} - \mathcal{I}||_{\sup}$ *be defined as* $||\mathsf{r} - \mathcal{I}||_{\sup} = \sup_{t \in I} |\mathsf{r}(t) - t|$. *Given two traces* $\pi : I_\pi \mapsto \mathcal{O}$ *and* $\pi' : I_{\pi'} \mapsto \mathcal{O}$, *where* $\mathcal{O}$ *is a metric space with the associated metric* $\mathcal{D}_{\mathcal{O}}$, *and a retiming* $\mathsf{r} : I_\pi \mapsto I_{\pi'}$, *let* $\|\pi - \pi' \circ \mathsf{r}\|_{\sup}$ *be defined as:*

$$\|\pi - \pi' \circ \mathsf{r}\|_{\sup} = \sup_{t \in I_\pi} \mathcal{D}_{\mathcal{O}}\big(\pi(t),\ \pi'(\mathsf{r}(t))\big).$$

The Skorokhod distance[3] *between the traces* $\pi()$ *and* $\pi'()$ *is defined to be:*

$$\mathcal{D}_{\mathcal{S}}(\pi, \pi') = \inf_{r \in \mathsf{R}_{I_\pi \mapsto I_{\pi'}}} \max(||\mathsf{r} - \mathcal{I}||_{\sup}\,,\ ||\pi - \pi' \circ \mathsf{r}||_{\sup}). \qquad \square \tag{1}$$

Intuitively, the Skorokhod distance incorporates two components: the first component quantifies the *timing discrepancy* of the timing distortion required to "match" two traces, and the second quantifies the *value mismatch* (in the metric space $\mathcal{O}$) of the values under the timing distortion. In the retimed trace $\pi \circ \mathsf{r}$, we see exactly the same values as in π, in exactly the same order, but the times at which the values are seen can be different.

The following theorem shows that the Skorokhod distance between polygonal traces can be computed efficiently. We remark that after retiming, the retimed version $\pi \circ \mathsf{r}$ of a polygonal trace π need not be polygonal (see e.g., [24]).

Theorem 1 (Computing the Distance Between Polygonal Traces [25]). *Let* $\pi : I_\pi \mapsto \mathbb{R}^n$ *and* $\pi' : I_{\pi'} \mapsto \mathbb{R}^n$ *be two polygonal traces with* m_π *and* $m_{\pi'}$ *affine segments respectively. Let the Skorokhod distance between them (for the* L_2 *norm on* $\mathbb{R}^n$*) be denoted as* $\mathcal{D}_{\mathcal{S}}(\pi, \pi')$.

1. *Given* $\delta \geq 0$, *it can be checked whether* $\mathcal{D}_{\mathcal{S}}(\pi, \pi') \leq \delta$ *in time* $O(m_\pi \cdot m_{\pi'} \cdot n)$.

[3] The two components of the Skorokhod distance (the retiming, and the value difference components) can be weighed with different weights – this simply corresponds to a change of scale.

2. *Suppose we restrict retimings to be such that the i-th affine segment of π can only be matched to π' affine segments $i - W$ through $i + W$ for all i, where $W \geq 1$. Under this retiming restriction, we can determine, with a streaming algorithm, whether $\mathcal{D}_{\mathcal{S}}(\pi, \pi') \leq \delta$ in time $O((m_\pi + m_{\pi'}) \cdot n \cdot W)$.* □

Let us denote by $\mathcal{D}_{\mathcal{S}}^W(\pi, \pi')$ the Skorokhod difference between π, π' under the retiming restriction of the second part of Theorem 1, *i.e.*, the value obtained by restricting the retimings in Eq. 1[4]. The value $\mathcal{D}_{\mathcal{S}}^W(\pi, \pi')$ is an upper bound on $\mathcal{D}_{\mathcal{S}}(\pi, \pi')$. In addition, for $W' < W$, we have $\mathcal{D}_{\mathcal{S}}^W(\pi, \pi') \leq \mathcal{D}_{\mathcal{S}}^{W'}(\pi, \pi')$.

3 Transference of Logical Properties

In this section, we demonstrate a transference result for the Skorokhod metric for a version of the timed linear time logic TLTL [4]. The logic we consider generalizes MTL and STL. We show that if the Skorokhod distance between two traces is small, they satisfy close TLTL formulae. Given a formula ϕ of TLTL satisfied by trace π_1, we can compute a "relaxation" of ϕ that will be satisfied by the "close" trace π_2. We first present the results in a propositional framework, and then extend to $\mathbb{R}^n$-valued spaces for a logic generalizing STL.

3.1 The Logic TLTL

Let $\mathcal{P}$ be a set of propositions. A *propositional trace* π over $\mathcal{P}$ is a trace where the topological space is $2^{\mathcal{P}}$, with the associated metric $\mathcal{D}_{\mathcal{P}}(\sigma, \sigma') = 0$ if $\sigma = \sigma'$, and ∞ otherwise, for $\sigma, \sigma' \in 2^{\mathcal{P}}$. We restrict our attention to propositional traces with finite variability: we require that there exists a finite partition of $\mathsf{tdom}(\pi)$ into disjoint subintervals $I_0, I_1, \ldots, I_m$ such that π is constant on each subinterval. The set of all timed propositional traces over $\mathcal{P}$ is denoted by $\Pi(\mathcal{P})$.

Definition 2 (TLTL($\mathcal{F}_{\mathsf{T}}$) **Syntax).** *Given a set of propositions $\mathcal{P}$, a set of (time) variables V_{T}, and a set $\mathcal{F}_{\mathsf{T}}$ of functions from $\mathbb{R}_+^l$ to $\mathbb{R}$, the formulae of* TLTL*($\mathcal{F}_{\mathsf{T}}$) are defined by the following grammar.*

$$\phi := p \mid true \mid f_{\mathsf{T}}(\overline{x}) \sim 0 \mid \neg\phi \mid \phi_1 \wedge \phi_2 \mid \phi_1 \vee \phi_2 \mid \phi_1 \mathcal{U} \phi_2 \mid x.\phi \quad \textit{where}$$

- *$p \in \mathcal{P}$ and $x \in V_{\mathsf{T}}$, and $\overline{x} = (x_1, \ldots, x_l)$ with $x_i \in V_{\mathsf{T}}$ for all $1 \leq i \leq l$;*
- *$f_{\mathsf{T}} \in \mathcal{F}_{\mathsf{T}}$ is a real-valued function, and $\sim$ is one of $\{\leq, <, \geq, >\}$.* □

The quantifier "$x.$" is known as the *freeze quantifier*, and binds variable x to the current time. A variable x is defined to be *free* in ϕ as follows. The variable x is *not* free in $x.\Psi$, or in p (a proposition), or in *true*, or in $f_{\mathsf{T}}(x_1, \ldots, x_l) \sim 0$ where $x_i \neq x$ for all i. It is also not free in ϕ if ϕ does not contain an occurrence of x. It is free in $\neg\psi$ iff x is free in ψ; and it is free in $\phi_1 \mathbin{\substack{\wedge \\ \vee}} \phi_2$, or in $\phi_1 \mathcal{U} \phi_2$, iff x is free in either ϕ_1 or in ϕ_2. Finally, variable x is free in $f_{\mathsf{T}}(x_1, \ldots, x_l) \sim 0$ if some x_i is x. A formula is *closed* if it has no free variables.

[4] $\mathcal{D}_{\mathcal{S}}^W$ is not a metric over traces (the triangle inequality fails).

Definition 3 (TLTL($\mathcal{F}_\mathsf{T}$) **Semantics).** *Let $\pi : I \mapsto 2^\mathcal{P}$ be a timed propositional trace, and let $\mathcal{E} : V_\mathsf{T} \mapsto I$ be the time environment mapping the variables in V_T to time values in I. The satisfaction of the trace π with respect to the* TLTL*($\mathcal{F}_\mathsf{T}$) formula ϕ in the time environment $\mathcal{E}$ is written as $\pi \models_\mathcal{E} \phi$, and is defined inductively as follows (denoting $t_0 = \min \mathsf{tdom}(\pi)$).*

$\pi \models_\mathcal{E} p$ *for* $p \in \mathcal{P}$ *iff* $p \in \pi(t_0)$; $\pi \models_\mathcal{E}$ *true*; $\pi \models_\mathcal{E} \neg\Psi$ *iff* $\pi \not\models_\mathcal{E} \Psi$;

$\pi \models_\mathcal{E} \phi_1 \wedge \phi_2$ *iff* $\pi \models_\mathcal{E} \phi_1$ *and* $\pi \models_\mathcal{E} \phi_2$; $\pi \models_\mathcal{E} \phi_1 \vee \phi_2$ *iff* $\pi \models_\mathcal{E} \phi_1$ *or* $\pi \models_\mathcal{E} \phi_2$;

$\pi \models_\mathcal{E} f_\mathsf{T}(x_1, \ldots, x_l) \sim 0$ *iff* $f_\mathsf{T}(\mathcal{E}(x_1), \ldots, \mathcal{E}(x_l)) \sim 0$ *for* $\sim \in \{\leq, <, \geq, >\}$;

$\pi \models_\mathcal{E} x.\psi$ *iff* $\pi \models_{\mathcal{E}[x:=t_0]} \psi$ *where* $\mathcal{E}[x:=t_0]$ *agrees with* $\mathcal{E}$ *for all* $x_i \neq x$, *and maps* x *to* t_0;

$\pi \models_\mathcal{E} \phi_1 \mathcal{U} \phi_2$ *iff* $\pi^t \models_\mathcal{E} \phi_2$ *for some* $t \in I$ *and* $\pi^{t'} \models_\mathcal{E} \phi_1 \vee \phi_2$ *for all* $t_0 \leq t' < t$.

A timed trace π is said to satisfy the closed formula ϕ (written as $\pi \models \phi$) if there is some environment $\mathcal{E}$ such that $\pi \models_\mathcal{E} \phi$. □

We define additional temporal operators in the standard way: the "eventually" operator $\Diamond\phi$ stands for $true\,\mathcal{U}\,\phi$; and the "always" operator $\Box\phi$ stands for $\neg\Diamond\neg\phi$. TLTL($\mathcal{F}_\mathsf{T}$) provides a richer framework than MTL [23] for expressing timing constraints as: (i) freeze quantifiers allow specification of constraints between distant contexts, which the bounded temporal operators in MTL cannot do; and (ii) the predicates $f_\mathsf{T}() \sim 0$ for $f_\mathsf{T} \in \mathcal{F}_\mathsf{T}$ allow the specification of complex timing requirements not expressible in MTL. Note that even if the predicates $f_\mathsf{T}() \sim 0$ are restricted to be of the form $x_1 - x_2 + c \sim 0$, where x_1, x_2 are freeze variables, and c is a constant, TLTL($\mathcal{F}_\mathsf{T}$) is more expressive than MTL [6] (and hence more expressive than MITL on which STL is based).

Example 1 (TLTL($\mathcal{F}_\mathsf{T}$) *Subsumes* MTL**).** Let $\mathcal{F}_\mathsf{T}$ be the set of two variable functions of the form $f(x, y) = x - y + c$ where c is a rational constant. Then TLTL($\mathcal{F}_\mathsf{T}$) subsumes MTL. The MTL formula $p\mathcal{U}_{[a,b]}q$ can be written as

$$x.\Big(p\mathcal{U}\, y.\big(\,(y \leq x + b) \wedge (y \geq x + a) \wedge q\big)\Big).$$

We explain the formula as follows. We assign the "current" time t_x to the variable x, and some future time t_y to the variable y. The values t_x and t_y are such that at time t_y, we have q to be true, and moreover, at all times between t_x and t_y, we have $p \vee q$ to be true. Furthermore, t_y must be such that $t_y \in [t_x + a, t_x + b]$, which is specified by the term $(y \leq x + b) \wedge (y \geq x + a)$. □

Example 2 (Temporal Constraints). Suppose we want to express that whenever the event p occurs, it must be followed by a response q, and then by r. In addition, we have the following timing requirement: if $\varepsilon_{pq}, \varepsilon_{qr}, \varepsilon_{pr}$ are the time delays between p and q, between q and r, and between p and r, respectively, then: we must have $\varepsilon_{pq}^2 + \varepsilon_{qr}^2 + \varepsilon_{pr}^2 \leq d$ for a given positive constant d. This can be written using freeze quantifiers as the TLTL formula ϕ:

$$x.\left(p \rightarrow \Diamond\left(y.\left(q \wedge \Diamond\left[z.\left(r \wedge \left((y-x)^2 + (z-y)^2 + (z-x)^2 \leq d\right)\right)\right]\right)\right)\right). \qquad \Box$$

3.2 Transference of TLTL Properties for Propositional Traces

We now show that if a timed propositional trace π satisfies a TLTL($\mathcal{F}_\mathsf{T}$) formula ϕ, then any timed trace π' that is at most δ distance away from π satisfies a slightly relaxed version of the formula ϕ, the degree of relaxation being governed by δ; and the variance of the functions in $\mathcal{F}_\mathsf{T}$ over the time interval containing the time domains of π and π'.

We define the distance $\mathcal{D}_\mathcal{S}$ between two propositional traces as the Skorokhod distance, where we use $\mathcal{D}_\mathcal{P}$ as the distance between two sets of propositions.

Next, we define relaxations of TLTL($\mathcal{F}_\mathsf{T}$) formulae. The relaxations are defined as a syntactic transformation on formulae in negation-normal form, *i.e.*, in which negations only appear at the propositions. It can be showed that every TLTL($\mathcal{F}_\mathsf{T}$) formula can be rewritten in negation-normal form, when we additionally use the waiting for operator, $\mathcal{W}$, defined as:

$\pi \models_\mathcal{E} \phi_1 \mathcal{W} \phi_2$ iff either (1) $\pi^t \models_\mathcal{E} \phi_1$ for all $t \in I_\pi$; or (2) $\pi^t \models_\mathcal{E} \phi_2$ for some $t \in I_\pi$; and $\pi^{t'} \models_\mathcal{E} \phi_1 \vee \phi_2$ for all $\min I_\pi \leq t' < t$.

Definition 4 (δ-relaxation of TLTL($\mathcal{F}_\mathsf{T}$) Formulae). *Let ϕ be a TLTL($\mathcal{F}_\mathsf{T}$) formula in which negations appear only on the propositional symbols. The δ relaxation of ϕ (for $\delta \geq 0$) over a closed interval J, denoted $\mathsf{rx}^\delta_J(\phi)$, is defined as:*

$$
\begin{array}{ll|ll}
\mathsf{rx}^\delta_J(p) & = p & \mathsf{rx}^\delta_J(true) & = true \\
\mathsf{rx}^\delta_J(\neg p) & = \neg p & \mathsf{rx}^\delta_J(false) & = false \\
\mathsf{rx}^\delta_J(\phi_1 \wedge \phi_2) & = \mathsf{rx}^\delta_J(\phi_1) \wedge \mathsf{rx}^\delta_J(\phi_2) & \mathsf{rx}^\delta_J(\phi_1 \vee \phi_2) & = \mathsf{rx}^\delta_J(\phi_1) \vee \mathsf{rx}^\delta_J(\phi_2) \\
\mathsf{rx}^\delta_J(x.\psi) & = x.\mathsf{rx}^\delta_J(\psi) & & \\
\mathsf{rx}^\delta_J(\phi_1 \mathcal{U} \phi_2) & = \mathsf{rx}^\delta_J(\phi_1) \mathcal{U} \mathsf{rx}^\delta_J(\phi_2) & \mathsf{rx}^\delta_J(\phi_1 \mathcal{W} \phi_2) & = \mathsf{rx}^\delta_J(\phi_1) \mathcal{W} \mathsf{rx}^\delta_J(\phi_2)
\end{array}
$$

$$
\mathsf{rx}^\delta_J\left(f_\mathsf{T}(x_1, \ldots, x_l)) \sim 0\right) = \begin{cases} f_\mathsf{T}(x_1, \ldots, x_l) + K_J^{f_\mathsf{T}}(\delta) \sim 0 & \text{if } \sim \in \{>, \geq\} \\ f_\mathsf{T}(x_1, \ldots, x_l) - K_J^{f_\mathsf{T}}(\delta) \sim 0 & \text{if } \sim \in \{<, \leq\}, \end{cases}
$$

where $K_J^{f_\mathsf{T}} : [0, \max \mathsf{tdom}(J) - \min \mathsf{tdom}(J)] \mapsto \mathbb{R}_+$, *and*

$$
K_J^{f_\mathsf{T}}(\delta) \stackrel{\text{def}}{=} \sup_{\substack{t_1, \ldots, t_l \in J \\ t'_1, \ldots, t'_l \in J}} \left\{ \left| \begin{array}{c} f_\mathsf{T}(t_1, \ldots, t_l) \\ - \\ f_\mathsf{T}(t'_1, \ldots, t'_l) \end{array} \right| \quad s.t.\ |t_i - t'_i| \leq \delta \text{ for all } i \right\} \tag{2}
$$

Thus, instead of comparing the $f_\mathsf{T}()$ values to 0, we relax by comparing instead to $\pm K_J^{f_\mathsf{T}}(\delta)$. The other cases recursively relax the subformulae. The functions $K_J^{f_\mathsf{T}}(\delta)$ define the maximal change in the value of f_T that can occur when the input variables can vary by δ. The role of J is to restrict the domain of the freeze quantifier variables to the time interval J (from $\mathbb{R}_+$) in order to obtain the least possible relaxation on a given trace π (e.g., we do not care about the values of a function in $\mathcal{F}_\mathsf{T}$ outside of the domain $\mathsf{tdom}(\pi)$ of the trace).

Example 3 (δ-relaxation for Bounded Temporal Operators – MTL*).* We demonstrate how δ-relaxation operates on bounded time constraints. Consider again the MTL formula $\phi = p\mathcal{U}_{[a,b]}q$. When written as a TLTL formula and relaxed using the $\mathsf{rx}^\delta_{\mathbb{R}_+}$ function, the relaxed TLTL formula is equivalent to the MTL formula $p\mathcal{U}_{[a-2\cdot\delta\,,\,b+2\cdot\delta]}q$. □

Theorem 2 (Transference for Propositional Traces). *Let π, π' be two timed propositional traces such that $\mathfrak{D}_{\mathcal{S}}(\pi, \pi') < \delta$ for some finite δ. Let ϕ be a closed* TLTL($\mathcal{F}_\mathsf{T}$) *formula in negation-normal form. If $\pi \models \phi$, then $\pi' \models \mathsf{rx}^{\delta}_{I_{\pi,\pi'}}(\phi)$ where $I_{\pi,\pi'}$ is the convex hull of* $\mathsf{tdom}(\pi) \cup \mathsf{tdom}(\pi')$. □

Theorem 2 relaxes the freeze variables over the entire signal time-range $I_{\pi,\pi'}$; it can be strengthened by relaxing over a smaller range: if $\pi \models \phi$, and $t_1, \ldots, t_k$ are time-stamp assignments to the freeze variables $x_1, \ldots, x_k$ which witness π satisfying ϕ, then x_i only needs to be relaxed over $[t_i - \delta, t_i + \delta]$ rather than the larger interval $I_{\pi,\pi'}$. These smaller relaxation intervals for the freeze variables can be incorporated in Eq. 2. We omit the details for ease of presentation.

Example 4. Recall Example 2, and the formula ϕ presented in it. Suppose a trace π satisfies ϕ; and let $\mathfrak{D}_{\mathcal{S}}(\pi, \pi') < \delta$ (using the Skorokhod metric for propositional traces). Our transference theorem ensures that (i) π' will satisfy the same untimed formula $p \to \Diamond(q \wedge \Diamond r)$; and (ii) it gives a bound on how much the timing constraints need to be relaxed in ϕ in order to ensure satisfaction by π'; it states that π' satisfies the following relaxed formula ϕ'.

$$\pi' \models x.\left(p \to \Diamond\left(y.\left(q \wedge \Diamond\left[z.\left(r \wedge \left((y-x)^2 + (z-y)^2 + (z-x)^2 \leq d^\dagger\right)\right)\right]\right)\right)\right)$$

where $d^\dagger = d + 12 \cdot \delta^2 + 4\sqrt{3} \cdot \delta \cdot \sqrt{d}$ (see [13]). □

3.3 Transference of TLTL Properties for $\mathbb{R}^n$-valued Signals

A *timed $\mathbb{R}^n$-valued trace* π is a function from a closed interval I of $\mathbb{R}_+$ to $\mathbb{R}^n$. For $\overline{\alpha} = (\alpha^0, \ldots, \alpha^n) \in \mathbb{R}^n$, we denote the k-th dimensional value α^k as $\overline{\alpha}[k]$. The π projected function onto the k-th $\mathbb{R}$ dimension is denoted by $\pi_k : I \mapsto \mathbb{R}$.

To define the semantics of TLTL formulae over timed $\mathbb{R}^n$-valued sequences, we use booleanizing predicates $\mu : \mathbb{R}^n \mapsto \mathbb{B}$, as in STL [15], to transform $\mathbb{R}^n$-valued sequences into timed propositional sequences. These predicates are part of the logical specification. In this work, we restrict our attention to traces and predicates such that each predicate varies only finitely often on the finite time traces under consideration. Since we also have freeze variables, TLTL with predicates is strictly more expressive than STL[5] (as in the propositional case [6]).

Definition 5 (TLTL($\mathcal{F}_\mathsf{T}, \mathcal{F}_\mathsf{S}$) **Syntax).** *Given a set of variables V_T (the freeze variables), a set of* ordered *variables V_S (the signal variables), and two sets $\mathcal{F}_\mathsf{T}, \mathcal{F}_\mathsf{S}$ of functions, the formulae of* TLTL($\mathcal{F}_\mathsf{T}, \mathcal{F}_\mathsf{S}$) *are defined by the grammar:*

$$\phi := true \mid f_\mathsf{T}(\overline{x}) \sim 0 \mid f_\mathsf{S}(\overline{y}) \sim 0 \mid \neg\phi \mid \phi_1 \wedge \phi_2 \mid \phi_1 \vee \phi_2 \mid \phi_1 \,\mathcal{U}\, \phi_2 \mid x.\phi \quad where$$

- *$x \in V_\mathsf{T}$, and $\overline{x} = (x_1, \ldots, x_l)$ with $x_i \in V_\mathsf{T}$ for all $1 \leq i \leq l$;*
- *$\overline{z} = (z_1, \ldots, z_d)$ with $z_j \in V_\mathsf{S}$ for all $1 \leq j \leq d$ (with $d \leq n$);*
- *V_T and V_S are disjoint;*
- *$f_\mathsf{T} \in \mathcal{F}_\mathsf{T}$ and $f_\mathsf{S} \in \mathcal{F}_\mathsf{S}$ are real-valued functions, and $\sim$ is $\leq, <, \geq$, or $>$.* □

[5] STL is MITL enriched with booleanzing predicates, *i.e.*, STL is MITL($\mathcal{F}_\mathsf{S}$).

The semantics of TLTL($\mathcal{F}_\mathsf{T}, \mathcal{F}_\mathsf{S}$) is straightforward and similar to the propositional case (Definition 3). The only new ingredients are the booleanizing predicates $f_\mathsf{S}(\overline{z}) \sim 0$: we define $\pi \models_\mathcal{E} f_\mathsf{S}(z_1, \ldots, z_d) \sim 0$ iff $f_\mathsf{S}(\pi_{j_1}[t_0], \ldots, \pi_{j_d}[t_0]) \sim 0$ for any freeze variable environment $\mathcal{E}$, where $t_0 = \min \mathsf{tdom}(\pi)$, and z_i is the j_i-th variable in V_S (*i.e.*, z_i refers to the j_i-th dimension in the signal trace). We require that for a timed $\mathbb{R}^n$-valued trace π to satisfy ϕ, the arity of the functions in $\mathcal{F}_\mathsf{S}$ occurring in ϕ should not be more than n, that is, functions should not refer to dimensions greater than n for an $\mathbb{R}^n$ trace.

δ relaxation of TLTL($\mathcal{F}_\mathsf{T}, \mathcal{F}_\mathsf{S}$). Let $\mathbf{J}_{V_\mathsf{S}}$ be a mapping from V_S to closed intervals of $\mathbb{R}$, thus $\mathbf{J}_{V_\mathsf{S}}(z)$ denotes a sub-domain of $z \in V_\mathsf{S}$. The relaxation function $\mathsf{rx}^\delta_{J,\mathbf{J}_{V_\mathsf{S}}}$ which operates on TLTL($\mathcal{F}_\mathsf{T}, \mathcal{F}_\mathsf{S}$) formulae is defined analogous to the relaxation function rx^δ_J in Definition 4. We omit the similar cases, and only present the new case for the predicates formed from $\mathcal{F}_\mathsf{S}$.

$$\mathsf{rx}^\delta_{J,\mathbf{J}_{V_\mathsf{S}}}(f_\mathsf{S}(z_1, \ldots, z_l)) \sim 0) = \begin{cases} f_\mathsf{S}(z_1, \ldots, z_l) + K^{f_\mathsf{S}}_{J,\mathbf{J}_{V_\mathsf{S}}}(\delta) \sim 0 & \text{if } \sim \in \{>, \geq\}; \\ f_\mathsf{S}(z_1, \ldots, z_l) - K^{f_\mathsf{S}}_{J,\mathbf{J}_{V_\mathsf{S}}}(\delta) \sim 0 & \text{if } \sim \in \{<, \leq\} \end{cases}$$

where $K^{f_\mathsf{S}}_{J,\mathbf{J}_{V_\mathsf{S}}} : \left[0,\ \max_{z \in V_\mathsf{S}} |\max \mathbf{J}_{V_\mathsf{S}}(z) - \min \mathbf{J}_{V_\mathsf{S}}(z)|\right] \mapsto \mathbb{R}_+$ is a function s.t.

$$K^{f_\mathsf{S}}_{J,\mathbf{J}_{V_\mathsf{S}}}(\delta) = \sup_{\substack{u_i \in \mathbf{J}_{V_\mathsf{S}}(z_i);\ u'_i \in \mathbf{J}_{V_\mathsf{S}}(z'_i) \\ \text{for all } i}} \left\{ \left| \begin{array}{c} f_\mathsf{S}(u_1, \ldots, u_l) \\ - \\ f_\mathsf{S}(u'_1, \ldots, u'_l) \end{array} \right| \text{ s.t. } |u_i - u'_i| \leq \delta \text{ for all } i \right\}.$$

The functions $K^{f_\mathsf{S}}_{J,\mathbf{J}_{V_\mathsf{S}}}(\delta)$ define the maximal change in the value of f_S that can occur when the input variables can vary by δ over the intervals in $\mathbf{J}_{V_\mathsf{S}}(z)$ and J. The role of $\mathbf{J}_{V_\mathsf{S}}$ in the above definition is to restrict the domain of the signal variables in order to obtain the least possible relaxation bounds on the signal constraints; as was done in Definition 4 for the freeze variables.

Theorem 3 (Transference for $\mathbb{R}^n$-valued Traces). *Let π, π' be two $\mathbb{R}^n$-valued traces such the Skorokhod distance between them is less than δ for some finite δ. Let ϕ be a closed* TLTL($\mathcal{F}_\mathsf{T}, \mathcal{F}_\mathsf{S}$) *formula in negation-normal form. If $\pi \models \phi$, then $\pi' \models \mathsf{rx}^\delta_{I_{\pi,\pi'}, \mathbf{I}_{V_\mathsf{S}}}(\phi)$, where*

- *$I_{\pi,\pi'}$ is the convex hull of $\mathsf{tdom}(\pi) \cup \mathsf{tdom}(\pi')$; and*
- *$\mathbf{I}_{V_\mathsf{S}}(z)$ is the convex hull of $\{\pi(t)[k] \mid t \in \mathsf{tdom}(\pi)\} \cup \{\pi'(t)[k] \mid t \in \mathsf{tdom}(\pi')\}$; where z is the k-th variable in the ordered set V_S.* □

Theorem 3 can be strengthened similar to the strengthening mentioned for Theorem 2 by relaxing the variables over smaller intervals obtained from assignments to variables which witness $\pi \models \phi$.

Example 5 (Spatial Constraints and Transference). Recall Example 2, suppose that the events p, q, and r are defined by the following predicates over real variables α_1 and α_2. Let $p \equiv \alpha_1 + 10{\cdot}\alpha_2 \geq 3$; the predicate $q \equiv |\alpha_1| + |\alpha_2| \leq 20$; and $r \equiv |\alpha_1| + |\alpha_2| \leq 15$. Let π satisfy this formula with these predicates, and let π' be δ close to π, for a finite δ under the Skorokhod metric for $\mathbb{R}^2$. Our robustness theorem ensures that π' will satisfy the relaxed formula

$$x.\left(p^\delta \to \Diamond\left(y.\left(q^\delta \wedge \Diamond\left[z.\left(r^\delta \wedge \left((y-x)^2 + (z-y)^2 + (z-x)^2 \leq d + 12{\cdot}\delta^2\right)\right)\right]\right)\right)\right).$$

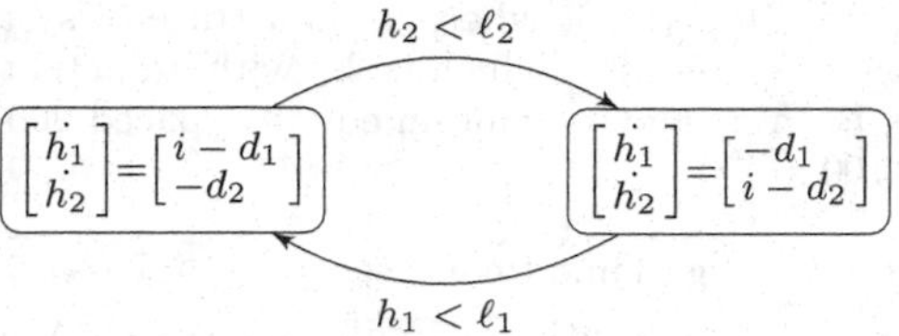

Fig. 1. System $\mathfrak{A}_1$ used for benchmarking Skorokhod Distance computation. Inflow rate i, Drain rate d_1 for tank 1 and d_2 for tank 2 are all inputs to the system.

where the relaxed predicates $p^\delta, q^\delta, r^\delta$ are defined as follows: $p^\delta \equiv \alpha_1 + 10{\cdot}\alpha_2 \geq 3 - 22{\cdot}\delta$; $q^\delta \equiv |\alpha_1| + |\alpha_2| \leq 20 + 4{\cdot}\delta$; and $r^\delta \equiv |\alpha_1| + |\alpha_2| \leq 15 + 4{\cdot}\delta$. □

4 Experimental Evaluation

We have implemented a streaming, sliding window-based monitoring routine which checks, given a fixed δ, whether the linear interpolations of two time-sampled traces are at Skorokhod distance at most δ away from each other. The least such δ value is then computed by binary search over the monitoring routine. The upper limit of the search range is set to the pointwise metric (i.e., assuming the identity retiming) between the two traces. The traces to the monitoring routine are pre-scaled, each dimension (and the time-stamp) is scaled by a different constant. The constants are chosen so that after scaling, one unit of deviation in one dimension is as undesirable as one unit of jitter in other dimensions.

We have integrated the monitoring routine in an adaptive testing procedure for Simulink blocks based on Algorithm 1. The output of Algorithm 1 is compared against tolerance levels (e.g., maximum allowed jitter) given by the engineering requirements. In the following, we evaluate the effectiveness of the Skorokhod metric in conformance testing of Simulink applications.

Skorokhod Distance Computation Benchmark. We first show that the window-based implementation is efficient using the following benchmark. Figure 1 shows a hybrid dynamical system $\mathfrak{A}_1$ consisting of two water tanks, each with an outlet from which water drains at a constant rate d_j. Both tanks share a single inlet pipe that is switched between the tanks, filling only one tank at any given time at a constant inflow rate of i. When the water-level in tank j falls below level ℓ_j, the pipe switches to fill it. The drain and inflow rates d_1, d_2 and i are assumed to be inputs to the system. Now consider a version $\mathfrak{A}_2$ that incorporates an actuation delay that is a function of the inflow rate. This means that after the level drops to ℓ_j for tank j, the inlet pipe starts filling it only after a finite time. $\mathfrak{A}_1$ and $\mathfrak{A}_2$ have the same initial water level. We perform a fixed number of simulations by systematically choosing drain and inflow rates d_1, d_2, i to generate traces (water-level vs. time) of both systems and compute their Skorokhod distance. We summarize the results in Table 1.

Recall that the Skorokhod distance computation involves a sequence of monitoring calls with different δ values picked by a binary-search procedure. Thus, the total time to compute $\mathcal{D}_\mathcal{S}$ is the sum over the computation times for individual monitoring calls plus some bookkeeping. In Table 1, we make a distinction

Table 1. Computation of $\mathfrak{D}_{\mathcal{S}}(\pi_1, \pi_2)$, where π_1 is a trace of system $\mathfrak{A}_1$ described in Fig. 1, and π_2 is a trace of system $\mathfrak{A}_2$, which is $\mathfrak{A}_1$ with an actuation delay. $\mathfrak{D}_2$ is the pointwise L_2 distance. Both π_1 and π_2 contain equally spaced 2001 time points over a simulation horizon of 100 s.

Window size	Avg. $\mathfrak{D}_{\mathcal{S}}$	Avg. Time taken (secs)		$\frac{\mathfrak{D}_2 - \mathfrak{D}_{\mathcal{S}}}{\mathfrak{D}_2}$		
		Computation	Monitoring	Max.	Avg.	Std. dev.
20	8.58	0.81	0.13	0.11	0.03	0.03
40	8.35	1.55	0.26	0.23	0.06	0.06
60	8.09	2.31	0.39	0.34	0.1	0.09
80	7.88	3.05	0.52	0.38	0.1	0.11
100	7.72	3.77	0.64	0.38	0.1	0.11

between the average time to monitor traces (given a δ value), and the average time to compute $\mathfrak{D}_{\mathcal{S}}$. There are an average of 6 monitoring calls per $\mathfrak{D}_{\mathcal{S}}$ computation. We ran 64 simulations by choosing different input values, and then computing $\mathfrak{D}_{\mathcal{S}}$ for increasing window sizes. As the window size increases, the average $\mathfrak{D}_{\mathcal{S}}$ decreases and the computation time increases linearly, as expected from Theorem 1. Finally, the Skorokhod distance can be significantly smaller than the simpler metric $\mathfrak{D}_2$ (defined as the maximum of the pointwise L_2 norm). This discrepancy becomes more prominent with increased window size. With a window size of 100, the variation between $\mathfrak{D}_{\mathcal{S}}$ and $\mathfrak{D}_2$ was up to 38 % (mean difference of 10 % with std. deviation of 11 %).

Case Study I: LQR-Based Controller. The first case study for conformance testing is an aircraft pitch control application taken from the openly accessible control tutorials for Matlab and Simulink [27]. The authors describe a linear dynamical system of the form: $\dot{\mathbf{x}} = (A - BK)\mathbf{x} + B\theta_{des}$. Here, $\mathbf{x}$ describes the vector of continuous state variables and θ_{des} is the desired reference provided as an external input. One of the states in the $\mathbf{x}$ vector is the pitch angle θ, which is also the system output. The controller gain matrix K is computed using the linear quadratic regulator method [5], a standard technique from optimal control. We are interested in studying a digital implementation of the continuous-time controller obtained using the LQR method. To do so, we consider sampled-data control where the controller samples the plant output, computes, and provides the control input to the plant every Δ s. To model sensor delay, we add a fixed delay element to the system; thus, the overall system now represents a delay-differential equation.

Control engineers are typically interested in the step response of a system. In particular, quantities such as the overshoot/undershoot of the output signal (maximum positive/negative deviation from a reference value) and the settling time (time it takes for transient behaviors to converge to some small region around the reference value) are of interest. Given a settling time and overshoot for the first system, we would like the second system to display similar characteristics. We remark that both of these properties can be expressed in STL (and hence in TLTL($\mathcal{F}_{\mathsf{T}}, \mathcal{F}_{\mathsf{S}}$)), see [21] for details. We quantify system conformance (and thereby adherence to requirements) in terms of the Skorokhod distance, or, in other words, maximum permitted time/space-jitter value δ. For this system,

Table 2. Variation in Skorokhod Distance with changing sampling time for an aircraft pitch control system with an LQR-based controller. Time taken indicates the total time spent in computing the upper bound on the Skorokhod distance across all simulations. We choose a window size chosen of 150 samples and simulate the system for 5 s with a variable-step solver.

Controller Sample-Time (seconds)	Skorokhod distance	Time taken (seconds) to compute $\mathfrak{D}_{\mathcal{S}}$	Number of simulations
0.01	0.012	232	104
0.05	0.049	96	104
0.1	0.11	70	106
0.3	0.39	45	104
0.5	1.51	40	101

we know that at nominal conditions, the settling time is approximately 2.5 s, and that we can tolerate an increase in settling time of about 0.5 s. Thus, we chose a time-scaling factor of $2 = \frac{1}{0.5}$. We observe that the range of θ is about 0.4 radians, and specify an overshoot of 20 % of this range as being permissible. Thus, we pick a scaling factor of $\frac{1}{0.08}$ for the signal domain. In other words, Skorokhod distance $\delta = 1$ corresponds to either a time-jitter of 0.5 s, or a space-discrepancy of 0.08 radians.

We summarize the results of conformance testing for different values of sampling time Δ in Table 2. As expected, the conformance increases with increasing Δ. The time taken to compute the Skorokhod distance decreases with increasing Δ, as the number of time-points in the two traces decreases.

Case Study II: Air-Fuel Ratio Controller. In [21], the authors present three systems representing an air-fuel ratio (λ) controller for a gasoline engine, that regulate λ to a given reference value of $\lambda_{\text{ref}} = 14.7$. Of interest to us are the second and the third systems. The former has a continuous-time plant model with highly nonlinear dynamics, and a discrete-time controller model. In [22], the authors present a version of this system where the controller is also continuous. We take this to be $\mathfrak{A}_1$. The third system in [21] is a continuous-time closed-loop system where all the system differential equations have right-hand-sides that are polynomial approximations of the nonlinear dynamics in $\mathfrak{A}_1$. We call this polynomial dynamical system $\mathfrak{A}_2$. The rationale for these system versions is as follows: existing formal methods tools cannot reason about highly nonlinear dynamical systems, but tools such as Flow* [10], C2E2 [16], and CORA [3] demonstrate good capabilities for polynomial dynamical systems. Thus, the hope is to analyze the simpler systems instead. In [21], the authors comment that the system transformations are not accompanied by formal guarantees. By quantifying the difference in the system behaviors, we hope to show that if the system $\mathfrak{A}_2$ satisfies the temporal requirements φ presented in [21], then $\mathfrak{A}_1$ satisfies a relaxation of φ. We pick a scaling factor of 2 for the time domain, as a time-jitter of 0.5 s is the maximum deviation we wish to tolerate in the settling time, and pick $0.68 = \frac{1}{0.1 * \lambda_{\text{ref}}}$ as the scaling factor for λ (which corresponds to the worst case tolerated discrepancy in the overshoot).

Table 3. Conformance testing for closed-loop A/F ratio controller at different engine speeds. We scale the signals such that 0.5 s of time-jitter is treated equivalent to 10 % of the steady-state value (14.7) of the A/F ratio signal. The simulation traces correspond to a time horizon of 10 s and the window size is 300.

Engine speed (rpm)	Skorokhod distance	Computation Time (secs)	Total Time taken (secs)	Number of simulations
1000	0.31	218	544	700
1500	0.20	240	553	700
2000	0.27	223	532	700

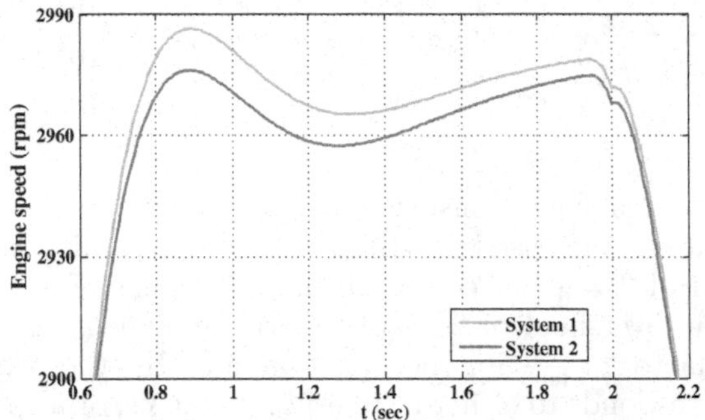

Fig. 2. Outputs showing a Skorokhod distance of 1.04.

Table 3 summarizes the results of conformance testing for these systems. In [14], the authors posed a challenge problem for conformance testing. They reported that the original nonlinear system and the approximate polynomial system both satisfy the STL requirements specifying overshoot/undershoot and settling time. We, however, found an input that causes the outputs of the two systems to have a high Skorokhod distance. Thus, comparing the two systems by considering equi-satisfaction of a given set of STL requirements such as overshoot/undershoot and settling time may not always be sufficient. Our experiment indicates that the Skorokhod metric may be a better measure of conformance.

Case Study III: Engine Timing Model. The Simulink demo palette from Mathworks [26] contains a system representing a four-cylinder spark ignition internal combustion engine based on a model by Crossley and Cook [11]. This system is then enhanced by adding a proportional plus integral (P+I) control law. The integrator is used to adjust the steady-state throttle as the desired engine speed set-point changes, and the proportional term compensates for phase lag introduced by the integrator. In an actual implementation of such a system, such a P+I controller is implemented using a discrete-time integrator. Such integrator blocks are typically associated with a particular numerical integration technique, e.g., forward-Euler, backward-Euler, trapezoidal, etc. It is expected that different numerical techniques will produce slight variation in the results. We wish to quantify the effect of using different numerical integrators in a closed-loop setting. We checked if the user-provided tolerance of $\delta = 1.0$ is satisfied by systems $\mathfrak{A}_1$ and $\mathfrak{A}_2$, where $\mathfrak{A}_1$ is the original system provided in [26] and $\mathfrak{A}_2$ is a modified system that uses the backward Euler method to compute the discrete-time integral in the controller. We scale the outputs in such a way that a value discrepancy of 1 % of the the output range ($\sim$ 1000) is equivalent to a time discrepancy of 0.1 s. These values are chosen to bias the search towards finding signals that have a small time jitter. This is an interesting scenario for this case study where the two systems are equivalent except for the underlying numerical integration solver. We find the signal shown in Fig. 2, for which we find output traces with Skorokhod distance 1.04. The experiment uses 296 simulations and the total time taken to find the counterexample is 677 s.

5 Conclusion

We argue that the Skorokhod metric provides a robust basis for checking conformance between dynamical systems. We showed that it provides transference of a rich class of temporal logic properties and that it can be computed efficiently, both in theory and in practice. Our experiments indicate that conformance checking using the Skorokhod metric can be integrated into a testing flow for Simulink models and can find non-conformant behaviors effectively, allowing for independent weighing of time and value distortions.

References

1. Abbas, H., Fainekos, G.E.: Formal property verification in a conformance testing framework. In: MEMOCODE (2014, To appear)
2. Abbas, H., Hoxha, B., Fainekos, G.E., Deshmukh, J.V., Kapinski, J., Ueda, K.: Conformance testing as falsification for cyber-physical systems. CoRR, abs/1401.5200 (2014)
3. Althoff, M.: Reachability analysis of nonlinear systems using conservative polynomialization and non-convex sets. HSCC **13**, 173–182 (2013)
4. Alur, R., Henzinger, T.A.: A really temporal logic. J. ACM **41**(1), 181–204 (1994)
5. Anderson, B.D.O.: Optimal Control: Linear Quadratic Methods Dover Books on Engineering. Dover Publications, Mineola (2007)
6. Bouyer, P., Chevalier, F., Markey, N.: On the Expressiveness of TPTL and MTL. In: Sarukkai, S., Sen, S. (eds.) FSTTCS 2005. LNCS, vol. 3821, pp. 432–443. Springer, Heidelberg (2005)
7. Branicky, M.S.: Studies in hybrid systems: modeling, analysis, and control. Ph.D. thesis, Massachusetts Institute of Technology, Cambridge, MA, USA (1995)
8. Broucke, M.: Regularity of solutions and homotopic equivalence for hybrid systems. IEEE Conf. Decis. Control **4**, 4283–4288 (1998)
9. Caspi, P., Benveniste, A.: Toward an approximation theory for computerised control. In: Sangiovanni-Vincentelli, A.L., Sifakis, J. (eds.) EMSOFT 2002. LNCS, vol. 2491. Springer, Heidelberg (2002)
10. Chen, X., Ábrahám, E., Sankaranarayanan, S.: Flow*: an analyzer for non-linear hybrid systems. In: Sharygina, N., Veith, H. (eds.) CAV 2013. LNCS, vol. 8044, pp. 258–263. Springer, Heidelberg (2013)
11. Crossley, P.R., Cook, J.A.: A nonlinear engine model for drivetrain system development. In: International Conference on Control, pp. 921–925. IET (1991)

12. Davoren, J.M.: Epsilon-tubes and generalized skorokhod metrics for hybrid paths spaces. In: Majumdar, R., Tabuada, P. (eds.) HSCC 2009. LNCS, vol. 5469, pp. 135–149. Springer, Heidelberg (2009)
13. Deshmukh, J.V., Majumdar, R., Prabhu, V.S.: Quantifying conformance using the Skorokhod metric. CoRR, abs/1505.05832 (2015)
14. Jinand, X., Deshmukh, J., Kapinski, J., Ueda, K., Butts, K.: Benchmarks for model transformations and conformance checking. In: ARCH (2014)
15. Donzé, A., Maler, O.: Robust satisfaction of temporal logic over real-valued signals. In: Chatterjee, K., Henzinger, T.A. (eds.) FORMATS 2010. LNCS, vol. 6246, pp. 92–106. Springer, Heidelberg (2010)
16. Duggirala, P.S., Mitra, S., Viswanathan, M.: Verification of annotated models from executions. In: EMSOFT, p. 26 (2013)
17. Girard, A., Pola, G., Tabuada, P.: Approximately bisimilar symbolic models for incrementally stable switched systems. IEEE Trans. Automat. Contr. **55**(1), 116–126 (2010)
18. Haghverdi, E., Tabuada, P., Pappas, G.J.: Bisimulation relations for dynamical, control, and hybrid systems. Theor. Comput. Sci. **342**(2–3), 229–261 (2005)
19. Hennessy, M., Milner, R.: Algebraic laws for nondeterminism and concurrency. J. ACM **32**(1), 137–161 (1985)
20. Henzinger, M.R., Henzinger, T.A., Kopke, P.W.: Computing simulations on finite and infinite graphs. In: FOCS: Foundations of Computer Science, pp. 453–462. IEEE Computer Society (1995)
21. Jin, X., Deshmukh, J.V., Kapinski, J., Ueda, K., Butts, K.: Powertrain control verification benchmark. In: HSCC, pp. 253–262 (2014)
22. Kapinski, J., Deshmukh, J.V., Sankaranarayanan, S., Arechiga, N.: Simulation-guided lyapunov analysis for hybrid dynamical systems. In: HSCC 2014, pp 133–142. ACM (2014)
23. Koymans, R.: Specifying real-time properties with metric temporal logic. Real Time Syst. **2**(4), 255–299 (1990)
24. Majumdar, R., Prabhu, V.S.: Computing the Skorokhod distance between polygonal traces. CoRR, abs/1410.6075 (2014)
25. Majumdar, R., Prabhu, V.S.: Computing the Skorokhod distance between polygonal traces. In: HSCC (2015)
26. The Mathworks. Engine timing model with closed loop control
27. Messner, W., Tilbury, D.: Control tutorials for matlab and simulink
28. Milner, R. (ed.): A Calculus of Communicating Systems. LNCS. Springer, Heidelberg (1980)
29. Sangiorgi, D., Rutten, J.: Advanced Topics in Bisimulation and Coinduction. Cambridge University Press, Cambridge (2011)
30. Tabuada, P.: Verification and Control of Hybrid Systems - A Symbolic Approach. Springer, Heidelberg (2009)

Pareto Curves of Multidimensional Mean-Payoff Games

Romain Brenguier(✉) and Jean-François Raskin

Université Libre de Bruxelles (U.L.B.), Brussel, Belgium
romain.brenguier@ulb.ac.be

Abstract. In this paper, we study the set of thresholds that the protagonist can force in a zero-sum two-player multidimensional mean-payoff game. The set of maximal elements of such a set is called the *Pareto curve*, a classical tool to analyze *trade-offs*. As thresholds are vectors of real numbers in multiple dimensions, there exist usually an infinite number of such maximal elements. Our main results are as follow. First, we study the geometry of this set and show that it is definable as a finite union of convex sets given by linear inequations. Second, we provide a $\Sigma_2\mathsf{P}$ algorithm to decide if this set intersects a convex set defined by linear inequations, and we prove the optimality of our algorithm by providing a matching complexity lower bound for the problem. Furthermore, we show that, under natural assumptions, i.e. fixed number of dimensions and polynomially bounded weights in the game, the problem can be solved in deterministic polynomial time. Finally, we show that the Pareto curve can be effectively constructed, and under the former natural assumptions, this construction can be done in deterministic polynomial time.

1 Introduction

Two-player zero-sum games played on graphs are adequate models for open reactive systems [12], i.e. systems maintaining a continuous interaction with their environment. In such model, `Eve` (the protagonist) models the system, `Adam` (the antagonist) models the environment, and a winning strategy for `Eve` in this game represents a controller that enforces a good property (modeled as the winning condition in the game) against all possible behaviors of the environment. Recently, there has been a large effort to study quantitative extensions of those graph games, see e.g. [6]. Those extensions are useful to model quantitative aspects of reactive systems such as mean energy or peak energy consumption, mean response time, etc. In practice, a system is most often exhibiting several such quantitative aspects, and they may be conflicting, e.g. one may need to consume more energy in order to ensure of a lower mean response time. This is why there is a clear need to study multi-dimensional quantitative games.

In [15], the *threshold problem* for multi-dimensional mean-payoff games is studied, i.e. given a d-dimensional value vector $v \in \mathbb{R}^d$, does `Eve` have a strategy

Work supported by ERC Starting Grant inVEST (279499).

D. Kroening and C.S. Păsăreanu (Eds.): CAV 2015, Part II, LNCS 9207, pp. 251–267, 2015.
DOI: 10.1007/978-3-319-21668-3_15

against all strategies of Adam to enforce values larger or equal to v. As weights in the game are given as vectors in multiple dimensions, there are usually an infinite number of incomparable thresholds that Eve is able to enforce. The set of maximal thresholds that Eve can enforce is called the *Pareto curve*, it is the classical tool to analyze *trade-offs*. Another application of the Pareto curve is the study of multiplayer games. For instance to compute Nash equilibria, a multiplayer game with mean-payoff objectives is transformed into a multidimensional mean-payoff two-player game [2], and the Pareto curve of this multidimensional game allows us to compute the equilibria of the original multiplayer game. In this paper, we study the Pareto curve and the set of thresholds that Eve can enforce in a multidimensional mean-payoff games.

Contributions. To effectively analyze the trade-offs in systems formalized by multidimensional mean-payoff games, we need algorithms to answer queries about Pareto curves or to compute an effective representation of them. This is the subject of this paper. Our main contributions are as follows.

First, we characterize the geometry of the set of thresholds that Eve can force: we show that this infinite set can be effectively represented as a (finite) union of convex sets defined by linear inequations. We obtain this result both for games where the mean-payoff is given dimension by dimension using lim inf (Theorem 4), and for a mixture of lim inf and lim sup (Theorem 10). Using this symbolic representation as a finite union of convex sets, it is now possible for instance to optimize linear functions by calls to linear programming.

Second, we study the computational complexity of natural associated decision problems. We provide a $\Sigma_2\mathsf{P}$ algorithm to decide if this set of thresholds intersects a convex set defined by linear inequations, and we prove the optimality of our algorithm by providing a matching complexity lower bound for the problem (Theorem 6). To obtain this result and several others in our paper, we extensively use techniques from discrete geometry [9] but we also need to establish new non-trivial results. In particular, we provide new results on the complexity of manipulating and querying linear sets defined by sets of linear inequations (Theorem 3). We believe that those results are of interest on their own. Equipped with those new results, we show that, even if the Pareto curve is represented by an exponential number of convex sets, each of them being defined by an exponential number of linear inequations, they are well behaved. Indeed, all the inequations that are needed to represent the Pareto curve and its downward closure (the set of thresholds that can be forced by Eve), have encoding that are bounded by polynomial functions in the size of the game.

Third, we show that it is possible to answer queries on the set thresholds that Eve can force (Theorem 7) and to construct the Pareto curve (Theorem 8) in *deterministic polynomial time* for fixed number of dimensions and polynomially bounded weights. Those results are of practical relevance as the number of dimension while multiple is often quite low in practice, and polynomially bounded weight is also a reasonable assumption, see [4,8,16] for papers where those two properties are exploited.

Related Works. In [1], Alur et al. consider languages of infinite words definable by Boolean queries over multidimensional mean-payoff automata. They study the accumulation points of infinite runs as a way to define an acceptance condition. They do not consider the construction of the Pareto curves associated to languages. Here, we show how to construct the Pareto curves in the more general and challenging setting of multidimensional mean-payoff games.

In [11], Papadimitriou et al. define a general procedure to construct *approximations* of Pareto curves. For models with *fixed* number of dimensions, they identify conditions that are sufficient to ensure that this approximation can be constructed in polynomial time. This technique has been used e.g. to provide approximate constructions of the Pareto curves for discounted sum Markov decision processes [7]. With the technique of [11], we can obtain approximations of the Pareto curves of multidimensional mean-payoff games in polynomial time for fixed number of dimensions. Here we provide a stronger result as we show how to construct *exact* representations of the Pareto curves (and not only approximations!) of multidimensional mean-payoff games in deterministic polynomial time for fixed number of dimensions.

Structure of the Paper. Section 2 defines the problems that we solve. Section 3 establishes general complexity results on the geometric objects that we use in the core of our paper. Section 4 solves the lim inf case. We concentrate on this case first as it exhibits all the difficulties of the general case with simpler notations. Section 5 deals with the construction of a concrete representation of the Pareto curve. In Sect. 6 we solve the general problem in which lim inf and lim sup are mixed.

For lack of space, the technical proofs are omitted, and can be found in [3].

2 Preliminaries

Arenas. We define *arenas* for two players that we call Eve and Adam. An *arena* $\mathcal{A}$ is a tuple $\langle \mathsf{States}_\exists, \mathsf{States}_\forall, \mathsf{Edges} \rangle$, where:

- $\mathsf{States} = \mathsf{States}_\exists \uplus \mathsf{States}_\forall$ is a finite set of *states* partitioned between the states of Eve and those of Adam;[1]
- $\mathsf{Edges} \subseteq \mathsf{States} \times \mathsf{States}$ is the set of *edges*. W.l.o.g. we assume that for all $s \in \mathsf{States}$, there exists $s' \in \mathsf{States}$ such that $(s, s') \in \mathsf{Edges}$.

A play proceeds as follows. Whenever we arrive at a state s: if $s \in \mathsf{States}_\exists$, then Eve selects a state s' such that $(s, s') \in \mathsf{Edges}$; if $s \in \mathsf{States}_\forall$, then Adam selects a state s' such that $(s, s') \in \mathsf{Edges}$. The game then continues from s' and this is repeated to form an infinite sequence of states. Formally, a *play* in the arena $\mathcal{A}$ is an infinite sequence of states $\rho = \rho_0 \rho_1 \cdots$ such that for all $i \geq 0$, $(\rho_i, \rho_{i+1}) \in \mathsf{Edges}$. We write $\rho{\leq}\, n$ for the prefix $\rho_0 \cdots \rho_n$. A *history* h of the arena $\mathcal{A}$ is a (finite and non-empty) prefix of a play, i.e. an element of $\mathsf{States}^* \cdot \mathsf{States}$.

[1] We will write $|\mathsf{States}|$ for the cardinal of States.

Strategies. Let $\mathcal{A}$ be an arena, a *strategy* for Eve maps histories ending in a state of $\mathsf{States}_\exists$ to a successor of that state. Formally, it is a function $\sigma_\exists \colon \mathsf{States}^* \cdot \mathsf{States}_\exists \to \mathsf{States}$, such that for all histories h and states s, $(s, \sigma_\exists(h \cdot s)) \in \mathsf{Edges}$. Similarly, a *strategy* for Adam is a function $\sigma_\forall \colon \mathsf{States}^* \cdot \mathsf{States}_\forall \to \mathsf{Actions}$, such that for all for all histories h and states s, $(s, \sigma_\forall(h \cdot s)) \in \mathsf{Edges}$. A strategy $\sigma_\forall$ is *memoryless* if for all histories h and h', and all states s, $\sigma_\forall(h \cdot s) = \sigma_\forall(h' \cdot s)$. We write $\mathbb{M}$ for the (finite) set of memoryless strategies of Adam. Let $\sigma_\exists$ be a strategy for Eve, a play ρ is *compatible* with the strategy $\sigma_\exists$ if, for all $k \geq 0$, if $\rho_k \in \mathsf{States}_\exists$ then $\rho_{k+1} = \sigma_\exists(\rho \leq k)$. We write $\mathsf{Outcome}_\mathcal{A}(s, \sigma_\exists)$ for the set of plays in $\mathcal{A}$ that are compatible with strategy $\sigma_\exists$ and have initial state s (i.e. ρ such that $\rho_0 = s$). These plays are called *outcomes* of $\sigma_\exists$ from s. We simply write $\mathsf{Outcome}(s, \sigma_\exists)$ when $\mathcal{A}$ is clear from context. The set of outcomes $\mathsf{Outcome}_\mathcal{A}(s, \sigma_\forall)$ of a strategy of Adam is defined symmetrically.

Weighted Game. A *weighted game* $\mathcal{G} = \langle \mathcal{A}, w, I, J \rangle$ is an arena $\mathcal{A}$ equipped with a *weight function* $w \colon \mathsf{Edges} \mapsto \mathbb{Z}^d$, and a partition of the set of dimensions $[\![1, d]\!] = \{1, 2, \ldots, d\}$ into $I \uplus J = [\![1, d]\!]$. We call d the dimension of $\mathcal{G}$. Given a weight function w, we write w_i for the projection to the i-th dimension of the function w. We write $W_\mathcal{G}$ for the maximal absolute value appearing in the weights: $W_\mathcal{G} = \max\{|w_i(e)| \mid i \in [\![1, d]\!], e \in \mathsf{Edges}\}$. The *mean-payoff inferior* and *mean-payoff superior* over dimension i of a play ρ are given by:

$$\underline{\mathsf{MP}}_i(\rho) = \liminf_{n \to \infty} \frac{1}{n} \sum_{0 \leq k < n} w_i(\rho_k, \rho_{k+1}),$$

$$\overline{\mathsf{MP}}_i(\rho) = \limsup_{n \to \infty} \frac{1}{n} \sum_{0 \leq k < n} w_i(\rho_k, \rho_{k+1}).$$

The goal of Eve is to maximize the mean-payoff inferior for the dimensions in I, and the mean-payoff superior for the dimensions in J. Let $\mathcal{G}$ be a weighted game, s a state of $\mathcal{G}$, and $v \in \mathbb{R}^d$, we say that a strategy $\sigma_\exists$ *ensures thresholds* v from state s if for all outcomes $\rho \in \mathsf{Outcome}_\mathcal{A}(s, \sigma_\exists)$, for all dimensions $i \in I$, $\underline{\mathsf{MP}}_i(\rho) \geq v_i$, and for all dimensions $j \in J$, $\overline{\mathsf{MP}}_j(\rho) \geq v_j$.

Pareto Optimality. We are interested in strategies of Eve that ensure thresholds as high as possible on all dimensions. However, since the weights are multidimensional, there is not a unique maximal threshold in general. We use the concept of *Pareto optimality* to identify the most interesting thresholds. To define the set of Pareto optimal thresholds, we first define the set of thresholds that Eve can force:

$$\mathtt{value}(\mathcal{G}, s) = \left\{ v \in \mathbb{R}^d \mid \exists \sigma_\exists \cdot \forall \rho \in \mathsf{Outcome}(s, \sigma_\exists) \cdot \begin{array}{c} \forall i \in I : \underline{\mathsf{MP}}_i(\rho) \geq v_i \\ \wedge \forall j \in J : \overline{\mathsf{MP}}_j(\rho) \geq v_j \end{array} \right\}.$$

A threshold $v \in \mathbb{R}^d$ is *Pareto optimal* from s if is maximal in the set $\mathtt{value}(\mathcal{G}, s)$. So the set of Pareto optimal thresholds is defined as:

$$\mathsf{PO}(\mathcal{G}, s) = \{v \in \mathtt{value}(\mathcal{G}, s) \mid \neg \exists v' \in \mathtt{value}(\mathcal{G}, s) : v' > v\}.$$

We refer to this set as the *Pareto curve* of the game. Our goal is to compute a representation of this curve. Note that the set of thresholds that Eve can force is exactly equal to the downward closure of the Pareto optimal thresholds, i.e. $\texttt{value}(\mathcal{G}, s) = \downarrow \mathsf{PO}(\mathcal{G}, s)$.

Linear Inequations. Let $a \in \mathbb{Q}^d$ be a vector in d dimensions. The associated *linear function* $\alpha_a : \mathbb{R}^d \mapsto \mathbb{R}$ is the function $\alpha_a(x) = \sum_{i \in [\![1,d]\!]} a_i \cdot x_i$ that computes the weighted sum relative to a. A *linear inequation* is a pair (a, b) where $a \in \mathbb{Q}^d \setminus \{\mathbf{0}\}$ and $b \in \mathbb{Q}$. The *half-space* satisfying (a, b) is the set $\frac{1}{2}\texttt{space}(a, b) = \{x \in \mathbb{R}^d \mid \alpha_a(x) \geq b\}$. A *linear equation* is also given by a pair (a, b) where $a \in \mathbb{Q}^d \setminus \{\mathbf{0}\}$ and $b \in \mathbb{Q}$ but we associate to it the *hyperplane* $\texttt{hplane}(a, b) = \{x \in \mathbb{R}^d \mid \alpha_a(x) = b\}$. If $H = \frac{1}{2}\texttt{space}(a, b)$ is a half-space, we sometimes write $\texttt{hplane}(H)$ for the *associated hyperplane* $\texttt{hplane}(a, b)$. A *system of linear inequations* is a set $\lambda = \{(a_1, b_1), \ldots, (a_l, b_l)\}$ of linear inequations. The *polyhedron* generated by λ is the set $\texttt{polyhedron}(\lambda) = \bigcap_{(a,b) \in \lambda} \frac{1}{2}\texttt{space}(a, b)$.

A natural problem, is to try to optimize the threshold we can ensure with respect to a linear function $\alpha : \mathbb{R}^d \mapsto \mathbb{R}$. We are looking for a strategy $\sigma_\exists$ which ensures a threshold $v \in \mathbb{R}^d$, and such that there is no $\sigma'_\exists$ which ensures a threshold $v' \in \mathbb{R}^d$, with $\alpha(v') > \alpha(v)$. To make this into a decision problem, we fix a real b, and ask if it is possible to ensure threshold v such that $\alpha(v) \geq b$. We consider a generalization of this problem which considers a set of linear inequations instead of a single one.

Polyhedron Value Problem. Given a mean-payoff game $\mathcal{G}$, a set of linear inequations λ over elements of $\mathbb{R}^d$, the *polyhedron value problem* asks whether there is a strategy $\sigma_\exists$ and a value $v \in \texttt{polyhedron}(\lambda)$ such that $\sigma_\exists$ ensures v. Note that this is equivalent to ask whether $\texttt{polyhedron}(\lambda)$ intersects $\texttt{value}(\mathcal{G}, s)$.

Remark 1. Other works ([8,15] for instance) focus on the 0-value problem, which is a special case of the polyhedron value problem (take as polyhedron the set $\mathbb{R}^d_+$). This special case is simpler: we will show that the polyhedron value problem is Σ_2P-complete while the 0-value problem is coNP-complete [15].

Consider a system with n resources $R_1, \ldots, R_n$ that are shared among d agents $A_1, \ldots, A_d$. Two agents cannot access the same resource at the same time and can request one resource at any time. We want to control the access to the resources in a way that minimizes the time that is spent during the waiting period by the different agents. This situation can be seen as a d dimensional game, in which if A_i is waiting then the reward is -1 on the i-th dimension and 0 otherwise. A situation with two agents and one resource is represented in Fig. 1.

On each dimension, the average corresponds to the opposite of the average waiting time of each agent. For limit inferior objectives the controller cannot ensure a payoff of 0 on all dimensions. However, it can ensure thresholds like $(-1, 0)$, $(0, -1)$, or $(-\frac{1}{2}, -\frac{1}{2})$, and in fact all the thresholds on the line segment from point $(-1, 0)$ to $(0, -1)$, or below it (this set is the set of *feasible thresholds*).

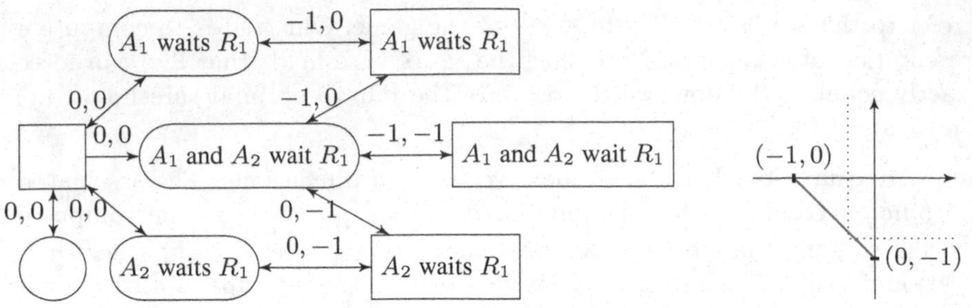

Fig. 1. A two-dimensional mean-payoff game. Rounded states belong to Eve and rectangles to Adam.

Fig. 2. Pareto curve of the game of Fig. 1.

Figure 2 shows the Pareto curve of the game. To illustrate the polyhedron value problem, assume we want a strategy which gives at least $-\frac{1}{3}$ on the first dimension, at least $-\frac{3}{4}$ on the second one: this corresponds to solution of the problems with $\lambda = ((1,0), -\frac{1}{3}), ((0,1), -\frac{3}{4})$. The frontier of this polyhedron is represented by dotted lines on the figure. This polyhedron has a non-empty intersection with the set of feasible thresholds, which means the problem has a solution.

3 Geometrical Representations

Since our typical reader may not be familiar with all the notions of discrete geometry that we need, we summarize in this section useful notions and properties related to convex sets which are useful for our characterization of the sets $\mathsf{PO}(\mathcal{G}, s)$ and $\mathtt{value}(\mathcal{G}, s)$. For an introduction to discrete geometry, we refer the interested reader to [9]. We also prove new results in Theorems 1, 2 and 3 on manipulating and querying polytopes and systems of linear inequations. Those results are necessary to prove the main theorems of our paper, and we believe that they are of interest on their own.

To allow computational complexity measure, the size of the representations of geometrical objects is relevant. We give here the number of bits required to represent the objects that we manipulate. The *size* of a rational number $r = \frac{p}{q} \in \mathbb{Q}$ where $p \in \mathbb{Z}, q \in \mathbb{N}$, p and q are relatively prime, is: $||r|| = 1 + \lceil \log_2(|p|+1) \rceil + \lceil \log_2(q+1) \rceil$. The size of a vector $v = (r_1, \dots, r_d)$ is $||v|| = d + \sum_{i \in [\![1,d]\!]} ||r_i||$. The size of an equation (a, b) is $||(a,b)|| = ||a|| + ||b||$ and the size of a system of equations λ is $||\lambda|| = \sum_{(a,b)\in\lambda} ||(a,b)||$.

A bounded polyhedron is called a *polytope*. A *face* F of P is a subset of P of the form $F = P \cap H_F$, where H_F is a half-space such that $P \subseteq H_F$. In that case, say that H_F *defines face* F of P. A face of dimension 1 is called a *vertex*. If P has dimension d', then a face of dimension $d' - 1$ is called a *facet*. Given a polytope P, a *complete set of facet-defining half-spaces* $\mathcal{F}$ contains for each facet F a half-space $H_F = \frac{1}{2}\mathtt{space}(a_F, b_F)$ such that $P \cap \mathtt{hplane}(a_F, b_F) = F$ and $P \subseteq H_F$.

We will write $\mathcal{F}(P)$ for such a set. The *convex hull* of a set of points $X \subseteq \mathbb{R}^d$ is the set $\text{conv}(X) = \{\sum_{x \in X} t_x \cdot x \mid \forall x \in X.\ t_x \in [0,1] \wedge \sum_{x \in X} t_x = 1\}$. The *downward closure* of a set of points $X \subseteq \mathbb{R}^d$, is the set $\downarrow X = \{x \mid \exists x' \in X.\ \forall i \in [\![1,d]\!].\ x_i \leq x'_i\}$.

If X is a finite set of points, the convex hull $P = \text{conv}(X)$ can be written as a finite intersection of half-spaces [9], it is therefore a polytope. It can be represented either by its extremal points or as the intersection of its facet-defining half-spaces.

For our algorithms, it is important to be able to go from the half-space representation to the extremal point representation and vice-versa. We need also to bound the complexity of the objects that we obtain, i.e. we want to ensure that the half-spaces are defined with inequations of polynomial size and the extremal points to be representable with polynomial encodings. We will show in Theorem 3 that this is possible.

Small Solutions of Large Systems of Equations. The following theorem establishes that if a system of linear equations has a solution, then it also has a solution with a small encoding.

Theorem 1. *There is a polynomial function P_1 such that for all system of equations λ of $\mathbb{R}^d$, if $\bigcap_{(a,b)\in\lambda} \textit{hplane}(a,b) \neq \varnothing$, then there exists $x \in \bigcap_{(a,b)\in\lambda} \textit{hplane}(a,b)$ whose representation has size smaller than $P_1(d) \cdot (1 + \max\{||(a,b)|| \mid (a,b) \in \lambda\})$.*

The proof given in long version of this paper relies on a result of [10] that we extend to non-singular, and non-square matrices of rational numbers rather than integers. Note also that our bound depends on the number of dimension d but not on the number of equations as in [10].

Small Witnesses of Large Systems of Inequations. To decide the polyhedron value problem, our algorithm nondeterministically constructs solutions of large systems of inequations. We show in Theorem 2 that we can restrict the guesses to points whose representation is of polynomial size. The proof relies on Lemma 1 that says that if a system of inequations has a solution, then there is one at the intersections of at most d of the hyperplanes defined by the associated equations. This is illustrated in Fig. 3: in two dimensions, if a collection of half-spaces (i.e. half-planes here) intersect (green shaded area in the picture), then either there is a point at the intersection of two boundary lines which is in the intersection (this is the case in our example for the blue points), or one of these lines is included in the intersection (this would be the case for instance if we only took parallel lines).

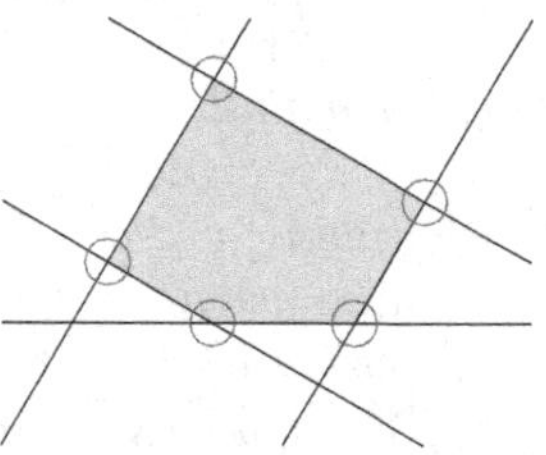

Fig. 3. Illustration of Lemma 1 in the case of two dimensions: In this example, the possible witnesses of the property are circled.

Lemma 1. *Let $H_1, \ldots, H_n$ be n inequations of $\mathbb{R}^d$. If $\bigcap_{i=1}^n \frac{1}{2}\mathtt{space}(H_i) \neq \varnothing$ then there are $k \leq d$ indexes $i_1, \ldots, i_d$ such that:*

1. $\bigcap_{j=1}^k \mathtt{hplane}(H_{i_j}) \neq \varnothing$*, and*
2. $\bigcap_{j=1}^k \mathtt{hplane}(H_{i_j}) \subseteq \bigcap_{i=1}^n \frac{1}{2}\mathtt{space}(H_i)$.

From Lemma 1, we conclude that small solutions always exists for systems of linear inequations independently of the number of inequations. Note that the main difference between the next theorem and Theorem 1 is that we consider here systems of inequations rather than equations.

Theorem 2. *There is a polynomial function P_1 such that for all systems of inequations λ of $\mathbb{R}^d$, if $\mathtt{polyhedron}(\lambda) \neq \varnothing$ then there is a point $x \in \mathtt{polyhedron}(\lambda)$ whose representation has size smaller than $P_1(d) \cdot (1 + \max\{||(a,b)|| \mid (a,b) \in \lambda\})$.*

Size Obtained When Changing the Representation of Polyhedra. As already recalled, it is well known that we can represent a polytope either as the intersection of half-spaces (solutions of a system of inequations) or by the finite set of its vertices (extremal points). Theorem 3 characterizes the complexity of one representation w.r.t. the other. Point 1 tells us how to bound the size of the inequations in the half-spaces representation as a function of the size of the representation of the points in the vertices representation. Point 2 does the same for the downward closure of the convex hull of the set of points. Point 3 tells us how to bound the size of the representation of the vertices as a function of the size of the inequations in the half-space representation. Proofs can be found in the long version of this paper.

Theorem 3. *There are polynomial functions P_2 and P_3 such that:*

1. *given a finite set of points $V = \{v_1, \ldots, v_n\}$, there are $k \leq n^d$ inequations $(a_1, b_1), \ldots, (a_k, b_k)$ whose representations have size smaller than $P_2(d) \cdot (2 + \log_2(\max\{||v|| \mid v \in V\}))$ and such that $\bigcap_{i \in [\![1,k]\!]} \frac{1}{2}\mathtt{space}(a_i, b_i) = \mathtt{conv}(V)$.*
2. *given a finite set of points $V = \{v_1, \ldots, v_n\}$, there are $k \in \mathbb{N}$ inequations $(a_1, b_1), \ldots, (a_k, b_k)$ whose representations have size smaller than $P_2(d) \cdot (2 + \log_2(\max\{||v|| \mid v \in V\}))$ and such that $\bigcap_{1 \leq i \leq k} \frac{1}{2}\mathtt{space}(a_i, b_i) = \downarrow \mathtt{conv}(V)$.*
3. *given a polytope P (i.e. a bounded polyhedron) represented by a system of inequations λ, such that $P = \bigcap_{(a,b) \in \lambda} \frac{1}{2}\mathtt{space}(a,b)$, there is a finite set V of points whose representations have size smaller than $P_3(d) \cdot (2 + \log_2(\max\{||(a,b)|| \mid (a,b) \in \lambda\}))$ and such that $\mathtt{conv}(V) = P$.*

4 The Limit Inferior Case

Let us fix for this section a weighted game $\mathcal{G} = \langle \mathsf{States}_\exists, \mathsf{States}_\forall, \mathsf{Edges}, w, I, J \rangle$ with $J = \emptyset$, i.e. the averages for all dimensions are defined using $\liminf$. In this case, the set of thresholds that can be ensured by $\mathtt{Eve}$ from state $s \in \mathsf{States}$ is:

$$\mathtt{value}(\mathcal{G}, s) = \left\{ v \in \mathbb{R}^d \mid \exists \sigma_\exists.\ \forall \rho \in \mathsf{Outcome}(s, \sigma_\exists).\ \forall i \in [\![1,d]\!].\ \underline{\mathsf{MP}}_i(\rho) \geq v_i \right\}.$$

To obtain a geometrical characterization of this set, we first study the set of thresholds that Eve can ensure when Adam plays according to a fixed memoryless strategy. Then, we show that the set $\mathtt{value}(\mathcal{G}, s)$ is the intersection of those sets for all the memoryless strategies of Adam. With the results of previous section, we deduce that if there is a solution to the *polyhedron value problem*, then there is one of bounded size which allows us to justify the correctness of a Σ_2P-algorithm for this problem. Finally, we show that this algorithm has optimal worst-case complexity by providing a matching Σ_2P-lower bound.

Playing Against Memoryless Strategies of Adam. Memoryless strategies for Adam are important as they are optimal for the threshold problem [15], i.e. if Adam has a strategy to prevent Eve from ensuring some threshold v then he has a memoryless one to do so. Our analysis relies on simple cycles. Let $S \subseteq \mathsf{States}$ be a subset of states of the arena of $\mathcal{G}$. A *simple cycle* within S is a finite sequence of states $s_0 \cdot s_1 \cdots s_n \in S^*$, such that $s_0 = s_n$, and for all i and j, $0 \leq i < j < n$, $s_i \neq s_j$. We write $\mathbb{C}(S)$ for the set of simple cycles of $\mathcal{A}$ within S. Let $\sigma_\forall \in \mathbb{M}$ be a memoryless strategy for Adam, this strategy induces the graph $\mathcal{G}(\sigma_\forall) = \langle \mathsf{States}, \mathsf{Edges}_{\sigma_\forall} \rangle$ where $\mathsf{Edges}_{\sigma_\forall} = \{(s, s') \in \mathsf{Edges} \mid s \in \mathsf{States}_\exists \vee (s \in \mathsf{States}_\forall \wedge \sigma_\forall(s) = s')\}$ which is a subgraph of the game arena in which Adam plays according to the memoryless strategy $\sigma_\forall$. We denote by $\mathsf{SCC}(s, \sigma_\forall)$ the set of *strongly connected components* accessible from s in $\mathcal{G}(\sigma_\forall)$.

Lemma 2. *For all $\sigma_\forall \in \mathbb{M}$, for all infinite paths $\rho = \rho_0\rho_1 \ldots \rho_n \ldots$ in $\mathcal{G}(\sigma_\forall)$, let $S \in SCC(\rho_0, \sigma_\forall)$ be such that $\mathsf{Inf}(\rho) \subseteq S$, then*

$$\underline{\mathsf{MP}}(\rho) \in \downarrow \mathit{conv}\left(\left\{\frac{1}{|c|} \cdot w(c) \mid c \in \mathbb{C}(S)\right\}\right).$$

Proof. An *accumulation point* of a sequence $x_0, x_1, \ldots, x_n, \ldots$ of vectors in $\mathbb{R}^d$ is a vector $x \in \mathbb{R}^d$ such that for every open set containing x, there are infinitely many elements in the sequence which belong to the open set. It is proved in [1] that if a run ρ gets trapped for ever in the SCC S (i.e. $\mathsf{Inf}(\rho) \subseteq S$) the set of accumulation points of the sequence $(\frac{1}{n} \cdot w(\rho_{\leq} n))_{\leq n}$ is included in $\mathtt{conv}\left(\left\{\frac{1}{|c|} \cdot w(c) \mid c \in \mathbb{C}(S)\right\}\right)$. Now, let us show that $\underline{\mathsf{MP}}(\rho)$ is smaller than any accumulation point of the infinite sequence of vectors $(\frac{1}{n} \cdot w(\rho_{\leq} n))_{\leq n}$. Indeed, if x be an accumulation point of that sequence, then for all dimension i the sequence $\frac{1}{n} w_i(\rho_{\leq} n)$ comes infinitely often arbitrarily close to x_i. This implies that $\liminf \frac{1}{n} w_i(\rho_{\leq} n)$ is smaller than x_i for all dimensions i. Therefore $\underline{\mathsf{MP}}(\rho) \leq x$ and $\underline{\mathsf{MP}}(\rho) \in \downarrow \{x\} \subseteq \downarrow \mathtt{conv}\left(\left\{\frac{1}{|c|} \cdot w(c) \mid c \in \mathbb{C}(S)\right\}\right)$. □

Note that it is not always the case that $\underline{\mathsf{MP}}(\rho)$ is in the convex hull of $\left\{\frac{1}{|c|} \cdot w(c) \mid c \in \mathbb{C}(S)\right\}$. The example Fig. 4 shows that the downward closure operator is necessary. In this example, the sequence of vectors $(1,0)^{2^1} \cdot (0,1)^{2^2} \cdot (1,0)^{2^3} \cdot (0,1)^{2^4} \cdots$ which can be obtained with a path ρ that cycles on state s_1 is such that $\underline{\mathsf{MP}}(\rho) = (0,0)$ which is not in the convex hull of $(1,0)$ and $(0,1)$ (this convex hull is the set of points $(t, 1-t)$ with $t \in [\![0,1]\!]$).

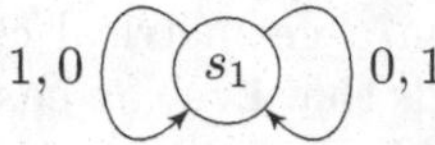

Fig. 4. Example of a game where $\underline{\mathsf{MP}}(\rho)$ does not belong to $\mathbf{conv}\left(\left\{\frac{1}{|c|} \cdot w(c) \mid c \in \mathbb{C}(S)\right\}\right)$ for all path ρ.

Lemma 3. *For all $\sigma_\forall \in \mathbb{M}$, for all $s \in$ States, for all $S \in \mathit{SCC}(s, \sigma_\forall)$, for all $v \in \mathbf{conv}\left(\left\{\frac{1}{|c|} \cdot w(c) \mid c \in \mathbb{C}(S)\right\}\right)$, there exists an infinite path ρ of $\mathcal{G}(\sigma_\forall)$ starting from s such that $\underline{\mathsf{MP}}(\rho) = v$.*

Proof. Let $\{c_1, c_2, \ldots, c_n\}$ be a set of simple cycles in S such that $v = \sum_{i=1}^{n} \lambda_i \frac{1}{|c_i|} \cdot w(c_i)$, with $\sum_{i=1}^{n} \lambda_i = 1$, and $\lambda_i \in [0,1]$, i.e. v is a linear combination of the average weights of the simple cycles. It is proved in [15, Lemma 11], that we can build a path ρ that starts in s, reaches the SCC S and then cycles within S between the simple cycles $c_1, c_2, \ldots, c_n$ in such a way that the $\underline{\mathsf{MP}}$ on each dimension j, $1 \leq j \leq d$ is equal to $v_j = \sum_{i=1}^{n} \lambda_i \frac{1}{|c_i|} \cdot w(c_i)_j$. □

Characterizing the Feasible Thresholds. As Adam can play optimally with memoryless strategies, the set of feasible thresholds that Eve can force is obtained by considering the intersection of all the sets of thresholds that she can enforce against those memoryless strategies of Adam.

Theorem 4. *Let $\mathcal{G}$ be a game and s a state of $\mathcal{G}$:*

$$\mathit{value}(\mathcal{G}, s) = \bigcap_{\sigma_\forall \in \mathbb{M}} \bigcup_{S \in \mathit{SCC}(s,\sigma_\forall)} \downarrow \mathbf{conv}\left(\left\{\frac{1}{|c|} \cdot w(c) \mid c \in \mathbb{C}(S)\right\}\right)$$

Proof. For the left to right inclusion. Assume that $\sigma_\exists$ is a winning strategy of Eve for the threshold v. For all memoryless strategies $\sigma_\forall \in \mathbb{M}$ of Adam, we have that $\rho = \mathsf{Outcome}(s, \sigma_\exists, \sigma_\forall)$ is such that $\underline{\mathsf{MP}}(\rho) \geq v$. By Lemma 2, $\underline{\mathsf{MP}}(\rho)$ belongs to the set $\downarrow \mathsf{conv}\left(\left\{\frac{1}{|c|} \cdot w(c) \mid c \in \mathbb{C}(S)\right\}\right)$, and as this set is downward closed it contains v.

For the right to left inclusion. Take any v in the set on the right. By Lemma 3, for all memoryless strategy $\sigma_\forall \in \mathbb{M}$ of Adam, we know that there exists an infinite path ρ starting from s in the graph $\mathcal{G}(\sigma_\forall)$ and such that $\underline{\mathsf{MP}}(\rho) = v$. This is equivalent to say that there exists a strategy $\sigma_\exists$ for Eve such that $\underline{\mathsf{MP}}(\mathsf{Outcome}(s, \sigma_\exists, \sigma_\forall)) = v$. So, this means that memoryless strategies of Adam cannot force from s an outcome with $\underline{\mathsf{MP}}$ which is not at least equal to v. As memoryless strategies of Adam are optimal, it means that Adam cannot obtain from s an outcome with $\underline{\mathsf{MP}}$ which is not at least equal to v, no matter the strategy that he plays. As multidimensional mean-payoff games are determined [15], it means that Eve has a strategy to force outcomes from s with a $\underline{\mathsf{MP}}$ at least equal to v, which in turn implies that $v \in \mathtt{value}(\mathcal{G}, s)$. □

Remark 2. As a corollary of Theorem 4, notice that the set $\mathtt{value}(\mathcal{G}, s)$ is closed.

Small Witnesses for Polyhedron Value Problem. We now show that if $\mathtt{value}(\mathcal{G}, s) \cap \mathtt{polyhedron}(\lambda) \neq \varnothing$, then there is a *witness* whose representation is polynomial.

Theorem 5. *There is a polynomial function P_4 such that, for all weighted game $\mathcal{G}$, for all states s, and system of linear inequations λ, if $value(\mathcal{G}, s) \cap polyhedron(\lambda) \neq \varnothing$ then there exists $x \in \mathbb{Q}^d$ such that:*

1. $x \in value(\mathcal{G}, s) \cap polyhedron(\lambda)$
2. $||x|| \leq P_4(d) \cdot (2 + \max\{||(a_j, b_j)|| \mid (a_j, b_j) \in \lambda\} + \log_2((W_{\mathcal{G}} + 1) \cdot (|\mathsf{States}| + 1)))$.

Proof. It follows from Theorem 4 that $\mathtt{value}(\mathcal{G}, s) \cap \mathtt{polyhedron}(\lambda) \neq \varnothing$ if, and only if, there is a function $f \colon \mathbb{M} \mapsto 2^{\mathsf{States}}$, such that $f(\sigma_\forall) \in \mathtt{SCC}(s, \sigma_\forall)$ for all strategy $\sigma_\forall$ and $\mathtt{polyhedron}(\lambda)$ intersects $\bigcap_{\sigma_\forall \in \mathbb{M}} \downarrow \mathtt{conv}\left(\left\{\frac{1}{|c|} \cdot w(c) \mid c \in \mathbb{C}(f(\sigma_\forall))\right\}\right)$. The values $\frac{1}{|c|} \cdot w(c)$ such that $c \in \mathbb{C}(S)$ for some SCC S, are such that their numerator is smaller in absolute value than $W_{\mathcal{G}} \cdot (|\mathsf{States}| + 1)$ and their denominator is smaller in absolute value than $|\mathsf{States}| + 1$. Let $a = (W_{\mathcal{G}} + 1) \cdot (|\mathsf{States}| + 1)$. We know by Theorem 3.3 that the set $\downarrow \mathtt{conv}\left(\left\{\frac{1}{|c|} \cdot w(c) \mid c \in \mathbb{C}(S)\right\}\right)$ can be written as the intersection of half-spaces $H_1, \ldots, H_k$ whose representation have size smaller than $P_2(d) \cdot (2 + \log_2(a))$. We conclude using Theorem 2 that there is a value $x \in \mathtt{value}(\mathcal{G}, s) \cap \mathtt{polyhedron}(\lambda)$ whose representation have size smaller than $d \cdot P_1(d) \cdot (1 + \max\{||H_i||, ||(a_j, b_j)|| \mid i \in [\![1, k]\!], (a_j, b_j) \in \lambda\})$ which is smaller than $d \cdot P_1(d) \cdot (1 + P_2(d) \cdot (2 + \log_2(a) + \max\{||(a_j, b_j)|| \mid (a_j, b_j) \in \lambda\}))$. We obtain the result for $P_4(d) = d \cdot P_1(d) \cdot (1 + P_2(d))$. □

Based on this property, we design a non-deterministic algorithm and characterize the complexity of our decision problem.

Theorem 6. *The polyhedron value problem is $\Sigma_2\mathsf{P}$-complete for mean-payoff inferior.*

Proof. **Easiness.** Based on Theorem 5, our algorithm is: 1. guess in polynomial time a value v; 2. check in deterministic polynomial time that it satisfies the set of linear equations λ (see e.g. [14, Theorem 3.3]); and 3. check in *non-deterministic* polynomial time that v belong to $\mathtt{value}(\mathcal{G}, s)$. This last check is based on the following result for the threshold problem: it is proved in [15, Theorem 7.2] that given a weighted game $\mathcal{G}$, a state s, and a threshold $v \in \mathbb{Q}^d$, the problem of deciding whether Eve has a winning strategy for the objective $\{\rho \mid \underline{\mathsf{MP}}(\rho) \geq v\}$ is coNP-complete. Our algorithm is thus in $\Sigma_2\mathsf{P} = \mathsf{NP}^{\mathsf{NP}} = \mathsf{NP}^{\mathsf{coNP}}$.

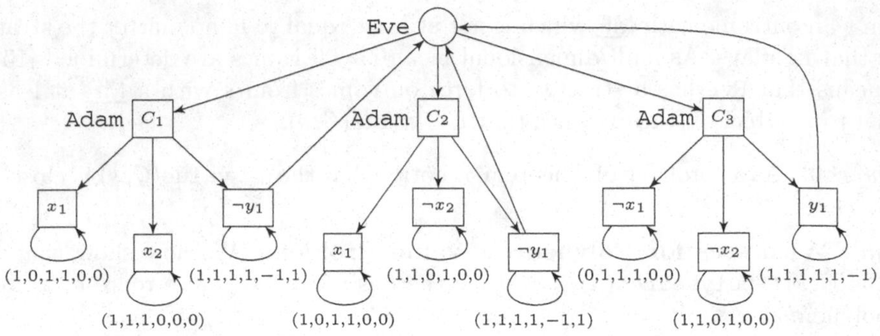

Fig. 5. Example of the encoding of QSAT_2 into the polyhedron value problem, for formula $\phi = \exists x_1.\exists x_2.\forall y_1.\ (x_1 \wedge x_2 \wedge \neg y_1) \vee (x_1 \wedge \neg x_2 \wedge \neg y_1) \vee (\neg x_1 \wedge \neg x_2 \wedge y_1)$. In a vector $(v_1, v_2, v_3, v_4, v_5, v_6)$, v_1 is associated to x_1, v_2 to $\neg x_1$, v_3 to x_2, v_4 to $\neg x_2$, v_5 to y_1, and v_6 to $\neg y_1$.

Hardness. We illustrate the reduction on an example. The full proof that the polyhedron value problem is Σ_2P-hard can be found in the long version of this paper.

Consider a QSAT_2 formula: $\phi = \exists x_1.\ \cdots \exists x_n.\ \forall y_1.\ \cdots \forall y_m.\ C_1 \vee \cdots \vee C_p$ where each C_i is the conjunction of at most three literals $C_i = \ell_{i,1} \wedge \ell_{i,2} \wedge \ell_{i,3}$ and literals are of the form: x_j, $\neg x_j$, y_j, or $\neg y_j$. The construction of the game is illustrated in Fig. 5. There is one dimension for each literal of the formula. We consider the constraint λ that enforces than on each dimension associated to a literal y_j or $\neg y_j$ the mean-payoff should be greater than 0, and the sum on the dimension associated to x_j and $\neg x_j$ (for j fixed) should be 1. It is possible to show that the polyhedron value problem is true if, and only if, the formula ϕ is valid.

Intuitively, if ϕ is valid, there is a partial valuation of the x variables that makes the remainder of the formula hold. From this partial valuation, we define a vector v that is 1 on dimensions associated to x literals that are true and 0 on the other dimensions. Such a vector satisfies the constraints λ. For each memoryless strategy of `Adam`, we can construct a counter strategy of `Eve` that is winning, and this is enough to show that `Eve` has a winning strategy. To construct this strategy, first notice that if the strategy of `Adam` chooses one literal in some clause and its negation in another clause, `Eve` can win by alternating between the two (this ensures 0 for this literal and 1 for the others). We can now assume that the strategy of `Adam` defines a valuation for the literals y, by setting those that are reachable to true. Then because ϕ is valid, `Eve` can choose a clause that holds under the valuation that we defined. Then `Adam` will always chose a literal that is true under this valuation and this ensures a payoff above v. □

Polynomial Time Algorithm for Fixed Number of Dimensions. We have seen in the previous paragraphs that the polyhedron value problem is Σ_2P-complete. Now, we show that the problem has a much better worst-case complexity for fixed number of dimensions and polynomially bounded weights, two hypotheses which are reasonable in practice.

Theorem 7. *The polyhedron value problem is solvable in polynomial time for mean-payoff inferior with fixed number of dimensions, polynomially bounded weights and a system a linear constraints with polynomially bounded numerators and denominators.*

Proof. Thanks to Theorem 5, for the polyhedron value problem, there are no more than $2^{P_4(d)\cdot(2+\max\{||(a,b)|||(a,b)\in\lambda\}+\log_2((W_{\mathcal{G}}+1)\cdot(|\mathsf{States}|+1)))}$ candidate witnesses. This quantity is equal to $(4 \cdot 2^{\max\{||(a,b)|||(a,b)\in\lambda\}} \cdot ((W_{\mathcal{G}}+1)\cdot(|\mathsf{States}|+1)))^{P_4(d)}$. Note that the size of equations in λ are logarithmic in the values of numerators and denominators that appear in it, so $2^{\max\{||(a,b)|||(a,b)\in\lambda\}}$ is polynomial with respect to these values (but exponential with respect to d). The bound on the number of candidates is polynomial when the number of dimensions d is fixed and W is polynomially bounded. As the threshold problem for multidimensional weight mean-payoff games is solvable in polynomial time when the number of dimensions is fixed and the weights are polynomially bounded [8, Theorem 1], we obtain a polynomial time algorithm by simply testing all the polynomially many witnesses. □

5 Constructing the Pareto Curve

Let $\mathcal{G}$ be a game of dimension d, we define the set of half-spaces $\mathcal{H}_{\mathcal{G}}$ and points $V_{\mathcal{G}}$ that are *relevant* for the representation of $\mathtt{value}(\mathcal{G}, s)$. $\mathcal{H}_{\mathcal{G}}$ and $V_{\mathcal{G}}$ are defined as the set of half-spaces and points with representation size bounded by $P_2(d)\cdot(2+\log_2((W_{\mathcal{G}}+1)\cdot(|\mathsf{States}|+1)))$. The following lemma explains why those sets are relevant.

Lemma 4. *Let $\mathcal{G}$ be a game of dimension d and s a state of $\mathcal{G}$. The set $\mathtt{value}(\mathcal{G}, s)$ can be written as a finite union of polyhedra, each of them definable as the intersection of half-spaces $H_1, \ldots, H_k \in \mathcal{H}_{\mathcal{G}}$. Moreover if $H_1, \ldots, H_k$ are half-spaces of $\mathcal{H}_{\mathcal{G}}$ and $\bigcap_{1\leq j\leq k} H_j \neq \varnothing$ then the intersection $\bigcap_{1\leq j\leq k} H_j$ contains a point of $V_{\mathcal{G}}$.*

Equivalence Classes. We say that two points x and y are equivalent with respect to the set of half-spaces $\mathcal{H}$, written $x \sim_{\mathcal{H}} y$, if they satisfy the same set of equations and inequations defined by $\mathcal{H}$. Formally $x \sim_{\mathcal{H}} y$ if for all $H \in \mathcal{H}$, $x \in H \Leftrightarrow y \in H$ and $x \in \mathtt{hplane}(H) \Leftrightarrow y \in \mathtt{hplane}(H)$. Given a point x, we write $[x]_{\mathcal{H}} = \{y \mid x \sim_{\mathcal{H}} y\}$ the equivalence class containing x. These equivalence classes are known in geometry as *cells* [13]. We write $C(\mathcal{H})$ the set of cells defined by $\mathcal{H}$. The following lemma, says that cells which intersect $\mathtt{value}(\mathcal{G}, s)$ are included in it.

Lemma 5. *Let $c \in C(\mathcal{H}_\mathcal{G})$ be a cell, $c \cap \mathtt{value}(\mathcal{G}, s) \neq \varnothing$ if, and only if, $c \subseteq \mathtt{value}(\mathcal{G}, s)$.*

From this we deduce a method to compute a representation of the set $\mathtt{value}(\mathcal{G}, s)$ as a finite union of cells in $C(\mathcal{H}_\mathcal{G})$. Given a tuple of at most $d+1$ points $X \subseteq V_\mathcal{G}$ with $|X| \leq d+1$, we consider the geometrical center $b(X) = \sum_{x \in X} \frac{1}{d+1} \cdot x$. We write $B(V_\mathcal{G})$ the set of all these point, it contains at most $|V_\mathcal{G}|^{d+1}$ points. The following lemma states that $\mathtt{value}(\mathcal{G}, s)$ can be represented as the union of all cells that contain a point in $B(V_\mathcal{G})$ which is in $\mathtt{value}(\mathcal{G}, s)$. Note that the fact that we do not need many points to cover each cell is coherent with Buck's theorem [5,13].

Lemma 6. *Let $\mathcal{G}$ be a game of dimension d, s a state of $\mathcal{G}$, We have that:*

$$[-W_\mathcal{G}, W_\mathcal{G}]^d \cap \mathtt{value}(\mathcal{G}, s) = [-W_\mathcal{G}, W_\mathcal{G}]^d \cap \bigcup_{x \in B(V_\mathcal{G}) \cap \mathtt{value}(\mathcal{G}, s)} [x]_{\mathcal{H}_\mathcal{G}}$$

As a corollary, we obtain an effective procedure to compute a representation of the set $\mathtt{value}(\mathcal{G}, s)$. The complexity of this procedure is given in the following theorem both for the general case, and for fixed number of dimensions and polynomially bounded weights.

Theorem 8. *There is a deterministic exponential time algorithm that given a game $\mathcal{G}$ and a state s, constructs a effective representation of $[-W_\mathcal{G}, W_\mathcal{G}]^d \cap \mathtt{value}(\mathcal{G}, s)$ as a union of cells. Moreover, when the dimension d is fixed and weights are polynomially bounded in the size of $\mathcal{G}$, then the algorithm works in deterministic polynomial time.*

Proof. The algorithm is based on the result of Lemma 6. We enumerate all subsets of $d+1$ points in $V_\mathcal{G}$. Because of their size, the number of points in $V_\mathcal{G}$ is bounded by $2^{P_4(d) \cdot (2 + \log_2((W_\mathcal{G}+1) \cdot (|\mathsf{States}|+1)))}$ which equals $(4 \cdot (W_\mathcal{G}+1) \cdot (|\mathsf{States}|+1))^{P_4(d)}$. The number of subsets of $d+1$ points is thus bounded by $(4 \cdot (W_\mathcal{G}+1) \cdot (|\mathsf{States}|+1))^{P_4(d) \cdot (d+1)}$. Note that it is exponential in general, but with polynomially bounded weights, $W_\mathcal{G}$ is polynomial in the sizes of the input, so that with d fixed this number of subsets is polynomially bounded.

Now for each of these subsets, we compute the geometrical center x, and test whether it is in $\mathtt{value}(\mathcal{G}, s)$. Thanks to [8, Theorem 1], there is an algorithm that works in time $O(|\mathsf{States}|^2 \cdot |\mathsf{Edges}| \cdot d \cdot W_\mathcal{G} \cdot (d \cdot |\mathsf{States}| \cdot W_\mathcal{G})^{d^2+2 \cdot d+1})$ to determine whether a point is in $\mathtt{value}(\mathcal{G}, s)$. This is exponential in general, but polynomial when the number of dimension is fixed and weights are polynomially bounded.

Then, to determine the cell corresponding to the geometrical center x, we test for each $H \in \mathcal{H}_\mathcal{G}$ whether $x \in H$: the intersection of the half-spaces that contain x and the complement of those that do not contain is equal to the cell containing x. Since the sizes of the half-spaces in $\mathcal{H}$ are bounded by $P_2(d) \cdot (2 + \log_2((W_\mathcal{G}+1) \cdot (|\mathsf{States}|+1)))$, we can test that x belongs to one of them in polynomial time and there are no more than $(4 \cdot (W_\mathcal{G}+1) \cdot (|\mathsf{States}|+1))^{P_2(d)}$ such half-spaces. Therefore testing all half-spaces can be done in exponential time in general, and in polynomial time with fixed dimension and polynomially bounded weights. □

Pareto Curve. The Pareto curve is composed of the maximal points in $[-W_\mathcal{G}, W_\mathcal{G}]^d \cap \texttt{value}(\mathcal{G}, s)$. To describe this curve, we need to refine the cells in $C(\mathcal{H}_\mathcal{G})$: we add to $\mathcal{H}_\mathcal{G}$ the half-spaces that are necessary to represent the downward closure of cells in $C(\mathcal{H}_\mathcal{G})$ (details can be found in the long version of this paper).

Theorem 9. *There is a deterministic exponential algorithm, that given a game $\mathcal{G}$ and a state s, computes an effective representation of $\mathsf{PO}(\mathcal{G}, s)$ as a union of cells. Moreover, when the dimension d is fixed and the weights are polynomially bounded then the algorithm works in deterministic polynomial time.*

Proof (Sketch). The algorithm works by computing a representation of $\texttt{value}(\mathcal{G}, s)$ as a union of cells. Then, for each of these cells we check that there is no cell above by using the downward closure operator: this is where refining the cells is required. The number of those cells is exponential so these checks can be done in exponential time. Moreover in the case where the dimension is fixed and weights are polynomially bounded, this number is polynomial so the algorithm works in polynomial time. □

6 General Case

We now consider the general case in which the average of dimensions in $I \subset [\![1, d]\!]$ are defined using lim inf and the average of dimensions in $J \subseteq [\![1, d]\!]$ are defined using lim sup. We give a characterization of the feasible thresholds as we did in Theorem 4. While the main ideas are similar, the characterization here is substantially more complicated and relies on a notion of subgame defined as follows. A *subarena for* $\texttt{Eve}$ is a tuple $\langle \mathsf{States}'_\exists, \mathsf{States}'_\forall, \mathsf{Edges}' \rangle$ with $\mathsf{States}' \subseteq \mathsf{States}$, $\mathsf{Edges}' \subseteq \mathsf{Edges}$ and such that $\forall s \in \mathsf{States}'_\forall.\ (s, s') \in \mathsf{Edges} \Rightarrow (s, s') \in \mathsf{Edges}'$ (i.e. it does not restrict actions of $\texttt{Adam}$). The game $\langle \mathcal{A}', w', I', J' \rangle$ is a subgame for $\texttt{Eve}$ of $\langle \mathcal{A}, w, I, J \rangle$ if $\mathcal{A}'$ is a subarena for $\texttt{Eve}$ of $\mathcal{A}$ and $w' = w$, $I' = I$, and $J' = J$. We write $\mathsf{Sub}(\mathcal{G}, s)$ the set of subgames for $\texttt{Eve}$ which contain the state s.

Theorem 10. *Let $\mathcal{G}$ be a weighted game and s a state of $\mathcal{G}$, then $\texttt{value}(\mathcal{G}, s)$ equals:*

$$\bigcup_{\mathcal{G}' \in \mathsf{Sub}(\mathcal{G}, s)} \bigcap_{s' \in \mathsf{States}'} \uparrow_J \left(\bigcap_{\sigma_\forall \in \mathbb{M}} \bigcup_{S' \in \mathsf{SCC}(s', \mathcal{G}'(\sigma_\forall))} \downarrow \mathit{conv}\left(\left\{ \frac{1}{|c|} \cdot w(c) \mid c \in \mathbb{C}(S') \right\} \right) \right)$$

where $\uparrow_J X = \{ x \in \mathbb{R}^d \mid \forall j \in J.\ \exists x' \in X.\ \forall i \in I \cup \{j\}.\ x_i = x'_i \}$.

Example 1. Consider the example of Fig. 6. We choose $J = \{1, 2\}$ and $I = \{3\}$, i.e. we consider the limit superior of the weights for the two first coordinate and the limit inferior for the last one. There is only one strategy of the adversary and one strongly connected component in this game. There are two simple cycles

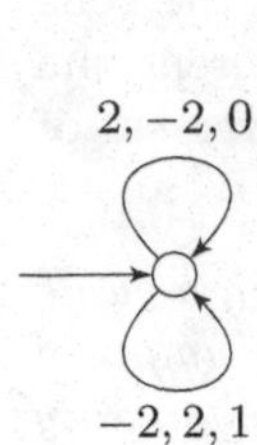

Fig. 6. A one-state 3-dimensional mean-payoff game, controlled by Eve. We refer to the 3 dimensions by x, y and z respectively.

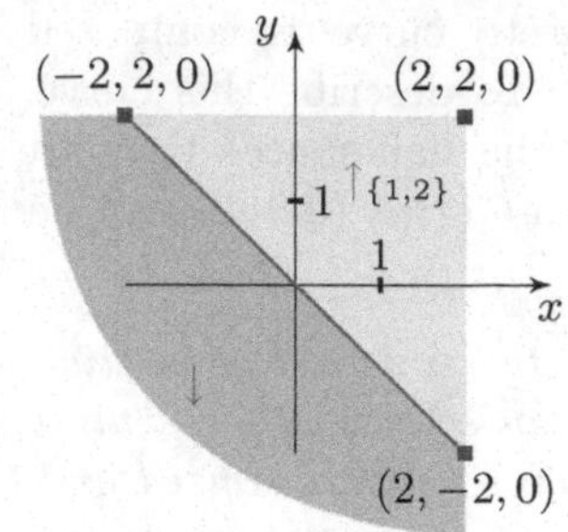

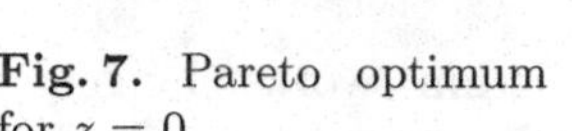

Fig. 7. Pareto optimum for $z = 0$.

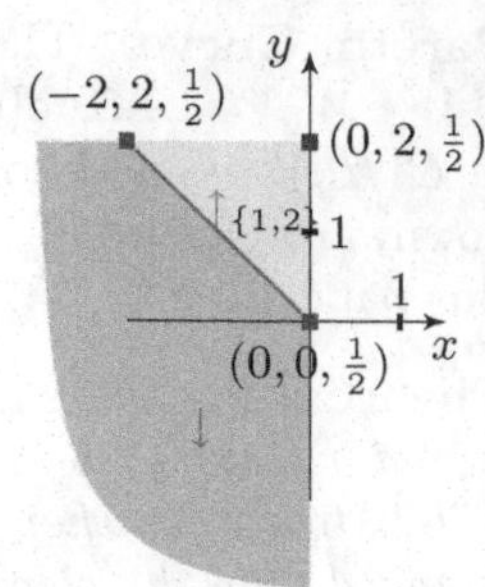

Fig. 8. Pareto optimum for $z = \frac{1}{2}$.

and their weight are $(2, -2, 0)$ and $(-2, 2, 1)$. We represented in Figs. 7 and 8 the feasible thresholds we can ensure with $z = 0$ and $z = \frac{1}{2}$.

For $z = 0$ the line segment between $(-2, 2, 0)$ and $(2, -2, 0)$ is below the convex hull of $(2, -2, 0)$ and $(-2, 2, 1)$. The downward closure this segment is the area that is below and left of this segment. The operator $\uparrow_{\{1,2\}}$ gives the whole area below of $(2, 2, 0)$ which is the Pareto optimum for $z = 0$. For $z = 1$ only $(-2, 2, 1)$ is below the weight of a simple cycle therefore it will be the Pareto optimum for $z = 1$. The convex hull of $(-2, 2, 1)$ and $(2, -2, 0)$ is above the plane $z = \frac{1}{2}$ for coordinates of x and y between $(0, 0)$ and $(-2, 2)$. The operator $\uparrow_{\{1,2\}}$ will give the whole area below $(0, 2, \frac{1}{2})$ which is the Pareto optimum for $z = 0$.

Thanks to the characterization of Theorem 10, we can express the value problem in terms of intersection of convex sets with a small description and using techniques similar to the ones used in the case of limit inferior we can show the following:

Theorem 11. *The polyhedron value problem is* $\Sigma_2\mathsf{P}$*-complete.*

The algorithm uses Theorem 10 and relies on the same principle as for lim inf.

References

1. Alur, R., Degorre, A., Maler, O., Weiss, G.: On omega-languages defined by mean-payoff conditions. In: de Alfaro, L. (ed.) FOSSACS 2009. LNCS, vol. 5504, pp. 333–347. Springer, Heidelberg (2009)
2. Bouyer, P., Brenguier, R., Markey, N., Ummels, M.: Concurrent games with ordered objectives. In: Birkedal, L. (ed.) FOSSACS 2012. LNCS, vol. 7213, pp. 301–315. Springer, Heidelberg (2012)

3. Brenguier, R., Raskin, J.-F.: Optimal values of multidimensional mean-payoff games. Research report, Université Libre de Bruxelles (U.L.B.), Belgium, October 2014. https://hal.archives-ouvertes.fr/hal-00977352
4. Brim, L., Chaloupka, J., Doyen, L., Gentilini, R., Raskin, J.-F.: Faster algorithms for mean-payoff games. Formal Methods Syst. Des. **38**(2), 97–118 (2011)
5. Buck, R.: Partition of space. Am. Math. Monthly **50**, 541–544 (1943)
6. Chakrabarti, A., de Alfaro, L., Henzinger, T.A., Stoelinga, M.: Resource interfaces. In: Alur, R., Lee, I. (eds.) EMSOFT 2003. LNCS, vol. 2855, pp. 117–133. Springer, Heidelberg (2003)
7. Chatterjee, K., Majumdar, R., Henzinger, T.A.: Markov decision processes with multiple objectives. In: Durand, B., Thomas, W. (eds.) STACS 2006. LNCS, vol. 3884, pp. 325–336. Springer, Heidelberg (2006)
8. Chatterjee, K., Velner, Y.: Hyperplane separation technique for multidimensional mean-payoff games. In: D'Argenio, P.R., Melgratti, H. (eds.) CONCUR 2013 – Concurrency Theory. LNCS, vol. 8052, pp. 500–515. Springer, Heidelberg (2013)
9. Matoušek, J.: Lectures on Discrete Geometry, vol. 212. Springer, New York (2002)
10. Papadimitriou, C.H.: On the complexity of integer programming. J. ACM (JACM) **28**(4), 765–768 (1981)
11. Papadimitriou, C.H., Yannakakis, M.: On the approximability of trade-offs and optimal access of web sources. In: 41st Annual Symposium on Foundations of Computer Science, Proceedings, pp. 86–92. IEEE (2000)
12. Pnueli, A., Rosner, R.: On the synthesis of a reactive module. In: POPL 1989, pp. 179–190. ACM Press (1989)
13. Sack, J.-R., Urrutia, J.: Handbook of Computational Geometry. Elsevier, Amsterdam (1999)
14. Schrijver, A.: Theory of Linear and Integer Programming. Wiley, Chichester (1998)
15. Velner, Y., Chatterjee, K., Doyen, L., Henzinger, T.A., Rabinovich, A., Raskin, J.-F.: The complexity of multi-mean-payoff and multi-energy games. CoRR, abs/1209.3234 (2012)
16. Zwick, U., Paterson, M.: The complexity of mean payoff games on graphs. TCS **158**(1), 343–359 (1996)

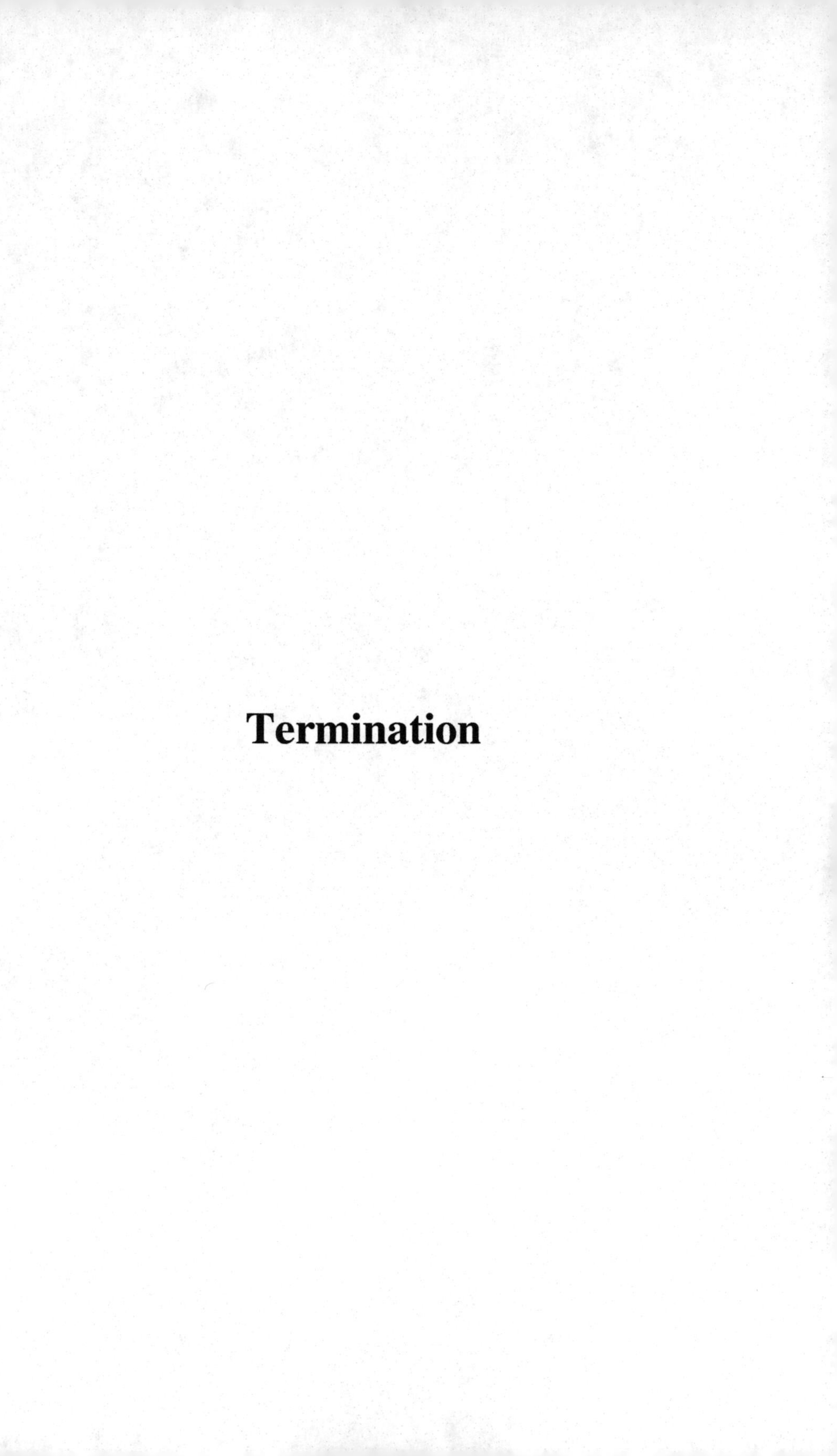

Termination

Conflict-Driven Conditional Termination

Vijay D'Silva[1] and Caterina Urban[2](✉)

[1] Google Inc., San Francisco, USA
[2] École Normale Supérieure, Paris, France
urban@di.ens.fr

Abstract. Conflict-driven learning, which is essential to the performance of SAT and SMT solvers, consists of a procedure that searches for a model of a formula, and refutation procedure for proving that no model exists. This paper shows that conflict-driven learning can improve the precision of a termination analysis based on abstract interpretation. We encode non-termination as satisfiability in a monadic second-order logic and use abstract interpreters to reason about the satisfiability of this formula. Our search procedure combines decisions with reachability analysis to find potentially non-terminating executions and our refutation procedure uses a conditional termination analysis. Our implementation extends the set of conditional termination arguments discovered by an existing termination analyzer.

1 Conflict-Driven Learning for Termination

Conflict-driven learning procedures are integral to the performance of SAT and SMT solvers. Such procedures combine search and refutation to determine if a formula is satisfiable. Conflicts discovered by search drive refutation, and search learns from refutation to avoid regions of the search space without solutions.

Our work is driven by the observation that discovering a small number of disjunctive termination arguments is crucial to the performance of certain termination analyzers [27]. Figure 1 summarizes our lifting of conflict-driven learning to termination analysis. We use reachability analysis to find a set of states that constitute potentially non-terminating execution. We apply a conditional termination analysis to this set to eliminate states from which all executions terminate. Unlike termination analysis, which solves a decision problem and returns a YES or NO answer, conditional termination analysis is concerned with discovering sufficient conditions for termination. Sufficient conditions for termination play the role of learned clauses in our analysis. They prevent subsequent runs of reachability analysis from revisiting states from which termination is guaranteed.

Our conflict driven conditional termination procedure (CDCT) can be viewed as a sound but incomplete solver for a family of monadic, second-order formulae. Büchi's theorem shows that the language of a Büchi automaton is non-empty exactly if a formula in the monadic second-order theory of one successor (S1S) is satisfiable [5]. This theorem can be viewed encoding non-termination of a finite-state program as satisfiability in S1S. We introduce S1S(T), an extension of S1S

D. Kroening and C.S. Păsăreanu (Eds.): CAV 2015, Part II, LNCS 9207, pp. 271–286, 2015.
DOI: 10.1007/978-3-319-21668-3_16

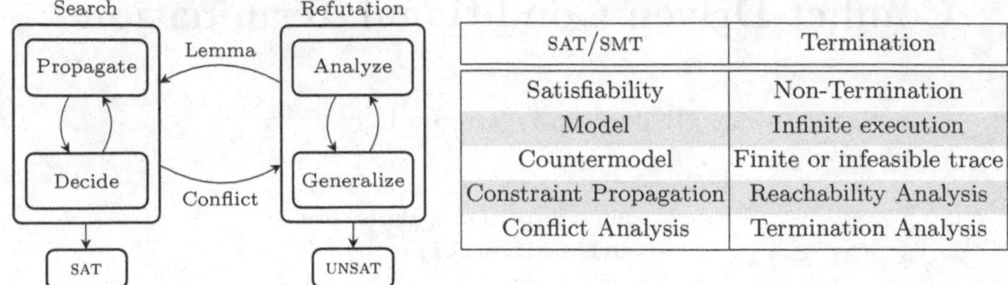

SAT/SMT	Termination
Satisfiability	Non-Termination
Model	Infinite execution
Countermodel	Finite or infeasible trace
Constraint Propagation	Reachability Analysis
Conflict Analysis	Termination Analysis

Fig. 1. Conflict driven learning as applied to termination

to sequences of first-order structures, and encode non-termination in a control-flow graph (CFG) as satisfiability in S1S(T). A model of a formula is an infinite execution that respects the transition constraints in the CFG.

Formulating non-termination as satisfiability provides a clear route for lifting CDCL to non-termination. We combine decisions with reachability in an abstract domain to construct and refine assignments to second-order variables in the same way that SAT solvers construct and refine partial assignments. A notable difference to standard abstract interpretation is that our assignments are neither over- nor under-approximations of the set of reachable states. Our conflict analysis uses backwards abstract interpretation to enlarge the set of states from which termination is guaranteed. We present a generalized unit rule for combining ranking functions with reachability analysis. These components are combined in our new analysis, which we have implemented and evaluated against state-of-the-art termination provers.

2 Non-Termination as Second-Order Satisfiability

The two contributions of this section are the logic S1S(T), which extends the monadic second-order logic of one successor (S1S) with a theory and an encoding of program non-termination as satisfiability in this theory.

2.1 Monadic Second-Order Theories of One Successor

We use $\hat{=}$ for definition. Let $\mathcal{P}(S)$ be the powerset of S. For $f : A \to B$, the function $f[a \mapsto b]$ maps a to b and c distinct from a to $f(c)$. The symbols x, y, z range over first-order variables in *Vars*, f, g, h over functions in *Fun*, and P, Q, R over predicates in *Pred*. We use a set *Pos* of first-order *position variables* whose elements are i, j, k, a set *SVar* of monadic second-order variables denoted X, Y, Z, a unary successor function *suc* and a binary successor predicate *Suc*.

Our logic consists of three families of formulae called state, transition and trace formulae, which are interpreted over first-order structures, pairs of first-order structures and infinte sequences of first-order structures respectively. The formulae are named after how they are interpreted over programs.

$$
\begin{array}{ll}
t ::= x \mid f(t_0, \ldots, t_n) & \text{Term} \\
\varphi ::= P(t_0, \ldots, t_n) \mid \varphi \wedge \varphi \mid \neg\varphi & \text{State Formula} \\
\psi ::= suc(x) = t \mid \psi \wedge \psi \mid \neg\psi & \text{Transition Formula} \\
\Phi ::= X(i) \mid Suc(i,j) \mid \varphi(i) \mid \psi(i) & \\
\quad \mid \Phi \wedge \Phi \mid \neg\Phi \mid \exists i : Pos.\Phi & \text{Trace formula}
\end{array}
$$

A first-order interpretation (Val, I) defines functions $I(f)$ and relations $I(P)$ over values in Val. The value $[\![t]\!]_s$ of a term t in a *state* $s : Vars \to Val$, is $s(x)$ if t is x, and $I(f)([\![t_0]\!]_s, \ldots, [\![t_n]\!]_s)$ if t is $f(t_0, \ldots, t_n)$. The interpretation of a state formula is the standard first-order semantics. A transition formula is interpreted at a *transition*, that is, a pair of states (r, s). A formula φ in which the symbol suc does not occur is interpreted at the state r, while $suc(x) = t$ compares the value of the term t in r with the value of x in the successor state s.

$$
\begin{array}{ll}
(r,s) \models P(t_0, \ldots, t_n) \text{ if } ([\![t_0]\!]_r, \ldots, [\![t_n]\!]_r) \in I(P) & \\
(r,s) \models \varphi \wedge \psi \text{ if } (r,s) \models \varphi \text{ and } (r,s) \models \psi & \\
(r,s) \models \neg\varphi \text{ if } (r,s) \not\models \varphi & (r,s) \models suc(x) = t \text{ if } [\![x]\!]_s = [\![t]\!]_r
\end{array}
$$

A *trace* $\tau : \mathbb{N} \to (Vars \to Val)$ is an infinite sequence of states and $\tau(m)$ is the *state at position* m. A *position assignment* $\sigma : (Pos \to \mathbb{N}) \uplus (SVar \to \mathcal{P}(\mathbb{N}))$ maps position variables to $\mathbb{N}$ and second-order variables to subsets of $\mathbb{N}$ such that $\{\sigma(X) \mid X \in SVar\}$ partitions $\mathbb{N}$. We explain this partition condition shortly. A trace formula is interpreted with respect to an S1S(T) *structure* (τ, σ).

Note that there are first-order variables of two sorts in a trace formula. A trace formula Φ asserting that the transition formula $\psi(x,y) \mathrel{\hat=} suc(x) = y+1$ is true at the trace position denoted by i has the form $\psi(x,y)(i)$. The predicate $Suc(i,j)$ asserts that the position j occurs immediately after i.

$$
\begin{array}{ll}
(\tau,\sigma) \models Suc(i,j) \text{ if } \sigma(i) + 1 = \sigma(j) & (\tau,\sigma) \models \varphi(i) \text{ if } \tau(\sigma(i)) \models \varphi \\
(\tau,\sigma) \models \psi(i) \text{ if } (\tau(\sigma(i)), \tau(\sigma(i)+1)) \models \psi & (\tau,\sigma) \models X(i) \text{ if } \sigma(i) \in \sigma(X) \\
(\tau,\sigma) \models \Phi \wedge \Psi \text{ if } (\tau,\sigma) \models \Phi \text{ and } (\tau,\sigma) \models \Psi & (\tau,\sigma) \models \neg\Phi \text{ if } (\tau,\sigma) \not\models \Phi \\
(\tau,\sigma) \models \exists i : Pos.\Phi \text{ if } (\tau, \sigma[i \mapsto n]) \models \Phi & \text{for some } n \text{ in } \mathbb{N}
\end{array}
$$

An S1S(T) structure (τ, σ) is a *model* of Φ if $(\tau, \sigma) \models \Phi$, and is a *countermodel* otherwise. A trace formula is *satisfiable* if it has a model. An S1S(T) structure is defined using an infinite trace, so finite traces cannot be models of a formula.

2.2 Encoding Non-Termination in S1S(T)

We now recall control flow graphs (CFGs) and encode non-termination as satisfiability. A *command* in *Cmd* is an assignment $x := t$ of a term t to a first-order variable x, or is a condition $[\varphi]$, where φ is a state formula. A CFG $G = (Loc, E, \mathtt{in}, \mathtt{ex}, stmt)$ consists of a finite set of locations Loc including an

$$
\begin{aligned}
&(\forall i.First(i) \Rightarrow X_{\mathtt{in}}(i)) \wedge (\forall i.X_{\mathtt{ex}}(i) \Rightarrow Last(i)) \\
\wedge\ &\forall i.\forall j.X_{\mathtt{in}}(j) \wedge Suc(i,j) \Rightarrow (suc(x) = x-1)(i) \wedge X_{\mathtt{a}}(i) \\
\wedge\ &\forall i.\forall j.X_{\mathtt{a}}(j) \wedge Suc(i,j) \ \Rightarrow (x \neq 0 \Rightarrow suc(x) = x)(i) \wedge X_{\mathtt{in}}(i) \\
\wedge\ &\forall i.\forall j.X_{\mathtt{ex}}(j) \wedge Suc(i,j) \Rightarrow (x = 0 \Rightarrow suc(x) = x)(i) \wedge X_{\mathtt{in}}(i)
\end{aligned}
$$

Fig. 2. A formula encoding non-termination of the program shown in the monadic second-order theory of one successor over integer arithmetic.

initial location in, an exit location ex, edges $E \subseteq Loc \times Loc$, and a labelling $stmt : E \longrightarrow Cmd$ of edges with commands. To assist the presentation, we assume that the exit location ex has no successors.

The formula $Trans_c$ below defines the semantics of commands using the condition $Same_V \mathrel{\hat{=}} \bigwedge_{x \in V} suc(x) = x$, that variables in V are not modified. The set of models of $Trans_c$ is the transition relation Rel_c. We write $Trans_e$ and Rel_e for the transition formula and relation of the command $stmt(e)$. The formula Inf_G extends the translation of Büchi automata to S1S to encode CFGs in S1S(T). We write $First(i) \mathrel{\hat{=}} \forall j.\neg Suc(j,i)$ for the first position on a trace and $Last(i) \mathrel{\hat{=}} \forall j.\neg Suc(i,j)$ for a position that cannot be on an infinite trace.

$$
Trans_c \mathrel{\hat{=}} \begin{cases} b \implies Same_{Vars} & \text{if } c = [b] \\ suc(x) = t \wedge Same_{Vars \setminus \{x\}} & \text{if } c = x := t \end{cases}
$$

$$
\begin{aligned}
Inf_G \mathrel{\hat{=}}\ & (\forall i.First(i) \implies X_{\mathtt{in}}(i)) \wedge (\forall j.X_{\mathtt{ex}}(j) \implies Last(j)) \\
& \wedge \bigwedge_{\mathtt{v} \in Loc} \forall i.\forall j.X_{\mathtt{v}}(j) \wedge Suc(i,j) \implies \bigvee_{(\mathtt{u},\mathtt{v}) \in E} Trans_{(\mathtt{u},\mathtt{v})}(i) \wedge X_{\mathtt{u}}(i)
\end{aligned}
$$

The formula Inf_G encodes program behaviour as follows. Consider an S1S(T) structure (τ, σ). The interpretation $\sigma(X_\ell)$ of a second-order variable X_ℓ represents positions on the trace when execution is at location ℓ. Such an interpretation partitions $\mathbb{N}$ because each position on a trace corresponds to a unique location. The *entry constraint* on $First(i)$ ensures execution begins at in. The *exit constraint* implying $Last(j)$ enforces that an infinite execution does not visit ex. The conditions involving $Suc(i,j)$ are called *transition constraints* and express that consecutive states on a trace must respect the transition relation of G. Theorem 1 expresses non-termination as satisfiability.

Theorem 1. *A* CFG *G has a non-terminating execution iff Inf_G is satisfiable.*

We believe this is a simple yet novel encoding of non-termination that allows the duality between search and refutation to be exploited for termination analysis. In contrast, the second-order encoding of termination in [13] uses a predicate for disjunctive well-foundedness and is solved in a different manner.

Example 1. A CFG G and the formula Inf_G for a program with a variable x of type $\mathbb{Z}$ are shown in Fig. 2. We write a trace as a sequence of values of x. Let τ

be the trace $-1, -1, -2, -2, \ldots$ and σ the assignment mapping $X_{\mathtt{ex}}$ to the empty set, and $X_{\mathtt{in}}$ and $X_{\mathtt{a}}$ to even and odd positions, respectively. The structure (τ, σ) is a model of Inf_G. Every structure (τ, δ), with τ as before, in which $\delta(X_{\mathtt{ex}})$ is not empty is a countermodel of Inf_G because ex is not reachable if x is initially -1, so some transition in τ must violate a transition constraint in Inf_G. Every structure (τ', δ') with x non-negative in $\tau'(0)$ is also a countermodel of Inf_G because executions with x initially non-negative terminate. Since τ' is infinite by definition, some transition in τ' must be infeasible. Terminating executions cannot be models of Inf_G because traces in S1S(T) structures are infinite. $\triangleleft$

The formula Inf_G is a conjunction of formulae in which second-order variables and first-order program variables are free but first-order position variables are bound. We exploit this structure in our analysis.

3 Conflict-Driven Conditional Termination

The conflict-driven conditional termination procedure (CDCT) in Algorithm 1 generalizes CDCL from SAT to termination analysis. The input is the formula Inf_G. The output $(\mathsf{result}, \Delta, \Theta)$ is a result concerning a set of structures Δ and a set Θ of piecewise-defined ranking functions (PDRFs).

The value of result is one of divergent, terminates, or unknown. CDCT returns divergent if the traces represented by Δ do not reach the exit location, which could be due to non-termination or undefined behaviour; It returns terminates if Δ is empty and Θ guarantees termination for all states. It returns unknown if CDCT cannot prove termination and cannot progress. This happens if the abstract domain cannot accurately represent non-terminating executions, if the ranking functions used cannot express a termination argument, or a bound on the number of decisions has been exceeded.

CDCT maintains four global data structures. The *trail* tr is a sequence of assignments to second-order variables. The *explanation array* exp contains in each element $exp[i]$, the decision or constraint used by propagation to add $tr[i]$ to the trail. The set of PDRFs Θ, generated by conditional termination analysis, are our analogue of learned clauses. The *blocking constraints* Ψ contain constraints representing two types of states, which need not be revisited. One is states from which all executions terminate. The other is states for which CDCT could neither prove termination nor demonstrate non-termination.

Each execution of the CDCT loop begins with a call to Search(), which attempts to find a non-terminating execution. If Search() returns divergent, CDCT returns. If Search() returns unknown, the trail represents a *potential conflict* because it has discovered a set of states from which some execution terminates. The conflict is potential because the trail may also contain models of Inf_G. This is a difference to SAT and SMT solvers where a conflict contradicts a formula.

The conflict analysis procedure Analyze()extracts from a potential conflict a definite conflict θ, expressed as a ranking function. The domain of θ represents

Algorithm 1. CDCT(Inf_G)

```
Trail: tr ← ε
Explanations: exp ← ε
Blocking constraints: Ψ ← ∅
PDRFs: Θ ← ∅
while true do
    result ← Search()
    if result = divergent or
    (result = unknown and exceeded()) then
        return (result, [tr], Θ)
    θ ← Analyze()
    Θ ← Θ ∪ {θ}
    Ψ ← Ψ ∪ Learn([tr], θ)
    if Backtrack() = false then
        return (terminates, [ε], Θ)
```

```
ℤ step(ℤ x) {
  if (x>20)
    return 3;
  else if (x>10)
    return 2;
  else
    return 1;
}
void main() {
      y, i : ℤ
[a] if (y>0)
        i = −step(y);
    else
        i = step(−y);
[b] while(y<−3||y>3)
        y = y+i;
[ex]}
```

states from which all executions terminate. The learning step Learn() generates a blocking constraint to drive subsequent search away from these states. Learning also generates a blocking constraint if CDCT cannot make progress analyzing $[tr]$. This happens if no more decisions can be made and no ranking function can be extracted. CDCT then backtracks if possible.

An Example Run. A program is shown in C-like syntax alongside Algorithm 1. The location a is reached after the variables are initialized, b is the loop head, and ex is the exit location. The program terminates but the abstract interpretation-based tool FuncTion [32] cannot prove termination. CDCT enables FuncTion to prove termination while also avoiding case explosion. Even though other tools may be able to prove termination, we believe CDCT is interesting because similar ideas could be used to expand the programs handled by those tools.

In this example, we use an interval abstract domain and affine ranking functions. Search() uses reachability analysis to derive the intervals $y{:}[-3,3], i{:}[-3,3]$ at ex but termination analysis fails. Decisions restrict the range of a variable at a location: for example, Search() heuristically uses conditions from the code to make the decisions $y{:}[1,\infty]$ and $y{:}[-\infty,10]$ at location a. Reachability derives the range $y{:}[1,3], i{:}[-1,-1]$ at ex, which is a conflict, because no trace with these states at ex satisfies Inf_G. Analyze() represents this conflict as $X_{\mathsf{ex}} \mapsto \{y{:}[1,3], i{:}[-1,-1] \to 0\}$, which assigns a PDRF to the second-order variable X_{ex} and expresses that the program terminates in 0 steps for the states shown. The PDRF is propagated backwards through the program by an abstract interpreter [31] to derive the second-order assignments below. We omit the interval on i, which is unchanged.

$$X_{\mathsf{ex}} \mapsto y{:}[1,3] \to 0, X_{\mathsf{b}} \mapsto y{:}[1,3] \to 1, X_{\mathsf{b}} \mapsto y{:}[4,4] \to 3, X_{\mathsf{b}} \mapsto y{:}[5,5] \to 5$$

If these assignments are propagated to location b, we could only prove that the program terminates for $y{:}[1,5]$ at a. Instead, we apply widening to the PDRFs to derive $X_b \mapsto \{y{:}[1,3] \to 1, y{:}[4,10] \to 2x+5\}$, which bounds the number of steps to termination at the loop head for y in the ranges shown. We heuristically expand the piece $y{:}[4,10]$ of the PDRF to $y{:}[1,\infty]$ and check if the $2x+5$ is still a ranking function. Since it is, we have proved termination for executions with $y{:}[1,\infty], i{:}[-1,-1]$ at b, despite having explicitly only analyzed the range $y{:}[0,5]$.

The learning step complements the decision $y{:}[1,\infty]$ and uses $X_{\mathtt{a}} \mapsto y{:}[-\infty,0]$ to restrict future search. Learnt constraints typically have more structure. A similar run of CDCT can show termination when y is initially non-positive.

Consider the program with the loop condition changed to $(y > -3)$. Now, the program does not always terminate. Decisions and learning can infer a ranking function for positive y as before. Decisions can also discover that for $X_{\mathtt{a}} \mapsto y{:}[-1,-1]$, ex is unreachable, indicating non-termination (as all locations lead to ex). In this way, CDCT proves conditional termination using disjunctions of ranking functions and also identifies non-terminating executions.

4 Search for a Conflict

We now show how a trail, a data structure used by SAT solvers, can be used to make explicit the incremental progress made by an abstract interpreter.

Abstract Domains. A bounded lattice $(L, \sqsubseteq, \sqcap, \sqcup)$ is a partially ordered set with a meet $\sqcap$, a join $\sqcup$, a greatest element $\top$ (top), and a least element $\bot$ (bottom). A concrete domain for forward analysis $(\mathcal{P}(State), \subseteq, F)$ is a lattice of states with a set $F = \{post_c \mid c \in Cmd\}$ of monotone functions called *transformers*, where $post_c(S)$ is the image of S under the transition relation for c. An *abstract domain* is a bounded lattice $(A, \sqsubseteq, G, \triangledown)$ with a set of abstract transformers $G = \{post_c^A \mid c \in Cmd\}$ and a *widening operator* $\triangledown : A \times A \to A$. There is a monotone *concretization* function $\gamma : A \to \mathcal{P}(State)$ satisfying that $\gamma(\top) = State$ and $\gamma(\bot) = \emptyset$. The transformers satisfy the soundness condition $post_c(\gamma(a)) \subseteq \gamma(post_c^A(a))$ that abstract transformers overapproximate concrete transformers.

Literals are essential for propagation and conflict analysis in SAT. The analogue of literals in abstract domains are complementable meet-irreducibles [11]. A lattice element c is a *meet-irreducible* if $a \sqcap b = c$ implies that $a = c$ or $b = c$. Let $\mathcal{M}_A$ be the meet-irreducibles of A. An abstract element a has a *concrete complement* if there exists an $\overline{a}$ in A such that $\gamma(a) = \neg\gamma(\overline{a})$. A *meet decomposition* of an element a is a finite set $mdc(a) \subseteq \mathcal{M}_A$ satisfying that $\bigsqcap mdc(a) = a$ and that there is no strict subset $S \subset mdc(a)$ with $\bigsqcap S = a$. A has *complementable meet irreducibles* if every $m \in \mathcal{M}_A$ has a concrete complement $\overline{m} \in \mathcal{M}_A$.

Example 2. The interval lattice has elements $[a,b]$, where $a \leq b \in \mathbb{Z} \cup \{-\infty, \infty\}$. The intervals $[-\infty,k], [k,\infty]$ are meet-irreducibles, unlike $[0,2]$. The set $S = \{[-\infty,2],[0,\infty],[-5,\infty]\}$ satisfies $\bigsqcap S = [0,2]$ but is not a meet decomposition because $\{[-\infty,2],[0,\infty]\} \subset S$. The concrete complements of $[-\infty,k]$ and $[k,\infty]$ are $[k+1,\infty]$ and $[-\infty,k-1]$, while $[0,2]$ has no concrete complement. $\lhd$

Algorithm 2. Search()

```
while true do
    Propagate()
    if tr(X_ex) = ⊥ then
        return divergent
    d ← dec(Inf_G, Ψ, tr)
    if [tr] ⊑ [tr·d] then
        return unknown
```

	Trail *tr*	*exp*	Modification
1	ϵ		Initial state
2	$X_{\mathtt{ex}}$:$[-\infty, 0]$, $X_{\mathtt{ex}}$:$[0, \infty]$	$\{\mathtt{in}, \mathtt{a}, \mathtt{ex}\}$	Propagation
3a	$\hookrightarrow X_{\mathtt{in}}$:$[9, \infty]$ $X_{\mathtt{in}}$:$[0, \infty]$	dec	Decision
4a	X_a:$[1, \infty]$	$\{\mathtt{a}, \mathtt{in}\}$	Propagation
5a	$X_{\mathtt{in}}$:$[-\infty, 0]$	dec	Decision
6a	$X_{\mathtt{a}}$:$\bot$	$\{\mathtt{a}, \mathtt{in}\}$	Propagation
3b	$X_{\mathtt{in}}$:$[-\infty, -7]$	dec	Decision
4b	X_a:$[-\infty, -7]$, $X_{\mathtt{ex}}$:$\bot$	$\{\mathtt{a}, \mathtt{in}\}$	Propagation

Abstract Assignments. SAT solvers use partial assignments to incrementally construct a model. We introduce abstract assignments, which use abstract domains to represent S1S(T) structures. Let *Struct* be the set of S1S(T) structures. The *lattice* of *abstract assignments* $(Asg_A, \sqsubseteq)$ contains the set $Asg_A \mathrel{\hat{=}} SVar \to A$ with the *pointwise order*: $asg \sqsubseteq asg'$ if $asg(X) \sqsubseteq asg'(X)$ for all X in $SVar$. The meet and join are also defined pointwise. An abstract assignment *asg* represents a set of S1S(T) structures as defined by the concretization $conc : Asg_A \to \mathcal{P}(Struct)$.

$$conc(asg) \mathrel{\hat{=}} \{(\tau, \sigma) \mid \text{for all}\, X \in SVar.\, \{\tau(i) \mid i \in \sigma(X)\} \subseteq \gamma(asg(X))\}$$

An abstract assignment *asg* is a *definite conflict* for Φ if no model of Φ is in $conc(asg)$ and is a *potential conflict* if $conc(asg)$ contains a countermodel of Φ.

Trail. We introduce a trail, which contains meet-irreducibles as in [4,10] and in which a second-order variable can appear multiple times. A *trail* over A is the empty sequence ϵ or the concatenation $tr{\cdot}(X{:}m)$, where X is a second-order variable and m is a complementable meet-irreducible. A trail *tr* defines the assignment $[tr]$ where $[\epsilon] \mathrel{\hat{=}} \lambda Y.\top$ and $[tr{\cdot}(X{:}m)]$ maps X to $[tr](X) \sqcap m$ and all other Y to $[tr](Y)$. A trail *tr* is in potential/definite conflict with Φ if $[tr]$ is. We write $tr(X)$ for $[tr](X)$. An *explanation exp* for a trail of length n is a function from $[0, n-1]$ to constraints in Inf_G or learnt clauses.

Search(). Algorithm 2 extends a trail *tr* by propagating constraints from the CFG, making decisions, or applying a generalized unit rule. It returns divergent if $tr(X_{\mathtt{ex}})$ is $\bot$, meaning that ex is unreachable. It returns unknown if $tr(X_{\mathtt{ex}})$ is not $\bot$ and no decisions can be made. This trail is a potential conflict because every structure in $conc([tr])$ with a non-empty assignment to $X_{\mathtt{ex}}$ violates the constraint $X_{\mathtt{ex}}(i) \implies Last(i)$, hence is a countermodel of Inf_G.

Example 3. The table alongside Algorithm 2 illustrates the construction of *tr* and *exp* during interval analysis of the program in Fig. 2. The *exp* column shows the locations of the propagated constraints. The rows $1, 2, 3a, 4a, 5a, 6a$ represent a run of Search(). The trail is initially empty and the result of standard interval analysis is the trail $X_{\mathtt{ex}}$:$[-\infty, 0]$, $X_{\mathtt{ex}}$:$[0, \infty]$ in step 2, representing the assignment $\{X_{\mathtt{in}} \mapsto \top, X_{\mathtt{a}} \mapsto \top, X_{\mathtt{ex}} \mapsto [0, 0]\}$. An arbitrary decision $X_{\mathtt{in}}$:$[9, \infty]$ in step $3a$ is not sound (see Example 3) and the smallest sound decision containing it is $[0, \infty]$. Propagation yields $X_{\mathtt{a}}$:$[1, \infty]$ in step $4a$. The decision $X_{\mathtt{in}}$:$[-\infty, 0]$ in step $5a$

Algorithm 3. Propagate()

```
asg ← [tr]
foreach S ∈ scc(Inf_G) do
    asg' ← Reach(S, asg)
    foreach X_v:m ∈ mdiff(asg', asg) do
        tr ← tr·(X_v:m)
foreach ψ ∈ Ψ do
    tr ← gunit(tr, ψ)
```

Algorithm 4. Analyze()

```
dc ← {j ↦ ⊤ | 0 ≤ j ≤ |tr|}
dc[|tr|] ← {|tr| ↦ [tr](X_ex) → 0}
i ← |tr|
repeat
    if dc[i] = ⊤ or exp[i] = nil then
        continue
    rk ← Term(exp[i], dc[i])
    dc[i] ← ⊤
    i ← i − 1
    Update(dc, tr, rk)
until Unique Implication Point
return [dc]
```

is sound, and when propagated, yields a conflict in step 6a, so search returns unknown. An alternative run is $1, 2, 3b, 4b$. A decision $X_{\mathtt{in}}$:$[-\infty, -7]$ is sound, and propagation yields $X_{\mathtt{a}}$:$[-\infty, -7]$ and $X_{\mathtt{ex}}$:$\bot$, so search returns divergent. ◁

Propagate(). Algorithm 3 calls an abstract interpreter and stores the results in the trail in a form amenable to conflict analysis and learning. The notion of *meet-difference* makes explicit the incremental change between two calls to the abstract interpreter. Formally, the *meet-difference* of $a, b \in A$ $\mathit{mdiff}(a, b) = \mathit{mdc}(a) \backslash \mathit{mdc}(b)$. The meet-difference of two abstract assignments is the pointwise lift $\mathit{mdiff}(asg, asg') = \{X_{\mathtt{v}}{:}m \mid m \in \mathit{mdiff}(asg(X_{\mathtt{v}}), asg'(X_{\mathtt{v}})), X_{\mathtt{v}} \in \mathit{SVar}\}$.

In a transition constraint $\psi \mathrel{\hat{=}} \forall i.\forall j.X_{\mathtt{v}}(j) \wedge \mathit{Suc}(i, j) \Rightarrow \ldots$, we write $\mathit{sink}(\psi)$ for $X_{\mathtt{v}}$. A *strongly connected component* (SCC) *of* Inf_G is a set of transition constraints T such that the set of locations $\{v \mid \psi \in T, X_{\mathtt{v}} = \mathit{sink}(\psi)\}$ is an SCC of G. The set of SCCs of Inf_G is $\mathit{scc}(\mathit{Inf}_G)$. Propagate() calls a standard abstract interpreter on each SCC and uses a meet-difference calculation to extend the trail with new information. Propagate() also applies a generalized unit rule *gunit*, explained in §conflicts. Propagation is sound in the sense that it does not eliminate models of the constraints involved.

Lemma 1. *If* (τ, σ) *satisfies* Inf_G *and* Ψ *and is in* $\mathit{conc}([tr])$, *it is also in* $\mathit{conc}([tr])$ *after invoking* Propagate().

Decisions. The abstract assignment computed by (the abstract interpreter used by) Propagate() can be refined using decisions. Boolean decisions make variables true or false and first-order decisions use values [7,24] but our decisions, like those in [11], use abstract domain elements.

A *decision* is an element $X{:}m$ that can be on a trail. A decision is *sound* if $\mathit{conc}(X{:}m) \cup \mathit{conc}(X{:}\overline{m}) = \mathit{Struct}$. That is, considering the structures in m and $\overline{m}$ amounts to considering all possible structures.

Example 4. Recall the unsound decision $X_{\mathtt{in}}$:$[9, \infty]$ from Example 3. The structure (τ, σ) with $\tau = 9, 9, 8, 8, \ldots$ and σ partitioning $X_{\mathtt{in}}$ and $X_{\mathtt{a}}$ into even and odd values is not in $\mathit{conc}(X_{\mathtt{in}}{:}[9, \infty])$ as x cannot be 8 at in. Similarly, it is not in $\mathit{conc}(X_{\mathtt{in}}{:}[-\infty, 8])$ so $\mathit{conc}(X_{\mathtt{in}}{:}[9, \infty]) \cup \mathit{conc}(X_{\mathtt{in}}{:}[-\infty, 8]) \neq \mathit{Struct}$. ◁

The unsoundness arises because pointwise lifting does not preserve concrete complements. Though $\overline{m}$ is the concrete complement of m in A, $[X_v{:}\overline{m}]$ need not be the concrete complement of $[X_v{:}m]$ in Asg_A. Unsound decisions can be extended by propagation to a post-fixed point to cover all structures. All decisions on variables X_v in singleton SCCs with no self-loops are sound.

A *decision rule* $\mathsf{dec}(Inf_G, \Psi, tr)$ returns an abstract domain element d such that $[tr{\cdot}(X_v{:}d)] \sqsubseteq [tr]$. The decision rule *makes progress* if this order is strict. Unlike in SAT the decision rule can cause divergence of CDCT because an infinite series of decisions like $[0, \infty], [1, \infty], \ldots$ may not change the result of propagation.

5 Conflict Analysis

Unlike SAT and SMT solvers, which generate definite conflicts, $\mathsf{Search}()$ generates potential conflicts. We apply backwards abstract interpretation with ranking functions to extract definite conflicts, and use widening to generalize them.

Ranking Function Domains. Due to space limitations, we only briefly recall the concrete domain of ranking functions, which provides the intuition for conflict analysis, and discuss the abstract domain informally. See [8,31] for details.

We write $f : A \twoheadrightarrow B$ for a partial function whose domain is $dom(f)$. A *ranking function* $f : State \twoheadrightarrow \mathbb{O}$ for a relation R is a map from states to ordinals satisfying that for all s in $dom(f)$ and (s, t) in R, t is in $dom(f)$ and $f(t) < f(s)$. A concrete domain for termination analysis $(Rank, \preccurlyeq, B)$ is a lattice of ranking functions with backwards transformers $B = \{bkw_c \mid c \in Cmd\}$ defined below. Informally $f \preccurlyeq g$ if f is defined on a state when g is and yields a lower rank: $f \preccurlyeq g \mathrel{\hat{=}} dom(f) \supseteq dom(g)$ and for all x in $dom(g)$, $f(x) < g(x)$. The transformer bkw_c maps a ranking function f to one defined on states with all their successors in $dom(f)$. Recall that Rel_c is the transition relation for a command c.

$$bkw_c(f) \mathrel{\hat{=}} \lambda s. \begin{cases} 0 & \text{if } Rel_c(s) = \emptyset \\ \sup\{f(r) \mid r \in Rel_c(s)\} + 1 & \text{if} Rel_c(s) \subseteq dom(f) \\ \text{undefined} & \text{otherwise} \end{cases}$$

A subset $P \subseteq A$ of a domain A is an *abstract partition* if $\{\gamma(a) \mid a \in P\}$ partitions $State$. Let $Fun \subseteq Rank$ be a lattice of functions, for example, affine functions.

A *piecewise defined ranking function* (PDRF) over Fun and A is a set $\rho \mathrel{\hat{=}} \{a_1 \mapsto f_1, \ldots, a_k \mapsto f_k\}$ such that $\{a_1, \ldots, a_k\}$ is an abstract partition, and each f_i is in Fun. The abstract domain of PDRFs $(aRank, \preccurlyeq, Abd)$ is a lattice $aRank$ with *abduction transformers* Abd. The concretization $\gamma^r : aRank \rightarrow Rank$ of a ρ as above maps states to ranking functions: $\gamma^r(\rho) \mathrel{\hat{=}} \{s \mapsto f_i \mid s \in \gamma(a_i)\}$. The order and lattice operations are defined in terms of partition refinement and unification [31]. To compare ρ_1 and ρ_2, we consider the coarsest abstract partition that refines the abstract partitions of both and compare the ranking functions in each block pointwise.

Conflict analysis starts with a precondition for termination and finds a weaker precondition for termination, hence performs abduction. The abduction transformers satisfy the soundness condition: $\gamma^r(abd_c(\rho)) \preccurlyeq bkw_c(\gamma^r(\rho))$, which states that the termination bounds obtained with PDRFs are weaker than those that could be obtained in the concrete domain. A sound abduction transformer is underapproximating. A *ranking assignment* $rk : SVar \to aRank$ associates a PDRF with each second-order variable. Ranking assignments form a lattice with point-wise meet and join and have a special order $\leqslant$ for fixed point checks [31]. To exchange information between Analyze() and Search() we extract a meet-irreducible representation of the domains of PDRFs. The *meet-projection* of a PDRF $\rho \mathrel{\hat{=}} \{a_i \mapsto f_i\}$ is the set of sets of meet-irreducibles $mpr(\rho) \mathrel{\hat{=}} \{mdc(a_i)\}$ and provides a DNF-like representation of the abstract partition in ρ.

Analyze(). Algorithm 4 uses an array dc to construct and generalize a definite conflict. Each $dc[i]$ represents termination conditions for states in the trail. Executions from states at ex terminate immediately so the last element of dc is $\{X_{\mathsf{ex}} \mapsto \{[tr](X_{\mathsf{ex}}) \mapsto 0\}\}$ and all other elements are $\top$. The conflict analysis loop walks backwards through the trail and extends $dc[i]$. Forward propagation through the SCC $exp[i]$ added $tr[i]$ to the trail, so $dc[i]$ is propagated backwards through $exp[i]$ to generalize the conflict to a ranking assignment rk. New PDRFs are added to dc by the procedure Update(). Specifically, for each X_v modified by Term(), and $m \in mpr(rk(X_v))$, Update() finds trail indices with $tr[j] \sqsubseteq X_v{:}m$ and sets $dc[j]$ to the appropriate PDRF. Analyze() continues until a *unique implication point* is reached, which is typically a dominator in the CFG at which a decision was made. Analyze() returns $[dc]$, a representation of the PDRFs in dc.

Learn() ***and the Generalized Unit Rule.*** Information computed by Search() is communicated to Analyze() using the trail, while information from Analyze() is represented within Search() by a blocking constraint and is incorporated in search using generalized unit rule. We describe these very briefly.

A set $C = \{X_1{:}m_1, \ldots, X_k{:}m_k\}$ of elements can be complemented element-wise to obtain $\overline{C} = \{X_1{:}\overline{m}_1, \ldots, X_k{:}\overline{m}_k\}$. If C is viewed as a conjunction of literals representing a conflict, $\overline{C}$ is a clause the procedure can learn. Learn() applies meet-projection to a PDRF and complements this projection to obtain a *blocking constraint.* In practice, we simplify the partitions of the PDRF to avoid an explosion of blocking constraints, analogous to subsumption in SAT.

The generalized unit rule [10] extends a trail using a blocking constraint. Assume that Ψ has the form $\{X_0{:}m_0, \ldots, X_k{:}m_k\}$. The trail $gunit(tr, \Psi)$ is $tr \cdot (X_k{:}m_k)$ if $[tr](X_i) \sqcap m_i = \bot$ for $0 \leq i < k$ and is tr otherwise. The generalized unit rule refines a trail in the sense that $[gunit(tr, \Psi)] \sqsubseteq [tr]$. If tr is inconsistent with Ψ, $[tr]$ will represent $\bot$. Having presented all components of the procedure, we now investigate how it works in practice.

6 Implementation

We have incorporated CDCT in our prototype static analyzer FuncTion (http://www.di.ens.fr/~urban/FuncTion.html), which is based on piecewise-defined

(a)

	Tot	Time	Timeouts
FuncTion+cdct	200	1.5s	15
AProVE [29]	256	15.9s	24
FuncTion [32]	175	0.7s	5
HIPTnT+ [22]	246	1.2s	4
Ultimate [18]	226	15.3s	35

(b)

	FuncTion+cdct			
	■	▲	×	○
AProVE [29]	15	71	185	17
FuncTion [32]	25	0	175	88
HIPTnT+ [22]	22	68	178	20
Ultimate [18]	41	67	159	21

Fig. 3. Overview of the experimental evaluation.

ranking functions [31]. A version without cdct [32] participated in the *4th International Competition on Software Verification (SV-COMP 2015)*.

FuncTion+cdct accepts (non-deterministic) programs in a C-like syntax. It is implemented in OCaml and uses the APRON library [20]. The pieces of a pdrf can be represented with intervals, octagons or convex polyhedra, and ranking functions within the pieces are represented by affine functions. The precision of the analysis can also be controlled by adjusting the widening delay.

Experimental Evaluation. We evaluated our tool against 288 terminating C programs from the termination category of *SV-COMP 2015*. In particular, we compared FuncTion+cdct with other tools from the termination category of *SV-COMP 2015*: AProVE [29], FuncTion without cdct [32], HIPTnT+ [22], and Ultimate Automizer [18]. The experiments were performed on a system with a 1.30 GHz 64-bit Dual-Core CPU (Intel i5-4250U) and 4 GB of RAM. For the other tools, since we did not have access to their competition version, we used the *SV-COMP 2015* results obtained on more powerful systems with a 3.40 GHz 64-bit Quad-Core CPU (Intel i7-4770) and 33 GB of RAM.

Figure 3 summarizes our evaluation. The first column is the number of programs each tool could prove terminating. The second column reports the average running time in seconds, and the last column reports the number of time outs, which was set to 180 seconds. In Fig. 3b, the first column (■) lists the number of programs that FuncTion+cdct proved terminating and the tool could not, the second column (▲) reports the number of programs that the tool proved terminating and FuncTion+cdct could not, and the last two columns report the number of programs that the tool and FuncTion+cdct were both able (×) or unable (○) to prove terminating. The same symbols are used in Fig. 4.

Figure 3a shows that cdct causes a 9 % improvement in FuncTion+cdct compared to FuncTion without cdct. The increase in runtime is not evenly distributed, and about 2 % of the test cases require more than 20 seconds to be analyzed by FuncTion+cdct (cf. Fig. 4a). In these cases the decision heuristics do not quickly isolate sets of states on which the abstract interpreter makes progress. Figure 4a shows that, as expected, FuncTion without cdct terminates with an unknown result earlier. Figures 4b and 4d show that though AProVE and Ultimate Automizer were run on more powerful machines, FuncTion+cdct is generally faster but proves termination of respectively 19 % and 9 % fewer programs (cf. Fig. 3a). HIPTnT+ proves termination of 16 % more

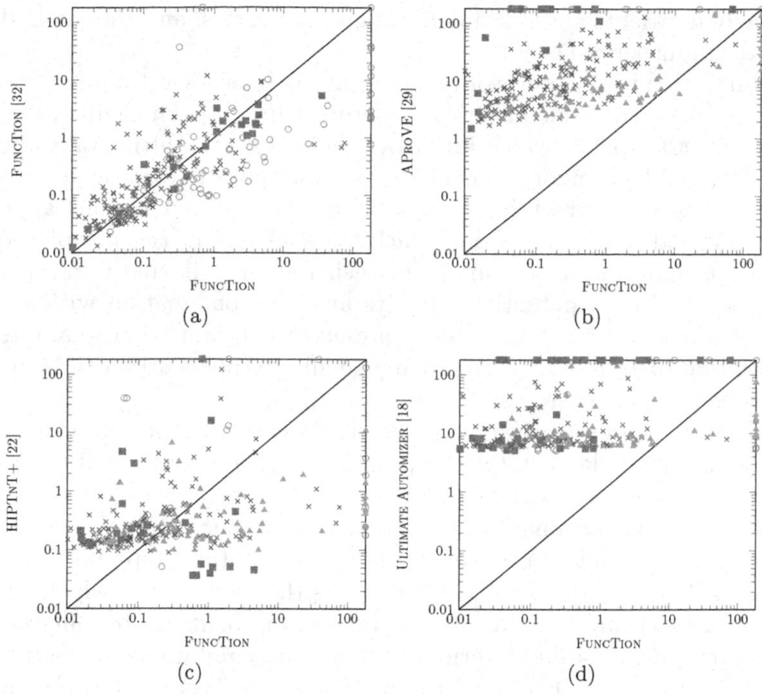

Fig. 4. Detailed comparison of FuncTion against its previous version [32] (a), AProVE [29] (b), HIPTnT+ [22] (c), and Ultimate Automizer [18] (d).

programs than FuncTion+cdct (cf. Fig. 4a), but FuncTion+cdct proves termination of 52 % of the program that HIPTnT+ is not able to prove terminating (8 % of the total test cases, cf. Fig. 3b). When comparing with FuncTion without cdct [32], we observed a 2x speedup in the *SV-COMP 2015* machines, so the runtime comparison of FuncTion+cdct and HIPTnT+ is inconclusive. Finally, thanks to the support for piecewise-defined ranking functions, 1 % of the programs could be proved terminating only by FuncTion+cdct (2.7 % by AProVE, 1 % by HIPTnT+, and 1.7 % by Ultimate Automizer). No tool could prove termination for 0.7 % of the programs.

7 Related Work and Conclusion

Büchi's work relating automata and logic [5] is the basis for automata-based verification and synthesis. We depart from most work in this tradition in two ways. One is the use of sequences of first-order structures as in first-order temporal logics [19] and the other is to go from a graph-based representation to a formula, which is opposite of the translation used in automata-theoretic approaches. The use of s1s for pointer analysis [26], and termination [25] is restricted to decidable cases, as is [9]. Program analysis questions have been formulated with set-constraints [1] and second-order Horn clauses [13], but solutions to these formulae are typically invariants and ranking functions, not errors, and the methods used to solve them differ from CDCT.

A key intuition behind our work is to lift algorithmic ideas from SAT solvers to program analysis. The same intuition underlies SMPP [17], which lifts DPLL(T) to programs, ACDCL [10,11], which lifts CDCL to lattices, the lifting of Stålmarck's method [30], and lazy annotation, which uses interpolants for learning [23]. The idea of guiding an abstract interpreter away from certain regions appears in DAGGER [14] and VINTA [2], from which CDCT differs in the use of a trail in search and a unit rule in learning. Our generalized unit rule is from ACDCL, but the use of S1S(T), potential conflicts and the combination with PDRFs is all new. The widening used in CDCT preserves a termination guarantee and we believe that algorithms for generating small interpolants [3] can help design better widening operators.

Finally, termination analysis is a thriving area with more approaches than we can discuss. A fundamental problem is the efficient discovery of disjunctions of ranking functions [27]. We use backward analysis, as in [8,12], and our combination of conditional termination [6] with non-termination [15,21] is crucial. The approach of [22] is similar ours with a different refutation step and information exchange mechanism. At a high level, CDCT is the dual of [16], which underapproximates non-terminating executions and overapproximates terminating ones, while we overapproximate non-termination and underapproximate termination. We believe CDCT can be extended to transition-based approaches [28], but the challenge is to develop search and learning.

References

1. Aiken, A.: Introduction to set constraint-based program analysis. Sci. Comput. Program. **35**, 79–111 (1999). Elsevier
2. Albarghouthi, A., Gurfinkel, A., Chechik, M.: Craig interpretation. In: Miné, A., Schmidt, D. (eds.) SAS 2012. LNCS, vol. 7460, pp. 300–316. Springer, Heidelberg (2012)
3. Albarghouthi, A., McMillan, K.L.: Beautiful interpolants. In: Sharygina, N., Veith, H. (eds.) CAV 2013. LNCS, vol. 8044, pp. 313–329. Springer, Heidelberg (2013)
4. Brain, M., D'silva, V., Griggio, A., Haller, L., Kroening, D.: Deciding floating-point logic with abstract conflict driven clause learning. Formal Methods Syst. Des. **45**(2), 213–245 (2014). Springer
5. Büchi, J.R.: On a decision method in restricted second order arithmetic. In: Logic, Methodology and Philosophy of Science, pp. 1–11. Stanford University Press (1960)
6. Cook, B., Gulwani, S., Lev-Ami, T., Rybalchenko, A., Sagiv, M.: Proving conditional termination. In: Gupta, A., Malik, S. (eds.) CAV 2008. LNCS, vol. 5123, pp. 328–340. Springer, Heidelberg (2008)
7. Cotton, S.: Natural domain SMT: a preliminary assessment. In: Chatterjee, K., Henzinger, T.A. (eds.) FORMATS 2010. LNCS, vol. 6246, pp. 77–91. Springer, Heidelberg (2010)
8. Cousot, P., Cousot, R.: An abstract interpretation framework for termination. In: Field, J., Hicks, M. (eds.) POPL, pp. 245–258. ACM (2012)

9. David, C., Kroening, D., Lewis, M.: Unrestricted termination and non-termination arguments for bit-vector programs. In: Vitek, J. (ed.) ESOP 2015. LNCS, vol. 9032, pp. 183–204. Springer, Heidelberg (2015)
10. D'Silva, V., Haller, L., Kroening, D.: Abstract conflict driven learning. In: Giacobazzi, R., Cousot, R. (eds.) POPL, pp. 143–154. ACM (2013)
11. D'Silva, V., Haller, L., Kroening, D., Tautschnig, M.: Numeric bounds analysis with conflict-driven learning. In: Flanagan, C., König, B. (eds.) TACAS 2012. LNCS, vol. 7214, pp. 48–63. Springer, Heidelberg (2012)
12. Ganty, P., Genaim, S.: Proving termination starting from the end. In: Sharygina, N., Veith, H. (eds.) CAV 2013. LNCS, vol. 8044, pp. 397–412. Springer, Heidelberg (2013)
13. Grebenshchikov, S., Lopes, N.P., Popeea, C., Rybalchenko, A.: Synthesizing software verifiers from proof rules. In: Vitek, J., Lin, H., Tip, F. (eds.) PLDI, pp. 405–416. ACM (2012)
14. Gulavani, B.S., Chakraborty, S., Nori, A.V., Rajamani, S.K.: Automatically refining abstract interpretations. In: Ramakrishnan, C.R., Rehof, J. (eds.) TACAS 2008. LNCS, vol. 4963, pp. 443–458. Springer, Heidelberg (2008)
15. Gupta, A., Henzinger, T.A., Majumdar, R., Rybalchenko, A., Xu, R.-G.: Proving non-termination. In: Necula, G.C., Wadler, P. (eds.) POPL, pp. 147–158. ACM (2008)
16. Harris, W.R., Lal, A., Nori, A.V., Rajamani, S.K.: Alternation for termination. In: Cousot, R., Martel, M. (eds.) SAS 2010. LNCS, vol. 6337, pp. 304–319. Springer, Heidelberg (2010)
17. Harris, W.R., Sankaranarayanan, S., Ivančić, F., Gupta, A.: Program analysis via satisfiability modulo path programs. In: Hermenegildo, M., Palsberg, J. (eds.) POPL, pp. 71–82. ACM (2010)
18. Heizmann, M., Dietsch, D., Leike, J., Musa, B., Podelski, A.: ULTIMATE AUTOMIZER with array interpolation (Competition Contribution). In: Baier, C., Tinelli, C. (eds.) TACAS 2015. LNCS, vol. 9035, pp. 455–457. Springer, Heidelberg (2015)
19. Hodkinson, I.M., Wolter, F., Zakharyaschev, M.: Decidable and undecidable fragments of first-order branching temporal logics. In: LICS, pp. 393–402. IEEE Computer Society (2002)
20. Jeannet, B., Miné, A.: APRON: a library of numerical abstract domains for static analysis. In: Bouajjani, A., Maler, O. (eds.) CAV 2009. LNCS, vol. 5643, pp. 661–667. Springer, Heidelberg (2009)
21. Larraz, D., Nimkar, K., Oliveras, A., Rodríguez-Carbonell, E., Rubio, A.: Proving non-termination using max-SMT. In: Biere, A., Bloem, R. (eds.) CAV 2014. LNCS, vol. 8559, pp. 779–796. Springer, Heidelberg (2014)
22. Le, T.-C., Qin, S., Chin, W.-N.: Termination and non-termination specification inference. In: Grove, D., Blackburn, S. (eds.) PLDI. ACM (2015)
23. McMillan, K.L.: Lazy annotation for program testing and verification. In: Touili, T., Cook, B., Jackson, P. (eds.) CAV 2010. LNCS, vol. 6174, pp. 104–118. Springer, Heidelberg (2010)
24. McMillan, K.L., Kuehlmann, A., Sagiv, M.: Generalizing DPLL to richer logics. In: Bouajjani, A., Maler, O. (eds.) CAV 2009. LNCS, vol. 5643, pp. 462–476. Springer, Heidelberg (2009)
25. Mesnard, F., Payet, É.: A second-order formulation of non-termination. In: CoRR (2014)
26. Møller, A., Schwartzbach, M.I.: The pointer assertion logic engine. In: Burke, M., Soffa, M.L. (eds.) PLDI, pp. 221–231. ACM (2001)

27. Podelski, A., Rybalchenko, A.: Transition invariants. In: LICS, pp. 32–41. IEEE Computer Society (2004)
28. Podelski, A., Rybalchenko, A.: Transition invariants and transition predicate abstraction for program termination. In: Abdulla, P.A., Leino, K.R.M. (eds.) TACAS 2011. LNCS, vol. 6605, pp. 3–10. Springer, Heidelberg (2011)
29. Ströder, T., Aschermann, C., Frohn, F., Hensel, J., Giesl, J.: AProVE: Termination and memory safety of C programs (Competition Contribution). In: Baier, C., Tinelli, C. (eds.) TACAS 2015. LNCS, vol. 9035, pp. 417–419. Springer, Heidelberg (2015)
30. Thakur, A., Reps, T.: A generalization of Stålmarck's method. In: Miné, A., Schmidt, D. (eds.) SAS 2012. LNCS, vol. 7460, pp. 334–351. Springer, Heidelberg (2012)
31. Urban, C.: The abstract domain of segmented ranking functions. In: Logozzo, F., Fähndrich, M. (eds.) Static Analysis. LNCS, vol. 7935, pp. 43–62. Springer, Heidelberg (2013)
32. Urban, C.: FuncTion: an abstract domain functor for termination (Competition Contribution). In: Baier, C., Tinelli, C. (eds.) TACAS 2015. LNCS, vol. 9035, pp. 464–466. Springer, Heidelberg (2015)

Predicate Abstraction and CEGAR for Disproving Termination of Higher-Order Functional Programs

Takuya Kuwahara[1(✉)], Ryosuke Sato[2], Hiroshi Unno[3], and Naoki Kobayashi[2]

[1] Knowledge Discovery Research Laboratories, NEC, Minato, Japan
t-kuwahara@me.jp.nec.com
[2] The University of Tokyo, Bunkyo, Japan
{ryosuke,koba}@kb.is.s.u-tokyo.ac.jp
[3] University of Tsukuba, Tsukuba, Japan
uhiro@cs.tsukuba.ac.jp

Abstract. We propose an automated method for disproving termination of higher-order functional programs. Our method combines higher-order model checking with predicate abstraction and CEGAR. Our predicate abstraction is novel in that it computes a mixture of under- and overapproximations. For non-determinism of a source program (such as random number generation), we apply underapproximation to generate a subset of the actual branches, and check that some of the branches in the abstract program is non-terminating. For operations on infinite data domains (such as integers), we apply overapproximation to generate a superset of the actual branches, and check that every branch is non-terminating. Thus, disproving non-termination reduces to the problem of checking a certain branching property of the abstract program, which can be solved by higher-order model checking. We have implemented a prototype non-termination prover based on our method and have confirmed the effectiveness of the proposed approach through experiments.

1 Introduction

We propose an automated method for disproving termination of higher-order functional programs (i.e., for proving that a given program does not terminate for *some* input). The method plays a role complementary to the automated method for proving termination of higher-order programs (i.e., for proving that a given program terminates for *all* inputs) [18]. Several methods have recently been proposed for proving non-termination of programs [7–9,11,13,14,19], but most of them have focused on *first-order* programs (or, while programs) that can be represented as finite control graphs. An exception is work on term rewriting systems (TRS) [9,11]; higher-order programs can be encoded into term rewriting systems, but the definition of non-termination is different: TRS is non-terminating if there exists a term that has a non-terminating rewriting sequence, not necessarily the initial term.

D. Kroening and C.S. Păsăreanu (Eds.): CAV 2015, Part II, LNCS 9207, pp. 287–303, 2015.
DOI: 10.1007/978-3-319-21668-3_17

Our approach is based on a combination of higher-order model checking [15,21] with predicate abstraction and CEGAR (counterexample-guided abstraction refinement). Values of a base type (such as integers) are abstracted to (tuples of) Booleans by using predicates, and higher-order functions are abstracted accordingly. Higher-order model checking is then used to analyze the abstracted program. A combination of predicate abstraction and higher-order model checking has been previously proposed for verifying safety properties of higher-order programs (i.e., for proving that a program does not reach an error state in *all* execution paths) [16]. With respect to that work, the approach of the present paper is novel in that we combine *over*approximation and *under*approximation. Note that predicate abstraction [3,12,16] usually yields an overapproximation, i.e., an abstract program that contains a *superset* of possible execution paths of the original program. With such an abstraction, non-termination of the abstract program (the existence of a non-terminating path) does not imply that of the original program. To address this problem, we use both under- and overapproximations. For a deterministic computation step of the original program, we apply overapproximation but check that *every* branch of the overapproximation has a non-terminating path. For a non-deterministic branch of the original program (such as random number generation and an input from the environment), we apply *under*-approximation, and check that *some* branch of the underapproximation has a non-terminating path.

Figure 1 illustrates how under- and overapproximations are combined. The program considered here is of the form:

$$\textbf{let } x = * \textbf{ in let } y = x + 1 \textbf{ in let } z = * \textbf{ in } \cdots .$$

Here, $*$ generates a random integer. Thus, the program has the execution tree shown on the top of Fig. 1. The first and third steps are non-deterministic, while the second step (corresponding to $y = x + 1$) is deterministic. Suppose that the predicates used for abstracting the values of x, y, and z are $x > 0$, $y > 0$, and $0 \leq z < x + y$ (these predicates do not necessarily yield a good abstraction, but are sufficient for explaining the combination of under- and overapproximations). Then, the abstract program has the execution tree shown on the bottom of the figure. Due to the predicate abstraction, the infinitely many branches on the value of x have been replaced by two branches $x > 0$ and $\neg x > 0$. The node $\exists$ means that only one of the branches needs to have an infinite path (for the original program having a non-terminating path). The deterministic path from $x = n$ to $y = n + 1$ has now been replaced by non-deterministic branches $y > 0$ and $\neg y > 0$. The node $\forall$ indicates that *every* child of the node must have an infinite path. Below the node $x > 0$, however, we do not have a node for $\neg y > 0$, as $x > 0$ and $y = x + 1$ imply $y > 0$. The infinite branches on z have been replaced by non-deterministic branches on $\neg(0 \leq z < x + y)$ or $0 \leq z < x + y$. As is the case for x, the branches are marked by $\exists$, meaning that one of the branches needs to have an infinite path. Note that below the node $\neg x > 0$, we only have a branch for $\neg(0 \leq z < x + y)$. This is because, when $x \leq 0$, there may be no z that satisfies $0 \leq z < x + y$; so, even if there may be an infinite execution sequence along that path, we cannot conclude that the source program is non-terminating. Thus, this part of the tree provides an *under*-approximation of the source program.

An abstract program is actually represented as a tree-generating program that generates an execution tree like the one shown on the bottom of Fig. 1. Higher-order model checking is then used for checking, informally speaking, that *every* child of each ∀-node has a non-terminating path, and that *some* child of each ∃-node has a non-terminating path.

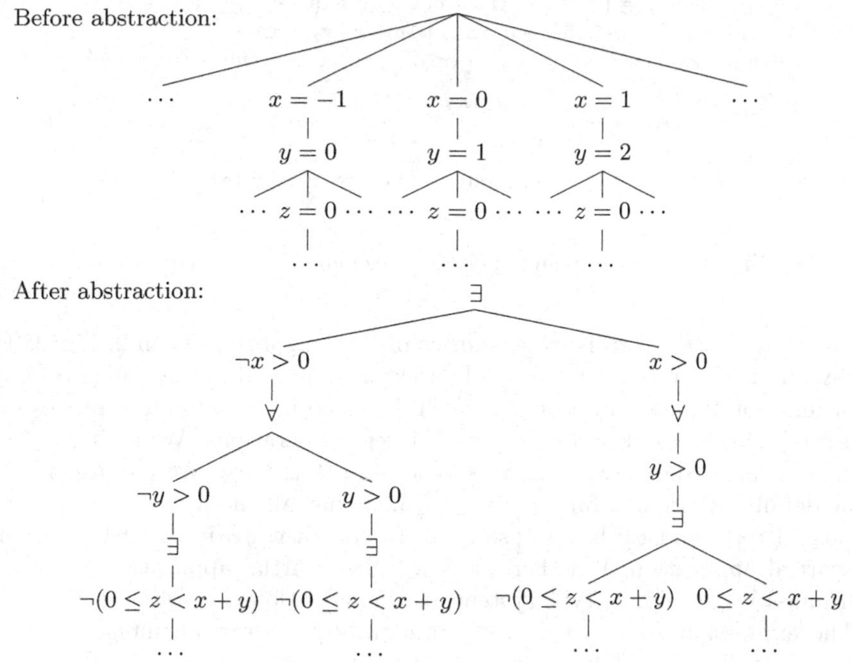

Fig. 1. Execution trees before/after abstraction

The use of overapproximation for disproving termination has also been proposed recently by Cook et al. [8]. Although their theoretical framework is general, their concrete method for automation is limited to first-order programs. They also propose a restricted form of combination of underapproximation and overapproximation, but underapproximation can be followed by overapproximation, but not vice versa.

The rest of this paper is structured as follows. Section 2 defines the language used as the target of our verification. Sections 3 and 4 describe predicate abstraction and CEGAR respectively. Section 5 reports experiments. Section 6 discusses related work and Sect. 7 concludes the paper.

2 Language

In this section, we introduce the language of source programs, used as the target of non-termination verification. It is a simply typed, call-by-value higher-order functional language. Throughout the paper, we often use the following abbreviations: $\widetilde{e}$ for a possibly empty sequence $e_1, \dots, e_n$, and $\{e_i\}_{i\in\{1,\dots,n\}}$ for the set $\{e_1, \dots, e_n\}$.

$$
\begin{array}{l}
P \text{ (programs)} := \{f_i\, \widetilde{x}_i = e_i\}_{i\in\{1\dots n\}} \\
e \text{ (expressions)} := () \mid y\,\widetilde{v} \mid \texttt{if } a \texttt{ then } e_1 \texttt{ else } e_2 \\
\qquad\qquad \mid \texttt{let } x = a \texttt{ in } e \mid \texttt{let } x = *_{\texttt{int}} \texttt{ in } e \\
a \text{ (simple expressions)} ::= x \mid n \mid \mathrm{op}(\widetilde{a}) \qquad v \text{ (values)} := n \mid y\,\widetilde{v}
\end{array}
$$

$$
\frac{f\,\widetilde{x} = e \in P \quad |\widetilde{x}| = |\widetilde{v}|}{f\,\widetilde{v} \longrightarrow_P [\widetilde{v}/\widetilde{x}]e} \qquad \frac{[\![a]\!] = n}{\texttt{let } x = a \texttt{ in } e \longrightarrow_P [n/x]e} \qquad \texttt{let } x = *_{\texttt{int}} \texttt{ in } e \longrightarrow_P [n/x]e
$$

$$
\texttt{if } n \texttt{ then } e_0 \texttt{ else } e_1 \longrightarrow_P e_0 \text{ if } n \neq 0 \qquad \texttt{if } 0 \texttt{ then } e_0 \texttt{ else } e_1 \longrightarrow_P e_1
$$

Fig. 2. The syntax and operational semantics of the language

The syntax and operational semantics of the language is given in Fig. 2. The meta-variable f_i ranges over a set of function names, and x, y range over the set of function names and ordinary variables. The meta-variable n ranges over the set of integers, and op over a set of integer operations. We omit Booleans and regard a non-negative integer as true, and 0 as false. We require that $y\,\widetilde{v}$ in the definition of e is a full application, i.e., that all the necessary arguments are passed to y, and $y\,\widetilde{v}$ has a base type. In contrast, $y\,\widetilde{v}$ in the definition of v is a partial application. Whether $y\,\widetilde{v}$ is a full or partial application is actually determined by the simple type system mentioned below.

The expression `let` $x = *_{\texttt{int}}$ `in` e randomly generates an integer, binds x to it, and evaluates e. The meanings of the other expressions should be clear. A careful reader may notice that we have only tail calls. This is for the simplicity of the presentation. Note that it does not lose generality, because we can apply the standard continuation-passing-style (CPS) transformation to guarantee that all the function calls are in this form. We assume that for every program $\{f_i\, \widetilde{x}_i = e_i\}_{i\in\{1\dots n\}}$, `main` $\in \{f_1, \dots, f_n\}$.

We assume that programs are simply-typed. The syntax of types is given by: $\tau ::= \mathbf{int} \mid \star \mid \tau_1 \to \tau_2$. The types **int** and $\star$ describe integers and the unit value $()$ respectively. The type $\tau_1 \to \tau_2$ describes functions from τ_1 to τ_2. The typing rules for expressions and programs are given in the full version [17], which are standard except that the body of each function definition can only have type $\star$. This does not lose generality since the CPS transformation guarantees this condition.

The one-step reduction relation $e_1 \longrightarrow_P e_2$ is defined by the rules in Fig. 2, where $[\![a]\!]$ stands for the value of the simple expression a. A program P is *non-terminating* if there is an infinite reduction sequence `main` $\to_P e_1 \to_P e_2 \to_P \dots$.

$$D \text{ (programs)} := \{f_i\ \widetilde{x}_i = M_i\}_{i\in\{1\dots n\}}$$
$$M \text{ (expressions)} := c(M_1,\dots,M_k) \mid y\,\widetilde{V} \mid \texttt{let}\ x = (b_1,\dots,b_k)\ \texttt{in}\ M$$
$$\mid \texttt{br}_\forall\,\{\psi_1 \to M_1,\dots,\psi_k \to M_k\} \mid \texttt{br}_\exists\,\{\psi_1 \to M_1,\dots,\psi_k \to M_k\}$$
$$b \text{ (Booleans)} ::= \texttt{true} \mid \texttt{false} \qquad V \text{ (values)} ::= (b_1,\dots,b_k) \mid y\,\widetilde{V}$$
$$\psi \text{ (Boolean expressions)} ::= b \mid \#_i(x) \mid \psi_1 \vee \psi_2 \mid \neg\psi$$

$$E[f\,V_1 \cdots V_k] \longrightarrow_D E[[V_1/x_1,\dots,V_k/x_k]M] \text{ if } f\,x_1 \cdots x_k = M \in D$$

$$E[\texttt{let}\ x = (b_1,\dots,b_k)\ \texttt{in}\ M] \longrightarrow_D E[[(b_1,\dots,b_k)/x]M]$$

$$E[\texttt{br}_\forall\,\{\psi_1 \to M_1,\dots,\psi_k \to M_k\}] \longrightarrow_D E[\texttt{br}_\forall(M_{i_1},\dots,M_{i_\ell})]$$
$$\text{if } \{\psi_i \mid i \in \{1,\dots,k\}, [\![\psi_i]\!] = \texttt{true}\} = \{\psi_{i_1},\dots,\psi_{i_\ell}\}$$

$$E[\texttt{br}_\exists\,\{\psi_1 \to M_1,\dots,\psi_k \to M_k\}] \longrightarrow_D E[\texttt{br}_\exists(M_{i_1},\dots,M_{i_\ell})]$$
$$\text{if } \{\psi_i \mid i \in \{1,\dots,k\}, [\![\psi_i]\!] = \texttt{true}\} = \{\psi_{i_1},\dots,\psi_{i_\ell}\}$$

$$E \text{ (evaluation contexts)} ::= [\,] \mid c(M_1,\dots,M_{i-1},E,M_{i+1},\dots,M_n)$$

Fig. 3. The syntax and semantics of the target language

3 Predicate Abstraction

3.1 Target Language

The target language of predicate abstraction is a higher-order simply-typed functional language having Booleans and special tree constructors as primitives. The syntax is given in Fig. 3. We assume that for every program $\{f_i\ \widetilde{x}_i = M_i\}_{i\in\{1\dots n\}}$, $\texttt{main} \in \{f_1,\dots,f_n\}$. Each expression generates a possibly infinite tree, describing possible executions of a source program. The expression $c(M_1,\dots,M_k)$ generates a node labeled with c, having the trees generated by $M_1,\dots,M_k$ as its children. Here, c ranges over the set $\{\texttt{end},\texttt{call},\texttt{br}_\forall,\texttt{br}_\exists\}$ of tree constructors. The constructors `end` and `call` have arities 0 and 1 respectively, while $\texttt{br}_\forall$ and $\texttt{br}_\exists$ may have arbitrarily many children. We just write `end` for `end()`. The expression $\texttt{let}\ x = (b_1,\dots,b_k)\ \texttt{in}\ M$ binds x to the tuple $(b_1,\dots,b_k)$, and evaluates M. The expression $\texttt{br}_\forall\,\{\psi_1 \to M_1,\dots,\psi_k \to M_k\}$ ($\texttt{br}_\exists\,\{\psi_1 \to M_1,\dots,\psi_k \to M_k\}$, resp.) generates the node $\texttt{br}_\forall$ ($\texttt{br}_\exists$, resp.), and adds the tree generated by M_i as a child of the node if ψ_i evaluates to `true`, where the order of children does not matter. The Boolean expression $\#_i x$ denotes the i-th element of the tuple x. For example, $\texttt{let}\ x = (\texttt{true},\texttt{false})\ \texttt{in}\ \texttt{br}_\forall\{\#_1(x) \to \texttt{end}, \#_2(x) \to \texttt{call}(\texttt{call}(\texttt{end})), \#_1(x) \vee \#_2(x) \to \texttt{call}(\texttt{end})\}$ generates the tree:

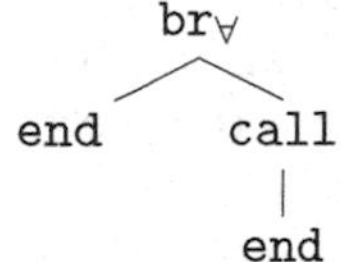

The formal semantics is given through the reduction relation $M \longrightarrow_D M'$, defined in Fig. 3. The tree generated by a program D, written $\textbf{Tree}(D)$, is the "limit" of the trees obtained from a (possibly infinite) reduction sequence

$\mathtt{main} \longrightarrow_D M_1 \longrightarrow_D M_2 \longrightarrow_D \cdots$. For example, the program $\{\mathtt{main} = \mathtt{call}(\mathtt{main})\}$ generates an infinite (linear) tree consisting of infinitely many `call` nodes.

Intuitively, the tree generated by a program of the target language describes possible execution sequences of a source program. The property that a source program has a non-terminating execution sequence is transformed to the property of the tree that (i) every child of each $\mathtt{br}_\forall$ node has an infinite path, and (ii) some child of each $\mathtt{br}_\exists$ node has an infinite path. More formally, the set of (infinite) trees that represent the existence of a non-terminating computation is the largest set **NonTermTrees** such that for every $T \in$ **NonTermTrees**, T satisfies one of the following conditions.

1. $T = \mathtt{call}(T')$ and $T' \in$ **NonTermTrees**
2. $T = \mathtt{br}_\forall(T_1, \ldots, T_k)$ and $T_i \in$ **NonTermTrees** for all $i \in \{1, \ldots, k\}$.
3. $T = \mathtt{br}_\exists(T_1, \ldots, T_k)$ and $T_i \in$ **NonTermTrees** for some $i \in \{1, \ldots, k\}$.

The property above can be expressed by MSO (the monadic second order logic; or equivalently, modal μ-calculus or alternating parity tree automata); thus whether the tree generated by a program of the target language belongs to **NonTermTrees** can be decided by higher-order model checking [15,21].

3.2 Abstraction

We now formalize predicate abstraction for transforming a source program to a program (of the target language) that generates a tree that approximately represents the possible execution sequences of the source program. Following Kobayashi et al. [16], we use *abstraction types* for expressing which predicate should be used for abstracting each value. The syntax of abstraction types is:

$$\sigma\text{(abstraction types)} ::= \star \mid \mathbf{int}[Q_1, \ldots, Q_k] \mid x : \sigma_1 \to \sigma_2$$
$$Q \text{ (predicates)} ::= \lambda x.\varphi \qquad \varphi ::= n_1 x_1 + \cdots + n_k x_k \leq n \mid \varphi_1 \vee \varphi_2 \mid \neg\varphi$$

The type $\star$ describes the unit value, and $\mathbf{int}[Q_1, \ldots, Q_k]$ describes an integer that should be abstracted by using the predicates $Q_1, \ldots, Q_k$. For example, given an abstraction type $\mathbf{int}[\lambda x.x \leq 1, \lambda x.2x - 1 \leq 0]$, the integer 1 is abstracted to $(\mathtt{true}, \mathtt{false})$. In the syntax above, we list only linear inequalities as primitive constraints, but we can include other constraints (such as those on uninterpreted function symbols) as long as the underlying theory remains decidable. The type $x : \sigma_1 \to \sigma_2$ describes a function whose argument and return value should be abstracted according to σ_1 and σ_2 respectively. In σ_2, the argument can be referred to by x if x has an integer type $\mathbf{int}[Q_1, \ldots, Q_k]$. For example, $x : \mathbf{int}[\lambda x.x \leq 0] \to \mathbf{int}[\lambda y.y - x \leq 0]$ describes a function from integers to integers whose argument should be abstracted using the predicate $\lambda x.x \leq 0$ and whose return value should be abstracted using $\lambda y.y - x \leq 0$. Thus, the successor function (defined by $f\, x = x + 1$) will be abstracted to a Boolean function $\lambda b.\mathtt{false}$ (because the return value $x + 1$ is always greater than x, no matter whether $x \leq 0$ or not).

The predicate abstraction for expressions and programs is formalized using the relations $\Gamma \vdash e : \sigma \rightsquigarrow M$ and $\vdash P : \Gamma \rightsquigarrow D$, where Γ, called an *abstraction type environment*, is of the form $x_1 : \sigma_1, \ldots, x_n : \sigma_n$. Intuitively, $\Gamma \vdash e : \sigma \rightsquigarrow M$ means that under the assumption that each free variable x_i of e is abstracted according to σ_i, the expression e is abstracted to M according to the abstraction type σ. In the judgment $\vdash P : \Gamma \rightsquigarrow D$, Γ describes how each function defined in P should be abstracted.

The relations are defined by the rules in Fig. 4. Here, we consider, without loss of generality, only if-expressions of the form $\texttt{if}\ x\ \texttt{then}\ e_1\ \texttt{else}\ e_2$. Also, function arguments are restricted to the syntax: $v ::= y\ \widetilde{v}$. (In other words, constants may not occur; note that $x\,c$ can be replaced by $\texttt{let}\ y = c\ \texttt{in}\ x\,y$.) We assume that each let-expression is annotated with an abstraction type that should be used for abstracting the value of the variable. Those abstraction types, as well as those for functions are automatically inferred by the CEGAR procedure described in Sect. 4.

$$\frac{}{\Gamma \vdash () : \star \rightsquigarrow \texttt{end}} \quad \text{(PA-UNIT)}$$

$$\frac{\begin{array}{c}\models b_1Q_1(a) \land \cdots \land b_kQ_k(a) \Rightarrow \theta_\Gamma \psi_{(b_1,\ldots,b_k)}\ \text{(for each } b_1,\ldots,b_k \in \{\texttt{true},\texttt{false}\})\\ \Gamma, x : \textbf{int}[Q_1,\ldots,Q_k] \vdash e : \star \rightsquigarrow M\end{array}}{\begin{array}{c}\Gamma \vdash \texttt{let}\ x : \textbf{int}[Q_1,\ldots,Q_k] = a\ \texttt{in}\ e : \star \rightsquigarrow \\ \texttt{br}_\forall \left\{\psi_{(b_1,\ldots,b_k)} \to \texttt{let}\ x = (b_1,\ldots,b_k)\ \texttt{in}\ M \mid b_1,\ldots,b_k \in \{\texttt{true},\texttt{false}\}\right\}\end{array}} \quad \text{(PA-SEXP)}$$

$$\frac{\models x \neq 0 \Rightarrow \theta_\Gamma \psi_1 \qquad \models x = 0 \Rightarrow \theta_\Gamma \psi_2 \qquad \Gamma \vdash e_1 : \star \rightsquigarrow M_1 \qquad \Gamma \vdash e_2 : \star \rightsquigarrow M_2}{\Gamma \vdash \texttt{if}\ x\ \texttt{then}\ e_1\ \texttt{else}\ e_2 : \star \rightsquigarrow \texttt{br}_\forall \{\psi_1 \to M_1, \psi_2 \to M_2\}} \quad \text{(PA-IF)}$$

$$\frac{\begin{array}{c}\models \theta_\Gamma \psi_{(b_1,\ldots,b_k)} \Rightarrow \exists x. b_1Q_1(x) \land \cdots \land b_kQ_k(x)\ \text{(for each } b_1,\ldots,b_k \in \{\texttt{true},\texttt{false}\})\\ \Gamma, x : \textbf{int}[Q_1,\ldots,Q_k] \vdash e : \star \rightsquigarrow M\end{array}}{\begin{array}{c}\Gamma \vdash \texttt{let}\ x : \textbf{int}[Q_1,\ldots,Q_k] = *_{\texttt{int}}\ \texttt{in}\ e : \star \rightsquigarrow \\ \texttt{br}_\exists \left\{\psi_{(b_1,\ldots,b_k)} \to \texttt{let}\ x = (b_1,\ldots,b_k)\ \texttt{in}\ M \mid b_1,\ldots,b_k \in \{\texttt{true},\texttt{false}\}\right\}\end{array}} \quad \text{(PA-RAND)}$$

$$\frac{\begin{array}{c}\Gamma(y) = x_1 : \sigma_1 \to \cdots \to x_k : \sigma_k \to \sigma\\ \Gamma \vdash v_i : [v_1/x_1,\ldots,v_{i-1}/x_{i-1}]\sigma_i \rightsquigarrow V_i \text{ for each } i \in \{1,\ldots,k\}\end{array}}{\Gamma \vdash y\,v_1 \cdots v_k : [v_1/x_1,\ldots,v_k/x_k]\sigma \rightsquigarrow y\,V_1 \cdots V_k} \quad \text{(PA-APP)}$$

$$\frac{\{f_i : \widetilde{x} : \widetilde{\sigma}_i \to \star\}_{i \in \{1,\ldots,k\}}, \widetilde{x} : \widetilde{\sigma}_j \vdash e_i : \star \rightsquigarrow M_i \text{ for each } j \in \{1,\ldots,k\}}{\vdash \{f_i\,\widetilde{x}_i = e_i\}_{i \in \{1,\ldots,k\}} : \{f_i : \widetilde{x} : \widetilde{\sigma}_i \to \star\}_{i \in \{1,\ldots,k\}} \rightsquigarrow \{f_i\,\widetilde{x}_i = \texttt{call}(M_i)\}_{i \in \{1,\ldots,k\}}} \quad \text{(PA-PROG)}$$

Fig. 4. Predicate abstraction rules

The rule PA-UNIT just replaces the unit value with **end**, which represents termination. The rule PA-SEXP overapproximates the value of a simple expression a. Here, θ_Γ is the substitution that replaces each variable x of type $\textbf{int}[Q'_1,\ldots,Q'_n]$ in Γ with $(Q'_1(x),\ldots,Q'_n(x))$. For example, if $\Gamma =$

$x : \mathbf{int}[\lambda x.x \leq 0, \lambda x.x \leq 2], y : \mathbf{int}[\lambda y.y \leq x]$, then $\theta_\Gamma(\#_2(x) \wedge \#_1(y))$ is $\#_2(x \leq 0, x \leq 2) \wedge \#_1(y \leq x)$, i.e., $x \leq 2 \wedge y \leq x$. The formula $b_i Q_i(a)$ stands for $Q_i(a)$ if $b_i = \mathtt{true}$, and $\neg Q_i(a)$ if $b_i = \mathtt{false}$. Basically, the rule generates branches for all the possible values $(b_1, \dots, b_k)$ for $(Q_1(a), \dots, Q_k(a))$, and combines them with node $\mathtt{br}_\forall$ (which indicates that this branch has been obtained by an overapproximation). To eliminate impossible values, we compute a necessary condition $\psi_{(b_1,\dots,b_k)}$ for $(Q_1(a), \dots, Q_k(a)) = (b_1, \dots, b_k)$ to hold, and guard the branch for $(b_1, \dots, b_k)$ with $\psi_{(b_1,\dots,b_k)}$. The formula $\psi_{(b_1,\dots,b_k)}$ can be computed by using an SMT solver, as in ordinary predicate abstraction [3,16]. (The rule generates 2^k branches, leading to code explosion. This is for the sake of simplicity; the eager splitting of branches is avoided in the actual implementation.) The rule PA-IF is similar: branches for the then- and else-clauses are generated, but they are guarded by necessary conditions for the branches to be chosen.

The rule PA-RAND for random number generation is a kind of dual to PA-SEXP. It applies an *underapproximation*, and generates branches for all the possible values $(b_1, \dots, b_k)$ for $(Q_1(x), \dots, Q_k(x))$ under the node $\mathtt{br}_\exists$. Each branch is guarded by a *sufficient* condition for the existence of a value for x such that $(Q_1(x), \dots, Q_k(x)) = (b_1, \dots, b_k)$, so that for each branch, there must be a corresponding execution path of the source program. The rule PA-APP for applications is the same as the corresponding rule of [16]. Finally, the rule PA-PROG for programs just transforms the body of each function definition, but adds a special node `call` to keep track of function calls. Note that a program is non-terminating if and only if it makes infinitely many function calls.

Example 1. Let us consider the following program **LOOP**.

$$\begin{array}{l} \mathit{loop}\ h\ x = \mathtt{let}\ b = (x > 0)\ \mathtt{in} \\ \qquad\qquad \mathtt{if}\ b\ \mathtt{then}\ \mathtt{let}\ d = *_{\mathtt{int}}\ \mathtt{in}\ \mathtt{let}\ y = x + d\ \mathtt{in}\ h\ y\ (\mathit{loop}\ \mathit{app})\ \mathtt{else}\ () \\ \mathit{app}\ m\ k = k\ m \qquad\qquad \mathtt{main} = \mathtt{let}\ r = *_{\mathtt{int}}\ \mathtt{in}\ \mathit{loop}\ \mathit{app}\ r \end{array}$$

LOOP is non-terminating; in fact, if $*_{\mathtt{int}}$ is always evaluated to 1, then we have:

$$\mathtt{main} \longrightarrow^* \mathit{loop}\ \mathit{app}\ 1 \longrightarrow^* \mathit{app}\ 2\ (\mathit{loop}\ \mathit{app}) \longrightarrow^* \mathit{loop}\ \mathit{app}\ 2 \longrightarrow^* \cdots$$

Let $\Gamma_{\mathbf{LOOP}}$ be an abstraction type environment:

$$\begin{array}{l} \mathit{loop} : (\mathbf{int}[\lambda\nu.\nu > 1] \rightarrow (\mathbf{int}[\lambda\nu.\nu > 1] \rightarrow \star) \rightarrow \star) \rightarrow \mathbf{int}[\lambda\nu.\nu > 1] \rightarrow \star \\ \mathit{app} : \mathbf{int}[\lambda\nu.\nu > 1] \rightarrow (\mathbf{int}[\lambda\nu.\nu > 1] \rightarrow \star) \rightarrow \star \end{array}$$

By using $\Gamma_{\mathbf{LOOP}}$ and the following abstraction types for b, d, and r:

$$b : \mathbf{int}[\lambda\nu.\nu \neq 0], d : \mathbf{int}[\lambda\nu.x + \nu > 1], r : \mathbf{int}[\lambda\nu.\nu > 1],$$

the program **LOOP** is abstracted to the following program $D_{\mathbf{LOOP}}$.

$$\begin{aligned}
&loop\ h\ x = \mathtt{call}(\mathtt{br}_\forall\{\mathtt{true} \to \mathtt{let}\ b\,\mathtt{=}\,\mathtt{true}\ \mathtt{in}\ M_1,\\
&\qquad\qquad\qquad \neg x \to \mathtt{let}\ b\,\mathtt{=}\,\mathtt{false}\ \mathtt{in}\ M_1\})\\
&app\ m\ k = \mathtt{call}(k\ m)\\
&\mathtt{main} = \mathtt{call}(\mathtt{br}_\exists\{\mathtt{true} \to \mathtt{let}\ r\,\mathtt{=}\,\mathtt{true}\ \mathtt{in}\ loop\ app\ r,\\
&\qquad\qquad \mathtt{true} \to \mathtt{let}\ r\,\mathtt{=}\,\mathtt{false}\ \mathtt{in}\ loop\ app\ r\})\\
&\text{where}\\
&M_1 = \mathtt{br}_\forall\,\{b \to M_2, \neg b \to \mathtt{end}\}\\
&M_2 = \mathtt{br}_\exists\,\{\mathtt{true} \to \mathtt{let}\ d\,\mathtt{=}\,\mathtt{true}\ \mathtt{in}\ M_3, \mathtt{true} \to \mathtt{let}\ d\,\mathtt{=}\,\mathtt{false}\ \mathtt{in}\ M_3\}\\
&M_3 = \mathtt{br}_\forall\{d \to \mathtt{let}\ y\,\mathtt{=}\,\mathtt{true}\ \mathtt{in}\ h\,y\,(loop\ app),\\
&\qquad \neg d \to \mathtt{let}\ y\,\mathtt{=}\,\mathtt{false}\ \mathtt{in}\ h\,y\,(loop\ app)\}.
\end{aligned}$$

For example, $\mathtt{let}\ b : \mathbf{int}[\lambda\nu.\nu \neq 0]\,\mathtt{=}\,x > 0\ \mathtt{in}\ e$ is transformed by PA-SEXP as follows:

$$\frac{\models (x > 0) \neq 0 \Rightarrow \mathtt{true} \qquad \models \neg((x > 0) \neq 0) \Rightarrow \neg(x > 1)(= \theta_\Gamma(\neg x)) \qquad \Gamma, b : \mathbf{int}[\lambda\nu.\nu = 0] \vdash e : \star \rightsquigarrow M_1}{\begin{array}{c}\Gamma \vdash \mathtt{let}\ b : \mathbf{int}[\lambda\nu.\nu = 0]\,\mathtt{=}\,x > 0\ \mathtt{in}\ e\\ \rightsquigarrow \mathtt{br}_\forall\,\{\mathtt{true} \to \mathtt{let}\ b\,\mathtt{=}\,\mathtt{true}\ \mathtt{in}\ M_1, \neg x \to \mathtt{let}\ b\,\mathtt{=}\,\mathtt{false}\ \mathtt{in}\ M_1\}\end{array}}$$

where

$$\Gamma = \Gamma_{\mathbf{LOOP}}, h : (\mathbf{int}[\lambda\nu.\nu > 1] \to (\mathbf{int}[\lambda\nu.\nu > 1] \to \star) \to \star), x : \mathbf{int}[\lambda\nu.\nu > 1].$$

Here, recall that a non-zero integer is treated as `true` in the source language; thus, $\neg((x > 0) \neq 0)$ means $x \leq 0$. Since $\mathbf{Tree}(D_{\mathbf{LOOP}}) \in \mathbf{NonTermTrees}$, we can conclude that the program **LOOP** is non-terminating (based on Theorem 1 below). □

The soundness of predicate abstraction is stated as follows (see the full version [17] for a proof).

Theorem 1. *Suppose* $\vdash P : \Gamma \rightsquigarrow D$. *If* $\mathbf{Tree}(D) \in \mathbf{NonTermTrees}$, *then* P *is non-terminating.*

4 Counterexample-Guided Abstraction Refinement (CEGAR)

This section describes our CEGAR procedure to refine abstraction based on a counterexample. Here, a *counterexample* output by a higher-order model checker is a finite subtree T of $\mathbf{Tree}(D)$, obtained by removing all but one branches of each $\mathtt{br}_\forall$ node. Figure 5 illustrates $\mathbf{Tree}(D)$ and a corresponding counterexample (showing $\mathbf{Tree}(D) \notin \mathbf{NonTermTrees}$). In the figure, "$\cdots$" indicates an infinite path. For each $\mathtt{br}_\forall$ node, a model checker picks one branch containing a finite path, preserving the branches of the other nodes ($\mathtt{br}_\exists$, `call`, and `end`).

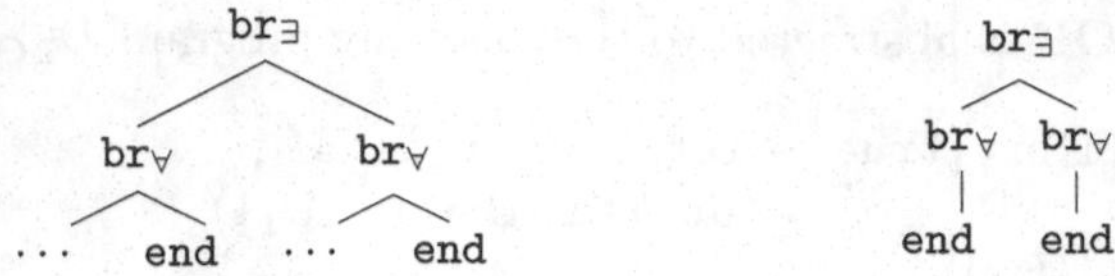

Fig. 5. **Tree**(D) (left) and a corresponding counterexample (right)

We analyze each path of the counterexample tree to infer new abstraction types for refining abstraction. To that end, we need to distinguish between two types of paths in the counterexample tree: one that has been introduced due to overapproximation, and the other due to underapproximation. Figure 6 illustrates the two types. For each type, the lefthand side shows the computation tree of a source program, and the righthand side shows the tree generated by the abstract program. Thick lines show a path of a counterexample tree. In the example of Type I, the computation of a source program takes the then-branch and falls into a non-terminating computation, but predicate abstraction has introduced the spurious path taking the else branch, which was detected as a part of the counterexample. In the example of Type II, a source program generates a random number and non-deterministically branches to a non-terminating computation or a terminating computation. After predicate abstraction, the two branches by the random number generation have been merged; instead, the next deterministic computation step has been split into two by an overapproximation. This situation occurs, for example, for

$$\texttt{let}\ x : \mathbf{int}[\,] = *_{\texttt{int}}\ \texttt{in let}\ y : \mathbf{int}[\lambda y.y \neq 0] = x\ \texttt{in if}\ y\ \texttt{then}\ loop()\ \texttt{else}\ ().$$

The program generated by the abstraction is

$$\begin{aligned}\texttt{br}_\exists\{\texttt{true} \to \texttt{br}_\forall\{&\texttt{true} \to \texttt{let}\ y = \texttt{true in}\ \cdots,\\ &\texttt{true} \to \texttt{let}\ y = \texttt{false in}\ \cdots\}\}.\end{aligned}$$

Thus, the branches at $*_{\texttt{int}}$ in the original program have been moved to the branches at $\texttt{br}_\forall$. The classification of the paths of a counterexample into Type I or II can be performed according to the feasibility of the path, i.e., whether there is a corresponding computation path in the source program. An infeasible path is Type I, since it has been introduced by an overapproximation, and a feasible path is Type II; it has a corresponding computation path, but the two kinds of non-determinism (expressed by $\texttt{br}_\exists$ and $\texttt{br}_\forall$) have been confused by predicate abstraction. We need to refine the predicates (or, abstraction types) used for overapproximation for a Type I path, and those used for underapproximation for a Type II path. In the example program above, by refining the abstraction type for x to $\mathbf{int}[\lambda x.x \neq 0]$, we obtain

$$\begin{aligned}\texttt{br}_\exists\{&\texttt{true} \to \texttt{let}\ x = \texttt{true in br}_\forall\,\{x \to \texttt{let}\ y = \texttt{true in}\ \cdots\},\\ &\texttt{true} \to \texttt{let}\ x = \texttt{false in br}_\forall\,\{\neg x \to \texttt{let}\ y = \texttt{false in}\ \cdots\}\}.\end{aligned}$$

Thus, the branches on terminating/non-terminating paths are moved to the node $\mathtt{br}_\exists$.

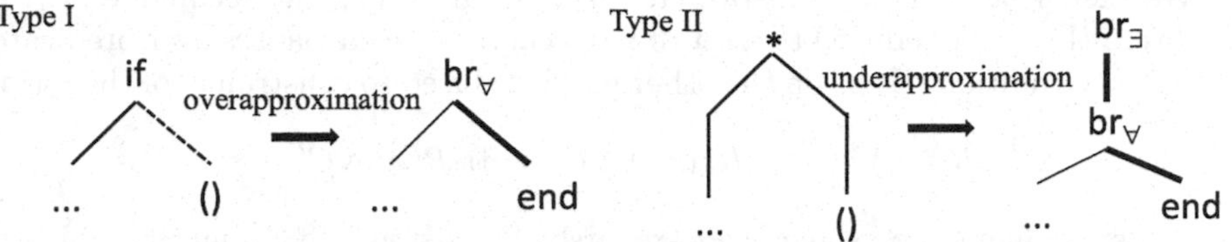

Fig. 6. Two types of paths in a counterexample

The refinement of abstraction types based on Type I (i.e., infeasible) paths can be performed in the same way as our previous work [16]. Thus, we focus below on how to deal with a Type II path.

4.1 Dealing with Type II Paths

Given a program P and a Type II path π, we first prepare fresh predicate variables $R_1, \ldots, R_k$ (called *separating predicates*), and replace each expression for random number generation $\mathtt{let}\ r_i = *_{\mathtt{int}}\ \mathtt{in}\ e_i$ with:[1]

$$\mathtt{let}\ r_i = *_{\mathtt{int}}\ \mathtt{in}\ \mathtt{assume}(R_i(r_i)); e_i.$$

Here, an expression $\mathtt{assume}(\phi); e$ evaluates to e only if ϕ is $\mathtt{true}$. Then, we instantiate R_i's so that the following conditions hold.

(C1) P has no longer an execution path along π.
(C2) If the execution along π reaches $\mathtt{let}\ r_i = *_{\mathtt{int}}\ \mathtt{in}\ \mathtt{assume}(R_i(r_i)); e_i$, there is at least one value for r_i such that $R_i(r_i)$ holds.

Condition C1 is for separating the path π at $\mathtt{br}_\exists$ node (recall Fig. 6; the problem of a Type II path has been that terminating/non-terminating paths are merged at $\mathtt{br}_\exists$ node). Condition C2 ensures that the paths separated from π are not empty. By C2, for example, an absurd assume statement like $\mathtt{assume(false)}$ is excluded out. We then add the instantiations of $R_1, \ldots, R_k$ to the abstraction types for $r_1, \ldots, r_k$.

For the example

$$\mathtt{let}\ x : \mathbf{int}[\,] = *_{\mathtt{int}}\ \mathtt{in}\ \mathtt{let}\ y : \mathbf{int}[\lambda y.y \neq 0] = x\ \mathtt{in}\ \mathtt{if}\ y\ \mathtt{then}\ loop()\ \mathtt{else}\ ()$$

discussed above, we insert an assume statement as follows.

$$\mathtt{let}\ x = *_{\mathtt{int}}\ \mathtt{in}\ \mathtt{assume}(R(x)); \mathtt{let}\ y = x\ \mathtt{in}\ \mathtt{if}\ y\ \mathtt{then}\ loop()\ \mathtt{else}\ ().$$

[1] Actually, we apply the replacement to each *instance* of $\mathtt{let}\ r_i = *_{\mathtt{int}}\ \mathtt{in}\ e_i$ along the execution path π, so that different assume conditions can be used for different instances of the same expression; we elide the details here.

Here, the Type II path π is the one that goes through the else-branch. Thus, a condition $R(x)$ that makes it infeasible is $x \neq 0$. As a result, $\lambda x.x \neq 0$ is added to the abstraction type for x.

We sketch below how to instantiate $R_1, \ldots, R_k$. Using the technique of [16] condition (I) can be reduced to a set of non-recursive Horn clauses over predicate variables. Condition (II) is, on the other hand, reduced to constraints of the form

$$R_1(\widetilde{x}_1) \wedge \cdots \wedge R_n(\widetilde{x}_n) \wedge C \Rightarrow \exists x.R(x) \wedge C'.$$

Thus, it remains to solve (non-recursive) existentially quantified Horn clauses [4]. To solve them, we first remove existential quantification by using a Skolemization-based technique similar to [4]. We prepare a linear template of Skolem function and move existential quantifiers out of universal quantifiers. For example, given

$$\forall r.\,(\exists \nu.\nu \leq 1 \wedge R(\nu)) \wedge \forall r.\,(R(r) \wedge \neg(r > 0) \Rightarrow \mathtt{false}),$$

we prepare the linear template $c_0 + c_1 r$ and transform the constraints into:

$$\exists c_0, c_1.\forall \nu.r.\,(\nu = c_0 + c_1 r \Rightarrow \nu \leq 1 \wedge R(\nu)) \wedge \forall\,(R(r) \wedge \neg(r > 0) \Rightarrow \mathtt{false}).$$

We then remove predicate variables by resolution, and get:

$$\forall \nu.r.\nu = c_0 + c_1 r \Rightarrow \nu \leq 1 \wedge \nu > 0$$

Finally, we solve constraints in the form of $\exists \widetilde{x}.\forall \widetilde{y}.\phi$ and obtain coefficients of linear templates that we introduced in the first step. We adopt the existing constraint solving technique based [24] on Farkas' Lemma. For the running example, we obtain $c_0 = 2, c_1 = 0$ as a solution of the constraints.

Now that we have removed existential quantification, we are left with non-recursive Horn clause constraints, which can be solved by using the existing constraint solving technique [23]. For the example above, we get

$$\forall \nu.r.\,(\nu = 2 \Rightarrow \nu \leq 1 \wedge R(\nu)) \wedge (R(r) \wedge \neg(r > 0) \Rightarrow \bot)$$

and obtain $R = \lambda \nu.\nu > 0$ as a solution.

5 Implementation and Experiments

We have implemented a non-termination verifier for a subset of OCaml, as an extension of MoCHi [16], a software model checker for OCaml programs. We use HorSat [5] as the backend higher-order model checker, and Z3 [20] as the backend SMT solver. The web interface of our non-termination verification tool is available online [1]. We evaluated our tool by experiments on two benchmark sets: (1) test cases consisting of higher-order programs and (2) a standard benchmark set on non-termination of first-order programs [7,19]. Both experiments were conducted on a machine with Intel Xeon E3-1225 V2 (3.20GHz, 16GB of memory)

Table 1. The result of the first benchmark set

Program	Cycle	Time (msec)	Program	Cycle	Time (msec)
`loopHO`	2	1,156	`unfoldr_nonterm`	3	13,540
`indirect_e`	1	111	`passing_cond`	2	9,202
`indirectHO_e`	1	112	`inf_clos`	2	12,264
`foldr_nonterm`	4	20,498	`fib_CPS_nonterm`	1	133
`alternate`	1	95	`fixpoint_nonterm`	2	168

with timeout of 60 seconds. The first benchmark set and an online demo page are available from our website [1].

Table 1 shows the result of the first evaluation. The columns 'program', 'cycle', and 'time' show the name of each test case, the number of CEGAR cycles, and the elapsed time (in milliseconds), respectively. For `foldr_nonterm`, we have used a different mode for a backend constraint solver; with the default mode, our verifier has timed out. All the programs in the first benchmark set are higher-order programs; so, they cannot be directly verified by previous tools. Our tool could successfully verify all the programs to be non-terminating (except that we had to change the mode of a backend constraint solver for `foldr_nonterm`).

We explain below two of the programs in the first benchmark set: `inf_clos` and `alternate`. The program `inf_clos` is:

$$\begin{array}{ll} \mathit{is\_zero}\ n = (n = 0) & \mathit{succ\_app}\ f\ n = f\ (n+1) \\ \multicolumn{2}{l}{f\ n\ \mathit{cond} = \mathtt{let}\ b = \mathit{cond}\ n\ \mathtt{in}\ \mathtt{if}\ b\ \mathtt{then}\ (\,)\ \mathtt{else}\ f\ n\ (\mathit{succ\_app}\ \mathit{cond})} \\ \multicolumn{2}{l}{\mathtt{main} = f\ *_{\mathtt{int}}\ \mathit{is\_zero}.} \end{array}$$

It has the following non-terminating reduction sequence:

$$\begin{array}{l} \mathtt{main} \longrightarrow^* f\,1\,\mathit{is\_zero} \longrightarrow^* f\,1\,(\mathit{succ\_app}\,\mathit{is\_zero}) \longrightarrow^* f\,1\,(\mathit{succ\_app}^2\,\mathit{is\_zero}) \\ \longrightarrow^* f\,1\,(\mathit{succ\_app}^m\,\mathit{is\_zero}) \longrightarrow^* \cdots. \end{array}$$

Note that $\mathit{succ\_app}^m\ \mathit{is\_zero}\ n$ is equivalent to $n+m=0$; hence b in the function f always evaluates to `false` in the sequence above. For proving non-termination, we need to reason about the value of the higher-order argument *cond*, so the previous methods for non-termination of first-order programs are not applicable.

The following program `alternate` shows the strength of our underapproximation.

$$\begin{array}{l} f\ g\ h\ z = \mathtt{let}\ x = *_{\mathtt{int}}\ \mathtt{in}\ \mathtt{if}\ x > 0\ \mathtt{then}\ g\ (f\ h\ g)\ \mathtt{else}\ h\ (f\ h\ g) \\ \mathit{proceed}\ u = u\ (\,) \qquad \mathit{halt}\ u = (\,) \qquad \mathtt{main} = f\ \mathit{proceed}\ \mathit{halt}\ (\,) \end{array}$$

It has the following non-terminating reduction sequence:

$$\begin{array}{l} \mathtt{main} \longrightarrow^* f\,\mathit{proceed}\,\mathit{halt}\,(\,) \\ \longrightarrow^* \mathtt{if}\ 1 > 0\ \mathtt{then}\ \mathit{proceed}(f\,\mathit{halt}\,\mathit{proceed})\ \mathtt{else}\ \cdots \longrightarrow^* f\,\mathit{halt}\,\mathit{proceed}\,(\,) \\ \longrightarrow^* \mathtt{if}\ -1 > 0\ \mathtt{then}\ \cdots\ \mathtt{else}\ \mathit{proceed}(f\,\mathit{proceed}\,\mathit{halt}) \longrightarrow^* f\,\mathit{proceed}\,\mathit{halt}\,(\,) \\ \longrightarrow^* \cdots. \end{array}$$

Here, since the arguments g and h are swapped for each recursive call, the program does not terminate only if positive and negative integers are created alternately by $*_{\texttt{int}}$. Thus, the approach of Chen et al. [7] (which underapproximates a program by inserting assume statements and then uses a safety property checker to prove that the resulting program never terminates) would not be applicable. In our approach, by using the abstraction type $\mathbf{int}[\lambda x.x > 0]$ for x, f is abstracted to:

$$f\ g\ h\ z = \texttt{br}_{\exists}\{\texttt{true} \rightarrow \texttt{let}\ x\,\texttt{=}\,\texttt{true}\ \texttt{in}\ \texttt{br}_{\forall}\{x \rightarrow g(f\ h\ g)\},\\ \texttt{true} \rightarrow \texttt{let}\ x\,\texttt{=}\,\texttt{false}\ \texttt{in}\ \texttt{br}_{\forall}\{\neg x \rightarrow h(f\ h\ g)\}\}.$$

Thus, both branches of the if-expression are kept in the abstract program, and we can correctly conclude that the program is non-terminating.

For the second benchmark, we have borrowed a standard benchmark set consisting of 78 programs categorized as "known non-terminating examples" [7,19]. (Actually, the original set consists of 81 programs, but 3 of them turned out to be terminating.) The original programs were written in the input language for T2 [2]; we have automatically converted them to OCaml programs. Our tool could verify 48 programs to be non-terminating in the time limit of 60 seconds. According to Larraz et al. [19], CppInv [19], T2-TACAS [7], AProVE [6,10], Julia [22], and TNT [13] could verify 70, 51, 0, 8, and 19 programs respectively, with the same limit but under a different environment. Thus, our tool is not the best, but competitive with the state-of-the-art tools for proving non-termination of first-order programs, despite that our tool is not specialized for first-order programs. As for the comparison with T2-TACAS [7], our tool could verify 7 programs for which T2-TACAS failed, and ours failed for 10 programs that T2-TACAS could verify.

6 Related Work

Methods for disproving termination have recently been studied actively [7,8, 13,19]. Most of them, however, focused on programs having *finite* control-flow graphs with numerical data. For example, the state-of-the-art method by Larraz et al. [19] enumerates a strongly connected subgraph (SCSG), and checks whether there is a computation that is trapped in the SCSG using a SMT solver. Thus, it is not obvious how to extend those techniques to deal with recursion and higher-order functions. Note that unlike in safety property verification, we cannot soundly overapproximate the infinite control-flow graph of a higher-order program with a finite one.

Technically, the closest to our work seems to be the series of recent work by Cook et al. [7,8]. They apply an underapproximation by inserting assume statements, and then either appeal to a safety property checker [7], or apply an overapproximation [8] to prove that the underapproximated program is non-terminating for all execution paths. A problem of their underapproximation [7] is that when an assume statement $\mathit{assume}(P)$ is inserted, all the computations such that $\neg P$ are discarded; so if P is wrongly chosen, they may overlook a non-terminating computation present in the branch where $\neg P$ holds. As in the case for `alternate` discussed in Sect. 5, in the presence of higher-order functions, there may be no proper way for inserting assume conditions. In contrast, with our predicate abstraction, given a predicate P, we basically keep both branches for P and $\neg P$, and apply an underapproximation only if the satisfiability of P or $\neg P$ is not guaranteed (recall Fig. 1). In Cook et al.'s method [8], underapproximation cannot be applied after overapproximation, whereas under- and overapproximation can be arbitrarily nested in our method. Furthermore, although the framework of Cook et al. [8] is general, their concrete method can be applied to detect only non-termination in the form of lasso for programs having finite control-flow graphs. Harris et al. [14] also combine under- and overapproximation, but in a way different from ours: they use under- and overapproximation for disproving and proving termination respectively, not both for disproving termination.

There have also been studies on non-termination of term rewriting systems (TRS). Higher-order programs can be encoded into term rewriting systems, but the resulting analysis would be too imprecise. Furthermore, as mentioned in Sect. 1, the definition of non-termination is different.

Higher-order model checking has been recently applied to program verification [15,16]. Predicate abstraction has been used for overapproximation for the purpose of safety property verification, but the combination of under- and overapproximation is new. Kuwahara et al. [18] have proposed a method for proving termination of higher-order programs; our new method for disproving termination plays a complementary role to that method.

The constraints generated in our CEGAR phase can be regarded as special instances of "existentially quantified Horn clauses" considered by Beyene et al. [4], where only acyclic clauses are allowed. Our constraint solving algorithm is specialized for the case of acyclic clauses. Incidentally, Beyene et al. [4] used existentially quantified clauses for verifying CTL properties of programs. Since non-termination can be expressed by the CTL formula $EG\neg terminated$, their technique can, in principle, be used for verifying non-termination. Like other methods for non-termination, however, the resulting technique seems applicable only to programs with finite control-flow graphs.

7 Conclusion

We have proposed an automated method for disproving termination of higher-order programs. The key idea was to combine under- and overapproximations by using predicate abstraction. By representing the approximation as a tree-generating higher-order program, we have reduced non-termination verification to higher-order model checking. The mixture of under- and overapproximations has also required a careful analysis of counterexamples, for determining whether and how under- or overapproximations are refined. We have implemented the proposed method and confirmed its effectiveness. Future work includes optimizations of the implementation and integration with the termination verifier [18].

Acknowledgments. We would like to thank Carsten Fuhs for providing us with their experimental data and pointers to related work, and anonymous referees for useful comments. This work was partially supported by Kakenhi 23220001 and 25730035.

References

1. MoCHi(Non-termination): Model Checker for Higher-Order Programs. http://www-kb.is.s.u-tokyo.ac.jp/~kuwahara/nonterm/
2. T2 temporal prover. http://research.microsoft.com/en-us/projects/t2/
3. Ball, T., Majumdar, R., Millstein, T., Rajamani, S.K.: Automatic predicate abstraction of C programs. In: PLDI 2001, pp. 203–213. ACM (2001)
4. Beyene, T.A., Popeea, C., Rybalchenko, A.: Solving existentially quantified horn clauses. In: Sharygina, N., Veith, H. (eds.) CAV 2013. LNCS, vol. 8044, pp. 869–882. Springer, Heidelberg (2013)
5. Broadbent, C., Kobayashi, N.: Saturation-based model checking of higher-order recursion schemes. In: CSL 2013. LIPIcs, vol. 23, pp. 129–148 (2013)
6. Brockschmidt, M., Ströder, T., Otto, C., Giesl, J.: Automated detection of non-termination and `NullPointerExceptions` for Java bytecode. In: Beckert, B., Damiani, F., Gurov, D. (eds.) FoVeOOS 2011. LNCS, vol. 7421, pp. 123–141. Springer, Heidelberg (2012)
7. Chen, H.-Y., Cook, B., Fuhs, C., Nimkar, K., O'Hearn, P.: Proving nontermination via safety. In: Ábrahám, E., Havelund, K. (eds.) TACAS 2014 (ETAPS). LNCS, vol. 8413, pp. 156–171. Springer, Heidelberg (2014)
8. Cook, B., Fuhs, C., Nimkar, K., O'Hearn, P.W.: Disproving termination with overapproximation. In: FMCAD 2014, pp. 67–74. IEEE (2014)
9. Emmes, F., Enger, T., Giesl, J.: Proving non-looping non-termination automatically. In: Gramlich, B., Miller, D., Sattler, U. (eds.) IJCAR 2012. LNCS, vol. 7364, pp. 225–240. Springer, Heidelberg (2012)
10. Giesl, J., et al.: Proving termination of programs automatically with aprove. In: Demri, S., Kapur, D., Weidenbach, C. (eds.) IJCAR 2014. LNCS, vol. 8562, pp. 184–191. Springer, Heidelberg (2014)
11. Giesl, J., Thiemann, R., Schneider-Kamp, P.: Proving and disproving termination in the dependency pair framework. In: Deduction and Applications, No. 05431. Dagstuhl Seminar Proceedings (2006)
12. Graf, S., Saidi, H.: Construction of abstract state graphs with PVS. In: Grumberg, O. (ed.) CAV 1997. LNCS, vol. 1254, pp. 72–83. Springer, Heidelberg (1997)
13. Gupta, A., Henzinger, T.A., Majumdar, R., Rybalchenko, A., Xu, R.G.: Proving non-termination. In: POPL 2008, pp. 147–158. ACM (2008)
14. Harris, W.R., Lal, A., Nori, A.V., Rajamani, S.K.: Alternation for termination. In: Cousot, R., Martel, M. (eds.) SAS 2010. LNCS, vol. 6337, pp. 304–319. Springer, Heidelberg (2010)
15. Kobayashi, N.: Model checking higher-order programs. J. ACM 60(3) (2013)
16. Kobayashi, N., Sato, R., Unno, H.: Predicate abstraction and CEGAR for higher-order model checking. In: PLDI 2011, pp. 222–233. ACM (2011)
17. Kuwahara, T., Sato, R., Unno, H., Kobayashi, N.: Predicate abstraction and CEGAR for disproving termination of higher-order functional programs. Full version, available from the last author's web page (2015)
18. Kuwahara, T., Terauchi, T., Unno, H., Kobayashi, N.: Automatic Termination Verification for Higher-Order Functional Programs. In: Shao, Z. (ed.) ESOP 2014 (ETAPS). LNCS, vol. 8410, pp. 392–411. Springer, Heidelberg (2014)

19. Larraz, D., Nimkar, K., Oliveras, A., Rodríguez-Carbonell, E., Rubio, A.: Proving non-termination using Max-SMT. In: Biere, A., Bloem, R. (eds.) CAV 2014. LNCS, vol. 8559, pp. 779–796. Springer, Heidelberg (2014)
20. de Moura, L., Bjørner, N.S.: Z3: an efficient SMT solver. In: Ramakrishnan, C.R., Rehof, J. (eds.) TACAS 2008. LNCS, vol. 4963, pp. 337–340. Springer, Heidelberg (2008)
21. Ong, C.H.L.: On model-checking trees generated by higher-order recursion schemes. In: LICS 2006, pp. 81–90. IEEE (2006)
22. Spoto, F., Mesnard, F.: Étienne payet: a termination analyzer for Java bytecode based on path-length. ACM Trans. Prog. Lang. Syst. **32**(3), 8:1–8:70 (2010)
23. Unno, H., Kobayashi, N.: Dependent type inference with interpolants. In: PPDP 2009, pp. 277–288. ACM (2009)
24. Unno, H., Terauchi, T., Kobayashi, N.: Automating relatively complete verification of higher-order functional programs. In: POPL 2013, pp. 75–86. ACM (2013)

Complexity of Bradley-Manna-Sipma Lexicographic Ranking Functions

Amir M. Ben-Amram[1] and Samir Genaim[2(✉)]

[1] School of Computer Science, The Tel-Aviv Academic College, Tel Aviv, Israel
[2] DSIC, Complutense University of Madrid (UCM), Madrid, Spain
genaim@gmail.com

Abstract. In this paper we turn the spotlight on a class of lexicographic ranking functions introduced by Bradley, Manna and Sipma in a seminal CAV 2005 paper, and establish for the first time the complexity of some problems involving the inference of such functions for linear-constraint loops (without precondition). We show that finding such a function, if one exists, can be done in polynomial time in a way which is sound and complete when the variables range over the rationals (or reals). We show that when variables range over the integers, the problem is harder—deciding the existence of a ranking function is coNP-complete. Next, we study the problem of minimizing the number of components in the ranking function (a.k.a. the dimension). This number is interesting in contexts like computing iteration bounds and loop parallelization. Surprisingly, and unlike the situation for some other classes of lexicographic ranking functions, we find that even deciding whether a two-component ranking function exists is harder than the unrestricted problem: NP-complete over the rationals and Σ_2^P-complete over the integers.

1 Introduction

Proving that a program will not go into an infinite loop is one of the most fundamental tasks of program verification, and has been the subject of voluminous research. Perhaps the best known, and often used, technique for proving termination is the *ranking function*. This is a function ρ that maps the program states into the elements of a well-founded ordered set, such that $\rho(s) > \rho(s')$ holds for any consecutive states s and s'. This implies termination since infinite descent in a well-founded order is impossible.

We focus on *numerical loops*, where a state is described by the values of a finite set of numerical variables; we consider the setting of integer-valued variables, as well as rational-valued (or real-valued) variables. We ignore details of the programming language; we assume that we are provided an abstract description of the loop as a finite number of alternatives, that we call *paths*, each one

This work was funded partially by the EU project FP7-ICT-610582 ENVISAGE: Engineering Virtualized Services (http://www.envisage-project.eu), by the Spanish MINECO project TIN2012-38137, and by the CM project S2013/ICE-3006.

D. Kroening and C.S. Păsăreanu (Eds.): CAV 2015, Part II, LNCS 9207, pp. 304–321, 2015.
DOI: 10.1007/978-3-319-21668-3_18

defined by a finite set of *linear constraints* on the program variables $x, y, \ldots$ and the primed variables $x', y', \ldots$ which refer to the state following the iteration. The following is such a loop consisting of four paths, $\mathcal{Q}_1, \ldots, \mathcal{Q}_4$:

$$\begin{array}{lllll}
\mathcal{Q}_1 = \{x \geq 0, x' \leq x - 1, & & y' = y, & & z' = z\} \\
\mathcal{Q}_2 = \{x \geq 0, x' \leq x - 1, & & y' = y, & z \geq 0, & z' \leq z - 1\} \\
\mathcal{Q}_3 = \{ & x' = x, & y \geq 0, y' \leq y - 1, & z \geq 0, & z' \leq z - 1\} \\
\mathcal{Q}_4 = \{ & x' = x, & y \geq 0, y' \leq y - 1, & & z' = z\}
\end{array}$$

Note that $\mathcal{Q}_i$ are convex polyhedra. A transition from a state $\bar{x}$ to $\bar{x}'$ is possible iff $(\bar{x}, \bar{x}')$ is a point in some path $\mathcal{Q}_i$. We remark that our results hold for arbitrarily-complex control-flow graphs (CFGs), we prefer to use the loop setting for clarity.

A popular tool for proving the termination of such loops is *linear ranking functions* (LRFs). An LRF is a function $\rho(x_1, \ldots, x_n) = a_1x_1 + \cdots + a_nx_n + a_0$ such that any transition $(\bar{x}, \bar{x}')$ satisfies (i) $\rho(\bar{x}) \geq 0$; and (ii) $\rho(\bar{x}) - \rho(\bar{x}') \geq 1$. E.g., $\rho(x, y, z) = x$ is an LRF for a loop that consists of only $\mathcal{Q}_1$ and $\mathcal{Q}_2$ above, $\rho(x, y, z) = y$ is an LRF for $\mathcal{Q}_3$ and $\mathcal{Q}_4$, and $\rho(x, y, z) = z$ is an LRF for $\mathcal{Q}_2$ and $\mathcal{Q}_3$. However, there is no LRF that satisfies the above conditions for all paths $\mathcal{Q}_1, \ldots, \mathcal{Q}_4$. An algorithm to find an LRF using linear programming (LP) has been found by multiple researchers in different places and times and in some alternative versions [1,10,14,21,23,26]. Since LP has a polynomial-time complexity, most of these methods yield polynomial-time algorithms. These algorithms are complete for loops with rational-valued variables, but not with integer-valued variables. Indeed, [4] shows loops that have LRFs over the integers but do not even terminate over the rationals. In a previous work [4] we considered the integer setting, where complete algorithms were proposed and a complexity classification was proved: to decide whether an LRF exists is *coNP-complete.*

LRFs do not suffice for all loops (e.g., the 4-path loop above), and thus, a natural question is what to do when an LRF does not exist; and a natural answer is to try a richer class of ranking functions. Of particular importance is the class of *lexicographic-linear ranking functions* (LLRFs). An LLRF is a d-tuple of affine-linear functions, $\langle \rho_1, \ldots, \rho_d \rangle$, required to descend lexicographically. Interestingly, Alan Turing's early demonstration [28] of how to verify a program used an LLRF for the termination proof. *Algorithms* to find LLRFs for linear-constraint loops (or CFGs) can use LP techniques, extending the work on LRFs. Alias et al. [1] extended the polynomial-time LRF algorithm to LLRFs and gave a complete solution for CFGs. As for LRFs, the solution is incomplete for integer data, and in [4] we established for LLRFs over the integers results that parallel those for LRFs, in particular, to decide whether an LLRF exists is *coNP-complete.*

Interestingly, when trying to define the requirements from a numeric "lexicographic ranking function" (corresponding to the conditions (i) and (ii) on an LRF, above), different researchers had come up with different definitions. In particular, the definition in [1] is more restrictive than the definition in [4]. Furthermore, an important paper [5] on LLRF generation that preceded both works gave yet a different definition. We give the precise definitions in Sect. 2; for the purpose of introduction, let us focus on the LLRFs of [5] (henceforth, BMS-LLRFs, after the authors), and illustrate the definition by an example.

Consider the above loop defined by $\mathcal{Q}_1, \ldots, \mathcal{Q}_4$. A possible BMS-LLRF for this loop is $\rho(x, y, z) = \langle x, y \rangle$. The justification is this: in $\mathcal{Q}_1$ and $\mathcal{Q}_2$, the function $\rho_1(x, y) = x$ is ranking (non-negative and decreasing by at least 1). In $\mathcal{Q}_3$ and $\mathcal{Q}_4$, $\rho_2(x, y) = y$ is ranking, while ρ_1 is non-increasing. This is true over the rationals and *a fortiori* over the integers. The following points are important: (1) for each path we have an LRF, which is one of the components of the BMS-LLRF; and (2) previous (lower-numbered) components are only required to be non-increasing on that path. Note that this LLRF does not satisfy the requirements of [1] or [4].

The goal of this paper is to understand the *computational complexity* of some problems related to BMS-LLRFs, starting with the most basic problem, whether a given loop has such LLRF. We note that [5] does not provide an answer, as a consequence of attempting to solve a much harder problem—they consider a loop given with a precondition and search for a BMS-LLRF together with a supporting linear invariant. We do not know if this problem is even decidable when parameters like the number of constraints in the invariants are not fixed in advance (when they are, the approach of [5] is complete, but only over the reals, and at a high computational cost – even without a precondition).

We consider the complexity of finding a BMS-LLRF for a given loop, without preconditions. We prove that this can be done in polynomial time when the loop is interpreted over the rationals, while over the integers, deciding the existence of a BMS-LLRF is coNP-complete. An exponential-time synthesis algorithm is also given. These results are similar to those obtained for the previously studied classes of LLRFs [4], but are shown for the first time for BMS-LLRFs.

Next, we consider the number of components d in a BMS-LLRF $\langle \rho_1, \ldots, \rho_d \rangle$. This number is informally called the *dimension* of the function. It is interesting for several reasons: An upper bound on the dimension is useful for fixing the template in the constraint-solving approach, and plays a role in analyzing the complexity of corresponding algorithms. In addition, an LLRF can be used to infer bounds on the number of iterations [1]; assuming linear bounds on individual variables, a polynomial bound of degree d is clearly implied, which motivates the desire to minimize the dimension, to obtain tight bounds. A smaller dimension also means better results when LLRFs are used to guide parallelization [15].

Importantly, the algorithms of Alias et al. [1] and Ben-Amram and Genaim [4] are optimal w.r.t. the dimension, i.e., they synthesize LLRFs of minimal dimension for the respective classes. We note that it is possible for a loop to have LLRFs of all three classes but such that the minimal dimension is different in each (see Sect. 4). We also note that, unlike the case for the previous classes, our synthesis algorithm for BMS-LLRFs is *not* guaranteed to produce a function of minimal dimension. This leads us to ask: (1) what is the best *a priori* bound on the dimension, in terms of the number of variables and paths; and (2) how difficult it is to find an LLRF of minimal dimension. As a relaxation of this optimization problem, we can pose the problem of finding an LLRF that satisfies a given bound on the dimension. Our results are summarized in Table 1. There is a striking difference of BMS-LLRFs from other classes w.r.t. to the minimum dimension problem: the complexity jumps from PTIME (resp. coNP-complete) to NPC (resp. Σ_2^P-complete) over rationals (resp. integers). This holds for any fixed dimension larger than one (dimension one is an LRF).

Table 1. Summary of results, considering a loop of k paths over n variables. Those in the third row are new, the others are from previous works or follow by minor variations.

LLRF type	Dimension bound	Existence		Fixed dimension	
		over $\mathbb{Q}$	over $\mathbb{Z}$	over $\mathbb{Q}$	over $\mathbb{Z}$
ADFG [1]	$\min(n, k)$	PTIME	coNP-complete	PTIME	coNP-complete
BG [4]	n	PTIME	coNP-complete	PTIME	coNP-complete
BMS [5]	k	PTIME	coNP-complete	NP-complete	Σ_2^P-complete

2 Preliminaries

Polyhedra. A *rational convex polyhedron* $\mathcal{P} \subseteq \mathbb{Q}^n$ (*polyhedron* for short) is the set of solutions of a set of inequalities $A\mathbf{x} \leq \mathbf{b}$, namely $\mathcal{P} = \{\mathbf{x} \in \mathbb{Q}^n \mid A\mathbf{x} \leq \mathbf{b}\}$, where $A \in \mathbb{Q}^{m\times n}$ is a rational matrix of n columns and m rows, $\mathbf{x} \in \mathbb{Q}^n$ and $\mathbf{b} \in \mathbb{Q}^m$ are column vectors of n and m rational values respectively. We say that $\mathcal{P}$ is specified by $A\mathbf{x} \leq \mathbf{b}$. We use calligraphic letters, such as $\mathcal{P}$ and $\mathcal{Q}$ to denote polyhedra. For a given polyhedron $\mathcal{P} \subseteq \mathbb{Q}^n$ we let $I(\mathcal{P})$ be $\mathcal{P} \cap \mathbb{Z}^n$, i.e., the set of integer points of $\mathcal{P}$. The *integer hull* of $\mathcal{P}$, commonly denoted by $\mathcal{P}_I$, is defined as the convex hull of $I(\mathcal{P})$. It is known that $\mathcal{P}_I$ is also a polyhedron. An *integer polyhedron* is a polyhedron $\mathcal{P}$ such that $\mathcal{P} = \mathcal{P}_I$. We also say that $\mathcal{P}$ is *integral.*

Multipath Linear-Constraint Loops. A *multipath* linear-constraint loop (MLC loop) with k paths has the form: $\bigvee_{i=1}^{k} A_i\binom{\mathbf{x}}{\mathbf{x}'} \leq \mathbf{c}_i$ where $\mathbf{x} = (x_1, \ldots, x_n)^T$ and $\mathbf{x}' = (x_1', \ldots, x_n')^T$ are column vectors, and for $q > 0$, $A_i \in \mathbb{Q}^{q\times 2n}$, $\mathbf{c}_i \in \mathbb{Q}^q$. Each path $A_i\binom{\mathbf{x}}{\mathbf{x}'} \leq \mathbf{c}_i$ is called an *abstract transition.* The loop is a *rational loop* if $\mathbf{x}$ and $\mathbf{x}'$ range over $\mathbb{Q}^n$, and it is an *integer loop* if they range over $\mathbb{Z}^n$. We say that there is a transition from a state $\mathbf{x} \in \mathbb{Q}^n$ to a state $\mathbf{x}' \in \mathbb{Q}^n$, if for some $1 \leq i \leq k$, $\binom{\mathbf{x}}{\mathbf{x}'}$ satisfies the i-th abstract transition. In such case we say that $\mathbf{x}$ is an enabled state. We use $\mathbf{x}''$ as a shorthand for a transition $\binom{\mathbf{x}}{\mathbf{x}'}$, and consider it as a point in $\mathbb{Q}^{2n}$. The set of transitions satisfying a particular abstract transition is a polyhedron in $\mathbb{Q}^{2n}$, denoted $\mathcal{Q}_i$, namely $A_i\mathbf{x}'' \leq \mathbf{c}_i$. In our work it is convenient to represent an MLC loop by its transition polyhedra $\mathcal{Q}_1, \ldots, \mathcal{Q}_k$, which we often write with explicit equalities and inequalities. These are sometimes referred to as the *paths* of the multipath loop.

Ranking Functions. An affine linear function $\rho : \mathbb{Q}^n \mapsto \mathbb{Q}$ is of the form $\rho(\mathbf{x}) = \boldsymbol{\lambda} \cdot \mathbf{x} + \lambda_0$ where $\boldsymbol{\lambda} \in \mathbb{Q}^n$ and $\lambda_0 \in \mathbb{Q}$. We define $\Delta\rho : \mathbb{Q}^{2n} \mapsto \mathbb{Q}$ as $\Delta\rho(\mathbf{x}'') = \rho(\mathbf{x}) - \rho(\mathbf{x}')$. Given a set $T \subseteq \mathbb{Q}^{2n}$, representing transitions, we say that ρ is an LRF for T if for every $\mathbf{x}'' \in T$ we have (i) $\rho(\mathbf{x}) \geq 0$; and (ii) $\Delta\rho(\mathbf{x}'') \geq 1$. We say that ρ is an LRF for a rational (resp. integer) loop, specified by $\mathcal{Q}_1, \ldots, \mathcal{Q}_k$, when it is an LRF for $\bigcup_{i=1}^k \mathcal{Q}_i$ (resp. $\bigcup_{i=1}^k I(\mathcal{Q}_i)$). For a rational loop, there is a polynomial-time algorithm to either find an LRF or determine that none exists [23]. Its essence is that using *Farkas' Lemma* [25, p. 93], it is possible to set up an LP problem whose feasibility is equivalent to the existence of ρ that satisfies (i) and (ii) over $\mathcal{Q}_1, \ldots, \mathcal{Q}_k$.

A *d-dimensional affine function* $\tau : \mathbb{Q}^n \to \mathbb{Q}^d$ is expressed by a d-tuple $\tau = \langle \rho_1, \ldots, \rho_d \rangle$, where each component $\rho_i : \mathbb{Q}^n \to \mathbb{Q}$ is an affine linear function. The number d is informally called the *dimension* of τ. Next we define when such a function is BMS-LLRF [5] for a given rational or integer MLC loop. We then compare with ADFG-LLRFs (due to [1]) and BG-LLRFs (due to [4]).

Definition 1 (BMS-LLRF). *Given k sets of transitions $T_1, \ldots, T_k \subseteq \mathbb{Q}^{2n}$, we say that $\tau = \langle \rho_1, \ldots, \rho_d \rangle$ is a* BMS-LLRF *for $T_1, \ldots, T_k$ iff for every $1 \le \ell \le k$ there is $1 \le i \le d$ such that the following hold for any $\mathbf{x}'' \in T_\ell$:*

$$\forall j < i \,.\, \Delta\rho_j(\mathbf{x}'') \ge 0\,, \tag{1}$$

$$\rho_i(\mathbf{x}) \ge 0\,, \tag{2}$$

$$\Delta\rho_i(\mathbf{x}'') \ge 1\,. \tag{3}$$

We say that T_ℓ is ranked by *ρ_i.*

We say that τ is a BMS-LLRF for a rational (resp. integer) loop, specified by $\mathcal{Q}_1, \ldots, \mathcal{Q}_k$, when it is a BMS-LLRF for $\mathcal{Q}_1, \ldots, \mathcal{Q}_k$ (resp. $I(\mathcal{Q}_1), \cdots, I(\mathcal{Q}_k)$). It is easy to see that the existence of a BMS-LLRF implies termination.

Definition 2 (BG-LLRF). *Given a set of transitions $T \subseteq \mathbb{Q}^{2n}$, we say that $\tau = \langle \rho_1, \ldots, \rho_d \rangle$ is a* BG-LLRF *for T iff for every $\mathbf{x}'' \in T$ there is $1 \le i \le d$ such that the following hold:*

$$\forall j < i \,.\, \Delta\rho_j(\mathbf{x}'') \ge 0\,, \tag{4}$$

$$\forall j \le i \,.\quad \rho_j(\mathbf{x}) \ge 0\,, \tag{5}$$

$$\Delta\rho_i(\mathbf{x}'') \ge 1\,. \tag{6}$$

We say that $\mathbf{x}$ is ranked by *ρ_i.*

We say that τ is a BG-LLRF for a rational (resp. integer) loop, specified by $\mathcal{Q}_1, \ldots, \mathcal{Q}_k$, when it is a BG-LLRF for $\mathcal{Q}_1 \cup \cdots \cup \mathcal{Q}_k$ (resp. $I(\mathcal{Q}_1) \cup \cdots \cup I(\mathcal{Q}_k)$). It is easy to see that the existence of a BG-LLRF implies termination.

Note the differences between the definitions: in one sense, BG-LLRFs are more flexible because of the different quantification — for every transition $\mathbf{x}''$ there has to be a component ρ_i that ranks it, but i may differ for different $\mathbf{x}''$, whereas in BMS-LLRFs, all transitions that belong to a certain T_ℓ have to be ranked by the same component. In another sense, BMS-LLRFs are more flexible because components ρ_j with $j < i$ can be negative (compare (2) with (5)). Thus, there are loops that have a BMS-LLRF and do not have a BG-LLRF (see loop in Sect. 1); and vice versa (see [4, Ex. 2.12]). A third type of LLRFs is attributed to [1], hence we refer to it as ADFG-LLRF. It is similar to BG-LLRFs but requires all components to be non-negative in every enabled state. That is, condition (5) is strengthened. Interestingly, the completeness proof in [1] shows that the above-mentioned flexibility of BG-LLRFs adds no power in this case; therefore, ADFG-LLRFs are a special case of both BG-LLRFs and BMS-LLRFs.

The decision problem *Existence of a* BMS-LLRF deals with deciding whether a given MLC loop admits a BMS-LLRF, we denote it by BMS-LexLinRF($\mathbb{Q}$) and BMS-LexLinRF($\mathbb{Z}$) for rational and integer loops respectively. The corresponding decision problems for ADFG- and BG-LLRFs are solved in [1] and [4], respectively, over the rationals; the case of integers is only addressed in [4] for BG-LLRFs, but the complexity results apply to ADFG-LLRFs as well.

3 Synthesis of BMS-LLRFs

In this section we describe a complete algorithm for synthesizing BMS-LLRFs for rational and integer MLC loops; and show that the decision problems BMS-LexLinRF($\mathbb{Q}$) and BMS-LexLinRF($\mathbb{Z}$) are PTIME and coNP-complete, respectively. We assume a given MLC loop $\mathcal{Q}_1, \ldots, \mathcal{Q}_k$ where each $\mathcal{Q}_i$ is given as a set of linear constraints, over $2n$ variables (n variables and n primed variables).

Definition 3. *Let $T_1, \ldots, T_k$ be sets of transitions such that $T_i \subseteq \mathbb{Q}^{2n}$. We say that an affine linear function ρ is a* BMS *quasi-*LRF *(*BMS-QLRF *for short) for $T_1, \ldots, T_k$ if every transition $\mathbf{x}'' \in T_1 \cup \cdots \cup T_k$ satisfies $\Delta\rho(\mathbf{x}'') \geq 0$, and for at least one T_ℓ, ρ is an* LRF *(such T_ℓ is said to be ranked by ρ).*

Example 1. The following are BMS-QLRFs for the loop consisting of $\mathcal{Q}_1, \ldots, \mathcal{Q}_4$ presented in Sect. 1: $f_1(x,y,z){=}x$, which ranks $\{\mathcal{Q}_1, \mathcal{Q}_2\}$; $f_2(x,y,z){=}y$ which ranks $\{\mathcal{Q}_3, \mathcal{Q}_4\}$; and $f_3(x,y,z){=}z$ which ranks $\{\mathcal{Q}_2, \mathcal{Q}_3\}$.

Lemma 1. *There is a polynomial-time algorithm that finds a* BMS-QLRF *ρ, if there is any, for $\mathcal{Q}_1, \ldots, \mathcal{Q}_k$.*

Proof. The algorithm iterates over the paths $\mathcal{Q}_1, \ldots, \mathcal{Q}_k$. In the i-th iteration it checks if there is an LRF ρ for $\mathcal{Q}_i$ that is non-increasing for all other paths, stopping if it finds one. The algorithm makes at most k iterations. Each iteration can be implemented in polynomial time using Farkas' Lemma (as in [23]). □

Our procedure for synthesizing BMS-LLRFs is depicted in Algorithm 1. In each iteration (i.e., call to `LLRFSYN`): it finds a BMS-QLRF ρ for the current paths (Line 2); it eliminates all paths that are ranked by ρ (Line 3); and calls recursively to handle the remaining paths (Line 4). The algorithm stops when all paths are ranked (Line 1), or when it does not find a BMS-QLRF (Line 6).

Example 2. Consider the MLC loop example in Sect. 1. Procedure `LLRFSYN` is first applied to $\langle \mathcal{Q}_1, \mathcal{Q}_2, \mathcal{Q}_3, \mathcal{Q}_4 \rangle$, and at Line 2 we can choose the BMS-QLRF x which ranks $\mathcal{Q}_1$ and $\mathcal{Q}_2$. Hence these are eliminated at Line 3, and at Line 4 `LLRFSYN` is applied recursively to $\langle \emptyset, \emptyset, \mathcal{Q}_3, \mathcal{Q}_4 \rangle$. Then at Line 2 we can choose the BMS-QLRF y which ranks $\mathcal{Q}_3$ and $\mathcal{Q}_4$. The next recursive call receives empty polyhedra, and thus the check at Line 1 succeeds and the algorithm returns $\langle x, y \rangle$.

Algorithm 1. Synthesizing BMS-LLRFs

LLRFSYN($\langle \mathcal{Q}_1, \ldots, \mathcal{Q}_k \rangle$)
begin
  if $\langle \mathcal{Q}_1, \ldots, \mathcal{Q}_k \rangle$ *are all empty* **then return nil**
  if $\mathcal{Q}_1, \ldots, \mathcal{Q}_k$ *has a* BMS-QLRF ρ **then**
    $\forall 1 \le i \le k.\ \mathcal{Q}'_i := \emptyset$ if $\mathcal{Q}_i$ is ranked by ρ, otherwise $\mathcal{Q}'_i = \mathcal{Q}_i$
    $\tau \leftarrow$ LLRFSYN($\langle \mathcal{Q}'_1, \ldots, \mathcal{Q}'_k \rangle$)
    if $\tau \neq$ NONE **then return** $\rho{::}\tau$
  return NONE

Lemma 2. *If* LLRFSYN($\langle \mathcal{Q}_1, \ldots, \mathcal{Q}_k \rangle$) *returns* τ *different from* NONE, *then* τ *is a* BMS-LLRF *for the rational loop* $\mathcal{Q}_1, \ldots, \mathcal{Q}_k$.

The proof of the above lemma is straightforward. Thus, Algorithm 1 is a sound algorithm for BMS-LLRFs. The following proposition shows completeness.

Proposition 1. *There is a* BMS-LLRF *for* $\mathcal{Q}_1, \ldots, \mathcal{Q}_k$ *if and only if every subset of* $\{\mathcal{Q}_1, \ldots, \mathcal{Q}_k\}$ *has a* BMS-QLRF.

Proof. The "if" direction is implied by the LLRFSYN procedure, in such case it will find a BMS-LLRF. For the "only if" direction, let $\tau = \langle \rho_1, \ldots, \rho_d \rangle$ be a BMS-LLRF for $\mathcal{Q}_1, \ldots, \mathcal{Q}_k$, and let $\mathcal{Q}_{\ell_1}, \ldots, \mathcal{Q}_{\ell_j}$ be an arbitrary subset of the loop's paths. Since τ is a BMS-LLRF for $\mathcal{Q}_1, \ldots, \mathcal{Q}_k$, each $\mathcal{Q}_{\ell_i}$ is ranked by some ρ_{l_i}. Let $l = \min\{l_1, \ldots, l_j\}$, then ρ_l is a BMS-QLRF for $\mathcal{Q}_{\ell_1}, \ldots, \mathcal{Q}_{\ell_j}$. □

Lemma 3. *Procedure* LLRFSYN *can be implemented in polynomial time.*

Proof. Procedure LLRFSYN makes at most k steps (since at least one path is eliminated in every step). Further, all steps are elementary except checking for a BMS-QLRF which can be done in polynomial time as stated by Lemma 1. □

Corollary 1. BMS-LexLinRF($\mathbb{Q}$) $\in$ *PTIME.*

So far we have considered only rational loops, next we consider integer loops.

Lemma 4. *There is a complete algorithm for synthesizing a* BMS-QLRF *for* $I(\mathcal{Q}_1), \ldots, I(\mathcal{Q}_k)$.

Proof. The algorithm computes the integer hull $\mathcal{Q}_{1I}, \ldots, \mathcal{Q}_{kI}$, and then proceeds as in the rational case (Lemma 1). Correctness follows from the fact that for integral polyhedra the implied inequalities over the rationals and integers coincide, i.e., $\mathcal{Q}_{1I}, \ldots, \mathcal{Q}_{kI}$ and $I(\mathcal{Q}_1), \ldots, I(\mathcal{Q}_k)$ have the same BMS-QLRFs. □

Lemma 5. *When procedure* LLRFSYN *is applied to the integer hulls* $\mathcal{Q}_{1I}, \ldots, \mathcal{Q}_{kI}$, *it finds a* BMS-LLRF *for* $I(\mathcal{Q}_1), \ldots, I(\mathcal{Q}_k)$, *if one exists.*

Proof. Soundness follows from the fact that $\mathcal{Q}_I$ contains $I(\mathcal{Q})$; for completeness, note that: (i) Proposition 1 holds also for integer loops; and (ii) Line 3 of LLRFSYN does not change the transition polyhedra, it only eliminates some, which means that they remain integral throughout the recursive calls. Thus, in each iteration the check at Line 2 is complete (see Lemma 4). □

In the general case this procedure has an exponential time complexity since computing the integer hull requires an exponential time. However, for special cases in which the integer hull can be computed in polynomial time [4, Sect. 4] it has polynomial time complexity. The following lemma implies (assuming P≠NP) that the exponential time complexity is unavoidable in general.

Theorem 1. BMS-LexLinRF($\mathbb{Z}$) *is a coNP-complete problem.*

Proof. The coNP-hardness follows from the reduction in [4, Sect. 3.1], since it constructs a loop that either does not terminate or has an LRF. The inclusion in coNP is based on arguments similar to those in [4, Sect. 5]; briefly, we use the generator representation of the transition polyhedra to construct a polynomial-size witness against existence of an LLRF (see [2]). □

4 The Dimension of BMS-LLRFs

Ben-Amram and Genaim [4, Cor. 5.12,p. 32] showed that if a given MLC loop has a BG-LLRF, then it has one of dimension at most n, the dimension of the state space. The same proof can be used to bound the dimension of ADFG-LLRFs by n as well. Hence for ADFG-LLRFs the bound $\min(n, k)$ holds (k is the number of paths), due to the fact that associating LLRF components with paths is no loss of generality for ADFG-LLRFs [1]. In the case of BMS-LLRFs, the bound k clearly holds, and the next example shows that it is tight.

Example 3. Define an MLC loop $\mathcal{Q}_1, \ldots, \mathcal{Q}_k$ for some $k > 0$, over variables x, y, where each $\mathcal{Q}_i = \{x' \leq x,\ x' + i \cdot y' \leq x + i \cdot y - 1,\ x + i \cdot y \geq 0\}$. Define $f_i(x, y) = x + i \cdot y$. It is easy to check that (i) f_i is an LRF for $\mathcal{Q}_i$, and is non-increasing for any $\mathcal{Q}_j$ with $i < j \leq k$; and (ii) there are no distinct $\mathcal{Q}_i$ and $\mathcal{Q}_j$ that have a common LRF. From (i) it follows that $\langle f_1, \ldots, f_k \rangle$ is a BMS-LLRF for this loop, and from (ii) it follows that any BMS-LLRF must have (at least) dimension k, since different paths cannot be ranked by the same component. We remark that this loop has no BG-LLRF (hence, also no ADFG-LLRF).

The above discussion emphasizes the difference between the various definitions of LLRFs, when considering the dimension. The next example emphasizes this difference further, it shows that there are loops, having LLRFs of all three kinds, for which the minimal dimension is different according to each definition. This also means that the implied bounds on the number of iterations (assuming, for simplicity, that all variables have the same upper bound) are different.

Example 4. Consider an MLC loop specified by the following paths

$$
\begin{array}{l}
\mathcal{Q}_1 = \left\{ \begin{array}{lllllll} r \geq 0, & & t \geq 0, & x \geq 0, & & z \geq 0, & w \geq 0, \\ r' < r, & & t' < t, & & & & \end{array} \right\} \\
\mathcal{Q}_2 = \left\{ \begin{array}{lllllll} r \geq 0, & s \geq 0, & t \geq 0, & x \geq 0, & & z \geq 0, & w \geq 0, \\ r' = r, & s' < s, & t' < t, & & & & \end{array} \right\} \\
\mathcal{Q}_3 = \left\{ \begin{array}{lllllll} r \geq 0, & s \geq 0, & t' = t & x \geq 0, & & z \geq 0, & w \geq 0, \\ r' = r, & s' = s, & & x' < x, & & & \end{array} \right\} \\
\mathcal{Q}_4 = \left\{ \begin{array}{lllllll} r \geq 0, & s \geq 0, & t' = t & x \geq 0, & y \geq 0, & z \geq 0, & w \geq 0, \\ r' = r, & s' = s, & & x' = x, & y' < y, & z' < z, & \end{array} \right\} \\
\mathcal{Q}_5 = \left\{ \begin{array}{lllllll} r \geq 0, & s \geq 0, & t' = t & x \geq 0, & y \geq 0, & z \geq 0, & w \geq 0, \\ r' = r, & s' = s, & & x' = x, & y' < y, & z' = z, & w' < w \end{array} \right\}
\end{array}
$$

where, for readability, we use $<$ for the relation "smaller at least by 1". This loop has the BMS-LLRF $\langle t, x, y \rangle$, which is neither a BG-LLRF or ADFG-LLRF because t is not lower-bounded on all the paths. Its shortest BG-LLRF is of dimension 4, e.g., $\langle r, s, x, y \rangle$, which is not an ADFG-LLRF because y is not lower-bounded on all the paths. Its shortest ADFG-LLRF is of dimension 5, e.g., $\langle r, s, x, z, w \rangle$. This reasoning is valid for both integer and rational variables.

Next, we consider the problem of minimal dimension. We ask (1) whether our algorithms return an LLRF with minimal dimension; and (2) what do we gain (or lose?) in terms of computational tractability if we fix a bound on the dimension in advance. Importantly, the algorithms of [1,4] are optimal w.r.t. the dimension, i.e., they synthesize LLRFs of minimal dimension. In both cases the optimal result is obtained by a greedy algorithm, that constructs the LLRF by adding one dimension at a time, taking care in each iteration to rank as many transitions as possible. The next example shows that a greedy choice in Algorithm 1 fails to guarantee optimality, for both rational and integer loops. Intuitively, the greedy approach worked in [1,4] because the classes of quasi-LRFs used to construact LLRFs are closed under conic combinations, so there is always an optimal choice that dominates all others. This is not true for BMS-QLRFs.

Example 5. Consider the MLC loop of Sect. 1. If at Line 2 of Algorithm 1 we seek a BMS-QLRF that ranks a maximal number of the paths, we can use any of those derived in Example 1: $f_1 = x$; $f_2 = y$; or $f_3 = z$. However, these alternatives lead to BMS-LLRFs of different dimensions: (i) choose f_1 to rank $\{\mathcal{Q}_1, \mathcal{Q}_2\}$, and then f_2 to rank $\{\mathcal{Q}_3, \mathcal{Q}_4\}$. (ii) choose f_2 to rank $\{\mathcal{Q}_3, \mathcal{Q}_4\}$, and then f_1 to rank $\{\mathcal{Q}_1, \mathcal{Q}_2\}$. (iii) choose f_3 to rank $\{\mathcal{Q}_2, \mathcal{Q}_3\}$, but then there is no single function that ranks $\{\mathcal{Q}_1, \mathcal{Q}_4\}$. Take f_1 to rank $\mathcal{Q}_1$ and then f_2 to rank $\mathcal{Q}_4$. The dimension of the BMS-LLRF in the first two cases is 2, and in the last one it is 3.

Since Algorithm 1 is not guaranteed to find a BMS-LLRF of minimal dimension, it is natural to ask *how hard is the problem of finding a* BMS-LLRF *of minimal dimension?* This can be posed as a decision problem: *does a given MLC loop have a* BMS-LLRF *with dimension at most* d? This decision problem is denoted by BMS-LexLinRF$(d, \mathbb{Q})$ and BMS-LexLinRF$(d, \mathbb{Z})$ for rational and integer loops respectively. Note that d is a constant, however, it will be clear that accepting

d as an input does not change the complexity class of these problems. Also note that for $d = 1$ it is just the LRF problem. Similar problems can be formulated for ADFG- and BG-LLRFs, of course. In these two settings, the imposition of a dimension bound does not change the complexity class.

Theorem 2. *Given a rational MLC loop, and $d \geq 1$, it is possible to determine in polynomial time if there is an* ADFG-LLRF *(resp.* BG-LLRF*s) for the loop of dimension at most d. For integer MLC loops, the problem is coNP-complete.*

Proof. The case of rational loops is straightforward since the corresponding synthesis algorithms find LLRFs with minimal dimension, and are in PTIME. The integer case follows easily from the techniques of [4] (see [2]). □

5 Complexity of BMS-LexLinRF $(d, \mathbb{Q})$

In this section we show that BMS-LexLinRF$(d, \mathbb{Q})$ is NP-complete.

Theorem 3. *For $d \geq 2$,* BMS-LexLinRF$(d, \mathbb{Q})$ *is an NP-complete problem.*

For inclusion in NP, a non-deterministic algorithm for the problem works as follows. First, it *guesses* a partition of $\{1, \dots, k\}$ into d sets $J_1, \dots, J_d$, of which some may be empty (we can assume they are last). Then it proceeds as in Algorithm 1 but insists that the paths indexed by J_r be ranked at the r-th iteration. This may fail, and then the algorithm rejects. If a BMS-LLRF of dimension at most d exists, there will be an accepting computation.

For NP-hardness we reduce from the NP-complete problem *d-Colorability of 3-Uniform Hypergraphs* [20,22]. An instance of this problem is a set H of m sets $F_1, \dots, F_m$ (hyperedges, or "faces"), where each F_i includes exactly 3 elements from a set of vertices $V = \{1, \dots, n\}$, and we are asked whether we can choose a color (out of d colors) for each vertex such that every face is not monocolored.

We construct a rational MLC loop in $3m$ variables and n paths. The variables are indexed by vertices and faces: variable $x_{i,j}$ corresponds to $i \in F_j \in H$. For each vertex $1 \leq i \leq n$ we define $\mathcal{Q}_i$ as a conjunction of the following:

$$\sum_{k:\, i \in F_k} x_{i,k} - \sum_{k:\, i \in F_k} x'_{i,k} \geq 1 \tag{7}$$

$$\sum_{k:\, j \in F_k} x_{j,k} - \sum_{k:\, j \in F_k} x'_{j,k} \geq 0 \quad \text{for all vertex } j \neq i \tag{8}$$

$$x_{i,k} \geq 0 \quad \text{for all face } F_k \text{ s.t. } i \in F_k \tag{9}$$

$$x_{j,k} \geq 0 \quad \text{for all vertex } j \text{ and face } F_k \text{ s.t. } j \in F_k \wedge i \notin F_k \tag{10}$$

$$x_{i,k} + x_{j,k} \geq 0 \quad \text{for all vertex } j \neq i \text{ and face } F_k \text{ s.t. } i, j \in F_k \tag{11}$$

We claim that a rational loop that consists of these n paths has a BMS-LLRF of dimension d iff there is a valid d-coloring for the vertices V.

Assume given a d-coloring, namely a division of the vertices in d disjoint sets $V = C_1 \cup \cdots \cup C_d$, such that the vertices of each C_i are assigned the same color. We construct a BMS-LLRF $\langle g_1, \ldots, g_d \rangle$ such that g_ℓ ranks all paths Q_i with $i \in C_\ell$. We assume that each C_ℓ is non-empty (otherwise we let $g_\ell(\mathbf{x}) = 0$).

We start with C_1. For each $F_k \in H$, define a function f_k as follows: if $F_k \cap C_1 = \emptyset$ we let $f_k(\mathbf{x}) = 0$; if $F_k \cap C_1 = \{i\}$ we let $f_k(\mathbf{x}) = x_{i,k}$; and if $F_k \cap C_1 = \{i, j\}$ we let $f_k(\mathbf{x}) = x_{i,k} + x_{j,k}$. We claim that $g_1(\mathbf{x}) = \sum_k f_k$ is a BMS-QLRF for $\mathcal{Q}_1, \ldots, \mathcal{Q}_n$ that ranks all paths $\mathcal{Q}_i$ with $i \in C_1$, which we justify as follows:

1. g_1 is non-increasing on all $\mathcal{Q}_j$, and decreasing for each $\mathcal{Q}_i$ with $i \in C_1$. To see this, rewrite $g(\mathbf{x})$ as $\sum_{\iota \in C_1} \sum_{k:\, \iota \in F_k} x_{\iota,k}$. As each inner sum is non-increasing by (7, 8), we conclude that g_1 is non-increasing on all paths. Moreover, for $i \in C_1$, the sum $\sum_{k:\, i \in F_k} x_{i,k}$ appears in g_1 and is decreasing according to (7), thus g_1 is decreasing for each $\mathcal{Q}_i$ with $i \in C_1$.
2. g_1 is non-negative for all $\mathcal{Q}_i$ with $i \in C_1$, because all f_k are non-negative on these paths. To see this, pick an arbitrary $i \in C_1$ and an arbitrary face F_k: if $i \in F_k$, and it is the only vertex from C_1 in F_k, then $f_k(\mathbf{x}) = x_{i,k}$ is non-negative on $\mathcal{Q}_i$ by (9); if $i \in F_k$ but there is another vertex $j \in C_1$ in F_k, then $f_k(\mathbf{x}) = x_{i,k} + x_{j,k}$ is non-negative on $\mathcal{Q}_i$ by (11); if $i \notin F_k$, then for any $j \in F_k$ we have $x_{j,k} \geq 0$ by (10), and then f_k is non-negative since it is a sum of such variables. Note that g_1 can be negative for $\mathcal{Q}_j$ with $j \notin C_1$.

Similarly, we construct BMS-QLRFs $g_2, \ldots, g_d$ such that g_ℓ ranks $\mathcal{Q}_i$ for $i \in C_\ell$. Clearly $\langle g_1, \ldots, g_d \rangle$ is a BMS-LLRF for this loop.

Now suppose we have a BMS-LLRF of dimension d; we analyze what paths $\mathcal{Q}_i$ can be associated with each component, and show that for any face F_k, the three paths that are indexed by its vertices, i.e., $\mathcal{Q}_i$ for $i \in F_k$, cannot be all associated with the same component. Which clearly yields a d-coloring.

Suppose that for some face $F_k = \{i_1, i_2, i_3\}$, the paths $\mathcal{Q}_{i_1}, \mathcal{Q}_{i_2}$ and $\mathcal{Q}_{i_3}$ are associated with the same component, i.e., all ranked by the same function, say g. Thus $\Delta g(\mathbf{x}'') \geq 1$ must be implied by the constraints of $\mathcal{Q}_{i_1}, \mathcal{Q}_{i_2}$ and $\mathcal{Q}_{i_3}$, independently. Now since, in each path, the only constraint with a non-zero free coefficient is (7), it follows that the coefficients of variables $x_{i_1,k}$, $x_{i_2,k}$ and $x_{i_3,k}$ in $g(\mathbf{x})$ are positive, i.e., $g(\mathbf{x}) = a_1 \cdot x_{i_1,k} + a_2 \cdot x_{i_2,k} + a_3 \cdot x_{i_3,k} + h(\mathbf{x})$ where $h(\mathbf{x})$ is a combination of other variables, and $a_1, a_2, a_3 > 0$. Similarly, $g(\mathbf{x}) \geq 0$ must be implied by the constraints of each of three paths independently. For this to hold, g must be a positive linear combination of functions constrained to be non-negative by these paths, and do not involve primed variables. Now consider variables $x_{i_1,k}$, $x_{i_2,k}$ and $x_{i_3,k}$, and note that they participate only in the following constraints in $\mathcal{Q}_{i_1}$ (left), $\mathcal{Q}_{i_2}$ (middle) and $\mathcal{Q}_{i_3}$ (right):

$$
\begin{array}{rrr}
x_{i_1,k} \geq 0 & x_{i_2,k} \geq 0 & x_{i_3,k} \geq 0 \\
x_{i_1,k} + x_{i_2,k} \geq 0 & x_{i_1,k} + x_{i_2,k} \geq 0 & x_{i_2,k} + x_{i_3,k} \geq 0 \\
x_{i_1,k} + x_{i_3,k} \geq 0 & x_{i_2,k} + x_{i_3,k} \geq 0 & x_{i_1,k} + x_{i_3,k} \geq 0
\end{array}
$$

This means that the corresponding coefficients in g, i.e., $\bar{a} = (a_1\ a_2\ a_3)$, must be equal to linear combinations of the corresponding coefficients in the above constraints. Namely, there exist $b_1, \ldots, b_9 \geq 0$ such that

$$\bar{a} = (b_1\ b_2\ b_3) \cdot \begin{pmatrix} 1\,0\,0 \\ 1\,1\,0 \\ 1\,0\,1 \end{pmatrix} \qquad \bar{a} = (b_4\ b_5\ b_6) \cdot \begin{pmatrix} 0\,1\,0 \\ 1\,1\,0 \\ 0\,1\,1 \end{pmatrix} \qquad \bar{a} = (b_7\ b_8\ b_9) \cdot \begin{pmatrix} 0\,0\,1 \\ 0\,1\,1 \\ 1\,0\,1 \end{pmatrix}$$

From these nine equations, and the constraints $b_i \geq 0$ for all i, we necessarily get $a_1 = a_2 = a_3 = 0$, which contradicts $a_1, a_2, a_3 > 0$ as we concluded before, and thus paths corresponding to $\{i_1, i_2, i_3\}$ of F_k cannot be all associated with the same component. This concludes the proof of Theorem 3.

6 Complexity of BMS-LexLinRF $(d, \mathbb{Z})$

In this section we turn to the problem BMS-LexLinRF$(d, \mathbb{Z})$, and show that it is harder than BMS-LexLinRF$(d, \mathbb{Q})$, specifically, it is Σ_2^P-complete. The class Σ_2^P is the class of decision problems that can be solved by a standard, non-deterministic computational model in polynomial time assuming access to an oracle for an NP-complete problem. I.e., $\Sigma_2^P = NP^{NP}$. This class contains both NP and coNP, and is likely to differ from them both (this is an open problem).

Theorem 4. *For $d \geq 2$, BMS-LexLinRF$(d, \mathbb{Z})$ is a Σ_2^P-complete problem.*

The rest of this section proves Theorem 4. For inclusion in Σ_2^P we use a non-deterministic procedure as in the proof of Theorem 3. Note that the procedure needs to find (or check for existence of) BMS-QLRFs over the integers, so it needs a coNP oracle. For Σ_2^P-hardness we reduce from the canonical Σ_2^P-complete problem (follows from [27, Theorem 4.1]): evaluation of sentences of the form

$$\exists X_1 \ldots X_n\ \forall X_{n+1} \ldots X_{2n}\ \neg\phi(X_1, \ldots, X_{2n}) \qquad (*)$$

where the variables X_i are Boolean and the formula ϕ is in 3CNF form. Thus, ϕ is given as a collection of m clauses, $C_1, \ldots, C_m$, each clause C_i consisting of three literals $L_i^j \in \{X_1, \ldots, X_{2n}, \neg X_1, \ldots, \neg X_{2n}\}$, $1 \leq j \leq 3$. The reduction is first done for $d = 2$, and later extended to $d > 2$ as well.

Let us first explain a well-known approach for reducing satisfiability of a Boolean formula ϕ to satisfiability of integer linear constraints. We first associate each literal L_i^j with an integer variables $x_{i,j}$. Note that the same Boolean variable (or its complement) might be associated with several constraint variables. Let C be the set of (1) all conflicting pairs, that is, pairs $((i,j),(r,s))$ such that L_i^j is the complement of L_r^s; and (2) pairs $((i,j),(i,j'))$ with $1 \leq j < j' \leq 3$, i.e., pairs of literals that appear in the same clause. We let $\mathcal{F}$ be a conjunction of the constraints: $x_{i,j} + x_{r,s} \leq 1$ for each $((i,j),(r,s)) \in C$; and $0 \leq x_{i,j} \leq 1$ for each $1 \leq i \leq m$ and $1 \leq j \leq 3$. An assignment for $x_{i,j}$ that satisfies $\mathcal{F}$ is called a *non-conflicting assignment*, since if two variables correspond to conflicting literals (or to literals of the same clause) they cannot be assigned 1 at the same time. The next Lemma relates integer assignments with assignments to the Boolean variables of $(\star)$. Given a literal L, i.e., X_v or $\neg X_v$, we let $\texttt{lsum}(L)$ be the sum of all $x_{i,j}$ where $L_i^j \equiv L$ (we use 0 and 1 for *false* and *true*).

Lemma 6. *(A) If σ is a satisfying assignment for ϕ, then there is a non-conflicting assignment for $\mathcal{F}$ such that (1) $x_{i,1}+x_{i,2}+x_{i,3}=1$ for all $1 \le i \le m$; (2) $\sigma(X_v)=1 \Rightarrow \texttt{lsum}(\neg X_v)=0$; and (3) $\sigma(X_v)=0 \Rightarrow \texttt{lsum}(X_v)=0$.* ***(B)*** *If ϕ is unsatisfiable, then for any non-conflicting assignment for $\mathcal{F}$ there is at least one $1 \le i \le m$ such that $x_{i,1}+x_{i,2}+x_{i,3}=0$.*

Proof. **(A)** If σ satisfies ϕ, we construct a satisfying assignment for $\mathcal{F}$: first every $x_{i,j}$ is assigned the value of L_i^j, and then we turn some $x_{i,j}$ from 1 to 0 so that at most one variable of each clause is set to 1. Since we only turn 1s to 0s, when $\sigma(X_v)=1$ (resp. $\sigma(X_v)=0$) all constraint variables that correspond to $\neg X_v$ (resp. X_v) have value 0, and thus $\texttt{lsum}(\neg X_v)=0$ (resp. $\texttt{lsum}(X_v)=0$). **(B)** If $\mathcal{F}$ has a non-conflicting assignment in which $x_{i,1}+x_{i,2}+x_{i,3}=1$ for all $1 \le i \le m$, then we can construct a satisfying assignment σ for ϕ in which $\sigma(X_v)$ is $\max\left(\{x_{i,j} | L_j^i \equiv X_v\} \cup \{1-x_{i,j} | L_j^i \equiv \neg X_v\}\right)$, so ϕ is satisfiable. $\square$

Next we proceed with the reduction, but first we give an outline. We build an integer loop, call it $\mathcal{T}$, with $2n+2$ abstract transitions: $2n$ transitions named $\Psi_{v,a}$, for $1 \le v \le n$ and $a \in \{0,1\}$; plus two named Φ and Ω. These are defined so that existence of a BMS-LLRF $\langle f_1, f_2 \rangle$ for $\mathcal{T}$ implies: (1) $\Psi_{v,0}$ and $\Psi_{v,1}$, for each $1 \le v \le n$, cannot be ranked by the same f_i, and the order in which they are ranked will represent a value for the existentially-quantified variable X_v; (2) Φ cannot be ranked by f_1, and it is ranked by f_2 iff $\forall X_{n+1} \ldots X_{2n}\, \neg\phi(X_1,\ldots,X_{2n})$ is true assuming the values induced for $X_1,\ldots,X_n$ in the previous step; and (3) Ω is necessarily ranked by f_1, its only role is to force Φ to be ranked by f_2. All these points will imply that ($\star$) is true. For the other direction, if ($\star$) is true we show how to construct a BMS-LLRF $\langle f_1, f_2 \rangle$ for $\mathcal{T}$. Next we formally define the variables and abstract transitions of $\mathcal{T}$, and prove the above claims.

Variables: Loop $\mathcal{T}$ includes $4m+2n+1$ variables: (1) every literal L_i^j contributes a variable $x_{i,j}$; (2) for each $1 \le i \le m$, we add a control variable $x_{i,0}$ which is used to check if clause C_i is satisfied; (3) for each $1 \le v \le n$, we add variables $z_{v,0}$ and $z_{v,1}$ which help in implementing the existential quantification; and (4) variable w, which helps in ranking the auxiliary transition Ω.

Transitions: First we define Φ, the transition that intuitively checks for satisfiability of $\phi(X_1,\ldots,X_{2n})$. It is a conjunction of the following constraints

$$0 \le x_{i,j} \le 1 \ \wedge\ x'_{i,j} = x_{i,j} \qquad \text{for all } 1 \le i \le m,\ 1 \le j \le 3 \quad (12)$$
$$x_{i,j} + x_{r,s} \le 1 \qquad \text{for all } ((i,j),(r,s)) \in C \quad (13)$$
$$x_{i,0} \ge 0 \ \wedge\ x'_{i,0} = x_{i,0} + x_{i,1} + x_{i,2} + x_{i,3} - 1 \qquad \text{for all } 1 \le i \le m \quad (14)$$
$$z_{v,0} \ge 0 \ \wedge\ z'_{v,0} = z_{v,0} - \texttt{lsum}(X_v) \qquad \text{for all } 1 \le v \le n \quad (15)$$
$$z_{v,1} \ge 0 \ \wedge\ z'_{v,1} = z_{v,1} - \texttt{lsum}(\neg X_v) \qquad \text{for all } 1 \le v \le n \quad (16)$$
$$w' = w \quad (17)$$

Secondly, we define $2n$ transitions which, intuitively, force a choice of a Boolean value for each of $X_1,\ldots,X_n$. For $1 \le v \le n$ and $a \in \{0,1\}$, transition $\Psi_{v,a}$ is defined as a conjunction of the following constraints

$$z_{v,a} \geq 0 \ \wedge \ z'_{v,a} = z_{v,a} - 1 \tag{18}$$
$$z_{u,b} \geq 0 \qquad \text{for all } 1 \leq u \leq n, b \in \{0,1\},\ u \neq v \tag{19}$$
$$z'_{u,b} = z_{u,b} \qquad \text{for all } 1 \leq u \leq n,\ b \in \{0,1\},\ (u,b) \neq (v,a) \tag{20}$$
$$x'_{i,0} \geq 0 \ \wedge \ x'_{i,0} = x_{i,0} \qquad \text{for all } 1 \leq i \leq m \tag{21}$$
$$w \geq 0 \ \wedge \ w' = w \tag{22}$$

Finally we define the abstract transition Ω, which aids in forcing a desired form of the BMS-LLRF, and it is defined as a conjunction of the following constraints

$$w \geq 0 \ \wedge \ w' = w - 1 \tag{23}$$
$$z_{u,b} \geq 0 \ \wedge \ z'_{u,b} = z_{u,b} \qquad \text{for all } 1 \leq u \leq n,\ b \in \{0,1\} \tag{24}$$

Now, we argue that in order to have a two-component BMS-LLRF for $\mathcal{T}$, the transitions have to be associated to the two components in a particular way.

Lemma 7. *Suppose that $\langle f_1, f_2 \rangle$ is a* BMS-LLRF *for $\mathcal{T}$. Then, necessarily, the correspondence between the* BMS-LLRF *components and transitions is as follows: (i) Ω is ranked by f_1; (ii) Φ is ranked by f_2; (iii) for $1 \leq v \leq n$, one of $\Psi_{v,0}$ and $\Psi_{v,1}$ is ranked by f_1, and the other by f_2.*

Proof. An LRF for Ω must involve w, since it is the only decreasing variable, and cannot involve any $x_{i,j}$ since they change randomly. Similarly, an LRF for Φ cannot involve w as it has no lower bound, and it must involve at least one $x_{i,j}$ since no function that involves only $z_{v,a}$ variable(s) decreases for an initial state in which all $x_{i,j}$ are assigned 0. Note that such LRF cannot be non-increasing for Ω since $x_{i,j}$ change randomly in Ω. Thus, we conclude that Ω must be associated with f_1 and Φ with f_2. For the last point, for each $1 \leq v \leq n$, transitions $\Psi_{v,0}$ and $\Psi_{v,1}$ must correspond to different positions because variables that descend in one (namely $z_{v,a}$ of $\Psi_{v,a}$) are not bounded in the other (since (19) requires $u \neq v$). □

Lemma 8. *A* BMS-LLRF *of dimension two exists for $\mathcal{T}$ iff ($\star$) is true.*

Proof. Assume that a BMS-LLRF $\langle f_1, f_2 \rangle$ exists for $\mathcal{T}$, we show that ($\star$) is true. By Lemma 7 we know how the transitions are associated with the positions, up to the choice of placing $\Psi_{v,0}$ and $\Psi_{v,1}$, for each $1 \leq v \leq n$. Suppose that, for each $1 \leq v \leq n$, the one which is associated with f_2 is Ψ_{v,a_v}, i.e., $a_v \in \{0,1\}$, and let $\bar{a}_v$ be the complement of a_v. By construction we know that: (i) in Ψ_{v,a_v} the variables $z_{v,\bar{a}_v}$ and $x_{i,j}$ with $j \geq 1$ change randomly, which means that f_2 cannot involve them; and (ii) in Φ the variable w is not lower bounded, which means that f_2 cannot involve w. Since these transitions must be ranked by f_2, we can assume that f_2 has the form $f_2(\mathbf{x}, \mathbf{z}, w) = \sum_i c_i \cdot x_{i,0} + \sum_v c_v \cdot z_{v,a_v}$ where c_i and c_v are non-negative rational coefficients. We claim that ($\star$) is necessarily true; for that purpose we select the value a_v for each X_v, and next we show that this makes it is impossible to satisfy $\phi(X_1, \ldots, X_{2n})$. Assume, to the contrary, that there is a satisfying assignment σ for ϕ, such that $\sigma(X_v) = a_v$ for all $1 \leq v \leq n$. By Lemma 6 we know that we can construct an assignment to the variables $x_{i,j}$

such that (i) $x_{i,1} + x_{i,2} + x_{i,3} = 1$, for each $1 \leq i \leq m$, which means that $x'_{i,0} = x_{i,0}$ at (14); and (ii) for each $1 \leq v \leq m$, if $a_v = 0$ (resp. $a_v = 1$), then $\mathtt{lsum}(X_v) = 0$ (resp. $\mathtt{lsum}(\neg X_v) = 0$), which means that $z'_{v,a_v} = z_{v,a_v}$ at (15) (resp. (16)). Hence f_2 as described above does *not* rank Φ since none of its variables change, contradicting our assumption. We conclude that ($\star$) is true.

Now assume that ($\star$) is true, we construct a BMS-LLRF of dimension two. The assumption means that there are values $a_1, \ldots, a_n$ for the existentially-quantified variables to satisfy the sentence. Let $f_1(\mathbf{x}, \mathbf{z}, w) = w + \Sigma_{v=1}^{n} z_{v,\bar{a}_v}$ and $f_2(\mathbf{x}, \mathbf{z}, w) = \Sigma_{i=1}^{m} x_{i,0} + \sum_v z_{v,a_v}$. We claim that $\langle f_1, f_2 \rangle$ is a BMS-LLRF such that: (i) f_1 is an LRF for Ω and $\Psi_{v,\bar{a}_v}$, and non-increasing for Ψ_{v,a_v} and Φ; and (ii) f_2 is an LRF for Ψ_{v,a_v} and Φ. All this is easy to verify, except possibly that f_2 is an LRF for Φ, for which we argue in more detail. By assumption, $\phi(a_1, \ldots, a_n, X_{n+1}, \ldots, X_{2n})$ is unsatisfiable. Consider a state in which Φ is enabled; by (12, 13), this state may be interpreted as a selection of non-conflicting literals. If one of the selected literals does not agree with the assignment chosen for $X_1, \ldots, X_n$, then by (15, 16) the corresponding variable z_{v,a_v} is decreasing. Otherwise, there must be an unsatisfied clause, and the corresponding variable $x_{i,0}$ is decreasing. All other variables involved in f_2 are non-increasing, all are lower bounded, so f_2 is an LRF for Φ. □

Σ_2^P-hardness of BMS-LexLinRF$(d, \mathbb{Z})$ for $d = 2$ follows from Lemma 8. For $d > 2$, we add to $\mathcal{T}$ additional $d-2$ paths as those of Example 3; and to each original path in $\mathcal{T}$ we add $x'{=}x$ and $y'{=}y$ (x, y are used in Example 3). Then, the new loop has a BMS-LLRF of dimension d iff ($\star$) is true. This concludes the proof of Theorem 4.

7 Related Work

LLRFs appear in the classic works of Turing [28] and Floyd [16]. Automatic generation of LRFs and LLRFs for linear-constraint loops begins, in the context of logic programs, with Sohn and van Gelder [26]. For imperative programs, it begins with Colón and Sipma [10,11]. The work of Feautrier on scheduling [14,15] includes, in essence, generation of LRFs and LLRFs. All these works gave algorithms that yield polynomial time complexity (inherited from LP), except for Colón and Sipma's method which is based on LP duality and polars. The polynomial-time LP method later reappeared in [21,23]. These methods are complete over the rationals and can be used in an integer setting by relaxing the loop from integer to rational variables, sacrificing completeness. This completeness problem was pointed out (but not solved) in [21,24], while [12,14] pointed out the role of the integer hull in ensuring completeness. Bradley et al. [7] use a bisection search over the space of coefficients for inferring LRFs over the integers, which yields completeness at exponential cost (as argued in [4]).

Alias et al. [1] extended the LP approach to LLRFs, obtaining a polynomial-time algorithm which is sound and complete over the rationals (for their notion of LLRF). The (earlier) work of Bradley et al. [5] introduced BMS-LLRFs and used a "constraint-solving method"that finds such LLRFs along with supporting invariants. The method involves an exponential search for the association of paths to LLRF components, and is complete over the reals. Subsequent work used more complex extensions of the LLRF concept [6,8]. Harris et al. [17] demonstrate that it is advantageous, to a tool that is based on a CEGAR loop, to search for LLRFs instead of LRFs only. The LLRFs they use are BMS-LLRFs. Similar observations have been reported in [13] (also using BMS-LLRFs), [9] (using ADFG-LLRFs) and [19] (using a an iterative construction that extends BMS-LLRFs). Heizmann and Leike [18] generalize the constraint-based approach by defining the concept of a "template" for which one can solve using a constraint solver. They also provide a template for ADFG-LLRFs (of constant dimension). Ben-Amram [3] shows that *every* terminating monotonicity-constraint program has a *piecewise* LLRF of dimension at most $2n$. Piecewise LLRFs are also used in [29], with no completeness result, there they are inferred by abstract interpretation.

8 Conclusion

This work contributes to understanding the design space of the ranking-function method, a well-known method for termination analysis of numeric loops, as well as related analyses (iteration bounds, parallelization schedules). This design space is inhabited by several kinds of "ranking functions" previously proposed. We focused on BMS-LLRFs and compared them to other proposals of a similar nature. We characterized the complexity of finding, or deciding the existence of, BMS-LLRF for rational and integer MLC loops. We also compared these three methods regarding the dimension of the LLRF, and the complexity of optimizing the dimension, which turns out to be essentially harder for BMS-LLRFs. Given our reductions, it is easy to show that it is impossible to approximate the minimal dimension of BMS-LLRFs, in polynomial time, within a factor *smaller than* $\frac{3}{2}$, unless $P{=}NP$ for rational loops, and $\Sigma_2^P{=}\Delta_2^P$ for integer loops (see [2]).

We conclude that none of the three methods is universally preferable. Even ADFG-LLRFs, which in principle are weaker than both other methods, have an advantage, in that the algorithm for computing them may be more efficient in practice (due to solving smaller LP problems). If this is not a concern, they can be replaced by BG-LLRFs, so we are left with two, incomparable techniques. This incomparability stems from the fact that BG-LLRFs and BMS-LLRFs relax the restrictions of ADFG-LLRFs in two orthogonal directions: the first in quantifying over concrete transitions rather than abstract ones, and the second in allowing negative components. By making both relaxations, we get a new type of LLRF [19], which is as in Definition 2 but relaxing condition (5) to hold only for $j = i$, but for which the computational complexity questions are still open.

References

1. Alias, C., Darte, A., Feautrier, P., Gonnord, L.: Multi-dimensional rankings, program termination, and complexity bounds of flowchart programs. In: Cousot, R., Martel, M. (eds.) SAS 2010. LNCS, vol. 6337, pp. 117–133. Springer, Heidelberg (2010)
2. Ben-Amram, A., Genaim, S.: Complexity of Bradley-Manna-Sipma lexicographic ranking functions. In: CoRR, abs/1504.05018 (2015)
3. Ben-Amram, A.M.: Monotonicity constraints for termination in the integer domain. Logical Methods in Comput. Sci. 7(3) (2011)
4. Ben-Amram, A.M., Genaim, S.: Ranking functions for linear-constraint loops. J. ACM **61**(4), 26:1–26:55 (2014)
5. Bradley, A.R., Manna, Z., Sipma, H.B.: Linear ranking with reachability. In: Etessami, K., Rajamani, S.K. (eds.) CAV 2005. LNCS, vol. 3576, pp. 491–504. Springer, Heidelberg (2005)
6. Bradley, A.R., Manna, Z., Sipma, H.B.: The polyranking principle. In: Caires, L., Italiano, G.F., Monteiro, L., Palamidessi, C., Yung, M. (eds.) ICALP 2005. LNCS, vol. 3580, pp. 1349–1361. Springer, Heidelberg (2005)
7. Bradley, A.R., Manna, Z., Sipma, H.B.: Termination Analysis of Integer Linear Loops. In: Abadi, M., de Alfaro, L. (eds.) CONCUR 2005. LNCS, vol. 3653, pp. 488–502. Springer, Heidelberg (2005)
8. Bradley, A.R., Manna, Z., Sipma, H.B.: Termination of polynomial programs. In: Cousot, R. (ed.) VMCAI 2005. LNCS, vol. 3385, pp. 113–129. Springer, Heidelberg (2005)
9. Brockschmidt, M., Cook, B., Fuhs, C.: Better termination proving through cooperation. In: Sharygina, N., Veith, H. (eds.) CAV 2013. LNCS, vol. 8044, pp. 413–429. Springer, Heidelberg (2013)
10. Colón, M., Sipma, H.: Synthesis of linear ranking functions. In: Margaria, T., Yi, W. (eds.) TACAS 2001. LNCS, vol. 2031, pp. 67–81. Springer, Heidelberg (2001)
11. Colón, M., Sipma, H.: Practical methods for proving program termination. In: Brinksma, D., Larsen, K.G. (eds.) CAV 2002. LNCS, vol. 2404, pp. 442–454. Springer, Heidelberg (2002)
12. Cook, B., Kroening, D., Rümmer, P., Wintersteiger, C.M.: Ranking function synthesis for bit-vector relations. Formal Methods in System Design **43**(1), 93–120 (2013)
13. Cook, B., See, A., Zuleger, F.: Ramsey vs. lexicographic termination proving. In: Piterman, N., Smolka, S.A. (eds.) TACAS 2013 (ETAPS 2013). LNCS, vol. 7795, pp. 47–61. Springer, Heidelberg (2013)
14. Feautrier, P.: Some efficient solutions to the affine scheduling problem. I. One-dimensional time. Int. J. Parallel Prog. **21**(5), 313–347 (1992)
15. Feautrier, P.: Some efficient solutions to the affine scheduling problem. II. Multi-dimensional time. Int. J. Parallel Prog. **21**(6), 389–420 (1992)
16. Floyd, R.W.: Assigning meanings to programs. Proc. Symp. Appl. Math. **XIX**, 19–32 (1967)
17. Harris, W.R., Lal, A., Nori, A.V., Rajamani, S.K.: Alternation for termination. In: Cousot, R., Martel, M. (eds.) SAS 2010. LNCS, vol. 6337, pp. 304–319. Springer, Heidelberg (2010)
18. Leike, J., Heizmann, M.: Ranking templates for linear loops. In: Ábrahám, E., Havelund, K. (eds.) TACAS 2014 (ETAPS). LNCS, vol. 8413, pp. 172–186. Springer, Heidelberg (2014)

19. Larraz, D., Oliveras, A., Rodríguez-Carbonell, E., Rubio, A.: Proving termination of imperative programs using Max-SMT. In: Formal Methods in Computer-Aided Design, FMCAD 2013, pp. 218–225. IEEE (2013)
20. László, L.: Coverings and colorings of hypergraphs. In: Proceedings of the 4th Southeastern Conference on Combinatorics, Graph Theory, and Computing, pp. 3–12 (1973)
21. Mesnard, F., Serebrenik, A.: Recurrence with affine level mappings is P-time decidable for CLP(R). TPLP **8**(1), 111–119 (2008)
22. Phelps, K.T., Rödl, V.: On the algorithmic complexity of coloring simple hypergraphs and steiner triple systems. Combinatorica **4**(1), 79–88 (1984)
23. Podelski, A., Rybalchenko, A.: A complete method for the synthesis of linear ranking functions. In: Steffen, B., Levi, G. (eds.) VMCAI 2004. LNCS, vol. 2937, pp. 239–251. Springer, Heidelberg (2004)
24. Rybalchenko, A.: Temporal verification with transition invariants. Ph.D. thesis, Universität des Saarlandes (2004)
25. Schrijver, A.: Theory of Linear and Integer Programming. John Wiley and Sons, New York (1986)
26. Sohn, K., Van Gelder, A.: Termination detection in logic programs using argument sizes. In: Rosenkrantz, D.J. (ed.) Symposium on Principles of Database Systems, pp. 216–226. ACM Press, New York (1991)
27. Stockmeyer, L.J.: The polynomial-time hierarchy. Theor. Comput. Sci. **3**(1), 1–22 (1976)
28. Turing, A.M.: Checking a large routine. In: Report of a Conference on High Speed Automatic Calculating Machines, pp. 67–69, 1948. reprinted. In: The early British computer conferences, Charles Babbage Institute Reprint Series For The History Of Computing, vol. 14. MIT Press (1989)
29. Urban, C., Miné, A.: An abstract domain to infer ordinal-valued ranking functions. In: Shao, Z. (ed.) ESOP 2014 (ETAPS). LNCS, vol. 8410, pp. 412–431. Springer, Heidelberg (2014)

Measuring with Timed Patterns

Thomas Ferrère[1], Oded Maler[1], Dejan Ničković[2], and Dogan Ulus[1(✉)]

[1] VERIMAG, CNRS and the University of Grenoble-Alpes, Gieres, France
[2] AIT Austrian Institute of Technology GmbH, Vienna, Austria
{thomas.ferrere,oded.maler,dogan.ulus}@imag.fr,
dejan.nickovic@ait.ac.at

Abstract. We propose a declarative measurement specification language for quantitative performance evaluation of hybrid (discrete-continuous) systems based on simulation traces. We use timed regular expressions with events to specify patterns that define segments of simulation traces over which measurements are to be taken. In addition, we associate measure specifications over these patterns to describe a particular type of performance evaluation (maximization, average, etc.) to be done over the matched signal segments. The resulting language enables expressive and versatile specification of measurement objectives. We develop an algorithm for our measurement framework, implement it in a prototype tool, and apply it in a case study of an automotive communication protocol. Our experiments demonstrate that the proposed technique is usable with very low overhead to a typical (computationally intensive) simulation.

1 Introduction

Verification consists in checking whether system behaviors, sequences of states and events, satisfy some specifications. These specifications are expressed in a formalism, for example temporal logic, with well-defined semantics such that the satisfaction or violation of a property φ by a behavior w can be computed based on φ and w. To perform exhaustive formal verification, property φ is typically converted into an automaton $\mathcal{A}_{\neg\varphi}$ that accepts only violating sequences which is later composed with the system model and checked for emptiness. Such specifications are also used in a more lightweight and scalable form of verification (known as *runtime verification* in software and *assertion checking* in hardware) where *individual* behaviors are checked for property satisfaction. In this context, the formal specification language can be used to automatically derive *property monitors* rather than inspect execution traces manually or program monitors by hand. The specification formalism allows us to focus on the observable properties of the system we are interested in and write them in a *declarative* way, separated from their implementation. It is this concept that we export from the qualitative to the quantitative world.

Properties offer a purely *qualitative* way to evaluate systems and their behaviors: correct or incorrect. There are many contexts, however, where we want also

D. Kroening and C.S. Păsăreanu (Eds.): CAV 2015, Part II, LNCS 9207, pp. 322–337, 2015.
DOI: 10.1007/978-3-319-21668-3_19

to associate *quantitative* measures with systems and their executions. Consider for example a real-time system with both safety-critical and non-critical aspects, evaluated according to the temporal distance between pairs of *request* and *service* events. Its safety-critical part will be evaluated according to whether some distance goes beyond a hard deadline. In contrast, its non-critical part is typically evaluated based on quality-of-service performance measures which are numerical in nature, such as the average response time or throughput.

Quantitative measures are used heavily in the design of cyber-physical systems involving heterogeneous components of computational and physical natures. Such systems exhibit continuous and hybrid behaviors and are often designed using modeling languages such as Simulink, Modelica or hardware description languages. These models are analyzed using a combination of numerical and discrete-event simulation, producing traces from which performance measures are extracted to evaluate design quality. Measures are computed by applying various operations such as summation/integration, arithmetical operations, max-min, etc. to certain segments of the simulation trace. The boundaries of these segments are defined according to the occurrence of certain *events* and *patterns* in the trace. When the measures are simple they are realized by inserting additional observer blocks to the system model but when they are more complex, they are extracted using manually-written (and error prone) procedural scripts that perform computations over the traces.

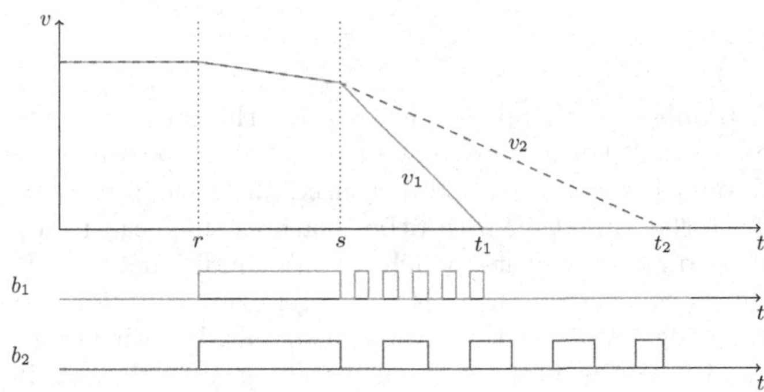

Fig. 1. Stopping distance measurement for anti-lock brake systems.

We illustrate how measurements can be used to compare two correct implementations of an anti-lock brake system (ABS), which prevents wheels from locking during heavy braking or on slippery roads. Figure 1 depicts braking control signals b_1 and b_2 and velocity signals v_1 and v_2 for two controller models C_1 and C_2. The driver starts to brake fully at $t = r$ and then the ABS takes control at $t = s$ and applies rapid pulsation to prevent locking. Both controllers C_1 and C_2 satisfy the anti-lock property but we also want to compare the distance covered during their respective breaking periods. These periods are identified as those where signal b matches some braking pattern, and are the intervals (r, t_1)

for C_1 and (r, t_2) for C_2. Integrating v_i over respective intervals (r, t_i) for $i = 1..2$ we get a numerical measure and conclude that C_1 performs better.

In this paper we propose a declarative and formal *measure specification language* for automatically extracting measures from hybrid discrete-continuous traces. The patterns that define the scope of measurements are expressed using a variant of the *timed regular expressions* (TRE) of [2,3], specially adapted for this purpose by adding preconditions, postconditions and events. An additional language layer is used to define the particular measures applied to the matching segments. The actual extraction of the measures takes advantage of the recent pattern matching procedure introduced in [19] for computing the set of segments of a Boolean signal that match a timed regular expression. In the general case, the number of such matches can be uncountable and the procedure of [19] represents them as a finite union of zones. In our language, where pattern boundaries are punctual events, we obtain a finite number of matches.

The resulting framework provides a step toward making the common practice of quantitative measurement extraction more rigorous, bridging the gap between qualitative verification and quantitative performance evaluation. We demonstrate the applicability of our approach using the Distributed System Interface (DSI3) standard protocol [15] developed by the automotive industry. We formalize in our language measurements of some features described in the standard, extract them from simulation traces and report the performance of our prototype implementation.

Related Work

The approach proposed in this paper builds upon the timed regular expressions introduced in [2,3] and shown there to be equivalent in expressive power to timed automata. We omit the renaming operator used for this expressivity theoretical result and enrich the formalism with other features that lead to a pattern language dedicated to measurements, which we call conditional TRE. Precondition and postcondition constraints allow us to express zero-duration events such as rising and falling edges of dense-time Boolean signals. Focusing on patterns that start and end with an event, the pattern matching algorithm of [19] returns a finite number of matching segments.

Our approach differs in several respects from monitoring procedures based on real-time temporal logics and their extensions to real-valued signals such as STL [16]. In a nutshell here is the difference between satisfaction in temporal logic and matching in regular expression. For any temporal logic with future operators, satisfaction of φ by a behavior w is defined as $(w, 0) \models \varphi$. To compute this satisfaction value of φ at 0 we need to compute $(w, t) \models \psi$ for some subformulas ψ of φ and some time $t \geq 0$, in other words determine whether some *suffix* of w satisfies ψ. This can be achieved by associating with every formula φ a satisfaction signal relative to w which is true for every t such that $(w, t) \models \varphi$. On the other hand, the matching of a regular expression φ in w is not defined relative to a single time point but to a *pair* of points (t, t') such that the segment of w between t and t' satisfies the expression. This property of regular expressions makes them ideal for defining intervals that match patterns.

The recent work on assertion-based features [7] is similar in spirit to ours. The authors propose an approach for quantitative evaluation of mixed-signal design properties expressed as regular expressions. In contrast to our work, the regular expressions are extended with local variables, which are used to explicitly store values of interest, such as the beginning and the end time of a matched pattern. This work addresses the problem of measuring properties (features) of hybrid automata models using formal methods. We also mention the extension to TRE proposed in [13] that combines specification of real-time events and states occurring in continuous-time signals. Their syntax and primitive constructs are inspired by and extend industrial standards PSL [10] and SVA [20]. This work focuses on a translation from TRE to timed automata acceptors, but does not address the problem of pattern matching an expression on a concrete trace.

In the context of modeling resource-constrained computations, quantitative languages [6] were studied as generalizations of formal languages in which traces are associated with a real number rather than a Boolean value. The authors use weighted automata to define several classes of quantitative languages and determine the trace values by computing maximum, limsup, liminf, limit average and discounted sum over a (possibly infinite) trace. The ideas of quantitative languages are further extended in [14], by defining the *model measuring* problem. The model checking problems of TCTL and LTL are extended in [1,11,21] to a model measuring paradigm by parameterizing the bounds of the temporal operators. The authors propose algorithms for identifying minimum and maximum parameter values for which the model satisfies the temporal formula. A similar extension is proposed in [4] for signal temporal logic (STL), where both the temporal bounds and real-valued thresholds are written as parameters and inferred from signals. Robust interpretation of temporal logic specifications [8,9,12] is another way to associate numbers with traces according to how strongly they satisfy or violate a property.

Hardware designers and others who use block diagrams for control and signal processing often realize measurement using additional observer blocks, but these are restricted to online measurements. As a result commercial circuit simulation suites offer scripting languages or built-in functions dedicated to measurement extraction, such as the `.measure` (Synopsys) and `.extract` (Mentor Graphics) libraries. The former is structured according to the notion of *trigger* and *target* events, the measurement being performed on the segment(s) of the trace in between. This is particularly suited for timing analysis such as rise-time or propagation time. The latter is more general but relies mostly on functional composition. Absolute time of events in the trace can be found by threshold crossing functions, and then passed on as parameters to other measurement primitives to apply an aggregating function over suitable time intervals. In the approach we propose, one gains the expressiveness of the language of timed regular expression, that allow to detect complex sequences of events and states in the trace.

This facilitates repeated measurements over a sequence of specified patterns, by clearly separating the behavior description from the measure itself.

2 Timed Regular Expression Patterns

In this section, we first recall the definition of the *timed regular expressions* (TRE) from [19]. Such expressions were defined over Boolean signals and in order to use them for real-valued signals we add predicates on real values to derive Boolean signals. This straightforward extension is still not entirely suitable for defining measurement segments, for the simple reason that an arbitrary regular expression may have infinitely many matches. For example an atomic proposition p is matched by all sub-segments of a dense-time Boolean signal where p continuously holds. Consequently in the second part of this section, we propose a novel extension that we call *conditional* timed regular expressions (CTRE). This extension enables to condition the match of a TRE to a prefix and suffix, and allows defining *events* of zero duration. We define a restriction to CTRE, that we call *event-bounded* timed regular expressions (E-TRE), which guarantees that the set of patterns matching a E-TRE is always finite. Thanks to this finiteness property, we will use E-TRE as the main building block in defining our measurement specification language.

2.1 Timed Regular Expressions

Let X and B be sets of *real* and *propositional* variables and $w\ :\ [0,d] \to \mathbb{R}^m \times \mathbb{B}^n$, where $m = |X|$ and $n = |B|$, a multi-dimensional signal of length d. For a variable $v \in X \cup B$ we denote by $\pi_v(w)$ the projection of w on its component v.

A propositional variable $b \in B$ admits a negation $\neg b$, which value at time t is the opposite of that of b. For θ a concrete predicate $\mathbb{R} \to \mathbb{B}$ we may create a propositional symbol $\theta(x)$ which interpretation at time t will be given by the evaluation of θ on the value of real variable x at time t. We define the projection of w on $\neg b$ by letting $\pi_{\neg b}(w)[t] = 1 - \pi_b(w)[t]$, and the projection of w on $\theta(x)$ by letting $\pi_{\theta(x)}(w)[t] = \theta(\pi_x(w)[t])$. A *proposition* p is taken to be either a variable $b \in B$, a predicate $\theta(x)$ over some real variable x, or their negation $\neg b$ and $\neg\theta(x)$ respectively. We assume a given set of real predicates and take P the set of propositions derived from real and propositional variables as described. A signal is said to have *finite variability* if for every proposition $p \in P$ the set of discontinuities of $\pi_p(w)$ is finite.

We now define the syntax of *timed regular expressions* according to the following grammar:

$$\varphi := \epsilon \mid p \mid \varphi_1 \cdot \varphi_2 \mid \varphi_1 \cup \varphi_2 \mid \varphi_1 \cap \varphi_2 \mid \varphi^* \mid \langle\varphi\rangle_I$$

where p is a proposition of P, and I is an interval of $\mathbb{R}_+$.

The semantics of a timed regular expression φ with respect to a signal w and times $t \leq t'$ in $[0,d]$ is given in terms of a satisfaction relation $(w,t,t') \models \varphi$

inductively defined as follows:

$$\begin{array}{ll}
(w,t,t') \models \epsilon & \leftrightarrow t = t' \\
(w,t,t') \models p & \leftrightarrow t < t' \text{ and } \forall t < t'' < t',\ \pi_p(w)[t''] = 1 \\
(w,t,t') \models \varphi_1 \cdot \varphi_2 & \leftrightarrow \exists t \leq t'' \leq t',\ (w,t,t'') \models \varphi_1 \text{ and } (w,t'',t') \models \varphi_2 \\
(w,t,t') \models \varphi_1 \cup \varphi_2 & \leftrightarrow (w,t,t') \models \varphi_1 \text{ or } (w,t,t') \models \varphi_2 \\
(w,t,t') \models \varphi_1 \cap \varphi_2 & \leftrightarrow (w,t,t') \models \varphi_1 \text{ and } (w,t,t') \models \varphi_2 \\
(w,t,t') \models \varphi^* & \leftrightarrow (w,t,t') \models \epsilon \text{ or } (w,t,t') \models \varphi \cdot \varphi^* \\
(w,t,t') \models \langle \varphi \rangle_I & \leftrightarrow t' - t \in I \text{ and } (w,t,t') \models \varphi
\end{array}$$

Following the definitions in [19], we characterize the set of segments of w that match an expression φ by their *match set.* The match set of expression φ over w is the set of all pairs (t, t') such that the segment of w between t and t' matches φ.

Definition 1 (Match Set). *For any signal w and expression φ, we define their match set as*

$$\mathcal{M}(\varphi, w) := \{(t,t') \in \mathbb{R}^2 \mid (w,t,t') \models \varphi\}$$

We recall that a match set is a subset of $[0, d] \times [0, d]$ confined to the upper triangle defined by $t \leq t'$ taking t, t' the first and second coordinates of $\mathbb{R}^2$. It has been established that such a set can always be represented as a finite union of *zones*. In $\mathbb{R}^n$, zones are a special class of convex polytopes definable by intersections of inequalities of the form $x_i \geq a_i$, $x_i \leq b_i$ and $x_i - x_j \leq c_{i,j}$ or corresponding strict inequalities. We say that a zone is *punctual* when the value of each variable is uniquely defined, with for instance $a_i = b_i$ for all $i = 1..n$. We use zones in $\mathbb{R}^2$ to describe the relation between t and t' in a match set.

Theorem 1 ([19]). *For any finite variability signal w and* TRE *φ, the set $\mathcal{M}(\varphi, w)$ is a finite union of zones.*

2.2 Conditional TRE

We propose in the sequel *conditional timed regular expressions* (CTRE) that extend TRE. This extension enables to condition the match of a TRE to a prefix or a suffix. We introduce in the syntax of CTRE two new binary operators, "?" for preconditions, and "!" for postconditions. For some expressions φ_1 and φ_2 a trace w matches the expression $\varphi_1 \mathbin{?} \varphi_2$ at (t, t') if it matches φ_2 and there is an interval ending at t where w matches φ_1. Symmetrically w matches the expression $\varphi_1 \mathbin{!} \varphi_2$ at (t, t') if it matches φ_1 and there is an interval beginning at t' where w matches φ_2. We define formally the semantics of these operators for φ_1, φ_2 arbitrary CTRE and w an arbitrary signal as follows:

$$\begin{array}{lll}
(w,t,t') \models \varphi_1 \mathbin{?} \varphi_2 & \leftrightarrow & (w,t,t') \models \varphi_2 \text{ and } \exists t'' \leq t,\ (w,t'',t) \models \varphi_1 \\
(w,t,t') \models \varphi_1 \mathbin{!} \varphi_2 & \leftrightarrow & (w,t,t') \models \varphi_1 \text{ and } \exists t'' \geq t',\ (w,t',t'') \models \varphi_2
\end{array}$$

A precondition φ_1 and a postcondition φ_3 can be associated to an expression φ_2 independently as we have $\varphi_1 \mathbin{?} (\varphi_2 \mathbin{!} \varphi_3) \equiv (\varphi_1 \mathbin{?} \varphi_2) \mathbin{!} \varphi_3$ so that such expressions may be noted $\varphi_1 \,?\, \varphi_2 \,!\, \varphi_3$ without ambiguity. Associating several conditions can form a sequential condition as with $(\varphi_1 \,?\, \varphi_2) \,?\, \varphi_3 \equiv (\varphi_1 \cdot \varphi_2) \,?\, \varphi_3$, or conjoint conditions as with $\varphi_1 \,?(\varphi_2 \,?\, \varphi_3) \equiv (\varphi_1 \,?\, \varphi_3) \cap (\varphi_2 \,?\, \varphi_3)$. There are further relationships with respect to other TRE operators, which we will not detail.

2.3 TRE with Events

Another important aspect of CTRE is that they enable defining *rise* and *fall events* of zero duration associated to propositional terms. The rise edge $\uparrow p$ associated to the propositional term p is obtained by syntactic sugar as $\uparrow p := \neg p \,?\, \epsilon \,!\, p$, while the fall edge $\downarrow p$ corresponds to $\downarrow p := \uparrow \neg p$. We now define a restriction of CTRE that we call TRE *with events.* This sub-class of CTRE consists of restricting the use of conditional operators to the definition of events. The introduction of events in TRE still guarantees the finite representation of their match set.

Corollary 1 (of Theorem 1). *For any finite variability signal w and* TRE *with events φ, the set $\mathcal{M}(\varphi, w)$ is a finite union of zones.*

Proof. By induction on the expression structure. For expressions of the form $\varphi = \uparrow p$, the match set $\mathcal{M}(\varphi, w)$ is of the form $\{(t,t) : t \in R\}$. By finite variability hypothesis R is finite as contained in the set of discontinuities of p, and in particular $\mathcal{M}(\varphi, w)$ is a finite union of punctual zones. All other operators are part of the grammar of timed regular expressions, and the proof of Theorem 1 grants us the property.

In what follows we consider events to be part of the syntax of timed regular expressions, and will just write TRE instead of TRE *with events.*

Remark. Our support for events is minimal as compared to the *real-time regular expressions* of [13] where the authors use special operators ##0 and ##1 for event concatenation. Their work extends discrete-time specification languages, which have the supplementary notion of *clocks* noted @($\uparrow c$) with c a Boolean variable, and the implicit notion of *clock context.* A clock @($\uparrow c$) can then be used in conjunction with a proposition p to form a clocked event noted @($\uparrow c$) p. Such an event allows to probe the value of p at the exact times where $\uparrow c$ occurs, which we did not consider. Assuming we dispose of atomic expressions @($\uparrow c$) p holding punctually at times such that $\uparrow c$ occurs and p is true, the event concatenation ##1 can be emulated by @($\uparrow c$) p ##1 @($\uparrow d$) $q \equiv$ @($\uparrow c$) $p \cdot d^* \cdot \neg d \cdot$ @($\uparrow d$) q.

We now say that a TRE is *event-bounded* when of the form $\uparrow p$, $\psi_1 \cdot \varphi \cdot \psi_2$, $\psi_1 \cup \psi_2$, or $\psi_1 \cap \varphi$ with p a proposition, and ψ_1, ψ_2 event-bounded TRE. Such expressions, that we call E-TRE for short, have an important "well-behaving" property as follows. Given an arbitrary finitely variable signal w, an E-TRE can be matched in w only a finite number of times. In the following lemma, we demonstrate that the match set for arbitrary finite signal w and E-TRE ψ consists of a finite number of points (t, t') with t an occurrence of a begin event and t' an occurrence of an end event.

Lemma 1. *Given an* E-TRE ψ *and a signal* w*, their associated match set* $\mathcal{M}(\psi, w)$ *is* finite.

Proof. By induction on the expression structure. Consider an arbitrary signal w and an event $\uparrow p$; by finite variability assumption there are finitely many time points in w where $\uparrow p$ occurs, so that its match set relatively to w is finite. Now let ψ be an E-TRE of the form $\psi = \psi_1 \cdot \varphi \cdot \psi_2$. The signal w matches ψ on the segment (t, t') if and only if there exists some times s and s' such that w matches ψ_1 on (t, s) and matches ψ_2 on (s', t'). By induction hypothesis there are finitely many such times t, t', s and s' so that ψ itself has a finite number of matches. One can easily see that the finiteness of the match set is also preserved by unions and intersections $\psi_1 \cup \psi_2$ and $\psi_1 \cap \varphi$, which concludes our proof.

3 Measuring with Conditional TRE

In this section, we propose a language for describing mixed-signal measures, and a procedure to compute such measures. In our approach, we will use *measure patterns* based on timed regular expressions to specify signal segments of interest. More precisely, a measure pattern consists of three parts: (1) the *main* pattern; (2) the *precondition*; and (3) the *postcondition*. The main pattern is an E-TRE that specifies the portion of the signal over which the measure is taken. Using E-TRE to express main patterns ensures the finiteness of signal segments, while pre- and post- conditions expressed as general TRE allow to define additional constraints. We formally define measure patterns as follows.

Definition 2 (Measure Pattern). *A measure pattern* φ *is a* CTRE *of the form* $\alpha\,?\,\psi\,!\,\beta$*, where* α *and* β *are* TRE*, while* ψ *is an* E-TRE.

Note that preconditions and postconditions can be made optional by using ϵ as we have $\epsilon\,?\,\varphi \equiv \varphi$ and $\varphi\,!\,\epsilon \equiv \varphi$. In what follows we may use simpler formulas to express their semantic equivalent, for instance writing φ to refer to the measure pattern $\epsilon\,?\,\varphi\,!\,\epsilon$.

According to previous definitions, the match set of a measure pattern $\alpha\,?\,\psi\,!\,\beta$ gives us the set of all segments of the signal, represented as couples (t, t'), such that $(w, t, t') \models \psi$, and w satisfies both the precondition α before t and the postcondition β after t'.

Proposition 1. *For any signal* w *and a pattern* $\varphi = \alpha\,?\,\psi\,!\,\beta$*, their associated match set set is given by*

$$\begin{aligned}\mathcal{M}(\varphi, w) = \{(t, t') \,:\, \exists s \leq t \leq t' \leq s',\ & (w, s, t) \models \alpha \\ \textit{and}\ & (w, t, t') \models \psi \\ \textit{and}\ & (w, t', s') \models \beta\}\end{aligned}$$

Theorem 2 (Match Set Finiteness). *For any signal* w *and measure pattern* $\varphi = \alpha\,?\,\psi\,!\,\beta$*, their associated match set* $\mathcal{M}(\varphi, w)$ *is* finite.

Proof. This is a direct consequence of Lemma 1. The set $\mathcal{M}(\varphi, w)$ is included in $\mathcal{M}(\psi, w)$, which makes it finite.

The match set of a measure pattern may be obtained by selecting the punctual zones of $\mathcal{M}(\psi, w)$ that meet a zone of $\mathcal{M}(\alpha, w)$ at the beginning, and a zone of $\mathcal{M}(\beta, w)$ at the end. Match sets of arbitrary TRE are computable following the proof of Theorem 1. The overall procedure to compute the match set of a measure pattern appears as Algorithm 1. It uses the procedure ZONES(φ, w) as appearing in [19] which returns a set of zones whose union is equal to $\mathcal{M}(\varphi, w)$ for any timed regular expression φ and signal w. For a zone z we denote by $\pi_1(z)$ and $\pi_2(z)$ projections on its first and second coordinates respectively.

Algorithm 1. Computation of the match set $\mathcal{M}(\varphi, w)$.

Require: measure pattern $\varphi = \alpha\,?\,\psi\,!\,\beta$, signal w
Ensure: $\mathcal{M}(\varphi, w)$

$\mathcal{M}(\varphi, w) \leftarrow \emptyset$
$Z_\alpha \leftarrow$ ZONES(α, w)
$Z_\beta \leftarrow$ ZONES(β, w)
$Z_\psi \leftarrow$ ZONES(ψ, w)
for all $\{(t, t')\} \in Z_\psi$ **do**
  for all $z \in Z_\alpha, z' \in Z_\beta$ **do**
    if $t \in \pi_2(z)$ and $t' \in \pi_1(z')$ **then**
      $\mathcal{M}(\varphi, w) \leftarrow \mathcal{M}(\varphi, w) \cup \{(t, t')\}$
    end if
  end for
end for
return $\mathcal{M}(\varphi, w)$

The computation of a match set for a measure pattern φ and a signal w enables powerful pattern-driven performance evaluation of hybrid or continuous systems. Once the associated match set $\mathcal{M}(\varphi, w)$ is computed, we propose a two stage analysis of signals.

In the first step, we compute a scalar value for each segment of w that matches φ, either from absolute times of that match, or from the values of a real signal x in w during that match. A measure is then written with the syntax $\text{op}(\varphi)$ with $\text{op} \in \{\mathsf{time}, \mathsf{value}_x, \mathsf{duration}, \mathsf{inf}_x, \mathsf{sup}_x, \mathsf{integral}_x, \mathsf{average}_x\}$ being some sampling or aggregating operator. The semantics $[\![\,]\!]_w$ of these operators is given in Table 1; it associates to a measure $\text{op}(\varphi)$ and trace w a multiset containing the scalar values computed over each matched interval.[1]

In the second step, we reduce the multiset of scalar values computed over the signal matched intervals in $\mathcal{M}(\varphi, w)$ to a single scalar. Typically, given the multiset $A = [\![\text{op}(\varphi)]\!]_w$ of scalar values associated with these signal segments, this

[1] We use *multiset* semantics as several patterns may have exactly the same measured value, in which case *set* semantics would not record its number of occurrences.

Table 1. Standard measure operators.

$$
\begin{aligned}
[\![\mathsf{time}(\uparrow p)]\!]_w &= \{t \,:\, (t,t) \in \mathcal{M}(\uparrow p, w)\}\\
[\![\mathsf{value}_x(\uparrow p)]\!]_w &= \{\pi_x(w)[t] \,:\, (t,t) \in \mathcal{M}(\uparrow p, w)\}\\
[\![\mathsf{duration}(\varphi)]\!]_w &= \{t' - t \,:\, (t,t') \in \mathcal{M}(\varphi, w)\}\\
[\![\mathsf{inf}_x(\varphi)]\!]_w &= \{\min_{t \le \tau \le t'} \pi_x(w)(\tau) : (t,t') \in \mathcal{M}(\varphi, w)\}\\
[\![\mathsf{sup}_x(\varphi)]\!]_w &= \{\max_{t \le \tau \le t'} \pi_x(w)(\tau) \,:\, (t,t') \in \mathcal{M}(\varphi, w)\}\\
[\![\mathsf{integral}_x(\varphi)]\!]_w &= \{\textstyle\int_t^{t'} \pi_x(w)(\tau)d\tau \,:\, (t,t') \in \mathcal{M}(\varphi, w)\}\\
[\![\mathsf{average}_x(\varphi)]\!]_w &= \{\textstyle\frac{1}{t'-t}\int_t^{t'} \pi_x(w)(\tau)d\tau \,:\, (t,t') \in \mathcal{M}(\varphi, w)\}
\end{aligned}
$$

phase consists in computing standard statistical indicators over A, such as the average, maximum, minimum or standard deviation. This final step is optional, the set of basic measurements sometimes provides sufficient information.

Anti-lock Brake System Example. We now refer back to our first example from Fig. 1 and propose measure pattern formalization to evaluate performance of the controller. We first formalize the pattern of a brake control signal b under a (heavy) braking situation. The main pattern ψ starts with a rise event on b and a braking period with the duration in I, continues with one or more pulses with duration in J, and ends with a fall event on b:

$$\psi := \uparrow b \cdot \langle b \rangle_I \cdot \langle \neg b \cdot b \rangle_J^+ \cdot \downarrow b$$

We also need to ensure that the speed should be zero at the end of braking situation, with the postcondition $\beta := (v \le 0)$. Finally, we can measure the stopping distance using the expression

$$\mathsf{integral}_v(\psi \,!\, \beta)$$

integrating v over intervals matching the measure pattern.

4 Case Study

4.1 Distributed Systems Interface

Distributed systems interface (DSI3) is a flexible and powerful bus standard [15] developed by the automotive industry. It is designed to interconnect multiple remote sensor and actuator devices to a controller. The controller interacts with the sensor devices via so-called *voltage* and *current lines*. In this paper we focus on two phases of the DSI3 protocol:

- the initialization phase called the *discovery mode*;
- one of the stationary phases called the *command and response mode*.

In the discovery mode, prior to any interaction the power is turned on, resulting in a voltage ramp from 0V to V_{high}. The communication is initiated by the controller that probes the presence/absence of sensors by emitting analog pulses on the voltage line. Connected sensor devices respond in turn with another pulse sent over the current line. At the end of this interaction, a final short pulse is sent to the sensors interfaces, marking the end of the discovery mode.

In the command and response mode, the controller sends a command to the sensor as a series of pulses (or pulse train) on the voltage line, which transmits its response by another pulse train on the current line. For power-demanding applications the command-response pairs are followed by a power pulse, which goes above V_{high}. This allows the sensor to load a capacitor used for powering its internal operation.

The DSI3 standard provides a number of ordering and timing requirements that determine correct communication between the controller and the sensor devices: (1) minimal time between the power turned on and first discovery pulse; (2) maximal duration of discovery mode; (3) expected time between two consecutive discovery pulses; (4) expected time between command and response. Figure 2 illustrates the discovery mode in the DSI3 protocol and provides a high-level overview of its ordering and timing requirements. In this example, the controller probes five sensor interfaces.

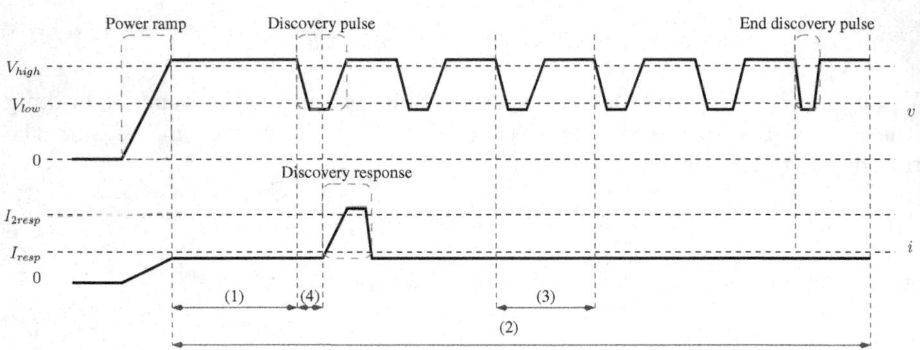

Fig. 2. DSI3 discovery mode – overview.

The correctness of a DSI3 protocol implementation in an automotive airbag system was studied in [17]. The above requirements were formalized as assertions expressed in *signal temporal logic* (STL) and the monitoring tool AMT [18] was used to evaluate the simulation traces. In this paper we do more than checking correctness, but evaluate the performance of a controller and sensor implementation. We use measure patterns to specify signal segments of interest and define several measures within the framework introduced in Sect. 3. We study two specific measures: (1) the time between consecutive discovery pulses; and (2) the amount of energy transmitted to the sensor through power pulses.

In order to generate simulation traces, we model our system as follows: the controller is a voltage-source, and the sensor is a current-source in parallel with a resistive-capacitive load. The schematic is shown in Fig. 3. During the discovery phase the load is disabled; the voltage source generates randomized pulses in which the time between two discovery pulses has a Gaussian distribution with a mean of 250μs and a standard deviation of 3.65μs. During the power pulses of the command and response mode, the load is enabled and randomized, with $C = 120$nF and R uniformly distributed in the range $[25\Omega, 35\Omega]$. Threshold levels are 4.6V low, 7.8V high, 8.3V power, and 11.5V idle.

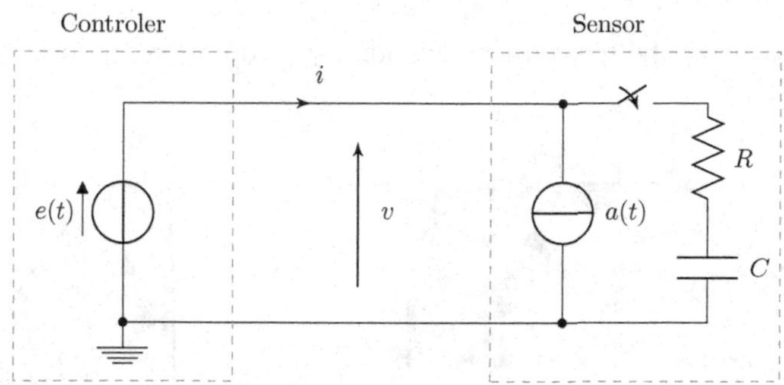

Fig. 3. Electrical model of the system.

4.2 Measurements

Time Between Consecutive Discovery Pulses. In order to characterize a discovery pulse, we first define three regions of interest – when the voltage v is (1) below V_{low}; (2) between V_{low} and V_{high}; and (3) above V_{high}. We specify these regions with the following predicates:

$$\begin{aligned} v_l &\equiv v \leq V_{low} \\ v_b &\equiv V_{low} \leq v \leq V_{high} \\ v_h &\equiv v \geq V_{high} \end{aligned}$$

Next, we describe the shape of a discovery pulse. Such a pulse starts at the moment when the signal v moves from v_h to v_b. The signal then must go into v_l, v_b and finally come back to v_h. In addition to its shape, the DSI3 specification requires the discovery pulse to have a certain duration between some d_{min} and d_{max}. This timing requirement allows distinguishing a discovery pulse from other pulses, such as the end-of-discovery pulse. We illustrate the requirements for a discovery pulse in Fig. 4-a and formalize it with the following E-TRE:

$$\psi_{dp} \equiv \downarrow(v_h) \cdot \langle v_b \cdot v_l \cdot v_b \rangle_{[d_{min}, d_{max}]} \cdot \uparrow(v_h)$$

In order to measure the time between consecutive discovery pulses, we need to characterize signal segments that we want to measure. The associated pattern shall start at the beginning of a discovery pulse and end at the beginning of the next one, as depicted by the ψ region in Fig. 4-a. It consists of a discovery pulse ψ_{dp}, followed by the voltage signal being in the v_h region, and terminating when the voltage leaves v_h. This description is not sufficient – we also need to ensure that this segment is effectively followed by another discovery pulse. Hence we add a postcondition that specifies this additional constraint. The measure pattern $\varphi_1 \equiv \alpha_1 \,?\, \psi_1 \,!\, \beta_1$ is formalized as follows.

$$\begin{aligned}\alpha_1 &\equiv \epsilon \\ \psi_1 &\equiv \psi_{dp} \cdot v_h \cdot \downarrow(v_h) \\ \beta_1 &\equiv \psi_{dp}\end{aligned}$$

Finally, we evaluate the measure expression $\mu_1 := \mathsf{duration}(\varphi_1)$ over signal w.

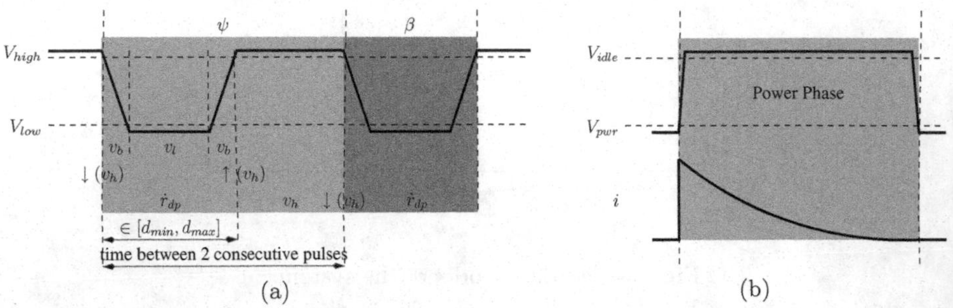

Fig. 4. (a) Consecutive discovery pulses with timing; (b) Power pulse and flow.

Energy Transfer from Controller to Sensor. In the DSI3 protocol, the discovery mode can be followed by a stationary command and respond mode. A command and respond mode sequence is a pulse train that consists of a command subsequence in the form of potential pulses between V_{high} and V_{low}, a response subsequence by means of current pulses between 0 and I_{resp}, and finishes by a power pulse rising to potential V_{idle} in which a large current can be drawn by the sensor. We first characterize the power pulse as depicted in Fig. 4-b. It occurs when the voltage goes from below V_{pwr} to above V_{idle}, and back under V_{pwr}. The three regions of interest are specified with the following predicates.

$$\begin{aligned}v_h &\equiv v \geq V_{pwr} \\ v_t &\equiv V_{pwr} \leq v \leq V_{idle} \\ v_p &\equiv v \geq V_{idle}\end{aligned}$$

Hence the pattern specifying a power pulse is expressed as

$$\psi_2 \equiv \uparrow(v_h) \cdot v_t \cdot v_p \cdot v_t \cdot \downarrow(v_h)$$

The measure pattern does not have pre- or post-conditions as all other communications occur with v below V_{idle}, hence $\alpha_2 = \beta_2 = \epsilon$. The measure pattern φ_2

is equivalent to its main pattern ψ_2. Given v the voltage and i the current on the communication line, the energy transfered to the sensor is given by the area under the signal $v \times i$ between the start and end of power pulse. We assume that such a signal is given in the simulation trace w, and evaluate the measure expression $\mu_2 := \mathsf{integral}_{v \times i}(\psi_2)$ over signal w.

4.3 Experimental Results

We extended the prototype tool developed in [19] with algorithms for matching zero-duration events and conditional TRE as appearing in measure patterns, and with the support of measure operations introduced in Sect. 3. The implementation was done in Python and uses the C library from IF [5] for computing operations on zones. For our experiment we apply a scenario according to which our electrical model is switched on/off 100 times in sequence to stress the discovery mode of DSI3. The set of traces we generate conform to the discovery, and command-and-response modes of the protocol. We then compute match sets for properties presented in Sect. 4.2 over these simulation traces using our prototype implementation. In Fig. 5, we depict measurement results using histograms. The distribution of the times between two discovery pulses follows a normal distribution according to the timing parameters used to generate it. The energy transfered to the sensor through power pulses has a flatter distribution as the result of a uniformly distributed load resistance value.

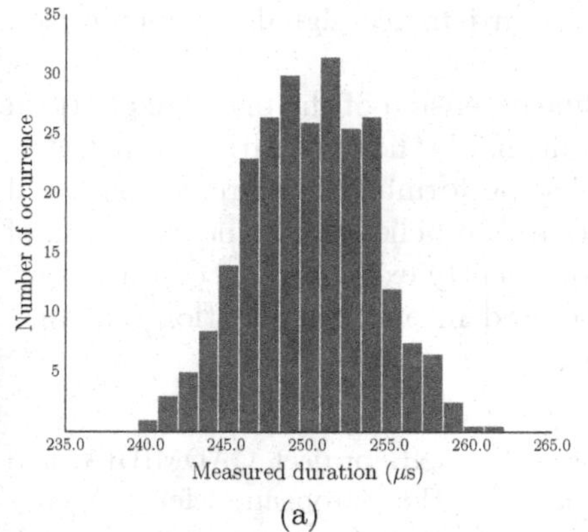

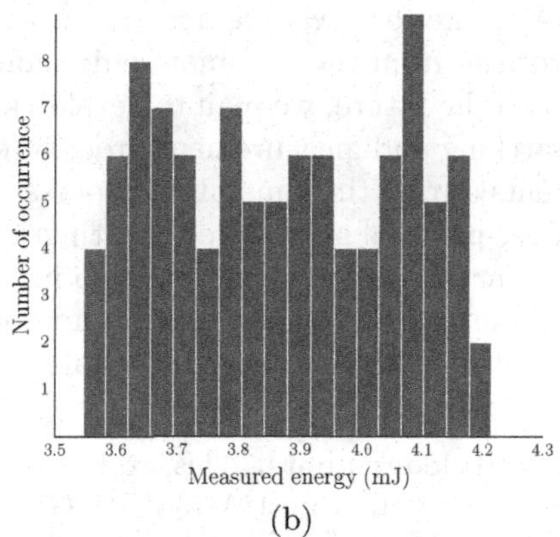

Fig. 5. (a) Distribution of μ_1, the time between two consecutive discovery pulses; (b) Distribution of μ_2, the energy transmitted per power pulse.

We then compared the execution times to compute measurements, using a periodic sampling with different sampling rates – note that our method supports variable step sampling without extra cost. The computation times are given in Table 2 with the detailed computation time needed for predicate evaluation (T_p), match set computation (T_m), measure aggregation (T_a) and total computation time (T). Computation of match sets does not depend on the number of samples but on the number of uniform intervals of atomic propositions; evaluation of real predicates by linear interpolation, and computing measures like integration can be done in time linear in the number of samples.

Table 2. Computation times (s)

	Measure μ_1				Measure μ_2			
# samples	T_p	T_m	T_a	T	T_p	T_m	T_a	T
1M	0.047	0.617	0.000	**0.664**	0.009	0.004	0.011	**0.024**
5M	0.197	0.612	0.000	**0.809**	0.050	0.005	0.047	**0.103**
10M	0.386	0.606	0.000	**0.992**	0.101	0.005	0.100	**0.216**
20M	0.759	0.609	0.000	**1.368**	0.203	0.005	0.260	**0.468**

5 Conclusion and Future Work

We presented a formal measurement specification language that can be used for evaluating cyber-physical systems based on their simulation traces. Starting from a declarative specification of the patterns that should be matched in the segments to be measured, we apply a pattern matching algorithm for timed regular expressions to find out the scope of measurements. The applicability of our framework was demonstrated on a standard mixed-signal communication protocol from the automotive domain.

In the future, we plan to develop an online extension of the presented pattern matching and measurement procedure. It will enable the application of measurements during the simulation process as well as performing measurements on real cyber-physical systems during their execution. We believe that the extension of regular expressions that we introduced is sufficiently expressive to capture common mixed signal properties, and could be used in other application domains, something that we intend to explore further.

Acknowledgements. This work was supported by ANR project CADMIDIA, and the MISTRAL project A-1341-RT-GP coordinated by the European Defence Agency (EDA) and funded by 8 contributing Members (France, Germany, Italy, Poland, Austria, Sweden, Netherlands and Luxembourg) in the framework of the Joint Investment Programme on Second Innovative Concepts and Emerging Technologies (JIP-ICET 2).

References

1. Alur, R., Etessami, K., La Torre, S., Peled, D.: Parametric temporal logic for model measuring. ACM Trans. Comput. Logic (TOCL) **2**(3), 388–407 (2001)

2. Asarin, E., Caspi, P., Maler, O.: A Kleene theorem for timed automata. In: Logic in Computer Science (LICS), pp. 160–171 (1997)
3. Asarin, E., Caspi, P., Maler, O.: Timed regular expressions. J. ACM **49**(2), 172–206 (2002)
4. Asarin, E., Donzé, A., Maler, O., Nickovic, D.: Parametric identification of temporal properties. In: Khurshid, S., Sen, K. (eds.) Runtime Verification. LNCS, vol. 7186, pp. 147–160. Springer, Heidelberg (2011)
5. Bozga, M., Graf, S., Mounier, L.: IF-2.0: a validation environment for component-based real-time systems. In: Brinksma, E., Larsen, K.G. (eds.) CAV 2002. LNCS, vol. 2404, pp. 343–348. Springer, Heidelberg (2002)
6. Chatterjee, K., Doyen, L., Henzinger, T.A.: Quantitative languages. ACM Trans. Comput. Logic (TOCL) **11**(4), 23 (2010)
7. Bruto da Costa, A.A., Dasgupta, P.: Formal interpretation of assertion-based features on AMS designs. IEEE Des. Test **32**(1), 9–17 (2015)
8. Donzé, A., Ferrère, T., Maler, O.: Efficient robust monitoring for STL. In: Sharygina, N., Veith, H. (eds.) CAV 2013. LNCS, vol. 8044, pp. 264–279. Springer, Heidelberg (2013)
9. Donzé, A., Maler, O.: Robust satisfaction of temporal logic over real-valued signals. In: Chatterjee, K., Henzinger, T.A. (eds.) FORMATS 2010. LNCS, vol. 6246, pp. 92–106. Springer, Heidelberg (2010)
10. Eisner, C., Fisman, D.: A Practical Introduction to PSL. Springer, New York (2006)
11. Emerson, E.A., Trefler, R.J.: Parametric quantitative temporal reasoning. In: Logic in Computer Science (LICS), pp. 336–343 (1999)
12. Fainekos, G.E., Pappas, G.J.: Robustness of temporal logic specifications for continuous-time signals. Theoret. Comput. Sci. **410**(42), 4262–4291 (2009)
13. Havlicek, J., Little, S.: Realtime regular expressions for analog and mixed-signal assertions. In: Formal Methods in Computer-Aided Design, FMCAD, pp. 155–162 (2011)
14. Henzinger, T.A., Otop, J.: From model checking to model measuring. In: D'Argenio, P.R., Melgratti, H. (eds.) CONCUR 2013 – Concurrency Theory. LNCS, vol. 8052, pp. 273–287. Springer, Heidelberg (2013)
15. Distributed System Interface. DSI3 Bus Standard. DSI Consortium
16. Maler, O., Nickovic, D.: Monitoring properties of analog and mixed-signal circuits. STTT **15**(3), 247–268 (2013)
17. Nguyen, T., Ničković, D.: Assertion-based monitoring in practice – checking correctness of an automotive sensor interface. In: Lang, F., Flammini, F. (eds.) FMICS 2014. LNCS, vol. 8718, pp. 16–32. Springer, Heidelberg (2014)
18. Nickovic, D., Maler, O.: AMT: a property-based monitoring tool for analog systems. In: Raskin, J.-F., Thiagarajan, P.S. (eds.) FORMATS 2007. LNCS, pp. 304–319. Springer, Heidelberg (2007)
19. Ulus, D., Ferrère, T., Asarin, E., Maler, O.: Timed pattern matching. In: Legay, A., Bozga, M. (eds.) FORMATS 2014. LNCS, vol. 8711, pp. 222–236. Springer, Heidelberg (2014)
20. Vijayaraghavan, S., Ramanathan, M.: A Practical Guide for SystemVerilog Assertions. Springer, New York (2006)
21. Wang, F.: Parametric timing analysis for real-time systems. Inf. Comput. **130**(2), 131–150 (1996)

Automatic Verification of Stability and Safety for Delay Differential Equations

Liang Zou[1], Martin Fränzle[2], Naijun Zhan[1(✉)], and Peter Nazier Mosaad[2]

[1] State Key Laboratory of Computer Science, Institute of Software, CAS, China
znj@ios.ac.cn

[2] Department of Computing Science, C. v. Ossietzky Universität, Oldenburg, Germany

Abstract. Delay differential equations (DDEs) arise naturally as models of, e.g., networked control systems, where the communication delay in the feedback loop cannot always be ignored. Such delays can prompt oscillations and may cause deterioration of control performance, invalidating both stability and safety properties. Nevertheless, state-exploratory automatic verification methods have until now concentrated on ordinary differential equations (and their piecewise extensions to hybrid state) only, failing to address the effects of delays on system dynamics. We overcome this problem by iterating bounded degree interval-based Taylor overapproximations of the time-wise segments of the solution to a DDE, thereby identifying and automatically analyzing the operator that yields the parameters of the Taylor overapproximation for the next temporal segment from the current one. By using constraint solving for analyzing the properties of this operator, we obtain a procedure able to provide stability and safety certificates for a simple class of DDEs.

1 Introduction

"Despite [...] very satisfactory state of affairs as far as [ordinary] differential equations are concerned, we are nevertheless forced to turn to the study of more complex equations. [...] the rate of change of physical systems depends not only on their present state, but also on their past history." [2, p. iii]

Ever since we first managed to make a children's swing oscillate with ourselves sitting happily on top, all of us are perfectly aware of the impact of feedback

Martin Fränzle—Work of this author has been supported by the Deutsche Forschungsgemeinschaft as part of the Transregional Collaborative Research Center SFB/TR 14 AVACS.

Naijun Zhan—Work of this author has been supported by "973 Program" under grant No. 2014CB340701, by NSFC under grants 91118007 and 91418204, and by the CAS/SAFEA International Partnership Program for Creative Research Teams.

Peter Nazier Mosaad—Work of this author has been supported by the Deutsche Forschungsgemeinschaft as part of the Research Training Group DFG GRK 1765 SCARE.

D. Kroening and C.S. Păsăreanu (Eds.): CAV 2015, Part II, LNCS 9207, pp. 338–355, 2015.
DOI: 10.1007/978-3-319-21668-3_20

delays on the performance of control loops. The same is true for more serious applications in automatic control, where digital implementation of the controller, though adding flexibility , comes at the price of introducing increasingly relevant delays into the feedback loop between controller and plant. The sources of such delays are manifold: conversions between analog and digital signal domains, complex digital signal-processing chains enhancing, filtering, and fusing sensory signals before they enter control, sensor networks harvesting multiple sensor sources before feeding them to control, or network delays in networked control applications physically removing the controller(s) from the control path. In each such application, describing the feedback dynamics of the controlled system by conjoining the ordinary differential equations (ODEs) describing the plant dynamics with the ODEs describing control may be misleading, as the delays introduced into the feedback loop may induce significantly deviating dynamics; cf. Fig. 1 for a simple example. Delays may prompt oscillations in otherwise convergently stable feedback loops or vice versa, they can destabilize otherwise stable orbits [40], can stretch dwell times, may induce residual error that never settles, or can cause transient overshoot into unsafe operational regimes (e.g. to negative values in Fig. 1), to name just a few of the various possible effects fundamentally altering system dynamics. Unmodeled delays in a control loop thus have the potential to invalidate any stability or safety certificate obtained on the delay-free model, as delays may significantly deteriorate control performance.

Given the omnipresence of such delays in modern control schemes, the apparent lack of tools permitting their safe automatic analysis surprises. While delay differential equations (DDEs) describing system dynamics as a function

$$\frac{\mathrm{d}}{\mathrm{d}t}\boldsymbol{x}(t) = f(\boldsymbol{x}(t), \boldsymbol{x}(t-\delta_1), \ldots, \boldsymbol{x}(t-\delta_n)), \text{ with } \delta_n > \ldots > \delta_1 > 0, \quad (1)$$

of past system states have long been suggested as an adequate means of modeling delayed feedback systems [2], their tool support still seems to be confined to numerical simulation based on integration from discontinuity to discontinuity, e.g. by Matlab's `dde23` algorithm. Such numerical simulation, despite being extremely useful in system analysis, nevertheless fails to provide reliable certificates of system properties, as it is numerically approximate only — in fact, error control even is inferior to ODE simulation codes as dynamic step-size control is much harder to attain for DDEs due to the non-local effects of step-size changes. Counterparts to the plethora of techniques for safely enclosing set-based initial value problems of ODEs, be it safe interval enclosures [25,27,37], Taylor models [3,28], or flow-pipe approximations based on polyhedra [6], zonotopes [13], ellipsoids [19], or support functions [22], are thus urgently needed for DDEs. As in the ODE case, such techniques would safely (and preferably tightly) overapproximate the set of states reachable at any given time point from the set of initial values. The reason for their current lack is that DDEs are in some respect much more complex objects than ODEs: DDEs belong to the class of systems with functional state, i.e., the future (and past) is not determined by a single temporal snapshot of the state variables, yet by a segment of a trajectory. This renders the systems infinite-dimensional; in fact, as can be seen from Eq. (1), transformed copies of the initial segment of duration δ_n will generally be found in higher-order derivatives of $\boldsymbol{x}(t)$ even after arbitrarily long time.

A safe enclosure method for DDEs therefore has to manipulate computational enclosures of sets of trajectory segments $\boldsymbol{x} : [a, b] \to \mathbb{R}^n$ rather than computational enclosures of sets of states $\boldsymbol{x} \in \mathbb{R}^n$, like interval boxes, zonotopes, ellipsoids, or support functions. A reasonable data structure could be interval-based Taylor forms, being able to enclose a set of functions by a parametric Taylor series with parameters in interval form. To avoid dimension explosion incurred by the ever-growing degree of the Taylor series along the time axis, following the idea of Taylor models [3,28], we employ Taylor series of fixed degree and move higher-degree terms into the parametric uncertainty. We use this data structure to iterate bounded degree Taylor overapproximations of the time-wise segments of the solution to a DDE, thereby identifying and automatically analyzing the operator that yields the parameters of the Taylor overapproximation for the next temporal segment from the current one. By using constraint solving for analyzing the properties of this operator, we obtain an automatic procedure providing stability and safety certificates for a simple class of DDEs of the form

$$\frac{\mathrm{d}}{\mathrm{d}t}\boldsymbol{x}(t) = f(\boldsymbol{x}(t - \delta)) \tag{2}$$

with linear or polynomial $f : \mathbb{R}^n \to \mathbb{R}^n$. While this form is very restrictive, in particular excluding immediate feedback between the state vector $\boldsymbol{x}(t)$ and its dynamics $\frac{\mathrm{d}}{\mathrm{d}t}\boldsymbol{x}(t)$ in the model of the physical plant, it serves well as an illustrative example for exposing the method, and can easily be generalized by combination with the well-developed techniques for flow-pipe approximations of ODEs.

2 Related Work

Driven by the demand for safety cases (in a broad sense) for safety-critical control systems, we have over the past decades seen a rapidly growing interest in automatic verification procedures for system models involving continuous quantities and dynamics described by, a.o., differential equations. Verification problems of primary interest are thereby invariance properties concerning the dynamically reachable states and stability properties describing the long-term behavior.

Invariance properties are a prototypical safety property. A natural approach to their automatic verification is state-space exploration aiming at computing the reachable state space. Unfortunately, only very few families of restrictive linear dynamic systems feature a decidable state reachability problem [16,20]. A more generally applicable option is to compute overapproximations of the state sets reachable under time-bounded continuous dynamics, and then to embed them, e.g., into depth-bounded automatic verification by bounded model checking, or into unbounded verification by theorem proving. Among the many abstraction techniques proposed for over-approximating reachable sets of continuous dynamics given as ordinary differential equations are use of interval arithmetic [25,27,33,37], Taylor models [3,28], flow-pipe approximations based on polyhedra [6], zonotopes [13], ellipsoids [19], or support functions [22], and abstraction based on discovering invariants [23,31,32,36]. There are several bounded model checkers available for continuous and hybrid systems, like iSAT-ODE [8], Flow* [5], and dReach [18], to name just a few. Theorem provers for ODE dynamics and hybrid systems are also available, e.g., KeYmaera [30] or HHL Prover [41].

Safety verification is complemented by automatic procedures for providing certificates of stability. Most such methods are based on the automatic construction of Lyapunov functions [4] or piecewise Lyapunov functions [29]. Again, such procedures can only be complete for restricted, mostly linear cases, though incomplete extensions to rather general classes exist, e.g. [24].

Delay differential equations (DDEs) [2] model continuous processes with delayed feedback, be it natural dynamic systems [1] or technical applications in automatic control, which increasingly feature feedback delay due to, a.o., communication networks. As the delay substantially alters system behavior, verification of properties of DDE is an independent area of research. Albeit there is extensive literature on the theory of DDEs, obviously also addressing the question of how to manually verify stability, fully automatic proof procedures for such models are currently lacking and thus provide an open area of research. To this end, it should be noted that DDE model a richer class of delay phenomena than sample-and-hold devices or sampled controllers, even if the latter come equipped with delayed output delivery. Such devices can well be modeled by hybrid automata, providing an infinite-state yet finite-dimensional Markovian model, and consequently can be analyzed by the corresponding verification tools. The functional state of DDE, in contrast, is infinite-dimensional.

3 Overview of Our Approach

A reasonably small delay does not affect the solution of a linear ordinary differential equation (ODE) much, such that analyzing the ODE derived from the DDE by ignoring the delays may be indicative of the overall behavior. Unfortunately, it is unclear how much delay can be ignored in general, as this depends on the property under investigation. The following example demonstrates the difference between a DDE and the related ODE obtained by neglecting delays.

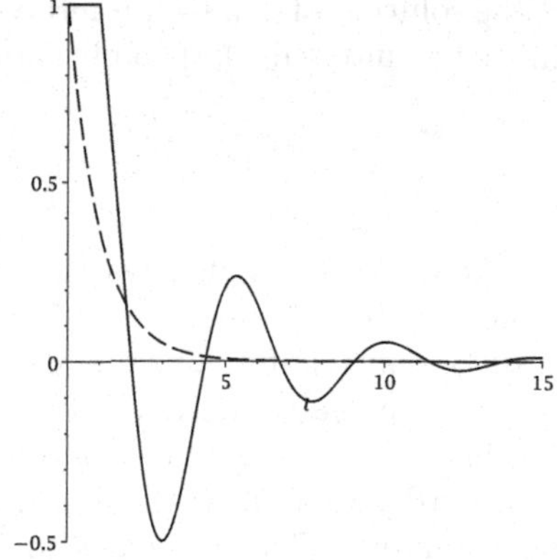

Fig. 1. Solutions to the ODE $\dot{x} = -x$ (dashed graph) and the related DDE $\dot{x}(t) = -x(t-1)$ (solid line), both on similar initial conditions $x(0) = 1$ and $x([0,1]) \equiv 1$, respectively.

In Fig. 1, the dashed and solid lines represent the solution of the ODE $\dot{x} = -x$ without delay and of the related DDE $\dot{x}(t) = -x(t-1)$ with 1 second delay, respectively. Both are given as initial value problems, where for the ODE we assume an initial value $x(0) = 1$, which we generalize for the DDE to $x([0,1]) \equiv 1$. Figure 1 demonstrates that the delay tremendously prolongs dwell times, as well as invalidates some safety properties: the dashed line (representing the ODE behavior) always stays above the horizontal axis whereas, in contrast, the solid line (representing the DDE solution) visits the negative range repeatedly. Even though the difference between the solutions of the ODE and the DDE becomes smaller when the delay turns smaller, it is in general hard to say how small a delay may ensure conservation of some safety property valid of the ODE. Hence, it is necessary to have native methods for analyzing the behaviour of DDE.

3.1 Computing Enclosures by Taylor Models

In the following, we will as a running example show how to analyze the DDE

$$\dot{x}(t) = -x(t-1) \tag{3}$$

with the initial condition $x([0,1]) \equiv 1$.

The solution to the DDE (3) can be computed segment-wise by integration, computing segments of duration 1 each. As we know the initial segment, we can set $f_0(t) = 1$ for $t \in [0,1]$, and can assume that the segment number $n \in \mathbb{N}$ satisfies $n \geq 1$ in what follows. Clearly, the solution of Eq. (3) over the time interval $(n, n+1]$ can be represented by using its solution over the previous 1 second interval (i.e., the solution on $(n-1, n]$) as follows:

$$x(n+t) = x(n) + \int_{n-1}^{n-1+t} -x(s)ds, \text{ for } t \in (0,1]. \tag{4}$$

We simplify Eq. (4) by renaming $x(n+t_1)$ to $f_n(t_1)$. Thus, $f_n(t) : (0,1] \to \mathbb{R}$ is the solution of Eq. (3) on interval $(n, n+1]$, but the domain of the solution is shifted to interval $(0,1]$ to obtain a normalized presentation, i.e.,

$$f_n(t) = f_{n-1}(1) + \int_0^t -f_{n-1}(s)ds, \qquad t \in (0,1] \tag{5}$$

From Eq. (5) it follows that the degree of the solution f_n over the n-th interval will be $n-1$, e.g., 3599 after one hour. Therefore, even if the DDE easily is solvable by polynomials, its representation rapidly gets too complex to be algorithmically analyzable due to excessive degrees and number of monomials. For instance, it is hard to calculate the reachable set of the DDE in Eq. (3).

In order to address this issue, we will propose a method based on bounded-degree interval Taylor models to over-approximate the solution by polynomials with fixed degree. For instance, suppose we are trying to over-approximate the solution by polynomials of degree 2. We can then predefine a template of the form $f_n(t) = a_{n0} + a_{n1}t + a_{n2}t^2$ on interval $[n, n+1]$, where a_{n0}, a_{n1}, and a_{n2} are interval parameters able to incorporate the approximation error necessarily incurred by bounding the degree of the polynomial. Thus, the solution on the next interval can be safely over-approximated using such a Taylor model.

To compute the Taylor model, we first need to obtain the first and second derivative $f_{n+1}^{(1)}(t)$ and $f_{n+1}^{(2)}(t)$ of solution segment $n+1$ based on the preceding segment. The first derivative $f_{n+1}^{(1)}(t)$ is computed directly from Eq. (3) as

$$f_{n+1}^{(1)}(t) = -f_n(t) = -a_{n0} - a_{n1}t - a_{n2}t^2 .$$

The second derivative $f_{n+1}^{(2)}(t)$ is computed based on $f_{n+1}^{(1)}(t)$ by

$$f_{n+1}^{(2)}(t) = \frac{d\,(f_{n+1}^{(1)}(t))}{dt} = -a_{n1} - 2a_{n2}t .$$

Note that while polynomial derivative rules do in general not lift to interval Taylor series, as the interval parameters permit to cover functions locally exhibiting larger derivatives, the generation process of the interval Taylor series for the first derivative avoids this fallacy here.

Using a Lagrange remainder with fresh variable $\xi_n \in [0,1]$, we hence obtain

$$\begin{aligned} f_{n+1}(t) &= f_n(1) + \frac{f_{n+1}^{(1)}(0)}{1!}t + \frac{f_{n+1}^{(2)}(\xi_n)}{2!}t^2 \\ &= (a_{n0} + a_{n1} + a_{n2}) - a_{n0}t - \frac{a_{n1} + 2a_{n2}\xi_n}{2}t^2. \end{aligned}$$

In order to proceed towards analysis of the asymptotic behavior of the system, we in a second step derive the operator expressing the relation between Taylor coefficients in the current and the next step. By replacing $f_{n+1}(t)$ with its parametric form $a_{n+1\,0}+a_{n+1\,1}t+a_{n+1\,2}t^2$ in the above equation, one therefore derives the operator

$$\begin{bmatrix} a_{n+1\,0} \\ a_{n+1\,1} \\ a_{n+1\,2} \end{bmatrix} = \begin{bmatrix} 1 & 1 & 1 \\ -1 & 0 & 0 \\ 0 & -\frac{1}{2} & -\xi_n \end{bmatrix} \begin{bmatrix} a_{n0} \\ a_{n1} \\ a_{n2} \end{bmatrix} \tag{6}$$

mapping the coefficients of the Taylor form at step f_n to the coefficients of the Taylor form of f_{n+1}. Hence, the coefficients change every second according to the above linear operator, which can be made time-invariant (yet interval-valued) by replacing ξ_n with its interval $[0,1]$.

Having obtained such a linear and time-invariant discrete system, we can in a third step determine whether this discrete dynamic system is *asymptotically* or *robustly stable* using the method proposed in [7]. If this holds, the sequence of coefficients finally converges to an equilibrium point, which in turn implies that the DDE in Eq. (3) is also *asymptotically* or *robustly stable.*

If we are interested in safety verification rather than stability, the above operator can be iterated within *bounded model checking* (BMC), using any BMC tool built on top of an arithmetic SMT solver being able to address polynomial arithmetic, e.g. iSAT [11]. For a given safety property like $S(x) \hat{=} -1 \leq x \leq 1$, the requirement in the n-th segment translates to $\forall t \in [0,1] : S(f_n(t))$, where f_n is the Taylor form stemming from the n-th iteration of the above linear operator. Hence, the safety property $S(x)$ for system (3) becomes safety property $\forall n \in \mathbb{N}, t \in [0,1] : S(f_n(t))$ in system (6). Discharging this proof obligation in BMC requires polynomial constraint solving due to the Taylor forms involved.

We can also conduct *unbounded safety verification* by means of pursuing BMC for sufficiently many steps k_s in case our DDE is stabilizing. The corresponding upper bound k_s on the number of steps can be computed via the following procedure (please refer to [7] for details): The *asymptotic* or *robust stability* of the linear time-invariant discrete dynamic system in Eq. (6) is guaranteed by solving a linear matrix inequality given by Theorem 1, which also gives a Lyapunov function $V(a_{n0}, a_{n1}, a_{n2}, \xi_n)$ (denoted by $V(\boldsymbol{A}(n), \xi_n)$ in the following, where $\boldsymbol{A}(n)$ represents a_{n0},a_{n1}, and a_{n2}). Using the Lyapunov function, we first compute by iSAT3 the largest c such that $V(\boldsymbol{A}(n), \xi_n) \leq c \wedge \neg\mathcal{S}(f_n(t))$ is unsatisfiable. Then we calculate the minimum reduction d_m on the condition $V(\boldsymbol{A}(n), \xi_n) \geq c$, i.e.

$$d_m = \min\{V(\boldsymbol{A}(n), \xi_n) - V(\boldsymbol{A}(n+1), \xi_{n+1}) \mid V(\boldsymbol{A}(n), \xi_n) \geq c\},$$

where the constraint can be eliminated by Lagrange multipliers and d_m can be calculated by Matlab function `fmincon`. The existence of such c implies that $V(\boldsymbol{A}(n), \xi_n) \leq c \rightarrow \mathcal{S}(f_n(t))$ holds, which implies that after $k_s = \frac{V(\boldsymbol{A}(0),\xi_0)-c}{d_m}$ steps we can be sure to reside inside the safety region $S(f_n(t))$. As $V(\boldsymbol{A}(0), \xi_0)$ is linear in ξ_0 (as explained in the next section), it follows that it is monotonic or antimonic in ξ_0 and thus $\max\left(\frac{V(\boldsymbol{A}(0),0)-c}{d_m}, \frac{V(\boldsymbol{A}(0),1)-c}{d_m}\right)$ provides an upper bound for k_s. Hence, all that remains to be done is to pursue BMC for k_s steps, as safety violations can only arise transiently during those first k_s steps.

In fact, there is no need to blindly unwind and compute the BMC problems up to depth k_s. Instead, it suffices to do so until the Lyapunov function decreases to below c—which is guaranteed after at most k_s steps, but maybe faster— and then stop. Hence, we may save a lot of computations by checking for the goal $\neg\mathcal{S}(f_n(t)) \vee V(\boldsymbol{A}, \xi) \leq c$ at each step in our BMC process. If the condition holds, the bounded model checking procedure terminates immediately. Then of course we need to disambiguate cases by determining which disjunct in $\neg\mathcal{S}(f_n(t)) \vee V(\boldsymbol{A}, \xi) \leq c$ is satisfied. If the first alternative $\neg\mathcal{S}(f_n(t))$ is satisfied, then a counter-example to the safety property is found, otherwise the safety property has been certified by the BMC in at most k_s steps.

In this example, no linear (i.e., Taylor order 1) enclosure for the DDE in Eq. (3) suffices to prove the safety property $-1 \leq x \leq 1$, but the enclosure computed for degree 2 guarantees it.

4 Formal Analysis of Polynomial DDEs

In this section, we will generalize the basic idea to a general technique for polynomial DDE of shape (2). The DDE under consideration thus are of the form

$$\dot{\boldsymbol{x}}(t+\delta) = \boldsymbol{g}(\boldsymbol{x}(t)), \ \forall t \in [0, \delta] : \boldsymbol{x}(t) = \boldsymbol{p}_0(t), \tag{7}$$

where $\boldsymbol{x}$ is a state vector in $\mathbb{R}^m$, $\boldsymbol{p}_0(t)$ is a vector of polynomials in $\mathbb{R}^m[\boldsymbol{x}]$ representing the initial condition as a trajectory of the DDE in the initial δ time units, and $\boldsymbol{g}$ is a vector of polynomials in $\mathbb{R}^m[\boldsymbol{x}]$.

In order to compute an enclosure for the trajectory defined by DDE (7), we predefine a template interval Taylor form of fixed degree k as

$$\boldsymbol{f}_n(t) = \boldsymbol{a}_{n_0} + \boldsymbol{a}_{n_1} t + \cdots + \boldsymbol{a}_{n_k} t^k, \tag{8}$$

where $\boldsymbol{a}_{n_0}, \ldots, \boldsymbol{a}_{n_k}$ are interval-vector parameters. As before, $\boldsymbol{f}_n$ is used to enclose the trajectory for time interval $[n\delta, (n+1)\delta]$. In what follows, we set $\boldsymbol{f}_0(t) = \boldsymbol{p}_0(t)$ and will compute the successive $\boldsymbol{f}_n$ recursively from it. For notational convenience, we denote $[\boldsymbol{a}_{n_0}, \ldots, \boldsymbol{a}_{n_k}]$ by a matrix $\boldsymbol{A}(n)$ in $\mathbb{R}^{m \times (k+1)}$.

4.1 Constraints on Interval Parameters

As explained in Sect. 3, the trajectory induced by the DDE in Eq. (7) can be represented by a piecewise function, with the duration of each piece being the feedback delay δ. In order to compute an enclosure for the whole trajectory of the DDE, we may calculate the relation between $\boldsymbol{A}(n)$ and $\boldsymbol{A}(n+1)$. In contrast to the linear case of the previous section, we now need to exploit different orders of Lie derivatives $\boldsymbol{f}_{n+1}^{(1)}, \boldsymbol{f}_{n+1}^{(2)}, \ldots, \boldsymbol{f}_{n+1}^{(k)}$, which can be computed as follows:

$$\boldsymbol{f}_{n+1}^{(1)}(t) = \boldsymbol{g}(\boldsymbol{f}_n(t)), \boldsymbol{f}_{n+1}^{(2)}(t) = \frac{d\,\boldsymbol{f}_{n+1}^{(1)}(t)}{dt}, \ldots, \boldsymbol{f}_{n+1}^{(k)}(t) = \frac{d\,\boldsymbol{f}_{n+1}^{(k-1)}(t)}{dt}, \tag{9}$$

i.e., the first-order Lie derivative is obtained directly from Eq. (7) and the $(i+1)$-st order Lie derivative is computed from the i-th order Lie derivative by symbolic differentiation. The Taylor expansion of $\boldsymbol{f}_{n+1}(t)$ is derived from this as

$$\boldsymbol{f}_{n+1}(t) = \boldsymbol{f}_n(\delta) + \frac{\boldsymbol{f}_{n+1}^{(1)}(0)}{1!} t + \cdots + \frac{\boldsymbol{f}_{n+1}^{(k-1)}(0)}{(k-1)!} t^{k-1} + \frac{\boldsymbol{f}_{n+1}^{(k)}(\boldsymbol{\xi}_n)}{k!} t^k, \tag{10}$$

where $\boldsymbol{\xi}_n$ is a vector ranging over $[0, \delta]^m$.

From Eq. (10), by comparing the coefficients of the monomials with the same degree at the two sides, a relation between $\boldsymbol{A}_n$ and $\boldsymbol{A}_{(n+1)}$ is obtained. It can be represented as a vector of polynomial equations possibly involving $\boldsymbol{\xi}_n$, say

$$\boldsymbol{A}(n+1) = \boldsymbol{R}(\boldsymbol{A}(n), \boldsymbol{\xi}_n) \tag{11}$$

where $\boldsymbol{R}$ is a vector of polynomial functions of overall type $\mathbb{R}^{m(k+2)} \to \mathbb{R}^{m(k+1)}$.

After substituting $\boldsymbol{\xi}$ with interval $[0, \delta]$, Eq. (11) again forms a time-invariant discrete dynamic system. The stability of this system can again be determined by existing approaches, as can the bounded and unbounded model-checking problems of the original system (7). We will elaborate on the approach subsequently.

4.2 Stability of the Time-Invariant Discrete Dynamic System

In this section, we discuss how to determine the stability of the resulting time-invariant discrete dynamic system in Eq. (11), which implies stabilization of the original system (7) to a stable orbit $\boldsymbol{f}_{\to\infty}$ which cycles through every δ time units. We distinguish a *linear* and a more general *polynomial case* concerning the right-hand side $\boldsymbol{g}$ of the DDE (as well as the initial condition).

Linear $\boldsymbol{g}$: In case $\boldsymbol{g}$ in (7) is a linear function, $\boldsymbol{f}^{(1)}_{n+1}(t), \ldots, \boldsymbol{f}^{(k)}_{n+1}(t)$ are all linear in the entries of $\boldsymbol{A}(n)$ according to Eq. (9). Using Eq. (10), the equation (11) can hence be reformulated as

$$\boldsymbol{A}(n+1) = T(\boldsymbol{\xi}_n)\boldsymbol{A}(n), \tag{12}$$

with $T(\boldsymbol{\xi}_n)$ an $m \times m$-matrix whose entries are linear in the components of $\boldsymbol{\xi}_n$.

The stability analysis for a linear time-invariant discrete dynamic system of form (12) can be pursued using the following theorem from [7]:

Theorem 1 (Stability Analysis [7]**).** *A system of the form*

$$\boldsymbol{x}(n+1) = T(\boldsymbol{\xi}_n)\boldsymbol{x}(n) \; T(\boldsymbol{\xi}_n) = \sum_{i=1}^{N} \boldsymbol{\lambda}_{ni} T_i \; \boldsymbol{\lambda}_{ni} \geq 0, \quad \sum_{i=1}^{N} \boldsymbol{\lambda}_{ni} = 1$$

is asymptotically/robustly stable *if and only if there exist symmetric positive definite matrices S_i, S_j and matrices G_i with appropriate dimensions such that*

$$\begin{bmatrix} G_i + G_i^T - S_i & G_i^T T_i^T \\ T_i G_i & S_j \end{bmatrix} > \mathbf{0}$$

for all $i = 1, \ldots, N$ and $j = 1, \ldots, N$. Moreover, the corresponding Lyapunov function is $V(\boldsymbol{x}(n), \boldsymbol{\xi}_n) = \boldsymbol{x}(n)^T (\sum_{i=1}^{N} \boldsymbol{\lambda}_{ni} S_i^{-1}) \boldsymbol{x}(n)$.

In order to exploit Theorem 1, we have to reformulate $T(\boldsymbol{\xi}_n)$ in Eq. (12) to

$$T(\boldsymbol{\xi}_n) = \sum_{i=1}^{N} \boldsymbol{\lambda}_{ni} T_i, \quad \text{where } \boldsymbol{\lambda}_{ni} \geq 0, \; \sum_{i=1}^{N} \boldsymbol{\lambda}_{ni} = 1. \tag{13}$$

From Eqs. (8) and (9), we recover that the degree of $\boldsymbol{f}^{(i)}_n(t)$ is $k+1-i$, for $i = 1, \cdots, k$. Furthermore, according to Eq. (12), each entry t_{ij} of $T(\boldsymbol{\xi}_n)$ is linear in the components of $\boldsymbol{\xi}_n$, written as $t_{ij}(\boldsymbol{\xi}_n)$, for $i = 1, \ldots, m$ and $j = 1, \ldots, m$. For each $t_{ij}(\boldsymbol{\xi}_n)$, we have

$$t_{ij}(\boldsymbol{\xi}_n) = (1 - \frac{\boldsymbol{\xi}_{n1}}{\delta}) t_{ij}(\boldsymbol{\xi}_n)[0/\boldsymbol{\xi}_{n1}] + \frac{\boldsymbol{\xi}_{n1}}{\delta} t_{ij}[\delta/\boldsymbol{\xi}_{n1}], \tag{14}$$

where $e[b/a]$ stands for substituting b for a in e. Hence,

$$T(\boldsymbol{\xi}_n) = (1 - \frac{\boldsymbol{\xi}_{n1}}{\delta}) T(\boldsymbol{\xi}_n)[0/\boldsymbol{\xi}_{n1}] + \frac{\boldsymbol{\xi}_{n1}}{\delta} T(\boldsymbol{\xi}_n)[\delta/\boldsymbol{\xi}_{n1}] \tag{15}$$

as $t_{ij}(\boldsymbol{\xi}_n)$ is linear in $\boldsymbol{\xi}_{n1}$. Obviously, $0 \leq 1 - \frac{\boldsymbol{\xi}_{n1}}{\delta} \leq 1$ and $0 \leq \frac{\boldsymbol{\xi}_{n1}}{\delta} \leq 1$, as $\boldsymbol{\xi}_{n1} \in [0,1]$. By repeating the above procedure m times, we obtain

$$T(\boldsymbol{\xi}_n) = \sum_{i=1}^{2^m} \lambda_i(\boldsymbol{\xi}_n) T_i, \;\; \lambda_i(\boldsymbol{\xi}_n) \geq 0, \;\; \sum_{i=1}^{2^m} \lambda_i(\boldsymbol{\xi}_n) = 1, \tag{16}$$

where T_i is a matrix, by substituting for each component of $\boldsymbol{\xi}_n$ either of the extremal values 0 or δ in $T(\boldsymbol{\xi}_n)$. This is sound due to the linearity in $\boldsymbol{\xi}_n$. Equation (16) constitutes a form where the stability of the time-invariant linear discrete dynamic system of Eq. (12) can be determined by the method of Theorem 1. Note that stabilization of the sequence of Taylor forms implies global stabilization of the underlying linear DDE (12), as the Taylor forms converge towards 0.

Polynomial $\boldsymbol{g}$: When $\boldsymbol{g}$ is *nonlinear*, the relation between $\boldsymbol{A}(n+1)$ and $\boldsymbol{A}(n)$ expressed in Eq. (11) becomes *nonlinear.* Thanks to existing methods on computing parametric Lyapunov functions, such as [24,34], we can apply such techniques to analyze the stability of a time-invariant *polynomial* discrete dynamic system of Eq. (11), as it arises for polynomial $\boldsymbol{g}$. In this paper, we build on the idea from [34] and adapt it to the discrete-time setting of Eq. (11).

A parametric polynomial in $\boldsymbol{y}$ of degree k is of the form $\sum_{(\sum \boldsymbol{\alpha}) \leq k} b_{\boldsymbol{\alpha}} \boldsymbol{y}^{\boldsymbol{\alpha}}$, where $\boldsymbol{y} = (y_1, \cdots, y_m), \boldsymbol{\alpha} = (\alpha_1, \cdots, \alpha_m), \boldsymbol{y}^{\boldsymbol{\alpha}} = y_1^{\alpha_1} \cdots y_m^{\alpha_m}, \sum \boldsymbol{\alpha} = \sum_{i=1}^m \alpha_i$. We will subsequently denote such a polynomial by $p(\boldsymbol{y}, \boldsymbol{b})$, where $\boldsymbol{b}$ stands the vector of the coefficients.

Definition 1. *Given a dynamic system as in Eq.* (11) *and state sets $\mathcal{A}$, $\mathcal{B}$ and $\mathcal{BA}$ with $\mathcal{BA} \subset \mathcal{A}$, a parametric polynomial $p((\boldsymbol{A}, \boldsymbol{\xi}), \boldsymbol{b})$ is called a relaxed Lyapunov function with respect to $\mathcal{A}$ and $\mathcal{BA}$ iff*

$$\begin{aligned} &\exists \boldsymbol{b} \in \mathcal{B}. \forall \boldsymbol{A}(n) \in \mathcal{A}. \forall \boldsymbol{\xi}_n, \boldsymbol{\xi}_{n+1} \in [0, \delta]^m. \\ &\boldsymbol{A}(n) \notin \mathcal{BA} \implies p((\boldsymbol{A}(n+1), \boldsymbol{\xi}_{n+1}), \boldsymbol{b}) - p((\boldsymbol{A}(n), \boldsymbol{\xi}_n), \boldsymbol{b}) < 0, \end{aligned} \tag{17}$$

where $\mathcal{A}$ and $\mathcal{B}$ are domain constraints on $\boldsymbol{A}(n)$ and $\boldsymbol{b}$ respectively, $\mathcal{BA}$ is a basin of attraction.

In Definition 1, for any $\boldsymbol{b}_0$ which satisfies (17), the *relaxed Lyapunov function* $p((\boldsymbol{A}, \boldsymbol{\xi}), \boldsymbol{b}_0)$ behaves like Lyapunov function in $\mathcal{A} \setminus \mathcal{BA}$ for the time-invariant discrete polynomial dynamic system in Eq. (11), abbreviated as $V(\boldsymbol{A}, \boldsymbol{\xi})$. Computing such $\boldsymbol{b}$ satisfying (17) can be achieved with interval arithmetic according to the method given in [34] as follows:

Step 1: Replace vector variables $\boldsymbol{A}(n)$, $\boldsymbol{\xi}_n$, and $\boldsymbol{\xi}_{n+1}$ in (17) respectively with the corresponding intervals ($\boldsymbol{A}(n)$ is bounded by $\mathcal{A}$), and simplify the formula with interval arithmetic.

Step 2: Solve the resulting constraints on $\boldsymbol{b}$, which are a set of linear interval inequalities (LIIs), by Rohn's approach [35] (will be elaborated below).

Step 3: If the LIIs do not have a solution, bisect the intervals for vector variables $\boldsymbol{A}(n)$, $\boldsymbol{\xi}_n$ and $\boldsymbol{\xi}_{n+1}$, and repeat the steps 1 and 2 until a solution of $\boldsymbol{b}$ is found or the length of intervals is smaller than a prescribed threshold ϵ.

LIIs can be solved almost exactly using Rohn's approach [35] as follows: first, replace each variable a by an expression $a_1 - a_2$, where $a_1 \geq 0$ and $a_2 \geq 0$; then, replace $Ia \rhd 0$ by $Ia_1 - Ia_2 \rhd 0$, which is equivalent to $I^+a_1 - I^-a_2 \rhd 0$, where $I^+ = \max I, I^- = \min I$ and $\rhd \in \{<, \leq\}$. One thus derives a system of linear inequalities that can be solved by linear programming. The only problem is that $(Ia_1 - Ia_2)$ is not equivalent to (Ia) in general. However, if $\mathcal{B}$ is symmetric with respect to the origin, i.e. $b_i \in [-\mathcal{B}_i, \mathcal{B}_i]$ for each b_i of $\boldsymbol{b}$, and I^+ and I^- have a same sign, then the two formulas are equivalent by interval arithmetic. In an actual implementation, it is easy to guarantee the above condition.

If the method succeeds, it proves that the parameters of the Taylor form will eventually converge from anywhere in region $\mathcal{A}$ into region $\mathcal{BA}$. This implies that DDE (7) will converge into a corresponding region of its state space defined by the range over $t = [0, \delta]$ of the Taylor polynomials with parameters in $\mathcal{BA}$, whenever the DDE is started on initial conditions defined by the Taylor polynomials with parameters in $\mathcal{A}$. It thus constitutes a proof of local stability of the DDE.

4.3 Guaranteeing Safety

Now, we show how to compute the upper bound k_s on steps potentially leaving the safety region, as needed for unbounded verification of a given invariant $\mathcal{S}(\boldsymbol{x})$ by means of bounded model checking (BMC). As computation of k_s for linear $\boldsymbol{g}$ has already been elaborated in the end of Sect. 3, the following discusses the computation of such k_s for polynomial $\boldsymbol{g}$ based on the above method.

When replacing the right-hand side constant 0 in (17) with a positive constant d_m, the above algorithm for computing relaxed Lyapunov functions will find a relaxed Lyapunov function that decreases by at least d_m for each step outside $\mathcal{BA}$. This can be used for unbounded safety verification, as it provides a computable bound for convergence into $\mathcal{BA}$, where for simplicity we here assume that $\mathcal{BA}$ is such that the range over $t = [0, \delta]$ of the Taylor polynomials with parameters in $\mathcal{BA}$ is a subset of our safety region $\mathcal{S}(\boldsymbol{x})$, i.e. the conjectured invariant.

Given such a minimum reduction d_m outside $\mathcal{BA}$, and thus outside the safety region $\mathcal{S}(\boldsymbol{x})$, we use iSAT to compute the largest c such that $V(\boldsymbol{A}(n), \boldsymbol{\xi}_n) \leq c \wedge \neg\mathcal{S}(\boldsymbol{f}_n(t)) \wedge t \in [0, \delta]$ is not satisfiable, where $S(\boldsymbol{x})$ is the invariant to be verified. Clearly, the existence of such c implies that $V(\boldsymbol{A}(n), \boldsymbol{\xi}_n) \leq c \rightarrow \mathcal{S}(\boldsymbol{f}_n)$ holds. Hence, after $k_s = \frac{V(\boldsymbol{x}(0), \boldsymbol{\xi}(0)) - c}{d_m}$ steps $S(\boldsymbol{f}_n)$ will necessarily hold, and safety violations can only occur transiently during the first k_s steps. Hence, using bounded model-checking for k_s steps yields an unbounded safety certificate in case no violation is detected before that step bound. Note that BMC here again requires polynomial SMT solving due to the Taylor forms. Again there is no need to always unwind the BMC problem to depth k_s, as checking the disjunctive goal $\neg\mathcal{S}(\boldsymbol{f}_n(t)) \vee V(\boldsymbol{A}(n), \boldsymbol{\xi}_n) \leq c$ and disambiguating the outcome probably permits early termination as in Sect. 3.

5 Implementation

The algorithms exposed in the previous section have been implemented in Matlab and C++, thereby taking advantage of the iSAT3 tool through its API. Given a DDE and the parameters relevant to the analysis, Matlab's symbolic computation is first employed for computing the Lie derivatives and thus identifying the discrete time-invariant operator connecting segments of the Taylor approximation. For the linear case, stability analysis is then conducted by the Matlab LMI solver, where actually synthesizing the pertinent Lyapunov function is done by Matlab matrix functions, and the minimum descent d_m outside the safety region is calculated by Matlab function `fmincon`. Polynomial stability analysis is based on Matlab and interval arithmetic packages `b4m` and `Profil`. Computation of a barrier value characterizing the safety region in terms of Lyapunov ranges is done by calling iSAT3. The same applies for bounded model checking.

6 Examples

In this section, we will introduce several examples to demonstrate how the approach works in practice. All these examples have been processed fully automatically by our prototype implementation.[1]

Example 1. Consider the linear DDE $\dot{x}(t) = -x(t-1)$ from Eq. (3)) with initial condition $x([0,1]) \equiv 1$ and check its stability as well as the safety property $\Box(-1 \leq x \leq 1)$.

Using a Taylor model with degree 1, we calculate the operator relating the parameters of successive Taylor forms to

$$\boldsymbol{A}(n+1) = \begin{bmatrix} 1 & 1 \\ -1 & -\xi_n \end{bmatrix} \boldsymbol{A}(n)\,.$$

This operator cannot be shown stable by the method of Theorem 1.

The operator automatically obtained for degree 2 has already been presented in Eq. (6). For this operator, stability verification by the method of Theorem 1 succeeds, as does (unbounded) safety verification for the property $\Box(-1 \leq x \leq 1)$ by bounded model checking.

Example 2. Consider the three-dimensional linear DDE

$$\dot{\boldsymbol{x}}(t) = \begin{bmatrix} -1 & \frac{1}{2} & 0 \\ \frac{1}{2} & -1 & \frac{1}{4} \\ 0 & \frac{1}{4} & -1 \end{bmatrix} \boldsymbol{x}(t - \frac{1}{100}) \tag{18}$$

with initial condition $\boldsymbol{x}([0,1]) \equiv [-\frac{125}{11}, -\frac{360}{11}, -\frac{90}{11}]$. This system, which has been inspired by [15, p. 585ff], models heat dissipation in a typical home with an

[1] The prototype implementation of the verification tool as well as the examples are available for download from https://github.com/liangdzou/isat-dde.

insulated ground floor, topped by an attic without significant insulation and supported by a basement surrounded by earth. Up to a coordinate shift introduced in order to move the equilibrium point to $(0, 0, 0)$, its three variables x_1 to x_3 model the temperatures in the basement, the ground floor, and the attic, respectively. The standard model usually encountered in introductory textbooks on modeling with differential equations takes the dissipation equations to be ODEs; it is, however, reasonable to assume that the heat transfer through the walls between the three compartments actually takes time (one could also add delays for convective heat transport within the rooms). A DDE model thus seems in place here. While the actual transport delays would be state dependent, any reasonably sized constant delay will already make the model better. Not yet being able to deal with state-dependent delays, we have set the delay to $\frac{1}{100}$h for the sake of demonstration.

For the resulting system, we have automatically checked stability as well as safety with respect to the invariance property $\Box(x_2 \leq \frac{25}{11})$, where x_2 denotes the (shifted) temperature in the ground floor.

Using Taylor models of degree 1, we compute the operator relating successive parameters of the Taylor forms to

$$\boldsymbol{A}(n+1) = \begin{bmatrix} 1 & \frac{1}{100} & 0 & 0 & 0 & 0 \\ -1 & -\xi_1 & \frac{1}{2} & \frac{\xi_1}{2} & 0 & 0 \\ 0 & 0 & 1 & \frac{1}{100} & 0 & 0 \\ \frac{1}{2} & \frac{\xi_2}{2} & -1 & -\xi_2 & \frac{1}{4} & \frac{\xi_2}{4} \\ 0 & 0 & 0 & 0 & 1 & \frac{1}{100} \\ 0 & 0 & \frac{1}{4} & \frac{\xi_3}{4} & -1 & -\xi_3 \end{bmatrix} \boldsymbol{A}(n) .$$

This operator has been shown stable by the method from Theorem 1 and the unbounded safety property has been verified by BMC.

Example 3. This example is an adaption of Gustafson's model of nutrient flow in an aquarium [15, p. 589f]. It deals with using a radioactive tracer for the food chain consisting of two aquatic plankton varieties drifting with the currents. The variables in this three-dimensional system reflect the isotope concentrations in the water, a phytoplankton species, and a zooplankton species, respectively. The original model was an ODE model; a concise model would presumably have to use PDE (partial differential equations) to model spacial variations and the necessary drifts of species in the predator-prey part of the food chain; our DDE model here is a compromise between these two extremes. Therefore consider the three-dimensional linear DDE

$$\dot{\boldsymbol{x}}(t) = \begin{bmatrix} -3 & 6 & 5 \\ 2 & -12 & 0 \\ 1 & 6 & -5 \end{bmatrix} \boldsymbol{x}(t - \frac{1}{100}) \tag{19}$$

with initial condition $\boldsymbol{x}([0, 1]) \equiv [0, 0, 10]$ and the conjectured invariant $\Box(x_1 - x_2 - x_3 \geq 5)$.

Beware that the eigenvalues of the matrix in this example are $0, -10-\sqrt{6}, -10+\sqrt{6}$, which implies that not even the corresponding ODE is asymptotically stable. Hence, it comes as no surprise that we are not able to find an asymptotically stable enclosure to the DDE. Using Taylor models of degree 1, we calculate the operator relating successive parameter vectors to

$$\boldsymbol{A}(n+1) = \begin{bmatrix} 1 & \frac{1}{100} & 0 & 0 & 0 & 0 \\ -3 & -3\xi_1 & 6 & 6\xi_1 & 5 & 5\xi_1 \\ 0 & 0 & 1 & \frac{1}{100} & 0 & 0 \\ 2 & 2\xi_2 & -12 & -12\xi_2 & 0 & 0 \\ 0 & 0 & 0 & 0 & 1 & \frac{1}{100} \\ 1 & \xi_3 & 6 & 6\xi_3 & -5 & -5\xi_3 \end{bmatrix} \boldsymbol{A}(n),$$

which cannot be proven stable by the method of Theorem 1. By translating above system into the form required for Theorem 1, we get a set of T_i. After calculation, we find out that the spectral radius of all the T_i is no more than 1, which at least shows that $\boldsymbol{A}(n)$ does not grow too fast. Using bounded model-checking on the Taylor approximation, we have been able to show the overapproximation unsafe in step 12 (corresponding to $t \in [0.12, 0.13]$s), while Simulink simulation confirms this for $t = 0.1452$s. Further exploiting iSAT3 for BMC on the Taylor-based overapproximation, we actually found the safe set $\{\boldsymbol{x} \mid x_1 - x_2 - x_e \geq 5\}$ itself (not its complement) being unreachable in step 18, i.e. for $t = 0.18$. This constitutes a rigorous automatic proof that the system actually is unsafe.

Example 4. Consider the polynomial DDE $\dot{x}(t) = -x(t-1)^3$ with initial condition $x([0,1]) \equiv c$, $c \in [3,6]$ arbitrary, and safety condition $\Box(-3000 < x < 3000)$.

This system is unsafe and Taylor approximations of arbitrary degree will thus eventually reach the complement of the safe set $S = \{x \mid -3000 < x < 3000\}$. Using a Taylor approximation of degree 5, we are able to show by BMC that the safe set S surely is left in the beginning of step 3, i.e., at $t = 3$, thus obtaining a rigorous automatic proof that the system actually is unsafe.

Execution times for each evaluation step in each example above are stated in Table 1, where the individual steps are calculating the Lyapunov function, the barrier c characterizing the safe set wrt. Lyapunov values, the minimum per-step reduction d_m of the Lyapunov function outside the safe set, and verifying the safety property, respectively. All benchmarks were performed on a 1.80GHz Intel Core-i5 processor with 4GB RAM running 64-bit Ubuntu 14.04.

Table 1. Analysis times for the sample problems.

	CLF(s)	CBV(s)	CSR(s)	VSP(s)
Ex. 1	1.9869	10.514	20.012	0.0302
Ex. 2	12.732	52.892	78.258	22.121
Ex. 3	55.053	skipped	skipped	0.0003
Ex. 4	timeout	skipped	skipped	0.0003

CLF = computing Lyapunov function
CBV = computing barrier value
CSR = computing per-step reduction
VSP = verifying/falsifying safety prop.

7 Conclusions and Future Work

In this paper, we have exposed an automatic method for the stability and safety verification of a simple class of delay differential equations (DDEs). The method is based on using interval Taylor forms for safely enclosing segments of the solutions of DDEs with point- or set-valued initial conditions. It thus complements the established methods for enclosing reachable state sets of ordinary differential equations (ODEs), lifting their power to DDEs. It consequently covers the situations actually encountered in many modern control applications, where the feedback dynamics entails delays due to communication networks etc. and thus can reasonably be described by DDEs. Relaxing these DDEs to ODEs in verification may yield misleading results due to the impact of delays on system dynamics. To provide verification and reliable certificates for system properties, e.g., stability and safety properties, we have thus established a safe enclosure method for DDEs. Interval-based Taylor forms are used as a suitable data structure, facilitating to enclose a set of trajectories by parametric Taylor series with parameters in interval form. This data structure is used to iterate bounded degree interval-based Taylor overapproximations of the time-wise segments of the solution to a DDE. Given a DDE, we thereby identify the operator that computes the parameters of the Taylor overapproximation for the next temporal segment from the current one, and we employ constraint solving for automatically analyzing its properties. Based on such analysis by numeric constraint solving as implemented in the iSAT tool [11], we were able to obtain an automatic procedure able to provide stability certificates for a simple class of DDE.

For this introductory exposition of the method, we assumed that the system dynamics is represented as a DDE with a single, constant delay, i.e., is of the restricted form given by Eq. (2). Several dynamical systems can be modeled by DDE with a single constant delay as in biology [14,26], optics [17], economics [38,39], ecology [10] . In control applications, one may however want to combine delayed feedback, as imposed by communication networks, with immediate state feedback as suggested by ODE models of the plant dynamics derived from, e.g., Newtonian models. Such cases can be addressed by a layered combination of Taylor-model computation for ODEs, e.g. [28], with the ideas exposed herein. The pertinent algorithms are currently under development and will be exposed in future work. Beyond that, we want to extend the method to still more general kinds of DDEs, like DDEs with multiple different discrete delays (cf. Eq. (1)), DDEs with randomly distributed delay, or DDEs with time-dependent or more generally state-dependent delay [21]. Likewise, this work can (and will) be extended to facilitate the automatic verification and analysis for hybrid systems featuring delays, extending Egger's method for integrating safe ODE enclosures into a SAT modulo theory (SMT) solver [8,9] from ODE enclosures to DDE enclosures. In this case, one will need to extend the enclosure methods for DDEs to a constraint propagator mutually narrowing intervals of pre- and post-states and integrate that propagator into the iSAT SMT solver as in [12].

References

1. Balachandran, B., Kalmár-Nagy, T., Gilsinn, D.E.: Delay Differential Equations. Springer, (2009)
2. Richard, B., Cooke, K.L.: Differential-difference equations. Technical report R-374-PR, The RAND Corporation, Santa Monica (1963)
3. Berz, M., Makino, K.: Verified integration of ODEs and flows using differential algebraic methods on high-order Taylor models. Reliable Comput. **4**(4), 361–369 (1998)
4. Stephen, B., El Ghaoui, L., Feron, E., Balakrishnan, V.: Linear matrix inequalities in system and control theory of studies in applied mathematics. Soc. Ind. Appl. Math. (SIAM) **15**, 215–249 (1994)
5. Chen, X., Ábrahám, E., Sankaranarayanan, S.: Flow*: an analyzer for non-linear hybrid systems. In: Sharygina, N., Veith, H. (eds.) CAV 2013. LNCS, vol. 8044, pp. 258–263. Springer, Heidelberg (2013)
6. Chutinan, A., Krogh, B.H.: Computing polyhedral approximations to flow pipes for dynamic systems. In: Proceedings of the 37th International Conference on Decision and Control (CDC 1998) (1998)
7. Daafouz, J., Bernussou, J.: Parameter dependent Lyapunov functions for discrete time systems with time varying parametric uncertainties. Sys. Control Lett. **43**(5), 355–359 (2001)
8. Eggers, A., Fränzle, M., Herde, C.: SAT Modulo ODE: a direct SAT approach to hybrid systems. In: Cha, S.S., Choi, J.-Y., Kim, M., Lee, I., Viswanathan, M. (eds.) ATVA 2008. LNCS, vol. 5311, pp. 171–185. Springer, Heidelberg (2008)
9. Andreas, E., Nacim, R., Nedialkov, N.S., Fränzle, M.: Improving the SAT modulo ODE approach to hybrid systems analysis by combining different enclosure methods. Software Systems Modeling **6**, 1–28 (2012)
10. Fort, J., Méndez, V.: Time-delayed theory of the neolithic transition in europe. Phys. Rev. Lett **82**(4), 867 (1999)
11. Fränzle, M., Herde, C., Ratschan, S., Schubert, T., Teige, T.: Efficient solving of large non-linear arithmetic constraint systems with complex boolean structure. J. Satisfiability Boolean Model. Comput. Spec. Issue SAT/CP Integr. **1**, 209–236 (2007)
12. Fränzle, M., Teige, T., Eggers, A.: Engineering constraint solvers for automatic analysis of probabilistic hybrid automata. J. Logic Algebraic Programm. **79**, 436–466 (2010)
13. Girard, A.: Reachability of uncertain linear systems using zonotopes. In: Morari, M., Thiele, L. (eds.) HSCC 2005. LNCS, vol. 3414, pp. 291–305. Springer, Heidelberg (2005)
14. Glass, L., Mackey, M.C.: From Clocks to Chaos: The Rhythms of Life. Princeton University Press, Princeton (1988)
15. Gustafson, G.B.: Systems of differential equations. In: Manuscript for Course Eng Math 2250–1 Spring 2014, ch 11. University of Utah, Department of Mathematics (2014)
16. Henzinger, T.A., Kopke, P.W., Puri, A., Varaiya, P.: What's decidable about hybrid automata? J. Comput. Syst. Sci. **57**(1), 94–124 (1998)
17. Ikeda, K., Matsumoto, K.: High-dimensional chaotic behavior in systems with time-delayed feedback. Physica D **29**(1–2), 223–235 (1987)
18. Kong, S., Gao, S., Chen, W., Clarke, E.: dReach: delta-reachability analysis for hybrid systems. In: TACAS (2015)

19. Kurzhanski, A.B., Varaiya, P.: Ellipsoidal techniques for hybrid dynamics: the reachability problem. In: Dayawansa, W.P., Lindquist, A., Zhou, Y. (eds.) New Directions and Applications in Control Theory. Lecture Notes in Control and Information Sciences, pp. 193–205. Springer, Heidelberg (2005)
20. Lafferriere, G., Pappas, G.J., Yovine, S.: Symbolic reachability computation for families of linear vector fields. J. Symbolic Comput. **32**(3), 231–253 (2001)
21. Lakshmanan, M., Senthilkumar, D.V.: Dynamics of Nonlinear Time-delay Systems. Springer Science Business Media. Springer, Heidelberg (2011)
22. Le Guernic, C., Girard, A.: Reachability analysis of linear systems using support functions. Nonlinear Anal. Hybrid Sys. **4**(2), 250–262 (2010)
23. Liu, J., Zhan, N., Zhao, H.: Computing semi-algebraic invariants for polynomial dynamical systems. In: EMSOFT 2011, pp. 97–106. ACM New York (2011)
24. Liu, J., Zhan, N., Zhao, H.: Automatically discovering relaxed Lyapunov functions for polynomial dynamical systems. Math. Comput. Sci. **6**(4), 395–408 (2012)
25. Lohner, R.: Einschließung der Lösung gewöhnlicher Anfangs- und Randwertaufgaben. Ph.D. thesis, Fakultät für Mathematik der Universität Karlsruhe, Karlsruhe (1988)
26. Mackey, M.C., Glass, L., et al.: Oscillation and chaos in physiological control systems. Science **197**(4300), 287–289 (1977)
27. Moore, R.E.: Automatic local coordinate transformation to reduce the growth of error bounds in interval computation of solutions of ordinary differential equations. In: Ball, L.B. (ed.) Error in Digital Computation. volume II, pp. 103–140. Wiley, New York (1965)
28. Neher, M., Jackson, K.R., Nedialkov, N.S.: On Taylor model based integration of ODEs. SIAM J. Numer. Anal. **45**(1), 236–262 (2007)
29. Oehlerking, J.: Decomposition of Stability Proofs for Hybrid Systems. Doctoral dissertation, Carl von Ossietzky Universität Oldenburg, Department of Computing Science (2011)
30. Platzer, A.: Differential-algebraic dynamic logic for differential-algebraic programs. J. Log. Comput. **20**(1), 309–352 (2010)
31. Platzer, A., Clarke, E.M.: Computing differential invariants of hybrid systems as fixedpoints. In: Gupta, A., Malik, S. (eds.) CAV 2008. LNCS, vol. 5123, pp. 176–189. Springer, Heidelberg (2008)
32. Prajna, S., Jadbabaie, A., Pappas, G.J.: A framework for worst-case and stochastic safety verification using barrier certificates. IEEE Trans. Autom. Control **52**(8), 1415–1428 (2007)
33. Ratschan, S., She, Z.: Safety verification of hybrid systems by constraint propagation based abstraction refinement. In: Morari, M., Thiele, L. (eds.) HSCC 2005. LNCS, vol. 3414, pp. 573–589. Springer, Heidelberg (2005)
34. Ratschan, S., She, Z.: Providing a basin of attraction to a target region by computation of Lyapunov-like functions. In: IEEE International Conference on Computational Cybernetics (ICCC 2006), pp. 1–5 (2006)
35. Rohn, J., Kreslová, J.: Linear interval inequalities. Linear Multilinear Algebra **38**(1–2), 79–82 (1994)
36. Sankaranarayanan, S., Sipma, H.B., Manna, Z.: Constructing invariants for hybrid systems. In: Alur, R., Pappas, G.J. (eds.) HSCC 2004. LNCS, vol. 2993, pp. 539–554. Springer, Heidelberg (2004)
37. Stauning, O.: Automatic Validation of Numerical Solutions. Ph.D .thesis, Technical University of Denmark, Lyngby (1997)
38. Szydłowski, M., Krawiec, A.: The stability problem in the kaldor-kalecki business cycle model. Chaos Solitons Fractals **25**(2), 299–305 (2005)

39. Szydłowski, M., Krawiec, A., Toboła, J.: Nonlinear oscillations in business cycle model with time lags. Chaos, Solitons Fractals **12**(3), 505–517 (2001)
40. Tang, X., Zou, X.: Global attractivity in a predator-prey system with pure delays. Proc. Edinburgh Math. Soc. **51**, 495–508 (2008)
41. Zou, L., Lv, J., Wang, S., Zhan, N., Tang, T., Yuan, L., Liu, Y.: Verifying chinese train control system under a combined scenario by theorem proving. In: Cohen, E., Rybalchenko, A. (eds.) VSTTE 2013. LNCS, vol. 8164, pp. 262–280. Springer, Heidelberg (2014)

Time Robustness in MTL and Expressivity in Hybrid System Falsification

Takumi Akazaki[1,2](✉) and Ichiro Hasuo[1]

[1] The University of Tokyo, Tokyo, Japan
ultraredrays@is.s.u-tokyo.ac.jp
[2] JSPS Research Fellow, Tokyo, Japan

Abstract. Building on the work by Fainekos and Pappas and the one by Donzé and Maler, we introduce **AvSTL**, an extension of metric interval temporal logic by *averaged* temporal operators. Its expressivity in capturing both space and time robustness helps solving *falsification* problems (searching for a critical path in hybrid system models); it does so by communicating a designer's intention more faithfully to the stochastic optimization engine employed in a falsification solver. We also introduce a sliding window-like algorithm that keeps the cost of computing truth/robustness values tractable.

1 Introduction

Model-Based Development of Hybrid Systems. The demand for quality assurance of *cyber-physical systems (CPS)* is ever-rising, now that computer-controlled artifacts—cars, aircrafts, and so on—serve diverse safety-critical tasks everywhere in our daily lives. In the industry practice of CPS design, deployment of *model-based development (MBD)* has become a norm. In MBD, (physical and costly) testing workbenches are replaced by (virtual and cheap) *mathematical models*; and this reduces by a great deal the cost of running a *development cycle*—design, implementation, evaluation, and redesign.

One of the distinctive features of CPS is that they are *hybrid systems* and combine discrete and continuous dynamics. For MBD of such systems the software *Simulink* has emerged as an industry standard. In Simulink a designer models a system using block diagrams—a formalism strongly influenced by *control theory*—and runs *simulation*, that is, numerical solution of the system's dynamics.

Falsification. The models of most real-world hybrid systems are believed to be beyond the reach of formal verification. While this is certainly the case with systems as big as a whole car, a single component of it (like automatic transmission or an engine controller) overwhelms the scalability of the state-of-art formal verification techniques, too.

What is worse, hybrid system models tend to have *black-box components*. An example is fuel combustion in an engine. Such chemical reactions are not easy to

D. Kroening and C.S. Păsăreanu (Eds.): CAV 2015, Part II, LNCS 9207, pp. 356–374, 2015.
DOI: 10.1007/978-3-319-21668-3_21

model with ODEs, and are therefore commonly represented in a Simulink model by a *look-up table*—a big table of values obtained by physical measurements [18,19]. The lack of structure in a look-up table poses a challenge to formal verification: each entry of the table calls for separate treatment; and this easily leads to state-space explosion.

Under such circumstances, *falsification* by stochastic optimization has proved to be a viable approach to quality assurance [7,18,19]. The problem is formulated as follows:

The falsification problem

Given: a *model* $\mathcal{M}$ (a function from an input signal to an output signal), and a *specification* φ (a temporal formula),

Answer: a *critical path*, that is, an input signal σ_{in} such that the output $\mathcal{M}(\sigma_{\text{in}})$ does not satisfy φ

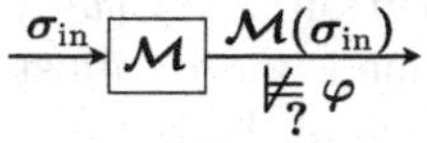

$$\xrightarrow{\sigma_{\text{in}}} \boxed{\mathcal{M}} \xrightarrow[\not\models_? \varphi]{\mathcal{M}(\sigma_{\text{in}})}$$

Unlike *testing* or *monitoring*—where input σ_{in} is given and we check if $\mathcal{M}(\sigma_{\text{in}}) \models \varphi$—a falsification solver employs stochastic optimization techniques (like the Monte-Carlo ones) and iteratively searches for a falsifying input signal σ_{in}.

Falsification is a versatile tool in MBD of hybrid systems. It is capable of searching for counterexamples, hence revealing potential faults in the design. One can also take, as a specification φ, the negation $\neg\psi$ of a desirable property ψ; then successful falsification amounts to *synthesis* of an input signal that satisfies ψ. Stochastic optimization used in falsification typically does not rely on the internal structure of models, therefore the methodology is suited for models with black-box components. Falsification is fairly scalable, making it a realistic option in the industrial MBD scenarios; see e.g. [18,19].

The current work aims at enhancing falsification solvers, notable among which are S-TaLiRo [7] and BREACH [11]. An obvious way to do so is via improvement of stochastic optimization; see e.g. [24,26]. Here we take a different, logical approach.

Robustness in Metric Temporal Logics. Let us turn to a formalism in which a specification φ is expressed. *Metric interval temporal logic* (**MITL**) [6], and its adaptation *signal temporal logic* (**STL**) [23], are standard temporal logics for (continuous-time) signals. However their conventional semantics—where satisfaction is Boolean—is not suited for falsification by stochastic optimization. This is because a formula φ, no matter if it is *robustly* satisfied and *barely* satisfied, yields the same truth value ("true"), making it not amenable to hill climb-style optimization.

It is the introduction of *robust semantics* of **MITL** [16] that set off the idea of falsification by optimization. In robust semantics, a signal σ and a formula φ are assigned a continuous truth value $[\![\sigma, \varphi]\!] \in \mathbb{R}$ that designates how robustly the formula is satisfied. Such "robustness values" constitute a sound basis for stochastic optimization.

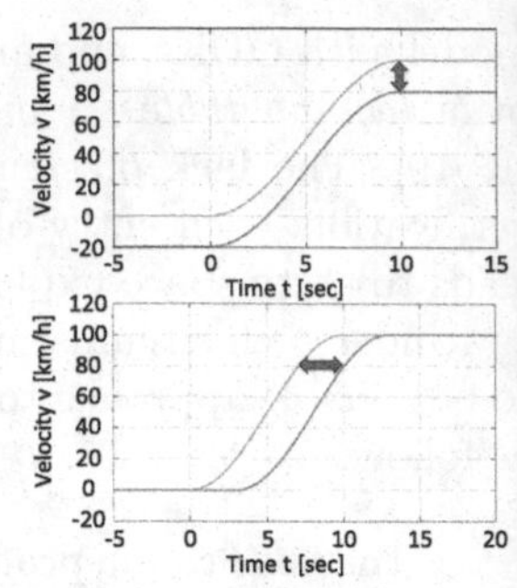

The original robust semantics in [16] is concerned with *space* robustness: for example, the truth values of $\Diamond_{[0,10]}(v \geq 80)$ ("the velocity reaches 80 km/h within 10 sec.") are 20 and 0, for the green and red signals on the right. Therefore space robustness is a "vertical margin" between a signal and a specification. An efficient algorithm is proposed in [12] for computing this notion of robustness.

The notion of robustness is extended in [13] to take *time* robustness also into account. Consider the same specification $\Diamond_{[0,10]}(v \geq 80)$ against the green and red signals on the right. The green one is more robust since it reaches 80 km/h much earlier than the deadline (10 s), while the red one barely makes the deadline.

The current work continues this line of work, with the slogan that *expressivity of temporal logic should help falsification.* With more expressivity, a designer's concerns that were previously ignored (much like time robustness was ignored in [16]) come to be reflected in the continuous truth value. The latter will in turn help stochastic optimization by giving additional "hints." We however are in a *trade-off* situation: the more expressive a logic is, the more expensive computation of truth values is in general.

Contributions. We aim at: a good balance in the last trade-off between expressivity and computational cost; and thereby enhancing falsification solvers by giving more "hints" to stochastic optimization procedures. Our technical contributions are threefold.

The Logic AvSTL. We introduce *averaged STL* (**AvSTL**); it is an extension of **STL** [23] by so-called *averaged temporal operators* like $\overline{\mathcal{U}}_I$ and $\overline{\Diamond}_I$. The (continuous) truth values of the new operators are defined by the average of truth values in a suitable interval. We show that this simple extension of **STL** successfully combines space and time robustness in [13, 16]; and that its expressivity covers many common specifications (expeditiousness, persistence, deadline, etc.) encountered in the context of CPS.

An Algorithm for Computing AvSTL Robustness. It is natural to expect that nonlocal temporal operators—like $\mathcal{U}_I$, $\Diamond_I$ and their averaged variants—incur a big performance penalty in computing truth values. For **STL** (without averaged modalities) an efficient algorithm is proposed in [12]; it employs the idea of the *sliding window minimum algorithm* [22] and achieves complexity that is linear with respect to the size of an input signal (measured by the number of timestamps).

We show that, under mild and realistic assumptions, the same idea as in [12] can be successfully employed to compute **AvSTL** truth values with linear complexity.

Enhancing S-TaLiRo: Implementation and Experiments. We use S-TaLiRo and demonstrate that our logic **AvSTL** indeed achieves a reasonable balance between expressivity and computational cost. We present our prototype implementation: it takes S-TaLiRo and lets the above algorithm (called the

AvSTL *evaluator*) replace TaLiRo, S-TaLiRo's original engine for computing **STL** truth values (see Fig. 7 in Sect. 4).

For its evaluation, we pick some benchmark models $\mathcal{M}$ and **STL** specifications φ—they are mostly automotive examples from [18]—and compare performance between:

- our prototype, run for $\mathcal{M}$ and the original **STL** specification φ,[1] and
- our prototype, run for $\mathcal{M}$ and a *refinement* of φ given as an **AvSTL** formula.

For benchmarks of a certain class we observe substantial performance improvement: sometimes the latter is several times faster; and in some benchmarks we even see the latter succeed in falsification while the former fails to do so.

Related Work. Besides those which are discussed in the above and the below, a closely related work is [2] (its abstract appeared in [3]). There a notion of *conformance* between two models $\mathcal{M}_1$, $\mathcal{M}_2$ is defined; and it is much like (an arity-2 variation of) combination of space and time robustness. Its use in falsification and comparison with the current approach is future work.

Organization of the Paper. In Sect. 2 we introduce the logic **AvSTL**: its syntax, semantics, some basic properties and examples of temporal specifications expressible in it. In Sect. 3, building on [12], an algorithm for computing **AvSTL** truth values is introduced and its complexity is studied. The algorithm is implemented and used to enhance a falsification solver S-TaLiRo, in Sect. 4, where experiment results are presented and discussed.

We used colors in some figures for clarity. Consult the electronic edition in case the colors are unavailable. Most of the proofs are deferred to an appendix in the extended version [4], where the other appendices are found, too.

2 Averaged Signal Temporal Logic AvSTL

We introduce *averaged STL* (**AvSTL**). It is essentially an extension of **MITL** [6] and **STL** [23] with so-called *averaged* temporal operators. We describe its syntax and its semantics (that is inspired by robust semantics in [13,16]). We also exemplify the expressivity of the logic, by encoding common temporal specifications like expeditiousness, persistence and deadline. Finally we will discuss the relationship to the previous robustness notions [13,16] for STL.

2.1 Syntax

We let $\equiv$ stand for the syntactic equality. We let $\mathbb{R}$ denote the set of real numbers, with $\mathbb{R}_{\geq 0}$ and $\mathbb{R}_{\leq 0}$ denoting its obvious subsets. We also fix the set **Var** of variables, each of which stands for a physical quantity (velocity, temperature, etc.).

[1] This is the control case of our experiments. We do not use S-TaLiRo itself, because we would like to disregard the potential disadvantage caused by the communication between the **AvSTL** evaluator (the additional component) and S-TaLiRo. We note that the **AvSTL** evaluator is capable of evaluating **STL** formulas, too.

Table 1. Definition of positive and negative robustness

$[\![\sigma, \top]\!]^{+} \triangleq \infty$	$[\![\sigma, \varphi_1 \mathcal{U}_I \varphi_2]\!]^{+} \triangleq \bigsqcup_{t \in I}([\![\sigma^{t}, \varphi_2]\!]^{+} \sqcap \bigsqcap_{t' \in [0,t)} [\![\sigma^{t'}, \varphi_1]\!]^{+})$
$[\![\sigma, \bot]\!]^{+} \triangleq 0$	$[\![\sigma, \varphi_1 \mathcal{R}_I \varphi_2]\!]^{+} \triangleq \bigsqcap_{t \in I}([\![\sigma^{t}, \varphi_2]\!]^{+} \sqcup \bigsqcup_{t' \in [0,t)} [\![\sigma^{t'}, \varphi_1]\!]^{+})$
$[\![\sigma, x < r]\!]^{+} \triangleq 0 \sqcup (r - \sigma(0)(x))$	$[\![\sigma, \varphi_1 \overline{\mathcal{U}}_I \varphi_2]\!]^{+} \triangleq$
$[\![\sigma, x \leq r]\!]^{+} \triangleq 0 \sqcup (r - \sigma(0)(x))$	$\begin{cases} \frac{1}{b-a}\int_a^b [\![\sigma, \varphi_1 \mathcal{U}_{I \cap [0,\tau]} \varphi_2]\!]^{+} d\tau & (I \text{ is bounded}) \\ [\![\sigma, \varphi_1 \mathcal{U}_I \varphi_2]\!]^{+} & (I \text{ is unbounded}) \end{cases}$
$[\![\sigma, x \geq r]\!]^{+} \triangleq 0 \sqcup (\sigma(0)(x) - r)$	
$[\![\sigma, x > r]\!]^{+} \triangleq 0 \sqcup (\sigma(0)(x) - r)$	
$[\![\sigma, \neg\varphi]\!]^{+} \triangleq -[\![\sigma, \varphi]\!]^{-}$	$[\![\sigma, \varphi_1 \overline{\mathcal{R}}_I \varphi_2]\!]^{+} \triangleq$
$[\![\sigma, \varphi_1 \vee \varphi_2]\!]^{+} \triangleq [\![\sigma, \varphi_1]\!]^{+} \sqcup [\![\sigma, \varphi_2]\!]^{+}$	$\begin{cases} \frac{1}{b-a}\int_a^b [\![\sigma, \varphi_1 \mathcal{R}_{I \cap [0,\tau]} \varphi_2]\!]^{+} d\tau & (I \text{ is bounded}) \\ [\![\sigma, \varphi_1 \mathcal{R}_I \varphi_2]\!]^{+} & (I \text{ is unbounded}) \end{cases}$
$[\![\sigma, \varphi_1 \wedge \varphi_2]\!]^{+} \triangleq [\![\sigma, \varphi_1]\!]^{+} \sqcap [\![\sigma, \varphi_2]\!]^{+}$	
$[\![\sigma, \top]\!]^{-} \triangleq 0$	$[\![\sigma, \varphi_1 \mathcal{U}_I \varphi_2]\!]^{-} \triangleq \bigsqcup_{t \in I}([\![\sigma^{t}, \varphi_2]\!]^{-} \sqcap \bigsqcap_{t' \in [0,t)} [\![\sigma^{t'}, \varphi_1]\!]^{-})$
$[\![\sigma, \bot]\!]^{-} \triangleq -\infty$	$[\![\sigma, \varphi_1 \mathcal{R}_I \varphi_2]\!]^{-} \triangleq \bigsqcap_{t \in I}([\![\sigma^{t}, \varphi_2]\!]^{-} \sqcup \bigsqcup_{t' \in [0,t)} [\![\sigma^{t'}, \varphi_1]\!]^{-})$
$[\![\sigma, x < r]\!]^{-} \triangleq 0 \sqcap (r - \sigma(0)(x))$	$[\![\sigma, \varphi_1 \overline{\mathcal{U}}_I \varphi_2]\!]^{-} \triangleq$
$[\![\sigma, x \leq r]\!]^{-} \triangleq 0 \sqcap (r - \sigma(0)(x))$	$\begin{cases} \frac{1}{b-a}\int_a^b [\![\sigma, \varphi_1 \mathcal{U}_{I \cap [0,\tau]} \varphi_2]\!]^{-} d\tau & (I \text{ is bounded}) \\ [\![\sigma, \varphi_1 \mathcal{U}_I \varphi_2]\!]^{-} & (I \text{ is unbounded}) \end{cases}$
$[\![\sigma, x \geq r]\!]^{-} \triangleq 0 \sqcap (\sigma(0)(x) - r)$	
$[\![\sigma, x > r]\!]^{-} \triangleq 0 \sqcap (\sigma(0)(x) - r)$	
$[\![\sigma, \neg\varphi]\!]^{-} \triangleq -[\![\sigma, \varphi]\!]^{+}$	$[\![\sigma, \varphi_1 \overline{\mathcal{R}}_I \varphi_2]\!]^{-} \triangleq$
$[\![\sigma, \varphi_1 \vee \varphi_2]\!]^{-} \triangleq [\![\sigma, \varphi_1]\!]^{-} \sqcup [\![\sigma, \varphi_2]\!]^{-}$	$\begin{cases} \frac{1}{b-a}\int_a^b [\![\sigma, \varphi_1 \mathcal{R}_{I \cap [0,\tau]} \varphi_2]\!]^{-} d\tau & (I \text{ is bounded}) \\ [\![\sigma, \varphi_1 \mathcal{R}_I \varphi_2]\!]^{-} & (I \text{ is unbounded}) \end{cases}$
$[\![\sigma, \varphi_1 \wedge \varphi_2]\!]^{-} \triangleq [\![\sigma, \varphi_1]\!]^{-} \sqcap [\![\sigma, \varphi_2]\!]^{-}$	

Definition 2.1. (Syntax). In **AvSTL**, the set **AP** of *atomic propositions* and the set **Fml** of *formulas* are defined as follows.

$$\begin{aligned} \mathbf{AP} \ni l &::= x < r \mid x \leq r \mid x \geq r \mid x > r \quad \text{where } x \in \mathbf{Var}, r \in \mathbb{R} \\ \mathbf{Fml} \ni \varphi &::= \top \mid \bot \mid l \mid \neg\varphi \mid \varphi \vee \varphi \mid \varphi \wedge \varphi \mid \varphi \mathcal{U}_I \varphi \mid \varphi \overline{\mathcal{U}}_I \varphi \mid \varphi \mathcal{R}_I \varphi \mid \varphi \overline{\mathcal{R}}_I \varphi \end{aligned}$$

Here I is a closed non-singular interval in $\mathbb{R}_{\geq 0}$, i.e. $I = [a, b]$ or $[a, \infty)$ where $a < b$. The overlined operator $\overline{\mathcal{U}}_I$ is called the *averaged-until* operator.

We introduce the following connectives as abbreviations, as usual: $\varphi_1 \rightarrow \varphi_2 \equiv (\neg\varphi_1) \vee \varphi_2$, $\Diamond_I \varphi \equiv \top \mathcal{U}_I \varphi$, $\Box_I \varphi \equiv \bot \mathcal{R}_I \varphi$, $\overline{\Diamond}_I \varphi \equiv \top \overline{\mathcal{U}}_I \varphi$ and $\overline{\Box}_I \varphi \equiv \bot \overline{\mathcal{R}}_I \varphi$. We omit subscripts I for temporal operators if $I = [0, \infty)$. The operators $\overline{\mathcal{R}}_I$, $\overline{\Diamond}_I$ and $\overline{\Box}_I$ are called the *averaged-release*, *averaged-eventually* and *averaged-henceforth* operators, respectively. We say a formula φ is *averaging-free* if it does not contain any averaged temporal operators.

2.2 Robust Semantics

AvSTL formulas, much like **STL** formulas in [13,16], are interpreted over (real-valued, continuous-time) *signals*. The latter stand for trajectories of hybrid systems.

Definition 2.2 (Signal). A *signal* over **Var** is a function $\sigma \colon \mathbb{R}_{\geq 0} \to (\mathbb{R}^{\mathbf{Var}})$; it is therefore a bunch of physical quantities indexed by a continuous notion of time.

For a signal σ and $t \in \mathbb{R}_{\geq 0}$, σ^{t} denotes the *t-shift* of σ, that is, $\sigma^{t}(t') \triangleq \sigma(t + t')$.

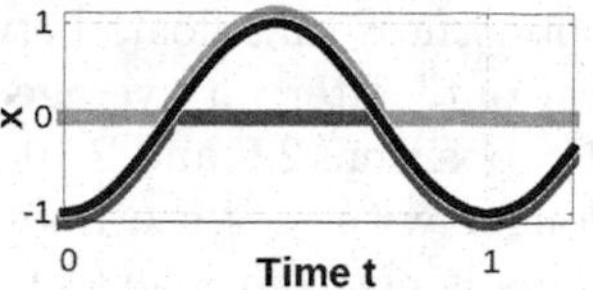

The interpretation of a formula φ over a signal σ is given by two different "truth values," namely *positive* and *negative robustness.* They are denoted by $[\![\sigma, \varphi]\!]^+$ and $[\![\sigma, \varphi]\!]^-$, respectively.

We will always have $[\![\sigma, \varphi]\!]^+ \geq 0$ and $[\![\sigma, \varphi]\!]^- \leq 0$. We will also see that, for averaging-free φ, it is never the case that $[\![\sigma, \varphi]\!]^+ > 0$ and $[\![\sigma, \varphi]\!]^- < 0$ hold at the same time. See the figure on the right for an example, where a sine-like (black) curve is a signal σ. The blue and red curves stand for the positive and negative robustness, of the formula $x \geq 0$ over the (t-shifted) signal σ^t, respectively.

Definition 2.3 (Positive/Negative Robustness). Let $\sigma\colon \mathbb{R}_{\geq 0} \to \mathbb{R}^{\mathbf{Var}}$ be a signal and φ be an **AvSTL** formula. We define the *positive robustness* $[\![\sigma, \varphi]\!]^+ \in \mathbb{R}_{\geq 0} \cup \{\infty\}$ and the *negative robustness* $[\![\sigma, \varphi]\!]^- \in \mathbb{R}_{\leq 0} \cup \{-\infty\}$ by mutual induction, as shown in Table 1. Here $\sqcap$ and $\sqcup$ denote infimums and supremums of real numbers, respectively.

The definition in Table 1 is much like the one for **STL** [12,13],[2] except for the averaged modalities on which a detailed account follows shortly. Conjunctions and disjunctions are interpreted by infimums and supremums, in a straightforward manner.

Figure 1 illustrates the semantics of averaged-temporal operators—the novelty of our logic **AvSTL**. Specifically, the black line designates a signal σ whose only variable is x; and we consider the "averaged-eventually" formula $\overline{\Diamond}_{[0,1]}(x \geq 0)$. For this formula, the definition in Table 1 specializes to:

$$[\![\sigma, \overline{\Diamond}_{[0,1]}(x \geq 0)]\!]^+ = \int_0^1 \Big(\bigsqcup_{\tau' \in [0,\tau]} 0 \sqcup \sigma(\tau')(x) \Big)\, d\tau, \quad \text{and} \quad [\![\sigma, \overline{\Diamond}_{[0,1]}(x \geq 0)]\!]^- = \int_0^1 \Big(\bigsqcup_{\tau' \in [0,\tau]} 0 \sqcap \sigma(\tau')(x) \Big)\, d\tau.$$

These values obviously coincide with the sizes of the blue and red areas in Fig. 1, respectively. Through this "area" illustration of the averaged-eventually operator we see that: the sooner φ is true, the more (positively) robust $\overline{\Diamond}_I\varphi$ is. It is also clear from Fig. 1 that our semantics captures space robustness too: the bigger a vertical margin is, the bigger an area is.

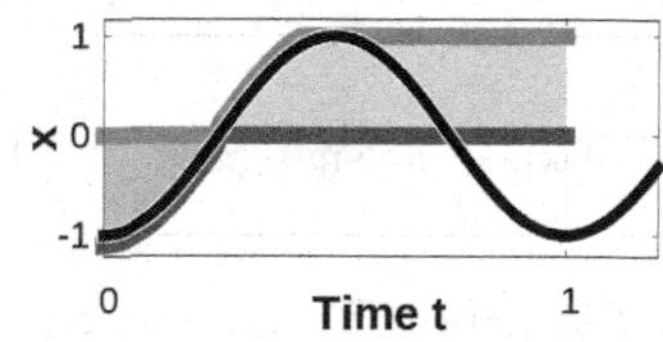

Fig. 1. The positive and negative robustness of $\overline{\Diamond}_{[0,1]}(x \geq 0)$ at $t = 0$.

Remark 2.4. Presence of averaged temporal operators forces separation of two robustness measures (positive and negative). Assume otherwise, i.e. that we have one robustness measure that can take both positive and negative values; then

[2] There is no distinction between strict inequalities ($<$) and non-strict ones ($\leq$). This is inevitable in the current robustness framework. This is also the case with **STL** in [12,13].

robustness that floats between positive and negative values over time can "cancel out" after an average is taken. This leads to the failure of *soundness* (see Propositions 2.9 and 2.10; also [13,16]), and then a positive robustness value no longer witnesses the Boolean truth of (the qualitative variant of) the formula. This is not convenient in the application to falsification.

2.3 Basic Properties of AvSTL

Lemma 2.5 (Temporal Monotonicity). *Let $0 \le t_0 < t \le t'$. The following hold.*

$$\llbracket \sigma, \varphi_1 \,\mathcal{U}_{[t_0,t]}\, \varphi_2 \rrbracket^+ \le \llbracket \sigma, \varphi_1 \,\mathcal{U}_{[t_0,t']}\, \varphi_2 \rrbracket^+ \quad \llbracket \sigma, \varphi_1 \,\mathcal{U}_{[t_0,t]}\, \varphi_2 \rrbracket^- \le \llbracket \sigma, \varphi_1 \,\mathcal{U}_{[t_0,t']}\, \varphi_2 \rrbracket^-$$
$$\llbracket \sigma, \varphi_1 \,\mathcal{R}_{[t_0,t]}\, \varphi_2 \rrbracket^+ \ge \llbracket \sigma, \varphi_1 \,\mathcal{R}_{[t_0,t']}\, \varphi_2 \rrbracket^+ \quad \llbracket \sigma, \varphi_1 \,\mathcal{R}_{[t_0,t]}\, \varphi_2 \rrbracket^- \ge \llbracket \sigma, \varphi_1 \,\mathcal{R}_{[t_0,t']}\, \varphi_2 \rrbracket^-$$

The inequalities hold also for the averaged temporal operators. □

We can now see well-definedness of Definition 2.3: we need that the integrals are defined; and the lemma shows that the integrated functions are monotone, hence Riemann integrable.

In Definition 2.3, the definitions for averaged operators with an infinite endpoint (like $\overline{\mathcal{U}}_{[0,\infty)}\varphi$) are given in terms of non-averaged operators. This is so that their well-definedness is immediate; the following lemma justifies those definitions.

Lemma 2.6. *For any $t_0 \in \mathbb{R}_{\ge 0}$, $\llbracket \sigma, \varphi_1 \,\mathcal{U}_{[t_0,\infty)}\, \varphi_2 \rrbracket^+ = \lim_{t\to\infty} \llbracket \sigma, \varphi_1 \,\overline{\mathcal{U}}_{[t_0,t]}\, \varphi_2 \rrbracket^+$. The same is true if we replace $\llbracket \_ \rrbracket^+$ with $\llbracket \_ \rrbracket^-$, and if we replace $\mathcal{U}$ with $\mathcal{R}$.* □

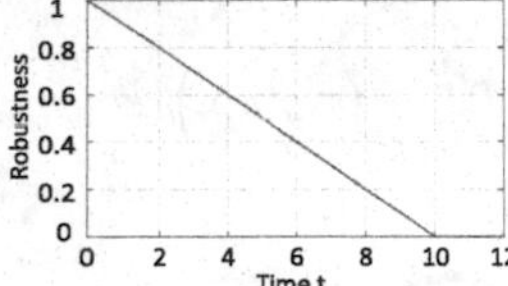

Fig. 2. Expeditiousness

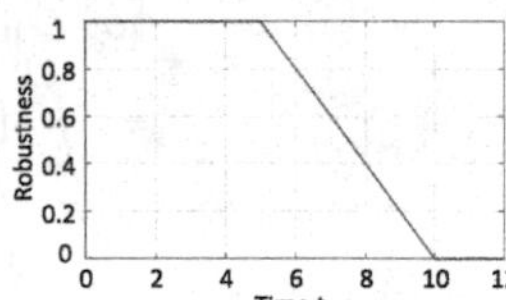

Fig. 3. Deadline

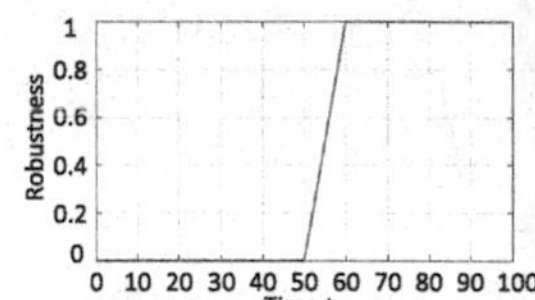

Fig. 4. Persistence

2.4 Common Temporal Specifications Expressed in AvSTL

Here we shall exemplify the expressivity of **AvSTL**, by encoding typical temporal specifications encountered in the model-based development of cyber-physical systems.

Remark 2.7. In what follows we sometimes use *propositional variables* such as `airbag` and $\mathtt{gear}_i$. For example, $\mathtt{gear}_2$ is a shorthand for the atomic formula $x_{\mathtt{gear}_2} \ge 0$ in **AvSTL**, where the variable $x_{\mathtt{gear}_2}$ is assumed to take a discrete value (1 or -1).

Expeditiousness ($\overline{\Diamond}_I \varphi$). Consider the following informal specification: *after heavy braking, the airbag must operate within 10 ms.* Its formalization in **STL** is straightforward by the formula $\Box(\texttt{heavyBraking} \rightarrow \Diamond_{[0,10]}\texttt{airbag})$. However, an airbag that operates after 1 ms. is naturally more desirable than one that operates after 9.99 ms. The **STL** formula fails to discriminate between these two airbags.

Such *expeditiousness* ("as soon as possible") requirements are more adequately modeled in **AvSTL**, using the averaged-eventually modality $\overline{\Diamond}_I$. See Fig. 2, where the horizontal axis is for time t. The vertical axis in the figure stands for the positive robustness value $[\![\sigma_t, \overline{\Diamond}_{[0,10]}\texttt{airbag}]\!]^+$ of the formula $\overline{\Diamond}_{[0,10]}\texttt{airbag}$, where σ_t is a signal in which $\texttt{airbag}$ operates (i.e. $x_{\texttt{airbag}}$ becomes from -1 to 1) at time t. We see that the formula successfully distinguishes an early-bird airbag from a lazy one.

Therefore the **AvSTL** formula $\Box(\texttt{heavyBraking} \rightarrow \overline{\Diamond}_{[0,10]}\texttt{airbag})$ formalizes a (refined) informal specification that: after heavy braking, the airbag must operate within 10 ms; *but the sooner the better.* It is not hard to expect that the latter is more faithful to the designer's intention than the original informal specification.

Deadline ($\Diamond_{[0,T]}\varphi \vee \overline{\Diamond}_{[T,T+\delta]}\varphi$). The expeditiousness-type requirement that we have discussed is sometimes too strict. Let us consider the following scenario: there is a deadline set at time T and arrival by then is rewarded no matter how late; and then there is a deadline extension by time δ and arrival between the deadline and the extended one is rewarded too, but with certain deduction.

Such a *deadline* specification is expressed in **AvSTL** by the formula $\Diamond_{[0,T]}\varphi \vee \overline{\Diamond}_{[T,T+\delta]}\varphi$, combining non-averaged and averaged eventually modalities. See Fig. 3, where the positive robustness of the formula $(\Diamond_{[0,5]}\texttt{airbag}) \vee (\overline{\Diamond}_{[5,5+5]}\texttt{airbag})$ is plotted, for the same signals σ_t as before (i.e. in σ_t the airbag operates at time t).

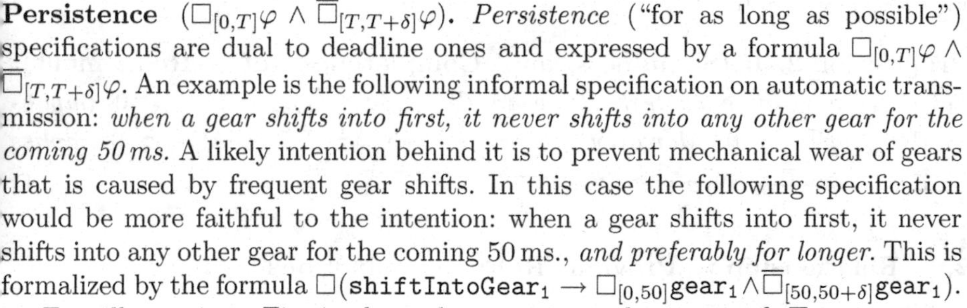

Persistence ($\Box_{[0,T]}\varphi \wedge \overline{\Box}_{[T,T+\delta]}\varphi$). *Persistence* ("for as long as possible") specifications are dual to deadline ones and expressed by a formula $\Box_{[0,T]}\varphi \wedge \overline{\Box}_{[T,T+\delta]}\varphi$. An example is the following informal specification on automatic transmission: *when a gear shifts into first, it never shifts into any other gear for the coming 50 ms.* A likely intention behind it is to prevent mechanical wear of gears that is caused by frequent gear shifts. In this case the following specification would be more faithful to the intention: when a gear shifts into first, it never shifts into any other gear for the coming 50 ms., *and preferably for longer.* This is formalized by the formula $\Box(\texttt{shiftIntoGear}_1 \rightarrow \Box_{[0,50]}\texttt{gear}_1 \wedge \overline{\Box}_{[50,50+\delta]}\texttt{gear}_1)$.

For illustration, Fig. 4 plots the positive robustness of $\Box_{[0,50]}\texttt{gear}_1 \wedge \overline{\Box}_{[50,60]}\texttt{gear}_1$ for signals σ'_t, where $\texttt{gear}_1$ is true in σ'_t from time 0 to t, and is false afterwards.

Other Temporal Specifications. Expressivity of **AvSTL** goes beyond the three examples that we have seen—especially after the extension of the language with *time-reversed* averaged temporal operators. The reversal of time here corresponds to the symmetry between *left* and *right* time robustness in [13]. Such an extension of **AvSTL** enables us to express specifications like *punctuality* ("no sooner, no later") and *periodicity.* The details will be reported in another venue.

2.5 Soundness of Refinements from STL to AvSTL

In Sect. 2.4 we have seen some scenarios where an **STL** specification is *refined* into an **AvSTL** one so that it more faithfully reflects the designer's intention. The following two are prototypical:

- **($\Diamond$-refinement)** the refinement of $\Diamond_I \varphi$ ("eventually φ, within I") into $\overline{\Diamond}_I \varphi$ ("eventually φ within I, but as soon as possible"); and
- **($\Box$-refinement)** the refinement of $\Box_{[a,b]} \varphi$ ("always φ throughout $[a, b]$") into $\Box_{[a,b]} \varphi \wedge \overline{\Box}_{[b,b+\delta]} \varphi$ ("always φ throughout $[a, b]$, and desirably also in $[b, b+\delta]$").

The following *soundness* results guarantee validity of the use of these refinements in falsification problems. *Completeness*, in a suitable sense, holds too.

Definition 2.8. A *positive context* is an **AvSTL** formula with a hole $[\,]$ at a positive position. Formally, the set of positive contexts is defined as follows:

$$\begin{aligned} \mathcal{C} ::= & [\,] \mid \mathcal{C} \vee \varphi \mid \varphi \vee \mathcal{C} \mid \mathcal{C} \wedge \varphi \mid \varphi \wedge \mathcal{C} \mid \mathcal{C}\, \mathcal{U}_I\, \varphi \mid \varphi\, \mathcal{U}_I\, \mathcal{C} \mid \mathcal{C}\, \overline{\mathcal{U}}_I\, \varphi \mid \varphi\, \overline{\mathcal{U}}_I\, \mathcal{C} \\ & \mid \mathcal{C}\, \mathcal{R}_I\, \varphi \mid \varphi\, \mathcal{R}_I\, \mathcal{C} \mid \mathcal{C}\, \overline{\mathcal{R}}_I\, \varphi \mid \varphi\, \overline{\mathcal{R}}_I\, \mathcal{C} \quad \text{where } \varphi \text{ is an } \textbf{AvSTL} \text{ formula.} \end{aligned}$$

For a positive context $\mathcal{C}$ and an **AvSTL** formula ψ, $\mathcal{C}[\psi]$ denotes the formula obtained by substitution of ψ for the hole $[\,]$ in $\mathcal{C}$.

Proposition 2.9 (Soundness and Completeness of $\Diamond$-Refinement). *Let $\mathcal{C}$ be a positive context. Then $[\![\sigma, \mathcal{C}[\overline{\Diamond}_{[a,b]} \varphi]]\!]^+ > 0$ implies $[\![\sigma, \mathcal{C}[\Diamond_{[a,b]} \varphi]]\!]^+ > 0$. Moreover, for any b' such that $b' < b$, $[\![\sigma, \mathcal{C}[\Diamond_{[a,b']} \varphi]]\!]^+ > 0$ implies $[\![\sigma, \mathcal{C}[\overline{\Diamond}_{[a,b]} \varphi]]\!]^+ > 0$.* □

Proposition 2.10 (Soundness and Completeness of $\Box$-Refinement). *Let $\mathcal{C}$ be a positive context. Then $[\![\sigma, \mathcal{C}[\Box_{[a,b]} \varphi \wedge \overline{\Box}_{[b,b+\delta]} \varphi]]\!]^+ > 0$ implies $[\![\sigma, \mathcal{C}[\Box_{[a,b]} \varphi]]\!]^+ > 0$. Moreover, for any $b' > b$, $[\![\sigma, \mathcal{C}[\Box_{[a,b']} \varphi]]\!]^+ > 0$ implies $[\![\sigma, \mathcal{C}[\Box_{[a,b]} \varphi \wedge \overline{\Box}_{[b,b+\delta]} \varphi]]\!]^+ > 0$.* □

2.6 Relationship to Previous Robustness Notions

Our logic **AvSTL** captures *space robustness* [16]—the first robustness notion proposed for **MITL/STL**, see Sect. 1—because the averaging-free fragment of **AvSTL** coincides with **STL** and its space robust semantics, modulo the separation of positive and negative robustness (Remark 2.4).

The relationship to *space-time robustness* proposed in [13] is interesting. In [13] they combine time and space robustness in the following way: for each time t and each space robustness value $c > 0$, *(right) time robustness relative to c*, denoted by $\theta_c^+(\varphi, \sigma, t)$, is defined by "how long after time t the formula φ maintains space robustness c." See the figure on the right, where the space-time robustness $\theta_c^+(x \geq 0, \sigma, 0)$ is depicted.

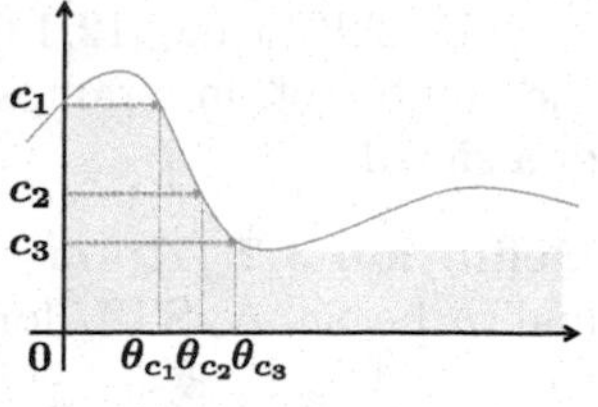

After all, space-time robustness in [13] is a function from c to $\theta_c^+(\varphi, \sigma, t)$; and one would like some real number as its characteristic. A natural choice of such is the *area* surrounded by the graph of the function (the shaded area in the figure), and it is computed in the same way as *Lebesgue integration*, as the figure suggests.

What corresponds in our **AvSTL** framework to this "area" characteristic value is the robustness of the formula $\overline{\Box}_{[0,\infty)}(x \geq 0)$ computed by Riemann integration (here we have to ignore the normalizing factor $\frac{1}{b-a}$ in Table 1). Therefore, very roughly speaking: our "averaged" robustness is a real-number characteristic value of the space-time robustness in [13]; and the correspondence is via the equivalence between Riemann and Lebesgue integration.

3 A Sliding-Window Algorithm for AvSTL Robustness

We shall present an algorithm for computing **AvSTL** robustness. It turns out that the presence of averaged modalities like $\overline{\Diamond}_I$—with an apparent nonlocal nature—does not incur severe computational overhead, at least for formulas in which averaged modalities are not nested. The algorithm is an adaptation of the one in [12] for **STL** robustness; the latter in turn relies on the *sliding window minimum algorithm* [22]. The algorithm's time complexity is linear with respect to the number of timestamps in the input signal; it exhibits a practical speed, too, as we will see later in Sect. 4.

Firstly we fix the class of signals to be considered.

Definition 3.1 (Finitely Piecewise-Constant/Piecewise-Linear Signal). A 1-dimensional signal $\sigma\colon \mathbb{R}_{\geq 0} \to \mathbb{R}$ is *finitely piecewise-constant (FPC)* if it arises from a finite sequence $\big[(t_0, r_0), (t_1, r_1), \dots, (t_n, r_n)\big]$ of timestamped values, via the correspondence $\sigma(t) = r_i$ (for $t \in [t_i, t_{i+1})$). Here $0 = t_0 < \cdots < t_n$, $r_i \in \mathbb{R}$, and t_{n+1} is deemed to be ∞.

Similarly, a 1-dimensional signal $\sigma\colon \mathbb{R}_{\geq 0} \to \mathbb{R}$ is *finitely piecewise-linear (FPL)* if it is identified with a finite sequence $\big[(t_0, r_0, q_0), \dots, (t_n, r_n, q_n)\big]$ of timestamped values, via the correspondence $\sigma(t) = r_i + q_i(t - t_i)$ (for $t \in [t_i, t_{i+1})$). Here $q_i \in R$ is the slope of σ in the interval $[t_i, t_{i+1})$.

The definitions obviously extend to many-dimensional signals $\sigma\colon \mathbb{R}_{\geq 0} \to \mathbb{R}^{\mathbf{Var}}$.

We shall follow [12,13] and measure an algorithm's complexity in terms of the number of timestamps (n in the above); the latter is identified with the *size* of a signal.

Definition 3.2 (Robustness Signal $[\varphi]_\sigma$). Let $\sigma : \mathbb{R}_{\geq 0} \to \mathbb{R}^{\mathbf{Var}}$ be a signal, and φ be an **AvSTL** formula. The *positive robustness signal* of φ over σ is the signal $[\varphi]^+_\sigma : \mathbb{R}_{\geq 0} \to \mathbb{R}$ defined by: $[\varphi]^+_\sigma(t) \triangleq [\![\sigma^t, \varphi]\!]^+$. Recall that $\sigma^t(t') = \sigma(t+t')$ is the t-shift of σ (Definition 2.2). The *negative robustness signal* $[\varphi]^-_\sigma$ is defined in the same way.

An averaged modality turns a piecewise-constant signal into a piecewise-linear one.

Lemma 3.3

1. *Let φ be an averaging-free **AvSTL** formula. If a signal σ is finitely piecewise-constant (or piecewise-linear), then so is $[\varphi]^+_\sigma$.*
2. *Let φ be an **AvSTL** formula without nested averaged modalities. If a signal σ is finitely piecewise-constant, then $[\varphi]^+_\sigma$ is finitely piecewise-linear.*

The above holds for the negative robustness signal $[\varphi]^-_\sigma$, too.

Proof. Straightforward by the induction on the construction of formulas. □

Our algorithm for computing **AvSTL** robustness $[\![\sigma, \varphi]\!]$ will be focused on: (1) a finitely piecewise-constant input signal σ; and (2) an **AvSTL** formula φ where averaged modalities are not nested. In what follows, for presentation, we use the (non-averaged and averaged) eventually modalities $\Diamond_I, \overline{\Diamond}_I$ in describing algorithms. Adaptation to other modalities is not hard; for complex formulas, we compute the robustness signal $[\varphi]_\sigma$ by induction on φ.

3.1 Donzé et al.'s Algorithm for STL Robustness

We start with reviewing the algorithm [12] for **STL** robustness. Our algorithm for **AvSTL** robustness relies on it in two ways: 1) the procedures for averaged modalities like $\overline{\Diamond}_I$ derive from those for non-averaged modalities in [12]; and (2) we use the algorithm in [12] itself for the non-averaged fragment of **AvSTL**.

Remark 3.4. The algorithm in [12] computes the **STL** robustness $[\![\sigma, \varphi]\!]$ for a finitely piecewise-*linear* signal σ. We need this feature e.g. for computing robustness of the formula $\Box(\texttt{heavyBraking} \to \overline{\Diamond}_{[0,10]}\texttt{airbag})$: note that, by Lemma 3.3, the robustness signal for $\overline{\Diamond}_{[0,10]}\texttt{airbag}$ is piecewise-linear even if the input signal is piecewise-constant.

Consider computing the robustness signal $[\Diamond_{[a,b]}\varphi]_\sigma$, assuming that the signal $[\varphi]_\sigma$ is already given.[3] The task calls for finding the supremum of $[\varphi]_\sigma(\tau)$ over

[3] In the rest of Sect. 3.1, for simplicity of presentation, we assume that $[\varphi]_\sigma$ is piecewise-constant. We note that the algorithm in [12] nevertheless extends to piecewise-linear $[\varphi]_\sigma$.

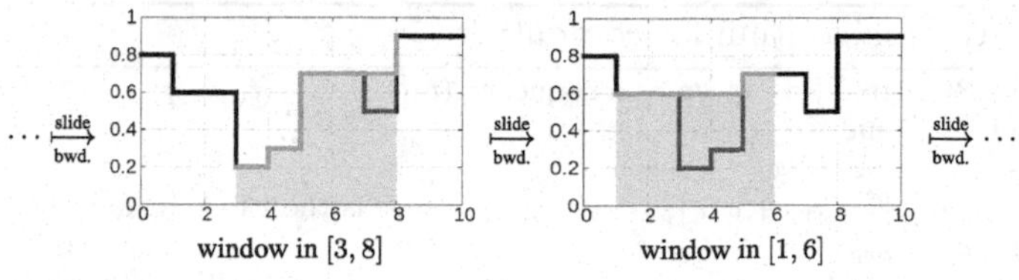

Fig. 5. A sliding window for computing $[\Diamond_{[0,5]}(x \geq 0)]^+_\sigma$; the black line is the signal σ

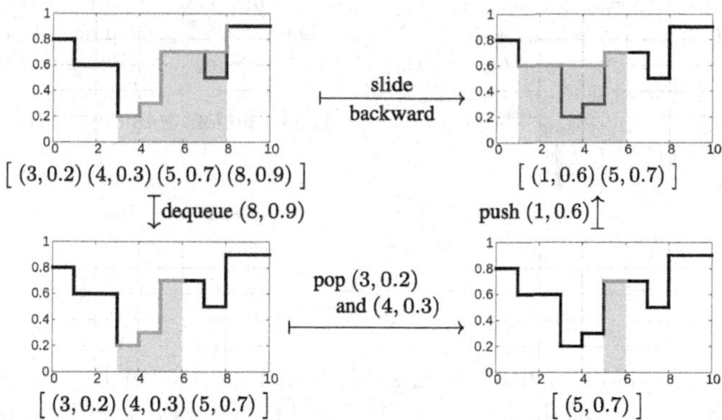

Fig. 6. Use of stackqueues and their operations, in the sliding window algorithm

$\tau \in [t+a, t+b]$; and this must be done for each t. Naively doing so leads to quadratic complexity.

Instead Donzé et al. in [12] employ a *sliding window* of size $b-a$ and let it scan the signal $[\varphi]_\sigma$ from right to left. The scan happens once for all, hence achieving linear complexity. See Fig. 5, where we take $[\Diamond_{[0,5]}(x \geq 0)]^+_\sigma$ as an example, and the blue shaded area designates the position of the sliding window. The window slides from $[3, 8]$ to the closest position to the left where its left-endpoint hits a new timestamped value of $[\varphi]_\sigma$, namely $[1, 6]$.

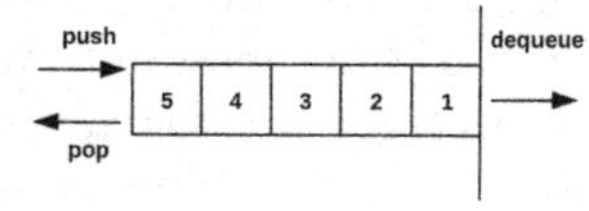

It is enough to know the shape of the blue (partial) signal in Fig. 5, at each position of the window. The blue signal denotes the (black) signal σ's local supremum within the window; more precisely, it denotes the value of the signal $[\![\sigma^t, \Diamond_{[0,\tau]}(x \geq 0)]\!]^+$ at time $t+\tau$, where $\tau \in [0, 5]$ and t is the leftmost position of the window. We can immediately read off the signal $[\Diamond_{[0,5]}(x \geq 0)]^+_\sigma$ from the blue signals: the former is the latter's value at the rightmost position of the window.

The keys in the algorithms in [12, 22] lie in:

- use of the *stackqueue* data structure (depicted above on the right) for the purpose of representing the blue (partial) signal in Fig. 5; and
- use of the operations *push*, *pop* and *dequeue* for updating the blue signal.

See Fig. 6, where each entry of a stackqueue is a timestamped value (t, r). We see that the slide of the window, from top-left to top-right in Fig. 6, is expressed by

Algorithm 1. An algorithm for computing $[\overline{\Diamond}_{[a,b]}\varphi]_\sigma$

Require: An FPC signal $[\varphi]_\sigma$ given as a sequence $(t_0, r_0), \ldots, (t_n, r_n)$
Ensure: The FPL signal $[\overline{\Diamond}_{[a,b]}\varphi]_\sigma$

$t_{\mathsf{temp}} := t_n - a;$
$F := \big[\, (t_{\mathsf{temp}} + a, [\varphi]_\sigma(t_{\mathsf{temp}} + a)) \,\big];$ ▷ F is the FPC signal $\tau \mapsto [\![\sigma^t, \Diamond_{[a,\tau]}\varphi]\!]$
$s := (b - a) \cdot [\varphi]_\sigma(t_{\mathsf{temp}} + a);$ ▷ The area of F
$G := \big[\, (t_{\mathsf{temp}}, s/(b-a), 0) \,\big];$ ▷ The FPC signal $[\overline{\Diamond}_{[a,b]}\varphi]_\sigma$
while $t_{\mathsf{temp}} \geq 0$ **do**
  $t_{\mathsf{old}} := t_{\mathsf{temp}};$
  $t_{\mathsf{temp}} :=$ the greatest t such that $t < t_{\mathsf{old}} \land \big(\exists t_i.\, t + a = t_i \lor \exists (t', r') \in F.\, t + b = t'\big);$
  $\mathsf{Deq} := \{(t, r) \in F \mid t > t_{\mathsf{temp}} + b\};$ $F := F \setminus \mathsf{Deq};$ ▷ Dequeue old elements in F
  $\mathsf{Pop} := \{(t, r) \in F \mid r \leq [\varphi]_\sigma(t_{\mathsf{temp}} + a)\};$ $F := F \setminus \mathsf{Pop};$ ▷ Pop small elements in F
  $t_{\mathsf{Pop}} := \min\{t \mid (t, r) \in F \text{ or } t = t_{\mathsf{temp}} + b\};$
  $F := \big[(t_{\mathsf{temp}} + a, [\varphi]_\sigma(t_{\mathsf{temp}} + a))\big] \cup F$ ▷ Push the left endpoint of the window to F
  $r_{\mathsf{left}} := \min\{r \mid (t, r) \in F\};$
  $r_{\mathsf{right}} := \max\{r \mid (t, r) \in F\};$
  $s := s - (t_{\mathsf{old}} - t_{\mathsf{temp}}) \cdot r_{\mathsf{right}} - \mathsf{area}(\mathsf{Pop}) + (t_{\mathsf{Pop}} - (t_{\mathsf{temp}} + a)) \cdot r_{\mathsf{left}}$
  $G := \{(t_{\mathsf{temp}}, s/(b-a), r_{\mathsf{right}} - r_{\mathsf{left}})\} \cup G$
end while

dequeue, pop and then push operations to stackqueues (in Fig. 6: from top-left to bottom-left, bottom-right and then top-right). Pseudocode for the algorithm can be found in [4, Appendix A.1].

3.2 An Algorithm for AvSTL Robustness

It turns out that the last algorithm is readily applicable to computing **AvSTL** robustness. Consider an averaged-eventually formula $\overline{\Diamond}_{[a,b]}\varphi$ as an example. What we have to compute is the size of the shaded areas in Fig. 5 (see also Fig. 1); and the shape of the blue signals in Fig. 5 carry just enough information to do so.

Pseudocode for the adaptation of the previous algorithm (in Sect. 3.1) to $\overline{\Diamond}_{[a,b]}\varphi$ is found in Algorithm 1. Its complexity is linear with respect to the number n of the timestamp values that represent the signal $[\varphi]_\sigma$.

An algorithm for the averaged-henceforth formula $[\overline{\Box}_{[a,b]}\varphi]_\sigma$ is similar. Extensions to averaged-until and averaged-release operators are possible, too; they use doubly-linked lists in place of stackqueues. See [4, Appendix A.2] for more details. Combining with the algorithm in Sect. 3.1 to deal with non-averaged temporal operators, we have the following complexity result. The complexity is the same as for **STL** [12].

Theorem 3.5. *Let φ be an **AvSTL** formula in which averaged modalities are not nested. Let σ be a finitely piecewise-constant signal. Then there exists an algorithm to compute $[\![\sigma, \varphi]\!]^+$ with time-complexity in $\mathcal{O}(d^{|\varphi|}|\varphi||\sigma|)$ for some constant d.*

The same is true for the negative robustness $[\![\sigma, \varphi]\!]^-$. □

Remark 3.6. The reason for our restriction to finitely piecewise-constant input signals is hinted in Remark 3.4; let us further elaborate on it. There the averaged modality $\overline{\Diamond}_{[0,10]}$ turns a piecewise-constant signal into a piecewise-linear one (Lemma 3.3); and then the additional Boolean connectives and non-averaged modalities (outside $\overline{\Diamond}_{[0,10]}$) are taken care of by the algorithm in [12], one that is restricted to piecewise-linear input.

It is not methodologically hard to extend this workflow to piecewise-*polynomial* input signals (hence to nested averaged modalities as well). Such an extension however calls for computing local suprema of polynomials, as well as their intersections—tasks that are drastically easier with affine functions. We therefore expect the extension to piecewise-polynomial signals to be computationally much more expensive.

4 Enhanced Falsification: Implementation and Experiments

We claim that our logic **AvSTL** achieves a good balance between expressivity—that communicates a designer's intention more faithfully to a falsification solver—and computational cost, thus contributing to the model-based development of cyber-physical systems. In this section we present our implementation that combines: (1) S-TaLiRo [7], one of the state-of-art falsification solvers that relies on robust MTL semantics and stochastic optimization; and (2) the **AvSTL** *evaluator*, an implementation of the algorithm in Sect. 3.2. Our experiments are on automotive examples of falsification problems; the results indicate that (refinement of specifications by) **AvSTL** brings considerable performance improvement.

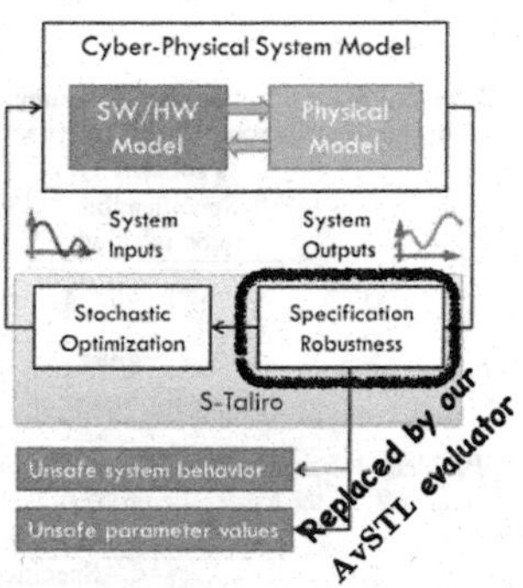

Fig. 7. An overview of S-TaLiRo (from [1]), with our modification

Implementation. S-TaLiRo [7] is "a Matlab toolbox that searches for trajectories of minimal robustness in Simulink/Stateflow" [1]. Recall the formalization of a falsification problem (Sect. 1). S-TaLiRo's input is: (1) a model $\mathcal{M}$ that is a Simulink/Stateflow model; and (2) a specification φ that is an **STL** formula.

S-TaLiRo employs stochastic simulation in the following *S-TaLiRo loop*:

1. Choose an input signal σ_{in} randomly.
2. Compute the output signal $\mathcal{M}(\sigma_{\mathsf{in}})$ with Simulink.
3. Compute the robustness $[\![\mathcal{M}(\sigma_{\mathsf{in}}), \varphi]\!]$.
4. If the robustness is ≤ 0 then return σ_{in} as a critical path. Otherwise choose a new σ_{in} (hopefully with a smaller robustness) and go back to Step 2.

Our modification of S-TaLiRo consists of: 1) changing the specification formalism from **STL** to **AvSTL** (with the hope that the robustness $[\![\mathcal{M}(\sigma_{\mathsf{in}}), \varphi]\!]^{+}$ carries

Table 2. Experiment results. Time is in seconds. The "Succ." columns show how many trials succeeded among the designated number of trials; the "Iter." columns show the average number of iterations of the S-TaLiRo loop, executed in each trial (max. 1000); and the "Time" columns show the average time that each trial took. For the last two we also show the average over *successful* trials.

Problem 1. Falsification means finding an input signal that keeps the engine speed ω below 2000 rpm, for T seconds. The bigger T is, the harder the problem is. We applied $\Diamond$-refinement.

Problem 1	$T = 20$			$T = 30$			$T = 40$		
Specification to be falsified	Succ. /**100**	Iter. (Succ.)	Time (Succ.)	Succ. /**100**	Iter. (Succ.)	Time (Succ.)	Succ. /**100**	Iter. (Succ.)	Time (Succ.)
$\Diamond_{[0,T]}(\omega \geq 2000)$	100	128.8	20.2	81	440.9	82.5	32	834.3	162.9
		128.8	20.2		309.7	59.0		482.2	94.4
$\overline{\Diamond}_{[0,T]}(\omega \geq 2000)$	100	123.9	22.9	98	249.8	46.1	81	539.6	110.9
		123.9	22.9		234.5	43.4		431.6	89.2

Problem 2. Falsification means finding an input signal that keeps ω within a range of 3500–4500 rpm for T consecutive seconds, at a certain stage. We applied $\Diamond$-refinement.

Problem 2	$T = 10$		
Specification to be falsified	Succ. /**100**	Iter. (Succ.)	Time (Succ.)
$\Box\Diamond_{[0,T]}(\omega \leq 3500 \vee \omega \geq 4500)$	45	625.4	209.1
		167.7	56.1
$\Box\overline{\Diamond}_{[0,T]}(\omega \leq 3500 \vee \omega \geq 4500)$	74	442.0	154.3
		245.9	86.6

Problem 3. Falsification means finding an input signal that shifts the gear into the fourth within T seconds. The smaller T is, the harder the problem is. Here $\mathbf{gear}_4$ is a propositional variable. We applied $\Box$-refinement.

Problem 3	$T = 4$			$T = 4.5$			$T = 5$		
Specification to be falsified	Succ. /**20**	Iter. (Succ.)	Time (Succ.)	Succ. /**20**	Iter. (Succ.)	Time (Succ.)	Succ. /**20**	Iter. (Succ.)	Time (Succ.)
$\Box_{[0,T]}\neg\mathbf{gear}_4$	0	1000	166.9	11	742.8	122.9	18	449.0	71.8
		–	–		532.3	87.5		387.7	61.9
$\Box_{[0,T]}\neg\mathbf{gear}_4$	17	570.1	94.0	20	250.5	40.3	20	107.5	17.6
$\wedge\overline{\Box}_{[T,10]}\neg\mathbf{gear}_4$		494.2	81.8		250.5	40.3		107.5	17.6

Problem 4. Falsification means finding input with which the gear never stays in the third consecutively for T seconds. The smaller T is, the harder the problem is. Here $\mathbf{gear}_3$ is a propositional variable. We applied $\Box$-refinement.

Problem 4	$T = 1$			$T = 2$		
Specification to be falsified	Succ. /**20**	Iter. (Succ.)	Time (Succ.)	Succ. /**20**	Iter. (Succ.)	Time (Succ.)
$\Diamond(\Box_{[0,T]}\mathbf{gear}_3)$	14	556.1	132.0	20	82.8	20.6
		365.8	87.1		82.8	20.6
$\Diamond(\Box_{[0,T]}\mathbf{gear}_3 \wedge \overline{\Box}_{[T,10]}\mathbf{gear}_3)$	20	105.1	36.3	20	29.7	10.2
		105.1	36.3	20	29.7	10.2

Problem 5. Falsification means finding input that violates the following requirement: *after the gear is shifted, it stays the same for T seconds.* (the smaller T, the harder). $\mathbf{gear}_1, \ldots, \mathbf{gear}_4$ are propositional variables. We applied $\Box$-refinement.

Problem 5 ($\varepsilon = 0.04$)	$T = 0.8$			$T = 1$			$T = 2$		
Specification to be falsified	Succ. /**20**	Iter. (Succ.)	Time (Succ.)	Succ. /**20**	Iter. (Succ.)	Time (Succ.)	Succ. /**20**	Iter. (Succ.)	Time (Succ.)
$\bigwedge_{i=1,\ldots,4}\Box\Big((\neg\mathbf{gear}_i \wedge \Diamond_{[0,\varepsilon]}\mathbf{gear}_i)$	2	972.5	402.5	19	356.8	155.6	20	27.4	11.8
$\rightarrow (\Box_{[\varepsilon,T+\varepsilon]}\mathbf{gear}_i)\Big)$		724.5	297.8		322.9	140.9		27.4	11.8
$\bigwedge_{i=1,\ldots,4}\Box\Big((\neg\mathbf{gear}_i \wedge \Diamond_{[0,\varepsilon]}\mathbf{gear}_i)$	12	561.1	349.1	20	93.1	57.8	20	42.7	26.9
$\rightarrow (\Box_{[\varepsilon,T+\varepsilon]}\mathbf{gear}_i \wedge \overline{\Box}_{[T+\varepsilon,5]}\mathbf{gear}_i)\Big)$		268.5	167.3		93.1	57.8		42.7	26.9

Problem 6. Falsification means finding an input signal that steers the vehicle speed v over 85 kph within T seconds, while keeping the engine speed ω below 4500 rpm. The smaller T is, the harder the problem is. We applied $\Box$-refinement.

Problem 6	$T = 10$			$T = 12$		
Specification to be falsified	Succ. /**20**	Iter. (Succ.)	Time (Succ.)	Succ. /**20**	Iter. (Succ.)	Time (Succ.)
$\Box_{[0,T]}(v \leq 85) \vee \Diamond(\omega \geq 4500)$	12	714.9	141.4	17	374.5	72.2
		524.9	108.1		264.1	51.2
$(\Box_{[0,T]}(v \leq 85) \wedge \overline{\Box}_{[T,20]}(v \leq 85))$	12	766.7	149.0	20	423.6	85.7
$\vee\Diamond(\omega \geq 4500)$		611.2	118.9		423.6	85.7

more information to be exploited in stochastic optimization); and 2) using, in Step 3 of the above loop, the **AvSTL** evaluator based on the sliding-window algorithm in Sect. 3. See Fig. 7.

Experiments. As a model $\mathcal{M}$ we used the automatic transmission model from [18], where it is offered "as benchmarks for testing-based falsification" [18]. The same model has been used in several works [15,20,25]. The model has two input ports (`throttle` and `brake`) and six output ports (the engine speed ω, the vehicle speed v, and four mutually-exclusive Boolean ports $\mathtt{gear}_1, \ldots, \mathtt{gear}_4$ for the current gear). See [4, Appendix C] for more details. As a specification φ to falsify, we took six examples from [18], sometimes with minor modifications. They constitute Problems 1–6 in Table 2.

Our goal is to examine the effect of our modification to S-TaLiRo. For the model $\mathcal{M}$ (that is fixed) and each of the six specifications φ, experiments are done with:

- $\mathcal{M}$ and the original **STL** formula φ, as a control experiment; and
- $\mathcal{M}$ and the **AvSTL** formula φ' that is obtained from φ as a refinement. The latter specifically involves $\Diamond$-*refinement* and $\Box$-*refinement* described in Sect. 2.5.

Faster, or more frequent, falsification in the latter setting witnesses effectiveness of our **AvSTL** approach. We note that falsifying φ' indeed means falsifying φ, because of the soundness of the refinement (Propositions 2.9 and 2.10).

A single falsification *trial* consists of at most 1000 *iterations* of the S-TaLiRo loop. For each specification φ (i.e. for each problem in Table 2) we made 20–100 falsification trials, sometimes with different parameter values T. We made multiple trials because of the stochastic nature of S-TaLiRo.

Experiment Results and Discussion. The experiment results are in Table 2. We used Matlab R2014b and S-TaLiRo ver.1.6 beta on ThinkPad T530 with Intel Core i7-3520M 2.90GHz CPU with 3.7 GB memory. The OS is Ubuntu14.04 LTS (64-bit).

Notable performance improvement is observed in Problems 3–5, especially in their harder instances. For example, our **AvSTL** enrichment made 17 out of 20 trials succeed in Problem 3 ($T = 4$), while no trials succeeded with the original **STL** specification. A similar extreme performance gap is observed also in Problem 5 ($T = 0.8$).

Such performance improvement in Problems 3–5 is not surprising. The specifications for these problems are concerned solely with the propositional variables $\mathtt{gear}_i$ (cf. Remark 2.7); and the space robustness semantics for **STL** assigns to these specifications only 0 or 1 (but no values in-between) as their truth values. We can imagine such "discrete" robustness values give few clues to stochastic optimization algorithms.

Both of $\Diamond$- and $\Box$-refinement in Sect. 2.5 turn out to be helpful. The latter's effectiveness is observed in Problems 3–5; the former improves a success rate from 32/100 to 81/100 in Problem 1 ($T = 40$).

Overall, the experiment results seem to support our claim that the complexity of (computing robustness values in) **AvSTL** is tractable. There is no big difference in the time each iteration takes, between the **STL** case and the **AvSTL** case.

5 Conclusions and Future Work

We introduced **AvSTL**, an extension of **STL** with *averaged* temporal operators. It adequately captures both space and time robustness; and we presented an algorithm for computing robustness that is linear-time with respect to the "size" of an input signal. Its use in falsification of CPS is demonstrated by our prototype that modifies S-TaLiRo.

As future work, we wish to compare our averaged temporal operators with other quantitative temporal operators, among which are the *discounting* ones [5,6]. The latter are closely related to *mean-payoff* conditions [10,14] as well as to *energy constraints* [8,9], all of which are studied principally in the context of automata theory.

Application of **AvSTL** to problems other than falsification is another important direction. Among them is *parameter synthesis*, another task that S-TaLiRo is capable of. We are now looking at application to *sequence classification* (see e.g. [21]), too, whose significant role in model-based development of CPS is widely acknowledged.

Acknowledgments. Thanks are due to Georgios Fainekos, Tomoyuki Kaga, Toshiki Kataoka, Hisashi Miyashita, Kohei Suenaga and Tomoya Yamaguchi for helpful discussions. The authors are supported by Grant-in-Aid for Young Scientists (A) No. 24680001, JSPS; and T.A. is supported by Grant-in-Aid for JSPS Fellows.

References

1. TaLiRo-tools. https://sites.google.com/a/asu.edu/s-taliro/s-taliro. Accessed 26 January 2015
2. Abbas, H., Hoxha, B., Fainekos, G.E., Deshmukh, J.V., Kapinski, J., Ueda, K.: Conformance testing as falsification for cyber-physical systems. In: CoRR, abs/1401.5200 (2014)
3. Abbas, H., Hoxha, B., Fainekos, G.E., Deshmukh, J.V., Kapinski, J., Ueda, K.: Wip abstract: conformance testing as falsification for cyber-physical systems. In: ACM/IEEE International Conference on Cyber-Physical Systems, ICCPS, Berlin, Germany, April 14–17, 2014, pp. 211. IEEE Computer Society (2014)
4. Akazaki, T., Hasuo, I.: Time robustness in MTL and expressivity in hybrid system falsification (extended version) (2015). http://arxiv.org/abs/1505.06307
5. Almagor, S., Boker, U., Kupferman, O.: Discounting in LTL. In: Ábrahám, E., Havelund, K. (eds.) TACAS 2014 (ETAPS). LNCS, vol. 8413, pp. 424–439. Springer, Heidelberg (2014)
6. Alur, R., Feder, T., Henzinger, T.A.: The benefits of relaxing punctuality. J. ACM **43**(1), 116–146 (1996)

7. Annpureddy, Y., Liu, C., Fainekos, G., Sankaranarayanan, S.: S-TaLiRo: a tool for temporal logic falsification for hybrid systems. In: Abdulla, P.A., Leino, K.R.M. (eds.) TACAS 2011. LNCS, vol. 6605, pp. 254–257. Springer, Heidelberg (2011)
8. Bouyer, P., Fahrenberg, U., Larsen, K.G., Markey, N., Srba, J.: Infinite runs in weighted timed automata with energy constraints. In: Cassez, F., Jard, C. (eds.) FORMATS 2008. LNCS, vol. 5215, pp. 33–47. Springer, Heidelberg (2008)
9. Brenguier, R., Cassez, F., Raskin, J.-F.: Energy and mean-payoff timed games. In: Fränzle, M., Lygeros, J. (eds.) Proceedings of the 17th International Conference on Hybrid Systems: Computation and Control, pp. 283–292. ACM, New York (2014)
10. Chatterjee, K., Henzinger, T.A., Jurdzinski, M.: Mean-payoff parity games. In: 20th IEEE Symposium on Logic in Computer Science, LICS, 26–29 June 2005, Chicago, IL, USA, pp. 178–187. IEEE Computer Society (2005)
11. Donzé, A.: Breach, a toolbox for verification and parameter synthesis of hybrid systems. In: Touili, T., Cook, B., Jackson, P. (eds.) CAV 2010. LNCS, vol. 6174, pp. 167–170. Springer, Heidelberg (2010)
12. Donzé, A., Ferrère, T., Maler, O.: Efficient robust monitoring for STL. In: Sharygina, N., Veith, H. (eds.) CAV 2013. LNCS, vol. 8044, pp. 264–279. Springer, Heidelberg (2013)
13. Donzé, A., Maler, O.: Robust satisfaction of temporal logic over real-valued signals. In: Chatterjee, K., Henzinger, T.A. (eds.) FORMATS 2010. LNCS, vol. 6246, pp. 92–106. Springer, Heidelberg (2010)
14. Ehrenfeucht, A., Mycielski, J.: Positional strategies for mean payoff games. Int. J. Game Theor. **8**(2), 109–113 (1979)
15. Fainekos, G.E., Sankaranarayanan, S., Ueda, K., Yazarel, H.: Verification of automotive control applications using S-TaLiRo. Am. Control Conf. (ACC) **2012**, 3567–3572 (2012)
16. Fainekos, G.E., Pappas, G.J.: Robustness of temporal logic specifications for continuous-time signals. Theor. Comput. Sci. **410**(42), 4262–4291 (2009)
17. Fränzle, M., Lygeros, J. (eds.) 17th International Conference on Hybrid Systems: Computation and Control (part of CPS Week), HSCC 2014, Berlin, Germany, April 15–17, 2014. ACM (2014)
18. Hoxha, B., Abbas, H., Fainekos, G.: Benchmarks for temporal logic requirements for automotive systems. In: Proceedings of Applied Verification for Continuous and Hybrid Systems (2014)
19. Jin, X., Deshmukh, J.V., Kapinski, J., Ueda, K., Butts, K.: Powertrain control verification benchmark. In: Fränzle, M., Lygeros, J. (eds.) Proceedings of the 17th international conference on Hybrid systems: computation and control, pp. 253–262. ACM, New York (2014)
20. Jin, X., Donzé, A., Deshmukh, J.V., Seshia, S.A.: Mining requirements from closed-loop control models. In: Belta, C., Ivancic, F. (eds.) Proceedings of the 16th International Conference on Hybrid Systems: Computation and Control, HSCC 2013, pp. 43–52. ACM, New York (2013)
21. Kong, Z., Jones, A., Ayala, A.M., Gol, E.A., Belta, C.: Temporal logic inference for classification and prediction from data. In: Fränzle, M., Lygeros, J. (eds.) Proceedings of the 17th international conference on Hybrid systems: computation and control, pp. 273–282. ACM, New York (2014)
22. Lemire, D.: Streaming maximum-minimum filter using no more than three comparisons per element. Nord. J. Comput. **13**(4), 328–339 (2006)
23. Maler, O., Nickovic, D.: Monitoring temporal properties of continuous signals. In: Lakhnech, Y., Yovine, S. (eds.) FORMATS 2004 and FTRTFT 2004. LNCS, vol. 3253, pp. 152–166. Springer, Heidelberg (2004)

24. Sankaranarayanan, S., Fainekos, G.: Falsification of temporal properties of hybrid systems using the cross-entropy method. In: Proceedings of the 15th ACM International Conference on Hybrid Systems: Computation and Control, HSCC 2012, pp. 125–134. ACM, New York, NY, USA (2012)
25. Yang, H., Hoxha, B., Fainekos, G.: Querying parametric temporal logic properties on embedded systems. In: Nielsen, B., Weise, C. (eds.) ICTSS 2012. LNCS, vol. 7641, pp. 136–151. Springer, Heidelberg (2012)
26. Zutshi, A., Deshmukh, J.V., Sankaranarayanan, S., Kapinski, J.: Multiple shooting, cegar-based falsification for hybrid systems. In: Proceedings of the 14th International Conference on Embedded Software, EMSOFT 2014, pp. 5:1–5:10, ACM, New York, NY, USA (2014)

Concurrency

Adaptive Concretization for Parallel Program Synthesis

Jinseong Jeon[1(✉)], Xiaokang Qiu[2], Armando Solar-Lezama[2], and Jeffrey S. Foster[1]

[1] University of Maryland, College Park, USA
{jsjeon,jfoster}@cs.umd.edu
[2] Massachusetts Institute of Technology, Cambridge, USA
{xkqiu,asolar}@csail.mit.edu

Abstract. Program synthesis tools work by searching for an implementation that satisfies a given specification. Two popular search strategies are *symbolic search*, which reduces synthesis to a formula passed to a SAT solver, and *explicit search*, which uses brute force or random search to find a solution. In this paper, we propose adaptive concretization, a novel synthesis algorithm that combines the best of symbolic and explicit search. Our algorithm works by partially concretizing a randomly chosen, but likely highly influential, subset of the unknowns to be synthesized. Adaptive concretization uses an online search process to find the optimal size of the concretized subset using a combination of exponential hill climbing and binary search, employing a statistical test to determine when one degree of concretization is sufficiently better than another. Moreover, our algorithm lends itself to a highly parallel implementation, further speeding up search. We implemented adaptive concretization for Sketch and evaluated it on a range of benchmarks. We found adaptive concretization is very effective, outperforming Sketch in many cases, sometimes significantly, and has good parallel scalability.

1 Introduction

Program synthesis aims to construct a program satisfying a given specification. One popular style of program synthesis is *syntax-guided synthesis*, which starts with a structural hypothesis describing the shape of possible programs, and then searches through the space of candidates until it finds a solution. Recent years have seen a number of successful applications of syntax-guided synthesis, ranging from automated grading [18], to programming by example [8], to synthesis of cache coherence protocols [22], among many others [6,14,20].

Despite their common conceptual framework, each of these systems relies on different synthesis procedures. One key algorithmic distinction is that some use

Supported in part by NSF CCF-1139021, CCF-1139056, CCF-1161775, and the partnership between UMIACS and the Laboratory for Telecommunication Sciences.

D. Kroening and C.S. Păsăreanu (Eds.): CAV 2015, Part II, LNCS 9207, pp. 377–394, 2015.
DOI: 10.1007/978-3-319-21668-3_22

explicit search—either stochastically or systematically enumerating the candidate program space—and others use *symbolic search*—encoding the search space as constraints that are solved using a SAT solver. The SyGuS competition has recently revealed that neither approach is strictly better than the other [1].

In this paper, we propose *adaptive concretization*, a new approach to synthesis that combines many of the benefits of explicit and symbolic search while also parallelizing very naturally, allowing us to leverage large-scale, multi-core machines. Adaptive concretization is based on the observation that in synthesis via symbolic search, the unknowns that parameterize the search space are not all equally important in terms of solving time. In Sect. 2, we show that while symbolic methods can efficiently solve for some unknowns, others—which we call *highly influential* unknowns—cause synthesis time to grow dramatically. Adaptive concretization uses explicit search to concretize influential unknowns with randomly chosen values and searches symbolically for the remaining unknowns. We have explored adaptive concretization in the context of the SKETCH synthesis system [19], although we believe the technique can be readily applied to other symbolic synthesis systems such as Brahma [12] or Rosette [21].

Combining symbolic and explicit search requires solving two challenges. First, there is no practical way to compute the precise influence of an unknown. Instead, our algorithm estimates that an unknown is highly influential if concretizing it will likely shrink the constraint representation of the problem. Second, because influence computations are estimates, even the highest influence unknown may not affect the solving time for some problems. Thus, our algorithm uses a series of trials, each of which makes an independent decision of what to randomly concretize. This decision is parameterized by a *degree of concretization*, which adjusts the probability of concretizing a high influence unknown. At degree 1, unknowns are concretized with high probability; at degree ∞, the probability drops to zero. The degree of concretization poses its own challenge: a preliminary experiment showed that across seven benchmarks and six degrees, there is a different optimal degree for almost every benchmark. (Section 3 describes the influence calculation, the degree of concretization, and this experiment.)

Since there is no fixed optimal degree, the crux of adaptive concretization is to estimate the optimal degree online. Our algorithm begins with a very low degree (i.e., a large amount of concretization), since trials are extremely fast. It then exponentially increases the degree (i.e., reduces the amount of concretization) until removing more concretization is estimated to no longer be worthwhile. Since there is randomness across the trials, we use a statistical test to determine when a difference is meaningful. Once the exponential climb stops, our algorithm does binary search between the last two exponents to find the optimal degree, and it finishes by running with that degree. At any time during this process, the algorithm exits if it finds a solution. Adaptive concretization naturally parallelizes by using different cores to run the many different trials of the algorithm. Thus a key benefit of our technique is that, by exploiting parallelism on big machines, it can solve otherwise intractable synthesis problems. (Section 4 discusses pseudocode for the adaptive concretization algorithm.)

We implemented our algorithm for SKETCH and evaluated it against 26 benchmarks from a number of synthesis applications including automated tutoring [18], automated query synthesis [6], and high-performance computing, as well as benchmarks from the SKETCH performance benchmark suite [19] and from the SyGuS'14 competition [1]. By running our algorithm over twelve thousand times across all benchmarks, we are able to present a detailed assessment of its performance characteristics. We found our algorithm outperforms SKETCH on 23 of 26 benchmarks, sometimes achieving significant speedups of 3× up to 14×. In one case, adaptive concretization succeeds where SKETCH runs out of memory. We also ran adaptive concretization on 1, 4, and 32 cores, and found it generally has reasonable parallel scalability. Finally, we compared adaptive concretization to the winner of the SyGuS'14 competition on a subset of the SyGuS'14 benchmarks and found that our approach is competitive with or outperforms the winner. (Section 5 presents our results in detail.)

2 Combining Symbolic and Explicit Search

To illustrate the idea of influence, consider the following SKETCH example:

```
bit[32] foo(bit[32] x) implements spec{
  if(??){
      return x & ??; // unknown m1
  }else{
      return x | ??; // unknown m2
} }
```

```
bit[32] spec(bit[32] x){
      return minus(x, mod(x, 8));
}
```

Here the symbol ?? represents an unknown constant whose type is automatically inferred. Thus, the ?? in the branch condition is a boolean, and the other ??'s, labeled as unknowns *m1* and *m2*, are 32-bit integers. The specification on the right asserts that the synthesized code must compute $(x - (x \; mod \; 8))$.

The sketch above has 65 unknown bits and 2^{33} unique solutions, which is too large for a naive enumerative search. However, the problem is easy to solve with *symbolic search*. Symbolic search works by symbolically executing the template to generate constraints among those unknowns, and then generating a series of SAT problems that solve the unknowns for well-chosen test inputs. Using this approach, SKETCH solves this problem in about 50 ms, which is certainly fast.

However, not all unknowns in this problem are equal. While the bit-vector unknowns are well-suited to symbolic search, the unknown in the branch is much better suited to explicit search. In fact, if we incorrectly concretize that unknown to *false*, it takes only 2 ms to discover the problem is unsatisfiable. If we concretize it correctly to *true*, it takes 30 ms to find a correct answer. Thus, enumerating concrete values lets us solve the problem in 32 ms (or 30 ms if in parallel), which is 35 % faster than pure symbolic search. For larger benchmarks this can make the difference between solving a problem in seconds and not solving it at all.

The benefit of concretization may seem counterintuitive since SAT solvers also make random guesses, using sophisticated heuristics to decide which variables to guess first. To understand why explicit search for this unknown is beneficial, we need to first explain how SKETCH solves for these unknowns. First, symbolic execution in SKETCH produces a predicate of the form $Q(x, c)$, where x is the 32-bit *input* bit-vector and c is a 65-bit *control* bit-vector encoding the unknowns. $Q(x, c)$ is true if and only if $foo(x) = x - (x \ mod \ 8)$ for the function *foo* described by c. Thus, SKETCH's goal is to solve the formula $\exists c. \forall x. Q(x, c)$. This is a doubly quantified problem, so it cannot be solved directly with SAT.

SKETCH reduces this problem to a series of problems of the form $\wedge_{x_i \in E} Q(x_i, c)$, i.e., rather than solving for all x, SKETCH solves for all x_i in a carefully chosen set E. After solving one of these problems, the candidate solution c is checked symbolically against all possible inputs. If a counterexample input is discovered, that counterexample is added to the set E and the process is repeated. This is the Counter-Example Guided Inductive Synthesis (CEGIS) algorithm, and it is used by most published synthesizers (e.g., [12,21,22]).

SKETCH's solver represents constraints as a graph, similar to SMT solvers, and then iteratively solves SAT problems generated from this graph. The graph is essentially an AST of the formula, where each node corresponds to an unknown or an operation in the theory of booleans, integer arithmetic, or arrays, and where common sub-trees are shared (see [19] for more details). For the simple example above, the formula $Q(x, c)$ has 488 nodes and CEGIS takes 12 iterations. On each iteration, the algorithm concretizes x_i and simplifies the formula to 195 nodes. In contrast, when we concretize the condition, $Q(x, c)$ shrinks from 488 to 391 nodes, which simplify to 82 nodes per CEGIS iteration. Over 12 iterations, this factor of two in the size of the problem adds up. Moreover, when we concretize the condition to the wrong value, SKETCH discovers the problem is unsatisfiable after only one counterexample, which is why that case takes only 2 ms to solve.

In short, unlike the random assignments the SAT solver uses for each individual sub-problem in the CEGIS loop, by assigning concrete values in the high-level representation, our algorithm significantly reduces the sub-problem sizes across *all* CEGIS loop iterations. It is worth emphasizing that the unknown controlling the branch is special. For example, if we concretize one of the bits in *m1*, it only reduces the formula from 488 to 486 nodes, and the solution time does not improve. Worse, if we concretize incorrectly, it will take almost the full 50 ms to discover the problem is unsatisfiable, and then we will have to flip to the correct value and take another 50 ms to solve, thus doubling the solution time. Thus, it is important to concretize only the most influential unknowns.

Putting this all together yields a simple, core algorithm for concretization. Consider the original formula $Q(x, c)$ produced by symbolic execution over the sketch. The unknown c is actually a vector of unknowns c_i, each corresponding to a different hole in the sketch. First, rank-order the c_i from most to least influence, $c_{j0}, c_{j1}, \cdots$. Then pick some threshold n smaller than the length of c, and concretize $c_{j0}, \cdots, c_{jn}$ with randomly chosen values. Run the previously described CEGIS algorithm over this partially concretized formula, and if a solution cannot be found, repeat the process with a different random assignment. Notice that this algorithm parallelizes trivially by running the same procedure on different cores, stopping when one core finds a solution.

This basic algorithm is straightforward, but three challenges remain: How to estimate the influence of an unknown, how to estimate the threshold of influence for concretization, and how to deal with uncertainty in those estimates. We discuss these challenges in the next two sections.

3 Influence and Degree of Concretization

An ideal measure of an unknown's influence would model its exact effect on running time, but there is no practical way to compute this. As we saw in the previous section, a reasonable alternative is to estimate how much we expect the constraint graph to shrink if we concretize a given node. However, it is still expensive to actually perform substitution and simplification.

Our solution is to use a more myopic measure of influence, focusing on the immediate neighborhood of the unknown rather than the full graph. Following the intuition from Sect. 2, our goal is to assign high influence to unknowns that select among alternative program fragments (e.g., used as guards of conditions), and to give low influence to unknowns in arithmetic operations. For an unknown n, we define $\mathit{influence}(n) = \sum_{d \in \mathit{children}(n)} \mathit{benefit}(d, n)$, where $\mathit{children}(n)$ is the set of all nodes that depend directly on n. Here $\mathit{benefit}(d, n)$ is meant to be a crude measure of how much the overall formula might shrink if we concretize the parent node n of node d. The function is defined by case analysis on d:

- *Choices.* If d is an ite node,[1] there are two possibilities. If n is d's guard ($d = \text{ite}(n, a, b)$) then $\mathit{benefit}(d, n) = 1$, since replacing a with a constant will cause the formula to shrink by at least one node. On the other hand, if n corresponds to one of the choices ($d = \text{ite}(c, n, b)$ or $d = \text{ite}(c, a, n)$), then $\mathit{benefit}(d) = 0$, since replacing n with a constant has no effect on the size of the formula.
- *Boolean nodes.* If d is any boolean node except negation, it has benefit 0.5. The intuition is that boolean nodes are often used in conditional guards, but sometimes they are not, so they have a lower benefit contribution than ite guards. If $d = \neg(n)$, then $\mathit{benefit}(d, n)$ equals $\mathit{influence}(d)$, since the benefit in terms of formula size of concretizing n and d is the same.
- *Choices among constants.* SKETCH's constraint graph includes nodes representing selection from a fixed sized array. If d corresponds to such a choice that is among an array of constants, then $\mathit{benefit}(d, n) = \mathit{influence}(d)$, i.e., the benefit of concretizing the choice depends on how many nodes depend on d.
- *Arithmetic nodes.* If d is an arithmetic operation, $\mathit{benefit}(d, n) = -\infty$. The intuition is that these unknowns are best left to the solver. For example, given ??+*in*, replacing ?? with a constant will not affect the size of the formula.

Note that while the above definitions may involve recursive calls to *influence*, the recursion depth will never be more than two due to prior simplifications. This pass also eliminates nodes with no children, and thus any unknown not involved in arithmetic will have at least one child and thus an influence of at least 0.5.

[1] $\text{ite}(a, b, c)$ corresponds to **if** *(a)* b **else** c, as in SMT-LIB.

Before settling on this particular influence measure, we tried a simpler approach that attempted to concretize holes that flow to conditional guards, with a probability based on the degree of concretization. However, we found that a small number of conditionals have a large impact on the size and complexity of the formula. Thus, having more refined heuristics to identify high influence holes is crucial to the success of the algorithm.

3.1 Degree of Concretization

The next step is to decide the threshold for concretization. We hypothesize the best amount of concretization varies—we will test this hypothesis shortly. Moreover, since our influence computation is only an estimate, we opt to incorporate some randomness, so that (estimated) highly influential unknowns might not be concretized, and (estimated) non-influential unknowns might be.

Thus, we parameterize our algorithm by a *degree of concretization* (or just *degree*). For each unknown n in the constraint graph, we calculate its estimated influence $N = \mathit{influence}(n)$. Then we concretize the node with probability

$$p = \begin{cases} 0 & \text{if } N < 0 \\ 1.0 & \text{if } N > 1500 \\ 1/(\max(2, \mathit{degree}/N)) & \text{otherwise} \end{cases}$$

To understand this formula, ignore the first two cases, and consider what happens when *degree* is low, e.g., 10. Then any node for which $N \geq 5$ will have a 1/2 chance of being concretized, and even if N is just 0.5—the minimum N for an unknown not involved in arithmetic—there is still a 1/20 chance of concretization. Thus, low degree means many nodes will be concretized. In the extreme, if *degree* is 0 then all nodes have a 1/2 chance of concretization. On the other hand, suppose *degree* is high, e.g., 2000. Then a node with $N = 5$ has just a 1/400 chance of concretization, and only nodes with $N \geq 1000$ would have a 1/2 chance. Thus, a high degree means fewer nodes will be concretized, and at the extreme of $\mathit{degree} = \infty$, no concretization will occur, just as in regular SKETCH.

For nodes with influence above 1500, the effect on the size of the formula is so large that we always find concretization profitable. Nodes with influence below zero are those involved in arithmetic, which we never concretize.

Overall, there are four "magic numbers" in our algorithm so far: the degree cutoff 1500 at which concretization stops being probabilistic, the ceiling of 0.5 on the probability for all other nodes, and the benefit values of 1 and 0.5 for boolean and choice unknowns, respectively. We determined these number in an ad hoc way using a subset of our benchmarks. For example, the 0.5 probability ceiling is the first thing we tried, and it worked well. On the other hand, we initially tried probability 0 for boolean unknowns, but found that some booleans also indirectly control choices; so we increased the benefit to 0.5, which seems to work well. We leave a more systematic analysis to future work.

Table 1. Expected running time (s) using empirical success rate. SIQR in small text. Fastest time in dark grey, second-fastest in light grey.

Benchmark	Degree 16		64		128		512		1024		4096	
p_button	∞		∞		∞		22	18	60	55	56	65
p_color	∞		∞		23	8	10	3	31	10	4	1
p_menu	∞		∞		∞		31	31	14	6	12	7
l_prepend	77	62	116	114	94	94	179	258	716	643	1,490	270
l_min	∞		23	274	59	2,388	1,440	2,711	5,770	3,387	7,434	2,177
a_mom_1	∞		1,176	620	308	1,376	1,655	1,476	3,883	3,000	1,433	2,514
a_mom_2	∞		∞		9,262	5,920	9,610	22,468	20,036	40,453	10,461	5,499

3.2 Preliminary Experiment: Optimal Degree

We conducted a preliminary experiment to test whether the optimal degree varies with subject program. We chose seven benchmarks across three different synthesis domains. The left column of Table 1 lists the benchmarks, grouped by domain. Section 5.1 describes the programs and experimental machine in more detail. We ran each benchmark with degrees varying exponentially from 16 to 4096. For each degree, we ran each benchmark 256 times, with no timeout.

For each benchmark/degree pair, we wish to estimate the time to success if we concretized the same benchmark many times at that degree. To form this estimate, for each such pair we compute the fraction of runs p that succeeded; this approximates the true probability of success. Then if a trial takes time t, we compute the *expected time to success* as t/p. While this is a coarse estimate, it provides a simple calculation we can also use in an algorithm (Sect. 4). If p is 0 (no trial succeeded), the expected time to success is ∞.

Results. Each cell in Table 1 contains the median expected run time in seconds, as computed for each degree. Since variance is high, we also report the semi-interquartile range (SIQR) of the running times, shown in small text. We highlight the fastest and second-fastest times.

The table shows that the optimal degree varies across all benchmarks; indeed, all degrees except 1024 were optimal for at least one benchmark. We also see a lot of variance across runs. For example, for `l_min`, degree 128, the SIQR is more than 40× the median. Other benchmarks also have high SIQRs. Importantly, if we visualize the median expected running times, they form a vee around the fastest time—performance gets worse the farther away from optimal in either direction. Thus, we can *search* for an optimal degree, as we discuss next.

4 Adaptive, Parallel Concretization

Figure 1 gives pseudocode for adaptive concretization. The core step of our algorithm, encapsulated in the **run_trial** function, is to run Sketch with the specified degree. If a solution is found, we exit the search. Otherwise, we return both

```
run_trial(degree)
  run SKETCH with specified degree
  if solution found then
    raise success
  else
    return (running time,
            concretization space size)

compare(deg_a, deg_b)
  dist_a ← ∅
  dist_b ← ∅
  while |dist_a| ≤ Max_dist ∧
      wilcoxon(dist_a, dist_b) > T do
    dist_a ∪← run_trial(deg_a)
    dist_b ∪← run_trial(deg_b)
  if wilcoxon(dist_a, dist_b) > T then
    return tie
  elsif avg(dist_a) < avg(dist_b) then
    return left
  else
    return right

climb()
  low, high ← 0, 1
  while high < Max_exp do
    case compare(2^low, 2^high) of
      left: break
      right:
        low ← high
        high ← high + 1
      tie: high ← high + 1
  return (low, high)

bin_search(low, high)
  mid ← (low + high) / 2
  case compare(low, mid) of
    left: return bin_search(low, mid)
    right: return bin_search(mid, high)
    tie: return mid

main()
  (low, high) ← climb()
  deg ← bin_search(2^low, 2^high)
  while (true) do run_trial(deg)
```

Fig. 1. Search Algorithm using Wilcoxon Signed-Rank Test.

the time taken by that trial and the size of the concretization space, e.g., if we concretized n bits, we return 2^n. We will use this information to estimate the time-to-solution of running at this degree.

Since SKETCH solving has some randomness in it, a single trial is not enough to provide a good estimate of time-to-solution, even under our heuristic assumptions. In Table 1 we used 256 trials at each degree, but for a practical algorithm, we cannot fix a number of trials, lest we run either too many trials (which wastes time) or too few (which may give a non-useful result).

To solve this issue, our algorithm uses the *Wilcoxon Signed-Rank Test* [24] to determine when we have enough data to distinguish two degrees. We assume we have a function **wilcoxon***(dist_a, dist_b)* that takes two equal-length lists of (time, concretization space size) pairs, converts them to distributions of estimated times-to-solution, and implements the test, returning a p-value indicating the probability that the means of the two distributions are different.

Recall that in our preliminary experiment in Sect. 3, we calculated the estimated time to success of each trial as t/p, where t was the time of the trial and p was the empirical probability of success. We use the same calculation in this algorithm, except we need a different way to compute p, since the success rate is always 0 until we find a solution, at which point we stop. Thus, we instead calculate p from the search space size. We assume there is only one solution, so if the search space size is s, we calculate $p = 1/s$.[2]

Comparing Degrees. Next, **compare** takes two degrees as inputs and returns a value indicating whether the **left** argument has lower expected running time, the **right** argument does, or it is a **tie**. The function initially creates two empty sets of trial results, *dist_a* and *dist_b*. Then it repeatedly calls **run_trial** to add a new trial to each of the two distributions (we write $x \cup\leftarrow y$ to mean adding y to set x). Iteration stops when the number of elements in each set exceeds some threshold *Max_dist*, or the **wilcoxon** function returns a p-value below some threshold T. Once the algorithm terminates, we return **tie** if the threshold was never reached, or **left** or **right** depending on the means.

In our experiments, we use $3 \times max(8, |cores|)$ for *Max_dist*. Thus, **compare** runs at most three "rounds" of at least eight samples (or the number of cores, if that is larger). This lets us cut off the **compare** function if it does not seem to be finding any distinction. We use 0.2 for the threshold T. This is higher than a typical p-value (which might be 0.05), but recall our algorithm is such that returning an incorrect answer will only affect performance and not correctness. We leave it to future work to tune *Max_dist* and T further.

Searching for the Optimal Degree. Given the **compare** subroutine, we can implement the search algorithm. The entry point is **main**, shown in the lower-right corner of Fig. 1. There are two algorithm phases: an *exponential climbing* phase (function **climb**) in which we try to roughly bound the optimal degree, followed by a binary search (function **bin_search**) within those bounds.

We opted for an initial exponential climb because binary search across the whole range could be extremely slow. Consider the first iteration of such a process, which would compare full concretization against no concretization. While the former would complete almost instantaneously, the latter could potentially take a long time (especially in situations when our algorithm is most useful).

The **climb** function aims to return a pair *low*, *high* such that the optimal degree is between 2^{low} and 2^{high}. It begins with *low* and *high* as 0 and 1, respectively. It then increases both variables until it finds values such that at degree 2^{high}, search is estimated to take a longer time than at 2^{low}, i.e., making things more symbolic than *low* causes too much slowdown. Notice that the initial trials of the **climb** will be extremely fast, because almost all variables will be concretized.

To perform this search, **climb** repeatedly calls **compare**, passing in 2 to the power of *low* and *high* as the degrees to compare. Then there are three cases. If **left** is returned, 2^{low} has better expected running time than 2^{high}. Hence we assume the true optimal degree is somewhere between the two, so we return them. Otherwise, if **right** is returned, then 2^{high} is better than 2^{low}, so we shift up to the next exponential range. Finally, if it is a **tie**, then the range is too narrow to show a difference, so we widen it by leaving *low* alone and incrementing *high*.

[2] Notice we can ignore the size of the symbolic space, since symbolic search will find a solution if one exists for the particular concretization.

We also terminate climbing if *high* exceeds some maximum exponent *Max_exp*. In our implementation, we choose *Max_exp* as 14, since for our subject programs this makes runs nearly all symbolic.

After finding rough bounds with **climb**, we then continue with a binary search. Notice that in **bin_search**, *low* and *high* are the actual degrees, whereas in **climb** they are degree exponents. Binary search is straightforward, maintaining the invariant that *low* has expected faster or equivalent solution time to *high* (recall this is established by **climb**). Thus each iteration picks a midpoint *mid* and determines whether *low* is better than *mid*, in which case *mid* becomes the new *high*; or *mid* is better, in which case the range shifts to *mid* to *high*; or there is no difference, in which case *mid* is returned as the optimal degree.

Finally, after the degree search has finished, we repeatedly run SKETCH with the given degree. The search exits when **run_trial** finds a solution, which it signals by raising an exception to exit the algorithm. (Note that **run_trial** may find a solution at any time, including during **climb** or **bin_search**).

Parallelization. Our algorithm is easy to parallelize. The natural place to do this is inside **run_trial**: Rather than run a single trial at a time, we perform parallel trials. More specifically, our implementation includes a worker pool of a user-specified size. Each worker performs concretization randomly at the specified degree, and thus they are highly likely to all be doing distinct work.

Timeouts. Like all synthesis tools, SKETCH includes a timeout that kills a search that seems to be taking too long. Timeouts are tricky to get right, because it is hard to know whether a slightly longer run would have succeeded. Our algorithm exacerbates this problem because it runs many trials. If those trials are killed just short of the necessary time, it adds up to a lot of wasted work. At the other extreme, we could have no timeout, but then the algorithm may also waste a lot of time, e.g., searching for a solution with incorrectly concretized values.

To mitigate the disadvantages of both extremes, our implementation uses an adaptive timeout. All worker threads share an initial timeout value of one minute. When a worker thread hits a timeout, it stops, but it doubles the shared timeout value. In this way, we avoid getting stuck rerunning with too short a timeout. Note that we only increase the timeout during **climb** and **bin_search**. Once we fix the degree, we leave the timeout fixed.

5 Experimental Evaluation

We empirically evaluated adaptive concretization against a range of benchmarks with various characteristics.[3] Compared to regular SKETCH (i.e., pure symbolic search), we found our algorithm is substantially faster in many cases; competitive in most of the others; and slower on a few benchmarks. We also compared adaptive concretization with concretization fixed at the final degree chosen by the adaption phase of our algorithm (i.e., to see what would happen if we

[3] Our testing infrastructure, benchmarks, and raw experimental data are open-sourced and explained at: http://plum-umd.github.io/adaptive-concretization/.

could guess this in advance), and we found performance is reasonably close, meaning the overhead for adaptation is not high. We measured parallel scalability of adaptive concretization of 1, 4, and 32 cores, and found it generally scales well. We also compared against the winner of the SyGuS'14 competition on a subset of the benchmarks and found that adaptive concretization is better than the winner on 6 of 9 benchmarks and competitive on the remaining benchmarks.

Throughout this section, all performance reports are based on 13 runs on a server equipped with forty 2.4 GHz Intel Xeon processors and 99 GB RAM, running Ubuntu 14.04.1. LTS. (We used the same machine for the experiments in Sect. 3.) For the pure SKETCH runs only, performance is also on 13 runs with a 2-hour timeout and 32 GB memory bound.

5.1 Benchmarks

The names of our benchmarks are listed in the left column of Table 2, with the size in the next column. The benchmarks are grouped by the synthesis application they are from. Each application domain's sketches vary in complexity, amount of symmetry, etc. We discuss the groups in order.

- PASKET. The first three benchmarks, beginning with `p_`, come from the application that inspired this work: PASKET, a tool that aims to construct executable code that behaves the same as a framework such as Java Swing, but is much simpler to statically analyze [11]. PASKET's sketches are some of the largest that have ever been tried, and we developed adaptive concretization because they were initially intractable with SKETCH. As benchmarks, we selected three PASKET sketches that aim to synthesize parts of Java Swing that include buttons, the color chooser, and menus.
- *Data Structure Manipulation.* The second set of benchmarks is from a project aiming to synthesize provably correct data-structure manipulations [13]. Each synthesis problem consists of a program template and logical specifications describing the functional correctness of the expected program. There are two benchmarks. `l_prepend` accepts a sorted singly linked list L and prepends a key k, which is smaller than any element in L. `l_min` traverses a singly linked list via a `while` loop and returns the smallest key in the list.
- *Invariants for Stencils.* The next sets of benchmarks, beginning with `a_mom_`, are from a system that synthesizes invariants and postconditions for scientific computations involving stencils. In this case, the stencils come from a DOE Miniapp called Cloverleaf [7]. These benchmarks involve primarily integer arithmetic and large numbers of loops.
- *SyGuS Competition.* The next sets of benchmarks, beginning with `ar_` and `hd_`, are from the first Syntax-Guided Synthesis Competition [1], which compared synthesizers using a common set of benchmarks. We selected nine benchmarks that took at least 10 s for any of the solvers in the competition, but at least one solver was able to solve it.

Table 2. Comparing SKETCH, adaptive, and non-adaptive concretization.

Benchmark	LoC	SKETCH		Adaptive				Non-Adaptive		
		Time (s)		Degree	# Trials	Time (s)		# Trials	Time (s)	
`p_button`	3,436	**50**	∞	4,160	639	51	8	249	21	6
`p_color`	3,194	**13**	0	3,072	551	33	6	109	12	4
`p_menu`	4,099	`OOM`		5,120	752	**84**	18	207	31	10
`l_prepend`	708	96	8	32	98	**20**	4	110	25	4
`l_min`	795	810	235	512	153	**59**	40	17	28	6
`a_mom_1`	229	336	35	256	316	**274**	76	331	285	16
`a_mom_2`	231	**1,000**	56	2,048	383	1,517	254	303	1,422	89
`ar_s_4`	313	6	1	16	18	**3**	0	25	3	0
`ar_s_5`	334	9	0	16	17	**4**	0	29	4	1
`ar_s_6`	337	17	2	32	23	**6**	0	33	9	1
`ar_s_7`	322	63	8	64	84	**50**	12	35	59	8
`ar_sum`	328	618	282	16	11	**50**	19	27	31	8
`hd_13_d5`	310	88	47	16	3	**11**	2	7	8	0
`hd_14_d1`	304	156	41	16	5	**29**	12	10	22	7
`hd_14_d5`	329	1,294	388	16	23	**229**	47	16	239	83
`hd_15_d5`	329	733	370	32	9	**177**	16	6	213	39
`s_cg`	124	18	4	64	161	**15**	2	160	14	0
`s_log2`	49	971	314	128	114	**349**	105	25	131	89
`s_logcnt`	30	225	206	32	90	**21**	26	84	16	6
`s_rev`	136	327	202	256	165	**53**	22	11	43	14
`deriv2`	1,444	28	4	16	15	**8**	0	20	8	2
`deriv3`	1,410	28	2	32	9	**7**	1	10	7	0
`deriv4`	1,410	14	0	16	7	**6**	0	20	5	0
`deriv5`	1,410	14	1	16	7	**6**	0	19	5	0
`q_noti`	262	12	6	32	100	**8**	2	79	6	1
`q_serv`	2,005	105	60	32	11	**22**	2	9	23	2

– SKETCH. The last three groups of benchmarks, beginning with `s_`, `deriv`, and `q_`, are from SKETCH's performance test suite, which is used to identify performance regressions in SKETCH and measure potential benefits of optimizations.

5.2 Performance Results

The right columns of Table 2 show our results. The columns that include running time are greyed for easy comparison, with the semi-interquartile range (SIQR) in a small font. (We only list the running times SIQR to save space.) The median is ∞ if more than half the runs timed out, while the SIQR is ∞ if more than one quarter of the runs timed out. The first grey column lists SKETCH's running time on one core. The next group of columns reports on adaptive concretization, run on 32 cores. The first column in the group gives the median of the final degrees chosen by adaptive concretization. The next column lists the median number of calls to **run_trial**. The last column lists the median running time. Lastly, the right group of columns shows the performance of our algorithm on 32 cores, assuming we skip the adaptation step and jump straight to running with the median degree shown in the table. For example, for `p_button`, these columns report results for running starting with degree 4,160 and never changing it. We again report the number of trials and the running time.

Comparing SKETCH and adaptive concretization, we find that adaptive concretization typically performs better. In the figure, we boldface the fastest time between those two columns. We see several significant speedups, ranging from 14× for `l_min`, 12× for `ar_sum`, and 11× for `s_logcnt` to 4× for `hd_15_d5` and `deriv3` and 3× for `ar_s_6` and `s_log2`. For `p_button`, regular SKETCH reaches the 2-hour timeout in 4 of 13 runs, while our algorithm succeeds, mostly within one minute. In another case, `p_menu`, SKETCH reliably exceeds our 32 GB memory bound and then aborts. Overall, adaptive concretization performed better in 23 of 26 benchmarks, and about the same on one benchmark.

On the remaining benchmarks (`p_color` and `a_mom_2`), adaptive concretization's performance was within about a factor of two. Comparing other similarly short-running benchmarks, such as `deriv4` and `deriv5`, where the final degree (16) was chosen very early, the degree search process needed to spend more time to reach bigger degree, resulting in the slowdown. Finally, `a_mom_2` is 1.5× slower. In this case, SKETCH's synthesis phase is extremely fast, hence parallelization has no benefit. Instead, the running time is dominated by the checking phase (when the candidate solution is checked symbolically against all possible inputs), and using adaptive concretization only adds overhead.

Next we compare adaptive concretization to non-adaptive concretization at the final degree. In 7 cases, the adaptive algorithm is actually faster, due to random chance. In the remaining cases, the adaptive algorithm is either about the same as non-adaptive or is at worst within a factor of approximately three.

5.3 Parallel Scalability and Comparison to SyGuS Solvers

We next measured how adaptive concretization's performance varies with the number of cores, and compare it to the winner of the SyGuS competition. Table 3 shows the results. The first two columns are the same as Table 2. The next five columns show the performance of adaptive concretization on 1, 4, and 32 cores. Real time is wall-clock time for the parallel run (the 32-core real-time column is the same as Table 2), and CPU time is the cumulative SKETCH back-end time summed over all cores. We discuss the rightmost column shortly. We boldface the fastest real time among SKETCH, 1, 4, and 32 cores.

The real-time results show that, in the one-core experiments, adaptive concretization performs better than regular SKETCH in 17 of 26 cases. Although adaptive concretization is worse or times out in the other cases, its performance improves with the number of cores. The 4-core runs are consistently close to

Table 3. Parallel scalability of adaptive concretization.

Bench mark	SKETCH Time (s)		# Cores (Time (s)) 1 Real		4 Real		4 CPU		32 Real		32 CPU		**Enum** Time(s)	
p_button	**50**	∞	818	∞	70	30	148	142	51	8	406	179		
p_color	**13**	0	∞		43	4	42	29	33	6	126	74		
p_menu	OOM		∞		304	275	501	589	**84**	18	780	300		
l_prepend	96	8	36	10	37	9	52	14	**20**	4	124	12		
l_min	810	235	∞		159	62	287	172	**59**	40	425	324		
a_mom_1	336	35	∞		455	97	1,545	460	**274**	76	3,055	802		
a_mom_2	**1,000**	56	∞		1,469	144	4,730	647	1,517	254	20,189	14,315		
ar_s_4	6	1	5	2	4	0	2	0	**3**	0	11	6	1,804	44
ar_s_5	9	0	6	2	8	2	9	2	**4**	0	9	4	∞	
ar_s_6	17	2	15	2	13	2	21	4	**6**	0	24	12	∞	
ar_s_7	63	8	131	61	62	36	97	90	**50**	12	340	221	∞	
ar_sum	618	282	97	46	103	70	168	60	**50**	19	74	31	∞	
hd_13_d5	88	47	**11**	5	13	2	8	4	**11**	2	7	2	8	0
hd_14_d1	156	41	48	32	53	23	28	20	**29**	12	26	18	8	0
hd_14_d5	1,294	388	∞		389	122	384	102	**229**	47	386	94	201	1
hd_15_d5	733	370	544	392	254	62	291	100	**177**	16	266	104	424	13
s_cg	18	4	**13**	4	15	2	19	4	15	2	42	17		
s_log2	971	314	∞		1,157	455	2,541	1,500	**349**	105	1,675	1,402		
s_logcnt	225	206	199	260	147	137	283	181	**21**	26	140	148		
s_rev	327	202	309	∞	117	102	176	106	**53**	22	107	144		
deriv2	28	4	19	7	12	4	14	7	**8**	0	18	4		
deriv3	28	2	**5**	2	8	2	6	2	7	1	11	4		
deriv4	14	0	**4**	2	6	0	3	1	6	0	6	2		
deriv5	14	1	**5**	1	6	0	4	0	6	0	8	2		
q_noti	12	6	**8**	4	19	9	14	8	**8**	2	21	4		
q_serv	105	60	34	16	33	6	29	14	**22**	2	45	26		

or better than 1-core runs; in some cases, benchmarks that time out on 1 core succeed on 4 cores. At 32 cores, we see the best performance in 20 of the 26 cases, with a speedup over 4-core runs ranging up to 7×. There is only one case where 4 cores is faster than 32: a_mom_2. However, as the close medians and large SIQR indicate, this is noise due to randomness in SKETCH.

Comparing real times and CPU time, we can see that our algorithm does fully utilize all cores. Investigating further, we found one source of overhead is that each trial re-loads its input file. We plan to eliminate this cost in the future by only reading the input once and then sharing the resulting data structure.

Finally, the rightmost column of Table 3 shows the performance of the Enumerative CEGIS Solver, which won the SyGuS'14 Competition [1]. As the Enumerative Solver does not accept problems in SKETCH format, we only compare on benchmarks from the competition (which uses the SyGuS-IF format, which is easily translated to a sketch). We should note that the enumerative solver is not parallelized and may be difficult to parallelize.

Adaptive concretization is faster for 6 of 9 benchmarks from the competition. It is also worth mentioning the Enumerative Solver actually won on the four benchmarks beginning with hd_. Our results show that adaptive concretization outperforms it on one benchmark and is competitive on the others.

6 Related Work

There have been many recent successes in sampling-based synthesis techniques. For example, Schkufza et al. use sampling-based synthesis for optimization [14,15], and Sharma et al. use similar techniques to discover complex invariants in programs [16]. These systems use Markov Chain Montecarlo (MCMC) techniques, which use fitness functions to prioritize sampling over regions of the solution space that are more promising. This is more sophisticated sampling technique than what is used by our method. We leave it to future work to explore MCMC methods in our context. Another alternative to constraint-based synthesis is explicit enumeration of candidate solutions. Enumerative solvers often rely on factoring the search space, aggressive pruning and lattice search. Factoring has been very successful for programming by example [8,10,17], and lattice search has been used in synchronization of concurrent data structures [23] and autotuning [2]. However, both factoring and lattice search require significant domain knowledge, so they are unsuitable for a general purpose system like SKETCH. Pruning techniques are more generally applicable, and are used aggressively by the enumerative solver compared against in Sect. 5.

Recently, some researchers have explored ways to use symbolic reasoning to improve sampling-based procedures. For example, Chaudhuri et al. have shown how to use numerical search for synthesis by applying a symbolic smoothing transformation [4,5]. In a similar vein, Chaganty et al. use symbolic reasoning to limit the sampling space for probabilistic programs to exclude points that will not satisfy a specification [3]. We leave exploring the tradeoffs between these approaches as future work.

Finally, there has been significant interest in parallelizing SAT/SMT solvers. The most successful of these combine a portfolio approach—solvers are run in parallel with different heuristics—with clause sharing [9,25]. Interestingly, these solvers are more efficient than solvers like PSATO [26] where every thread explores a subset of the space. One advantage of our approach over solver parallelization approaches is that the concretization happens at a very high-level of abstraction, so the solver can apply aggressive algebraic simplification based on the concretization. This allows our approach to even help a problem like p_menu that ran out of memory on the sequential solver. The tradeoff is that our solver loses the ability to tell if a problem is UNSAT because we cannot distinguish not finding a solution from having made incorrect guesses during concretization.

7 Conclusion

We introduced adaptive concretization, a program synthesis technique that combines explicit and symbolic search. Our key insight is that not all unknowns are equally important with respect to solving time. By concretizing high *influence* unknowns, we can often speed up the overall synthesis algorithm, especially when we add parallelism. Since the best *degree of concretization* is hard to compute, we presented an online algorithm that uses exponential hill climbing and binary search to find a suitable degree by running many trials. We implemented our algorithm for SKETCH and ran it on a suite of 26 benchmarks across several different domains. We found that adaptive concretization often outperforms SKETCH, sometimes very significantly. We also found that the parallel scalability of our algorithm is reasonable.

References

1. Alur, R., Bodík, R., Juniwal, G., Martin, M.M.K., Raghothaman, M., Seshia, S.A., Singh, R., Solar-Lezama, A., Torlak, E., Udupa, A.: Syntax-guided synthesis. In: Formal Methods in Computer-Aided Design, FMCAD 2013, Portland, OR, USA, October 20–23, 2013, pp. 1–17 (2013). http://ieeexplore.ieee.org/xpl/freeabs_all.jsp?arnumber=6679385
2. Ansel, J., Kamil, S., Veeramachaneni, K., Ragan-Kelley, J., Bosboom, J., O'Reilly, U., Amarasinghe, S.P.: Opentuner: an extensible framework for program autotuning. In: International Conference on Parallel Architectures and Compilation, PACT 2014, Edmonton, AB, Canada, August 24–27, 2014, pp. 303–316. (2014). http://doi.acm.org/10.1145/2628071.2628092
3. Chaganty, A., Nori, A.V., Rajamani, S.K.: Efficiently sampling probabilistic programs via program analysis. In: Proceedings of the Sixteenth International Conference on Artificial Intelligence and Statistics, AISTATS 2013, Scottsdale, AZ, USA, April 29 - May 1, 2013, pp. 153–160 (2013). http://jmlr.org/proceedings/papers/v31/chaganty13a.html
4. Chaudhuri, S., Clochard, M., Solar-Lezama, A.: Bridging boolean and quantitative synthesis using smoothed proof search. In: The 41st Annual ACM SIGPLAN-SIGACT Symposium on Principles of Programming Languages, POPL 2014, San Diego, CA, USA, January 20–21, 2014, pp. 207–220 (2014). http://doi.acm.org/10.1145/2535838.2535859
5. Chaudhuri, S., Solar-Lezama, A.: Smooth interpretation. In: Proceedings of the 2010 ACM SIGPLAN Conference on Programming Language Design and Implementation, PLDI 2010, Toronto, Ontario, Canada, June 5–10 2010, pp. 279–291 (2010). http://doi.acm.org/10.1145/1806596.1806629
6. Cheung, A., Solar-Lezama, A., Madden, S.: Optimizing database-backed applications with query synthesis. In: ACM SIGPLAN Conference on Programming Language Design and Implementation, PLDI 2013, Seattle, WA, USA, June 16–19, 2013, pp. 3–14 (2013). http://doi.acm.org/10.1145/2462156.2462180
7. Gaudin, W., Mallinson, A., Perks, O., Herdman, J., Beckingsale, D., Levesque, J., Jarvis, S.: Optimising hydrodynamics applications for the cray xc30 with the application tool suite. The Cray User Group, pp. 4–8 (2014)

8. Gulwani, S.: Automating string processing in spreadsheets using input-output examples. In: Proceedings of the 38th ACM SIGPLAN-SIGACT Symposium on Principles of Programming Languages, POPL 2011, Austin, TX, USA, January 26–28, 2011, pp. 317–330 (2011). http://doi.acm.org/10.1145/1926385.1926423
9. Hamadi, Y., Jabbour, S., Sais, L.: Manysat: a parallel SAT solver. JSAT **6**(4), 245–262 (2009). http://jsat.ewi.tudelft.nl/content/volume6/JSAT6_12_Hamadi.pdf
10. Harris, W.R., Gulwani, S.: Spreadsheet table transformations from examples. In: Proceedings of the 32nd ACM SIGPLAN Conference on Programming Language Design and Implementation, PLDI 2011, San Jose, CA, USA, June 4–8, 2011, pp. 317–328 (2011). http://doi.acm.org/10.1145/1993498.1993536
11. Jeon, J., Qiu, X., Foster, J.S., Solar-Lezama, A.: Synthesizing Framework Models for Symbolic Execution, under submission
12. Jha, S., Gulwani, S., Seshia, S.A., Tiwari, A.: Oracle-guided component-based program synthesis. In: Proceedings of the 32nd ACM/IEEE International Conference on Software Engineering, Vol. 1, ICSE 2010, pp. 215–224. ACM, New York (2010). http://doi.acm.org/10.1145/1806799.1806833
13. Qiu, X., Solar-Lezama, A.: Synthesizing Data-Structure Manipulations with Natural Proofs, under submission
14. Schkufza, E., Sharma, R., Aiken, A.: Stochastic superoptimization. In: Architectural Support for Programming Languages and Operating Systems, ASPLOS 2013, Houston, TX, USA - March 16–20, 2013, pp. 305–316 (2013). http://doi.acm.org/10.1145/2451116.2451150
15. Schkufza, E., Sharma, R., Aiken, A.: Stochastic optimization of floating-point programs with tunable precision. In: ACM SIGPLAN Conference on Programming Language Design and Implementation, PLDI 2014, Edinburgh, United Kingdom - June 09–11, 2014. p. 9 (2014). http://doi.acm.org/10.1145/2594291.2594302
16. Sharma, R., Aiken, A.: From invariant checking to invariant inference using randomized search. In: Computer Aided Verification - 26th International Conference, CAV 2014, Held as Part of the Vienna Summer of Logic, VSL 2014, Vienna, Austria, July 18–22, 2014, Proceedings, pp. 88–105 (2014). http://dx.doi.org/10.1007/978-3-319-08867-9_6
17. Singh, R., Gulwani, S.: Synthesizing number transformations from input-output examples. In: Computer Aided Verification - 24th International Conference, CAV 2012, Berkeley, CA, USA, July 7–13, 2012 , Proceedings, pp. 634–651 (2012). http://dx.doi.org/10.1007/978-3-642-31424-7_44
18. Singh, R., Gulwani, S., Solar-Lezama, A.: Automated feedback generation for introductory programming assignments. In: ACM SIGPLAN Conference on Programming Language Design and Implementation, PLDI 2013, Seattle, WA, USA, June 16–19 2013, pp. 15–26 (2013). http://doi.acm.org/10.1145/2462156.2462195
19. Solar-Lezama, A.: Program sketching. Int. J. Softw. Tools Technol. Transf. **15**(5–6), 475–495 (2013)
20. Solar-Lezama, A., Jones, C.G., Bodik, R.: Sketching concurrent data structures. In: Proceedings of the 2008 ACM SIGPLAN conference on Programming language design and implementation, PLDI 2008, pp. 136–148 (2008)
21. Torlak, E., Bodík, R.: A lightweight symbolic virtual machine for solver-aided host languages. In: ACM SIGPLAN Conference on Programming Language Design and Implementation, PLDI 2014, Edinburgh, United Kingdom - June 09–11, 2014, p. 54 (2014). http://doi.acm.org/10.1145/2594291.2594340

22. Udupa, A., Raghavan, A., Deshmukh, J.V., Mador-Haim, S., Martin, M.M.K., Alur, R.: TRANSIT: specifying protocols with concolic snippets. In: ACM SIGPLAN Conference on Programming Language Design and Implementation, PLDI 2013, Seattle, WA, USA, June 16–19, 2013, pp. 287–296 (2013). http://doi.acm.org/10.1145/2462156.2462174
23. Vechev, M.T., Yahav, E.: Deriving linearizable fine-grained concurrent objects. In: Proceedings of the ACM SIGPLAN 2008 Conference on Programming Language Design and Implementation, Tucson, AZ, USA, June 7–13, 2008, pp. 125–135 (2008). http://doi.acm.org/10.1145/1375581.1375598
24. Wilcoxon, F.: Individual comparisons by ranking methods. Biometrics Bull. **1**(6), 80–83 (1945)
25. Wintersteiger, C.M., Hamadi, Y., de Moura, L.M.: A concurrent portfolio approach to SMT solving. In: Computer Aided Verification, 21st International Conference, CAV 2009, Grenoble, France, June 26 - July 2, 2009, Proceedings, pp. 715–720 (2009). http://dx.doi.org/10.1007/978-3-642-02658-4_60
26. Zhang, H., Bonacina, M.P., Hsiang, J.: Psato: A distributed propositional prover and its application to quasigroup problems. J. Symb. Comput. **21**(4–6), 543–560 (1996). http://dx.doi.org/10.1006/jsco.1996.0030

Automatic Completion of Distributed Protocols with Symmetry

Rajeev Alur[1], Mukund Raghothaman[1], Christos Stergiou[1,2], Stavros Tripakis[2,3], and Abhishek Udupa[1(✉)]

[1] University of Pennsylvania, Philadelphia, USA
audupa@seas.upenn.edu
[2] University of California, Berkeley, USA
[3] Aalto University, Helsinki, Finland

Abstract. A distributed protocol is typically modeled as a set of communicating processes, where each process is described as an extended state machine along with fairness assumptions. Correctness is specified using safety and liveness requirements. Designing correct distributed protocols is a challenging task. Aimed at simplifying this task, we allow the designer to leave some of the guards and updates to state variables in the description of the protocol as unknown functions. The protocol completion problem then is to find interpretations for these unknown functions while guaranteeing correctness. In many distributed protocols, process behaviors are naturally symmetric, and thus, synthesized expressions are further required to obey symmetry constraints. Our counterexample-guided synthesis algorithm consists of repeatedly invoking two phases. In the first phase, candidates for unknown expressions are generated using the SMT solver Z3. This phase requires carefully orchestrating constraints to enforce the desired symmetry constraints. In the second phase, the resulting completed protocol is checked for correctness using a custom-built model checker that handles fairness assumptions, safety and liveness requirements, and exploits symmetry. When model checking fails, our tool examines a set of counterexamples to safety/liveness properties to generate constraints on unknown functions that must be satisfied by subsequent completions. For evaluation, we show that our prototype is able to automatically discover interesting missing details in distributed protocols for mutual exclusion, self stabilization, and cache coherence.

1 Introduction

Protocols for coordination among concurrent processes are an essential component of modern multiprocessor and distributed systems. The multitude of behaviors arising due to asynchrony and concurrency makes the design of such

This research was partially supported by NSF Expeditions award CCF 1138996 and by NSF award #1329759. The authors also acknowledge support from the Academy of Finland and the iCyPhy Research Center (Industrial Cyber-Physical Systems, supported by IBM and United Technologies).

D. Kroening and C.S. Păsăreanu (Eds.): CAV 2015, Part II, LNCS 9207, pp. 395–412, 2015.
DOI: 10.1007/978-3-319-21668-3_23

protocols difficult. Consequently, analyzing such protocols has been a central theme of research in formal verification for decades. Now that verification tools are mature enough to be applied to find bugs in real-world protocols, a promising area of research is *protocol synthesis*, aimed at simplifying the design process via more intuitive programming abstractions to specify the desired behavior.

Traditionally, a distributed protocol is modeled as a set of communicating processes, where each process is described by an extended state machine. The correctness is specified by both safety and liveness requirements. In *reactive synthesis* [5,24,26], the goal is to automatically derive a protocol from its correctness requirements specified in temporal logic. However, if we require the implementation to be distributed, then reactive synthesis is undecidable [13,20,25,31]. An alternative, and potentially more feasible approach inspired by *program sketching* [28], is to ask the programmer to specify the protocol as a set of communicating state machines, but allow some of the guards and updates to state variables to be unknown functions, to be completed by the synthesizer so as to satisfy all the correctness requirements. This methodology for protocol specification can be viewed as a fruitful collaboration between the designer and the synthesis tool: the programmer has to describe the structure of the desired protocol, but some details that the programmer is unsure about, for instance, regarding corner cases and handling of unexpected messages, will be filled in automatically by the tool.

In our formalization of the synthesis problem, processes communicate using input/output channels that carry typed messages. Each process is described by a state machine with a set of typed state variables. Transitions consist of (1) guards that test input messages and state variables and, (2) updates to state variables and fields of messages to be sent. Such guards and updates can involve *unknown* (typed) functions to be filled in by the synthesizer. In many distributed protocols, such as cache coherence protocols, processes are expected to behave in a symmetric manner. Thus, we allow variables to have *symmetric types* that restrict the read/write accesses to obey symmetry constraints. To specify safety and liveness requirements, the state machines can be augmented with acceptance conditions that capture incorrect executions. Finally, fairness assumptions are added to restrict incorrect executions to those that are *fair*. It is worth noting that in verification one can get useful analysis results by focusing solely on safety requirements. In synthesis, however, ignoring liveness requirements and fairness assumptions, typically results in trivial solutions. The protocol completion problem, then, is, given a set of extended state machines with unknown guards and update functions, to find expressions for the unknown functions so that the composition of the resulting machines does not have an accepting fair execution.

Our synthesis algorithm relies on a counterexample-guided strategy with two interacting phases: candidate interpretations for unknown functions are generated using the SMT solver Z3 and the resulting completed protocol is verified using a model checker. We believe that our realization of this strategy leads to the following contributions. First, while searching for candidate interpretations for unknown functions, we need to generate constraints that enforce symmetry in an accurate manner without choking current SMT solvers. Second, surprisingly there is no publicly available model checker that handles all the features that we critically need, namely, symmetry, liveness requirements, and fairness assumptions. So, we had to develop our own model checker, building on the known theoretical foundations. Third, we develop an algorithm that examines the counterexamples to safety/liveness requirements when model checking fails, and generates constraints on unknown functions that must be satisfied in subsequent completions. Finally, the huge search space for candidate expressions is a challenge for the scalability for any synthesis approach. As reported in Sect. 5, we experimented with many alternative strategies for prioritizing the search for candidate expressions, and this experience offers some insights regarding what information a user can provide for getting useful results from the synthesis tool. We evaluate our synthesis tool in completing a mutual exclusion protocol, a self stabilization protocol and a non-trivial cache coherence protocol. Large parts of the behavior of the protocol were left unspecified in the case of the mutual exclusion protocol and the self stabilization protocol, whereas the cache coherence protocol had quite a few tricky details left unspecified. Our tool synthesized the correct completions for these protocols in a reasonable amount of time.

Related Work. *Bounded synthesis* [14] and *genetic programming* [18,19] are other approaches for handling the undecidability of distributed reactive synthesis. In the first, the size of the implementation is restricted, and in the second the implementation space is sampled and candidates are mutated in a stochastic process. The problem of inferring extended finite-state machines has been studied in the context of active learning [6]. The problem of completing distributed protocols has been targeted by the works presented in [2,32] and *program repair* [17] addresses a similar problem. Compared to [2], our algorithm can handle extended state machines that include variables and transitions with symbolic expressions as guards and updates. Compared to [32], our algorithm can also handle liveness violations and, more importantly, can process counterexamples automatically. PSKETCH [29] is an extension of the *program sketching* work for concurrent data structures but is limited to safety properties. The work in [15] describes an approach based on QBF solvers for synthesizing a distributed self-stabilizing system, which also approximates liveness with safety and uses templates for the synthesized functions. Also, compared to all works mentioned above, our algorithm can be used to enforce symmetry in the synthesized processes.

2 An Illustrative Example

Consider Peterson's mutual exclusion algorithm, described in Fig. 1a, which manages two symmetric processes contending for access to a critical section. Each process is parameterized by `Pm` and `Po` (for "my" process id and "other" process id respectively), such that `Pm` $\neq$ `Po`. Both parameters `Pm` and `Po` are of type `processid` and they are allowed to take on values `P0` and `P1`. We therefore have two instances: P_0, where (`Pm` = `P0`, `Po` = `P1`), and P_1, where (`Pm` = `P1`, `Po` = `P0`). P_0 and P_1 communicate through the shared variables *turn* and *flag*. The variable

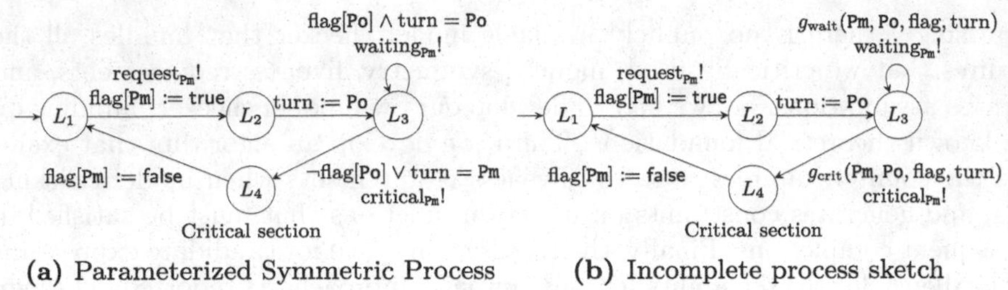

(a) Parameterized Symmetric Process **(b)** Incomplete process sketch

Fig. 1. Peterson's mutual exclusion algorithm. The non-trivial guards of the (L_3, L_3) and (L_3, L_4) transitions in Fig. 1(a) have been replaced in Fig. 1(b) by "unknown" functions g_{wait} and g_{crit} respectively.

turn has type processid. The *flag* variable is an array of Boolean values, with index type processid. The objective of the protocol is to control access to the critical section, represented by location L_4, and ensure that both of the processes P_0 and P_1 are never simultaneously in the critical section.

The liveness monitor shown in Fig. 2 captures the requirement that a process does not wait indefinitely to enter the critical section. The monitor accepts all undesirable runs where a process has requested access to the critical section but never reaches state L_4 after. The messages request, waiting, and critical inform the liveness monitor about the state of the processes, and the synchronization model here is that of communicating I/O automata [21]. Note that a run accepted by the monitor may be *unfair* with respect to some processes. Enforcing *weak* process fairness on P_0 and P_1 is sufficient to rule out unfair executions, but not necessary. Enforcing weak fairness on the transitions between (L_2, L_3), (L_3, L_4) and (L_4, L_1) suffices.

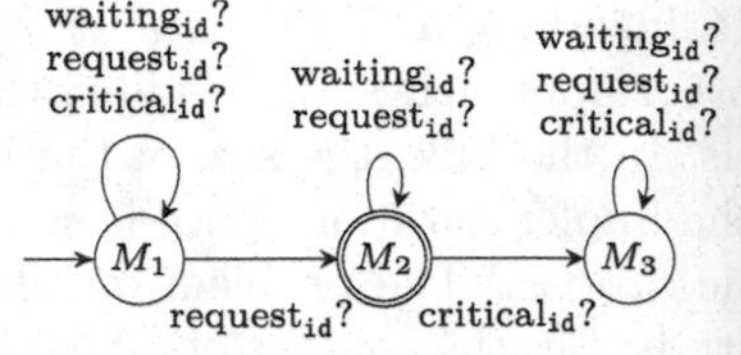

Fig. 2. Liveness monitor

Now, suppose the protocol developer has trouble figuring out the exact condition under which a process is allowed to enter the critical section, but knows the structure of the processes P_0 and P_1, and requires them to be symmetric. Figure 1b describes what the developer knows about the protocol. The functions g_{wait} and g_{crit} represent unknown Boolean valued functions over the state variables and the parameters of the process under consideration. Including the parameters as part of the domain of g_{wait} and g_{crit} indicates that the completions for processes P_0 and P_1 need to be symmetric. The objective is to assist the developer by automatically discovering interpretations for these unknown functions, such that the completed protocol satisfies the necessary mutual exclusion property, and the requirements imposed by the liveness monitor. We formalize this completion problem in Sect. 3, and present our completion algorithm in Sect. 4.

3 Formalization

3.1 Extended State Machine Sketches

We model processes using Extended State Machine Sketches (ESM-S). Fix a collection of types, such as the type *bool* of the Boolean values $\{\mathsf{true}, \mathsf{false}\}$, enumerated types such as $\{\mathsf{red}, \mathsf{green}, \mathsf{blue}\}$, or finite subsets $nat[x, y]$ of natural numbers $\{i \mid x \leq i \leq y\}$. Other examples include *symmetric types* (described in Sect. 3.2), array and record types. Note that each type is required to be finite.

The description of an ESM-S will mention several function symbols. Some of these have interpretations which are already known, while others have unknown interpretations. Each function symbol, both known and unknown, is associated with a signature, $d_1 \times \cdots \times d_n \to r$, where $d_1, \ldots, d_n$ are the types of its arguments and r is the return type. Expressions may then be constructed using these function symbols, state variables, and input channels. Formally, an ESM-S A is a tuple $\langle L, l_0, I, O, S, \sigma_0, U, T, \mathcal{F}_s, \mathcal{F}_w \rangle$ such that:

- L is a finite set of locations and $l_0 \in L$ is the initial location,
- I and O are finite sets of typed input and output channels, respectively,
- S is a finite set of typed state variables,
- σ_0 maps each variable $x \in S$ to its initial value $\sigma_0(x)$,
- U is a set of unknown function symbols,
- T is a set of transitions of the form $\langle l, c, \mathsf{guard}, \mathsf{updates}, l' \rangle$, where $c \in I$, $c \in O$ and $c = \epsilon$ for input, output and internal transitions respectively. The transition is guarded by the expression guard and updates are the updates to state variables,
- $\mathcal{F}_s, \mathcal{F}_w \subseteq 2^{T_\epsilon \cup T_O}$, are sets of strong and weak fairnesses respectively. Here T_O and T_ϵ are the sets of output and internal transitions respectively.

A guard description guard is a Boolean expression over the state variables S that can use unknown functions from U. Similarly, an update description updates is a sequence of assignments of the form $\mathsf{lhs} := \mathsf{rhs}$ where lhs is one of the state variables or an output channel in the case of an output transition, and rhs is an expression over state variables or state variables and an input channel in the case of an input transition, possibly using unknown functions from U.

Executions. To define the executions of an ESM-S, we first pick an *interpretation* R which maps each unknown function $u \in U$ to an interpretation of u. Given a set of variables V, a *valuation* σ is a function which maps each variable $x \in V$ to a value $\sigma(x)$ of the corresponding type, and we write Σ_V for the set of all such valuations. Given a valuation $\sigma \in \Sigma_V$, a variable x, and a value v of appropriate type, we write $\sigma[x \mapsto v] \in \Sigma_{V \cup \{x\}}$ for the valuation which maps all variables $y \neq x$ to $\sigma(y)$, and maps x to v.

The executions of A are defined by describing the updates to the state valuation $\sigma \in \Sigma_S$ during each transition. Note that each guard description guard naturally defines a set $[\![\mathsf{guard}, R]\!]$ of valuations $\sigma \in \Sigma_S$ which satisfy guard with the unknown functions instantiated with R. Similarly, each update description updates defines a function $[\![\mathsf{updates}, R]\!]$ of type $\Sigma_{S\cup\{x\}} \rightarrow \Sigma_S$ for input transitions on the channel x, $\Sigma_S \rightarrow \Sigma_{S\cup\{y\}}$ for output transitions on the channel y, and $\Sigma_S \rightarrow \Sigma_S$ for internal transitions respectively. A *state* of an ESM-S A is a pair (l, σ) where, $l \in L$ and $\sigma \in \Sigma_S$. We then write:

- $(l, \sigma) \xrightarrow{x?v} (l', \sigma')$ if A has an input transition from l to l' on channel x with guard guard and update updates such that $\sigma \in [\![\mathsf{guard}, R]\!]$ and $[\![\mathsf{updates}, R]\!](\sigma[x \mapsto v]) = \sigma'$;
- $(l, \sigma) \xrightarrow{y!v} (l', \sigma')$ if A has an output transition from l to l' on channel y with guard guard and update updates such that $\sigma \in [\![\mathsf{guard}, R]\!]$ and $[\![\mathsf{updates}, R]\!](\sigma) = \sigma'[y \mapsto v]$; and
- $(l, \sigma) \xrightarrow{\epsilon} (l', \sigma')$ if A has an internal transition from l to l' with guard guard and update guard such that $\sigma \in [\![\mathsf{guard}, R]\!]$ and $[\![\mathsf{updates}, R]\!](\sigma) = \sigma'$.

We write $(l, \sigma) \rightarrow (l', \sigma')$ if either there are x, v such that $(l, \sigma) \xrightarrow{x?v} (l', \sigma')$, there are y, v such that $(l, \sigma) \xrightarrow{y!v} (l', \sigma')$, or $(l, \sigma) \xrightarrow{\epsilon} (l', \sigma')$. A finite (infinite) *execution* of the ESM-S A under R is then a finite (resp. infinite) sequence: $(l_0, \sigma_0) \rightarrow (l_1, \sigma_1) \rightarrow (l_2, \sigma_2) \rightarrow \cdots$ where for every $j \geq 0$, (l_j, σ_j) is a state of A, (l_0, σ_0) is an initial state of A, and for $j \geq 1$, $(l_j, \sigma_j) \rightarrow (l_{j+1}, \sigma_{j+1})$. A state (l, σ) is *reachable* under R if there exists a finite execution that reaches that state: $(l_0, \sigma_0) \rightarrow \cdots \rightarrow (l, \sigma)$. We say that a transition from l to l' with guard guard is *enabled* in state (l, σ) if $\sigma \in [\![\mathsf{guard}, R]\!]$. A state (l, σ) is called a *deadlock* if no transition is enabled in (l, σ). The ESM-S A is called deadlock-free under R if no deadlock state is reachable under R. The ESM-S A is called *deterministic* under R if for every state (l, σ), if there are multiple transitions enabled at (l, σ), then they must be input transitions on distinct input channels.

Consider a weak fairness requirement $F \in \mathcal{F}_w$. An infinite execution of A under R is called *fair* with respect to a weak fairness F if either: (a) for infinitely many indices i, none of the transitions $t \in F$ is enabled in (l_i, σ_i), or (b) for infinitely many indices j one of the transitions in F is taken at step j. Thus, for example, the necessary fairness assumptions for Peterson's algorithm are $\mathcal{F}_w = \{\{\tau_{23}\}, \{\tau_{34}\}, \{\tau_{41}\}\}$, where τ_{23}, τ_{34}, and τ_{41} refer to the (L_2, L_3), (L_3, L_4) and (L_4, L_1) transitions respectively. Similarly, an infinite execution of A under R is fair with respect to a strong fairness $F \in \mathcal{F}_s$ if either: (a) there exists k such that for every $i \geq k$ and every transition $t \in F$, t is not enabled in (l_i, σ_i), or (b) for infinitely many indices j one of the transitions in F is taken at step j. Finally, an infinite execution of A is fair if it is fair with respect to each strong and weak fairness requirement in $\mathcal{F}_s$ and $\mathcal{F}_w$ respectively.

Composition of ESM Sketches. For lack of space, we only provide an informal definition of composition of ESM-S here. A formal definition can be found in the full version of this paper [3]. Informally, two ESM-S A_1 and A_2 are composed by synchronizing their output and input transitions on a given channel. If A_1 has an output transition on channel c from location l_1 to l'_1 with guard and updates guard_1 and $\mathsf{updates}_1$, and A_2 has an input transition on the same channel c from location l_2 to l'_2 with guard and updates guard_2 and $\mathsf{updates}_2$

then their product has an output transition from location (l_1, l_2) to (l_1', l_2') on channel c with guard $\mathsf{guard}_1 \wedge \mathsf{guard}_2$ and updates $\mathsf{updates}_1; \mathsf{updates}_2$. Note that by sequencing the updates, the value written to the channel c by A_1 is then used by subsequent updates of the variables of A_2 in $\mathsf{updates}_2$.

Specifications. An ESM-S can be equipped with error locations $L_e \subseteq L$, accepting locations $L_a \subseteq L$, or both. The composition of two ESM-S A_1, A_2 "inherits" the error and accepting locations of its components. A product location (l_1, l_2) is an error (accepting) location if either l_1 or l_2 are error (accepting) locations. An ESM-S A is called *safe* under R if for all reachable states (l, σ), l is not an error location. An infinite execution of A under R, $(l_0, \sigma_0) \rightarrow (l_1, \sigma_1) \rightarrow \cdots$, is called *accepting* if for infinitely many indices j, $l_j \in L_a$. A is called *live* under R if it has no infinite fair accepting executions.

3.2 Symmetry

It is often required that the processes of an ESM-S completion problem have some structurally similar behavior, as we saw in Sect. 2 in the case of Peterson's algorithm. To describe such requirements, we use *symmetric types*, which are similar to *scalarsets* used in the Murφ model checker [23].

A symmetric type T is characterized by: (a) its name, and (b) its cardinality $|T|$, which is a finite number. Given a collection of processes parameterized by a symmetric type T, such as P_0 and P_1 of Peterson's algorithm, the idea is that the system is invariant under permutations (i.e. renaming) of the parameter values. Let $\mathsf{perm}(T)$ be the set of all permutations $\pi_T : T \rightarrow T$ over the symmetric type T. For ease of notation, we define $\pi_T(v) = v$, for values v whose type is *not* T. Given the collection of all symmetric types $\mathcal{T} = \{T_1, T_2, \ldots, T_n\}$ of the system, we can then describe permutations over $\mathcal{T}$ as the composition of permutations over the individual types, $\pi_{T_1} \circ \pi_{T_2} \circ \cdots \circ \pi_{T_n}$. Let $\mathsf{perm}(\mathcal{T})$ be the set of such "system-wide" permutations over $\mathcal{T}$.

ESM sketches and input and output channels may thus be parameterized by symmetric values. The state variables and array variable indices of an ESM-S may also be of symmetric type. Given the symmetric types $\mathcal{T}$ and an interpretation R of the unknown functions in an ESM-S A, we say that A is *symmetric* with respect to $\mathcal{T}$ if every execution $(l_0, \sigma_0) \rightarrow (l_1, \sigma_1) \rightarrow \cdots \rightarrow (l_n, \sigma_n) \rightarrow \cdots$ of A under R also implies the existence of the permuted execution $(\pi(l_0), \pi(\sigma_0)) \rightarrow (\pi(l_1), \pi(\sigma_0)) \rightarrow \cdots (\pi(l_n), \pi(\sigma_n)) \rightarrow \cdots$ of A, where the channel identifiers along transitions are also suitably permuted, for every permutation $\pi \in \mathsf{perm}(\mathcal{T})$.

We therefore require that any interpretation R considered be such that the completed ESM-S A is symmetric with respect to $\mathcal{T}$ under R. For every unknown function f in A, requiring that $\forall d \in \mathsf{dom}(f), \pi(f(d)) = f(\pi(d)))$, for each permutation $\pi \in \mathsf{perm}(\mathcal{T})$, ensures that the behavior of f is symmetric. In Sect. 4, we will describe how these additional constraints are presented to the SMT solver. Note that while we have only discussed *full symmetry* here, other notions of symmetry such as *ring symmetry* and *virtual symmetry* [11] can also be accommodated in our formalization.

3.3 Completion Problem

In many cases, the designer has some prior knowledge about the unknown functions used in an ESM-S. For example, the designer may know that the variable *turn* is read-only during the (L_3, L_4) transition of Peterson's algorithm. The designer may also know that the unknown guard of a transition is independent of some state variable. Many instances of such "prior knowledge" can already be expressed using the formalism just described: the update expression of *turn* in the unknown transition can be set to the identity function (in the first case), and the designer can omit the irrelevant variable from the signature of the update function (in the second case). We also allow the designer to specify additional constraints on the unknown functions: she may know, as in the case of Peterson's algorithm for example, that $g_{\text{crit}}(\texttt{Pm}, \texttt{Po}, \mathit{flag}, \mathit{turn}) \vee g_{\text{wait}}(\texttt{Pm}, \texttt{Po}, \mathit{flag}, \mathit{turn})$, for every valuation of the function arguments Pm, Po, *flag*, and *turn*. This additional knowledge, which is helpful to guide the synthesizer, is encoded in the initial constraints Φ_0 imposed on candidate interpretations of U. Note that these constraints might refer to multiple unknown functions from the same or different ESM-S.

Formally, we can now state the completion problem as: Given a set of ESM-S $A_1, \ldots A_N$ with sets of unknown functions $U_1, \ldots, U_N$, an environment ESM-S E with an empty set of unknown functions, and a set of constraints Φ_0 on the unknown functions $U = U_1 \cup \cdots \cup U_N$, find an interpretation R of U, such that (a) $A_1, \ldots, A_N$ are deterministic under R, (b) the completed system $\Pi = A_1 \mid \cdots \mid A_N \mid E$ is symmetric with respect to $\mathcal{T}$ under R, where $\mathcal{T}$ is the set of symmetric types in the system, (c) R satisfies the constraints in Φ_0, and (d) the product Π under R is deadlock-free, safe, and live.

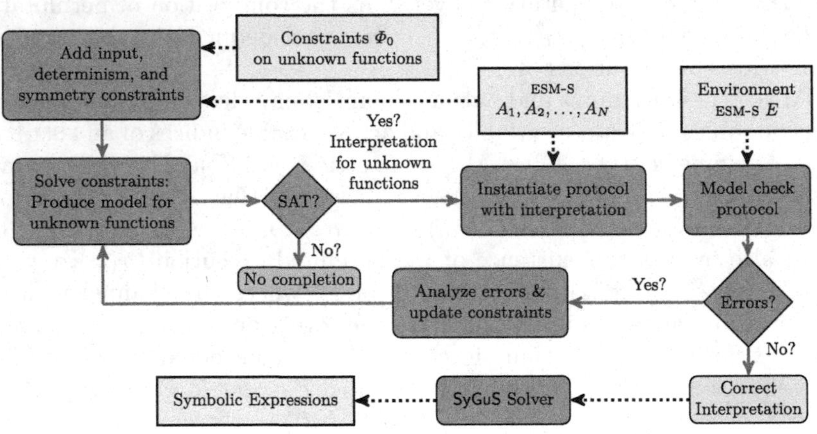

Fig. 3. Completion algorithm.

4 Solving the Completion Problem

The synthesis algorithm is outlined in Fig. 3. We maintain a set of constraints Φ on possible completions, and repeatedly query Z3 [22] for candidate interpretations satisfying all constraints in Φ. If the interpretation is certified correct by the model checker, we are done. Otherwise, counter-example executions returned by the model checker are analyzed, and Φ is strengthened with further constraints which eliminate all subsequent interpretations with similar erroneous executions. If a symbolic expression is required, we can submit the correct interpretation to a SyGuS solver [1]. A SyGuS solver takes a set of constraints $\mathcal{C}$ on an unknown function f together with the search space for the body of f — expressed as a grammar — and finds an expression in the grammar for f, such that it satisfies the constraints $\mathcal{C}$. In this section, we first describe the initial determinism and symmetry constraints expected of all completions. Next, we briefly describe the model checker used in our implementation, and then describe how to analyze counterexamples returned by the model checker. Finally, we describe additional heuristics to bias the SMT solver towards intuitively simpler completions first.

4.1 Initial Constraints

Determinism Constraints. Recall that an ESM-S is deterministic under an interpretation R if and only if for every state (l, σ) if there are multiple transitions enabled at (l, σ), then they must be input transitions on distinct input channels. We constrain the interpretations chosen at every step such that all ESM-S in the protocol are deterministic. Consider the ESM-S for Peterson's algorithm shown in Fig. 1b. We have two transitions from the location L_3, with guards $g_{\text{crit}}(\texttt{Pm}, \texttt{Po}, \mathit{flag}, \mathit{turn})$ and $g_{\text{wait}}(\texttt{Pm}, \texttt{Po}, \mathit{flag}, \mathit{turn})$. We ensure that these expressions never evaluate to true simultaneously with the constraint $\neg\exists v_1 v_2 v_3 v_4\, (g_{\text{crit}}(v_1, v_2, v_3, v_4) \wedge g_{\text{wait}}(v_1, v_2, v_3, v_4))$. Although this is a quantified expression, which can be difficult for SMT solvers to solve, note that we only support finite types, whose domains are often quite small. So our tool unrolls the quantifiers and presents only quantifier-free formulas to the SMT solver.

Symmetry Constraints. Suppose that the interpretation chosen for the guard g_{crit} shown in Fig. 1b, was such that $g_{\text{crit}}(\texttt{P0}, \texttt{P1}, \langle\bot, \top\rangle, \texttt{P0}) = \texttt{true}$. Then for the ESM-S to be symmetric under this interpretation, we require that $g_{\text{crit}}(\texttt{P1}, \texttt{P0}, \langle\top, \bot\rangle, \texttt{P1} = \texttt{true}$ as well, because the latter expression is obtained by applying the permutation $\{\texttt{P0} \mapsto \texttt{P1}, \texttt{P1} \mapsto \texttt{P0}\}$ on the former expression. Note that the elements of the *flag* array in the preceding example were flipped, because *flag* is an array indexed by the symmetric type processid. In general, given a function $f \in U_i$, we enforce the constraint $\forall \pi \in \mathsf{perm}(\mathcal{T}) \forall d \in \mathsf{dom}(f)(f(\pi(d)) \equiv \pi(f(d)))$, where $\mathcal{T}$ is the set of symmetric types that appear in A_i. As in the case of determinism constraints, we unroll the quantifiers here as well.

4.2 Model Checker

To effectively and repeatedly generate constraints to drive the synthesis loop, a model checker needs to: (a) support checking liveness properties, with algorithmic support for fine grained notions of strong and weak fairness, (b) dynamically prioritize certain paths over others (*cf.* Sect. 4.4), and (c) exploit symmetries inherent in the model. The fine grained notions of fairness over sets of transitions, rather than bulk process fairness are crucial. For instance, in the case of unordered channel processes, we often require that no message be delayed indefinitely, which cannot be captured by enforcing fairness at the level of the entire process. The ability to prioritize certain paths over others is also crucial so that candidate interpretations are exercised to the extent possible in one model checking run (*cf.* Sect. 4.4). Finally, support for symmetry-based state space reductions, while not absolutely crucial, can greatly speed up each model checking run.

Surprisingly, we found that none of the well-supported model checkers met all of our requirements. SPIN [16] only supports weak process fairness at an algorithmic level and does not employ symmetry-based reductions. Support for symmetry-based reductions is present in Murφ [10,23], but it lacks support for liveness checking. SMC [27] is a model checker with support for symmetry reduction and strong and weak process fairness. Unfortunately, it is no longer maintained, and has very rudimentary counterexample generation capabilities. Finally, NuSMV [8] does not support symmetry reductions, but supports strong and weak process level fairness. But bugs in the implementation of counterexample generation, left us unable to obtain counterexamples in some cases.

We therefore implemented a model checker based on the ideas used in Murφ [10] for symmetry reduction, and an adaptation of the techniques presented in earlier literature [12] for checking liveness properties under fairness assumptions. The model checking algorithm consists of the following steps: (1) construct the symmetry-reduced state graph, (2) find accepting strongly connected components (SCCs) in the reduced state graph, (3) delete unfair states from each SCC; repeat steps (2) and (3) until either a fair SCC is found or no more accepting SCCs remain. A more detailed description of the model checking algorithm is presented in the full version of the paper [3].

4.3 Analysis of Counterexamples

We now describe our algorithms for analyzing counterexamples by way of examples. A more formal description of the algorithms can be found in the full version of this paper [3].

Analyzing Deadlocks. In Fig. 1b, consider the candidate interpretation where both $g_{\text{crit}}, g_{\text{wait}}$ are set to be universally false. Two deadlock states are then reachable: $S_1 = ((L_3, L_3), \{\mathit{flag} \mapsto \langle \top, \top \rangle, \mathit{turn} \mapsto \texttt{P1}\}$ and $S_2 = ((L_3, L_3), \{\mathit{flag} \mapsto \langle \top, \top \rangle, \mathit{turn} \mapsto \texttt{P0}\}$. We strengthen Φ by asserting that these deadlocks do not occur in future interpretations: either S_1 is unreachable, or the system can make a transition from S_1 (and similarly for S_2). In this example, the reachability of both deadlock states is not dependent on the interpretation, *i.e.*, the execution that leads to the states does not exercise any unknown function, hence, we need to make sure that the states are not deadlocks. The possible transitions out of location (L_3, L_3) are the transitions from L_3 to L_3 (waiting transition) and from L_3 to L_4 (critical transition) for each of the two processes. In each deadlock state, at least one of the four guards has to be true: $g_{\text{wait}}(\texttt{P0}, \texttt{P1}, \langle \top, \top \rangle, \texttt{P1}) \lor g_{\text{crit}}(\texttt{P0}, \texttt{P1}, \langle \top, \top \rangle, \texttt{P1}) \lor g_{\text{wait}}(\texttt{P1}, \texttt{P0}, \langle \top, \top \rangle, \texttt{P1}) \lor g_{\text{crit}}(\texttt{P1}, \texttt{P0}, \langle \top, \top \rangle, \texttt{P1})$ for S_1, and $g_{\text{wait}}(\texttt{P0}, \texttt{P1}, \langle \top, \top \rangle, \texttt{P0}) \lor g_{\text{crit}}(\texttt{P0}, \texttt{P1}, \langle \top, \top \rangle, \texttt{P0}) \lor g_{\text{wait}}(\texttt{P1}, \texttt{P0}, \langle \top, \top \rangle, \texttt{P0}) \lor g_{\text{crit}}(\texttt{P1}, \texttt{P0}, \langle \top, \top \rangle, \texttt{P0})$ for S_2. The two disjuncts are added to the set of constraints, since any candidate interpretation has to satisfy them in order for the resulting product to be deadlock-free.

Analyzing Safety Violations. Consider now an erroneous interpretation where the critical transition guards are true for both processes when *turn* is P0, that is: $g_{\text{crit}}(\texttt{P0}, \texttt{P1}, \langle \top, \top \rangle, \texttt{P0})$ and $g_{\text{crit}}(\texttt{P1}, \texttt{P0}, \langle \top, \top \rangle, \texttt{P0})$ are set to true. Under this interpretation the product can reach the error location (L_4, L_4). We perform a weakest precondition analysis on the corresponding execution to obtain a necessary condition under which the safety violation is possible. In this case, the execution crosses both critical transitions and the generated constraint is $\neg g_{\text{crit}}(\texttt{P0}, \texttt{P1}, \langle \top, \top \rangle, \texttt{P0}) \lor \neg g_{\text{crit}}(\texttt{P1}, \texttt{P0}, \langle \top, \top \rangle, \texttt{P0})$. Note that the conditions obtained from this analysis are necessary; the product under any interpretation that does not satisfy them will exhibit the same safety violation.

Analyzing Liveness Violations. An interpretation that satisfies the constraints gathered above is one that, when *turn* is P0, enables both waiting transitions and disables the critical ones. Intuitively, under this interpretation, the two processes will not make progress if *turn* is P0 when they reach L_3. The executions in which the processes are at L_3 and either P_0 or P_1 continuously take the waiting transition is an accepting one. As with safety violations, we eliminate liveness violations by adding constraints generated through weakest precondition analysis of the accepting executions. In this case, this results in two constraints: $\neg g_{\text{wait}}(\texttt{P0}, \texttt{P1}, \langle \top, \top \rangle, \texttt{P0})$ and $\neg g_{\text{wait}}(\texttt{P1}, \texttt{P0}, \langle \top, \top \rangle, \texttt{P0})$. However, in the presence of fairness assumptions, these constraints are too strong. This is because removing an execution that causes a fair liveness violation is not the only way to resolve it: another way is to make it unfair. Given the weak fairness assumption on the transitions on the $\text{critical}_{\texttt{Pi}}$ channels, the correct constraint generated for the liveness violation of Process P_0 is: $\neg g_{\text{wait}}(\texttt{P0}, \texttt{P1}, \langle \top, \top \rangle, \texttt{P0}) \lor g_{\text{crit}}(\texttt{P0}, \texttt{P1}, \langle \top, \top \rangle, \texttt{P0}) \lor g_{\text{crit}}(\texttt{P1}, \texttt{P0}, \text{true}, \text{true}, \texttt{P0})$, where the last two disjuncts render the accepting execution unfair.

4.4 Optimizations and Heuristics

We describe a few key optimizations and heuristics that improve the scalability and predictability of our technique.

Not All Counterexamples are Created Equal. The constraint we get from a single counter-example trace is weaker when it exercises a large number of unknown functions. Consider, for example, a candidate interpretation for the incomplete Peterson's algorithm which, when *turn* = P0, sets both waiting transition guards g_{wait} to true, and both critical transition guards g_{crit} to

false. We have already seen that the product is not live under this interpretation. From the infinite execution leading up-to the location (L_3, L_3), and after which P_0 loops in L_3, we obtain the constraint $\neg g_{\text{wait}}(\texttt{P0}, \texttt{P1}, \langle \top, \top \rangle, \texttt{P0})$. On the other hand, if we had considered the longer self-loop at (L_3, L_3), where P_0 and P_1 alternate in making waiting transitions, we would have obtained the weaker constraint $\neg g_{\text{wait}}(\texttt{P0}, \texttt{P1}, \langle \top, \top \rangle, \texttt{P0}) \vee \neg g_{\text{wait}}(\texttt{P1}, \texttt{P0}, \langle \top, \top \rangle, \texttt{P0})$. In general, erroneous traces which exercise fewer unknown functions have the potential to prune away a larger fraction of the search space and are therefore preferable over traces exercising a larger number of unknown functions.

In each iteration, the model checker discovers several erroneous states. In the event that the candidate interpretation chosen is blatantly incorrect, it is infeasible to analyze paths to all error states. A naïve solution would be to analyze paths to the first n errors states discovered (where n is configurable). But depending on the strategy used to explore the state space, a large fraction these errors could be similar, and would only provide us with rather weak constraints. On the other hand, exercising as many unknown functions as possible, along different paths, has the potential to provide stronger constraints on future interpretations. In summary, we bias the model checker to *cover* as many unknown functions as possible, such that each path exercises as few unknown functions as possible.

Heuristics/Prioritizations to Guide the SMT Solver. As mentioned earlier, we use an SMT solver to obtain interpretations for unknown functions, given a set of constraints. When this set is small, as is the case at the beginning of the algorithm, there exist many satisfying interpretations. At this point the interpretation chosen by the SMT solver can either lead the rest of the search down a “good” path, or lead it down a futile path. Therefore the run time of the synthesis algorithm can depend heavily on the interpretations returned by the SMT solver, which we consider a non-deterministic black box in our approach.

To reduce the influence of non-determinism of the SMT solver on the run time of our algorithm, we bias the solver towards specific forms of interpretations by asserting additional constraints. These constraints associate a *cost* with interpretations and require an interpretation with a given bound on the cost, which is relaxed whenever the SMT solver fails to find a solution.

We briefly describe the most important of the heuristics/prioritization techniques: (1) We minimize the number of points in the domain of an unknown guard function at which it evaluates to true. This results in minimally permissive guards. (2) Based on the observation that most variables are unchanged in a given transition, we prioritize interpretations where update functions leave the value of the variable unchanged, as far as possible. (3) We can also try to minimize the number of arguments on which the value of an unknown function depends.

5 Experiments

5.1 Peterson's Mutual Exclusion Protocol

In addition to the missing guards g_{grit} and g_{wait}, we also replace the update expressions of flag[Pm] in the (L_1, L_2) and (L_4, L_1) transitions with unknown functions that depend on all state variables. In the initial constraints we require that $g_{\text{crit}}(\texttt{Pm}, \texttt{Po}, \mathit{flag}, \mathit{turn}) \vee g_{\text{wait}}(\texttt{Pm}, \texttt{Po}, \mathit{flag}, \mathit{turn})$. The synthesis algorithm returns with an interpretation in less than a second. Upon submitting the interpretation to a SyGuS solver, the synthesized expressions match the ones shown in Fig. 1b.

5.2 Self-stabilizing Systems

Our next case study is the synthesis of self-stabilizing systems [9]. A distributed system is self-stabilizing if, starting from an arbitrary initial state, in each execution, the system eventually reaches a global *legitimate* state, and only legitimate states are ever visited after. We also require that every legitimate state be reachable from every other legitimate state. Consider N processes connected in a line. Each process maintains two Boolean state variables x and up. The processes are described using guarded commands of the form, "`if` *guard* `then` *update*". Whether a command is enabled is a function of the variable values x and up of the process itself, and those of its neighbors. We attempted to synthesize the guards and updates for the middle two processes of a four process system P_1, P_2, P_3, P_4. Specifically, the ESM-S for P_2 and P_3 have two transitions, each with an unknown function as a guard and two unknown functions for updating its state variables. The guard is a function of x_{i-1}, x_i, x_{i+1}, up_{i-1}, up_i, up_{i+1}, and the updates of x_i and up_i are functions of x_i and up_i. We followed the definition in [15] and defined a state as being legitimate if exactly one guarded command is enabled globally. We also constrain the completions of P_2 and P_3 to be identical.

Due to the large number of unknown functions needed to be synthesized in this experiment and, in particular, because there were a lot of input domain points at which the guards had to be true, the heuristic that prefers minimally permissive guards, described in Sect. 4, was not effective. However, the heuristic that prioritizes interpretations in which the guards depend on fewer arguments of their domain was effective. For state variable updates, we applied the heuristic that prioritizes functions that leave the state unchanged or set it to a constant. After passing the synthesized interpretation through a SyGuS solver, the expressions we got were exactly the same as the ones found in [9].

5.3 Cache Coherence Protocol

A cache coherence protocol ensures that the copies of shared data in the private caches of a multiprocessor system are kept up-to-date with the most recent version. We describe the working of the German cache coherence protocol, which is often used as a case study in model checking research [7,30]. The protocol consists of a *Directory* process, n symmetric *Cache* processes and n symmetric *Environment* processes, one for each cache process. Each cache may be in the E, S or I state, indicating read-write, read, and no permissions on the data respectively. All communication between the caches and the directory is non-blocking, and occurs over buffered, unordered communication channels.

The environment issues *read* and *write* commands to its cache. In response to a *read* command, the cache C sends a *RequestS* command to the directory. The directory, sends C the most up-to-date copy of the data, after coordinating with other caches, and grants read access to C, and remembers C as a *sharer* of the data. In response to a *write* request from the environment, the cache C sends a *RequestE* command to the directory. The directory coordinates with every other cache C' that has read or write permissions to revoke their permissions and then grants C exclusive access to the data, and remembers C as the owner of the data. The complete German/MSI protocol, modeled as communicating extended state machines, is fairly complex, with a symmetry-reduced state space of about 20,000 states when instantiated with two cache processes and about 450,000 states when instantiated with three cache processes.

We consider a more complex variant of the German cache coherence protocol to evaluate the techniques we have presented so far, which we refer to as German/MSI. The main differences from the base German protocol are: (1) Direct communication between caches is possible in some cases, (2) A cache in the S state can silently relinquish its permissions, which can cause the directory to have out-of-date information about the caches which are in the S state. (3) A cache in the E state can coordinate with the directory to relinquish their permissions. A complete list of scenarios typically used when describing this protocol is presented in the full version of the paper [3]. These scenarios however, do not describe the protocol's behavior in several cases induced by concurrency.

Consider the scenario shown in Fig. 4, where initially, cache C1 is in the I state, in contrast, the directory records that C1 is in state S and is a sharer, due to C1 having silently relinquished its read permissions at some point in the past. Now, both caches C1 and C2 receive *write* commands from their respective environments. Cache C2 sends a *RequestE* message to the directory, requesting exclusive write permissions. The directory, under the impression that C1 is in state S, sends an *Inv* message to it, informing it that C2 has requested exclusive access and C1 needs to acknowledge that it has relinquished permissions to C2. Concurrently, cache C1 sends a *RequestE* message to the directory requesting write permissions as well, which gets delayed. Subsequently, the cache C1 receives an invalidation when it is in the state IM, which cannot happen in the base German protocol. The correct behavior for the cache in this situation (shown by dashed arrows), is to send an *InvAck* message to the cache C2. The guard, the state

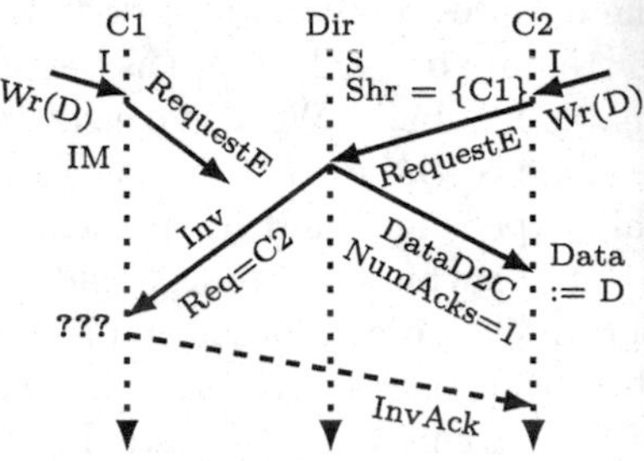

Fig. 4. A racy scenario

Table 1. Experimental results

Benchmark	# UF	Search space	# States	# Iters	SMT Time (s)	Total Time (s)
Peterson	3	2^{36}	60	14	0.1	0.13
Dijkstra	6	2^{192}	~2000	30	27	64
German/MSI-2	16	~2^{4700}	~20000 (symm. red.)	217	31	298
German/MSI-4	28	~2^{7614}	~20000 (symm. red.)	419	898	1545
German/MSI-5	34	~2^{9000}	~20000 (symm. red.)	525	2261	3410

variable updates, as well as the location update is what we have left unspecified in the case of this particular scenario. As part of the evaluation, we successfully synthesized the behavior of the German/MSI protocol in five such corner-case scenarios arising from concurrency. A description of the other corner-case scenarios can be found in the full version of the paper [3].

5.4 Summary of Experimental Results

Table 1 summarizes our experimental findings. All experiments were performed on a Linux desktop, with an Intel Core i7 CPU running at 3.4 GHz., with 8 GB of memory. The columns show the name of the benchmark, the number of unknown functions that were synthesized (# UF), the size of the search space for the unknown functions, the number of states in the complete protocol (# States), "symm. red." denotes symmetry reduced state space. The "# Iters." column shows the number of algorithm iterations, while the last two columns show the total amount of time spent in SMT solving and the end-to-end synthesis time.

The "German/MSI-n" rows correspond to the synthesizing the unknown behavior for the German/MSI protocol, with n out of the five unknown transitions left unspecified. In each case, we applied the heuristic to obtain minimally permissive guards and biased the search towards updates which leave the values of state variables unchanged as far as possible, except in the case of the Dijkstra benchmark, as mentioned in Sect. 5.2. Also, note that we ran each benchmark multiple times with different random seeds to the SMT solver, and report the worst of the run times in Table 1.

Programmer Assistance. In all cases, the programmer specified the kinds of messages to handle in the states where the behavior was unknown. For example, in the case of the German/MSI protocol, the programmer indicated that in the IM state on the cache, it needs to handle an invalidation from the directory (see Fig. 4). In general, the programmer specified *what* needs to be handled, but not the *how*. This was crucial to getting our approach to scale.

Overhead of Decision Procedures. We observe from Table 1 that for the longer running benchmarks, the run time is dominated by SMT solving. In all of these cases, a very large fraction of the constraints asserted into the SMT solver are constraints to implement heuristics which are specifically aimed at guiding the SMT solver, and reducing the impact of non-deterministic choices made by the solver. Specialized decision procedures that handle these constraints at an algorithmic level [4] can greatly speed up the synthesis procedure.

Synthesizing Symbolic Expressions. The interpretations returned by the SMT solver are in the form of tables, which specify the output of the unknown function on specific inputs. We mentioned that if a symbolic expression is required we can pass this output to a SyGuS solver, which will then return a symbolic expression. We were able to synthesize compact expressions in all cases using the enumerative SyGuS solver [1]. Further, although the interpretations are only guaranteed to be correct for the finite instance of the protocol, the symbolic expressions generated by the SyGuS solver were *parametric*. We found that they were general enough to handle larger instances of protocol.

6 Conclusions

We have presented an algorithm to complete symmetric distributed protocols specified as ESM sketches, such that they satisfy the given safety and liveness properties. A prototype implementation, which included a custom model checker, successfully synthesized non-trivial portions of Peterson's mutual exclusion protocol, Dijkstra's self-stabilizing system, and the German/MSI cache coherence protocol. We show that programmer assistance in the form of *what* needs to be handled is crucial to the scalability of the approach. Scalability is currently limited by the scalability of the SMT solver. As part of future work, we plan to investigate algorithms that do not depend as heavily on SMT solvers as a core decision procedure. We are hopeful that such an approach will improve the scalability of our algorithms.

References

1. Alur, R., Bodík, R., Juniwal, G., Martin, M.M.K., Raghothaman, M., Seshia, S.A., Singh, R., Solar-Lezama, A., Torlak, E., Udupa, A.: Syntax-guided Synthesis. In: FMCAD, pp. 1–17 (2013)
2. Alur, R., Martin, M., Raghothaman, M., Stergiou, C., Tripakis, S., Udupa, A.: Synthesizing finite-state protocols from scenarios and requirements. In: Yahav, E. (ed.) HVC 2014. LNCS, vol. 8855, pp. 75–91. Springer, Heidelberg (2014)
3. Alur, R., Raghothaman, M., Stergiou, C., Tripakis, S., Udupa, A.: Automatic completion of distributed protocols with symmetry. In: CoRR, arXiv:1505.0440 (2015). http://arxiv.org/abs/1505.04409
4. Bjorner, N., Phan, A.D.: νZ - maximal satisfaction with Z3. In: Kutsia, T., Voronkov, A. (eds.) SCSS 2014. EPiC Series, vol. 30, pp. 1–9. EasyChair (2014)
5. Bloem, R., Jobstmann, B., Piterman, N., Pnueli, A., Sa'ar, Y.: Synthesis of reactive(1) designs. J. Comput. Syst. Sci. **78**(3), 911–938 (2012)

6. Cassel, S., Howar, F., Jonsson, B., Steffen, B.: Learning extended finite state machines. In: Giannakopoulou, D., Salaün, G. (eds.) SEFM 2014. LNCS, vol. 8702, pp. 250–264. Springer, Heidelberg (2014)
7. Chou, C.-T., Mannava, P.K., Park, S.: A simple method for parameterized verification of cache coherence protocols. In: Hu, A.J., Martin, A.K. (eds.) FMCAD 2004. LNCS, vol. 3312, pp. 382–398. Springer, Heidelberg (2004)
8. Cimatti, A., Clarke, E., Giunchiglia, E., Giunchiglia, F., Pistore, M., Roveri, M., Sebastiani, R., Tacchella, A.: NuSMV 2: an open-source tool for symbolic model checking. In: CAV 2002. LNCS, vol. 2404, pp. 359–364. Springer, Heidelberg (2002)
9. Dijkstra, E.W.: Self-stabilizing Systems in spite of distributed control. Commun. ACM **17**(11), 643–644 (1974)
10. Dill, D.L.: The murφ verification system. In: Proceedings of the 8th International Conference on Computer Aided Verification, pp. 390–393, CAV 1996, Springer-Verlag, London, UK (1996)
11. Emerson, E.A., Havlicek, J.W., Trefler, R.J.: Virtual symmetry reduction. In: Proceedings of the Fifteenth Annual IEEE Symposium on Logic in Computer Science (LICS 2000), pp. 121–131, June 2000
12. Emerson, E.A., Sistla, A.P.: Utilizing symmetry when model-checking under fairness assumptions: an automata-theoretic approach. ACM Trans. Program. Lang. Syst. **19**(4), 617–638 (1997)
13. Finkbeiner, B., Schewe, S.: Uniform distributed synthesis. In: IEEE Symposium on Logic in Computer Science, pp. 321–330 (2005)
14. Finkbeiner, B., Schewe, S.: Bounded synthesis. Softw. Tools Technol. Transf. **15**(5–6), 519–539 (2013)
15. Gascón, A., Tiwari, A.: Synthesis of a simple self-stabilizing system. In: Proceedings 3rd Workshop on Synthesis, SYNT 2014, pp. 5–16, Vienna, Austria, July 23–24, 2014
16. Holzmann, G.J.: The model checker spin. IEEE Trans. Softw. Eng. **23**(5), 279–295 (1997)
17. Jobstmann, B., Griesmayer, A., Bloem, R.: Program repair as a game. In: Etessami, K., Rajamani, S.K. (eds.) CAV 2005. LNCS, vol. 3576, pp. 226–238. Springer, Heidelberg (2005)
18. Katz, G., Peled, D.A.: Model checking-based genetic programming with an application to mutual exclusion. In: Ramakrishnan, C.R., Rehof, J. (eds.) TACAS 2008. LNCS, vol. 4963, pp. 141–156. Springer, Heidelberg (2008)
19. Rich, A., Alexandron, G., Naveh, R.: An explanation-based constraint debugger. In: Namjoshi, K., Zeller, A., Ziv, A. (eds.) HVC 2009. LNCS, vol. 6405, pp. 52–56. Springer, Heidelberg (2011)
20. Lamouchi, H., Thistle, J.: Effective control synthesis for DES under partial observations. In: 39th IEEE Conference on Decision and Control, pp. 22–28 (2000)
21. Lynch, N.A.: Distributed Algorithms. Morgan Kaufmann, Burlington (1996)
22. de Moura, L., Bjørner, N.S.: Z3: an efficient SMT solver. In: Ramakrishnan, C.R., Rehof, J. (eds.) TACAS 2008. LNCS, vol. 4963, pp. 337–340. Springer, Heidelberg (2008)
23. Norris, I.P.: Better verification through symmetry. Formal Methods Syst. Des. **9**(1–2), 41–75 (1996)
24. Pnueli, A., Rosner, R.: On the synthesis of a reactive module. In: Proceedings of the 16th ACM Symposium on Principles of Programming Languages (1989)
25. Pnueli, A., Rosner, R.: Distributed Reactive Systems Are Hard to Synthesize. In: 31st Annual Symposium on Foundations of Computer Science. pp. 746–757 (1990)

26. Ramadge, P., Wonham, W.: The control of discrete event systems. IEEE Trans. Control Theory **77**, 81–98 (1989)
27. Sistla, A.P., Gyuris, V., Emerson, E.A.: SMC: a symmetry-based model checker for verification of safety and liveness properties. ACM Trans. Softw. Eng. Methodol. **9**(2), 133–166 (2000)
28. Solar-Lezama, A., Rabbah, R., Bodik, R., Ebcioglu, K.: Programming by sketching for bit-streaming programs. In: Proceedings of the 2005 ACM Conference on Programming Language Design and Implementation (2005)
29. Solar-Lezama, A., Jones, C.G., Bodik, R.: Sketching concurrent data structures. In: Proceedings of the 2008 ACM SIGPLAN Conference on Programming Language Design and Implementation, PLDI 2008 (2008)
30. Talupur, M., Tuttle, M.R.: Going with the flow: parameterized verification using message flows. In: Cimatti, A., Jones, R.B. (eds.) Formal Methods in Computer-Aided Design. FMCAD 2008, pp. 1–8. IEEE, Portland (2008)
31. Tripakis, S.: Undecidable problems of decentralized observation and control on regular languages. Inf. Process. Lett. **90**(1), 21–28 (2004)
32. Udupa, A., Raghavan, A., Deshmukh, J.V., Mador-Haim, S., Martin, M.M., Alur, R.: TRANSIT: specifying protocols with concolic snippets. In: Proceedings of the 34th ACM SIGPLAN Conference on Programming Language Design and Implementation, PLDI 2013, pp. 287–296 (2013)

An Axiomatic Specification for Sequential Memory Models

William Mansky(✉), Dmitri Garbuzov, and Steve Zdancewic

University of Pennsylvania, Philadelphia, PA, USA
wmansky@seas.upenn.edu

Abstract. Formalizations of concurrent memory models often represent memory behavior in terms of sequences of operations, where operations are either reads, writes, or synchronizations. More concrete models of (sequential) memory behavior may include allocation and free operations, but also include details of memory layout or data representation. We present an abstract specification for sequential memory models with allocation and free operations, in the form of a set of axioms that provide enough information to reason about memory without overly constraining the behavior of implementations. We characterize a set of "well-behaved" programs that behave uniformly on all instances of the specification. We show that the specification is both feasible—the CompCert memory model implements it—and usable—we can use the axioms to prove the correctness of an optimization that changes the memory behavior of programs in an LLVM-like language.

Keywords: Memory models · Optimizing compilers · Deep specifications

1 Introduction

Vhen reasoning about compilers and low-level code, it is not enough to treat nemory as an assignment of values to locations; memory management, concur-ency behavior, and many other factors complicate the picture, and without ıccounting for these factors our reasoning says nothing about the programs that ıctually run on processors. Memory models provide the necessary abstraction, ;eparating the behavior of a program from the behavior of the memory it reads ınd writes. There have been many formalizations of concurrent memory models, ɔeginning with sequential consistency [1] (in which memory must behave as if .t has received an ordered sequence of read and write operations) and extend-.ng to more relaxed memory models. Most of these models include a theorem ılong the lines of "well-synchronized programs behave as if the memory model .s sequentially consistent," characterizing a large class of programs that behave .he same regardless of the concurrent memory model [7].

What, then, is the behavior of a sequentially consistent memory model? When the only memory operations are reads and writes (and possibly synchro-ıization operations), the answer is simple: each read of a location reads the

D. Kroening and C.S. Păsăreanu (Eds.): CAV 2015, Part II, LNCS 9207, pp. 413–428, 2015.
DOI: 10.1007/978-3-319-21668-3_24

value that was last written to that location. In other words, the memory does in fact act as an assignment of values to locations. If we try to model other memory operations, however, the picture becomes more complicated. C and many related intermediate and low-level languages include at least allocation and free operations, and we might also want to include casts, structured pointers, overlapping locations, etc. Even restricting ourselves to sequential memory models, we can see that the space of possible models is much larger than "sequential consistency" suggests.

Formalizing memory models is a crucial step in compiler verification. Projects such as CompCert [4], CompCertTSO [9], Vellvm [11], and Compositional CompCert [8] specify memory models as part of the process of giving semantics to their various source, target, and intermediate languages, and use their properties in proving the correctness of optimizations and program transformations. The (in most cases sequential) memory models in these works include some of the complexity that more abstract formalisms lack, but they are also tightly tied to the particular languages and formalisms used in the projects. Compiler verification stands to benefit from memory model specifications that generalize away from the details of particular memory models, specifications which encompass most commonly used models and allow reasoning about programs without digging into the details of particular models. Generic specifications of memory models have the potential to lead to both simpler proofs—since all the reasoning about a particular model is encapsulated in a proof that it satisfies the specification—and more general ones—since a proof using a specification is true for any instance of that specification.

In this paper, we develop a specification for sequential memory models that support allocation and free operations as well as reads and writes, and demonstrate its use in reasoning about programs. We prove a sequential counterpart to the "well-synchronized programs are sequentially consistent" theorem, characterizing the set of programs that have the same behavior under any sequential memory model that meets our specification. We also show that CompCert's memory model is an instance of our specification, and verify a dead code elimination optimization for an LLVM-like language using the specification, resulting in a proof that is measurably simpler than the corresponding proof in Vellvm. All definitions and proofs have been formalized in the Coq proof assistant, so that our specification can be used for any application that requires mechanized proofs about programs with memory; the Coq development can be found online at http://www.seas.upenn.edu/~wmansky/meminterface.

2 An Abstract Sequential Memory Model

A memory model is a description of the allowed behavior of a set of memory operations over the course of a program. A memory model can be defined in various ways: as a set of functions that can be called along with some guarantees on their results, as a description of the set of valid traces of operations performed by the execution of a program, or as an abstract machine that receives and responds to messages. In each case, the memory model makes a set of operations available to programs and provides some guarantees on their behavior. These operations always include reading and writing, and in many models these are the only operations; however, there are many other memory-related operations used in real-world programs. The main question is one of where we draw the line between program and memory. Is the runtime system that handles memory allocation part of the memory, or a layer above it? Does a cast from a pointer to an integer involve the memory, or is it a computation within the program? Does the memory contain structured blocks in which different references may overlap, or are structured pointers program objects that must be evaluated to references to distinct locations before they are read or written?

Our goal is to formalize the interface that memory provides to a programming language. We aim to give an abstract specification for memory models that can be used to define the semantics of a language, and to prove useful properties of programs in that language independently of the implementation details of any particular memory model. Our specification should describe the assumptions about memory that programmers can make when writing their programs and verifiers can make while reasoning. Since from the program's perspective the runtime system and the memory model are not distinct, our specification should include the operations provided by the runtime system. It should be easy to use in defining operational semantics for programming languages, and it should provide as many axioms as are needed to make the behavior of memory predictable without overconstraining the set of possible implementations.

For our specification, we begin with four operations: read, write, alloc, and free. These operations appear in code at almost every level. They are, for instance, the operations supported by the CompCert memory model [5], which has been used to verify a compiler from C to machine code. Although CompCert's model provides a realistic and usable formalization of the semantics of these operations, it is not the *only* such formalization. Other choices, such as CompCertTSO's [9] or the quasi-concrete model [2], may allow more optimizations on memory operations or a cleaner formulation of some theorems. We may want to store values in memory other than those included in CompCert, or abstract away from the details of blocks and offsets.

Our aim is to give a simple specification of memory models such that:

- Most memory models that support read, write, alloc, and free can be seen as instances of the specification.
- The specification provides the guarantees on these operations needed to reason about programs.

Then we can use this specification to reason about programs independently of the particular memory model being used, and by proving that particular models (such as CompCert's) meet the specification, be assured that our reasoning is valid for those models.

2.1 Memory Model Axioms

Previously, we mentioned three main approaches to specifying memory models. In the functional approach (e.g. CompCert [5]), each operation is a function with its own arguments and return type, and restrictions are placed on the results of the functions. In the abstract-machine approach (e.g. CompCertTSO [9]), memory is a separate component from the program with its own transition system, and steps of the system are produced by combining program steps and memory steps. In the axiomatic approach (taken in most concurrent memory models), a set of rules are given that allow some sequences of memory operations and forbid others. A definition in one of these styles is often provably equivalent to a definition in another style, although the axiomatic approach can be used to formalize some models that cannot be expressed in other ways (i.e. non-operational models). Our axioms should be true for all (reasonable) memory models, and also provide enough information to prove useful properties of a language that uses the specification.

Our model begins with a set $\mathcal{L}$ of *locations* and a set $\mathcal{V}$ of *values*. Every memory operation targets exactly one location, and locations are *distinct*: we can check whether two locations are equal, and a change to one location should not affect any other location. Locations may be thought of as unique addresses or memory cells. Values are the data that are stored in the memory; for simplicity, each location is assumed to be able to hold a single value of any size (in future work, we intend to extend this model to account for the size of data).

Definition 1. Given a location $\ell \in \mathcal{L}$ and a value $v \in \mathcal{V}$, a *memory operation* is one of $\mathsf{read}(\ell, v)$, $\mathsf{write}(\ell, v)$, $\mathsf{alloc}(\ell)$, and $\mathsf{free}(\ell)$. The operations $\mathsf{write}(\ell, v)$, $\mathsf{alloc}(\ell)$, and $\mathsf{free}(\ell)$ *modify* the location ℓ. Over the course of execution, a program produces a series of memory operations. A memory model can be given as a predicate can_do on a sequence of memory operations $m = op_1 \ldots op_k$ (called the *history*) and an operation op, such that $\mathsf{can\_do}(m, op)$ holds if and only if, given that the operations in m have occured, the operation op can now be performed. A sequence of operations $op_1 \ldots op_k$ is *consistent* with a memory model if $\mathsf{can\_do}(op_1 \ldots op_{i-1}, op_i)$ for each $i < k$, i.e., each operation in the sequence was allowable given the operations that had been performed so far.

The axioms shown in Fig. 1 restrict the possible behavior of a can_do predicate. (We write $loc(op)$ for the location accessed by op.) The first two axioms state the distinctness of locations, requiring that operations on one location do not affect the operations possible on other locations. The remaining rules enforce (but do not completely determine) the intended semantics of each kind of memory operation: e.g., a $\mathsf{write}(\ell, v)$ operation must allow v to be read at ℓ. We do not completely constrain the semantics of the operations, but we attempt to capture the expectations of a programmer about each operation: it should be possible to allocate free memory and free allocated memory, write to allocated memory and read the last value written, etc., and it should not be possible to free memory that is already free, allocate memory that is already allocated, read values that have not been written, etc. Note that, while the axioms are meant to

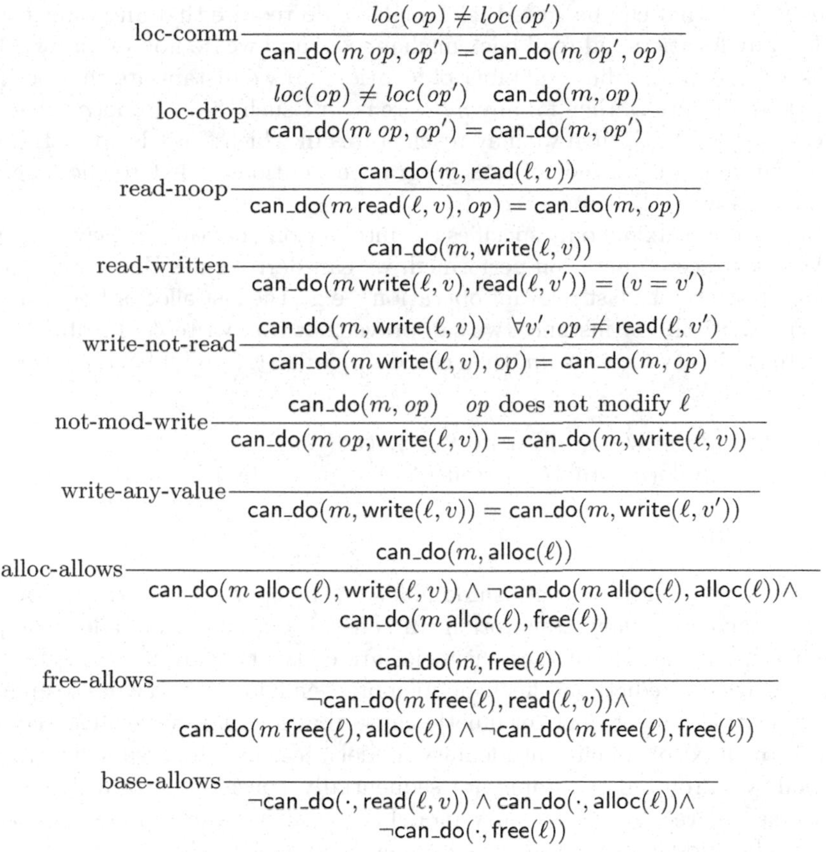

Fig. 1. The axioms of the memory model specification

lefine the possible semantics of memory models, they also coincide with the sorts of equivalences that are commonly used in compiler optimizations—reordering unrelated operations, propagating stored values forward to later reads, etc.

If a behavior is "implementation-dependent", or might vary across different memory models, then the axioms leave it unspecified. Two major kinds of operation are left unspecified: reads from locations that have been allocated but not written to (we call these locations "uninitialized"), and writes to locations that have not been allocated. Because these operations are unspecified, the specification admits instances in which they have a wide variety of interpretations: a write to an allocated location may fail, write a value that can be read later, unpredictably either allocate the location and write a value or do nothing at all, or any other (possibly empty) subset of the conceivable behaviors of a write, depending on the memory model. Parameterizing by the sets $\mathcal{L}$ and $\mathcal{V}$ also implicitly leaves some aspects of the memory model unspecified. We do not constrain the kinds or sizes of data that can be stored (although we do require that any value can be stored in any location and read back unchanged), and we do not specify whether there is a finite or an infinite number of locations. If we instantiate the specification with an infinite $\mathcal{L}$, then for any m there is an ℓ such that $\mathsf{can\_do}(m, \mathsf{alloc}(\ell))$; if we choose a finite $\mathcal{L}$, then we may reach states in which there is no such ℓ. The effect of running out of memory on program executions is left to the language semantics, as we will show in Sect. 4.1.

Although each axiom only specifies the interaction between the new operation and the most recent operation performed, we can derive rules that connect each new operation to "the last relevant operation", e.g., the last alloc or free of a location being written. For instance, we can prove that if $m\ \mathsf{write}(\ell, v)\ \mathsf{write}(\ell', v')$ is a consistent history for some m, then $\mathsf{can\_do}(m\ \mathsf{write}(\ell, v)\ \mathsf{write}(\ell', v'), \mathsf{read}(\ell, v))$ holds:

$$
\begin{aligned}
&\mathsf{can\_do}(m\ \mathsf{write}(\ell, v)\ \mathsf{write}(\ell', v'), \mathsf{read}(\ell, v)) \\
&= \mathsf{can\_do}(m\ \mathsf{write}(\ell, v), \mathsf{read}(\ell, v)) && \text{by loc-drop} \\
&= (v = v) && \text{by read-written} \\
&= \mathsf{true}
\end{aligned}
$$

In each step, the condition that can_do holds on the operations in the history follows from the consistency assumption. In general, our rules only allow complex reasoning about histories if those histories are consistent; an unspecified operation may have unpredictable effects on memory behavior (e.g., a write to an unallocated location may or may not quietly cause that location to be allocated).

In the context of concurrent memory models, it is usually assumed or proved that well-synchronized programs are sequentially consistent, regardless of the relaxations allowed by the memory model. This allows the complexities of the model to be hidden from the programmer, and means that verification of a certain (large) class of programs can be done independently of the relaxed model. Our axiomatization admits a similar property for sequential memory models.

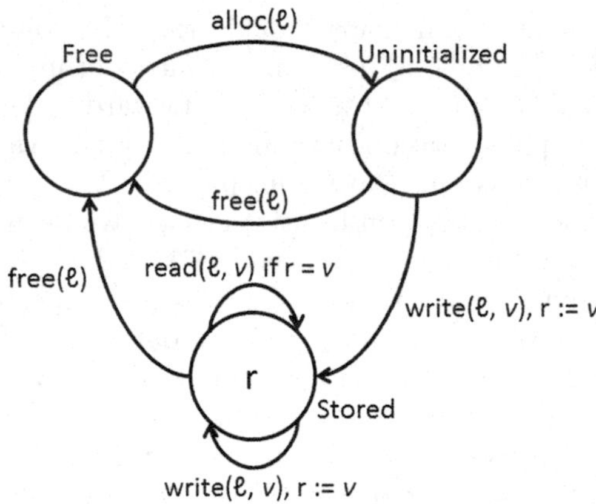

Fig. 2. The transition system for locations in the simple memory machine

Consider a simple abstract machine that associates each memory location with one of three states: free, uninit, or stored(v), where v is a value. Upon receiving a memory operation on a location, the machine's state for the location transitions as shown in the register automata of Fig. 2; any operation not shown leads to an error state.

Definition 2. The simple machine corresponding to a history m, written SM(m), is the machine reached by starting with each location in the Free state and applying the operations in m to their corresponding locations, in order. The can_do predicate induced by the simple machine is the one such that $\mathsf{can\_do}_{\mathsf{SM}}(m, op)$ when $loc(op)$ has a transition labeled with op in SM(m).

Then we can prove the following theorems:

Theorem 1. *The simple machine satisfies the memory model axioms.*

Theorem 2. *If a program never reads an uninitialized location and never writes to a free location, then for any* can_do *predicate that satisfies the axioms and any consistent history m and operation op,* can_do(m, op) *if and only if* $\mathsf{can\_do}_{\mathsf{SM}}(m, op)$.

This gives us a class of programs for which any model that satisfies the axioms is equivalent. For the (large) set of programs that take a principled approach to memory and avoid implementation-dependent behavior, we can reason using the simple machine and derive results that are applicable to any memory model that implements the specification; this has the potential to greatly simplify our proofs. On the other hand, many interesting programs may not meet the requirements of the theorem. In this case, we may still be able to reason using the specification: while we cannot turn to the fully defined simple machine, we can still use the axioms to draw conclusions about a program's memory behavior. Finally, if we expect that the correctness of our reasoning depends on a particular implementation, then we can go beneath the specification and work with the implementation directly. Having a reasoning principle for "well-behaved" programs simplifies our reasoning when it can be applied, but does not force us to give up on reasoning about programs that are not well-behaved.

3 Instantiating the Specification

The CompCert verified C compiler includes a C-like memory model [5], which is used to verify its transformations. In fact, it includes both a specification of a memory model and an implementation of that specification. Memory is modeled as a set of non-overlapping blocks, each of which behaves as an array of bytes; an *address* is a pair (b, o) of a block and an offset into the array. The specification defines four functions that can be called by programs (`alloc`, `free`, `load`, and `store`) and states properties on them. Most of these properties center around the *permissions* associated with each address, such as Readable, Writeable, and Freeable, which indicate which operations can be performed on the

$$\frac{(b, o) \text{ has permission Writeable in } M_1}{\exists M_2.\ \texttt{store}(M_1, b, o, v) = M_2}$$

$$\frac{\texttt{store}(M_1, b, o, v) = M_2 \quad (b', o') \text{ has permission } p \text{ in } M_1}{(b', o') \text{ has permission } p \text{ in } M_2}$$

$$\frac{\texttt{store}(M_1, b, o, v) = M_2 \quad (b', o') \text{ has permission } p \text{ in } M_2}{(b', o') \text{ has permission } p \text{ in } M_1}$$

$$\frac{\texttt{store}(M_1, b, o, v) = M_2}{(b, o) \text{ has permission Writeable in } M_1}$$

Fig. 3. A few of CompCert's `store` axioms

address. Figure 3 shows some of the properties for `store`; the other operations have similar axioms. CompCert's memory implementation manages the bounds, allocation state, and content of each block in a way that is shown to satisfy the axioms.

Although the CompCert memory specification abstracts away from some of the details of the implementation, it has some limitations as a generic memory model specification. It is tied to CompCert's particular definition of values and its notion of blocks. Furthermore, there is no uniformity across the different memory operations; each function takes different arguments and has a different result type, so that 44 axioms are used to express properties of the sort laid out in our specification. The CompCert memory model specification does not include an axiom that says "operations on different locations are independent"; indeed, it is difficult to state such an axiom, since "operations" are not quantifiable objects. Instead, we can look at the axioms stating that, e.g., a `store` to (b, o) does not change the permissions of another block and a `free` succeeds as long as the target address is Freeable, and conclude that a `free` can occur after a `store` to a different location if and only if it could occur before the `store`.

Using this sort of reasoning, we can show that the CompCert memory model specification satisfies our specification in turn. We "implement" each one of our memory operations with a call to the corresponding CompCert function, with one allocated block for each allocated memory location. Our specification does not include details about the size of values, so we restrict ourselves to 32-bit values (which includes most CompCert values).

Definition 3. Given CompCert memory states M and M', let $M \xrightarrow{op} M'$ if the function call corresponding to op can be applied to M to yield M'. Let $\mathsf{can\_do}_{\mathsf{CC}}(m, op)$ be true when there exist CompCert memory states M_1, M_2 such that $\texttt{empty} \xrightarrow{m}{}^{*} M_1$ and $M_1 \xrightarrow{op} M_2$, where `empty` is the initial CompCert memory state.

Theorem 3. $\mathsf{can\_do}_{\mathsf{CC}}$ *satisfies the axioms of our specification.*

Proof. The difficult axioms are loc-comm and loc-drop, since the other axioms refer to the interaction of particular operations. For each of loc-comm and loc-drop, we must break the proof into 16 cases, one for each ordered pair of memory operations. The cases involving `load` are straightforward, since it does not change the memory state. In each other case, we must show that the first operation does not change the permissions associated with the location of the second operation and vice versa. This allows us to conclude that each operation can still be performed after an operation to a different location is reordered/dropped.

This provides some evidence for the feasibility of our specification, since the CompCert memory model (when used in this restricted way) satisfies its axioms. By Theorem 2, we also know that on programs that do not read uninitialized locations or write to free locations, the CompCert memory model has the same behavior as the simple abstract machine. (The CompCert specification requires that reads of uninitialized locations return a special `undef` value and writes to free locations fail, which is just one point in the design space of memory models allowed by our specification; reads of uninitialized locations could also fail or return arbitrary values, for instance.)

Interestingly, while we choose the set of 32-bit CompCert values as our $\mathcal{V}$ for this instance, we do not need to choose a particular $\mathcal{L}$ in order to prove the above theorem. Each allocated location is mapped to a block, but the set of locations need not be the set of blocks itself. In the CompCert memory model, an `alloc` call always succeeds, implying that memory is infinite; however, the proof of implementation still applies even if we choose a finite $\mathcal{L}$. In this case, while CompCert's memory model is always willing to allocate more blocks, programs may still run out of distinct locations to request. Our specification's view of CompCert's infinite-memory model gives us an interface that can be either infinite-memory or finite-memory.

4 Using the Specification

From the perspective of a programming language, a memory model fills in the gaps in the semantics and provides some guarantees about the observable behavior of the memory. In this section, we show how our specification can be used for these tasks, by defining the semantics of a language using the specification and verifying an optimization against it.

4.1 MiniLLVM

Our example language is MiniLLVM, a language based on the LLVM intermediate representation [3]. The syntax of the language closely resembles LLVM, with the slight variation that labels are implicit in the structure of the control flow graph rather than explicitly present in the instructions.

$$\mathit{expr} ::= \%\mathrm{x} \mid @\mathrm{x} \mid \mathrm{c} \qquad\qquad \mathit{type} ::= \texttt{int} \mid \mathit{type}\ \texttt{pointer}$$

$$\begin{aligned} \mathit{instr} ::= {} & \%\mathrm{x} = \mathrm{op}\ \mathit{type}\ \mathit{expr},\ \mathit{expr} \mid \%\mathrm{x} = \texttt{icmp}\ \mathrm{cmp}\ \mathit{type}\ \mathit{expr}, \mathit{expr} \mid \\ & \texttt{br}\ \mathit{expr} \mid \texttt{br} \mid \texttt{alloca}\ \%\mathrm{x}\ \mathit{type} \mid \\ & \%\mathrm{x} = \texttt{load}\ \mathit{type}^*\ \mathit{expr} \mid \texttt{store}\ \mathit{type}\ \mathit{expr},\ \mathit{type}^*\ \mathit{expr} \mid \\ & \%\mathrm{x} = \texttt{cmpxchg}\ \mathit{type}^*\ \mathit{expr},\ \mathit{type}\ \mathit{expr},\ \mathit{type}\ \mathit{expr} \mid \\ & \%\mathrm{x} = \texttt{phi}\ [\mathit{node}_1, \mathit{expr}_1], ..., [\mathit{node}_k, \mathit{expr}_k] \mid \\ & \%\mathrm{x} = \texttt{call}\ \mathit{type}\ \mathit{expr}(\mathit{expr}, ..., \mathit{expr}) \mid \texttt{return}\ \mathit{expr} \mid \texttt{output}\ \mathit{expr} \end{aligned}$$

A MiniLLVM program P is a list of function definitions $(f, \ell, \mathit{params}, G)$, where f is the name of the function, ℓ is its location in memory, *params* is the list of the function's formal parameters, and G is the function's control-flow graph (CFG). (For simplicity, we assume that each node in a CFG contains exactly one instruction.) A *configuration* is either an error state Error or a tuple $(f, p_0, p, \mathit{env}, \mathit{st}, \mathit{al})$, where f is the name of the currently executing function, p_0 is the previously executed program point, p is the current program point, *env* is the environment giving values for thread-local variables, *st* is the call stack, and *al* is a record of the memory locations allocated by the currently executing function (the `alloca` instruction allocates space that is freed when the function returns). The semantics of MiniLLVM are given by a transition relation $P \vdash c \xrightarrow{a} c'$, where a is either a list of memory operations performed in the step or a value output by the `output` instruction. A few of the semantic rules for MiniLLVM instructions are shown in Fig. 4, where P_f is the CFG for the function f in P, $\mathsf{succ}(p)$ is the successor node of p in its CFG, Label extracts the instruction label for a node from the CFG, and $(e, \mathit{env}) \Downarrow v$ means that the expression e evaluates to v in the presence of the environment *env*. We make a point of allowing the `store` instruction to fail into an Error state so that in our example optimization—a dead store elimination—we can safely remove ill-formed stores.

Note that the interaction between the semantics of MiniLLVM and the memory model is restricted to the transition labels. We complete the semantics by combining the transitions of the language with an instance of the memory model specification, passing the memory operations to the can_do predicate and retaining the output values, if any:

$$\mathrm{mem-step}\frac{P \vdash c \xrightarrow{op_1,\ldots,op_n,v_1,\ldots,v_k} c' \quad \mathsf{can\_do}(m, op_1 \ldots op_n)}{P \vdash (c, m) \xrightarrow{v_1,\ldots,v_k} (c', m\ op_1\ \ldots\ op_n)}$$

So while, e.g., a `load` operation may produce $\mathsf{read}(\ell, v)$ for any v, the only v that will be allowed by the can_do predicate is the one stored at ℓ. To obtain MiniLLVM semantics for a particular memory model, we simply instantiate the rule with the can_do predicate for that model; we can also reason at the level of the specification and derive results that hold for every instance.

Finite Memory Semantics. In Sect. 2.1, we noted that our specification encompasses both infinite-memory and finite-memory models, and indeed our semantics for MiniLLVM works in either case. However, it is interesting to consider the way that finite memory is reflected in the semantics. If the set of locations is finite, then we may reach a state (c, m) in which $\mathsf{can\_do}(m, \mathsf{alloc}(\ell))$

$$\frac{\mathsf{Label}\ P_f\ p = (\%x = \text{op}\ ty\ e_1, e_2) \quad (e_1\ \text{op}\ e_2, env) \Downarrow v}{P \vdash (f, p_0, p, env, st, al) \rightarrow (f, p, \mathsf{succ}(p), env(x \mapsto v), st, al)}$$

$$\frac{\mathsf{Label}\ P_f\ p = (\texttt{alloca}\ \%x\ ty)}{P \vdash (f, p_0, p, env, st, al) \xrightarrow{\mathsf{alloc}(\ell)} (f, p, \mathsf{succ}(p), env(x \mapsto \ell), st, al \cup \{\ell\})}$$

$$\frac{\mathsf{Label}\ P_f\ p = (\%x = \texttt{load}\ ty^*\ e) \quad (e, env) \Downarrow \ell}{P \vdash (f, p_0, p, env, st, al) \xrightarrow{\mathsf{read}(\ell, v)} (f, p, \mathsf{succ}(p), env(x \mapsto v), st, al)}$$

$$\frac{\mathsf{Label}\ P_f\ p = (\texttt{store}\ ty_1\ e_1, ty_2{}^*\ e_2) \quad (e_1, env) \Downarrow v \quad (e_2, env) \Downarrow \ell}{P \vdash (f, p_0, p, env, st, al) \xrightarrow{\mathsf{write}(\ell, v)} (f, p, \mathsf{succ}(p), env, st, al)}$$

$$\frac{\begin{array}{c}\mathsf{Label}\ P_f\ p = (\texttt{store}\ ty_1\ e_1, ty_2{}^*\ e_2) \\ e_1 \text{ fails to evaluate in } env \text{ or } e_2 \text{ fails to evaluate to a pointer in } env\end{array}}{P \vdash (f, p_0, p, env, st, al) \rightarrow \mathsf{Error}}$$

$$\frac{\mathsf{Label}\ P_f\ p = (\texttt{output}(e)) \quad (e, env) \Downarrow v}{P \vdash (f, p_0, p, env, st, al) \xrightarrow{v} (f, p, \mathsf{succ}(p), env, st, al)}$$

$$\frac{}{P \vdash \mathsf{Error} \xrightarrow{a} \mathsf{Error}}$$

Fig. 4. Part of the transition semantics of MiniLLVM

does not hold for any ℓ. In this case, the mem-step rule cannot be applied, and (c, m) is stuck. In terms of optimizations, this means that `alloca` instructions may not be removed from programs, since this may enable behaviors that were previously impossible due to the out-of-memory condition.

An alternative approach is to treat out-of-memory as an error state. We can obtain this semantics by adding one more rule:

$$\frac{P \vdash c \xrightarrow{\mathsf{alloc}(\ell)} c' \quad \forall \ell.\ \neg\mathsf{can\_do}(m, \mathsf{alloc}(\ell))}{P \vdash (c, m) \rightarrow (\mathsf{Error}, m)}$$

Now the language semantics catches the out-of-memory condition and transitions to an error state rather than getting stuck. This new semantics allows `alloca` instructions to be removed but not inserted, since optimizations should not introduce new errors. (With a more sophisticated treatment of $\mathcal{L}$, we may be able to state a semantics that allows both adding and removing `alloca`.) We can choose whichever semantics is appropriate to the language or the application at hand; our specification implicitly makes the behavior of out-of-memory programs a question of language design rather than a feature of the memory model itself.

4.2 Verifying an Optimization

A good specification should allow us to abstract away from unnecessary details, so that we can separate reasoning about programs from reasoning about memory models. In this section, we will use the semantics of MiniLLVM with the memory model specification to prove the correctness of a dead store elimination optimization (under any memory model that satisfies the specification). We will assume that we have some analysis for finding dead stores, and prove that removing dead stores does not change the behaviors of a MiniLLVM program.

To begin, we need to state our notion of correctness. A correct optimization should *refine* the behaviors of a program; it may remove some behaviors (e.g. by collapsing nondeterminism), but it should never introduce new behaviors.

Definition 4. A configuration is *initial* if it is a tuple (f, p_0, p, env, st, al) such that st and al are empty and p is the start node of P_f. A *trace* of a program P is a sequence of values $v_1, \ldots v_n$ for which there is some initial configuration c_0 and some state (c', m') such that $(c_0, \cdot) \xrightarrow{v_1,\ldots,v_n}{}^{*} (c', m')$. A program P *refines* a program Q if every trace of P is a trace of Q.

We can prove refinement through the well-established technique of *simulation*. In particular, since dead store elimination removes an instruction from the program, we will use *right-option simulation*, in which the original program may take some externally unobservable steps that the transformed program omits.

Definition 5. A relation R on states is a *right-option simulation* between programs P and Q if the initial states of P and Q are in R and for any states C_P, C_Q in P and Q respectively, if $R(C_P, C_Q)$ and $P \vdash C_P \xrightarrow{k} C'_P$, then there is a state C'_Q such that $R(C'_P, C'_Q)$ and either

- $Q \vdash C_Q \xrightarrow{k} C'_Q$, or
- $\exists C''_Q.\ Q \vdash C_Q \rightarrow C''_Q$ and $Q \vdash C''_Q \xrightarrow{k} C'_Q$.

Theorem 4. *If there is a right-option simulation between P and Q, then P refines Q.*

We conservatively approximate dead stores by defining them as stores to locations that will never be read again.

Definition 6. An instruction `store` $ty_1\ e_1,\ ty_2{}^*\ e_2$ in a program P is *dead* if in all executions of P, if e_2 is evaluated to a location ℓ when the store is executed, then ℓ will not be the target of a read for the remainder of the execution.

The optimization itself, given a dead store, is simple: we remove the node containing the dead store from its CFG. The simulation relation R_{dse} relates a state (c', m') in the transformed program to a state (c, m) in the original program if m' can be obtained from m by dropping writes to locations that will not be read again, and c' can be obtained from c by replacing the removed node n with its immediate successor.

Definition 7. Let P be a graph in which the function f contains a node n whose successor is n'. The predicate skip_node holds on a pair of configurations (c, c') if either both c and c' are Error, or c' can be obtained from c by replacing all occurrences of n in the program point and the stack with n'. Let R_{dse} be the relation such that $R_{dse}((c', m'), (c, m))$ when either

- $c =$ Error, or
- m' can be obtained from m by removing writes to locations that will not be targeted by reads for the rest of the execution, and skip_node(c, c') holds.

The proof proceeds as follows. First, we show that any step in the transformed graph can occur in the original graph.

Lemma 1. *Let P' be the program obtained from P by removing a node n from a function f, and n' be the successor of n. If $P' \vdash (c', m) \xrightarrow{k} (c'_2, m_2)$, skip_node$(c, c')$, and c is not at n, then there exists c_2 such that $P \vdash (c, m) \xrightarrow{k} (c_2, m_2)$ and skip_node(c_2, c'_2).*

Proof. Because c is not at n, c and c' execute the same instruction and produce the same results, modulo the fact that n is present in P and absent in P' (giving us skip_node(c_2, c'_2)).

Next, we show that dropping writes to unread locations from a history does not change the operations it allows.

Lemma 2. *Let m and m' be consistent histories such that m is produced by a partial execution of a program P and m' can be obtained from m by removing* writes *to locations that are not targeted by* reads *for the rest of the execution. If P never reads uninitialized locations or writes to free locations, then* can_do(m, op) *if and only if* can_do(m', op).

Proof. By Theorem 2, can_do(m, op) iff $\text{can\_do}_{\text{SM}}(m, op)$ (and likewise for m'). We can show by induction that for any location ℓ, if SM(m) and SM(m') differ, then SM(m) is in the Stored state and SM(m') is not in the Freed state (and ℓ is not read again in the execution). This is sufficient to guarantee that any non-read operation has the same effect in SM(m) and SM(m'), and the conclusion follows directly.

We can use this lemma to show that the relationship between memories is preserved by program steps.

Lemma 3. *Let m and m' be consistent histories such that m is produced by a partial execution of a program P and m' can be obtained from m by removing* writes *to locations that are not targeted by* reads *for the rest of the execution. If P never reads uninitialized locations or writes to free locations and $P \vdash (c, m') \xrightarrow{k} (c_2, m'_2)$, then there exists m_2 such that $P \vdash (c, m) \xrightarrow{k} (c_2, m_2)$ and m'_2 can be obtained from m_2 by removing* writes *to locations that are not targeted by* reads *for the rest of the execution.*

Proof. Since we never observe the differences between m and m', we can take the same steps and produce the same operations under each history, preserving the relationship between them.

Lemmas 1 and 3 taken together, with a little reasoning about the effects of the dead store, allow us to conclude that R_{dse} is a simulation relation.

Theorem 5. *Let P' be the program obtained from P by removing a dead store, and suppose that P' never reads an uninitialized location and P never writes to a free location. Then R_{dse} is a right-option simulation between P' and P, and so P' refines P.*

Proof. The combination of Lemmas 1 and 3 give us all cases except the one in which P executes the removed `store`. In that last case, we can show that the effect of the `store` is to augment the history with a `write` to a location that is not the target of a `read` for the rest of the execution, and after executing the `store`, P is once again in lockstep with P'.

Note that since P' has fewer writes than P, it may have more uninitialized locations, and so the condition on reads must be checked on P' and the condition on writes must be checked on P. We can conclude that, for this class of well-behaved programs, the dead store elimination optimization is correct under any memory model that meets the specification.

Comparison with Vellvm. Using a more abstract specification should lead to simpler proofs, giving us a more concise formulation of the properties of the memory model and allowing us to avoid reasoning about details of the model. The Vellvm project [11] also included a dead store elimination for an LLVM-based language verified in Coq, using a variant of the CompCert memory model, and so provides us a standard with which to compare our proofs. While it is difficult to compare different proof efforts based on different formalizations, several metrics suggest that our specification did indeed lead to significantly simpler proofs. Vellvm's DSE verification consists of about 1860 lines (65 k characters) of definitions and proof scripts, while our verification is 890 lines (44 k characters). A separate section of Vellvm's code is devoted to lifting CompCert's memory axioms for use in the proofs—essentially the memory model specification for Vellvm—and this section is 1200 lines (38 k characters), while our memory model specification is 420 lines (17 k characters). To correct for the effects of different proof styles on line and character counts, we also compared the gzipped sizes of the developments; Vellvm's proof is 12.4 kb, our proof is 8.3 kb, Vellvm's specification is 6.7 kb, and our specification is 3.3 kb.

Although Vellvm's language is more featureful than MiniLLVM, this appears to account for little of the difference in the proofs, since most of these features are orthogonal to memory operations. Roughly speaking, our proof of correctness is 2/3 the size of Vellvm's and our specification is half the size, supporting the assertion that our specification lends itself to simpler proofs. Furthermore, our results hold not just for one model but for any instance of the specification.

5 Related Work

There have been many efforts to generically specify concurrent and relaxed memory models. The work of Higham et al. [1] is an early example of formalizing memory models in terms of sequences of read and write events; this approach is used to formalize models ranging from linearizability to TSO and PSO. Yang et al. [10] gave axiomatic specifications of six memory models, and used constraint logic programming and SMT solving to check whether specific executions adhered to the models. Saraswat et al. [7] gave a simple specification for concurrent memory models in terms of the "well-synchronized programs are sequentially consistent" property, and demonstrated that their specification could be instantiated with both models that prohibited thin-air reads and those that allowed them. In all these works, reads, writes, and synchronizations were assumed to be the only memory operations, and thus "sequential consistency" was taken to uniquely define the single-threaded memory model.

Owens et al. [6] defined the x86-TSO memory model, and showed that their axiomatic definition was equivalent to an abstract-machine model. This model formed the basis for the memory model of CompCertTSO [9], the main inspiration for our work. CompCertTSO's model includes `alloc` and `free` operations, and we follow its approach in giving semantics to our language by combining language steps and memory steps. CompCertTSO does not seek to give a general specification of a category of memory models, but rather a single instance with TSO concurrency and CompCert-specific allocation and free behavior. We know of no other work that attempts to give a generic, language-independent specification of memory models with operations beyond read and write.

6 Conclusions and Future Work

While much work has gone into formalizing the range of possibilities for concurrent memory models, less attention has been devoted to a truly generic description of sequential memory models. Our specification is a first step towards such an account, and we have highlighted the properties of generality, feasibility, and usability that make it a reasonable specification for sequential memory models with allocation and free operations. We have characterized the set of programs for which all such models are equivalent, proved that CompCert's memory model is an instance of our specification, and used it to verify an optimization with proofs demonstrably simpler than those written without such a specification.

Our memory model specification is currently based on the simplifying assumption that the size of data does not matter. Reflecting the size of data in the specification (e.g. by specifying the size of each allocation and allowing reads/writes to offsets within blocks) would allow us to more faithfully model CompCert's and other C-like memory models, and give us an angle from which to attack the problem of structured data. Another natural next step is to integrate our specification into a framework for concurrent memory models, allowing us to instantiate it with realistic models (such as CompCertTSO) that include allocation and free operations and verify optimizations with respect to those models. Ultimately, we aim to construct a unified specification for memory models that can be used to support and simplify any compiler verification effort.

Acknowledgements. This work is supported by NSF grants 1065166, 1116682, and 1337174. Any opinions, findings, and conclusions or recommendations expressed in this material are those of the authors and do not necessarily reflect the views of the NSF.

References

1. Higham, L., Kawash, J., Verwaal, N.: Defining and comparing memory consistency models. In: Proceedings of the 10th International Conference on Parallel and Distributed Computing Systems, pp. 349–356 (1997)
2. Kang, J., Hur, C., Mansky, W., Garbuzov, D., Zdancewic, S., Vafeiadis, V.: A formal C memory model supporting integer-pointer casts. In: ACM SIGPLAN Conference on Programming Language Design and Implementation, PLDI 2015 (to appear)
3. Lattner, C., Adve, V.: LLVM: A compilation framework for lifelong program analysis & transformation. In: Proceedings of the international symposium on Code generation and optimization: feedback-directed and runtime optimization, CGO 2004, p. 75. IEEE Computer Society, Washington, DC (2004). http://dl.acm.org/citation.cfm?id=977395.977673
4. Leroy, X.: A formally verified compiler back-end. J. Autom. Reason **43**(4), 363–446 (2009). http://dx.doi.org/10.1007/s10817-009-9155-4
5. Leroy, X., Blazy, S.: Formal verification of a C-like memory model and its uses for verifying program transformations. J. Autom. Reason **41**, 1–31 (2008). http://dl.acm.org/citation.cfm?id=1388522.1388533
6. Owens, S., Sarkar, S., Sewell, P.: A better x86 memory model: x86-TSO. In: Berghofer, S., Nipkow, T., Urban, C., Wenzel, M. (eds.) TPHOLs 2009. LNCS, vol. 5674, pp. 391–407. Springer, Heidelberg (2009)
7. Saraswat, V.A., Jagadeesan, R., Michael, M., von Praun, C.: A theory of memory models. In: Proceedings of the 12th ACM SIGPLAN Symposium on Principles and Practice of Parallel Programming, PPoPP 2007, pp. 161–172. ACM, New York, NY (2007). http://doi.acm.org/10.1145/1229428.1229469
8. Stewart, G., Beringer, L., Cuellar, S., Appel, A.W.: Compositional compcert. In: Proceedings of the 42Nd Annual ACM SIGPLAN-SIGACT Symposium on Principles of Programming Languages, POPL 2015, pp. 275–287. ACM, New York, NY (2015). http://doi.acm.org/10.1145/2676726.2676985
9. Ševčík, J., Vafeiadis, V., Zappa Nardelli, F., Jagannathan, S., Sewell, P.: CompCertTSO: a verified compiler for relaxed-memory concurrency. J. ACM **60**(3), 221–2250 (2013). http://doi.acm.org/10.1145/2487241.2487248
10. Yang, Y., Gopalakrishnan, G., Lindstrom, G., Slind, K.: Nemos: a framework for axiomatic and executable specifications of memory consistency models. In: Proceedings of 18th International Parallel and Distributed Processing Symposium, p. 31 (2004)
11. Zhao, J., Nagarakatte, S., Martin, M.M., Zdancewic, S.: Formalizing the LLVM intermediate representation for verified program transformations. SIGPLAN Not. **47**(1), 427–440 (2012). http://doi.acm.org/10.1145/2103621.2103709

Approximate Synchrony: An Abstraction for Distributed Almost-Synchronous Systems

Ankush Desai[1](✉), Sanjit A. Seshia[1], Shaz Qadeer[2], David Broman[1,3], and John C. Eidson[1]

[1] University of California at Berkeley, Berkeley, CA, USA
ankush@eecs.berkeley.edu
[2] Microsoft Research, Redmond, CA, USA
[3] KTH Royal Institute of Technology, Redmond, Sweden

Abstract. Forms of synchrony can greatly simplify modeling, design, and verification of distributed systems. Thus, recent advances in clock synchronization protocols and their adoption hold promise for system design. However, these protocols synchronize the distributed clocks only within a certain tolerance, and there are transient phases while synchronization is still being achieved. Abstractions used for modeling and verification of such systems should accurately capture these imperfections that cause the system to only be "almost synchronized." In this paper, we present approximate synchrony, a sound and tunable abstraction for verification of almost-synchronous systems. We show how approximate synchrony can be used for verification of both time synchronization protocols and applications running on top of them. We provide an algorithmic approach for constructing this abstraction for *symmetric, almost-synchronous* systems, a subclass of almost-synchronous systems. Moreover, we show how approximate synchrony also provides a useful strategy to guide state-space exploration. We have implemented approximate synchrony as a part of a model checker and used it to verify models of the Best Master Clock (BMC) algorithm, the core component of the IEEE 1588 precision time protocol, as well as the time-synchronized channel hopping protocol that is part of the IEEE 802.15.4e standard.

1 Introduction

Forms of synchrony can greatly simplify modeling, design, and verification of distributed systems. Traditionally, a common sense of time is established using *time-synchronization* (*clock-synchronization*) protocols or systems such as the global positioning system (GPS), network time protocol (NTP), and the IEEE 1588 [20] precision time protocol (PTP). These protocols, however, synchronize the distributed clocks only within a certain bound. In other words, at any time point, clocks of different nodes can have differing values, but time synchronization ensures that those values are within a specified offset of each other, i.e., they are *almost synchronized*.

Distributed protocols running on top of time-synchronized nodes are designed under the assumption that while processes at different nodes make independent

D. Kroening and C.S. Păsăreanu (Eds.): CAV 2015, Part II, LNCS 9207, pp. 429–448, 2015.
DOI: 10.1007/978-3-319-21668-3_25

progress, no process falls very far behind any other. Figure 1 provides examples of such real world systems. For example, *Google Spanner* [8] is a distributed fault tolerant system that provides consistency guarantees when run on top of nodes that are synchronized using GPS and atomic clocks, wireless sensor networks [27,28] use time synchronized channel hopping (TSCH) [1] as a standard for time synchronization of sensor nodes in the network, and IEEE 1588 precision time protocol (PTP) [20] has been adopted in industrial automation, scientific measurement [22], and telecommunication networks. Correctness of these protocols depends on having some synchrony between different processes or nodes.

When modeling and verifying systems that are almost-synchronous it is important to compose them using the right concurrency model. One requires a model that lies somewhere between completely synchronous (lock-step progress) and completely asynchronous (unbounded delay). Various such concurrency models have been proposed in the literature, including *quasi-synchrony* [7,18] and *bounded-asynchrony* [16]. However, we discuss in Sect. 7, these models permit behaviors that are typically disallowed in almost-synchronous systems. Alternatively, one can use formalisms for hybrid or timed systems that explicitly model clocks (e.g., [2,3]), but the associated methods (e.g., [17,21]) tend to be less efficient for systems with a huge discrete state space, which is typical for distributed software systems.

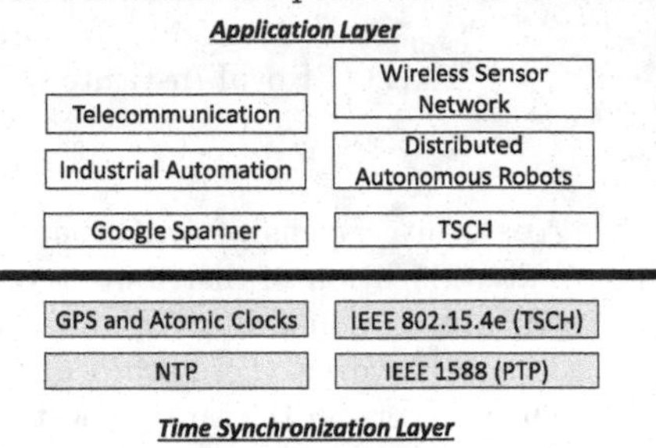

Fig. 1. Almost-synchronous systems comprise an application protocol running on top of a time-synchronization layer.

In this paper, we introduce *symmetric, almost-synchronous* (SAS) systems, a class of distributed systems in which processes have symmetric timing behavior. In our experience, protocols at both the application layer and the time-synchronization layer can be modeled as SAS systems. Additionally, we introduce the notion of *approximate synchrony (*AS*)* as a concurrency model for almost-synchronous systems, which also enables one to compute a sound discrete abstraction of a SAS system. Intuitively, a system is approximately-synchronous if the number of steps taken by any two processes do not differ by more than a specified bound, denoted Δ. The presence of the parameter Δ makes approximate synchrony a *tunable* abstraction method. We demonstrate three different uses of the approximate synchrony abstraction:

1. **Verifying Time-Synchronized Systems:** Suppose that the system to be verified runs on top of a layer that guarantees time synchronization throughout its execution. In this case, we show that there is a sound value of Δ which can be computed using a closed form equation as described in Sect. 3.2.
2. **Verifying Systems with Recurrent Logical Behavior:** Suppose the system to be verified does not rely on time synchronization, but its traces contain recurrent logical conditions — a set of global states that are visited repeatedly during the protocol's operation. We show that an iterative approach based

on model checking can identify such recurrent behavior and extract a value of Δ that can be used to compute a sound discrete abstraction for model checking (see Sect. 4). Protocols verifiable with this approach include some at the time-synchronization layer, such as IEEE 1588 [20].

3. **Prioritizing State-Space Exploration:** The approximate synchrony abstraction can also be used as a search prioritization technique for model checking. We show in Sect. 6 that in most cases it is more efficient to search behaviors for smaller value of Δ ("more synchronous" behaviors) first for finding bugs.

We present two practical case studies: (i) a time-synchronized channel hopping (TSCH) protocol that is part of the IEEE802.15.4e [1] standard, and (ii) the best master clock (BMC) algorithm of the IEEE 1588 precision time protocol. The former is system where the nodes are time-synchronized, while the latter is the case of a system with recurrent logical behavior. Our results show that approximate synchrony can reduce the state space to be explored by orders of magnitude while modeling relevant timing semantics of these protocols, allowing one to verify properties that cannot be verified otherwise. Moreover, we were able to find a so-called "rogue frame" scenario that the IEEE 1588 standards committee had long debated without resolution (see our companion paper written for the IEEE 1588 community [6] for details).

Our abstraction technique can be used with any finite-state model checker. In this paper we implement it on top of the ZING model checker [4], due to its ability to control the model checker's search using an external scheduler that enforces the approximate synchrony condition.

To summarize, this paper makes the following contributions:

- The formalism of *symmetric, almost synchronous* (SAS) systems and its use in modeling an important class of distributed systems (Sect. 2);
- A tunable abstraction technique, termed *approximate synchrony* (Sects. 2 and 3);
- Automatic procedures to derive values of Δ for sound verification (Sects. 3 and 4);
- An implementation of approximate synchrony in an explicit-state model checker (Sect. 5), and
- The use of approximate synchrony for verification and systematic testing of two real-world protocols, the BMC algorithm (a key component of the IEEE 1588 standard), and the time synchronized channel hopping protocol (Sect. 6).

2 Formal Model and Approach

In this section, we define clock synchronization precisely and formalize the notion of *symmetric almost-synchronous* (SAS) systems, the class of distributed systems we are concerned with in this paper.

2.1 Clocks and Synchronization

Each node in the distributed system has an associated (local) physical clock χ, which takes a non-negative real value. For purposes of modeling and analysis, we will also assume the presence of an ideal (global) reference clock, denoted t. The notation $\chi(t)$ denotes the value of χ when the reference clock has value t. Given this notation, we describe the following two basic concepts:

1. *Clock Skew:* The *skew* between two clocks χ_i and χ_j at time t (according to the reference clock) is the difference in their values $|\chi_i(t) - \chi_j(t)|$.
2. *Clock Drift:* The *drift* in the rate of a clock χ is the difference per unit time of the value of χ from the ideal reference clock t.

Time synchronization ensures that the skew between any two physical clocks in the network is bounded. The formal definition is as below.

Definition 1. *A distributed system is* time-synchronized *(or* clock-synchronized*) if there exists a parameter β such that for every pair of nodes i and j and for any t,*

$$|\chi_i(t) - \chi_j(t)| \leq \beta \tag{1}$$

For ease of exposition, we will not explicitly model the details of dynamics of physical clocks or the updates to them. We will instead abstract the clock dynamics as comprising arbitrary updates to χ_i variables subject to additional constraints on them such as Eq. 1 (wherever such assumptions are imposed).

Example 1. The IEEE 1588 precision time protocol [20] can be implemented so as to bound the physical clock skew to the order of sub-nanoseconds [22], and the typical clock drift to at most 10^{-4} [20].

2.2 Symmetric, Almost-Synchronous Systems

We model the distributed system as a collection of processes, where processes are used to model both the behavior of nodes as well as of communication channels. There can be one or more processes executing at a node.

Formally, the system is modeled as the tuple $\mathcal{M}_C = (\mathcal{S}, \delta, \mathcal{I}, \text{ID}, \boldsymbol{\chi}, \boldsymbol{\tau})$ where

- $\mathcal{S}$ is the set of discrete states of the system,
- $\delta \subseteq \mathcal{S} \times \mathcal{S}$ is the transition relation for the system,
- $\mathcal{I} \subseteq \mathcal{S}$ is the set of initial states,
- $\text{ID} = \{1, 2, \ldots, K\}$ is the set of process identifiers,
- $\boldsymbol{\chi} = (\chi_1, \chi_2, \ldots, \chi_K)$ is a vector of local clocks, and
- $\boldsymbol{\tau} = (\tau_1, \tau_2, \ldots, \tau_K)$ is a vector of process timetables. The timetable of the ith process, τ_i, is an infinite vector $(\tau_i^1, \tau_i^2, \tau_i^3, \ldots)$ specifying the time instants according to local clock χ_i when process i executes (steps). In other words, process i makes its jth step when $\chi_i = \tau_i^j$.

For convenience, we will denote the ith process by $\mathcal{P}_i$. Since in practice the dynamics of physical clocks can be fairly intricate, we choose not to model these details — instead, we assume that the value of a physical clock χ_i can vary arbitarily subject to additional constraints (e.g., Eq. 1).

The kth *nominal step size* of process $\mathcal{P}_i$ is the intended interval between the $(k-1)$th and kth steps of $\mathcal{P}_i$, viz., $\tau_i^k - \tau_i^{k-1}$. The *actual step size* of the process is the actual time elapsed between the $(k-1)$th and kth step, according to the ideal reference clock t. In general, the latter differs from the former due to clock drift, scheduling jitter, etc.

Motivated by our case studies with the IEEE 1588 and 802.15.4e standards, we impose two restrictions on the class of systems considered in this paper:

1. *Common Timetable:* For any two processes $\mathcal{P}_i$ and $\mathcal{P}_j$, $\tau_i = \tau_j$. Note that this does *not* mean that the process step synchronously, since their local clocks may report different values at the same time t. However, if the system is time synchronized, then the processes step "almost synchronously."
2. *Bounded Process Step Size:* For any process $\mathcal{P}_i$, its actual step size lies in an interval $[\sigma^l, \sigma^u]$. This interval is the same for all processes. This restriction arises in practice from the bounded drift of physical clocks.

A set of processes obeying the above restrictions is termed a *symmetric, almost-synchronous* (SAS) system. The adjective "symmetric" refers only to the timing behavior — note that the logical behavior of different processes can be very different. Note also that SAS systems may or may not be running on top of a time synchronization layer, i.e., SAS systems and time-synchronized systems are orthogonal concepts.

Example 2. The IEEE 1588 protocol can be modeled as a SAS system. All processes intend to step at regular intervals called the *announce time interval.* The specification [20] states the nominal step size for all processess as 1 second; thus the timetable is the sequence $(0, 1, 2, 3, \ldots)$. However, due to the drift of clocks and other non-idealities such as jitter due to OS scheduling, the step size in typical IEEE 1588 implementations can vary by $\pm 10^{-3}$. From this, the actual step size of processes can be derived to lie in the interval $[0.999, 1.001]$.

Traces and Segments. A *timed trace* (or simply *trace*) of the SAS system $\mathcal{M}_C$ is a timestamped record of the execution of the system according to the global (ideal) time reference t. Formally, a timed trace is a sequence $h_0, h_1, h_2, \ldots$ where each element h_j is a triple (s_j, χ_j, t_j) where $s_j \in \mathcal{S}$ is a discrete (global) state at time $t = t_j$ and $\chi_j = (\chi_{1,j}, \chi_{2,j}, \ldots, \chi_{K,j})$ is the vector of clock values at time t_j. For all j, at least one process makes a step at time t_j, so there exists at least one i and a corresponding $m_i \in \{0, 1, 2, \ldots\}$ such that $\chi_{i,j}(t_j) = \tau_i^{m_i}$. Moreover, processes step according to their timetables; thus, if any $\mathcal{P}_i$ makes its m_ith and l_ith steps at times t_j and t_k respectively, for $m_i < l_i$, then $\chi_{i,j}(t_j) = \tau_i^{m_i} < \tau_i^{l_i} = \chi_{i,k}(t_k)$. Also, by the bounded process step size restriction, if any $\mathcal{P}_i$ makes its m_ith and $m_i + 1$th steps at times t_j and t_k respectively (for all m_i), $|t_k - t_j| \in [\sigma^l, \sigma^u]$. Finally, $s_0 \in \mathcal{I}$ and $\delta(s_j, s_{j+1})$ holds for all $j \geq 0$ with the transition into s_j occuring at time $t = t_j$.A *trace segment* is a (contiguous) subsequence $h_j, h_{j+1}, \ldots, h_l$ of a trace of $\mathcal{M}_C$.

2.3 Verification Problem and Approach

The central problem considered in this paper is as follows:

Problem 1. Given an SAS system $\mathcal{M}_C$ modeled as above, and a linear temporal logic (LTL) property Φ with propositions over the discrete states of $\mathcal{M}_C$, verify whether $\mathcal{M}_C$ satisfies Φ.

One way to model $\mathcal{M}_C$ would be as a hybrid system (due to the continuous dynamics of physical clocks), but this approach does not scale well due to the extremely large discrete state space. Instead, we provide a sound discrete abstraction $\mathcal{M}_A$ of $\mathcal{M}_C$ that preserves the relevant timing semantics of the 'almost-synchronous' systems. (Soundness is formalized in Sect. 3).
There are two phases in our approach:

1. *Compute Abstraction Parameter:* Using parameters of $\mathcal{M}_C$ (relating to clock dynamics), we compute a parameter Δ characterizing the "approximate synchrony" condition, and use Δ to generate a sound abstract model $\mathcal{M}_A$.
2. *Model Checking:* We verify the temporal logic property Φ on the abstract model using finite-state model checking.

The key to this strategy is the first step, which is the focus of the following sections.

3 Approximate Synchrony

We now formalize the concept of *approximate synchrony (AS)* and explain how it can be used to generate a discrete abstraction of almost-synchronous distributed systems. Approximate synchrony applies to both (segments of) traces and to systems.

Definition 2. *(Approximate Synchrony for Traces) A trace (segment) of a SAS system $\mathcal{M}_C$ is said to satisfy* approximate synchrony *(is* approximately-synchronous*) with parameter Δ if, for any two processes $\mathcal{P}_i$ and $\mathcal{P}_j$ in $\mathcal{M}_C$, the number of steps N_i and N_j taken by the two processes in that trace (segment) satisfies the following condition:*

$$|N_i - N_j| \leq \Delta$$

Although this definition is in terms of traces of SAS systems, we believe the notion of approximate synchrony is more generally applicable to other distributed systems also. An early version of this definition appeared in [10].

The definition extends to a SAS system in the standard way:

Definition 3. *(Approximate Synchrony for Systems) A SAS system $\mathcal{M}_C$ satisfies* approximate synchrony *(is* approximately-synchronous*) with parameter Δ if* all traces *of that system satisfy approximate synchrony with parameter Δ.*

We refer to the condition in Definition 3 above as the *approximate synchrony (AS) condition* with parameter Δ, denoted AS(Δ). For example, in Fig. 2, executing step 5 of process *P1* before step 3 of process *P2* violates the approximate synchrony condition for $\Delta = 2$. Note that Δ quantifies the "approximation" in approximate synchrony. For example, for a (perfectly) synchronous system $\Delta = 0$, since processes step at the same time instants. For a fully asynchronous system, $\Delta = \infty$, since one process can get arbitrarily ahead of another.

3.1 Discrete Approximate Synchrony Abstraction

We now present a discrete abstraction of a SAS system. The key modification is to (i) remove the physical clocks and timetables, and (ii) include instead an explicit scheduler that constrains execution of processes so as to satisfy the approximate synchrony condition AS(Δ).

Formally, given a SAS system $\mathcal{M}_C = (\mathcal{S}, \delta, \mathcal{I}, \text{ID}, \chi, \tau)$, we construct an *$\Delta$-abstract model* $\mathcal{M}_A$ as the tuple $(\mathcal{S}, \delta^a, \mathcal{I}, \text{ID}, \rho_\Delta)$ where ρ_Δ is a scheduler process that performs an asynchronous composition of the processes $\mathcal{P}_1, \mathcal{P}_2, \ldots, \mathcal{P}_K$ while enforcing AS(Δ). Conceptually, the scheduler ρ_Δ maintains state counts N_i of the numbers of steps taken by each process $\hat{\mathcal{P}}_i$ from the initial state.[1] A configuration of $\mathcal{M}_A$ is a pair (s, N) where $s \in \mathcal{S}$ and $N \in \mathbb{Z}^K$ is the vector of step counts of the processes. The abstract model $\mathcal{M}_A$ changes its configuration according to its transition function δ^a where $\delta^a((s, N), (s', N'))$ iff (i) $\delta(s, s')$ and (ii) $N_i' = N_i + 1$ if ρ_Δ permits $\mathcal{P}_i$ to make a step and $N_i' = N_i$ otherwise.

Fig. 2. AS(Δ) violated for $\Delta = 2$

In an initial state, all processes $\mathcal{P}_i$ are enabled to make a step. At each step of δ^a, ρ_Δ enforces the approximate synchrony condition by only enabling $\mathcal{P}_i$ to step iff that step does not violate AS(Δ). Behaviors of $\mathcal{M}_A$ are *untimed traces*, i.e., sequences of discrete (global) states $s_0, s_1, s_2, \ldots$ where $s_j \in \mathcal{S}$, s_0 is an initial (global) state, and each transition from s_j to s_{j+1} is consistent with δ^a defined above.

Note that approximate synchrony is a *tunable timing abstraction*. Larger the value of Δ, more conservative the abstraction. The key question is: for a given system, what value of Δ constitutes a *sound* timing abstraction, and how do we automatically compute it? Recall that one model is a sound abstraction of another if and only if every execution trace of the latter (concrete model $\mathcal{M}_C$) is also an execution trace of the former (abstract model $\mathcal{M}_A$). In our setting, the Δ-abstract and concrete models both capture the protocol logic in an identical manner, and differ only in their timing semantics. The concrete model explicitly models the physical clocks of each process as real-valued variables as described in Sect. 2. The executions of this model can be represented as *timed traces* (sequences of timestamped states). On the other hand, in the Δ-abstract model, processes are interleaved asynchronously while respecting the approximate synchrony condition stated in Definition 3. An execution of the Δ-abstract model is an *untimed trace* (sequences of states). We equate timed and untimed traces using the "untiming" transformation proposed by Alur and Dill [3] — i.e., the traces must be identical with respect to the discrete states.

---

[1] The inclusion of step counts may seem to make the model infinite-state. We will show in Sect. 5 how the model checker can be implemented without explicitly including the step counts in the state space.

3.2 Computing Δ for Time-Synchronized Systems

We now address the question of computing a value of Δ such that the resulting $\mathcal{M}_A$ is a sound abstraction of the original SAS system $\mathcal{M}_C$. We consider here the case when $\mathcal{M}_C$ is a system running on a layer that guarantees time synchronization (Eq. 1) from the initial state. A second case, when nodes are not time-synchronized and approximate synchrony only holds for segments of the traces of a system, is handled in Sect. 4.

Consider a SAS system in which the physical clocks are always synchronized to within β, i.e., Eq. 1 holds for all time t and β is a tight bound computed based on the system configuration. Intuitively, if $\beta > 0$, then $\Delta \geq 1$ since two processes are not guaranteed to step at the same time instants, and so the number of steps of two processes can be off by at least one. The main result of this section is that SAS systems that are time-synchronized are also approximately-synchronous, and the value of Δ is given by the following theorem.

Theorem 1. *Any SAS system $\mathcal{M}_C$ satisfying Eq. 1 is approximately-synchronous with parameter $\Delta = \left\lceil \frac{\beta}{\sigma^l} \right\rceil$.* *(Proof in [12])*

Suppose the abstract model $\mathcal{M}_A$ is constructed as described in Sect. 3.1 with Δ as given in Theorem 1 and σ^l is the lower bound of the step size defined in Sect. 2.2. Then as a corollary, we can conclude that $\mathcal{M}_A$ is a sound abstraction of $\mathcal{M}_C$: every trace of $\mathcal{M}_C$ satisfies AS(Δ) and hence is a trace of $\mathcal{M}_A$ after untiming.

Example 3. The *Time-Synchronized Channel Hopping* (TSCH) [1] protocol is being adopted as a part of the low power Medium Access Control standard IEEE802.15.4e. It can be modeled as a SAS system since it has a time-slotted architecture where processes share the same timetable for making steps. The TSCH protocol has two components: one that operates at the application layer, and one that provides time synchronization, with the former relying upon the latter. We verify the application layer of TSCH that assumes that nodes in the system are always time-synchronized within a bound called the "guard time" which corresponds to β. Moreover, in practice, β is much smaller than σ^l and thus Δ is typically 1 for implementations of the TSCH.

4 Systems with Recurrent Logical Conditions

We now consider the case of a SAS system that does not execute on top of a layer that guarantees time synchronization (i.e., Eq. 1 may not hold). We identify behavior of certain SAS systems, called *recurrent logical conditions*, that can be exploited for abstraction and verification. Specifically, even though AS(Δ) may not hold for the system for any finite Δ, it may still hold for *segments* of every trace of the system.

Definition 4. *(Recurrent Logical Condition) For a SAS system $\mathcal{M}_C$, a* recurrent logical condition *is a predicate logicConv on the state of $\mathcal{M}_C$ such that $\mathcal{M}_C$ satisfies the LTL property* **G F** *logicConv.*

Our verification approach is based on finding a finite Δ such that, for every trace of $\mathcal{M}_C$, segments of the trace between states satisfying *logicConv* satisfy AS(Δ). This property of system traces can then be exploited for efficient model checking.

We begin with an example of a recurrent logical condition case in the context of the IEEE 1588 protocol (Sect. 4.1). We then present our verification approach based on inferring Δ for trace segments via iterative use of model checking (Sect. 4.2).

4.1 Example: IEEE 1588 Protocol

The IEEE 1588 standard [20], also known as the *precision time protocol (PTP)*, enables precise synchronization of clocks over a network. The protocol consists of two parts: the *best master clock (BMC)* algorithm and a *time synchronization phase*. The BMC algorithm is a distributed algorithm whose purpose is two-fold: (i) to elect a unique *grandmaster clock* that is the best clock in the network, and (ii) to find a unique *spanning tree* in the network with the grandmaster clock at the root of the tree. The combination of a grandmaster clock and a spanning tree constitutes the global stable configuration known as *logical convergence* that corresponds to the recurrent logical condition. The second phase, the time synchronization phase, uses this stable configuration to synchronize or correct the physical clocks (more details in [20]).

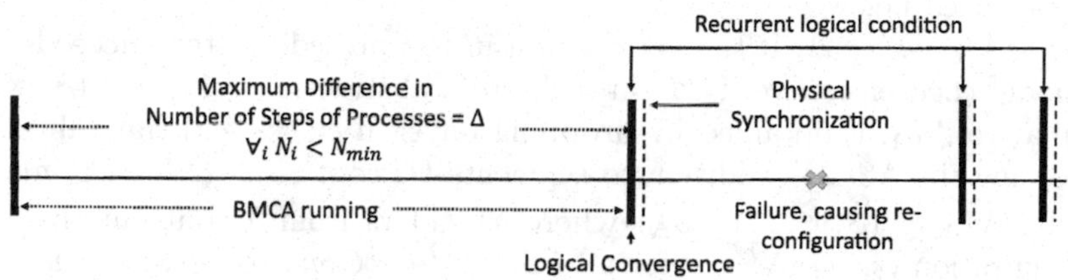

Fig. 3. Phases of the IEEE 1588 time-synchronization protocol

Figure 3 gives an overview of the phases of the IEEE 1588 protocol execution. The distributed system starts executing the first phase (e.g., the BMC algorithm) from an initial configuration. Initially, the clocks are not guaranteed to be synchronized to within a bound β. However, once logical convergence occurs, the clocks are synchronized shortly thereafter. Once the clocks have been synchronized, it is possible for a failure at a node or link to break clock synchronization. The BMC algorithm operates continually, with the goal of ensuring that, if time synchronization is broken, the clocks will be re-synchronized. Thus, a typical 1588 protocol execution is structured as a (potentially infinite) repetition of the two phases: logical convergence, followed by clock synchronization. We exploit this *recurrent* structure to show in Sect. 4.2 that we can compute a value of Δ obeyed by segments of any trace of the system. The approach operates by iterative model checking of a specially-crafted temporal logic formula.

Note that the time taken by the protocol to logically converge depends on various factors including network topology and clock drift. In Sect. 6, we demonstrate empirically that the value of Δ depends on the number of steps (length of the segment) taken by BMCA to converge which in turn depends on factors mentioned above.

4.2 Iterative Algorithm to Compute Δ-Abstraction for Verification

Given a SAS system $\mathcal{M}_C$ whose traces have a recurrent structure, and an LTL property Φ, we present the following approach to verify whether $\mathcal{M}_C$ satisfies Φ:

1. *Define recurrent condition:* Guess a *recurrent logical condition, logicConv*, on the global state of $\mathcal{M}_C$.
2. *Compute* $N_{\min}$*:* Guess an initial value of Δ, and compute, from parameters σ^l, σ^u of the processes in $\mathcal{M}_C$, a number $N_{\min}$ such that the AS(Δ) condition is satisfied on all trace segments where no process makes $N_{\min}$ or more steps. We describe the computation of $N_{\min}$ in more detail below.
3. *Verify if* Δ *is sound:* Verify using model checking on $\mathcal{M}_A$ that, every trace segment that starts in an initial state or a state satisfying *logicConv* and ends in another state in *logicConv* satisfies AS(Δ). This is done by checking that no process makes $N_{\min}$ or more steps in any such segment. Note that verifying $\mathcal{M}_A$ in place of $\mathcal{M}_C$ is sound as AS(Δ) is obeyed for up to $N_{\min}$ steps from *any* state. Further details, including the LTL property checked, are provided below.
4. *Verify* $\mathcal{M}_C$ *using* Δ*:* If the verification in the preceding step succeeds, then a model checker can verify Φ on a discrete abstraction $\widehat{\mathcal{M}_A}$ of $\mathcal{M}_C$, which, similar to $\mathcal{M}_A$, is obtained by dropping physical clocks and timetables, and enforcing the AS(Δ) condition to segments *between visits to logicConv*. Formally, $\widehat{\mathcal{M}_A} = (\mathcal{S}, \widehat{\delta^a}, \mathcal{I}, \text{ID}, \rho_\Delta)$ where $\widehat{\delta^a}$ differs from δ^a only in that for a configuration (s, N), $N'_i = 0$ for all i if $s' \in$ *logicConv* (otherwise it is identical to δ^a).

   However, if the verification in Step 3 fails, we go back to Step 2 and increment Δ and repeat the process to compute a sound value of Δ.

Figure 4 depicts this iterative approach for the specific case of the BMC algorithm. We now elaborate on Steps 2 and 3 of the approach.

Step 2: Computing $N_{\min}$ for a Given Δ. Recall from Sect. 2.2 that the actual step size of a process lies in the interval $[\sigma^l, \sigma^u]$. Let $\mathcal{P}_f$ be the fastest process (the one that makes the most steps from the initial state) and $\mathcal{P}_s$ be the slowest (the fewest steps). Denote the corresponding number of steps by N_f and N_s respectively. Then the approximate synchrony condition in Definition 3 is always satisfied if $N_f - N_s \leq \Delta$. We wish to find the smallest number of steps taken by the fastest process when AS(Δ) is violated. We denote this value as $N_{\min}$, and obtain it by formulating and solving a linear program.

Suppose first that $\mathcal{P}_s$ and $\mathcal{P}_f$ begin stepping at the same time t. Then, since the time between steps of $\mathcal{P}_f$ is at least σ^l and that between steps of $\mathcal{P}_s$ is at

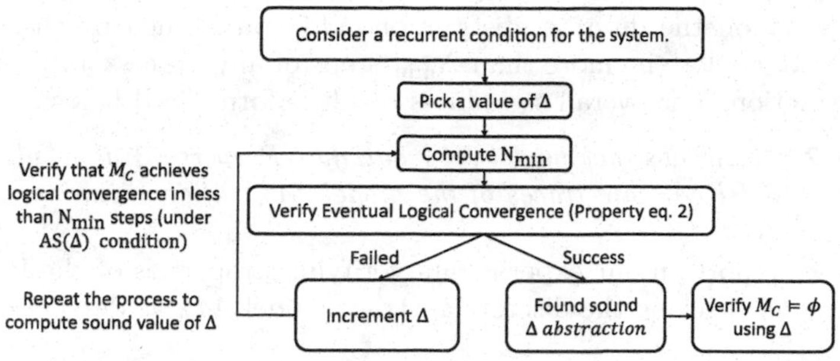

Fig. 4. Iterative algorithm for computing Δ exploiting logical convergence

most σ^u, the total elapsed must be at least $\sigma_l N_f$ and at most $\sigma^u N_s$, yielding the inequality $\sigma^l N_f \leq \sigma^u N_s$.

However, processes need not begin making steps simultaneously. Since each process must make its first step at least σ^u seconds into its execution, the maximum initial offset between processes is σ^u. The smallest value of N_f occurs when the fast process starts σ^u time units after the slowest one, yielding the inequality:

$$\sigma^l N_f + \sigma^u \leq \sigma^u N_s$$

We can now set up the following integer linear program (ILP) to solve for $N_{\min}$:

$$\min N_f \quad s.t.$$

$$N_f \geq N_s, \qquad N_f - N_s > \Delta, \qquad \sigma^l N_f + \sigma^u \leq \sigma^u N_s, \qquad N_f, N_s \geq 1$$

$N_{\min}$ is the optimal value of this ILP. In effect, it gives the fewest steps any process can take (smallest N_f) to violate the approximate synchrony condition AS(Δ).

Example 4. For the IEEE 1588 protocol, as described in Sect. 2.2, the actual process step sizes lie in $[0.999, 1.001]$. Setting $\Delta = 1$, solving the above ILP yields $N_{\min} = 1502$.

Step 3: Temporal Logic Property. Once $N_{\min}$ is computed, we verify on the discrete abstraction $\mathcal{M}_A$ whether, from any state satisfying $\mathcal{I} \vee logicConv$, the model reaches a state satisfying $logicConv$ in less than $N_{\min}$ steps. This also verifies that all traces in the BMC algorithm satisfy the recurrent $logicConv$ property and the segments between $logicConv$ satisfy AS(Δ). We perform this by invoking a model checker to verify the following LTL property, which references the variables N_i recording the number of steps of process $\mathcal{P}_i$:

$$(\mathcal{I} \vee logicConv) \implies \mathbf{F}\left[logicConv \wedge \left(\bigwedge_i (0 < N_i < N_{\min})\right)\right] \tag{2}$$

We show in Sect. 5 how to implement the above check without explicitly including the N_i variables in the system state. Note that it suffices to verify the above property on the discrete abstraction $\mathcal{M}_A$ constrained by the scheduler ρ_Δ because we explore no more than $N_{\min}$ steps of any process and so $\mathcal{M}_A$ is a sound abstraction. The overall soundness result is formalized below.

Theorem 2. *If the abstract model $\mathcal{M}_A$ satisfies Property 2, then all traces of the concrete model $\mathcal{M}_C$ are traces of the model $\widehat{\mathcal{M}}_A$ (after untiming) (Proof in [12])*

In Sect. 6, we report on our experiments verifying properties of the BMC algorithm by model checking the discrete abstract model $\widehat{\mathcal{M}}_A$ as described above.

5 Model Checking with Approximate Synchrony

We implemented approximate synchrony within ZING [4], an explicit state model checker. ZING performs a "constrained" asynchronous composition of processes, using an external scheduler to guide the interleaving. Approximate synchrony is enforced by an external scheduler that explores only those traces satisfying AS(Δ) by scheduling, in each state, only those processes whose steps will not violate AS(Δ).

Section 4 described an iterative approach to verify whether a Δ-abstract model of a protocol is sound. The soundness proof depends on verifying Property 2. A naïve approach for checking this property would be to include a local variable N_i in each process as part of the process state to keep track of the number of steps executed by each process, causing state space explosion. Instead, we store the values of N_i for each i external to the system state, as a part of the model checker explorer.

The algorithm in Fig. 5 performs systematic bounded depth first search for a state $s_{initial}$, belonging to the set of all possible initial states. To check whether all traces of length $N_{\min}$ satisfy eventual logical convergence under AS(Δ) constraint, we enforce two bounds: first, the final depth bound is $(N_{\min} + \Delta)$ and second, in each state a process is enabled only if executing that process does not violate AS(Δ). If a state satisfies $logicConv$ then we terminate the search along that path.

```
var StateTable : Dictionary⟨State, List⟨int⟩⟩;
BoundedDFS(s : State) {
    var i : int, s' : State, steps' : List⟨int⟩;
    i := 0;
    while (i <#Processes(s)){
        steps' :=IncElement(i, StateTable[s]);
        if ¬ CheckASCond(steps')
            ∨ steps'[i] > (N_min + Δ)
            ∨ s ⊨ logicConv then
            continue ;
        s' :=NextState(s, i);
        if steps'[i] = N_min then
            assert(s' ⊨ logicConv);
        if s' ∉ Domain(StateTable)
            ∨ ¬(steps' ≥_pt StateTable[s']) then
            StateTable[s'] := steps';
            BoundedDFS(s');
        i := i + 1; } }

Verify() {
    StateTable[s_initial] = newList⟨int⟩;
    BoundedDFS(s_initial);}
```

Fig. 5. Algorithm for Verification of Property 2

The BoundedDFS function is called recursively on each successor state and it explore only those traces that satisfy AS(Δ). If the steps executed by a process is N_{min} then the $logicConv$ monitor is invoked to assert if $s' \models logicConv$ (i.e. we have reached logical convergence state) and if the assertion fails we increment the value of Δ as described in Sect. 4.2. $N_{\min}$ and Δ values are derived as explained in Sect. 4.2.

StateTable is a map from reachable state to the tuple of steps with which it was last explored. *steps'* is the vector of number of steps executed by each process and is stored as a list of integers. #Processes(s) returns the number of enabled processes in the state s. IncElement(i, t) increments the ith element of tuple t and returns the updated tuple. CheckASCond(*steps'*) checks the following condition that $\forall s_1, s_2 \in steps'$ $|s_1 - s_2| \leq \Delta$.

To avoid re-exploring a state which may not lead to new states, we do not re-explore a state if it is revisited with *steps'* greater than what it was last visited with. The operator $\geq_{pt}$ does a pointwise comparison of the integer tuples. We show in the following section that we are able to obtain significant state space reduction using this implementation.

6 Evaluation

In this section, we present our empirical evaluation of the approximate synchrony abstraction, guided by the following goals:

- Verify two real-world standards protocols: (1) the best master clock algorithm in IEEE 1588 and (2) the time synchronized channel hopping protocol in IEEE 802.15.4e.
- Evaluate if we can verify properties that cannot be verified with full asynchrony (either by reducing state space or by capturing relevant timing constraints).
- Evaluate approximate synchrony as an iterative bounding technique for finding bugs efficiently in almost-synchronous systems.

6.1 Modeling and Experimental Setup

We model the system in P [11], a domain-specific language for writing event-driven protocols. A protocol model in P is a collection of state machines interacting with each other via asynchronous events or messages. The P compiler generates a model for systematic exploration by ZING [4]. P also provides ways of writing LTL properties as monitors that are synchronously composed with the model. Both the case studies, the BMC algorithm and the TSCH protocol, are modeled using P. Each node in the protocol is modeled as a separate P state machine. Faults and message losses in the protocol are modeled as non-deterministic choices.

All experiments were performed on a 64-bit Windows server with Intel Xeon ES-2440, 2.40GHz (12 cores/24 threads) and 160 GB of memory. ZING can exploit parallelism as its iterative depth-first search algorithm is completely parallelized. All timing results reported in this section are when ZING is run with 24 threads. We use the number of states explored and the time taken to explore them as the comparison metric.

Table 1. Temporal properties verified for the case studies

Protocol	Temporal property	Description
BMCA	**F G** (*logicConv*)	Eventually the BMC algorithm stabilizes with a unique spanning tree having the grandmaster at its root. The system is said to be in *logicConv* state when the system has converged to the expected spanning tree
TSCH	$\bigwedge_{i \in n} \mathbf{G}(\neg desynched_i)$	A node in TSCH is said to be *desynched* - if it fails to synchronize with its master within the threshold period. The desired property of a correct system is that the nodes are always synchronized

6.2 Verification and Testing Using Approximate Synchrony

We applied approximate synchrony in three different contexts: (1) Time synchronized Channel Hopping protocol (*time synchronized system*) (2) Best Master Clock Algorithm in IEEE 1588 (*exploiting recurrent logical condition*) (3) Approximate Synchrony as a bounding technique for finding bugs.

Verification of the TSCH Protocol. Time Synchronized Channel Hopping (TSCH) is a Medium Access Control scheme that enables low power operations in wireless sensor network using time-synchronization. It makes an assumptions that the clocks are always time-synchronized within a bound, referred to as the 'guard' time in the standard. The low power operation of the system depends on the sensor nodes being able to maintain synchronization (desynchronization property in Table 1). A central server broadcasts the global schedule that instructs each sensor node when to perform operations. Whether the system satisfies the desynchronization property depends on this global schedule, and the standard provides no recommendation on these schedules.

We modeled the TSCH as a SAS system and used Theorem 1 to calculate the value of Δ[2]. We verified the desynchronization property (Table 1) in the presence of failures like message loss, interference in wireless network, etc. For the experiments we considered three schedules (1) round-robin: nodes are scheduled in a round robin fashion, (2) shared with random back-off: all the schedule slots are shared and conflict is resolved using random back-off (3) Priority Scheduler: nodes are assigned fixed priority and conflict is resolved based on the priority.

We were able to verify if the property was satisfied for a given topology under the global schedule, and generated a counterexample otherwise (Table 2) which helped the TSCH system developers in choosing the right schedules for low power operation. Using sound approximate synchrony abstraction (with $\Delta = 1$), we could accurately capture the "almost synchronous" behavior of the TSCH system.

[2] For system of nodes under consideration, the maximum clock skew, $\epsilon = 120\mu s$ and nominal step size of $100ms$, the value of $\Delta = 1$.

Table 2. Verification results using Approximate Synchrony.

Verification of BMC Algorithm											
Network Topology (#Nodes)	Safety Property							Convergence Property			
	Fully Asynchronous Model			Model with Approximate Synchrony				Model with Approximate Synchrony			
	States Explored	Time (h:mm)	Property Proved	Δ	States Explored	Time (h:mm)	Property Proved	Δ	States Explored	Time (hh:mm)	Property Proved
Linear(5)	1.2 E+9	7:12	Yes	1	9.5 E+5	0:35	Yes	1	5.3 E+8	6:33	Yes
Star(5)	2.4 E+10	9:40	Yes	1	5.8 E+5	0:54	Yes	1	4.1 E+7	5:10	Yes
Random(5)	9.19 E+9	9:01	Yes	2	5.5 E+6	1:44	Yes	2	1.8 E+9	9:10	Yes
Ring(5)	7.1 E+12*	*	No	1	4.8 E+7	3:44	Yes	1	8 E+9	8:04	Yes
Linear(7)	1.4 E+13*	*	No	1	4.6 E+7	3:05	Yes	1	1.0 E+8	6:21	Yes
Star(7)	1.1 E+13*	*	No	2	3.7 E+8	5:06	Yes	2	3.3 E+10	13:34	Yes
Ring(7)	3.3 E+12*	*	No	2	6.8 E+8	8:04	Yes	2	2.1 E+10	11:11	Yes
Random(6)	1.1 E+13*	*	No	3	5.7 E+9	6:00	Yes	3	1.3 E+10	10:34	Yes
Random(7)	1.1 E+13*	*	No	3	8.1 E+8	7:11	Yes	3	9.9 E+10	10:11	Yes

Verification of TSCH Protocol									
Network Topology (#Nodes)	Round-Robin Scheduler			Shared with CSMA			Priority Scheduler		
	States Explored	Time (h:mm)	Property Satisfied	States Explored	Time (h:mm)	Property Satisfied	States Explored	Time (h:mm)	Property Satisfied
Linear(5)	4.4 E+4	0:20	Yes	1.2 E+2#	0:03	No	2.4E +3#	0:09	No
Random(5)	3.6 E+2#	0:05	No	6.2 E+3#	0:12	No	1.9E +6	0:35	Yes
Mesh(5)	1.7 E+7	4:05	Yes	9.1 E+6	2:01	Yes	9.3 E+5	0:31	Yes

** denotes end of exploration as model checker ran out of memory, # denotes property violated and counter example is reported*

Verification of BMC Algorithm. The BMC algorithm is a core component of the IEEE 1588 precision time protocol. It is a distributed fault tolerant protocol where nodes in the system perform operations periodically to converge on a unique hierarchical tree structure, referred to as the *logical convergence* state in Sect. 4. Note that the convergence property for BMCA holds *only in the presence of almost synchrony* — it does not guarantee convergence in the presence of unbounded process delay or message delay. Hence, it is essential to verify BMC using the right form of synchrony.

We generated various verification instances by changing the configuration parameters such as number of nodes, clock characteristics, and the network topology. The results in Table 2 for the BMC algorithm are for 5 and 7 nodes in the network with linear, star, ring, and random topologies. The Δ value used for verification of each of these configurations was derived by using the iterative approach described in Sect. 4.2. The results demonstrate that the value of Δ required to construct the sound abstraction varies depending on network topology, and clock dynamics. Table 2 shows the total number of states explored and time taken by the model checker for proving the safety and convergence property (Table 1) using the sound Δ-abstract model. Approximate synchrony abstraction is orders of magnitude faster as it explores the reduced state-space. BMCA algorithm satisfies safety invariant even in the presence of complete asynchrony. For demonstrating the efficiency of using approximate synchrony we also conducted the experiments with complete asynchronous composition, exploring all possible interleaving (for safety properties). The complete asynchronous model is simple to implement but fails to prove the properties for most of the topologies.

An upshot of our approach is that we are the *first* to prove that the BMC algorithm in IEEE 1588 achieves logical convergence to a unique stable state for some interesting configurations. This was possible because of the *sound and tunable* approximate synchrony abstraction. Although experiments with 5/7 nodes may seem small, networks of this size do occur in practice, e.g., in industrial automation where one has small teams of networked robots on a factory floor.

Endlessly Circulating (Rogue) Frames in IEEE 1588: The possibility of an endlessly circulating frame in a 1588 network has been debated for a while in the standards committee. Using formal model of BMC algorithm under approximate synchrony, we were able to reproduce a scenario were rogue frame could occur. Existence of a rogue frame can lead to network congestion or cause the BMC algorithm to never converge. The counter example was cross-validated using simulation and is described in detail in [6]. It was well received by the IEEE 1588 standards committee.

Table 3. Iterative Approximate Synchrony with bound Δ for finding bugs faster.

Buggy models	Iterative depth bounding with random search			Non-iterative AS			Iterative AS		
	Depth	States Explored	Time (h:mm)	Δ Δ	States Explored	Time (h:mm)	Δ Δ	States Explored	Time (h:mm)
BMCA_Bug_1	51	1.4 E+3	0:05	2	1.1 E+3	0:04	0	2.1 E+2	0:02
BMCA_Bug_2	64	5.9 E+5	0:15	2	6.1 E+4	0:14	0	1.6 E+3	0:04
BMCA_Bug_3	101	9.4 E+7	0:45	3	3.3 E+5	0:17	1	9.1 E+2	0:05
ROGUE_FRAME_Bug_1	44	3.9 E+5	0:18	2	9.7 E+6	0:29	1	5.6 E+4	0:12
ROGUE_FRAME_Bug_2	87	4.4 E+4	0:09	2	2.1 E+3	0:05	1	1.1 E+3	0:03
SPT_Bug_1	121	8.4 E+8	1:05	3	8.1 E+4	0:11	0	5.5 E+2	0:04

Approximate Synchrony as a Search Prioritization Technique. Approximate synchrony can also be used as a bounding technique to prioritize search. We collected buggy models during the process of modeling the BMC algorithm and used them as benchmarks, along with buggy instance of the Perlman's Spanning Tree Protocol [24] (SPT). We used AS as an iterative bounding technique, starting with $\Delta = 0$ and incrementing Δ after each iteration. For $\Delta = 0$, the model checker explores only synchronous system behaviors. Increasing the value could be considered as adding bounded asynchronous behaviors incrementally. Table 3 shows comparison between iterative AS, non-iterative AS with fixed value of Δ taken from Table 2 and iterative depth bounding with random search. Number of states explored and the corresponding time taken for finding the bug is used as the comparison metric. Results demonstrate that most of the bugs are found at small values of Δ (hence iterative search is beneficial for finding bugs). Some bugs like the rogue frame error, that occur only when there is asynchrony were found with minimal asynchrony in the system ($\Delta = 1$). These results confirm that prioritizing search based on approximate synchrony is beneficial in finding bugs. Other bounding techniques such as delay bounding [15] and context bounding [23] can be combined with approximate synchrony but this is left for future work.

7 Related Work

The concept of *partial synchrony* has been well-studied in the theory of distributed systems [13,14,25]. There are many ways to model partial synchrony depending on the type of system and the end goal (e.g., formal verification). Approximate synchrony is one such approach, which we contrast against the most closely-related work below.

Hybrid/Timed Modeling: The choice of modeling formalism greatly influences the verification approach. A time-synchronized system can be modeled as a hybrid system [2]. However, it is important to note that, unlike traditional hybrid systems examples from the domain of control, the discrete part of the state space for these protocols is very large. Due to this we observed that leading hybrid systems verification tools, such as SpaceEx [17], cannot explore the entire state space.

There has been work on modeling timed protocols using real-time formalisms such as *timed automata* [3], where the derivatives of all continuous-time variables are equal to one. While tools based on the theory of timed automata do not explicitly support modeling and verification of multi-rate timed systems [21], there do exist techniques for approximating multirate clocks. For instance, Huang *et al.* [19] propose the use of *integer clocks* on top of UPPAAL models. Daws and Yovine [9] show how multirate timed systems can be over-approximated into timed automata. Vaandrager and Groot [29] models a clock that can proceed with different rate by defining a clock model consisting of one location and one self transition. Such models only approximately represent multirate time systems. By contrast, our approach algorithmically constructs abstractions that can be refined to be more precise by tuning the value of Δ, and results in an *sound* untimed model that can be directly checked by a finite-state model checker.

Synchrony and Asynchrony: There have been numerous efforts devoted towards mixing synchronous and asynchronous modeling. Multiclock Esterel [26] and communicating reactive processes (CRP) [5] extend the synchronous language Esterel to support a mix of synchronous and asynchronous processes. *Bounded asynchrony* is another such modeling technique with applications to biological systems [16]. It can be used to model systems in which processes can have different but *constant* rates, and can be interleaved asynchronously (with possible stuttering) before they all synchronize at the end of a global "period." Approximate synchrony has no such synchronizing global period. The *quasi-synchronous (QS)* [7,18] approach is designed for communicating processes that are *periodic* and have almost the *same* period. QS [18] is defined as "Between any two successive activations of one period process, the process on any other process is activated either 0, 1, or at most 2 times". As a consequence, in both quasi-synchrony and bounded asynchrony, the difference of the absolute number of activations of two different processes can grow unboundedly. In contrast, the definition of AS does not allow this difference to grow unbounded.

8 Conclusion

This paper has introduced two new concepts: a class of distributed systems termed as *symmetric, almost-synchronous* (SAS) systems, and *approximate synchrony*, an abstraction method for such systems. We evaluated applicability of approximate synchrony for verification in two different contexts: (i) application-layer protocols running on top of time-synchronized systems (TSCH), and (ii) systems that do not rely on time synchronization but exhibit recurrent logical behavior (BMC algorithm). We also described an interesting search prioritization technique based on approximate synchrony with the key insight that, prioritizing synchronous behaviors can help in finding bugs faster.

In this paper, we focus on verifying protocols that fit the SAS formalism defined in Sect. 2.2. While other protocols whose behavior and correctness relies on using values of timestamps do not natively fit into the SAS formalism, they can be abstracted using the suitable methods (e.g., using a state variable to model a local timer for a process whose value is incremented on each step of that process — with approximate synchrony the timer values across different processes will not differ by more than Δ). Evaluating such abstractions for protocols like Google Spanner and others that use timestamps would be an interesting next step.

Acknowledgments. The first and second authors were supported in part by TerraSwarm, one of six centers of STARnet, a Semiconductor Research Corporation program sponsored by MARCO and DARPA. The fourth author was supported in part by the Swedish Research Council (#623-2013-8591) and the iCyPhy Research Center (Industrial Cyber-Physical Systems, supported by IBM and United Technologies).

References

1. 15.4e 2012. IEEE standard for local and metropolitan area networks-part 15.4: Low-rate wireless personal area networks (LR-WPANs) amendment 1: MAC sub-layer (2012)
2. Alur, R., Courcoubetis, C., Halbwachs, N., Henzinger, T.A., Ho, P.-H., Nicollin, X., Olivero, A., Sifakis, J., Yovine, S.: The Algorithmic Analysis of Hybrid Systems.Theoretical Computer Science. Kluwer Academic Publisher, The Netherlands (1995)
3. Alur, R., Dill, D.L.: A Theory of Timed Automata.Theoretical Computer Science. Kluwer Academic Publishers, The Netherlands (1994)
4. Andrews, T., Qadeer, S., Rajamani, S.K., Rehof, J., Xie, Y.: Zing: a model checker for concurrent software. In: Alur, R., Peled, D.A. (eds.) CAV 2004. LNCS, vol. 3114, pp. 484–487. Springer, Heidelberg (2004)
5. Berry, G., Ramesh, S., Shyamasundar, R.: Communicating reactive processes. In: Proceedings of POPL (1993)
6. Broman, D., Derler, P., Desai, A., Eidson, J.C., Seshia, S.A.: Endlessly circulating messages in IEEE 1588–2008 systems. In: Proceedings of the 8th International IEEE Symposium on Precision Clock Synchronization for Measurement, Control and Communication (ISPCS), September 2014

7. Caspi, P., Mazuet, C., Reynaud Paligot, N.: About the design of distributed control systems: the quasi-synchronous approach. In: Voges, U. (ed.) SAFECOMP 2001. LNCS, vol. 2187, p. 215. Springer, Heidelberg (2001)
8. Corbett, J.C., Dean, J., Epstein, M., Fikes, A., Frost, C., Furman, J.J., Ghemawat, S., Gubarev, A., Heiser, C., Hochschild, P., Hsieh, W., Kanthak, S., Kogan, E., Li, H., Lloyd, A., Melnik, S., Mwaura, D., Nagle, D., Quinlan, S., Rao, R., Rolig, L., Saito, Y., Szymaniak, M., Taylor, C., Wang, R., Woodford, D.: Spanner: google's globally-distributed database. In: Proceedings of OSDI (2012)
9. Daws, C., Yovine, S.: Two examples of verification of multirate timed automata with Kronos. In: Proceedings of RTSS (1995)
10. Desai, A., Broman, D., Eidson, J., Qadeer, S., Seshia, S.A.: Approximate synchrony: An abstraction for distributed time-synchronized systems. Technical report UCB/EECS-2014-136, University of California, Berkeley, June 2014
11. Desai, A., Gupta, V., Jackson, E.K., Qadeer, S., Rajamani, S.K., Zufferey, D.P.: Safe asynchronous event-driven programming. In: Proceedings of PLDI (2013)
12. Desai, A., Seshia, S.A., Qadeer, S., Broman, D., Eidson, J.: Approximate synchrony: An abstraction for distributed almost-synchronous systems. Technical report UCB/EECS-2015-158, EECS Department, University of California, Berkeley, May 2015
13. Dolev, D., Dwork, C., Stockmeyer, L.: On the minimal synchronism needed for distributed consensus. J. ACM **34**(1), 77–97 (1987)
14. Dwork, C., Lynch, N., Stockmeyer, L.: Consensus in the presence of partial synchrony. J. ACM **35**(2), 288–323 (1988)
15. Emmi, M., Qadeer, S., Rakamarić, Z.: Delay-bounded scheduling. In: Proceedings of POPL (2011)
16. Fisher, J., Henzinger, T.A., Mateescu, M., Piterman, N.: Bounded asynchrony: concurrency for modeling cell-cell interactions. In: Fisher, J. (ed.) FMSB 2008. LNCS (LNBI), vol. 5054, pp. 17–32. Springer, Heidelberg (2008)
17. Frehse, G., Le Guernic, C., Donzé, A., Cotton, S., Ray, R., Lebeltel, O., Ripado, R., Girard, A., Dang, T., Maler, O.: SpaceEx: scalable verification of hybrid systems. In: Gopalakrishnan, G., Qadeer, S. (eds.) CAV 2011. LNCS, vol. 6806, pp. 379–395. Springer, Heidelberg (2011)
18. Halbwachs, N., Mandel, L.: Simulation and verification of asynchronous systems by means of a synchronous model. In: Proceedings of ACSD (2006)
19. Huang, X., Singh, A., Smolka, S.A.: Using Integer Clocks to Verify the Timing-Sync Sensor Network Protocol. In: Proceedings of NFM (2010)
20. IEEE Instrumentation and Measurement Society. IEEE Standard for a Precision Clock Synchronization Protocol for Networked Measurement and Control Systems (2008)
21. Larsen, K.G., Pettersson, P., Yi, W.: UPPAAL in a nutshell. Int. J. STTT **1**(1–12), 134–152 (1997)
22. Lipinski, M., Wlostowski, T., Serrano, J., Alvarez, P., Gonzalez Cobas, J., Rubini, A., Moreira, P.: Performance results of the first white rabbit installation for cngs time transfer. In: Proceedings of ISPCS (2012)
23. Musuvathi, M., Qadeer, S.: Iterative context bounding for systematic testing of multithreaded programs. In: Proceedings of PLDI (2007)
24. Perlman, R.: An algorithm for distributed computation of a spanning tree in an extended LAN. In: Proceedings of SIGCOMM (1985)
25. Ponzio, S., Strong, R.: Semisynchrony and real time. In: Segall, A., Zaks, S. (eds.) Distributed Algorithms. Lecture Notes in Computer Science, vol. 647, pp. 120–135. Springer, Berlin Heidelberg (1992)

26. Rajan, B., Shyamasundar, R.: Multiclock esterel: a reactive framework for asynchronous design. In: IPDPS (2000)
27. Sundararaman, B., Buy, U., Kshemkalyani, A.D.: Clock synchronization for wireless sensor networks: a survey. Ad Hoc Netw. **3**, 281–323 (2005). (Elsevier, 2005)
28. Tinka, A., Watteyne, T., Pister, K.: A decentralized scheduling algorithm for time synchronized channel hopping. In: Zheng, J., Simplot-Ryl, D., Leung, V.C.M. (eds.) ADHOCNETS 2010. LNICST, vol. 49, pp. 201–216. Springer, Heidelberg (2010)
29. Vaandrager, F.W., de Groot, A.: Analysis of a biphase mark protocol with Uppaal and PVS. Formal Aspects Comput. **18**(4), 433–458 (2006)

Automated and Modular Refinement Reasoning for Concurrent Programs

Chris Hawblitzel[1], Erez Petrank[2], Shaz Qadeer[1], and Serdar Tasiran[3](✉)

[1] Microsoft, Redmond, USA
[2] Technion, Haifa, Israel
[3] Koç University, Istanbul, Turkey
stasiran@ku.edu.tr

Abstract. We present CIVL, a language and verifier for concurrent programs based on automated and modular refinement reasoning. CIVL supports reasoning about a concurrent program at many levels of abstraction. Atomic actions in a high-level description are refined to fine-grain and optimized lower-level implementations. A novel combination of automata theoretic and logic-based checks is used to verify refinement. Modular specifications and proof annotations, such as location invariants and procedure pre- and post-conditions, are specified separately, independently at each level in terms of the variables visible at that level. We have implemented CIVL as an extension to the BOOGIE language and verifier. We have used CIVL to refine a realistic concurrent garbage collection algorithm from a simple high-level specification down to a highly-concurrent implementation described in terms of individual memory accesses.

1 Introduction

We present a technique for verifying a refinement relation between two concurrent, shared-memory multithreaded programs. Our work is inspired by stepwise refinement [43], where a high-level description is systematically refined, potentially via several intermediate descriptions, down to a detailed implementation. Refinement checking is a classical problem in verification and has been investigated in many contexts, including hardware verification [11] and verification of cache-coherence protocols and distributed algorithms [32]. In the realm of sequential software, notable successes using the refinement approach include the work of Abrial et al. [2] and the proof of full functional correctness of the seL4 microkernel [30]. This paper presents the first general and automated proof system for refinement verification of shared-memory multithreaded software.

We present our verification approach in the context of CIVL, an idealized concurrent programming language. In CIVL, a program is described as a collection of procedures whose implementation can use the standard features such as assignment, conditionals, loops, procedure calls, and thread creation. Each procedure accesses shared global variables only through invocations of atomic actions. A subset of the atomic actions may be refined by new procedures and a new program is obtained by replacing the invocation of an atomic action by a call to the corresponding procedure refining the action. Several layers of refinement may

D. Kroening and C.S. Păsăreanu (Eds.): CAV 2015, Part II, LNCS 9207, pp. 449–465, 2015.
DOI: 10.1007/978-3-319-21668-3_26

be performed until all atomic actions in the final program are directly implementable primitives. Unlike classical program verifiers based on Floyd-Hoare reasoning [20,28] that manipulate a program and annotations, the CIVL verifier manipulates multiple operational descriptions of a program, i.e., several layers of refinement are specified and verified at once.

To prove refinement in CIVL, a simulation relation between a program and its abstraction is inferred from checks on each procedure, thus decomposing a whole-program refinement problem into per-procedure verification obligations. The computation inside each such procedure is partitioned into "steps" such that one step behaves like the atomic specification and all other steps have no effect on the visible state. This partitioning follows the syntactic structure of the code in a way similar in spirit to Floyd-Hoare reasoning. To express the per-procedure verification obligations in terms of a collection of per-step verification tasks, the CIVL verifier needs to address two issues. First, the notion of a "step" in the code implementing a procedure must be defined. The definition of a step can deeply affect the number of checks that need to be performed and the number of user annotations. Second, it is typically not possible to show the correctness of a step from an arbitrary state. A precondition for the step in terms of shared variables must be supplied by the programmer and mechanically checked by the verifier.

To address the first problem, CIVL lets the programmer define the granularity of a step, allowing the user to specify a semantics with larger atomic actions. A *cooperative* semantics for the program is explicitly introduced by the programmer through the use of a new primitive *yield* statement; in this semantics a thread can be scheduled out only when it is about to execute a yield statement. The *preemptive* semantics of the program is sequentially consistent execution; all threads are imagined to execute on a single processor and preemption, which causes a thread to be scheduled out and a nondeterministically chosen thread to be scheduled in, may occur before any instruction.[1] Given a program P, CIVL verifies that the safety of the cooperative semantics of P implies the safety of the preemptive semantics of P. This verification is done by computing an automata-theoretic simulation check [24] on an abstraction of P in which each atomic action of P is represented by only its mover type [17,35]. The mover types themselves are verified separately and automatically using an automated theorem prover [9].

To address the second problem that refinement verification for each step requires invariants about the program execution, CIVL allows the programmer to specify location invariants, attached either to a yield statement or to a procedure as its pre- or post-condition. Each location invariant must be correct for all executions and must continue to hold in spite of potential interference from concurrently executing threads. We build upon classical work [29,38] on reasoning about non-interference with two distinct innovations. First, we do not require the annotations to be strong enough to prove program correctness but only strong

[1] In this paper, we focus our attention on sequential consistency and leave consideration of weak memory models to future work.

enough to provide the context for refinement checking. Program correctness is established via a sequence of refinement layers from an abstract program that cannot fail. Second, to establish a postcondition of a procedure, we do not need to propagate a precondition through all the yield annotations in the procedure body. The correctness of an atomic action specification gives us a simple frame rule—the precondition only needs to be propagated across the atomic action specification. CIVL further simplifies the manual annotations required for logical non-interference checking by providing a linear type system [42] that enables logical encoding of thread identifiers, permissions [7], and disjoint memory [31].

Finally, CIVL provides a simple module system. Modules can be verified separately, in parallel or at different times, since the module system soundly does away with checks that pertain to cross-module interactions. This feature is significant since commutativity checks and non-interference checks for location invariants are quadratic, whole program checks involving all pairs of yield locations and atomic blocks, or all pairs of actions from a program. Using the module system, the number of checks is reduced; they become quadratic in the number of yields and atomic blocks within each module rather than the entire program.

We have implemented CIVL as a conservative extension of the BOOGIE verifier. We have used it to verify a collection of microbenchmarks and benchmarks from the literature [6,13–15,19,27]. The most challenging case study with CIVL was carried out concurrently with CIVL's development and served as a design driver. We verified a concurrent garbage collector, through six layers of refinement, down to atomic actions corresponding to individual memory accesses. The level of granularity of the lowest-level implementation distinguishes this verification effort, detailed in a technical report [23], from previous attempts in the literature.

In conclusion, CIVL is the first automated verifier for shared-memory multithreaded programs that provides the capability to establish a multi-layered refinement proof. This novel capability is enabled by two important innovations in core verification techniques for reducing the complexity of invariants supplied by the programmer and the verification conditions solved by the prover.

- Reasoning about preemptive semantics is replaced by simpler reasoning about cooperative operational semantics by exploiting automata-theoretic simulation checking. This is a novel technique that combines automata-based and logic-based reasoning.
- A linear type system establishes invariants about disjointness of permission sets associated with values contained in program variables. These invariants, communicated to the prover as free assumptions, significantly reduce the overhead of program annotations. We are not aware of any other verifier that combines type-based and logic-based reasoning in this style.

2 Overview

We present an overview of our approach to refinement on an example (Fig. 1) inspired by the write barrier in our concurrent garbage collector (GC). In a concurrent GC, each object in the heap has a color: `UNALLOC`, `WHITE`, `GRAY`, or `BLACK`.

The GC traverses reachable objects, marking the reached objects GRAY and then BLACK. At the end of the traversal, reached objects are BLACK, unreached objects are WHITE, and the GC deallocates the WHITE objects. The threads in the system must cooperate with the GC to ensure that the collection creates no dangling pointers (i.e., if object A is reachable and A points to object B, then B should not be deallocated). Therefore, before a mutator thread mutates an object A to point to an object B, the thread executes a write barrier to check the color of B. If B is WHITE, the write barrier darkens B's color to GRAY to ensure that the GC does not deallocate B. WB implements the write barrier. The write barrier is only invoked on allocated objects, thus, colors cannot be UNALLOC when WB is called. To simplify exposition, we consider a single object whose color is stored in the shared variable Color. WB first reads Color without holding a lock, to avoid when possible, the cost of acquiring and releasing a lock for each object encountered by a mutator. If Color <= WHITE, WB calls the more expensive procedure WBSlow to re-examine and possibly update Color while holding the lock. The annotation yield Color >= cNoLock is a local invariant expected to be preserved by the environment of WB. CIVL simplifies reasoning about WBSlow by allowing us to express its specification as the following atomic action:

```
var Color: int; // UNALLOC=0, WHITE=1,
                // GRAY=2, BLACK=3

procedure WB(linear tid:Tid)
atomic [if (Color == WHITE) Color := GRAY];
requires Color >= WHITE;
ensures Color >= GRAY;
{
  var cNoLock:int;
  yield Color >= WHITE;
  cNoLock := GetColorNoLock(tid);
  yield Color >= cNoLock;
  if (cNoLock <= WHITE)
    call WBSlow(tid);
  yield Color >= GRAY;
}

procedure WBSlow(linear tid:Tid)
atomic [if (Color <= WHITE) Color := GRAY];
{
  var cLock:int;
  call AcquireLock(tid);
  cLock := GetColorLocked(tid);
  if (cLock <= WHITE)
    call SetColorLocked(tid, GRAY);
  call ReleaseLock(tid);
}

procedure GetColorNoLock(linear tid:Tid)
  returns (cl:int) atomic [...];
procedure AcquireLock(linear tid:Tid)
  right [...];
procedure ReleaseLock(linear tid:Tid)
  left [...];
procedure GetColorLocked(linear tid:Tid)
  returns (cl:int) both [...];
procedure SetColorLocked(linear tid:Tid,
  cl: int) atomic [...];
```

Fig. 1. Write barrier

[if (Color <= WHITE) Color := GRAY] This specification indicates that regardless of how the environment interferes with its execution, to its caller it appears as if WBSlow atomically executes the code above.

Per-procedure Simulation, Non-interference via Invariants. The verification of WB illustrates a combination of techniques. We first explain how WB's post-condition is verified. To see that this task is not trivial, consider a scenario in which WB, not holding a lock, reads Color and sets cNoLock to GRAY and then yields. Another thread sets Color to WHITE. WB resumes, but because the local variable cNoLock is GRAY, does nothing and exits with Color being WHITE, violating WB's postcondition. But, in the GC this scenario is not possible. The yield predicate (location invariant) Color >= cNoLock expresses the fact that other threads can only modify Color to a higher (darker) value. CIVL verifies the correctness of this location invariant and rules out this undesirable scenario. Using this location invariant, WB's pre-condition, and WBSlow's atomic specification, CIVL is able to verify WB's post-condition.

In Fig. 1, we suppose for illustration's sake that WB and WBSlow have slightly different atomic specifications, one testing for `Color == WHITE` and the other for `Color <= WHITE`. In this case, verifying that the implementation of WB refines its atomic specification relies on `Color` not being `UNALLOC`. Otherwise, WBSlow would set `Color` to `GRAY` whereas WB would leave it unmodified, leading to a refinement violation. WB's precondition `Color >= WHITE` and the location invariant `Color >= cNoLock` imply that `Color` is never `UNALLOC` during the execution of WB. Given this constraint, CIVL checks atomicity refinement for WB by verifying the existence of a particular simulation-relation. Each control path through WB is analyzed as a sequence of code fragments, from one `yield` statement to the next. For each control path through a procedure, exactly one code fragment must be simulated by the atomic action specification while others do not modify global state. This refinement proof for WB makes use of (1) correct modeling of environment interference by the pre- and post-conditions, and the yield predicate, and (2) the atomic action specification for the called procedure WBSlow. The CIVL verifier automatically computes a logical verification condition capturing the proof obligations from the body and specification of WB.

Just as the verification of WB builds on the specification of WBSlow, the verification of WBSlow builds on other refinement proofs (not shown) of the procedures called in WBSlow; these procedures are shown at the bottom of the figure. This example shows only one procedure at this layer. In programs with many procedures with atomic specifications at each layer, CIVL combines the per-procedure refinement proofs soundly into a whole-program refinement proof.

Preemptive vs Cooperative Semantics. The verification of WBSlow highlights another important feature in CIVL. Refinement checking is performed on cooperative semantics in which a `yield-to-yield` execution fragment of code is executed atomically. However, in a real execution, control can switch between threads at any point in the code. A naive modeling of a real execution would put a yield statement before every instruction in the code. The absence of a yield statement before every instruction is justified by reasoning about mover types [17]. The procedures called in WBSlow have the mover types claimed in their declarations and verified by CIVL. For example, the mover type of `AcquireLock` is `right` which indicates that it commutes later in time against concurrently executing environment actions. These mover types are checked by constructing verification conditions from each pair of atomic actions.

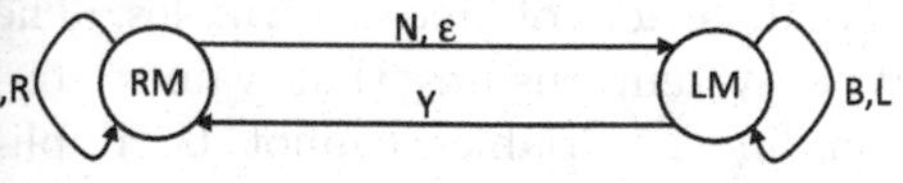

Fig. 2. Yield sufficiency automaton

Given verified mover types for actions, CIVL verifies the correctness of the placement of `yield` statements using a novel approach. A *yield sufficiency automaton* (Fig. 2) encodes all sequences of atomic actions (of **R**ight, **L**eft, **B**oth and **N**on-mover types) and yields for which safety of cooperative semantics is sufficient for safety of preemptive semantics. Each "transaction" starts with a sequence of right movers (or both movers) and ends with a sequence of left movers (or both movers). In the middle, it can have at most one non mover. Transactions must be separated by `yield` statements. CIVL then interprets the control-flow graph of each procedure as an automaton with mover types as edge labels. This abstraction for `WBSlow` is shown in Fig. 3. CIVL verifies that this automaton is simulated by the yield sufficiency automaton using an existing algorithm for computing simulation relations [24].

The use of commutativity reasoning is optional in CIVL, but beneficial in our experience. Commutativity reasoning may be avoided by annotating atomic action specifications with the mover type `atomic` and inserting a yield statement before every invocation of an atomic action. In our experience with CIVL, using more yield statements, each with an accompanying location invariant, can make proofs difficult in two ways. First, the annotation burden goes up because sophisticated ghost variables may need to be introduced in the program semantics.[2] Second, the computational cost of the pairwise mover reasoning is replaced by the cost of pairwise non-interference checks between yield predicates and concurrently executing atomic actions.

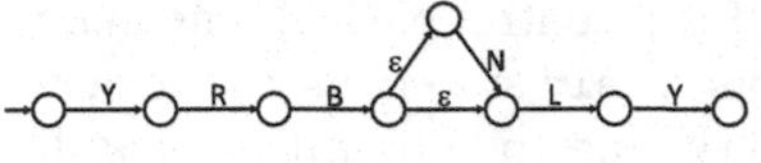

Fig. 3. Abstraction of `WBSlow`

Linear Variables. In Fig. 1, thread identifier (`tid`) variables are declared `linear` to indicate that two threads cannot possess the same thread identifier simultaneously. We now explain this feature of CIVL in more detail using the program in Fig. 4. This example contains a shared global array `a` indexed by an uninterpreted type `Tid` representing the set of thread identifiers. A collection of threads are executing procedure `P` concurrently. The identifier of the thread executing `P` is passed in as the parameter `tid`. A thread with identifier `tid` owns `a[tid]` and can increment it without danger of interference. The yield predicate `t == a[tid]` in `P` indicates this expectation, yet it is not possible to prove it unless the reasoning engine knows that the value of `tid` in one thread is distinct from its value in a different thread.

```
type Tid;
procedure Allocate()
  returns (linear tid:Tid);

var a:[Tid]int;

procedure main()
{
  while (true) {
    var linear tid:Tid := Allocate();
    async call P(tid);
    yield true;
  }
}
procedure P(linear tid: Tid)
  ensures a[tid] == old(a)[tid] + 1;
{
  var t:int := a[tid];
  yield t == a[tid];
  a[tid] := t + 1;
}
```

Fig. 4. Encoding thread identifiers

Instead of building a notion of thread identifiers into CIVL, we provide a more primitive and general notion of linear variables. The CIVL type system ensures that values contained in linear variables cannot be duplicated [42]. Consequently, the parameter `tid` of distinct concurrent calls to `P` are known to be distinct; the CIVL verifier exploits this invariant while checking

[2] Location invariants that cannot refer to the state of other threads are known to be incomplete, both in theory and in practice.

for non-interference and commutativity. Linearity is general enough to support much more than just fixed thread identifiers: CIVL also uses it to express separation of memory (as is done commonly in separation logic proofs [39]; see [31]) and to express permissions [7] that may be transferred but not duplicated between threads. Our verified GC, for example, expresses mutual exclusion during initialization and root scanning by temporarily transferring permissions from mutator threads to the GC thread.

Variable Hiding. The atomic action specification of `WBSlow` makes no reference to the lock variable, although its implementation involves a lock. When verifying refinement for `WBSlow`, the lock variable has been hidden. CIVL allows the programmer to both introduce and hide variables in each refinement step, thereby providing the capability to perform data refinement. The ability to introduce and hide variables and write yield predicates specific to each refinement step facilitates proofs spanning a large range of abstraction.

3 Verification

In this section, we present our verification method on a core concurrent programming language called CIVL (Fig. 5). Due to lack of space, we can only provide an overview of the design of the CIVL verifier. The full formalization of the language and detailed rules for all verification judgments is available in a technical report [23].

$s \in Stmt$	$::=$	*skip* | *yield e* | *call A* | *call P* | *async P* | *ablock* $\{e\}$ *s* | *s*; *s* | *if le then s else s* | *while* $\{e\}$ *le do s*
$F \in Frame$	$::=$	(P, L, s)
$T \in Thread$	$::=$	$(TL, \overrightarrow{F})$
$Prog \in Program$	$::=$	$(ps, as, G, \overrightarrow{T})$

Fig. 5. Syntax

A CIVL program *Prog* contains procedures *ps*, atomic actions *as*, global state G, and threads $\overrightarrow{T}$. Each thread T in $\overrightarrow{T}$ contains thread-local state TL and stack frames $\overrightarrow{F}$. Each stack frame F in $\overrightarrow{F}$ contains a procedure name P, procedure-local state L, and a statement s representing the code in P that remains to be executed. Thus, *Prog* contains all information to represent not only the static program written by the programmer but also the entire state of the program as it executes. The statements in CIVL contain the usual constructs such as sequencing, conditional control flow, and looping. In addition, it contains invocation of procedures (*call P*), execution of atomic actions (*call A*), and thread creation (*async P*). Each atomic action has a single-state *gate predicate* and a two-state *transition relation*. If a thread executes an atomic action in a state (disjoint union of global, thread-local, and procedure-local state) where its gate predicate does not hold, the program fails; otherwise, the state is modified according to its transition relation. The execution of *Prog* is modeled as the usual *preemptive* semantics in which a nondeterministically chosen thread may execute any number of steps. *Prog* is *unsafe* if some execution fails the gate of an atomic action; otherwise, *Prog* is *safe*.

Suppose a program $Prog^{hi}$ has been proved to be safe. However, it is implemented using atomic actions that are too coarse to be directly implementable. To carry over the safety of $Prog^{hi}$ to a realizable implementation $Prog^{lo}$, these coarse atomic actions must be refined down to lower-level actions. During refinement, a high-level atomic action A is implemented by a procedure P, which is itself implemented using lower-level atomic actions. In CIVL, the programmer can simultaneously refine many atomic actions by specifying a partial function RS from procedures to atomic actions; $Prog^{hi}$ is obtained from $Prog^{lo}$ by replacing each occurrence of *call* P for $P \in dom(RS)$ with *call* $RS(P)$. The main contribution of this paper is a verification method that allows us to validate such a refinement from $Prog^{hi}$ to $Prog^{lo}$ (or abstraction from $Prog^{lo}$ to $Prog^{hi}$) so that safety of $Prog^{hi}$ implies the safety of $Prog^{lo}$ as well.

While abstracting $Prog^{lo}$ to $Prog^{hi}$, it is often inconvenient to reason about $Prog^{lo}$ using its preemptive semantics, which allows potential interference at *every* control location in a thread from concurrently-executing threads. To make reasoning more convenient, CIVL provides the statement *yield* e, an annotation used to specify a cooperative semantics for the program. In this semantics, a thread executes continuously until it reaches a yield statement, at which point a different thread may be scheduled. To ensure that any reasoning performed on cooperative semantics is also sound for preemptive semantics, CIVL exploits commutativity reasoning. It allows the programmer to specify the commutativity type of atomic actions in the program—B for both mover, R for right mover, L for left mover, and N for non mover [17]. The CIVL verifier checks the correctness of these commutativity types by verifying each atomic action pairwise against every atomic action in the program. While it is sound to put a yield statement before and after every atomic action, the programmer may omit certain yield statements, e.g., a yield after a right mover or a yield before a left mover. In general, the *Yield Sufficiency Automaton* from Fig. 2 encodes all sequences of atomic actions and yield statements for which reasoning about cooperative semantics is sound. Given the commutativity types of atomic actions and the program code annotated with yield statements, the CIVL verifier checks modularly for each procedure that its implementation is connected to the yield sufficiency automaton via a simulation relation [24].

In addition to introducing a control location where interference is allowed to occur, a yield statement *yield* e also provides an invariant e to constrain the environment interference. The invariant e is similar to the location invariant in the method of Owicki and Gries [38]. It is expected to hold when the executing thread reaches the yield statement (sequential correctness) and also be preserved by concurrently-executing threads (non-interference). Each procedure is equipped with a precondition, a postcondition, and a set of (potentially) modified thread-local variables. CIVL uses these procedure annotations to verify the sequential correctness of location invariants for each procedure separately. To verify non-interference, it would suffice to check that each location invariant is preserved by each atomic action in the program. CIVL increases the precision of this check by allowing each location invariant to be preserved across an atomic block, introduced as the statement *ablock* $\{e\}$ s. The invariant e annotating the atomic block is expected to hold when this statement begins execution and is verified as part of sequential correctness. The CIVL type checker checks that the tatement s inside this atomic block does not have any yield statement or other tomic blocks inside it. Thus, non-interference of a location invariant e' against *block* $\{e\}$ s is achieved by proving the Floyd-Hoare triple $\{e \wedge e'\}s\{e'\}$.

Having verified sequential correctness and non-interference for location invarints, it remains to verify refinement, i.e., if $RS(P) = A$, then the atomic action A is correctly refined by the procedure P. This requirement means that any path rom entry to exit of P must contain exactly one atomic block that implements he action A; all other atomic blocks on the path must leave global and threadocal variables unchanged. To perform this check, the CIVL verifier introduces he following fresh local variables in P: (1) a *Boolean* variable b initialized to *alse* to track whether an atomic block along the current execution has modified global or thread-local variable, (2) variables to capture snapshot of global and hread-local variables at the beginning of each atomic block. By updating these uxiliary variables appropriately, the refinement check is reduced to a collection f assertions introduced into the body of P at the end of atomic blocks and at he exit of P.

Often, commutativity and non-interference checks require knowledge about listinctness of local program variables in different threads. For example, in Fig. 1, o prove that `AcquireLock` commutes to the right of `ReleaseLock`, the verifier must know that the input parameter `tid` to these atomic actions is different if hey are being executed by different threads. A similar situation arises in Fig. 4, vhen attempting to prove that the location invariant `t == a[tid]` is preserved y the atomic action `a[tid] := t + 1`. Information about distinctness of program variables in different threads is difficult to provide as a location invariant vhose scope is local to the context of the unique executing thread. As an alterative, we exploit reasoning based on a linear type system [42]. The programmer eclares certain variables as linear at input and output interfaces of procedures nd actions. Using this interface information, the CIVL type system computes set of *available* linear variables at each control location in a procedure. The vailability of a variable may change at an assignment or a procedure call, e.g., f `y` is available just before `x := y`, then `y` is not available and `x` is available ust afterwards. The CIVL type checker guarantees that the values contained in vailable linear variables, across all threads at their respective control locations, re distinct from each other. This fact is introduced as a logical assumption by he verifier when performing commutativity and non-interference checks.

The interaction between the linear type system and logical reasoning in CIVL s more general than the description above. In CIVL, the programmer may specify n arbitrary function *Perm* from a value to a set of values; the set $Perm(v)$ is he set of *permissions* associated with v. The example described in the previous aragraph corresponds to the special case when $Perm(v) = \{v\}$. The CIVL type hecker enforces a generalization of the distinctness invariant that the permission ets corresponding to the values in available variables across all threads are nutually disjoint.

3.1 Safety Guarantee

We can combine the verification techniques described above to verify the safety of a program $Prog^{lo}$. Specifically, we can guarantee that $Prog^{lo}$ is safe (i.e., all atomic actions will satisfy their gates when run) if the following conditions hold:

1. $Prog^{hi}$ is safe when executed with preemptive semantics.
2. $Prog^{lo}$ is a valid refinement of $Prog^{hi}$, according to the rules for refinement in CIVL. Specifically, for any atomic action A in $Prog^{hi}$ implemented by a procedure P in $Prog^{lo}$, any path from entry to exit of P must contain exactly one atomic block that implements the action A; all other atomic blocks on the path must leave the global and thread-local state unchanged. Furthermore, all calls to A in $Prog^{hi}$ are replaced by calls to P in $Prog^{lo}$.
3. The invariants of $Prog^{lo}$ satisfy sequential correctness and non-interference with respect to cooperative semantics.
4. $Prog^{lo}$ is *well-typed* with respect to linearity. Specifically, $Prog^{lo}$ does not try to duplicate any linear variables, and linear variables passed to procedures calls and atomic actions are available as expected by the type checker.
5. The atomic actions in $Prog^{lo}$ satisfy the pairwise commutativity checks.
6. The yield statements in $Prog^{lo}$ are sufficient, according to the yield sufficiency automaton in Fig. 2.
7. Any infinite execution of $Prog^{lo}$ must visit a yield statement infinitely often.

By themselves, conditions 1-4 guarantee that $Prog^{lo}$ will be safe when executed with cooperative semantics. Conditions 5-7 then additionally ensure that $Prog^{lo}$ will be safe when executed with preemptive semantics. The technical report [23], which includes formal definitions of all the conditions for an extension of the language in Fig. 5, formalizes this safety guarantee into a soundness theorem by establishing a simulation relation between $Prog^{lo}$ and $Prog^{hi}$. Since the theorem connects the safety of one program's preemptive semantics to another program's preemptive semantics, multiple applications of the theorem can be chained together to establish the safety of a low-level program: the lowest level $Prog^0$ is safe because $Prog^1$ is safe, $Prog^1$ is safe because $Prog^2$ is safe, and so on.

4 Modules

The technical report [23] describes a simple module system built on CIVL that allows separate verification of modules, allowing programmers to check a large program by breaking it into smaller pieces and checking the pieces independently. A key challenge for modular verification in CIVL is the checking of non-interference and commutativity. Naively, these are whole-program judgments, quadratically checking all pairs of actions or all pairs of yields and atomic blocks from an entire program. To check these judgments on a per-module basis rather for a whole program, we observe that commutativity and non-interference are trivially satisfied for operations that act on disjoint sets of global variables.

f an atomic block modifies only variables g_1 and g_2, it will not interfere with location invariant that refers only to variables g_3 and g_4. More generally, let ach module M own a set of global variables, such that each global variable is wned by exactly one module, and decree that only M's procedures and actions an access M's global variables. Statements in M's procedures can only read nd write M's own global variables, and M's actions and location invariants can nly refer to M's own global variables. (On the other hand, procedure assertions hat are not checked for non-interference, such as the e in *ablock* $\{e\}$ s, may nention global variables from other modules, since these assertions can neither nterfere with other modules' location invariants nor be interfered with by other nodules' statements.)

Note that ownership can change across refinement layers. For example, a ibrary module implementing locks may define a variable to represent the abstract tate of a lock; after the lock module is verified at a low layer, another module can ake ownership of the lock variable in a higher layer (see [23] for a detailed example of ownership transfer across three layers, from a lock module to a datatype nodule to a client module).

5 Implementation

Ve have implemented the method described in this section as a conservative xtension of the Boogie [4] language and verifier. Our implementation proides new language primitives for linear variables, asynchronous and parallel rocedure calls, yields, atomic actions as procedure specifications, expressing efinement layers, and hiding of global variables and procedures. At its core, 3oogie is an unstructured language comprising code blocks and goto statements.)ur implementation handles the complexity of unstructured control flow. To implify the exposition, our formalization uses Floyd-Hoare triples to present equential correctness and annotated atomic code blocks to present refinement nd non-interference checks. However, our implementation is considerably more utomated. All the annotations, except those at yields, loops, and procedure oundaries, are automatically generated using the technique of verification conitions [5]. Annotated atomic code blocks are also inferred automatically. Nonnterference checks are collected as inlined procedures invoked at appropriate laces within the code of a procedure for increased precision.

We automated the simulation relation check used for yield sufficiency in ect. 3 by adapting an algorithm by Henzinger et al. [24] for computing the imilarity relation of labeled graphs. The complexity of the algorithm is $O(n*m)$, vhere n and m are the number of control-flow graph nodes and edges. In practice, his part of the verification is fast.

A large proof usually comprises multiple layers of refinement chained together.)ur implementation allows the specification of multiple views of a program in single file by using the mechanism of *layers*. The programmer may attach a ositive layer number to each annotation and procedure; version i of the program s constructed from annotations labeled i and procedures labeled at least i.

We have implemented a type checker to make sure that layer numbers are used appropriately, e.g., it is illegal for a procedure with layer i to call a procedure with layer j greater than i.

6 Experience

The CIVL verifier has been under development for around two years. Over that period, we have developed a collection of 32 benchmarks, ranging in size from 17 to 539 LOC, to illustrate various features of CIVL and for regression testing as we evolved the verifier. In addition to microbenchmarks, this collection also includes standard benchmarks from the literature such as a multiset implementation [14], the ticket algorithm [15], Treiber stack [27], work-stealing queue [6], device cache [13], and lock-protected increment [19]. The CIVL verifier is fast; the entire benchmark set verifies in 20 s on a standard 4-core Windows PC (2.8GHz, 8GB) with no benchmark requiring more than a few seconds.

6.1 Garbage Collector

We have used CIVL to design and verify a realistic concurrent mark-sweep garbage collection (GC) algorithm (available at [22]). In particular, although our algorithm is based on an earlier algorithm by Dijkstra et al. [10], it extends the earlier algorithm with various modern optimizations and embellishments to improve generality and performance. These extensions include lower write barrier overhead, phase-based synchronization and handshaking, and coordination between the GC and mutator threads during root scanning; our use of linearity aids the proof of root scanning, while our rely-guarantee encoding aids management of colors inside the write barrier (which is similar to the barrier in Sect. 2). Furthermore, our encoding of the algorithm in CIVL spans a wide range of abstraction from low-level memory operations all the way up to high-level specifications; we used six layers of refinement to help hide low-level details from the high-level portions of the verification.

We believe that CIVL's combination of features makes practical, for the first time, verification across such a wide range of abstraction:

- The GC's lowest layers relied primarily on reduction to prove that operations on concurrent data structures and synchronization operations appear atomic to higher layers.
- The GC's higher layers relied primarily on invariant-based non-interference reasoning. This reasoning was simplified because reduction already made lower-layer operations atomic, reducing the amount of interference between higher-layer operations. In addition, the use of location invariants made certain layers of the proof more manageable compared to an earlier effort verifying the same GC where we used rely-guarantee reasoning and auxiliary variables to reason about non-interference.

- Linear variables were used throughout the proof to model the distinct thread identifiers for the garbage collector thread and mutator threads, but were most instrumental in expressing mutual exclusion during initialization and during root scanning. In initialization and root scanning, the mutator threads temporarily donate a fraction of their linear permissions to the GC thread. The distinctness invariant from Sect. 3 guarantees that the mutator threads and GC threads cannot simultaneously possess the same linear permissions; we leverage this guarantee to prove non-interference of mutator and GC actions during initialization and root scanning.

CIVL's support for refinement also enabled concise specifications of the GC's orrectness: a correct GC must implement Allocate, ReadField, and WriteField ctions that appear to act atomically, even though the implementations of these perations actually execute concurrently with the GC thread and with other rogram threads. The specification states that Allocate atomically adds new bjects to the heap, while ReadField and WriteField read and write heap object elds. Although the GC's Mark and Sweep code constitutes most of the GC code, hey are hidden in the high-level specification; they have detailed correctness pecifications in the middle layers of the proof, but the most important point t the high level is that their work not interfere with Allocate, ReadField, and VriteField. In particular, Mark must coordinate with WriteField's write barrier, nd Sweep must not remove objects reachable by ReadField and WriteField.

Overall, our GC implementation consists of about 2100 lines of Boogie code. he verification takes 60 s on the same PC used for microbenchmarks. The bulk f this time, 54 s, is taken by the verification of sequential correctness and non-nterference. The checks for linear variables, yield sufficiency, and commutativity ake the rest of the time and are insignificant in comparison.

Related Work

ur work is the first to provide a tool and theory to support automated, modu-ar whole-program refinement through multiple layers, as distinct from existing ork on single-layer atomicity refinement between procedure implementations nd specifications. CIVL combines a number of techniques in a novel manner to ecompose the refinement task following the syntactic structure of a program. elow, we first contrast CIVL with refinement verification techniques, and then ith tools and techniques for reasoning about concurrent programs in general.

.1 Refinement-Oriented Verification

tomic action specifications have been explored by the CALVIN [18,21] verifier. IVL carries out refinement verification on a procedure body with cooperative emantics as enabled by movers types and reduction. CALVIN attempts to ver-fy refinement directly on the preemptive semantics, making only limited use f movers at the lowest-level representation. CALVIN, unlike CIVL, does not sup-ort location invariants and linear variables but incorporates rely-guarantee rea-oning. CIVL supports both location invariants or rely-guarantee reasoning, and either technique can be used to prove non-interference. However, in certain cases, rely-guarantee reasoning requires use of auxiliary (shared) variables and makes interactive proofs difficult as was the case in our GC proof.

QED [13] is a simplifier for concurrent programs and is close in spirit to the refinement-oriented approach of CIVL. A key distinction between CIVL and QED is the fact that a proof step in QED is a small rewrite in the concurrent program that must be justified by potentially expensive reduction and invariant reasoning. In QED, procedures can be proven atomic only one procedure at a time, and only by transforming their bodies by reduction to be yield free. The number of small proof steps directly affect both programmer and computer effort. By contrast, CIVL supports large proof steps, in each of which the bodies of several procedures are automatically replaced by atomic actions, thereby lowering the cost of both interaction and automation. The non-interference reasoning in QED is even more limited than CALVIN. QED supports only global invariants and does not support rely-guarantee reasoning or linear variables.

Liang et al. [34] present a method for verifying that procedure bodies refine atomic specifications The key verification approach is rely-guarantee reasoning and the refinement (simulation) relation between a procedure and its specification is constrained so it is preserved under parallel composition. No tool support is provided. Authors present a (paper) GC proof, which is limited in scope compared to ours, as their proof corresponds to a few layers of our proof. In particular, the GC is not refined down to individual atomic memory accesses. Since this work uses different languages to describe the high-level and low-level programs, it is not immediately possible to carry out a multi-level stepwise refinement proof.

Turon and Wand [40] use ownership disciplines and separation logic to verify refinement of atomic specifications by concurrent data structure implementations. Rely-guarantee reasoning is supported to provide compositionality and non-interference arguments. This work targets a single refinement step between atomic specifications for methods and their implementations. No tool support for this verification method is provided.

Verifying linearizability of concurrent data structures (see, e.g., [12,25]) can be viewed as an instance of one-level of refinement in our setting. CIVL can be used for mechanical verification of linearizability, as we did for the Treiber stack. Tools and techniques specific to verifying linearizability cannot be easily generalized for stepwise refinement proofs through multiple levels.

Refinement proofs between implementations and specifications of protocols have been investigated using the TLA+ [32] specification language. Compositional refinement proofs [1] have also been investigated in this context. Modular refinement proofs for hardware systems have been investigated extensively (e.g., [11,26]) using the SMV [36] and Mocha [3] model checking tools. To verify a concurrent, shared-memory program using such tools, one must encode the program semantics as a state-transition system and express verification goals in terms of this system. For concurrent, shared-memory software, CIVL enables reasoning on the structured, imperative multithreaded program text rather than a logic description of the program's state-transition relation.

7.2 Reasoning About Concurrency

In this section, we discuss foundational techniques for combating the complexity of concurrent program verification. CIVL and refinement techniques discussed in the previous section have common ideas with tools and formalisms discussed in this section, however, the latter primarily target verification of a *single* program rather than refinement. Refinement in CIVL is orthogonal to these techniques, which can be aided by CIVL's ability to connect a complex concurrent program to a simpler abstraction.

VCC [8] is a tool for verifying concurrent C programs. Chalice [33] is a language and modular verification tool for concurrent programs. VCC does not support refinement and Chalice does so only for sequential programs. VCC and Chalice base their invariant reasoning on objects, object ownership, and type invariants. Invariant reasoning in CIVL is more primitive and based on predicates in yield statements. Although the approach in VCC and Chalice is more convenient when applicable, CIVL's approach is more flexible. VCC and Chalice can reason sequentially about objects exclusively owned by a thread; CIVL accomplishes the same using linear variables. Neither VCC nor Chalice support movers and reduction reasoning.

Concurrent separation logic [37] reasons about concurrency without explicitly checking for non-interference between threads. Recently, tools based on this logic that blend in explicit non-interference reasoning (but without support for reduction and mover reasoning) have been developed [16,41]. CIVL's combination of interference checking and linear variables is an extreme example of this trend, is very general and technique-agnostic. We supply very primitive abstractions and let programmers mix and match these abstractions freely to encode the non-interference reasoning style of their choice.

References

1. Abadi, M., Lamport, L.: Composing specifications. ACM Trans. Program. Lang. Syst. **15**(1), 73–132 (1993)
2. Abrial, J.-R., Butler, M., Hallerstede, S., Hoang, T.S., Mehta, F., Voisin, L.: Rodin: an open toolset for modelling and reasoning in Event-B. STTT **12**(6), 447–466 (2010)
3. Alur, R., Henzinger, T.A., Mang, F.Y.C., Qadeer, S., Rajamani, S.K., Tasiran, S.: MOCHA: modularity in model checking. In: Computer Aided Verification, 10th International Conference Proceedings, CAV 1998, pp. 521–525, Vancouver, June 28 - July 2 (1998)
4. Barnett, M., Chang, B.-Y.E., DeLine, R., Jacobs, B., Leino, K.R.M.: Boogie: a modular reusable verifier for object-oriented programs. In: de Boer, F.S., Bonsangue, M.M., Graf, S., de Roever, W.-P. (eds.) FMCO 2005. LNCS, vol. 4111, pp. 364–387. Springer, Heidelberg (2006)
5. Barnett, M., Leino, K.R.M.: Weakest-precondition of unstructured programs. In: PASTE (2005)
6. Blumofe, R.D., Leiserson, C.E.: Scheduling multithreaded computations by work stealing. J. ACM **46**(5), 720–748 (1999)

7. Boyland, J.: Checking interference with fractional permissions. In: Static Analysis: 10th International Symposium (2003)
8. Cohen, E., Dahlweid, M., Hillebrand, M., Leinenbach, D., Moskal, M., Santen, T., Schulte, W., Tobies, S.: VCC: a practical system for verifying concurrent C. In: Berghofer, S., Nipkow, T., Urban, C., Wenzel, M. (eds.) TPHOLs 2009. LNCS, vol. 5674, pp. 23–42. Springer, Heidelberg (2009)
9. de Moura, L., Bjørner, N.S.: Z3: an efficient SMT solver. In: Ramakrishnan, C.R., Rehof, J. (eds.) TACAS 2008. LNCS, vol. 4963, pp. 337–340. Springer, Heidelberg (2008)
10. Dijkstra, E.W., Lamport, L., Martin, A.J., Scholten, C.S., Steffens, E.F.M.: On-the-fly garbage collection An exercise in cooperation. Commun. ACM **21**(11), 280–294 (1978)
11. Eiríksson, A.T.: The formal design of 1M-gate ASICs. Form. Methods Syst. Des. **16**(1), 7–22 (2000)
12. Elmas, T., Qadeer, S., Sezgin, A., Subasi, O., Tasiran, S.: Simplifying linearizability proofs with reduction and abstraction. In: Esparza, J., Majumdar, R. (eds.) TACAS 2010. LNCS, vol. 6015, pp. 296–311. Springer, Heidelberg (2010)
13. Elmas, T., Qadeer, S., Tasiran, S.: A calculus of atomic actions. In: POPL, pp. 2–15 (2009)
14. Elmas, T., Tasiran, S., Qadeer, S..: VYRD: verifying concurrent programs by runtime refinement-violation detection. In: Proceedings of the ACM SIGPLAN 2005 Conference on Programming Language Design and Implementation, pp. 27–37, Chicago, 12–15 June 2005
15. Farzan, A., Kincaid, Z., Podelski, A.: Proofs that count. In: The 41st Annual ACM SIGPLAN-SIGACT Symposium on Principles of Programming Languages (POPL 2014), San Diego, pp. 151–164, 20–21, January 2014
16. Feng, X., Ferreira, R., Shao, Z.: On the relationship between concurrent separation logic and assume-guarantee reasoning. In: De Nicola, R. (ed.) ESOP 2007. LNCS, vol. 4421, pp. 173–188. Springer, Heidelberg (2007)
17. Flanagan, C., Freund, S.N., Lifshin, M., Qadeer, S.: Types for atomicity: Static checking and inference for java. ACM Trans. Program. Lang. Syst. **30**(4), 1–53 (2008)
18. Flanagan, C., Freund, S.N., Qadeer, S., Seshia, S.A.: Modular verification of multithreaded programs. Theor. Comput. Sci. **338**(1–3), 153–183 (2005)
19. Flanagan, C., Qadeer, S.: Thread-modular model checking. In: Ball, T., Rajamani, S.K. (eds.) SPIN 2003. LNCS, vol. 2648, pp. 213–224. Springer, Heidelberg (2003)
20. Floyd, R.: Assigning meaning to programs. In: Symposia in Applied Mathematics, vol. 19, pp. 19–32. American Mathematical Society (1967)
21. Freund, S.N., Qadeer, S.: Checking concise specifications for multithreaded software. J. Object Technol. **3**(6), 81–101 (2004)
22. Hawblitzel, C., Petrank, E., Qadeer, S., Tasiran, S.: Verified concurrent garbage collector. http://singularity.codeplex.com/SourceControl/latest#base/Imported/Bartok/runtime/verified/GCs/concur/GC.bpl
23. Hawblitzel, C., Petrank, E., Qadeer, S., Tasiran, S.: Automated and modular refinement reasoning for concurrent programs. Technical report MSR-TR-2015-8 Microsoft Research (2015). http://research.microsoft.com/apps/pubs/?id=238907
24. Henzinger, M.R., Henzinger, T.A., Kopke, P.W.: Computing simulations on finite and infinite graphs. In: FOCS (1995)
25. Henzinger, T.A., Sezgin, A., Vafeiadis, V.: Aspect-oriented linearizability proofs In: D'Argenio, P.R., Melgratti, H. (eds.) CONCUR 2013 – Concurrency Theory LNCS, vol. 8052, pp. 242–256. Springer, Heidelberg (2013)

6. Henzinger, T.A., Liu, X., Qadeer, S., Rajamani, S.K.: Formal specification and verification of a dataflow processor array. In: Proceedings 1999 IEEE/ACM International Conference on Computer-aided Design, (ICCAD 1999), pp. 494–499. IEEE Press (1999)
7. Herlihy, M., Shavit, N.: The Art of Multiprocessor Programming. Morgan Kaufmann Publishers Inc., San Francisco (2008)
8. Hoare, C.A.R.: An axiomatic basis for computer programming. Commun. ACM **12**(10), 576–580 (1969)
9. Jones, C.B.: Tentative steps toward a development method for interfering programs. ACM TOPLAS **5**(4), 596–619 (1983)
0. Klein, G., Andronick, J., Elphinstone, K., Murray, T., Sewell, T., Kolanski, R., Heiser, G.: Comprehensive formal verification of an OS microkernel. ACM Trans. Comput. Sys. **32**(1), 2:1–2:70 (2014)
1. Lahiri, S.K., Qadeer, S., Walker, D.: Linear maps. In: PLPV, pp. 3–14 (2011)
2. Lamport, L.: Specifying Systems: The TLA+ Language and Tools for Hardware and Software Engineers. Addison-Wesley, Boston (2004)
3. Leino, K.R.M., Müller, P.: A basis for verifying multi-threaded programs. In: Castagna, G. (ed.) ESOP 2009. LNCS, vol. 5502, pp. 378–393. Springer, Heidelberg (2009)
4. Liang, H., Feng, X., Fu, M.: Rely-guarantee-based simulation for compositional verification of concurrent program transformations. ACM Trans. Program. Lang. Syst. **36**(1), 3:1–3:55 (2014)
5. Lipton, R.J.: Reduction: A method of proving properties of parallel programs. Commun. ACM **18**(12), 717–721 (1975)
6. McMillan, K.L.: A methodology for hardware verification using compositional model checking. Sci. Comput. Program. **37**(1–3), 279–309 (2000)
7. O'Hearn, P.W.: Resources, concurrency, and local reasoning. Theor. Comput. Sci. **375**(1–3), 271–307 (2007)
8. Owicki, S.S., Gries, D.: An axiomatic proof technique for parallel programs i. Acta Inf. **6**, 319–340 (1976)
9. Reynolds, J.C.: Separation logic: a logic for shared mutable data structures. In: LICS, pp. 55–74 (2002)
0. Turon, A.J., Wand, M.: A separation logic for refining concurrent objects. In: Proceedings 38th ACM SIGPLAN-SIGACT Symposium on Principles of Programming Languages (POPL 2011), pp. 247–258. ACM, New York (2011)
1. Vafeiadis, V., Parkinson, M.: A marriage of rely/guarantee and separation logic. In: Caires, L., Vasconcelos, V.T. (eds.) CONCUR 2007. LNCS, vol. 4703, pp. 256–271. Springer, Heidelberg (2007)
2. Wadler, P.: Linear types can change the world!. In: Programming Concepts and Methods, North (1990)
3. Wirth, N.: Program development by stepwise refinement. Commun. ACM **14**(4), 221–227 (1971)

Author Index

Printed in the United States
By Bookmasters